Y0-ATG-823

Catalogue

of Medieval and Renaissance Manuscripts in the Houghton Library Harvard University

Volume 1: MSS Lat 3–179.

Medieval & Renaissance Texts & Studies

Volume 145

Catalogue

of Medieval and Renaissance Manuscripts in the Houghton Library Harvard University

Volume 1: MSS Lat 3–179

by

Laura Light

MEDIEVAL & RENAISSANCE TEXTS & STUDIES
Tempe, Arizona
1997

The publication of this volume has been supported by a grant from the National Endowment for the Humanities, an independent federal agency.

© Copyright 1995
Center for Medieval and Early Renaissance Studies
State University of New York at Binghamton

Second Printing
© Copyright 1997
Arizona Board of Regents for Arizona State University

Library of Congress Cataloging-in-Publication Data

Houghton Library.
Medieval and Renaissance manuscripts in the Houghton Library, Harvard University / compiled by Laura Light.
p. cm. — (Medieval & Renaissance Texts & Studies; v. 145)
Includes bibliographical references.
Contents: v. 1 MSS Lat 3–179
ISBN 0–86698–185–3 (v. 1 : alk. paper)
1. Manuscripts, Medieval—Massachusetts—Cambridge—Bibliography—Catalogs. 2. Manuscripts, Renaissance—Massachusetts—Cambridge—Bibliography—Catalogs. 3. Houghton Library—Catalogs. I. Light, Laura. II. Title. III. Series.
Z6621.H592M435 1995
011'.31'097444—dc20 95–21800
CIP

This book is made to last. It is set in Plantin, smythe-sewn and printed on acid-free paper to library specifications.

Printed in the United States of America

Contents

Acknowledgements

It is a special joy to thank the many scholars who generously shared their knowledge and time. Their contributions were invaluable; the errors that remain are my responsibility. Paul Meyvaert was a constant source of knowledge, inspiration and comfort. Consuelo Dutschke, Richard Rouse and Barbara Shailor were unstinting in their generosity. I owe them special thanks for the time they spent at Houghton, examining manuscripts and reviewing descriptions, as well as for the many queries they answered in correspondence. I would like to thank Richard Rouse in addition for his thoughtful guidance in helping us to structure the project as a whole.

Many other scholars patiently answered my questions; I have tried to acknowledge individual contributions in the text, and hope that I have not inadvertently omitted anyone. I owe them all my thanks, and would like to thank in particular those scholars who visited the library: Lilian Armstrong, Virginia Brown, Jane Carroll, Albinia de la Mare, Albert Derolez, Dennis Dutschke, the late Margaret Gibson, Michael Gullick, Hope Mayo, Paul Needham, Terry Nixon, Gude Sudkale-Redelfsen, and Bernard Rosenthal. I also owe thanks to the Harvard community, especially to James Hankins, Beverly Kienzle, Michael McCormick, Nicholas Pickwoad, Eckehard Simon, Richard Tarrant and Jan Ziolkowski.

If space permitted I would thank each of my colleagues at Houghton individually for their assistance and knowledge. Dennis Marnon assisted with conservation problems and gave advice on bindings. James Walsh shared his expertise in fifteenth century printed books. Leslie Morris, Curator of Manuscripts, and Betty Falsey, Associate Curator, contributed countless hours of administrative support and proofread the descriptions. Jennifer Lopez, Ken Marcus, William Mendelsohn, and Susan Shroff assisted the project for varying lengths of time and accomplished many thankless tasks gracefully. And finally, last in order, but first in importance, I thank Rodney Dennis,

Curator of Manuscripts Emeritus, who started this project and never wavered in his support. I am grateful both for his knowledge of the collection, which was an invaluable resource, and for his faith in the project, without which nothing could have been accomplished.

The volume also could not have been completed without the endless patience and support of my husband, Carroll, and to him and to our children, Maggie, Jane and Francis, I am deeply grateful.

Preface

Harvard's eclectic collection of medieval and Renaissance manuscripts has been the subject of study and scholarly publications over the years, but this volume inaugurates the first catalogue of this collection of more than 850 pre-1520 Western manuscripts. A catalogue is the foundation of all that a library does to make its collections accessible to scholars. It initiates a process of discovery, both for the library whose manuscripts are examined by the expert and sophisticated eyes of the cataloguer, and for the scholar who peruses the catalogue in search of fresh material and knowledge. During the preparation of this catalogue, unidentified texts have been newly identified, the contents of tract volumes have been analyzed for the first time, and the structure and history of the manuscripts themselves has been studied and recorded with meticulous detail. When one considers that many of these manuscripts have been housed at Harvard for almost 200 years, it is surprising how much new information is here made widely available for the first time.

Before Laura Light undertook this project, Houghton's documentation on its manuscripts was poor. There were few scholarly descriptions, the specialist literature on individual manuscripts had not been gathered, and the existing catalogue descriptions were so brief and incomplete as to offer practically no basis for expansion into a modern manuscript catalogue. Here, for the first time, a description of a Houghton manuscript tells the scholar what the manuscript is like in itself and what it contains. Both the Houghton Library and the scholarly community owe Laura Light a debt of thanks for undertaking this time-consuming and often difficult endeavor.

As the fortunate custodian of one of the largest collections of early manuscripts in the United States, Harvard has recognized the importance of ensuring that the scholarly community has access to this valuable resource. The present volume is the first part of a two-volume catalogue of MS Latin. MS Richardson and MS Typ will be described in volumes three and four. The fifth volume will describe the remaining medieval and Renaissance manuscripts in the collection, including the vernacular manuscripts shelved by language (MS Dutch, French, German, Italian, Portuguese, Spanish, and Greek), MS Riant and MS Judaica, and single leaves and fragments.

Our warmest thanks go to those who have provided financial support in this undertaking: the National Endowment for the Humanities, the Hunt Foundation, the Richard and Natalie Jacoff Foundation Inc., the late Professor Stanley J. Kahrl, John Heller, Mrs. Frederick B. Deknatel, Anne H. Van Buren, Mr. and Mrs. Gordon P. Getty, and an anonymous donor.

Leslie A. Morris
Curator of Manuscripts in the Harvard College Library
May 1995

Introduction

Harvard College has been collecting medieval and Renaissance manuscripts since the early nineteenth century, and now enjoys one of the major collections of early manuscripts in the United States. Since 1942, when Houghton Library was built to house the College's rare book and manuscript collections, these manuscripts have been available to scholars in its reading room.

The collection has grown to approximately 850 manuscripts in Western European languages dating before ca. 1525. These manuscripts are divided into a number of shelf classifications. Latin manuscripts from all periods are shelved as MS Lat; among these are 192 medieval and Renaissance codices and a number of leaves and fragments. The exceptional collection of manuscripts gathered by William King Richardson (1859–1951), including 46 medieval and Renaissance manuscripts, is known as MS Richardson. Manuscripts in the Department of Printing and Graphic Arts are classified as MS Typ; most of these manuscripts were acquired by Philip Hofer (1898–1984), the first curator of the department. This collection includes approximately 226 medieval and Renaissance manuscripts and a large collection of over 125 leaves and fragments. Other medieval and Renaissance manuscripts are found among the collections of English, French, German, Greek, Italian, Portuguese and Spanish manuscripts (MS Eng, MS Fr, MS Ger, MS Gr, MS Ital, MS Port, and MS Span), in the subject classification, MS Judaica, and among the manuscripts once owned by comte Paul Riant (1836–1888), MS Riant.

The present volume describes MS Lat 3 through MS Lat 179. The classification includes manuscripts in Latin from all periods, but the general rule has been to include only codices dating before ca. 1525 in this catalogue. A few later manuscripts are described because they are logically continuous with the earlier material, such as MS Lat 111, a Carthusian Breviary from the first half of the sixteenth century, and pfMS Lat 128, an Italian Gradual from the sixteenth century.[1] Excluded are sixteenth-century items such as autograph letters, diaries, private papers and copies of printed books, which must be understood as new ventures in the intellectual and cultural history of Europe.[2] Fragments and single leaves that had been given individual shelf marks are included, but boxed collections of fragments and leaves, many of them removed from printed books, will be included in a future volume.[3] The language of most of the manuscripts is Latin, although occasional phrases in the vernacular are present, and three manuscripts in French, Dutch and Italian, respectively, are described because they are shelved in this classification.[4]

MS Lat is a collection of manuscripts resulting from a long period of institutional collecting where the majority of the manuscripts were acquired one at a time, either by purchase or by gift. Harvard College owes its first gift of medieval manuscripts to Edward Everett (1794–1865), Eliot Professor of Greek Literature at Harvard. In 1819, after a trip to Constantinople, Everett gave the library six Greek and one Latin manuscript, fMS Lat 39, a fourteenth-century French copy of Aristotle's *Politics*, *Rhetoric*, and the *Magna Moralia* in Latin translation.[5] From this beginning the collection grew slowly, primarily by gifts, with only an occasional foray into the market.

---

[1] Other manuscripts dating after ca. 1525 include fMS Lat 182, Leonardo Bruni Aretino, *Historiarum florentini populi* (Italy, Florence, 154<2?>); MS Lat 197, St. Augustine, *Rule*; Hermits of St. Paul, *Constitutions* (Hungary, 1522); and fMS Lat 245, Thomas Aquinas, *Super tertio libro Sententiarum* (Germany, 1508).

[2] The criteria of selection used in De Ricci, *Census*, and Bond and Faye, *Supplement* were broader; these catalogues therefore include a number of later manuscripts and boxed collections of charters and fragments not described in the present volume.

[3] Excluded material includes MS Lat 10, Thirteen charters, 1235–1529, relating to the Cistercians of Bockland Abbey, Devonshire; pfMS Lat 53, boxed collection of Papal documents; bMS Lat 100, fragments of Latin manuscripts; bMS Lat 227, Charters; and bMS Lat 229, single leaves.

[4] MS Lat 256, *La doctrine aux simples gens* (France, 1410), MS Lat 268, David van Augsburg and St. Bernard in Dutch (June 28, 1466) and MS Lat 290, Cecco d'Ascoli, *L'acerba* in Italian (Northern Italy, Venice?, s. $\mathrm{XV}^{\mathrm{med}-3/4}$).

[5] The story of the formation of the collection of medieval and Renaissance manuscripts at Harvard has been told by Rodney Dennis in Dennis, "Collecting"; on Everett's gift, see Dennis, "Collecting," 286–87 and Edward Everett, "An account of Some Greek Manuscripts, procured at Constantinople in 1819, and now

This pattern of acquiring manuscripts remains the norm to the present day, but a few exceptions may be noted. In 1874, Charles Sumner bequeathed the library his collection of twenty-six medieval and Renaissance manuscripts; among these were Books of Hours, fifteenth-century Italian copies of classical texts and thirteenth-century Bibles.[6] In 1910 the Harvard Professor of Classical Philology, Morris Hicky Morgan (1859–1910), gave the library four manuscripts of the *Satires* of Persius (MSS Lat 135–137 and fMS Lat 138); three additional Persius manuscripts were purchased between 1926 and 1935 (MSS Lat 139, 145, and 155). The library acquired the Walter Arthur Copinger *Imitatio christi* collection in 1921, which included ten manuscripts, many of which were from the Carthusian monastery at Buxheim in Bavaria, diocese of Augsburg.[7] In 1949 Imrie de Vegh (1906–62), honorary curator of Eastern European History, gave the library ten distinguished manuscripts from his collection.[8] Among these manuscripts is an abbreviated copy of Maffeo Vegio, *De liberorum educatione*, which was copied for Poggio Bracciolini and includes corrections in his hand (MS Lat 190).[9]

The library's first major purchase was at the 1896 sale from the

belonging to the Library of the University at Cambridge," *Memoirs of the American Academy of Arts and Sciences* 4, part 2 (1821) 409–15, especially 414–15.

[6] Rodney Dennis, "The World of Madness and the World of Dreams: Charles Sumner and Philip Hofer as Collectors of Early Manuscripts," *Gazette of the Grolier Club* n.s. 42 (1990) 17–37.

[7] Walter Arthur Copinger, *Hand List of What is Believed to be the Largest Collection in the World of Editions of the "The Imitation" of Thomas à Kempis* (1908); the collection was acquired by Harvard as the gift of James Byrne in 1921; see James Walsh, "Attributions in a Manuscript of *Imitatio Christi* (MS Lat 246)," in *The Marks in the Fields. Essays on the Uses of Manuscripts*, eds. Rodney Dennis and E. Falsey (Cambridge, Mass. 1992) 62–65; the *Imitatio Christi* manuscripts are now shelved as MS Lat 236, MS Lat 237, MS Lat 238, MS Lat 239, MS Lat 241, MS Lat 242, MS Lat 244, fMS Lat 246, and fMS Lat 247; MS Lat 240, which also includes the *Imitatio Christi* was purchased in 1937.

[8] Eight of these manuscripts are now included in MS Lat: MS Lat 188, MS Lat 189, MS Lat 190, fMS Lat 192, fMS Lat 193, MS Lat 194, MS Lat 195 and MS Lat 196 were acquired in 1949. MS Lat 206 was acquired from de Vegh in 1953.

[9] The annotations were identified as Poggio's by Professor A. C. de la Mare. See also James Hankins, *Italian Humanists in Ten Manuscripts from the Houghton Library. An Exhibition on the Occasion of the Annual National Meeting of the Renaissance Society of America, 30 March–1 April 1989* (Cambridge, Mass. 1989) 3–4.

collection of Sir Thomas Phillipps, when it bought seven manuscripts of classical texts.[10] All of these manuscripts have a note signed by Harvard College librarian Justin Winsor, stating that they were to be used by faculty of the Classics Department for teaching and research. The focus on acquiring material for research and teaching continues to this day, and the Harvard faculty have often influenced acquisitions. In 1923, for example, Edward K. Rand (1871–1945), Pope Professor of Latin, recommended that the library purchase MS Lat 117, a copy of the Gospel of Nicodemus. Charles Eliot Norton (1827–1908), Professor of Art History, owned fifteen medieval manuscripts, which were purchased by the library in 1905.[11] Most of his manuscripts were, not surprisingly, illuminated, but he also collected manuscripts because of their text, such as the two manuscripts of Boethius, *De consolatio philosophiae*, MS Lat 178 and MS Lat 179. These served as a springboard, and Harvard librarians purchased three additional Boethius manuscripts between 1917 and 1920 (MSS Lat 51, 126, and 127).

MS Lat is thus a heterogenous collection of material, acquired from many different sources over a long period of time. The manuscripts range in date from the ninth through the fifteenth century. The collection includes two ninth-century manuscripts, a fragment of the "Arno Sacramentary," fMS Lat 156, from Salzburg, and a biblical fragment from Northern France, fMS Lat 272, which once belonged to E. K. Rand. The earliest complete manuscript is MS Lat 199, a distinguished copy of Horace from the end of the tenth or early eleventh century. There are sixteen complete manuscripts and a number of fragments from the twelfth century.[12] The new learning of the twelfth-century schools is illustrated by manuscripts such as MS Lat 44, a copy of Priscian, *Institutiones grammaticae* with glosses from the second quarter of the twelfth century, and MS Lat 334, a manuscript of Numbers with the Ordinary Gloss from Italy dating

---

[10] MS Lat 40, MS Lat 41, fMS Lat 42, MS Lat 43, MS Lat 44, MS Lat 46 and MS Lat 47.

[11] Ten of these manuscripts are now shelved in MS Lat (MS Lat 170, MS Lat 176, MS Lat 178, MS Lat 179, MS Lat 180, MS Lat 213, MS Lat 265, MS Lat 267, fMS Lat 270, and MS Lat 266).

[12] See Light, *The Bible in the Twelfth Century*, with a check-list of twelfth-century manuscripts at Houghton by Rodney Dennis.

from the third quarter of the century. Handsome, large-format monastic manuscripts are represented by such manuscripts as the collection of saints lives from Holme Cultram, fMS Lat 27.

The bulk of the collection dates from the later Middle Ages and the Renaissance.[13] It is especially strong in manuscripts from fifteenth-century Italy. Among the fifty-six Italian humanist manuscripts, many in their original bindings, are handsome, formal copies by known scribes and artists, such as MS Lat 43, copied by Piero Cennini, and MS Lat 163, illuminated either by the Florentine artist Francesco di Lorenzo Rosselli or by the Master of the Hamilton Xenophon. Other humanistic manuscripts, humbler in appearance, are of equal importance to the scholar. The codex that is now MS Lat 271 was assembled from three fifteenth-century Italian manuscripts. One of these manuscripts includes an unpublished speech to Borsio d'Este and a funeral speech on Lodovico Sanbonifacio, Count of Verona, probably by Ludovico Carbo.[14]

The collection also includes many liturgical manuscripts. Two of particular interest to historians of the liturgy are MS Lat 115, a portable Breviary from the second half of the thirteenth century probably meant to be used by Dominican nuns, and a notably full collection of prayers for exorcisms and benedictions, MS Lat 134 (Germany s. XIV^{2}). Many of the liturgical manuscripts are illuminated, for example the Book of Hours by the Master of the Burgundian Prelate, MS Lat 249, and the two Books of Hours attributed to the Maître François, MSS Lat 133 and 159. The few categories mentioned here do not adequately characterize this diverse collection. One could mention the thirteenth-century manuscripts, including a copy of St. Bonaventure with *pecia*-marks (MS Lat 265), and five Bibles (fMS Lat 36, MS Lat 261, MS Lat 262, MS Lat 264, and MS Lat 354); the copies of secular Latin texts, notably versions of the Alexander legend (MS Lat 34, fMS Lat 121, and MS Lat 122); and many others.

---

[13] See Roger S. Wieck, *Late Medieval and Renaissance Illuminated Manuscripts 1350–1525 in the Houghton Library* (Cambridge, Mass. 1983) including 42 manuscripts from MS Lat with illumination.

[14] Kristeller, *Iter* 5:227.

Previous Cataloguing

S. de Ricci's *Census of Medieval and Renaissance Manuscripts in the United States and Canada* (1935–40) and the *Supplement to the Census of Medieval and Renaissance Manuscripts in the United States and Canada* by W. H. Bond and C. U. Faye, published in 1962, are the main published sources of information on Houghton's manuscripts.[15] Additional information on some manuscripts is provided by exhibition catalogues and library records. When the *Census* was published, the manuscripts now shelved as MS Lat were divided into a number of different classifications. The manuscripts in these small classifications—the *Imitatio Christi* Collection, the Fearing Collection, the Folklore Collection, the Norton Collection and the Sumner Collection—were combined with MS Lat and given new shelf marks before the *Supplement* appeared. MS Lat is an open classification; twenty-nine manuscripts have been acquired since 1962 and it continues to grow.

Form of Entry

Heading: Each entry begins with the shelf mark, followed by a brief characterization of the contents (author and title or subject statement), with the place and date of origin of the manuscript; composite manuscripts may have several places and dates in the heading. Dates are listed according to accepted convention, using roman numerals with superscripts indicating the approximate years within a century, as follows: "in," "med" and "ex" used for the beginning, middle and end of a century; first and second half of the century indicated by superscript "1" or "2"; "1/4," "2/4," etc. used to indicate twenty-five year periods within each century; a diagonal slash between two centuries indicates a date around the turn of the century. References to the plates at the end of the volume are listed here when pertinent.

Text: This section is divided into articles, numbered in arabic numerals, corresponding to the textual divisions in the manuscript, or

[15] See note 2, above.

to divisions indicated by internal features such as headings or major decorative elements. Roman numerals are used to indicate that the manuscript is composite, assembled from a number of manuscripts of differing origins. Each entry includes a complete list of individual texts with the opening and closing words and the folios on which they occur. In especially lengthy entries only the opening words and beginning folios are listed. When the incipits and explicits of liturgical texts are too common to be useful, an identification of the text is given instead. The text of binding fragments and leaves from other manuscripts are described as a separate article in this section when they are large enough to contain a significant amount of text. The usual criteria were used to establish the liturgical use of the Hours of the Virgin and the Office of the Dead.[16]

Rubrics and decorative headings are in italics. Transcriptions of incipits and explicits retain the original orthography of the manuscript. Abbreviations are expanded silently. Capitalization attempts to follow the practice of the manuscript, except in rubrics written in capitals, which are transcribed with each word in the rubric beginning with a capital letter; punctuation is supplied sparingly. A double diagonal slash is used when a text begins or ends defectively. Corrections in the text are noted in square brackets, with *corr.*[1] indicating corrections made by the scribe, and *corr.*[2] indicating corrections made subsequently in another hand. Doubtful information is indicated by [?] immediately following the item queried; problems in transcription due to damage to the manuscript or other difficulties are indicated by angle brackets <?> placed in the position of the doubtful word or passage.

Identification of the texts and bibliographic citations, when available, accompany each item, together with a discussion of problems raised by the text. Contemporary and later notes and marginalia are discussed here when they are significant.

Physical description, arranged in discrete paragraphs: 1. Material, with description and identification of watermarks according to classi-

[16] F. Madan, "The Localization of Manuscripts," in *Essays in History Presented to Reginald Lane Poole*, ed. H. W. C. Davis (Oxford 1927) 21–29; I would like to thank Consuelo Dutschke for sharing her notes on the liturgical use of the Office of the Dead based on comparisons with early printed Books of Hours with stated use.

fications established in Briquet, Piccard, or elsewhere, if possible, when the manuscript is on paper; comments on the type or quality of the parchment are included when significant. Number of leaves, with the flyleaves designated by small roman numerals. Standard practice for Houghton manuscripts is to leave flyleaves unnumbered, and to foliate the manuscript in pencil in the bottom, inside margin. Foliation that does not follow this convention is noted in the descriptions. Dimensions of height and width of the leaves and of written space, in millimeters; dimension of the ruled space is also included if it differs significantly from that of the written space; number of lines and columns; instruments or materials used for ruling (hard point or dry point, crayon, lead, or ink); placement of bounding lines; and prickings. 2. Collation, catchwords, leaf and/or quire signatures. 3. Discussion of type of scripts used and number of scribes.

Decoration, beginning with the most elaborate and proceeding to the simplest: includes attributions to known artists or schools when possible or discussion of the style; iconography of all miniatures and historiated initials described with their location and function in the text.

Imperfections, if applicable.

Description of binding: leaves from other manuscripts used in the binding are described here if they have not been included as a separate item above.

Provenance: this section presents what is known of the manuscript's date, place of origin, circumstance of production and subsequent history, including all known previous owners, dates and locations of sales and auctions, and previous Harvard shelf marks. Houghton accession numbers are listed for manuscripts that were assigned these references. The opening words of the second folio are listed last.

Bibliography: initial references to the *Census* by De Ricci or the *Supplement* by Bond and Faye followed by works that refer to the manuscript as a whole in chronological order of publication. Bibliography pertaining to specific aspects of the manuscript, such as the text, scribes, or artists, are included in the body of the description in the appropriate section.

Plates: included are reproductions of all dated manuscripts, followed by selected undated material arranged according to place of origin and probable date.

Abbreviations

Alexander and de la Mare, *Italian Manuscripts . . . of Major J. R. Abbey*

J. J. G. Alexander and A. C. de la Mare, *The Italian Manuscripts in the Library of Major J. R. Abbey* (New York and London 1969)

Aristoteles latinus

Corpus philosophorum medii aevi academiarum consociatarum auspiciis et consilio editum, *Aristoteles latinus* (Bruges-Paris 1957–)

Aristoteles latinus: Codices

Aristoteles latinus. Codices descripsit, George Lacombe, with A. Birkenmajer, M. Dulong, and E. Francheschini (Rome 1939); emended and supplemented by Lorenzo Minio-Paluello in vol. 2 (Cambridge 1955) and *Supplementa altera* (Bruges and Paris 1961); all three volumes repr. (Leiden 1979)

Avril, "Review"

François Avril, review of Roger Wieck, *Late Medieval and Renaissance Illuminated Manuscripts, 1350–1525* (Cambridge, Mass. 1983) in *Bulletin du bibliophile* 3 (1984) 364–69

Axters, *Bibliotheca dominicana neerlandica*

Stephanus G. Axters, O.P., *Bibliotheca dominicana neerlandica manuscripta 1224–1500.* Bibliothèque de la revue d'histoire ecclésiastique 49 (Louvain 1970)

Baron, *Leonardo Bruni Aretino*

Hans Baron, *Leonardo Bruni Aretino: humanistisch-philosophische Schriften.* Quellen zur Geistesgeschichte des Mittelalters und der Renaissance 1 (Leipzig and Berlin 1928)

Bertalot

L. Bertalot, *Initia humanistica latina: Initienverzeichnis lateinischer Prosa und Poesie aus der Zeit des 14. bis 16. Jahrhunderts* (Tübingen 1985–)

BHL

Bibliotheca hagiographica latina, Socii Bollandiani, ed. (Brussels 1898–1901; Supplement, Brussels 1986)

Biblia sacra

Biblia sacra iuxta latinam vulgatam versionem ad codicum fidem, iussu Pii PP. XI cura studio monachorum Sancti Benedicti commissionis pontificiae a Pio PP. X institutae sodalium praesidae Aidano Gasquet S.R.E. cardinale edita (Rome 1926–87)

Biographie universelle

Biographie universelle ancienne et moderne (Paris 1811–62)

Bloomfield

Morton W. Bloomfield et. al., *Incipits of Latin Works on the Virtues and Vices, 1100–1500 AD* Medieval Academy of America Publications 88 (Cambridge, Mass. 1979)

Bond and Faye

C. U. Faye and W. H. Bond, *Supplement to the Census of Medieval and Renaissance Manuscripts in the United States and Canada* (New York 1962)

Branner, *Manuscript Painting*

Robert Branner, *Manuscript Painting in Paris during the Reign of St. Louis: A Study of Styles* (Berkeley 1977)

Brev. O.P.

Breviarium iuxta ritum sacri ordinis fratrum praedicatorum auctoritate apostolica approbatum reverendissimi patris Fr. Josephi Mariae Sanvito jussu editum (Tournai 1878)

Briquet

C. M. Briquet, *Les filigranes: dictionnaire historique des marques du papier . . . 1282 jusqu'à 1600*, facs. of the 1907 edition with supplementary material, ed. A. Stevenson (Amsterdam 1968)

Bruylants, *Oraisons*
P. Bruylants, *Les oraisons du missel romain.* Etudes liturgiques 1 (Louvain 1952)

de Bruyne, *Préfaces*
[Donatien de Bruyne], *Les préfaces de la Bible latine* (Namur 1920)

de Bruyne, *Sommaires*
[Donatien de Bruyne], *Les Sommaires, divisions, et rubriques de la Bible latine* (Namur 1914)

CC
Corpus christianorum: series latina (Turnhout 1954–)

Churchill
W. A. Churchill, *Watermarks in Paper in Holland, England, France, etc. in the Seventeenth and Eighteenth Centuries and Their Interconnection* (Amsterdam 1935)

Colophons
Colophons de manuscrits occidentaux des origines au XVIe *siècle* (Fribourg 1965–82)

Copinger
W. A. Copinger, *Supplement to Hain's Repertorium bibliographicum* (London 1895–1902)

Cosenza
M. E. Cosenza, *Biographical and Bibliographical Dictionary of the Italian Humanists and of the World of Classical Scholarship in Italy, 1300–1800* (Boston, Mass. 1962–67)

CPL
Eligius Dekkers and A. Gaar, eds., *Clavis patrum latinorum.* Sacris erudiri 3, 2nd. ed. (Steenbrugge 1961)

CTC
Virginia Brown, F. Edward Cranz, Paul O. Kristeller, eds., *Catalogus translationum et commentariorum: Mediaeval and Renaissance Latin Translations and Commentaries* (Washington, D.C. 1960–)

DBI
Dizionario biografico degli italiani (Rome 1960–)

de la Mare, "New Research"
Albinia de la Mare, "New Research on Humanistic Scribes in Florence," in Annarosa Garzelli, ed., *Miniatura fiorentina de Rinascimento 1440–1525*. Inventari e Cataloghi Toscani 18–19 (Florence 1985) 393–600

De Ricci
S. De Ricci, with the assistance of W. H. Wilson, *Census of Medieval and Renaissance Manuscripts in the United States and Canada* (New York 1935–40)

De Ricci, "Handlist"
S. De Ricci, "A Handlist of Latin Classical Manuscripts in American Libraries," *Philological Quarterly* 1 (1922) 100–108

Dennis, "Collecting"
Rodney G. Dennis, "Collecting Early Manuscripts at Harvard," *Harvard Library Bulletin* 31 (1983) 285–98

Destrez
Jean Destrez, *La Pecia dans les manuscrits universitaires du XIII*[e] *et du XIV*[e] *siècle* (Paris 1935)

Dogaer, *Flemish Miniature Painting*
Georges Dogaer, *Flemish Miniature Painting in the 15th and 16th Centuries* (Amsterdam 1987)

Dondaine and Shooner, *Codices*
H. F. Dondaine and H. V. Shooner, *Codices manuscripti operum Thomae de Aquino* (Rome 1967)

Dutschke, *Guide*
C. W. Dutschke, *Guide to Medieval and Renaissance Manuscripts in the Huntington Library*, with the assistance of R. H. Rouse and S. Hodson, V. Rust, H. Schulz and E. Compte (San Marino, California 1989)

EETS
Early English Text Society

Garzelli, "Le immagini"
Annarosa Garzelli, "Le immagini" in Annarosa Garzelli, ed., *Miniatura fiorentina del Rinascimento 1440–1525.* Inventari e Cataloghi Toscani 18–19 (Florence 1985) 1–391

GKW
Gesamtkatalog der Wiegendrucke (Leipzig and New York 1925–)

Gruys, *Cartusiana*
Albert Gruys, *Cartusiana: Un Instrument heuristique* (Paris 1976–78)

Hain
L. F. T. Hain, *Repertorium bibliographicum* (Stuttgart etc. 1826–38)

Hankins, "Bruni manuscripts"
J. Hankins, "Bruni Manuscripts in North America: A Handlist," in *Per Il Censimento dei Codici dell'Epistolario di Leonardo Bruni. Seminario Internazionale di Studi, Firenze, 30 ottobre 1987*, eds. Lucia Gualdo Rosa and Paolo Viti. Nuovi studi storici 10 (1991) 55–90

Harvard College Library, *Illuminated and Calligraphic Manuscripts*
Harvard College Library, *Illuminated and Calligraphic Manuscripts* (Cambridge, Mass. 1955)

HE
C. Wordsworth, ed., *Horae Eboracenses.* Surtees Society 132 (Durham and London 1920)

Houghton Library 1942–1967
Harvard College Library, *The Houghton Library 1942–1967. A Selection of Books and Manuscripts in Harvard Collections* (Cambridge, Mass. 1967)

Houghton Library Report
Harvard College Library, *The Houghton Library Report of Accessions* (Cambridge, Mass. 1942–)

Hourlier and du Moustier, "Le Calendrier cartusien"
Jacques Hourlier and Benôit du Moustier, "Le Calendrier cartusien," *Études Grégoriennes* 2 (1957) 151–61.

Kaeppeli, *SOPMA*
Thomas Kaeppeli, O.P., *Scriptores ordinis praedicatorum medii aevi* (Rome 1970–)

Ker, *MLGB*
N. R. Ker, *Medieval Libraries of Great Britain. A List of Surviving Books*, 2nd. ed. (London 1964)

Ker, *MMBL*
N. R. Ker, *Medieval Manuscripts in British Libraries* (Oxford 1969–)

Kottler, "The Vulgate Tradition"
Barnet Kottler, "The Vulgate Traditon of the *Consolatio Philosophiae* in the Fourteenth Century," *Mediaeval Studies* 17 (1955) 209–14

Krämer, *Handschriftenerbe*
Sigrid Krämer, *Handschriftenerbe des deutschen Mittelalters.* Mittelalterliche Bibliothekskataloge Deutschlands und der Schweiz, Ergänzungsband 1 (Munich 1989)

Kristeller, *Iter*
Paul Oskar Kristeller, *Iter italicum accedunt alia itinera* (London and Leiden 1963–90)

Lambert, *Bibliotheca Hieronymiana*
Bernard Lambert, O.S.B., *Bibliotheca hieronymiana manuscripta.* Instrumenta Patristica 4 (Steenbrugge 1969–72)

Leroquais, *LH*
V. Leroquais, *Les Livres d'heures manuscrits de la Bibliothèque Nationale* (Paris 1927–43)

Light, *Bible in the Twelfth Century*
Laura Light, *The Bible in the Twelfth Century. An Exhibition of Manuscripts at the Houghton Library* (Cambridge, Mass. 1988)

Lyell Cat.
Albinia de la Mare, *Catalogue of the Collection of Medieval Manuscripts Bequeathed to the Bodleian Library Oxford by James P. R. Lyell* (Oxford 1971)

Marks, *Library of the Charterhouse of St. Barbara in Cologne*
Richard Bruce Marks, *The Medieval Manuscript Library of the Charterhouse of St. Barbara in Cologne.* Analecta Cartusiana 21–22 (Salzburg 1974)

Meer, *Atlas de l'ordre cistercien*
Frédérick van der Meer, *Atlas de l'ordre cistercien* (Amsterdam-Brussels 1965)

MGH
Monumenta Germaniae historica

Morison, *Byzantine Elements*
S. Morison, *Byzantine Elements in Humanistic Script illustrated from the Aulus Gellius of 1445 in the Newberry Library* (Chicago 1952)

Morison, *Politics and Script*
S. Morison, *Politics and Script: Aspects of Authority and Freedom in the Development of Graeco-Latin Script from the Sixth Century BC to the Twentieth Century AD*, ed. N. Barber (Oxford 1972)

Munby, *Phillipps Studies*
A. N. L. Munby, *Phillipps Studies* (Cambridge 1951–60)

OCT
Oxford Classical Texts

Parkes, *Keble College*
M. B. Parkes, *The Medieval Manuscripts of Keble College Oxford* (London 1979)

Pellegrin
Elisabeth Pellegrin, J. Fohlen, C. Jeudy, Y.-F. Riou and A. Marucchi, *Les Manuscrits classiques latins de la Bibliothèque Vaticane*. Documents, Études et Répertoires publiés par l'Institut de Recherche et d'Histoire des Textes 21 (Paris 1975–82)

Perdrizet
Paul Perdrizet, *Le Calendrier parisien à la fin du moyen âge*. Publications de la faculté de lettres de l'Université de Strasbourg 63 (Paris 1933)

Phillipps Cat.
The Phillipps Manuscripts. Catalogus librorum manuscriptorum in bibliotheca D. Thomae Phillipps, B.T. impressum typis Medio-Montanis 1837–1871, reprint with intro by A. N. L. Munby (London 1968)

Piccard
G. Piccard, *Die Wasserzeichenkartei Piccard im Haupstaatsarchiv Stuttgart* (Stuttgart 1961–)

PL
J. P. Migne, *Patrologia latina*

Quentin, *Mémoire*
H. Quentin, *Mémoire sur l'établissement du texte de la Vulgate*. Collectanea Biblica Latina 6 (Rome and Paris 1922)

RH
Ulysse Chevalier, *Repertorium hymnologicum* (Louvain 1892–1912, Brussels 1920–21)

Rietstap
J. B. Rietstap, *Armorial général*, 2nd. ed. (Gouda 1884–87; plates 1903–26 and Supplements 1926–51 by V. Rolland and H. Rolland)

Robothan and Cranz
Dorothy Robothan and F. Edward Cranz, *A. Persius Flaccus*. CTC 3 (Washington, D.C. 1976)

Sarum Breviary
Franciscus Procter and Christopher Wordsworth, eds., *Breviarium ad usum insignis ecclesiae sarum* (Cambridge 1879–86)

Scarcia Piacentini
Paola Scarcia Piacentini, "Saggio di un censimento dei manoscritti contenenti il testo de Persio e gli scoli e i commenti al testo," *Studi sulla tradizione di Persio e la scoliastica persiana Serie II.* Studi su Persio e la Scoliastica Persiana 3.1 (Rome 1972)

Schneyer
Johannes Baptist Schneyer, *Repertorium der lateinischen Sermones des Mittelalters für die Zeit von 1150–1350.* Beiträge zur Geschichte der Philosophie und Theologie des Mittelalters 43 (Münster 1969–80)

Shailor, *Beinecke Cat.*
Barbara Shailor, *Catalogue of Medieval and Renaissance Manuscripts in the Beinecke Rare Book and Manuscript Library, Yale University.* Medieval and Renaissance Texts and Studies 34, 48, and 100 (Binghamton, N.Y. 1984, 1987, 1992)

Sonet
J. Sonet, *Répertoire d'incipit de prières en ancien français.* Société de publications romanes et françaises 54 (Geneva 1956)

Stegmüller
Fridericus Stegmüller, *Repertorium biblicum medii aevi* (Madrid 1950–61), and *Supplement*, with the assistance of N. Reinhardt (Madrid 1976–80)

Thorndike and Kibre
Lynn Thorndike and P. Kibre, *A Catalogue of Incipits of Mediaeval Scientific Writings in Latin.* Mediaeval Academy of America Publications 29, 2nd. ed. (Cambridge, Mass. 1963)

Ullman, *Humanistic Script*
B. L. Ullman, *The Origin and Development of Humanistic Script* (Rome 1960)

Van Dijk, *Ordinal*

Stephen J. P. Van Dijk and Joan Hazeldon Walker, *The Ordinal of the Papal Court from Innocent III to Boniface VIII and Related Documents.* Spicilegium friburgense 22 (Fribourg 1975)

Van Dijk, *SMRL*

Stephen J. P. Van Dijk, *Sources of the Modern Roman Liturgy.* Studia et documenta franciscana 1–2 (Leiden 1963)

Walters Art Gallery, *Calligraphy*

Baltimore, Museum of Art, Peabody Institute Library and Walters Art Gallery, *2,000 Years of Calligraphy* (Baltimore, Maryland 1965)

Walther, *Initia*

Hans Walther, *Initia carminum ac uersuum medii aevi poterioris latinorum.* Carmina medii aevi posterioris latina 1 (Göttingen 1959)

Walther, *Proverbia*

Hans Walther, *Proverbia sententiaeque latinitatis medii aevi. Lateinische Sprichwörter und Sentenzen des Mittelalters in alphabetischer Anordnung.* Carmina medii aevi posterioris latina 2 (Göttingen 1963–67, and new series in progress)

Wieck

Roger S. Wieck, *Late Medieval and Renaissance Illuminated Manuscripts, 1350–1525* (Cambridge, Mass. 1983)

Wilmart

A. Wilmart, *Auteurs spirituels et textes dévots du moyen âge latin* (Paris 1932; reprint 1971)

Winsor

Justin Winsor, ed., "The Collection of Books and Autographs Bequeathed to Harvard College Library by the Honorable Charles Sumner," *Harvard University Library. Bibliographical Contributions* 6 (Cambridge, Mass. 1879)

Wordsworth
Iohannes Wordsworth, Henricus Iulianus White, et al., eds., *Novum Testamentum domini nostri Iesu Christi latine* (Oxford 1889–1954)

Wright, ed., *Walter Mapes*
Thomas Wright, ed., *The Latin Poems Commonly Attributed to Walter Mapes*. Camden Society Publications 16 (London 1841)

List of Manuscripts

MS Lat 3: Angelus Callimachus, Libellus de oratione dominica
Northeastern Italy (Venice or Padua) s. XV^{ex} (1492–1516)

MS Lat 4: Book of Hours, fragment
Northern France s. XV/XVI

MS Lat 5: Conradus Holtnicker de Saxonia, O.F.M., Sermones de sanctis
Germany s. XIII^{ex}–XIV^{1}

fMS Lat 6: Sapiential Books with the Ordinary Gloss
Northeastern France or Flanders s. XIII$^{2/4}$

MS Lat 9: Jacobus de Voragine, Sermones de tempore
Germany (Cologne) 1452

fMS Lat 12: Walter Burley, Expositio super artem veterem, libri I et II
Italy (Padua) 1442

MS Lat 15: Henricus de Freimar, O.E.S.A.; Gerardus de Fracheto
Germany s. XV^{1} (?)

MS Lat 17: Book of Hours, use of Paris
Northern France s. XV/XVI

MS Lat 18: Ovid, Heroides
Italy (Florence) 1416

fMS Lat 27: Lives of Saints Anselm, Odo, Majolus, Odilo, and Hugh
England s. XII^{2}

MS Lat 34: Historia de preliis Alexandri Magni (recension J^{3})
Italy (Bologna?) s. XIII^{ex}–XIV^{1}

fMS Lat 35: Guido de Columnis, Historia destructionis troiae
Italy (Bologna or Venice?) 1353

fMS Lat 36: Bible
France (Paris) s. XIII/XIV

MS Lat 37: Ps. Cicero, Rhetorica ad Herennium
Northeastern Italy s. XV$^{2/4}$

fMS Lat 38: Aristotle, Logical Treatises in Latin Translation
Spain s. XIII$^{4/4}$–XIV$^{1/4}$
fMS Lat 39: Aristotle, Politica, Rhetorica et Magna Moralia in Latin Translation
France s. XIV^{1}
MS Lat 40: Juvenal, Saturae
Italy (Bologna) 1462
MS Lat 41: Cornelius Nepos, Vitae
Northeastern Italy s. XV^{2}
fMS Lat 42: Ovid, Works
Northern Italy (Verona) s. XV$^{3/4}$
MS Lat 43: Plautus, Comoediae VIII
Italy (Florence) s. XV$^{3/4}$
MS Lat 44: Priscian, Institutiones grammaticae
France s. XII$^{2/4}$
MS Lat 45: Terence, Comoediae
Germany s. XV^{2}
MS Lat 46: Tibullus, Carmina; Ovid, Epistula Sapphus, etc.
Italy (Florence) s. XV^{med}
MS Lat 47: Seneca, Tragoediae
Italy (Northeast?) 1432
MS Lat 48: Valerius Maximus, Factorum et dictorum memorabilium libri
Central Italy s. XIV$^{2/4}$
MS Lat 49: Ps. Plutarch, De liberis educandis
Northeastern Italy s. XV$^{2/4\text{–}med}$
MS Lat 50: Bible, part
Southern Germany s. XV$^{3/4}$
MS Lat 51: Boethius; Ps. Dionysius the Areopagite
Germany s. XIV^{1}
MS Lat 111: Carthusian Breviary for Terce, Sext and None
France s. XVI^{1} (after 1515)
MS Lat 112: Charter
England 1366
MS Lat 115: Dominican Portable Breviary
Germany s. XIII^{2}
MS Lat 116: Ranulf Higden, Polychronicon
England s. XIV^{2}; s. XV

MS Lat 117: Evangelium Nicodemi
France s. XIV^{2}
fMS Lat 119: Aristotle, Physica in Latin Translation, fragment
England s. XIII^{2}
MS Lat 120: Prosdocimo de' Beldomandi, Canones de motibus corporum supercoelestium
Italy (Northeast?) s. XV^{med}
fMS Lat 121: Miscellany
Austria 1433; s. XV^{1}
MS Lat 122: Extracts from Historia de preliis Alexandri Magni (recension J^{2}), and Godefridus de Viterbo, Pantheon
Germany s. XV
MS Lat 124: Humanist Anthology: Translations and Other Texts
Italy (Florence) s. XV$^{2/4}$; s. XV$^{3/4}$
MS Lat 125: Thomas of Cantimpré, Liber de natura rerum
England s. XIII^{ex}–s. XIV^{in}
MS Lat 126: Commentary on Boethius, Philosophiae consolatio
Italy s. XV
MS Lat 127: Boethius, Philosophiae consolatio
England s. XII$^{4/4}$
pfMS Lat 128: Gradual
Italy s. XVI
MS Lat 129: Breviary
Germany 1474–77
fMS Lat 130: Fragment of a Noted Breviary
Southern Italy s. XII^{2}
MS Lat 132: Book of Hours, use of Rome
Flanders s. XV$^{2/4}$
MS Lat 133: Book of Hours, use of Rouen
Northern France s. XV$^{4/4}$
MS Lat 134: Prayers for Exorcism; Benedictions, etc.
Germany s. XIV^{2}
MS Lat 135: Juvenal; Persius
Northern Italy s. XV^{2}
MS Lat 136: Juvenal; Persius
Italy (Northeast?) 1471
MS Lat 137: Persius, Saturae; Commentarius in Persii
Italy (Florence?) s. XV$^{1/4}$

MS Lat 138: Persius, Saturae
Northeastern Italy s. XV$^{3/4}$
fMS Lat 139: Persius, Saturae
France s. XV^{2}
MS Lat 143: Fragment of a Letter
England s. XVI
MS Lat 144: Franciscus Barbarus, De re uxoria
Italy (Venice?) s. XV$^{1/4}$
MS Lat 145: Juvenal; Perisus; Batrachomyomachia
Northeastern Italy s. XV$^{3/4}$
MS Lat 146: Poetry
Bohemia (Prague?) s. XV^{1}
MS Lat 150: Augustinus, Confessiones
Southern Europe s. XII$^{2/4}$
MS Lat 154: Geoffrey of Vinsauf, Poetria nova
Italy s. XIV
MS Lat 155: Persius, Saturae
Northern Italy (Venice?) s. XV^{ex}
fMS Lat 156: Sacramentary, fragment ("The Arno Sacramentary")
Austria (Salzburg) s. IX^{in}
fMS Lat 157: Fragment of a Noted Breviary
Southern Italy s. XII^{2}
MS Lat 158: Remigius of Auxerre, Expositio missae
Germany s. XII$^{3/4}$
MS Lat 159: Book of Hours, use of Paris
Northern France (Paris?) s. XV$^{3/4}$
MS Lat 160: Book of Hours, use of Paris
Northern France (Paris?) s. XVI$^{1/4}$
MS Lat 161: Book of Hours, use of Rome
Flanders (Bruges?) s. XV$^{3/4}$
MS Lat 162: University of Vienna, Theological Disputations
Austria (Vienna) s. XV$^{2/4\text{-}med}$
MS Lat 163: Franciscus Barbarus, De re uxoria
Italy (Florence) s. XV$^{4/4}$
MS Lat 165: Speculum humanae salvationis; Richard Rolle, etc.
England s. XV^{1}
MS Lat 167: Gregory the Great, Moralia in Job, books 23–29
Belgium or Germany s. XII$^{3/4}$

fMS Lat 168: Hieronymus, Commentariorum in Danielem
Italy (Central or Tuscany) s. XII$^{2/4}$

fMS Lat 169: Jacobus de Cessolis, De ludo scaccorum
Germany (Southwest) s. XV^{2}

MS Lat 170: Leonardo Bruni Aretino, De bello italico adversus gothos
Northern Italy s. XV$^{med-3/4}$

MS Lat 171: Franciscan Breviary
Italy (Florence?) 1465

fMS Lat 172: Thomas Aquinas, Catena aurea in Mattheum
Northeastern France or Germany s. XIV^{1}

MS Lat 173: Penitential psalms, litanies, etc. for Dominican use
Germany s. XV^{2}

MSS Lat 174–175: Ps. Cicero; Ps. Boethius
Italy (Venice?) s. XV^{1}

MS Lat 176: Cicero, Tusculanae disputationes
Italy (Florence) s. XV$^{4/4}$

MS Lat 177: Cicero, De officiis
Italy (Rome or Florence) s. XV^{med}

MS Lat 178: Boethius, Philosophiae consolatio
Northern Italy s. XV$^{1/4}$

MS Lat 179: Boethius, Philosophiae consolatio
Southern France or Spain s. XIV^{2}

MS Lat 3 NE Italy (Venice or Padua) s. XV^{ex} (1492–1516)
Angelus Callimachus, Libellus de oratione dominica Pl. 12

ff. 1–27 [Preface] *Ad Praestantissimum Patrem Et Meritissimum Rhavenatem Antistitem Philiam Roverellam Angeli Callimachi Sicvli In Libellvm De Oratione Praefatio.* Cvm multe [*sic*] et variae sint disciplinae pientissime pater illa profecto reiectis affectibus quibus mortales tantopere laborant ... et ea tuo celeberrimo nomini dedicabo. *Divinis Tantvm Sapientia Vera Refvlget Quam Svmmo Stvdio Qvi Cvpit Ille Sapit.* [f. 5 text] *Interlocvtores Petrvs Lvcerinus Praesvl Et Callimachvs Sicvlvs.* Qvm [*sic*] ex Pannonia in italiam rediissem post inclyti Regis Matthiae mortem que omne consilium meum et uitae rationes discussit ... et ita deum optimum maximum precamur. *Finis.* ΤΩ Θεωχλριε. [Ff. 27v–29v blank, but ruled.]

The text, written as a dialogue between the author, Angelo Callimaco (fl. s. XV^{med}–XVI^{in}) and Pietro Ransano, bishop of Lucera (d. 1492), and dedicated to Filasio Roverella, Bishop of Ravenna (1476–1516, d. 1521), has never been printed; see G. Schizzerotto, "Angelo Callimaco," *DBI* (Rome 1973) 16:754–57.

Marginal annotations in red by the scribe or contemporary in an italic script, more informal than the script of the main text, including names of authors in the text, or, infrequently, brief comments on the contents (cf. ff. 3v, 7v, etc.), added after the manuscript was rubricated (cf. f. 6, where this hand adds an 'h' to "Callimacus," written in blue). Quotations underlined and paragraph and nota marks (scalloped lines alongside text or pointing hands as on f. 9) added in red, likely by the same hand. Omission in text, f. 19v, supplied in a different contemporary hand, possibly by the scribe. Later note in a formal italic script, s. XVI, f. 19v: "non in solo pane uiuit. . ."

Parchment, ff. iii (paper with unidentified armorial watermark, surmounted by crown, obscured in gutter) + 30 (incorrectly foliated 1–29, with f. 10 bis) + iii (paper), 192 x 133 (122 x 70–68) mm. 24 long lines. Ruled lightly in brown ink; double full-length vertical bounding lines, sometimes used for the first majuscule of a new section of text.

1^{11} (structure uncertain) 2^{10} 3^{10} (–10, cancelled). Vertical catchwords, lower margin, written along the inner bounding line, decoratively encircled in red.

Written above the top line by one scribe in a sloping italic script, using straight 's' written on the line except in the last line of a page, and round 's' finally; possibly by the same scribe as Ravenna, Biblioteca Classense, MS 94, Raffaele Brandolini, *Proverbia* (see *DBI* 16:755).

Five-line gold initial, f. 1, on a dark maroon ground edged in gold and bronze, and infilled with stylized foliage in gold; bottom margin, the coat of arms of Filasio Roverella, Bishop of Ravenna (per pale: 1, or a demi-eagle displayed sable, crowned or; 2, or an uprooted tree proper fruited or; cf. Rietstap, v. 5, pl. 203), flanked by two winged putti, executed in pen and ink with careful shading, with touches of pink and yellow. Similar 2-line gold initials, ff. 5 and 6. Top margin, f. 1, opening rubric in gold epigraphic capitals on a deep blue scroll, edged in shaded gold or bronze; f. 4v, final words of preface in red epigraphic capitals, enclosed in crossed laurel branches in green and brown; rubric, f. 5, in gold epigraphic capitals on a rectangular blue ground, edged in gold and bronze. Opening words of the prologue and text, ff. 1 and 5, in square capitals with alternate lines in red and green, and red and blue, respectively. Text is written as a dialogue with the names of speakers in square capitals within the line of text, alternately red and blue. Rubrics in red. When the beginning of a new section of the text coincides with the beginning of a line, the first majuscule is placed between the outer bounding lines; remaining sections begin with a red paragraph mark.

Bound in English mottled calf, s. XVIII, gold-tooled with narrow double borders; author and title in gold on spine; edges dyed red; rebacked with spine laid down.

Written in the late fifteenth century, likely in Venice or Padua, as indicated by the script and decoration (we thank Professor A. C. de la Mare for this information; in correspondence March, 1983; August, 1987). The *Libellus* seems to have originally been dedicated to Pietro Ransano, bishop of Lucera. This manuscript can be dated after his death in 1492, since the work was subsequently dedicated to Filasio Roverella, Bishop of Ravenna (1476–1516), and this is the dedication copy (with his arms, f. 1). Unidentified shelf mark in brown ink, front flyleaf, f. ii: "0.5.14." In England s. XVIII, when the book was bound. Belonged to John Adrian Louis Hope, the seventh Earl of Hopetoun (1860–1908; armorial bookplate, inside front cover, with shelf mark in brown ink: "T–15"); his sale, London, Sotheby's, February 25 and three following days, 1889, no. 173 to Matthews (clipping glued on front flyleaf, f. i^{v}). Unidentified bookseller's note (?) in black ink, front flyleaf, f. ii: "- x." Belonged to Daniel B. Fearing (1859–1918; bookplate, front flyleaf, f.i); his gift to Morris Hickey Morgan (1859–1910; note in Fearing's hand, front flyleaf, f. i; Morgan's bookplate, front flyleaf, f. i^{v}). Purchased from his estate, July 7, 1910 (Salisbury fund; library stamp, f. 1v; bookplate, front flyleaf, f. i).

secundo folio: Liquido cognoscens

Bibliography: De Ricci, 976; Wieck, p. 107 and fig. 58 (reproducing f. 1); Kristeller, *Iter* 5:226.

MS Lat 4 — Northern France s. XV/XVI
Book of Hours, fragment — Pl. 30

ff. 1–16 Seven penitential psalms, followed immediately by the antiphon, f. 11: "Ne reminiscaris [printed *Sarum Breviary* 2:250]," and "Parce domine parce populo tuo redimisti precioso sanguine . . . [following the antiphon immediately, with no break]," and the litany, ff. 11v–15v, including Firminus, Quentin, Lucianus, patron of Beauvais, Denis, and Clarus among the martyrs, Eligius, Germar, and Ebrulf among the confessors, and Angadrisima among the Virgins. Concludes with prayers: f. 15v "Omnipotens sempiterne deus dirige actus nostros in bene placito tuo . . ."; f. 15v "Deus cui proprium est misereri semper et parcere suscipe deprecationem nostram . . . [printed *HE*, 97]"; ff. 15v–16 "Fidelium deus omnium conditor et redemptor animabus omnium fidelium defunctorum . . . [Bruylants, *Oraisons* 2: no. 567; printed *HE*, 30 and 98]"; f. 16 "Deus a quo sancta desideria recta consilia . . . [Bruylants, *Oraisons* 2: no. 201]." [F. 16v blank, but ruled.]

Parchment, ff. iii (paper) + 16 + i (paper), 195 x 133 (99–97 x 73–71) mm. 15 long lines. Ruled lightly in brown ink, with the top and bottom horizontal rules full across; single full-length vertical bounding lines. Prickings in the three outer margins.

$1–2^8$. Quire and leaf signatures in ink, bottom, outer margin, recto, with a letter designating the quire and an arabic numeral, the leaf.

Written below the top line by one scribe in a liturgical gothic script.

One 4-line blue initial, f. 1, with white highlights resembling three-dimensional ribbons, on a square gold-patterned brown ground, in-filled with a delicate red-brown vine, leaves, and small orange flowers on brushed gold; compartment panel borders, top and inside margins, with similar vines and orange and blue flowers on grounds of alternately brushed gold and black (tarnished silver?). 2- to 1-line gold initials throughout on square grounds, alternately blue and red-brown, edged with gold, with interiors of initials and grounds decorated with scrolls and other motifs in gold; similar bar line-fillers. Some majuscules in text highlighted with very pale yellow.

Bound, s. XIX (dated by De Ricci ca. 1850) in English brown calf, blind-tooled with an outer border of triple rules with rosettes in the corners, and a simple garland border along the inner rule; center ornament of a floral garland surrounding the title ("Psalmi Penitentiales Septem") in gilt; gilt edges. Rebacked with the spine laid down.

Written in Northern France in the late fifteenth or early sixteenth century for use in the diocese of Beauvais, as indicated by the saints in the litany, in particular Lucianus, Clarus, Germar, Ebrulf and Angadrisima. Most likely once part of a book of hours; these leaves were removed by the nineteenth century (date of the present binding). Front flyleaf, f. ii, initials, "G.A.S." in red ink, inscribed above a cross, with date, 1843. Booksellers' notes in pencil, back flyleaf: "F.," "xdc/-," and price, "1/1/-." Traces of paper remain, verso of back flyleaf, probably from a label or description. Purchased, June 30, 1868, by John Harvey Treat (1839–1908), historiographer, M. A. Harvard 1862 (bookplate, inside front cover, with date in ink, and price code[?], "AKEE"); his bequest to Harvard College, October 28, 1909 (library bookplate, inside front cover). Typed library description glued to front flyleaf, f. i.

Bibliography: De Ricci, 976.

MS Lat 5 Germany s. XIIIex–XIV[1]
Conradus Holtnicker de Saxonia, O.F.M., **Pl. 34**
Sermones de sanctis

ff. 1–17v [rubric omitted; *De sancto Johanne Baptista*] Multi in natiuitate eius gaudebunt. Luc. 1[:14]. Hoc in beatissimo Iohanne hodie et in omni anno impletur . . . sed corpora ad huc misera remanent . . . [f. 17 rubric omitted; *De Sancto Bartholomaeo*] Tulerunt pallium meum custodes murorum etc. Cant. 5[:7]. Ciuitas quedam est mundus . . . Similiter dico de aliis sanctis. S[?]//

Fragment of a larger manuscript including twenty-four sermons, beginning with John the Baptist (24 June) and ending imperfectly in the sermon for Bartholomew (24 August); Schneyer 1:767–69, nos. 296–97, 299–314, 316–17, 319–20, and 324–25; this manuscript not included among those listed by Schneyer 1:777–79; printed, Paris 1521 and Brescia 1596, where they are attributed to St. Bonaventure (editions not available for consultation). In general, see P. Samuele Girotto, O.F.M., *Corrado di Sassonia, predicatore e mariologo del sec. XIII.* Biblioteca di studi francescani 3 (Florence 1952) 32–46, and Conradus de Saxonia, O.F.M., *Speculum seu salutatio beatae mariae virginis ac sermones mariani*, ed. Petrus de Alcantara Martinez (Grottaferrata 1975) 17–57.

Contemporary marginal annotations listing the initials of authors cited in the text in red, possibly by the scribe (cf. ff. 3, 3v, 8v, etc.; in black, f. 17v). Infrequent brief notes on the contents in a cursive hand, s. XIV–XV (cf. ff. 3, 3v). F. 14v, bottom margin, contemporary note on the soul, here ascribed to Augustine. F. 17v, two verses in another contemporary hand (Walther, *Initia* 12385).

Parchment, ff. ii (unnumbered paper) + 16 (incorrect modern foliation in pencil, bottom inside corner, 1–12, *14–17) + ii (unnumbered paper), 225–224 x 167–164, unevenly trimmed (194–193 x 144–135) mm. Two columns, 40–38 lines. Ruled in brown ink with the top 2 or the top and third, and the bottom and penultimate or only the bottom horizontal lines full across on many folios; on other folios the horizontal rules are indiscernible (cf. ff. 1v–4 and 8v–12); single full-length vertical bounding lines. Prickings, outer margin, alongside the vertical bounding lines, and on some folios, in the top and bottom margins.

1^{12} 2^{4}.

Written above the top line, by at least two scribes, with the first scribe copying ff. 1–17 col. b, line 33 in a well-spaced gothic bookhand; the second scribe continued to the end in a gothic bookhand.

Two- to 1-line red initials (with 'I' extending up to 4 lines), usually plain, but a few with red pen flourishes in a style one would expect in an older manuscript (cf. ff. 2v and 16v); red paragraph marks. No rubrics.

Bound in modern black half sheepskin; in very poor condition, with both covers detached, and with only fragments of the spine remaining.

Written in Germany at the end of the thirteenth or the first half of the fourteenth century; almost certainly once part of a longer manuscript, presumably with the complete sermon cycle. Added top margin, f. 1, in ink, s. XIX–XX, "Commentarius in sacras scripturae, Cent. XIV." Purchased February 8, 1867 by John Harvey Treat (1839–1908), historiographer, M.A. Harvard 1862, for $3.10 (bookplate, inside front cover, with date and price, $3.10, in ink). His bequest, October 28, 1909 (bookplate, inside front cover; library stamp, bottom margin, f. 1v). Typed description pasted on the front flyleaf, f. i, probably dating after the acquisition of the book by Harvard, and an earlier handwritten note in ink, signed on the back by Bertha Magee describing the manuscript as an old book, 593 years old, containing six biblical commentaries; later note, dated 1913, states that this note was found in the book, and that the information cannot be verified.

secundo folio: magnus effectus est

Bibliography: De Ricci, 976.

fMS Lat 6 — NE France or Flanders s. XIII$^{2/4}$
Sapiential Books with the Ordinary Gloss — Pl. 24

1. ff. 1–49v Proverbs; f. 1 [prologue, written as a gloss] Jeronimus. Iungat epistola quos iungit sacerdotium . . . [Stegmüller 457]; f. 1 [first gloss] Parabole salomonis secundum hebraicam ueritatem translate . . . [Stegmüller 11802, listed third]; f. 1 [second gloss] Notandum quod uulgata editio parabolas que hebraice masloth patrohemias [*sic*] id est prouerbia dicit . . . [Stegmüller 11802, listed first; Bede, *PL* 91:938]; . . . f. 49rv [last gloss] "Date ei de fructu

manuum suarum etc. [Proverbs 31:31]," hoc uir ille de quo supra dictum est [Proverbs 31:28], uir eius et laudabit . . . et probante ac remunerante deo cui est honor et gloria in secula seculorum. Amen [Stegmüller 11802, last gloss; Bede, *PL* 91:1052].

2. ff. 49v–65 Ecclesiastes; f. 49v [first gloss] Jeronimus. Tribus nominibus uocatus est Salomon, id est pacificus . . . et nescit se regem esse [Stegmüller 11803, listed first; Jerome, *PL* 23:1063–65; related to Stegmüller 456]; f. 49v [prologue, written as a gloss] Memini me hoc ferme quinquennio cum adhuc rome essem . . . [Stegmüller 462]; f. 49v [second gloss] Gregorius. Quomodo hic liber sit legendus et exponendus sic dicit . . . [Stegmüller 11803, listed second; Gregory, *PL* 77:324–25; Alcuin, *PL* 100:670–71]; . . . f. 64v [concluding glosses] Legitur enim salomon deum offendisse . . . [Stegmüller 11803, listed eighth]; ff. 64v–65 Notandum etiam quod non omnes sententie que hic ponuntur . . . [Stegmüller 11803, listed ninth]; ff. 64v–65 [last gloss] Stabat amos supra morum litus [*sic*]. Et dixit dominus ad eum . . . in hoc libro loquitur ad populum iam penitentem [Stegmüller 11803, listed seventh]; f. 65 [chapter list to Wisdom, following immediately, copied in a glossing hand; not printed in *Biblia sacra* or de Bruyne, *Sommaires*, but with some similarities to *Biblia sacra*, 12:12–13, series B] De diligendo iusticia. De cogitationibus impiorum. De sanctis martiribus. De meritis impiorum . . . De bona hospitalitate.

3. ff. 65v–84 Canticles; f. 65v [first gloss] Salomon id est pacificus quia in regno eius pax per quam pax futura ecclesie figuratur [*sic*] . . . et quem [*sic*] in his profecisse uident ad theoricam usque perducunt [Stegmüller 11804, listed second]; f. 65v [second gloss] Materia sponsus et sponsa, id est caput et ecclesia . . . [Stegmüller 11804, listed third]; . . . ff. 83v–84 [last two glosses] "Assimilare [Canticles 8:14]." Ita fuge ut creberrime per gratiam compunctionis fidelium cordibus appareas . . . [Stegmüller 11804, penultimate gloss]; f. 84 [concluding gloss] Tria sunt oscula primum pedum [*sic*] . . . desiderat ab ipso osculum postulat. Osculetur me osculoris sui. [Ends top f. 84; remainder blank.]

4. ff. 84v–109 Wisdom; f. 84v [prologue, written as a gloss] Liber sapientie apud hebreos nusquam est . . . [Stegmüller 468]; f. 84v [first gloss] Rabanus. Hunc librum ieronimus asserit non a salo-

mone ut putatur [*sic*]... [Stegmüller 11805; listed first; Rabanus, *PL* 109:671–72]; ... f. 109 [last gloss] Misericors et miserator dominus semper adest fidelibus suis ... multe enim tribulationes iustorum et de omnibus his liberauit eos dominus [Stegmüller 11805; concluding gloss; Rabanus, *PL* 109:762; ends top f. 109; remainder blank.]

5. ff. 109v–167v Ecclesiasticus, lacking the biblical introduction "Multorum nobis"; f. 109v [prologue, written as a gloss] Librum ihesu filii sirach dicit se ieronimus apud hebreos repperisse ... [Stegmüller 473]; f. 109v [first gloss] Rabanus. "Omnis sapientia a domino deo, etc. [Ecclesiasticus 1:1]." Incipit ab eterna dei sapientia que christus est ... [Stegmüller 11806, listed first]; ... f. 167v [last gloss] Dum lucem habetis, credite in lucem ut sitis filii lucis. [f. 167v text with interlinear gloss (in parentheses)] ... et dabit uobis mercedem [Ecclesiasticus 51:38] (remunerationem eternam) uestram in tempore (iudicio) suo (metemus non deficientes). Amen [Stegmüller 11806, listed last]. *Expliciunt quinque libri salomonis* [added above in a later hand: *melius sapientiales*]. [Ends mid f. 167v; remainder blank.]

Sapiential Books with the *Glossa ordinaria*; printed in M.T. Gibson and K. Froehlich, eds., *Biblia latina cum glossa ordinaria* (Louvain 1992) [facsimile of the *editio princeps* of the Glossed Bible, 1480]. Text of the Gloss is generally similar to that described in Stegmüller 11802–11806, although the order of the glosses sometimes differs, and some passages are omitted. Includes prologues not listed by Stegmüller, copied in a glossing script before the biblical text. Prologues such as these were sometimes copied as text (cf. for example, Paris, Bibliothèque nationale, MS lat. 131, Glossed Canticles and Minor Prophets, Northern France, s. XII$^{4/4}$; and Paris, Bibilothèque nationale, MS lat. 1558, Glossed Matthew, Paris, s. XIII$^{1/4}$). Modern chapter divisions throughout.

Comments, usually brief, including frequent cross references to other books of the Bible, added throughout in a minute, neat noting hand, s. XIII; a skeletal distinction of "diluuium" in this hand, f. 159v. Occasional notes in later hands: cf. f. 64, s. XIV, in lead, and f. 167v, s. XIV–XV, in ink.

Parchment, ff. i (paper) + 167 + i (paper), 417 x 292 (text and gloss: 255–242 x 144–146) mm. 3 columns (two columns of equal size with a wider outer column), 53–49 lines. Ruled in lead with the top 2 (except f. 1, top 3) and bottom 2 horizontal lines full across; double full-length vertical bounding lines; some folios with an additional set of narrow double rules in the outer margin. Layout varies from 1 to 3 columns, depending on the ratio of text to gloss, using one basic ruling pattern for all pages. Biblical text copied in a larger script, every other line; the Gloss copied every line in a smaller script. Pages pricked in all four margins (used for ruling text and gloss). On the development of the "alternate line" layout, see Christopher de Hamel, *Glossed Books of the Bible and the Origins of the Paris Booktrade* (Woodbridge, Suffolk, and Dover, New Hampshire 1984) 23–27.

$1\text{–}4^{10}$ 5^{8} 6^{10} 7^{8} $8\text{–}10^{10}$ 11^{8} $12\text{–}17^{10}$ 18^{3} (1, f. 165, + conjugate pair). Horizontal catchwords, lower inside margin (lacking in quires 5, 16 and 17, ff. 48v, 154v, 164v); leaf and quire signatures in very faint lead in most quires, lower right margin, recto, with a letter designating the leaf and a sign designating the quire.

Text written in a formal gothic bookhand; the gloss is copied in a less formal gothic glossing script. Text copied below the top line; gloss begins below the top line, except when it is continued from the previous page. One scribe throughout.

Five 9- to 6-line (with the exception of 'P,' f. 1, 20-line) initials in blue and orange, orange, or pink and blue; with touches of yellow, edged with white dots and with white highlights, on geometrical grounds of polished gold, heavily edged in black and with interior vine scrolls, terminating in stylized leaves or animal heads at the beginning of the biblical books (except Ecclesiastes, with major initial at chapter l:2). Similar 6-line initial, f. 49v (Ecclesiastes 1:1) on a dark pink ground with white detailing, edged in black. The initials are well executed, but often seem too large for the page (cf. especially f. 84v). One 6-line parted red and blue initial with red and gray-green pen flourishes, f. 65v (Canticles, first gloss). 8- to 4-line blue initials with red pen flourishes, ff. 1 and 49v (prologue and first gloss, Proverbs and Ecclesiasticus). Chapters and smaller divisions within the biblical text begin with 2- to 1-line alternating red and blue initials with contrasting pen flourishes, usually simple, in red or gray-green. Chapter numbers, paragraph marks, and running headlines in red and blue. Tie marks used to indicate the continuation of a gloss. Some guide notes for running headlines and chapter numbers, in lead.

Chapter numbers added in brown ink, upper margin, recto, indicating the chapter of the Bible discussed on that opening.

Bound, s. XIX, possibly in Boston (see De Ricci) in half russia leather with pink-brown boards; title on spine in gold, with the initials "M. S. M." below. Slight stains (rust?), bottom, middle margin, f. 1, possibly from the metal fittings of an earlier binding.

Written in Northeastern France or Flanders in the second quarter of the thirteenth century. Although the style of the painted initials suggests the influence of Parisian work of about the same period (cf. Branner, *Manuscript Painting*, especially ateliers discussed on pp. 66–96), the colors, the polished gold grounds, the simplified shapes, and the size of the initials indicate that the book was likely not painted in Paris. The elaborate majuscules and the gray-green ink used for pen flourishes also suggest an origin outside of Paris. The large format of this manuscript is typical of thirteenth-century manuscripts of the *Glossa ordinaria*. Contents indicated, f. 1, in brown ink, s. XVII–XVIII, signed "R" or "B," possibly by an early owner. Given by the Massachusetts Historical Society to the Harvard Divinity School, November 24, 1908 (library note, front flyleaf, verso). Transferred to Harvard College Library, May 16, 1912 (library stamp, f. 1; bookplate, front flyleaf). No records exist of its earlier provenance (cf. the two letters pasted on the front flyleaf written to W. C. Lane from the Divinity School and the Massachusetts Historical Society in 1912, with negative responses to his inquiries about the provenance of the manuscript).

secundo folio: text: [tendicu]las contra
gloss: In fontem. Qui

Bibliography: De Ricci, 976; *Houghton Library 1942–1967*, 14 (with plate of f. 109v); Light, *Bible in the Twelfth Century*, 99–100, and plate 25 (of f. 77v); M. T. Gibson and K. Froehlich, eds., *Biblia latina cum glossa ordinaria* (Louvain 1992), plate 3 (of f. 84v).

MS Lat 9 Germany (Cologne) 1452
Jacobus de Voragine, O.P., Sermones de tempore Pls. 7, 63

ff. 1–200 [f. 1 Prologue] Humane labilis vite decursus salubri erudicione nos monet [*sic*] . . . et michi ad meritum pervenire [*sic*] concedat. [f. 1] *Dominica prima aduentus domini. Sermo primus.* "Preparare in occursum dei tui israel. Amos 4[:12]." Quando rex uel aliquis princeps maxime dignitatis ad ciuitatem aliquam est venturus . . . qui in celis est quo ad laudem operis ipse intrabit in regnum celorum . . . [f. 198v rubric omitted; 25th Sunday after Pentecost] "Ut autem impleti sunt, etc. [John 6:12]." Per istam ergo refectionem qua omnes sunt repleti intelligitur . . . sicut ipsa vita erit communis. Ad illum benedictum finem perducat nos ille que est principium et finis, qui sine fine viuit et regnat per infinita secula seculorum. Amen. *Expliciunt sermones dominicales per circulum anni a fratre Iacobo Ianuensis archiepiscopo editi ordinis fratrum predicatorum. Scripti per manus theodorici de alcmaria studentis in colonia, etc.* [F. 200v blank.]

Jacobus de Voragine, *Sermones de tempore*. Schneyer 3:221–35, not listing this manuscript. 160 sermons in the same order as those listed in Schneyer, from the first Sunday in Advent through the 25th Sunday after Pentecost. See also Kaeppeli, *SOPMA* 2156, listing additional manuscripts, not including this one. Printed Cologne 1467–69, and thereafter (cf. Kaeppeli, *SOPMA*, 364 and Copinger 6523–6546).

Corrections throughout by the scribe (for example, f. 51v) and by the hand supplying the red paragraph marks marking major divisions within the text and the red strokes marking the majuscules (for example ff. 5 and 74v, in red; f. 123v, supplying omitted word). Marginalia throughout including repetition of key ideas in the text (for example, ff. 123v–124), marking of *exempla* (for example, f. 149), and numbers indicating divisions within text and nota marks (cf. ff. 75–77).

Paper (heavily sized; watermark, similar to Piccard Traube I.189 and 190, Cologne, Rheinfelden 1445), ff. i (parchment pastedown, + 2 parchment stubs) + 200 + i (parchment pastedown, preceded by two parchment stubs), 282 x 209 (197–195 x 141–135) mm. 2 columns, 43–40 lines. Frame ruled in lead, with horizontal rules full across, and full-length vertical bounding lines. Prickings for each line in three outer margins.

1–5^{12} 6^{10} 7–16^{12} 17^{12} (–11, 12 cancelled with no loss of text; stubs remain). Horizontal catchwords, lower inside margins; carefully written quire and leaf signatures, lower outside margin, recto, with a letter on the first leaf only designating the quire, and arabic numerals designating the leaves (a1, 2, 3, . . . 6; b1, 2, 3, . . . 6, etc.); signatures trimmed in some quires.

Written below the top line in a small, very precise and controlled hybrida formata, using the *punctus* for all pauses.

Eight-line red initial, f. 1, with decorative void shapes within the body of the initial, and with purple pen flourishes and infilling forming a box around the initial, and extending into a border in the top and inner margins. Each sermon begins with 5- to 3-line (except 'I' up to 11 lines) red initials; initials executed by two hands: ff. 1–154v orange-red, usually plain, but occasionally with decorative void spaces within the body of the initial; ff. 155 (beginning quire 14)–end, darker red, with decorative finials, void spaces within the initial and sometimes with red pen flourishes. Rubrics supplied by the same two hands, consistently in orange-red through f. 154v, and sporadically in darker red from f. 155 to end. Majuscules within the text stroked with red. Names of biblical books and authors cited within the text underlined in red. Biblical lemmata at the beginning of each sermon usually underlined in red; divisions within each sermon marked by red paragraph marks. Notes to rubricator in pencil (cf. ff. 30, 83, 95v); scribe occasionally copied rubrics as part of the text at the conclusion of a sermon (for example ff. 14 and 17; also copied in red).

Bound, s. XV, in Germany, in wooden boards with a cushion bevel, covered with soft light brown tawed skin; spine with five raised bands; two brass and leather clasps (leather straps broken with stubs remaining), which once fastened to catches, upper board; edges dyed yellow; spine rebacked; detached register between ff. 145v–146 (long thin strip of tawed skin), once attached to the headband.

Written in Cologne by a student, Theodoric of Alkmaar (Netherlands; colophon, f. 200) for the Carthusian monastery of St. Barbara, Cologne (Gruys 2:267–69; Krämer, *Handschriftenerbe* 2:426; founded 1334; suppressed 1796) at the request of the prior, John Castor (alias

Schunde de Dottechem, Hollandus, 1434–57) in 1452, after the fire that destroyed the library of St. Barbara's in 1451 (contemporary ex libris, inside front cover in a formal hand: "Sermones magistri Iacobi de voragine ordinis predicatorum Archiepiscopi Ianuensis per anni circulum dominicales pertinentes ad domum sancte Barbare in colonia ordinis Carthusiensis. Quos venerabilis pater dominus Iohannes de deuthechem prefate domus prior scribi fecit. Anno domini 1452 [corrected from 1432]"; Marks, *Library of the Charterhouse of St. Barbara in Cologne*, 10, note 43; and 225–26, and *Colophons* 9462, transcribing date as 1432). Theoderic also copied Cologne, Dombibliothek, MS 90, Gregory, *Dialogues* and *Pastoralia* in 1459, still describing himself as a student from Cologne (*Colophons* 17676).

Identifiable in the new catalogue of the library of St. Barbara's as no. 0 107 (Marks, *Library of the Charterhouse of St. Barbara in Cologne*, 410; cf. p. 414, suggesting an alternative identification as 0 171; this is corrected by Sigrid Krämer, who suggests in her review of Marks that 0 171 is Manchester, John Rylands Library, MS Lat 410; see "Die mittelalterliche Bibliothek der Kartause St. Barbara in Köln," *Buchhandelgeschichte, hg. von der Historischen Kommission des Börsenvereins 2/3, Börsenblatt f. d. Deutschen Buchhandel—Frankfürter Ausgabe* 71 [1979] B158–B168, especially B160 and B164). Belonged to Leander van Ess (1772–1847; in general see Hermann Knaus, "Die Handschriften des Leander van Ess," *Archiv für Geschichte des Buchwesens* 1 [1958] 331–36; *Sammlung und Verzeichnis handschriftlicher Bücher . . . welche besitzt Leander van Ess* [Darmstadt 1823] no. 208); sold in 1824 to Sir Thomas Phillipps (see Munby, *Phillipps Studies* 3:29–30). Phillipps MS 592 (note in black ink, bottom margin, f. 1) or Phillipps MS 594 (inside front cover, stamp with crest, with "594" altered to "592"); the description of Phillipps MS 594: "*Sermones Dominicales per annum.* fol." may describe this manuscript more accurately than that of MS 592: "Jacobi de Voragine, *Sermones.* quarto" (see *Phillipps Cat.*, 7). Phillipps sale, London, Sotheby's, June 6–9, 1910, no. 470 (Kl. Löffler, *Kölnische Bibliotheksgeschichte im Umriss* [Cologne 1923] 72, no. 236); note that neither no. 818 in this sale, also from St. Barbara's, nor London, Sotheby's, April 24–28, 1911, no. 600, can be identified as our manuscript as has been suggested (cf. Marks, *Library of the Charterhouse of St. Barbara's in Cologne*, 450; these two items probably describe the same manuscript; cf. Löffler, *Kölnische Bibliotheksgeschichte* 73, nos. 261 and 271). Ellis

Cat. 138 [London, 1911] no. 81, for £7.10s (cf. notes in pencil, inside front cover, recording the price and author, written diagonally); purchased from Ellis, November 22, 1911 (Treat fund; library stamp, f. 1; bookplate, inside front cover).

secundo folio: dictis sum etenim

Bibliography: De Ricci, 976; Marks, *Library of the Charterhouse of St. Barbara in Cologne*, 225–26.

fMS Lat 12 **Italy (Padua) 1442**
Walter Burley, Expositio super artem veterem, libri I et II **Pl. 6**

1. ff. 2–14 [Prologue] Quia de dictis in logica intendo quoddam compendium compilare, videnda sunt . . . Ita vnde iste v. intenciones sunt v. genera respectu illorum de quibus predicantur de nominatiue. [ff. 3v–14 text] *Cum sit necessarium grisarori.* Iste liber qui est primus in ordine doctrine inter omnes libros logice continet . . . accidit [*corr. add.* sed] secundum maius et minus. *Et in hoc finitur breuis sententia huius libri edita ab universali magistro burleo.*

   Walter Burley, *Commentary on Boethius's Translation of the Isagoge of Porphyry.*

2. ff. 14–54v [Prologue] Circa librum predicamentorum est sciendum quod subiectum contentiuum tocius scientie tradite in libro predicamentorum est . . . vel diuidendum extrema ab inuicem. [ff. 16–54v text] *Equiuoca dicuntur solum nomen metaphysice est.* Iste liber est de decem predicamentis [*add. in marg.* ut eis] insunt intenciones secunde et continet tres tractatus . . . sunt alis [*sic*] a quolibet modo predicatorum ut satis liquet homini[?] intuenti, *etc. etc. etc. Explicit scripta egregii ac famosissimi doctoris magistri Burley supra librum predicamentorum. Scripta per me fratrem Iohannem de francia conuentus theonis uille filii* [*corr.*[2]*: filius*] *eiusdem* [*expunged: temporis*] *conuentus tempore principii mei studii* [*expunged: tunc temporis studens*] *padue. Sub anno domini 1442 ac completa in eadem conuentu ad sanctum philippum et iacobum. Ad laudem omnipotentis dei sueque genitrici* [*corr.*[2]*: genitricis*] *Uirginis marie, omnique successorum meorum et in hoc libro proficiencium. etc., etc., etc.* [f. 54v scribal colophon] *Libro fine dato do laudes virgine nato/ <C>ui dedit explevi laudem mentem*

fideli/ Acto fine pia laude virgo Maria/ Nomen scriptoris Iohannes est miles amoris/ O maria pia summis super me philosophya/ Pro tanto precio aliis numquam scibere uolo/ Heu non bene finiui qui non bene scribere sciui/ Grates inmensas laudes inferam intensas./ Datori munerum super guttas fluvium etc. etc. etc.

Walter Burley, *Commentary on the Praedicamenta of Aristotle.* (Arts. 1 and 2) Books one and two of Walter Burley's *Expositio super artem veterem* (final form 1337); see Charles Lohr, "Medieval Latin Aristotle Commentaries: Authors G–I," *Traditio* 24 (1968) 174–76, no. 4, not listing this manuscript. First printed Venice 1476–78; *GKW* 5765–72. In this manuscript the commentary is accompanied only by lemmata from the texts of Porphyry and Aristotle.

Infrequent contemporary corrections, possibly by the scribe (for example f. 14v, supplying an omitted phrase, f. 4v, f. 5 col. b, and f. 25); contemporary annotations in a formal hand, again possibly the scribe, including nota marks and indications of the type and number of arguments in the text (for example, f. 29rv). F. 2rv heavily annotated in three hands, s. XV (?); comments in these hands are also found infrequently throughout the manuscript; it has been suggested that the notes found on f. 2 in a good cursive script, s. XV, written carefully with a thin nib (cf. also f. 15v) are by the Venetian nominalist, Paul of Pergula (d. 1451), who is mentioned on the medieval flyleaf, f. 1 (unverified; see provenance, below). Pointing hands throughout.

Paper (at least two unidentified watermarks, bell and mountain, obscured by the text), ff. iii (paper) + i (medieval flyleaf, numbered f. 1) + 53 (ff. 2–54, with modern foliation in pencil, bottom, inside corner and early modern foliation in ink, middle bottom margin), 303 x 210 mm. Layout varies: ff. 2–33v, written space (217–215 x 147–145) mm. 2 columns. Begins with a fairly compressed layout, ff. 2–10v, 54–42 lines; continues with larger script and with more space between the lines, ff. 10–22v, 39–37 lines; progressively more compressed (note decreased size of script, f. 23, mid-col. b; f. 23, 41 lines, f. 23v, 46 lines) ff. 24–33 col. a, 59–52 lines. F. 33, col. b, 44 lines (new hand, line 7). Ff. 34–54v, written space (212–210 x 145) mm. 56–45 lines, with script decreasing in size and layout becoming more compressed. Quickly frame ruled in lead, usually with all four bounding lines full across (except f. 33, col. b, and ff. 33v–34, frame ruled in lead, but with horizontal rules in ink). No prickings remain.

1^{12} (beginning f. 2; structure uncertain, but possibly resewn and glued; now with sewing between 3 and 4, ff. 4 and 5) 2^{12} 3^{8} 5^{12} 6^{12} (–10 through 12 following f. 54, cancelled with no loss of text). Horizontal catchwords, bottom, inner margin (partially trimmed, quires 3–5).

Written by two scribes, the second, Johannes de Francia, who identified himself in the colophon, beginning on f. 33, col. b, line 7. The first scribe copied the commentary in a small cursive gothic script, with some loops; the appearance of the script varies depending on how hurried the scribe was and the degree of compression; as the script gets smaller, it also tends to lose its loops and become very precise; this scribe copied the lemmata in a larger formal gothic text script. The second scribe used a more informal, open gothic cursive script for the commentary, and a much larger, bold gothic text script for the lemmata.

Text begins, f. 2, with a 6-line blank space for an initial; 4-line red initial infilled with a simple red flower, added later. Type of decoration changes when scribe changes. Ff. 2–33 (scribe 1), blank spaces for 5- to 3-line initials at major divisions within the text (initials often supplied by a later hand, brown ink). Red paragraph marks; majuscules within the text often slashed with red; red line-fillers. Ff. 33–54v (scribe 2), 7- to 3-line blank spaces for initials (often supplied later in brown ink). Lemmata highlighted above and below with a red line; opening letter slashed, and sometimes decorated in red. Red paragraph marks; majuscules within the text slashed with red throughout.

Fragile; ff. 1–2, cracking along reinforcement and almost completely detached.

Bound in England, s. XIX, in half roan; title on spine in gilt.

Written in part and completed in Padua in 1442 by Johannes de Francia, who explains in the colophon that he is a brother from a convent in Thionville, France (northeast), who was then studying in Padua (see above, f. 54v; *Colophons* 9693); he followed his colophon by nine lines of verse (see above, f. 54v; cf. *Colophons* 22487, listing Vatican, Biblioteca Apostolica Vaticana, MS Reg. lat. 28, f. 135v, which apparently also includes the first line of this verse colophon).

Also owned, s. XV, by Johannes de sancto nabore (clipping from another flyleaf, glued on medieval flyleaf, f. 1): "Iste liber est fratris iohannis de sancto nabore [now St. Avold, Moselle, France, near Thionville] ordinis fratrum <. . .>"; this clipping also includes notes in two other hands, and a rough sketch of a man's profile. Another note, medieval flyleaf, f. 1, mentions Paul of Pergula, possibly the Venetian nominalist (d. 1451): "1450, magister paulus de pergula fecit principium studii uidelicet die 4 nouembris in quo quidem principio incepit Burleum regulas dubia et sophismata, et tanquam nouus operam dedi magno studio"; the opinions of "magister Paulus venetus" are mentioned in two notes clipped from another medieval flyleaf and also glued on f. 1. Other early owners or readers filled the remaining space on f. 54v; additions include a 12-line erotic note in German, "Got grussze die czoneste un[d] libe/ ... Die stoussze suldent sich/ woil verdragen"; a 2-line note on logic; a 3-line note mentioning biblical men who had difficulty with women (Adam, Samson, David, etc.); and "Malo rodere fabam quam rodi perpetue cura." Ex-libris note, s. XV (?), in a formal gothic hand, f. 54v: "Liber iste est monasterii sanctorum quadraginta martyrum prope et extra taruisium," an Augustinian house in Treviso, Italy (Paul F. Kehr, *Italia pontificia.* Regesta pontificum romanum [Berolini 1923] 7, part 1:110–11). Top margin, f. 2, in red-brown pencil: "4 CE7." Given to the library by J. G. Marwin of Towanda, Pennsylvania, September 7, 1844, who was then a Harvard law student (f. iii, presentation note; library bookplate, inside front cover). Note on contents with transcription of colophon by Charles Peirce (1839–1914), logician, AB Harvard 1859, laid in between front flyleaves, ff. ii and iii. Original Harvard shelf mark: Phil 5000.1.

secundo folio: [f. 3] Et si dicitur

Bibliography: De Ricci, 977.

MS Lat 15 — Germany s. XV[1](?)
Henricus de Friemar, O.E.S.A; Gerardus de Fracheto — Pls. 36, 65

1. ff. 1–5v [Added subject index] *Sermones pulcherrimi.* Abrahe imitatio, 46g. Accedendam est ad deum propter u<irtus?; hole in parchment> . . . Zizania dicuntur errores, 41k.

Entries are arranged alphabetically through the first two letters; references consist of arabic numerals indicating the folio number and letters showing the location on the opening.

The scribe of this index also foliated art. 2 using arabic numerals, upper margin, verso, of each opening, and added reference letters, a–z, corresponding to major sections of the text of each sermon, with the length and number of these divisions therefore varying; series begin again with 'a' following 'z'. This same scribe may also have added the parchment scrap following f. 14v discussing the Second Coming (referring to the sermon beginning f. 15 for the second Sunday in Advent, Schneyer 13).

2. ff. 6–173v [Henricus de Friemar, O.E.S.A., *Sermones de tempore*] *Dominica prima in aduentv domini sermo de epistola.* "Scientes quia hora est iam nos de sompno surgere. Ro. xiii[:11]." In ewangelio annuntiatur nobis aduentus magni regis inquam pauperis ... de sompno peccati surgere debemus. Quod nobis prestet dominus qui uiuit et regnat deus.... [f. 171 25th Sunday after Pentecost] *De ewangelio.* "Hic est uere propheta qui uenturus est in mundum. Joh. vi b [6:14]." Consuetudo pauperum et humilium est quod benefactores suos et magnificant et laudant ... Hic est uere propheta qui uenturus est in mundum, non solum ad condempnandum impios ut dicit glosa super psalmos, Cum exurgeret munditio deus sed etiam ad saluandum pios. [added in margin: *Finis sermonis.*] [f. 173 Prayer by the compiler] Ihesu ergo pie quia ad honorem et gloriam et laudem super excellentissime trinitatis et unitatis et tue gloriosissime matris ... et te ipsum mihi in premium totaliter tribuendo. Qui cum patre et spiritu sancto viuis et regnas deus per omnia secula seculorum. Amen.

Schneyer, 2:640–49, series 1, listing 17 manuscripts (this manuscript not listed); Adolar Zumkeller, *Manuskripte von Werken der Autoren des Augustiner-Eremitenordens in mitteleuropäischen Bibliotheken.* Cassiciacum 20 (Würzburg 1966) 158–59, no. 332. These sermons are attributed to Henricus de Friemar, senior (d.1340) by Schneyer (2:369). Zumkeller notes that they may instead be by Henricus de Friemar, junior (d.1354); the works of these two authors are still confused (Zumkeller, 125).

Some variation in the order listed by Schneyer, and with six additional unidentified sermons, as follows: Schneyer no. 1; 2; 6; 8; 3; 4–5; 7; 9–10; 12–13; 11; f. 17rv [2nd Sunday in Advent] *Alius sermo de epistola.* "Christus suscepit vos in honorem dei. Ro. xv[:7]." Ut ad aduentum domini in carnem auctoritatem istam referamus ... et simus [*sic*] immortales cum ipso ut dicit glosa super illud suscepit nos in honorem dei; 14; f. 19rv *Dominica iii* [*in adventu*] *sermo de epistola.* "Sic nos existimet homo ut ministros christi. 1 Cor. iv[:1]." Cum magna sollicitudine aliquis pauper artem addiscit ... Item quia rependum nobis uicem in seruiendo. Lu. xii. Seruiens mi illis. Quod nobis prestet dominus; 15; f. 21rv [3rd Sunday in Advent] *Sermo de ewangelio unde supra.* "Ecce ego mitto angelum meum ante faciem tuam qui preparabit uiam tuam ante te. Mat. xi c [11:10]." Et est sumptum de malachia iii c [3:1]. Moraliter in ista auctore innuitur aduentus domini spiritualiter ad animam ... secundo ut eam illuminet, tercio ut eam perficiat. Quod nobis prestet dominus; 16; 17; ff. 23v–26 [3rd Sunday in Advent] *Alius sermo de ewangelio.* "Cum audisset iohannes in uinculis opera christi. Math. xi[:12]." Sed que opera? Opera namque que operatus est ... Hii sunt vii digiti missi in aures peccatoris. Septem panes reficientes, Mt. xv[:36?] et Marci viii[:20]; vii sporte, Mat. xv[:37] ... [19 lines of biblical references] ... vii. candelabra, apo. 1[:12 or 20]. Quibus nos illuminare dignetur. Qui uiuet; ff. 26–27 [3rd Sunday in Advent] "Quid existis in desertum uidere arundinem vento agitatam. Mt. xi[:7]." Commendatur hic beatus iohannes de constantia [expunged: Commendatur hic]. Tria hic considera. Primum quid sit constantia ... Bonum est constantem esse in deo. Quod nobis prestare deo; 18–19; 21; 20; 22–24; f. 36rv [Sunday within the octave of the Epiphany] *De eodem.* "Nolite conformari huic seculo sed reformamini in nouitate sensus uestri. Ro. xii a [12:2]." Nota fidelis pedagogus primi sunt ... Talis renouatio debet fieri in nouitate sensus uestri non corporis uestri. Quod ipse per; 25–141.

F. 32rv is blank but ruled; Schneyer no. 20, the last of a series of four sermons for the 4th Sunday in Advent, ends f. 31v, three lines from the bottom; text resumes, f. 33, with Schneyer 22, a sermon for the Sunday during the Octave of the Nativity; the page may have been left blank because the scribe noted the absence of sermons for Christmas and its vigil.

Throughout, contemporary marginal annotations referring to the subjects in the text (cf. ff. 13 and 93v, etc.) and to the biblical books cited (cf. ff. 172, 172v, 173, etc.); occasional longer notes (cf. ff. 30, 59rv, 64, 101, etc.) and notes that may be cross-references to other sections of the text (cf. ff. 114v, 118rv, 120v, etc.). Annotations in later hands: f. 137v, citing Cicero; and f. 160, a series of notes in Latin and German.

3. f. 173v [Short gloss added in another hand at the end of art. 2] Job vlt. [42:16] "Et mortuus est senex et plenus dierum." Glosa Gre. Vacuus dierum est qui et quodlibet multum uixerit . . . et postquam transacti sunt uel fuerunt reseruantur. [Added in another hand: *Explicit soliensis* [*or: Doliensis?*].

4. ff. 174–179 [Extracts from Gerardus de Fracheto, *Vitae fratrum ordinis praedicatorum*] *De corpore Christi.* Anno ab incarnacione domini mccxxx predicante magistro Chunrado Theutonico contra hereticos et ab ipsis passo . . . narrauit qui et hoc fratribus multociens recitauit tacitis nominibus personarum . . . *De v. marcis mirabiliter oblatis.* Cum creditor quidam expeteret . . . Unde fratres ex pia suspicione hoc beate marie matri misericordie asscripserunt [*sic*].

   Benedictus Maria Reichert, O.P., ed. Monumenta ordinis fratrum praedicatorum historica 1 (Louvain 1896); Kaeppeli, *SOPMA* 1282, not listing this manuscript; includes the following extracts: *De corpore christi* (ed. 4:23.1, p. 211); *De cruce* (ed. 4:23.3, p. 213); *Consolaco* [*sic*] *spiritualis* (ed. 4:24.12, p. 217); *De medicina spirituali* (ed. 4:24.12, p. 217); *De horribili visione dyaboli* (ed. 4:24.14, p. 220); *De obitu lectoris cuiusdam* (ed. 5:2.9, p. 252); *De obitu fratris cuiusdam petri* (ed. 5:3.2, p. 258); *De obitu fratris sui arnoldi* (ed. 5:3.3, p. 258); *Amici defuncti subenveniunt amicis morituris* (ed. 5:3.6e, p. 261); *Quod demon in morte bonorum aliqundo adest* (ed. 5:3.7, p. 264); *De presencia christi in obitu bonorum* (ed. 5:3.9, p. 264); *Quid contigit cuiusdam fratri spirituales consolationes petenti* (ed. 4:3.2, p. 156); *Quomodo demon exivit de obsesso abdventu fratris Vincentis conpiscenciam* (ed. 4:4.1, p. 158); *De confessione* (ed. 4:7.4, p. 167); *De tractu fratris* (ed. 4:7.2, p. 166); *De confessione* (ed. 4:7.5, p. 167); *De confessione* (ed. 4:7.6, p. 168); *Quomodo ordo contrarius est demonibus* (ed. 4:15.1, p. 194); *Quomodo dyabolus persecutus est quandam fratrem propter bibliam* (ed. 4:15.4, p. 195); *Quod angeli a demonibus nos defendunt* (ed. 4:15.6, p. 197; concludes, f. 177, with 19 lines of text not identified in the edition); *Quod sompnia interdum verificantur* (ed. 4:17.5, p. 202); *De fratre a temptatione liberato miraculo s. petri martyri* (ed. 4:17.6, p. 202); *De temptatione fratris* (ed. 4:17.7, p. 203); *De sanctis dominico et francisco* (ed. 1:1.4, p. 9); *De oratione pro fratribus dicenda* (ed. 1:5.7, p. 32); *De miluo ostendente uiam fratribus* (ed. 1:5.8, p. 33); *De tribus angelis apparentibus in spem fratrem* (ed. 1:5.11, p. 35); *De temptato* [*sic*] *fratre quomodo stetit* (ed. 1:6.9, p. 45); *De fratre retento in ordine per febres* (ed. 1:6.10, p. 46); *De v. marcis mirabliliter oblatis* (ed. 1:6.11, p. 47).

5. ff. 179–182v [Unidentified sermons] "Homo fecit cenam magnam. [Luke 14:16]." Nota quod sacramenta ecclesie sunt vii et evcharistia est fons omnium . . . Vide ergo hostiam que est paruam etc. sicut in sermone abiit ihesus. [f. 181] "Memor esto iudicii mei sic enim erit et tuum [Ecclesiasticus 38:23]." Dominus habet duo iudicia. Vnum particulare quod fit cotidie in morte <c. . .?>. Reliquum uniuersale quod fit in fine mundi . . . quia uado per regionem meorum hostium et bene fa<tuus?> est qui per terram inimicorum uadit sine tutore angeleuten.

Parchment (velvety), ff. 182 (medieval foliation, 1–167, art. 2, added in the top middle margin in arabic numerals on the verso of each opening beginning on f. 6v and continuing through f. 172v; modern foliation in pencil, bottom inside margin, 1–182, cited), 221 x 160 (163–158 x 110–105) mm. 2 columns, 34 lines. Ruled in brown ink with the top, third, and bottom two lines full across, with many variations and sometimes also with the antepenultimate line full across; single full-length vertical bounding lines. Prickings in three outer margins.

1^{6} (added quire; –1, probably cancelled with no loss of text) 2^{12} (small parchment scrap sewn in after 9, f. 14) $3–15^{12}$ (through f. 173v) 16^{10} (added quire; –10, cancelled with no loss of text). Quires 2 through 15 signed at the end of each quire, middle, lower margin, with a roman numeral (i–xii).

The original text (art. 2) was written below the top line in very dark brown ink in a careful gothic bookhand; letter forms betray no influence of current scripts (bottom lines, ff. 30v–31v were copied in lighter brown ink, but likely by the same scribe). Sermons begin with plain 2-line initials, alternately red and blue, set within the text space; paragraph marks, alternately red and blue, mark some sections within the sermons; red rubrics.

Additions to the manuscript were made by three hands, as follows. (1) Art. 1 (ff. 1–5v): ruled space, 160–3 x 127–6 mm. 2 columns, 34 lines. Ruled lightly in lead; single vertical bounding lines. Prickings, three outer margins. Written below the top line in a quick gothic noting hand; long 's' drops below the line. Plain 2-line red initials at the beginning of each letter of the alphabet; first majuscule of remaining entries stroked with red. (2) Art. 4 (ff. 174–179): written space, (170 x 112–110) mm. 2 columns, 35 lines. Ruled in dark brown ink, with the top 2 and bottom 2 horizontal rules full across; single full-length vertical bounding lines. Written below the top line in a gothic bookhand. Two-line red initials within the text space; red rubrics. (3) Art. 5 (ff. 179–182v), added on the blank folios following art. 4, in a less formal gothic bookhand.

Bound in Germany, s. XV, in dark brown calf over wooden boards; blind-tooled with two sets of double rules forming a border surrounding intersecting double diagonal rules; two isolated small floral stamps, lower board; formerly fastened back to front with a strap-and-pin fastening (hole in upper board and indentation and nails, lower); two of the five brass bosses remain, lower board; remains of title, front board, "Sermones pulcerrimi," and fragment of paper label on spine; rebacked with spine laid down; leather rubbed and in poor condition. Red "4" on spine (modern addition).

Written in Germany in the later Middle Ages, probably in the first half of the fifteenth century (we thank Susan Shroff for her extensive research on this manuscript). Inside back cover, pious notes in Latin, and notes in Latin using the Greek alphabet, s. XV. Belonged to the Cistercian abbey of St. Mary of Oliva (now Oliwa; near Gdánsk, Poland; founded 1175; secularized 1831; Krämer, *Handschriftenerbe*, 639; Meer, *Atlas de l'ordre cistercien*, 290); ex libris note, f. 1 (in two hands): "Fratrum B. Mariae de Oliva. 1636; Ord. Cist. in Prussia." Ownership note, s. XVIII, f. 1, top margin, mostly illegible: "Ecclesie star<. . .?> 1797" (there is a Stargard in Poland, not far from Oliwa, but no positive identification with this town is possible). No. 68 in a catalogue, s. XIX, in French (cutting pasted inside front cover). Inside front cover in pencil, unidentified dealer's note: "66/" and illegible notation (a price code?). Belonged to William Gibbons Medlicott (1816–83), collector and scholar of English literature; *Catalogue of a Collection of Books formed by William G. Medlicott of Longmeadow, Mass...* (Boston 1878) no. 2730 (in general, see J. R. Hall, "William G. Medlicott [1816–83]: An American Book Collector and His Collection," *Harvard Library Bulletin* N.S. 1 [1990] 13–46). Purchased September 2, 1878 for $7.50 (James Walker fund; bookplate and library note, inside front cover).

secundo folio: [added text:] diuicie et delicie sunt vitandum;
[now f. 7:] [subar]//rauit me et lilia

Bibliography: De Ricci, 977.

MS Lat 17 — Northern France s. XV/XVI
Book of Hours, use of Paris — Pl. 31

Bound out of order, but described in what was probably the original order:

1. ff. 1–10v Calendar in French in red and black, now lacking two folios with February and March after f. 1; generally similar to the type printed by Perdrizet. Major feasts in red include Genevieve (3 January), Eligius (translation, 25 June), King Louis (25 August), and Denis (9 October). Among the remaining feasts are Salvius, bishop of Amiens (10 January), Souplice, bishop of Bourges (17 January), Cassianus, bishop of Autun (5 August), Romanus, bishop of Auxerre (7 October), Mellonius, bishop of Rouen (22 October), and Maximus, bishop of Mainz (18 November).

2. ff. 99rv, 124–126v Gospel pericopes; pericope from John (1:1–14), now begins imperfectly with John 1:11: "[recepe]//runt. Quotquot autem receperunt eum dedit . . . ," followed by antiphon, response, and prayer: "Protector in te sperantium deus sine quo nichil est .. [Perdrizet, 25]"; pericope from Luke (1:26–38), begins f. 99v; text continues with no breaks on f. 124v, where it ends abruptly, Luke 1:35: ". . . Et respondens angelus dixit//"; pericope from Matthew (2:1–12) begins imperfectly at the top of f. 125, with Matthew 2:3:

"//illo. Et congregans omnes principes sacerdotum et scribas populi scicitabatur [*sic*] . . . ," and continues, with no break in the text, through f. 126; pericope from Mark (16:14–20), begins on f. 126, and ends abruptly, f. 126v, with Mark 16:17: ". . . In nomine meo demonia eicient linguis loquentur//".

3. ff. 65rv, 135–141v Prayers; the prayer "Obsecro te domina . . . Et michi famula tua . . . [feminine forms; Leroquais, *LH*, ii:346]," begins imperfectly, "//plenissima summi regis filia mater gloriosissima mater orphanorum consolacio desolatorum . . ." on f. 65, and continues through f. 138, with no breaks; ff. 138–141 *Oratio deuotissima ad beatissimam uirginem mariam.* O intemerata . . . orbis terrarum. Inclina mater misericordie aures tue pietatis . . . Et esto michi miserrimo peccatori pia . . . [Wilmart, 488–90]; f. 141rv *Oratio beate marie uirgine* [*sic*]. Saluto te sancta uirgo maria domina celorum et regina ea salutacione . . . [similar to *Lyell Cat.*, 394, no. 347], followed by the "Pater noster" and "Ave Maria," both with cues only.

4. Hours of the Virgin, use of Paris; text of each hour is complete, despite the severely misordered state of the manuscript: ff. 116–123v, 41–45 matins; ff. 45v–48v, 27–34v, 127rv lauds; ff. 128–133v prime; ff. 134rv, 81–84 terce; ff. 84v–88v sext; ff. 49–53 none; ff. 53v–56v, 89–92v vespers; ff. 93–98v compline; matins with one nocturn of three psalms and three lessons; lauds through compline conclude with the prayers usual for use of Paris; lauds concludes "Deus qui corda fidelium sancti spiritus . . . [Bruylants, *Oraisons* 2: no. 349; printed *Sarum Breviary* 1:ix]," "Deus qui de beate marie uirginis utero uerbum tuum . . . [Bruylants, *Oraisons* 2: no. 230]," and "Ecclesiam tuam quesumus domine benignus illustra ut beati iohannis . . ."; prime concludes "Deus qui apostolis tuis sanctum dedisti spiritum concede . . . ," "Famulorum tuorum quesumus domine delictis ignosce . . . ," "Ecclesiam tuam quesumus domine . . . [as above]"; terce followed by "Assit nobis quesumus domine uirtus spiritus sancti . . . ," "Concede nos famulos tuos quesumus domine deus perpetua mentis . . . [Bruylants, *Oraisons* 2: no. 122; printed *HE*, 44 and 51]," "Ecclesiam tuam quesumus domine . . . [as above]"; sext followed by "Mentes nostras quesumus domine spiritus paraclitus qui a te proccedit . . ," "Concede misericors deus fragilitati nostre presidium . . . ," "Eccle-

siam tuam quesumus domine . . . [as above]"; none followed by "Mentibus nostris quesumus domine spiritum sanctum benignus infunde . . . ," "Protege famulos tuos subsidiis pacis . . . [printed *Brev. O.P.*, p. lxxxiv]," "Ecclesiam tuam quesumus domine . . . [as above]"; vespers followed by "Deus qui corda fidelium sancti spiritus . . . [Bruylants, *Oraisons* 2: no. 349]," "Deus qui salutis eterne beate marie uirginitate fecunda . . . [Bruylants, *Oraisons* 2: no. 440]," "Ecclesiam tuam quesumus domine . . . [as above]"; compline followed by prayers, "Ure igne sancti spiritus renes nostros et cor nostrum domine . . . [Van Dijk, *Ordinal*, 177]," "Gratiam tuam quesumus domine mentibus nostris infunde . . . [printed *HE*, 61]," "Ecclesiam tuam quesumus domine. . . . [as above]."

5. ff. 66–68v Hours of the Cross, short form, beginning imperfectly with the conclusion of the opening hymn ("Patris sapientia ueritas diuina . . . [*RH* 14726]"): "//Et afflictus."

6. ff. 69–72v Hours of the Holy Spirit, short form.

7. ff. 108–115v, 11–21v Penitential psalms and litany (ff. 16v–21v) including Denis, George, and Arnulph among the martyrs, Marcellus, King Louis, Dominic, Benedict and Bernard among the confessors, and Genevieve among the Virgins; concludes, f. 21v, with prayers: "Deus cui proprium est misereri semper et parcere suscipe deprecationem . . . [printed *HE*, 97]," and "*Alia oratio, etc.* Fidelium deus omnium conditor et redemptor animabus famulorum famularumque . . . [printed *HE*, 30 and 98; Bruylants, *Oraisons* 2: no. 567]."

8. ff. 22–26v, 100–107v, 57–64v, 73–80v, 35rv Office of the Dead; matins with one nocturn of three lessons: Parce michi domine nichil . . . , [R.] Qui lazarum resuscitasti . . .; Tedet animam meam uite mee . . . , [R.] Credo quod redemptor meus . . .; Manus tue domine fecerint me . . . , [R.] Libera me domine de morte eterna . . .; vespers concludes on f. 102 with prayers: "Inclina domine aurem tuam ad preces nostras . . . [printed *HE*, 101]," "Deus uenie largitor et humane salutis amator . . . [printed *HE*, 111]," and "*Oracio generalis.* Fidelium deus omnium conditor et redemptor . . . [Bruylants, *Oraisons* 2: no. 567; printed *HE*, 30 and 98]."

Text is misbound, beginning with vespers on ff. 22–26v, ending with Psalm 137:8, then continuing with no break, ff. 100–107v, ending in matins, Psalm 7:12; continuing on ff. 57–64v, ending in lauds, Psalm 64:12, continuing, with no break, ff. 73–80v, ending in the Canticle of Zachary [Luke 1:76], and then concluding on f. 35rv, where the text breaks off imperfectly in Psalm 129:2 of lauds.

9. ff. 36–40v Suffrages of Michael, Peter and Paul, Lawrence, Sebastian, Nicholas and Barbara, followed, f. 40rv, by the prayers, "*P*[*ri*]-*mierement tu diras au matin quant tu te lieueras de to*[*n*] *lit.* In matutinis domine meditabor in te quia adiutor meus. *Oratio.* Gracias tibi ago omnipotens pater qui me in hac nocte custodire. . . . [these same prayers are found in Oxford, Keble College, MS 44, f. 146; see Parkes, *Keble College*, 203]"; although the text of the first suffrage is complete, it was likely once preceded by two folios with additional suffrages.

Parchment, ff. ii (paper) + 141 (modern foliation in pencil, top, outer corner, recto, 1–141, cited; remains of older pagination, s. XVIII–XIX, in ink, top, outer corner of the recto only, as follows [with corresponding references to the modern foliation]: pp. 1–19, with p. 16 bis [quires 1 and 2, ff. 1–10v], pp. 20–35 [quire 8, ff. 49–56v], pp. 36–66 [quires 3 and 4, ff. 11–26]; manuscript is seriously misbound, and neither set corresponds to the original order of the manuscript, reconstructed above in description of contents) + ii (paper), 189 x 128 (99–98 x 60–59) mm. 15 long lines. Ruled in red ink, with the top and bottom horizontal rules full across; single full-length vertical bounding lines. Calendar (ff. 1–10v): written space (99–96 x 61–60) mm. 4 columns (one broad for main entry and 3 narrow columns), 17 lines. Ruled in red ink, with the top and bottom horizontal rules full across; inner and outer vertical bounding lines are single, and full-length; remaining vertical bounding lines extend only the length of the written space, and are double between the third and fourth columns.

1^6 (–2,3 after f. 1, with loss of text) 2^6 3^8 4^8 (2 and 7 are single) 5^8 6^8 (–2, 3, following f. 35, stubs remain, with loss of text) $7–8^8$ 9^8 (+1, f. 65, added after 8) 10^8 (–1, before f. 66, with loss of text) $11–12^8$ 13^{10} 14^8 (+1, f. 99, misbound from quire 17, where it should precede f. 124) $15–16^8$ 17^6 (–1, now f. 99 in quire 14; -3, following f. 124, with loss of text; –6, following f. 126, with loss of text) 18^8 19^8 (–8, following f. 141, cancelled with no loss of text).

Written in a gothic bookhand in two sizes depending on liturgical function.

Eleven large miniatures in a style showing the influence of contemporary workshops active in Tours, especially that of Jean Bourdichon, but of mediocre quality. The scenes are reduced to the main figures, usually shown 1/2- to 3/4-length, cut off by the frames, and frozen in their actions; brush-strokes are broad, figures full and rounded, with blunt and muddy features; predominant colors include soft rose, blue, violet, light green, gray and brown, with gold highlights used copiously in draperies. Miniatures are set above 4- to 3-lines of text, fully enclosed in narrow red and gold arched frames; text and miniatures bounded on all sides except the top by a black or red ink rule; full outer borders, edged with black rules, of two types: either with red and blue acanthus placed at the corners, and naturalistic plants, including stawberries, violets and other flowers, on brushed-gold grounds (ff. 116, 128, 108, 69, 22); or with blue and gold acanthus and plants, as above, with gold balls and scattered black ink sprays on natural parchment grounds, intersected by geometric sections in a variety of shapes, including triangles, diagonal bands, and fleur-de-lis, of rose, dark blue, and brown, with floral and geometrical brushed-gold highlights (ff. 45v, 134, 84v, 49, 53v, 93).

Miniatures are now misbound; subjects as follows, listed in reconstructed order: f. 116 (Hours of the Virgin; matins) Annunciation, with Mary, 3/4-length, kneeling in the foreground before a simple table with an open book; Gabriel, partly cut off by the frame, on the left; f. 45v (lauds) Visitation, with Mary and Elizabeth shown frontally, 3/4-length; f. 128 (prime) Nativity, with Mary, 3/4-length, in the foreground, and Joseph, head and shoulders only, behind; Jesus and the heads of an ox and ass on the right; f. 134 (terce) Annunciation to the shepherds, set in a landscape, with a blue angel in the sky; f. 84v (sext) Adoration of the Magi, with Mary seated under a simple canopy on the left; the three kings on the right, with a crowd behind them; f. 49 (none) Presentation in the Temple, with Simeon holding Christ on a cloth which covers his hands; Joseph carries the basket of offerings; f. 53v (vespers) Flight into Egypt, showing Mary, 1/2-length, holding the Child, and Joseph; the donkey mostly cut off by the frame; f. 93 (compline) Coronation of the Virgin, with Mary, crowned, kneeling before Christ, who blesses her; [leaf excised before f. 66, with miniature for the hours of the Cross]; f. 69 (Hours of the Holy Spirit) Pentecost, set in an interior, with Mary kneeling in front of the apostles, who are depicted in green, and the dove entering through a window on tongues of fire and rays of gold; f. 108 (Penitential psalms and litany) David, dressed in mail, praying; f. 22 (Office of the Dead) Job on dunghill, shown with two companions.

Two smaller rectangular miniatures, equivalent to four lines of text, set into the text space and simply bounded by black ink rules, on f. 126, text and miniature are bounded by double pink rules; both with full borders: f. 126 (Gospel pericope, Mark) Mark with scroll and lion, in a landscape; f. 99v (Gospel pericope, Luke) Luke with scroll and ox, in a landscape; [pericopes from John and Matthew, now beginning ff. 99 and 125, possibly once preceded by miniatures].

Traced panel borders in outer margins of each page of text, with blue and liquid gold acanthus and naturalistic flowers, strawberries and leaves, with black dots; some borders with urns, bare branches, or solid color bands highlighted with liquid gold. Major initials on folios with miniatures, 3-line (except f. 22, 4-line), white-patterned blue on dark red grounds, highlighted with brushed gold, infilled with gold floral designs on dark red; similar 5-line initial used before the prayer "O intemerata," f. 138. 2-line "KL" monograms, alternately dark red and gray. 1-line gold initials within the text on square grounds, alternately dark red and gray or dark red and blue, with gold highlights; similar bar line-fillers. Red rubrics. Majuscules within the text daubed with yellow.

Bound, s. XVIII, in panelled calf, possibly in the United States as suggested by De Ricci, blind-tooled with outer borders of narrow double rules, and a rectangular center panel bordered by two sets of double rules, with a simple garland pattern between; floral stamps in each of the outer corners; gilt edges.

Written in Northern France, possibly in the northeast as indicated by the decoration and the saints included in the calendar, at the end of the fifteenth century or the beginning of the sixteenth century; the calendar is mixed, including some feasts especially associated with Paris (3 January, Genevieve in red; 24 August, King Louis, in red; 9 October, Denis in red), but also including Saints associated with northeastern France (Cassianus, bishop of Autun, 5 August, Romanus, Bishop of Auxerre, observed in Auxerre on the 7 October, and in the roman martyrology on the 6th, here on 7 October, and Maximus, bishop of Mainz).

Belonged to André Le Mercier (fl. s. XVIII): his ex libris note, f. 1, in brown ink: "Ex libris Andreae Le Mercier Ecclesiae Gallicanae Bostonensis Minister [*sic*]"; the same note recopied in a later hand on the front flyleaf, f. ii^{v}; front flyleaf f. i, reversed signature, likely an impression from a facing page, now missing: "Rev. <seigneur?> Le Mercier." Note in pencil, front flyleaf, f. i, states that the manuscript was given to Harvard College Library by Le Mercier's daughter (cf. library bookplate, inside front cover). Date of acquisition unknown. Inside front cover, paper label with "Dr. 71," probably from Harvard College; previous Harvard shelf mark: Arg 3.15 (front flyleaf, f. ii^{v}, in pencil).

Bibliography: De Ricci, 977; Charles Arthur Lynch, "Horarii saec. XV Manuscripti Harvardiani Lat. 17 . . . ," (typescript [Cambridge] 1931) now Houghton bMS Lat 315(14); Wieck, p. 107 and fig. 17 (reproducing f. 22).

MS Lat 18 — Italy (Florence) 1416
Ovid, Heroides — Pl. 2

ff. 1–49: f. 1 [Ep. 1] *Hanc epistolam mictit* [*sic*] *penelope vl*[*ixi*]. Hanc tua penolope [*sic*] lento tibi mictit ulixe./ . . . Protinus ut redeas facta uidebor anus; f. 2v [Ep. 2] *Hanc epistolam mictit phyllis demophonti.* Hospita demofon tua te rodopeia phyllis/ . . . Ille nescis causam prebuit illa manum; f. 5 [Ep. 3, with verses 6–15, 43, 48–51, 75–88 now partly cut away on ff. 5 and 6] *Hanc epistolam mictit briseis achilli.* Quam legis arapta [*sic*] briseide littera [*corr.*^{2}: litera] uenit/ . . . Siue manes domini more uenire iube.; f. 7v [Ep. 4] *Hanc epistolam mictit phedra ypolito.* Quam nisi tu dederis caritura est [*corr.*^{2}: *add.* ipsa] salutem/ . . . Per legis, et lacrimas finge uidere meas.; f. 10v [Ep. 5] *Hanc epistolam mictit oenoe paridi.* Perlegis? an coniux [*sic*] prohibet noua? perlege non est/ . . . Et tua quod superest temporis esse precor.; f. 13 [Ep. 6] *Hanc epistolam mictit ysiphyle Iasoni.* Lictora tesalie reduci tetigisse carina/ . . . Viuite deuoto nuptaque uirque thoro.; f. 15v [Ep. 7] *Hanc epistolam mictit dido*

Enee. Sic ubi fata uocant udis abiectus in herbis/ . . . Ipsa sua dido concidit usa manu.; f. 19 [Ep. 8] *Hanc epistolam mictit Ermione Horesti.* Pirrus achileides animosus imagine patris/ . . . A [effaced: ut ego] tantalide tantalis uxor ero.; f. 20v [Ep. 9] *Hanc epistolam mictit deyanira herculi.* Gratulor oetoliam titulis accedere nostris/ . . . Virque, sed o possis, et puer ile [*corr.*[2]: ille] uale.; f. 23v [Ep. 10] *Hanc epistolam mictit adriana teseo.* Mitius inueni quam te genus omne ferarum./ . . . Si prius occidero, tu tamen ossa feres.; f. 26 [Ep. 11, verses 1–119] *Hanc epistolam mictit canace machareo.* Siqua tamen cecis errabunt scripta lituris/ . . . Ipsa quoque infantis cum uulnere prosequar umbras//; f. 28 [Ep. 12, beginning imperfectly at verse 115] //Quod facere ausa mea est non audet scribere dextra/ . . . Nescio quid certe mens mea maius habet.; f. 29v [Ep. 13] *Hanc epistolam mictit Laudomia pthesilao* [*sic*] *viro suo.* Mictit et optat amans quo mictitur [rewritten by a later hand] ire salutem/ . . . Sit [*sic*] tibi cura mei sit [*sic*] tibi cura tui.; f. 32 [Ep. 14] *Hanc epistolam mictit ypermestra Lino viro suo.* Mictit hipermestra de tot modo fratribus uni/ . . . Est manus et uires subtrait ipse timor.; f. 34 [Ep. 16] *Hanc epistolam mictit paris helene.* Hanc tibi priamides micto ledea salutem/ . . . Exige cum plena munera pacta fide.; f. 38v [Ep. 17, lacking f. 42 with verses 197–258] *Hanc epistolam rescribit helena paridi.* Nunc oculos tua cum uiolaret epistola nostros/ . . . Que mihi sunt comites consilumque due.; f. 43 [Ep. 18] *Hanc epistolam mictit Leander hero [sic].* Mittit abideus quam mallet ferre salutem/ . . . Quam precor ut minima persequar [*sic*] ipse mora.; f. 46v [Ep. 19, verses 1–81] *Hanc epistolam rescribit hero Leandro.* Quam mihi misisti uerbis leandre salutem/ . . . Certe ego tum ventos audirem leta sonantes//; f. 48 [Ep. 20, beginning imperfectly at verse 119, and ending abruptly at verse 180] //Seruentur vultus ad nostra incendia nati./ . . . Fac modo polliciti conscia templa colas.//; f. 49 [Ep. 21, beginning imperfectly at verse 2] //Iuraret ne quos inscia lingua deos/ . . . Quos vereor paucos ne uelit esse mihi. *Explicit ouidius* [*sic*] *epistolarum die quinta decima augusti anno domini 1416 a domino niccholao ser Guidi de castro franco superiori comitatus Florentie, scolas regente florentie. Inceptus per bartholomeum laurentii de fighino eius tunc discipulum.* [F. 49v blank, except for later notes.]

Epistles 1–14, 16–20, and 21.2–12 (does not include the Letter of

Sappho to Phaonis; epistle 16 lacks verses 39–144); Henricus Dörrie, ed., *P. Ovidii Nasonis Epistulae Heroidum.* Texte und Kommentare; eine Altertumswissenschaftliche Reihe 6, eds. O. Gigon, F. Heinimann, and O. Luschnat (Berlin and New York 1971) 45–275. Although Dörrie counted introductory distichs as verses 1–2 in Epistles 7, 8, 11, 12, 17, 20 and 21, the traditional line numbers have been used in this description.

Contemporary marginal and interlinear glosses throughout, in a number of hands, including a neat gothic script, ff. 1–3 and occasionally elsewhere in the beginning portion of the manuscript (for example, f. 2v [ep. 2] "Hanc epistolam mictit phyllis filia lirgi regis tracie demophon qui cum rediret a captione troye ab ea susceptum est hospitio. . . ."); a more cursive script, throughout (for example, bottom margin f. 1 (badly rubbed) "Diuiditur autem[?] libros iste principaliter in duas partes . . ."; and f. 1v, bottom margin, "Sed mihi quod prodest. Superius domina penelope probavit troyam fuisse destructam per adventum grecorum. . . . Et diuidere pars hec in partes duas. . . ."). Two lines omitted by the first scribe, supplied by the second, margin, f. 37 (Ep. 16, lines 278–79). Occasional notes in later hands (for example, f. 4v, s. XVI (?), explaining "fructiosa").

Parchment, ff. iv (unnumbered paper) + 49 + iv (unnumbered paper), 220 x 149 (177–175 x 95–78) mm., trimmed, with glosses and later notes partly cut away on all three sides. 31 lines of verse. Ruled in lead, usually very faintly, with the 2 top and single bottom horizontal rules full across; full-length vertical bounding lines, double in the left margin, used for the first majuscule of each line of verse.

$1–3^8$ 4^8 (–4, 5, conjugate pair after f. 27, with loss of text) 5^8 6^8 (–4, f. 42, with loss of text; stub remains) 7^8 (–2 through 5 following f. 47; and –7 following f. 48, with loss of text).

Written by two scribes (colophon f. 49); ff. 1–46v were copied by Bartholomeus Laurentii of Fighino in a well-spaced gothic bookhand, influenced by humanistic script; the manuscript was then completed (ff. 47–49) by Niccholaus ser Guidi in a similar, although more angular gothic script.

One 4-line parted blue initial, f. 1; remaining poems begin with 3-line red initials set into the text space. Rubrics in red. Poems numbered in inner or outer margins in red arabic numerals. Each line of verse begins with a majuscule written between the bounding lines in brown ink. Guide letters for the initials sometimes visible.

Ff. 5–6 partly cut away, with loss of text (epistle 3); f. 42 excised, stub remains; outer margin, f. 48, partly cut away, with loss of glosses; many leaves stained by damp, making glosses difficult to read; initials rubbed throughout.

Bound in diced russia leather with simple gold-tooled borders, s. XIX (dated by De Ricci, ca. 1820), probably in the United States; "Ovidii Her. Latine MS.," lettered in gilt on spine; marbled end papers.

Written in Florence in 1416; completed on August 15th by Nicchòlaus ser Guidi [transcribed as "Gerini" by De Ricci], who describes himself as regent master ("*scolas regente*") in Florence, and begun by his pupil Bartholomeus Laurentii of Fighino (*Colophons* 14280); Bartholomeus also copied London, British Library, Additional MS 39844, Ps.-Aristotle, *Secretum secretorum* and *Le Livre du Trésor* of Brunetto Latini, both in Italian, with colophon, f. 143v: "Questo libro e scripto di mano di sere Bartolomeo di Lorenzo da Fighine compiuto a di xvi di Marzo MCCCCXXV" (*Colophons* 1793; see British Museum, *Catalogue of Additions to the Manuscripts 1916–1920* [London 1933] 212–16, suggesting, p. 214, that Fighine may be Figline Val d'Arno between Florence and Arezzo).

Owned, s. XVI, by Antonius di Matteo di giovanni foresi da bibbiena, who left numerous marginal annotations: f. 30, top margin: "Io antonio di matteo di giovanni foressi [*sic*] da bibbiena casato sichi//"; f. 47, top margin: "carissimo mio ma amatissimo fratello salute . . ."; f. 47v, top margin: "Di matteo di giouanni foresi da bibbiena casato de natibus"; f. 49, "Questo libro sie[?] di antonio <quarti?> fratello salu<ti?>," and "Questo libro sie di antonio dispose chi lo trovo . . . <two lines, partially effaced> . . . a di 26 iugno 153[3]"; f. 49v, note mentioning Antonio; cf. also f. 14, top margin, erased. This man may be related to the owner of a treatise on arithmetic in Italian with the inscription, "Questo libro è Giovanni di Forese Bizeri el quale scrisse Niccolò suo zio" (formerly Florence, Biblioteca Riccardiana, MS R.III.XXVI; see J. Lamius, *Catalogus codicum manuscriptorum qui in Bibliotheca Riccardiana Florentiae adservantur* [Livorno 1756] 43 and 190; *Colophons* 13981). The manuscript bears many signs of long use as a school book, including numerous crude marginal drawings, pen trials and other miscellaneous additions (for example, ff. 2, 5, 5v, 6, 6v, and 18). Large "3" in pencil, f. 49v, from an unidentified modern owner or bookseller. Date and source of acquisition by Harvard uncertain, but library records suggest it was acquired in 1915. Original Harvard shelf mark: APq 3.18 (as reported by Gragg, see below; once written in blue on Harvard College Library bookplate, inside front cover).

secundo folio: Nos pilon

Bibliography: De Ricci, 978; Florence Alden Gragg, "Manuscript of Ovid's Heroides in the Harvard Library," unpublished manuscript (Cambridge, June 27, 1906) now Houghton, bMS Lat 315(4); De Ricci, "Handlist," 105; John Petersen Elder, "A Description of Harvard University Library MS 18, 1416. Ovid's Heroides," unpublished typescript (Cambridge, January 13, 1936) now Houghton bMS Lat 315(31); Kristeller, *Iter* 5:226.

fMS Lat 27 — England s. XII²

Lives of Saints Anselm, Odo, Majolus, Odilo and Hugh — Pl. 19

1. ff. 1–38v [*Vita sancti anselmi (d. 1109) eadmeri monachi cantuariensis*] *Incipit prologus in uita sancti anselmi cantuariensis archiepiscopi.* Qvoniam multas et antecessorum nostrorum temporibus insolitas rerum mutationes nostris diebus in anglia accidisse et coaluisse conspeximus . . . [f. 1 text] *Incipit uita uenerabilis patris nostri anselmi cantuariensis archiepiscopi angelorum.* Instituta uitae et conuersationis anselmi cantuariensis archiepiscopi litterarum memoriae traditurus primo omnium uocata in auxilium meum summa dei clementia et maiaestate quaedam breui dicam . . . libens parui sperans eum insita sibi beniuolentia quae corrigenda//

   BHL 526; R. W. Southern, ed. and trans., *The Life of St. Anselm Archbishop of Canterbury by Eadmer.* Nelson Medieval Texts (London 1962), printing the Latin text with facing translation; this manuscript listed as 'J' and classified as belonging to group II, the long version (see p. xxii).

   Text now ends imperfectly in book 2, chapter 72 (ed., p. 150, line 10), and lacks the following sections: f. 5v concludes in book

1, chapter 9 (ed., p. 16, line 6), "... Uerum ut clareat quo pacto id prouenerit unum ex ipsis exempli gratia ponam quatinus//"; f. 6 begins in book 1, chapter 18 (ed., p. 28, line 1), "//Sturio unus en tibi defertur et animus tuus de deliciarum inopia queritur? ..."; text then continues, with no breaks, through f. 28v, ending in book 2, chapter 27 (ed., p. 103, line 1), "... Cvm autem lugdunum uenisset//"; and resumes abruptly, f. 29, in book 2, chapter 35 (ed., p. 113, line 12), "//-changeli. Quod anselmus agnoscens ilico lugdunum ire [*sic*] uolebat ..."

2. ff. 39–65v [*Vita sancti odonis abbatis cluniacensis (d. 942) auctore iohanne monacho cluniacense*] //excubias diligenter menti suae suggestum est ... erat animus et terrena iam oblitus puro mentis intuitu tanquam uerus martini uer-//

   BHL 6292–96; *PL* 133:43–86, here beginning imperfectly in book 1, chapter 5 (ed., col. 46C, line 38), and ending abruptly in book 3, chapter 45 (ed., col. 84C, line 52).

   Divided into 4 books, beginning on ff. 49, 56, and 60. Conclusion of book 2, ff. 49–56, agrees with *BHL* 6294: "Multis calamitati [*corr.*: calamitatibus] et crebris languoribus affecto pauca uobis mihi licuit ... Sed quia satis iam in his immorati sumus, hunc librum debito iam fine concludamus." Book 2, chapters 14–22 of the edition (cols. 69–73) are here found on ff. 59–62, between chapters 6 and 7 of book 3 (ed., col. 79D; cf. *BHL* 6296).

3. ff. 66–73 [*Vita maioli abbatis cluniacensis (d. 994) auctore odilone abbatis cluniacense*] //deuotissimum studium beatorum martirum triumphus aecclesie sancte commendatur ... [f. 71v] ... redit ad propria sospes et letus, prestante domino nostro ihesu christo qui uiuit et regnat in unitate spiritus deus per omnia secula seculorum. amen. [f. 71v appendix] Cvm enim huic sententiae finem imponem [*corr.*: imponere] uellem ... qui est uia ueritas et uita dominus uidelicet ihesus christus qui uiuit et regnat per omnia secula seculorum. amen. *Explicit uita sancti maioli abbatis.*

   BHL 5182–83; *PL* 142:943–62, here beginning imperfectly in book 1 (ed., col. 945A, line 6); includes the appendix, here beginning with a major initial (cf. col. 959B).

4. ff. 73–81v [*Vita sancti odilonis abbatis cluniacensis (d. 1049) auctore*

petro damiano] [*I*]*ncipit prologus in uita beati odilonis abbatis.* Petrus damianus sanctis aecclesiis quae sunt . . . Hugo cluniacensis monasterii rector et spiritualis militiae dux ac precipuus informator. Hoc mihi laboris iniunxit . . . [f. 73v text] *Incipit uita beati odilonis abbatis.* Beatus igitur odilo auernie oriundus ex equestri quidem ordine genus dixit . . . Proxima quoque quadragesima succendete sanctae ac uenerandae memoriae laurentius amalfitanae se-//

BHL 6282; *PL* 144:925–44, here ending imperfectly (ed., col. 944A, line 13). Divided into numerous short chapters that do not correspond with the divisions of the edition.

5. ff. 82–84v [*Vita hugonis abbatis cluniacensis (d. 1109) a domino hugone monacho cluniacense*] //Iniquirenti denique sancto de cuius esset episcopatu ille homo inuenit . . . et reprehendo comonuit [*sic*] ut ridiculosa quae male consueuerat//

BHL 4012; Martin Marrier and André Duchesne, eds., *Bibliotheca Cluniacensis* (Paris 1614; reprint Maçon 1915) cols. 437–48, here beginning imperfectly (ed., col. 440D, line 49) and ending abruptly (ed., col. 444D, line 52). Divided into numerous short chapters which do not correspond with those of the edition.

(Articles 1–5) Remains of tabs and other place markers, ff. 9, 19, 20v, and 24. Later notes are rare, but include a few marginal notations in an early hand (ff. 6, 14, 57v, 73, etc.), indications of subjects in lead point or brown crayon (for example, f. 26v), and nota marks (ff. 7, 7v, 21, etc.).

Parchment (repaired with slips of parchment, set into notched holes, and glued with half the slip on the recto and half on the verso; many now lack glue; cf. ff. 9, 12, 21, 30, 38, 46, 52, 54, 63, 65, 66 etc.), ff. i (paper) + 84 + i (paper), 297 x 205 (198–195 x 140–132) mm. 2 columns, 29 lines. Ruled in brown crayon, with the first, third, last, antepenultimate, and the middle three horizontal lines full across; single full-length vertical bounding lines. Horizontal rules are continued between the columns (on ff. 79–84v only the horizontal rules which are full across continue between the columns). Prickings in all margins, including the inside; bottom prickings are about halfway between the bottom of the written space and lower edge; double prickings in the outer margin for the middle three horizontal rules.

1^8 (–6 through 8, after f. 5, with loss of text) 2^8 (–1, before f. 6, with loss of text) $3–4^8$ 5^8 (–1 through 3, before f. 29, with loss of text) 6^8 (–6 and 7, after f. 38, with loss of text) $7–9^8$ 10^8 (–3, after f. 65, with loss of text) 11^8 12^8 (–4, and 5, after f. 81, with loss of text); ends imperfectly and therefore once included an additional quire(s). Manuscript now consists of singletons glued on stubs; signatures, roman numerals, often flourished, verso of last leaf, center, lower margin, many now excised completely or in part: ff. 12v ("II"), 20v, 28v, 33v, 47v, 55v, 63v ("IX"), 70v ("X"), 78v ("XI").

Written above the top line by one scribe in a conservative upright twelfth-century minuscule; e-cedilla used for 'ae' and incorrectly for 'e'; punctuation includes the *punctus flexus*.

Eight 6- to 4-line (except "I," f. 1v, 18-line) initials in red-orange, green or light-blue, infilled with decorative scrolls and other motifs in contrasting colors, used at the beginning of works and at the major divisions within each work; similar initials in New Haven, Conn., Yale University, Beinecke Library, MS 154, Robert of Bridlington, England, s. XII^2 (Shailor, *Beinecke Cat.*, 1:206–7, plate 17, and Barbara Shailor, *The Medieval Book: Illustrated from the Beinecke Rare Book and Manuscript Library*. Medieval Academy Reprints for Teaching 28 [Toronto 1991] 15, no. 14, with plate; we thank Michael Gullick for this information). Articles 1, 2, 4, and 5 divided into chapters with 2-line green, light-blue, and orange-red initials, often parted (one color), or terminating with decorative flourishes. Rubrics at the beginning of works and major divisions in orange-red or blue, often with the opening words of the text copied in majuscules in contrasting colors.

Rebound in 1954 in dark blue morocco by Arno Werner, replacing an American half calf binding, s. XIX; the manuscript was described as misbound in this earlier binding; when the manuscript was rebound, W. H. Bond entered notes on its contents and collation, inside back cover.

Written in England in the second half of the twelfth century (we thank Michael Gullick and Mary Carruthers for their comments on this manuscript). Belonged to the Cistercian abbey of St. Mary at Holme Cultram, Cumberland (founded 1151; Meer, *Atlas de l'ordre cistercien*, 283; this manuscript listed in Ker, *MLGB*, 102); ex libris note, s. XIII, f. 1, lower margin: "Liber sancte Marie de holmo," and later medieval pressmark, upper margin: "Liber cxcix"; manuscripts with similar ex libris notes and pressmarks include Oxford, Bodleian Library, MS Lyell 2, Jerome, *Letters*, England, s. XII^{ex} (de la Mare, *Lyell Cat.*, 2–4, and plate 1c) and San Marino, California, Huntington Library, HM 19915, Augustine, Pomerius, etc., England, s. XII/XIII (Dutschke, *Guide*, 602–4). Belonged to Nathaniel G. Snelling by 1845 when the manuscript was shown to the Harvard College librarian, John Langdon Sibley (1804–85; cf. Dennis, "Collecting," 287). In correspondence with Snelling, Sibley noted that the manuscript was incomplete and misbound, with portions of Eadmer's *Life of Anselm* (now art. 1) at the end (see the letters from Sibley to Snelling, December 1845, and December 18, 1846, once housed in the manuscript, now kept in the Autograph File, Houghton Library). Given to the library by Winslow Lewis, M.D. (1799–1875), probably on May 18, 1861, given the date of Lewis' death (date accepted by De Ricci, following a later pencil note in the manuscript), although other sources record the date as 1881 (library records and bookplate, inside front cover).

secundo folio: hoc sepius animo

Bibliography: De Ricci, 978; Harvard College Library, *Illuminated and Calligraphic Manuscripts*, 12, no. 17, plate 6 (reproducing f. 73); *Houghton Library 1942–1967*, 13 (with plate of f. 73); Light, *Bible in the Twelfth Century*, 107 (checklist).

MS Lat 34 — Italy (Bologna?) s. XIII^{ex}– XIV^{1}
Historia de preliis Alexandri Magni (recension J^{3}) — Pl. 39

ff. 1–12v [Text is misbound; correct order: ff. 1–3v, 7–10v, 4–6v, 11–12v] Sapientissimi quippe egiptii scientes mensuram terre undasque maris et celestium ordinem cognoscentes id est stellarum cursum motum etiam firmamenti tradiderunt . . . Duodecima alexandria est que dicitur Egyptus. *Explicit liber prudentissimi Alexandri, amen./ Fortis Alexander sapiens, robustus in armis/ Laudandus deus est in cunctis actibus eius.*

Karl Steffens, ed., *Die Historia de preliis Alexandri Magni; Rezension J^{3}*. Beiträge zur Klassischen Philologie 73 (Meisenheim am Glan

1975) 4–198, line 28, lacking the prohemium (ed., pp. 2–3) and the final chapter (ed., pp. 198–219), found in some manuscripts; this manuscript listed p. XVIII, no. 14, as '(H)' (the lacunae in the text incorrectly described); Francis P. Magoun, "Harvard MS. Latin 34, 'Historia de preliis' (J³ Recension)," *Harvard Library Notes* 2 (1928) 172–75; this manuscript also listed in F. Magoun, *The Gests of King Alexander of Macedon* (Cambridge, Mass. 1929) 51, note 3; and in A. Hilka and F. P. Magoun, "A List of Manuscripts containing texts of the 'Historia de preliis Alexandri Magni,' Recensions I¹, I², I³," *Speculum* 9 (1934) 84–86, p. 85, as 'H'.

Text is bound in incorrect order: ff. 1–3v, ending ed., p. 30, line 11; resumes, with no break, f. 7, and continues through f. 10v, ending ed., p. 64, line 32; resumes, with no break, f. 4, and continues through f. 6v, ending imperfectly, ". . . Spondemus enim uobis quod unicuique militi uestrum [*sic*] in nostrum//," ed., p. 90, line 11; resumes abruptly, f. 11, "//Alexandri et eorum clippeos transfforabant [*sic*] . . . ," ed., p. 182, line 6, and continues, with no break, to the end, f. 12v, ed., p. 198, line 28. Blank spaces remain for rubrics. Marginal annotations throughout in a running Italian hand, s. XIV, usually tied to the text and supplying captions lacking in this manuscript, for example, f. 8, "Epistola Alexandri ad darium," or, infrequently, correcting the text or supplying alternate readings (for example, f. 9). Pointing fingers, and nota marks throughout, s. XIV–XV.

On this recension (not mentioning this manuscript), see also: Friedrich Pfister, "Die Historia de preliis und das Alexanderepos des Quilichinus," *Münchener Museum für Philologie des Mittelalters und der Renaissance* 1 (1912) 249–301; and Hermann-Josef Bergmeister, ed., *Die Historia de preliis Alexandri Magni (Der lateinische Alexanderroman des Mittelalters); Synoptische Edition der Rezensionen des Leo Archipresbyter und der interpolierten Fassungen J¹, J², J³, (Buch I und II)*. Beiträge zur Klassischen Philologie 65 (Meisenheim am Glan 1975), basing his text of J³ on Quilichinus de Spoleto, *Historia Alexandri Magni nebst dem Text der Zwickauer Handschrift der Historia de preliis Alexandri Magni, Rezension J³*, W. Kirsch, ed. (Skopje 1971).

Parchment (prepared in the manner of southern Europe), ff. 12, 287–280 x 200 (211–207 x 139) mm. 2 columns, 52 lines. Ruled in dark lead; double vertical bounding lines at the far inside and outside and between the columns. Prickings, top and bottom margins.

Now misbound as: 1^{6} 2^{4} (ff. 7–10 misbound; originally 4, 5, 6, 7 of quire 1) 3^{2} (singletons, glued on stubs); originally 1^{10} (misbound, so that 10 is now f. 6) 2^{10} (–1 through 8, following f. 6, with loss of text).

Written below the top line by one scribe in a rounded southern gothic bookhand, with some use of decorative hairlines and flourishes, especially on the majuscule letters; opening two lines of text following painted initial, f. 1, in decorative majuscules, brown ink.

One 12-line historiated initial, f. 1, depicting Alexander, wearing robes over chain mail (?), and holding orb and sceptre, seated on a throne against a canopy; gray-brown initial on a polished gold ground, edged in black, terminating in curling acanthus leaves, with a full-length border, extending partly into the upper and lower margins, of blue, green, gray, pink and orange acanthus entwined around a thin stem, punctuated by knots and gold balls, finishing in spirals in the margins. Secondary divisions within the text marked by 2–line alternately red and blue initials, set within the text space, with violet and red pen flourishes respectively; guide letters visible alongside these initials. Blank lines remain for rubrics.

Bound in Italy, s. XV (?) in angled wooden boards, sewn on three bands (cf. note in an Italian hand, s. XV^{2}–XVI, inside back cover); rounded spine with three raised bands; four leather straps, tooled with simple flowers, with metal clasps, upper board (two missing the metal clasps), and four trefoil metal catches, lower board; boards are uncovered, except for leather back, probably added later, blind-tooled with crude diagonal lines.

Written in Italy, probably in Bologna, at the end of the thirteenth or in the first half of the fourteenth century. Belonged to Guglielmo Libri (1803–69); his sale, London, Sotheby's, March 28, 1859, no. 35 to Morton. Belonged to John Eliot Hodgkin (d. 1912; bookplate, inside front cover); not described in his *Classified Hand-list of Books, Prints, Coins, Pottery, etc., Collected by J*[*ohn*]. *E*[*liot*]. *H*[*odgkin*]., *F.S.A., 1858–85* (n.d., n.p.), or in *Rariora, being notes of some of the printed books, manuscripts, historical documents, medals, engravings, pottery, etc. collected 1858–1900 by J. E. Hodgkin* (London 1902), but listed in John C. Jeaffreson, *The Manuscripts of J. Eliot Hodgkin, Esq.,*

F.S.A. Historical Manuscripts Commission, Fifteenth Report, Appendix, Part 2 (London 1897) 2, 4. Hodgkin sale, London, Sotheby's, May 12, 1914, no. 27 to Ellis. Unidentified bookseller's or owner's notation, inside back cover, in pencil: "n/i/." Purchased, December 14, 1914 from Ellis, Cat. 156 (Winter 1914–15) no. 251 (Charles Minot Fund; library stamp, bottom margin, f. 1, and bookplate, inside front cover).

secundo folio: [pecca]sti inquam et non

Bibliography: De Ricci, 979.

fMS Lat 35 **Italy (Bologna or Venice?) 1353**
Guido de Columnis, Historia destructionis troiae **Pl. 1**

1. ff. 1–119 [Prologue] Si et cotidie uetera recentibus obruant ... [f. 1v Book 1] *De Rege peleo inducente Iasonem Ire ad acquirendum aureum Velus.* In regno thesalie de predicte scilicet prouinciis romanie ... Diomedes uero interfecit regem Antipum, regem Esterionem, regem Prothenorem, regem Optomenum et Sagitarium. [f. 118] *De eo qui fecit et compilauit hunc librum.* Et ego Guido de columpnis predictum ditem grecum in omnibus sum sequutus ... Quod quidem opus factum est Anno dominice incarnationis m cc octuagesimo septimo, prime indictionis. *Explicit liber de casu troie, deo gratias, amen.* [f. 118v chronology] Troia vrbs capta fuit a grecis, Anno tercio Labdon Iudicis israel qui tempore Iudicum gubernabat populum israel ... et ante romam conditam cc cxiiii anni et ante natiuitatem christi mlxx anni. [f. 118v colophon] Tempus quo ego perfinere./ Iniui et expleui presens opus/ Sidere quod tauri scribens surgentis Iniui/ Ego libra peregit opus/ Coeperat at phebus domini tunc mille trecentis./ Annis iuncta tribus uoluere lustra decem. *Finis libri troiani et grecii.* [f. 119 Epitaph for Hector; Walther, *Initia* 19461; Bertalot 6374] *Epitaphium hectoris.* [added: Troum protector Daneum [*sic*] metus, hic iacet Hector./] Defensor patrie Iuuenum fortissimus Hector,/ ... Condidit et merens hac tumulauit [*sic*] humo./ [f. 119 Epitaph for Achilles; Walther, *Initia* 13917] *Epithafium* [*sic*] *Achillis.* [*added: Achillis*] Pellides ego sum, Thetidis notissima proles,/ ... Cum pressi hostilem fraude peremptus humum./

Nathaniel E. Griffin, ed., The Medieval Academy of America Publications 26 (Cambridge, Mass. 1936), citing this manuscript as "C," p. xii. Not mentioned in Hugo Buchtal, *Historia troiana. Studies in the History of Medieval Secular Illustration.* Studies of the Warburg Institute 32, ed. E. Gombrich (London 1971). Divided into numerous, unnumbered sections rather than the 35 books of the edition. Manuscript is misbound, with the following sections of the text out of order: f. 24, containing the beginning of book 8 (Griffin, ed., p. 80, line 3–p. 82, line 1) should be between the present ff. 34 and 35; f. 29, book 10 (Griffin, ed., p. 91, line 18–p. 93, line 24) should be between ff. 38 and 39. The Epitaphs for Hector and Achilles, here found after the author's epilogue, are printed before it in the edition (Griffin, ed., p. 275).

Sparse marginalia, including scattered nota marks ("no") in red, possibly original (ff. 87, 93, etc.), and the comment "deo gracias," enclosed in a red paragraph mark (ff. 88v, 89v). A longer note on f. 39, added by an early reader, citing Ovid, *Metamorphoses*, on Prometheus. Occasional pointing hands added later.

(Articles 2–4) ff. 119v–120 Epitaphs added in another hand.

2. f. 119v [Epitaph of King Robert of Sicily, d. 1343] *Epitaphyum regis Ruberti* [*sic*]. Hic sacra magnanimi requiesschunt [*sic*] ossa Roberti/ . . . Eternumque canet nullum tacitura per euum.

   Walther, *Initia* 8091; Bertalot 2273; cf. Bertalot 2618; printed in Francisci Petrarchae, *Poemata Minora quae exstant omnia* (Milan 1831) 2:286–89.

3. f. 119v [Menghino Mezzani, Epitaph of Dante Alighieri, 1265–1321] *Epitaphyum dantis.* Inclita fama cuius uniuerssum [*sic*] penetrat orbem/ . . . Septembris Idibus presentis clauditur aulla.

   Walther, *Initia* 9236; Bertalot 2689; printed in Carlo del Balzo, *Poesie di mille autori intorno a Dante Alighieri* (Rome 1889) 1:269, no. XLII.

4. f. 120 [Gabrius de Zamoreis, Epitaph of Iohannes Vicecomitis, archbishop of Milan, 1342–54] *Epitaphyum domini Archiepiscopi Vicecomitis Mediolanensis domini.* Quam fasstus [*sic*], quam ponpa [*sic*] leuis, quam gloria mundi/ . . . Cum michi sufficiat, quod paruoque [expunged: in] marmore claudor./ Et clauxi [*sic*] diem meum m°cccliiii [*sic*] quinto octubris.

Walther, *Initia* 15138; Bertalot 4653; printed in Ferdinandus Ughelli, *Italia sacra sive de episcopis Italiae*, 2nd. ed. (Venice 1719) 4: col. 249–50; see also Helmut Boese, *Die Lateinischen Handschriften der Sammlung Hamilton zu Berlin* (Wiesbaden 1966) 128.

5. ff. 120v–121v Miscellaneous notes in a number of Italian hands, s. XV–XVI, including a series of proverbs and other short mottos, some written several times by the same scribe in different scripts, including among others, Walther, *Proverbia* 120, 25000, 25010b, "Vir virtuosus semper erat plurimis . . . ," "Amichus causa utilitas assumptus tam diu placebit quam diu utilitas," and "Nuptie sumptuose dampnum sine honore conferunt"; a minim exercise ("id minimum minimoque minus"); the date, m°ccccxvi, in a hand appearing elsewhere on these folios; f. 120 [fragment of an unidentified epitaph; text partially obscured by later repair] *Epitaphium regis teutre, regis civitatis.* Molose me se amici . . .; f. 120 [*Septem versus orationem dominicam exprimentes*] O pater alme tuum sit nomen sanctificatum/ Adueniatque tuum regnum per secula beatum/ . . . Et tutela malo nos deffendat ab omni. [Bloomfield 8641; Walther, *Initia* 12835]; f. 121 [short discussion of the seven deadly sins] Dicuntur peccata fore mortalia septem. Prima quia peccata sic esse superbia fertur . . . Ergo vitemus illam que ducit ad ortum.; and various signatures of early users and owners of the manuscript (see below, provenance).

Parchment (well washed palimpsest, apparently a Latin legal document, Italy, s. XIII, with the text running parallel with the present text), ff. i (paper) + i (early modern paper) + 121 (medieval foliation, possibly original, upper left margin, verso, in roman numerals, brown ink, reflecting the original order of the text as follows: 1–23, 33 [now f. 24v], 24–27, 38 [now f. 29v], 28–32, 34–37, 39–118; two sets of continuous modern foliation: in pencil, upper right corner, recto, 1–118, + 3 unnumbered folios, cited; and center lower margin, recto, 1–119, incorrectly foliated with unnumbered folios following ff. 75 and 110) + i (paper), 299 x 220 (225–215 x 147–145) mm. 36–33 long lines. Ruled in lead, usually with all horizontal rules full across; single full-length vertical bounding lines, except quire 3 (ff. 21–32v), with double full-length vertical bounding lines in the outer margin.

$1–2^{10}$ 3^{10} (+4 and 9, ff. 24 and 29, conjugate pair misbound from quire 4) 4^{10} (–3 and 8, following ff. 33 and 37, conjugate pair, now ff. 24 and 29 in quire 4) $5–9^{10}$ 10^{8} $11–12^{10}$ 13^{2} (+3, f. 121, singleton). Vertical catchwords, center lower margin, boxed in brown ink.

Written by one scribe in a quick mercantesca script. Articles 2–4 (ff. 119–20) added by a near contemporary, using a similar script.

Three 5- to 3-line historiated initials, ff. 1, 1v, 17v; initials are pink (except f. 1v, where figure serves as initial) with white highlights on rectangular grounds of polished gold, edged in black; on f. 1, with a C-shaped border extending into the outer margin of blue and gray-green acanthus leaves on a rigid stem, with touches of bright and dark red and pink and scattered large gold balls heavily circled in black ink; top margin, center, a miniature of a mounted knight, in full armor with shield; horse robed in a heraldic cloth, badly rubbed, possibly with red lions rampant on gold; bottom margin, roundel with effaced coat of arms. Remaining initials with short extensions of similar acanthus leaves and large gold balls scattered in the margins. Subjects include: f. 1 Troy, depicted as a walled town, in shades of orange and gray, with a blue sky, on a dark gray ground; f. 1v a bust of a King (Peleus?), crowned, in a blue robe and pink mantle; f. 17v (beginning of book 5, Griffin, ed., p. 43) a man, possibly King Priam, although without a crown, in green robe and red mantle, standing before Troy, against a blue background. Numerous 3-line intitials, alternating red and blue, with pen flourishes in violet or red respectively, at the beginning of each section of the text. Red rubrics; red paragraph marks used sporadically within the text.

Bound in half vellum and marbled paper, s. XIX–XX; title and date (s. XII) written on spine in ink.

Written in Italy in 1353 (dated by the scribe, f. 119), probably in Bologna or Venice (we thank Professor Lilian Armstrong for her assistance, January, 1989). Effaced arms of original owner, f. 1, and miniature of a mounted knight with shield, f. 1, suggest the manuscript was made for a patrician. In Italy, s. XIV–XV; names of early readers or owners, ff. 120v–121v, include Jachomollus de Fortamella, Guidollus, Antoginus filius quondam Melchionis de Guasto (Vasto, once Istonio, pr. Chieti), [f. 121v read under ultraviolet] "Geo<?>grus de sancto Julliana scripsi," and below, "Iste liber est meus Granoli e latue<?>." Unidentified marks of modern owners or booksellers: inside front cover, in pencil "M.R."; inside back cover:

"L.M."; front flyleaf, f. ii^{v}: "5864/ 5.S." Belonged to Katherine Petersen, Brooklyn, New York (pencil note, front flyleaf, f. ii^{v}); her gift, January 6, 1898 (library stamp, front flyleaf, f. ii^{v}; bookplate, inside front cover). Letter identifying Dante's Epitaph tipped in between ff. 119–120, March 27, 1898, from Theo[dore] W. Koch, Cornell University Library to William Hopkins Tillinghast, A.B. Harvard 1877, Assistant Librarian, Harvard. Original Harvard shelf mark: 27282.67.6*.

secundo folio: totum uulgus

Bibliography: De Ricci, p. 979 and 2302; S. Harrison Thomson, *Latin Bookhands of the Later Middle Ages, 1100–1500* (Cambridge 1969), no. 73, reproducing f. 25; Émile Van Balberghe, "Un Album Paléographique de Manuscrits Datés," [review of Thomson] *Scriptorium* 25 (1971) 309; Wieck, p. 107, fig. 75 (reproducing f.1v).

fMS Lat 36 — France (Paris) s. XIII/XIV
Bible — Pl. 25

The order of the books and the choice of prologues conform to the pattern commonly found in Bibles from northern France and especially Paris dating after c. 1230 (cf. Ker, *MMBL* 1:96–7), with four additional prologues: Stegmüller 674 (Romans), 631 (Acts), 834 and 829 (Apocalypse). A test of selected passages from the Octateuch (cf. Quentin, *Mémoire*, 385) and the Gospels indicates that textually it is related to the Paris Bible. Modern chapter divisions throughout.

Five folios with the following portions of text excised: f. 3, general prologue (Stegmüller 284), ending imperfectly, prologue (Stegmüller 285) and Genesis 1:1–2:12; f. 97, 1 Kings 31:7–2 Kings 3:12; f. 128, 4 Kings ending imperfectly at 25:14, prologue (Stegmüller 328) and 1 Chronicles 1:1–1:53; f. 173, 2 Ezra (=3 Ezra, Stegmüller 94,1) ending imperfectly at 9:28, prologue (Stegmüller 332) and Tobit 1:1–3:5; f. 222, Proverbs ending imperfectly at 30:18, prologue (Stegmüller 462) and Ecclesiastes 1:1–3:4.

1. [3 unnumbered folios added before f. 1] Epistle and Gospel lections for the liturgical year, identified by book, chapter number and opening and closing words; including the temporale from the

first Sunday in Advent through the twenty-fourth Sunday after Pentecost, the sanctorale, rather brief, from the vigil of Andrew through All Saints, including Anthony of Padua, Apollinaris, and Francis, and concluding with the common of the saints from many apostles through the dedication of a church, and concluding, "in agenda defunctorum."

2. ff. 1–346v Old Testament: f. 1 *Incipit epistola sancti ieronimi presbiteri ad paulinum de omnibus diuine hystorie libris.* Frater ambrosius mihi tua munuscula perferens detulit ... Petenti datur pulsanti aperitur querens inuenit. Discamus// [Stegmüller 284, ending imperfectly]; [f. 3 with Stegmüller 285, excised]; f. 4 Genesis, beginning imperfectly at 2:12: "//illius optimum est. Ibique inuenitur bdellium et lapis onichinus. . . ."; f. 19v Exodus; f. 33 Leviticus; f. 42v Numbers; f. 55v Deuteronomy; f. 66 *Incipit prologus in libro iosue.* Tandem finito pentatheuco moysi velut grandi fenore ... [Stegmüller 311]; f. 66v Joshua; f. 74v Judges; f. 83 Ruth; f. 84v *Incipit prologus in libro regum.* Viginti et duas litteras esse apud hebreos ... [Stegmüller 323]; f. 85 1 Kings, ending imperfectly at 31:7: ". . . Veneruntque philistiim et habi-//"; [f. 97 excised]; f. 98 2 Kings, beginning imperfectly at 3:12: "//ad dauid in ebron pro se dicentes. Cuius est terra. . . ."; f. 106v 3 Kings; f. 117v 4 Kings, ending imperfectly at 25:14: ". . . et trullas et tridentes et syphos [*sic*] et mortariola et omnia//"; [f. 128 with Stegmüller 328, excised]; f. 129 1 Chronicles, beginning imperfectly at 1:53: "//-non dux cenez dux theman dux mabsan [*sic*] dux madihel dux iram. Hii duces edom ..."; f. 137v *Incipit prologus in ii libro paralipomenon.* Eusebius Ieronimus dominioni [*corr.*[2]: dominiani] et rogationo [*sic*] suis in ihesu christo salutem. Quomodo grecorum hystorias magis intelligunt ... [Stegmüller 327 with salutation]; f. 138 2 Chronicles, followed immediately by the Prayer of Manasses: "Domine deus omnipotens patrum nostrorum abraham ysaac et iacob ..." [Stegmüller 93,2]; [incorrectly foliated so that f. 149 is followed by f. 160]; f. 160 *Incipit prologus in libro esdre.* Utrum difficilius sit facere quod poscitis an negare ... [Stegmüller 330]; f. 160v 1 Ezra; f. 163v Nehemiah; f. 168 2 Ezra [=3 Ezra; Stegmüller 94, 1], ending imperfectly at 9:28: "Et ex filii [*corr.*[2]: filiis] zathom eliadas//"; [f. 173 with Stegmüller 332, excised]; f. 174 Tobit, beginning imperfectly at 3:5: "//quia non egimus secundum

precepta tua et non amblerauimus [*sic*] . . ."; f. 176v *Incipit prologus in libro iudith.* Apud hebreos liber iudith inter agyographa legitur . . . [Stegmüller 335]; f. 176v Judith; f. 181 *Incipit prologus in libro hester.* Librum hester variis translationibus [*sic*] constat esse uiciatum . . .; Rursum in libro hester alphabetum . . . [Stegmüller 341 and 343 written as one prologue]; f. 181 Esther; f. 185 *Incipit prologus in libro iob.* Cogor per singulos scripture diuine libros . . . [Stegmüller 344]; f. 185v *Item alius prologus.* Si aut ficellam [*corr.*[2]: fiscellam] iunco texerem aut palmarum . . . [Stegmüller 357]; f. 185v Job; f. 194 Psalms [Stegmüller 21]; f. 215 *Incipit prologus in libro prouerbiorum.* Ivngat epistola quos iungit sacerdocium . . . [Stegmüller 457]; f. 215 Proverbs, ending imperfectly at 30:18: ". . . effodiant eum corui de torrentibus et comedant eum filii aquile. Tria//"; [f. 222 with Stegmüller 462, excised]; f. 223 Ecclesiastes, beginning imperfectly at 3:4: "//plangendi et tempus saltandi. Tempus spargendi lapides et tempus colligendi . . ."; f. 224v Song of Songs; f. 226 *Incipit prologus in libro sapientie.* Liber sapientie apud hebreos nusquam est . . . [Stegmüller 468]; f. 226 Wisdom; f. 231 *Incipit prologus ecclesiastici.* Multorum nobis et magnorum per legem . . . [biblical introduction to Ecclesiasticus treated as a prologue]; f. 231 Ecclesiasticus; f. 244v *Incipit prologus sancti ieronimi in ysaie propheta.* Nemo cum prophetas uersibus uiderit esse . . . [Stegmüller 482]; f. 244v Isaiah; f. 261 *Incipit prologus ieremie prophete.* Iheremias propheta cui hic [*corr.*[2] *add.* prologus] scribitur . . . [Stegmüller 487]; f. 261 Jeremiah; f. 281 Lamentations; f. 283 *Prologus in libro baruhc* [*sic*]. Liber iste qui baruch nomine prenotatur . . . [Stegmüller 491]; f. 283 Baruch; f. 285v *Prologus in ezechielis. Rubrica.* Ezechiel propheta cum ioachim rege iuda . . . [Stegmüller 492]; f. 286 Ezechiel; f. 304 *Incipit prologus in libro Danielis prophete.* Danielem prophetam iuxta septuaginta interpretres [*sic*] . . . [Stegmüller 494]; f. 304v Daniel; f. 311v *Prologus xii prophetarum.* Non idem ordo est duodecim prophetarum . . . [Stegmüller 500]; f. 311v *Alius prologus.* Temporibus ozie et ioathe achaz . . . [Stegmüller 507]; f. 312 Hosea; f. 314 *Prologus ioel* [*sic*]. Sanctus iohel apud hebreos post osee ponitur . . . [Stegmüller 511]; f. 314v [rubric omitted] Ioel fatuel filius describit terram . . . [Stegmüller 510]; f. 314v Joel; f. 315v *Incipit prologus amos. Rubrica.* Ozias rex cum dei religionem sollicite emularetur . . . [Stegmüller 515]; f. 315v *Alius prologus.* Amos [expunged by a later hand: propheta] pastor et rusticus et ruborum moros distringuens [*sic*] ... [Stegmüller 512]; f. 315v [rubric omitted] Hic amos propheta [*om.* et pastor] non fuit pater ysaie ... [Stegmüller 513]; f. 315v Amos; f. 317v *Incipit prologus abdie prophete.* Iacob patriarcha fratrem habuit ...; Hebrei hunc dicunt esse ... [Stegmüller 519 and 517, written as one prologue]; f. 317v Obadiah; f. 318 *Incipit prologus in iona propheta* [*sic*]. Sanctum ionam hebrei affirmant filium ...; Iona [*sic*] columba et dolens filius amathi ... [Stegmüller 524 and 521 written without a break]; f. 318 Jonah; f. 319 *Incipit prologus michee prophete. Rubrica.* Temporibus ioathe et achaz et ezechie ... [Stegmüller 526]; f. 319 Micah; f. 320v *Incipit prologus naum prophete. Rubrica.* Naum prophetam ante aduentum regis ... sicut in consequentibus libri huius demonstrabitur.// [Stegmüller 528, ending imperfectly; completed in a later hand, bottom margin]; f. 320v Nahum; f. 321 *Incipit prologus abacuch prophete. Rubrica.* Quatuor prophete in xii prophetarum .. [Stegmüller 531]; f. 321v Habakkuk; f. 322 *Incipit prologus sophonie prophete.* Tradunt hebrei cuiuscumque prophete ... [Stegmüller 534]; f. 322v Zephaniah; f. 323 *Incipit prologus aggei. Rubrica.* Ieremias propheta ob causam periurii ... [Stegmüller 538]; f. 323v Haggai; f. 324 *Incipit prologus in libro zacharie.* In anno secundo darii regis medorum ... [Stegmüller 539]; f. 324 Zachariah; f. 327 *Incipit prologus in libro malachie prophete.* Deus per moysen populo Israeli [*sic*] preceperat ... [Stegmüller 543]; f. 327 Malachai; f. 328 *Incipit prologus in libro machabeorum primo.* Domino excellentissimo et in cultu christiane ... Cum sim promptus animo ... [Stegmüller 547]; f. 328 *Item alius prologus. Rubrica.* Reuerentissimo [*om.* domino] et omni ... Memini me in palacio uuangionum ... [Stegmüller 553]; f. 328v *Incipit prologus alius. Rubrica. Rubrica. Rubrica.* Machabeorum libri duo prenotant [prenotant: written twice; corrected by a later hand] prelia ... [Stegmüller 551]; f. 328v 1 Maccabees; f. 339v 2 Maccabees.

3. ff. 346v–433v New Testament: f. 346v *Incipit prologus mathei euangeliste.* Matheus ex iudea [*sic*] sicut in ordine primus ponitur ... [Stegmüller 590]; f. 346v *Alius prologus.* Matheus cum primo predicasset euangelium ... [Stegmüller 589]; f. 347 Matthew; f. 357v *Incipit prologus in libro marci euangeliste.* Marcus euangelista dei electus a [*sic*] petri ... [Stegmüller 607]; f. 357v Mark; f. 364v

Incipit prologus in euangelium secundum lucam. Quoniam quidem multi conati sunt . . . [Luke 1:1–4, treated as a prologue]; f. 364v *Item alius prologus.* Lucas syrus nacione antiochensis arte medicus discipulus apostolorum . . . [Stegmüller 620]; f. 365 Luke; f. 376 *Incipit prologus Iohannis euangeliste.* Hic est iohannes euangelista unus ex discipulis domini . . . [Stegmüller 624]; f. 376v John; f. 386v *Incipit prologus Ieronimi in epistola pauli ad romanos.* Romani sunt qui ex iudeis gentibusque crediderunt . . . ad pacem et concordiam cohortatur. [Stegmüller 674]; f. 387 *Alius prologus.* Romani sunt [*om.* in] partis [*sic*] ytalie. Hii preuenti sunt a falsis apostolis . . . [Stegmüller 677]; f. 387 Romans; f. 391 *Incipit prologus Ieronimi epistole prime beati pauli ad Corinthios.* Corinthii sunt achaici. Et hii similiter ab apostolo . . . per timotheum discipulum suum. [Stegmüller 685]; f. 391v 1 Corinthians; f. 395v *Incipit prologus in epistola secunda ad corinthios.* Post actam penitentiam consolatoriam . . . emendatos ostendens. [Stegmüller 699]; f. 395v 2 Corinthians; f. 398v *Incipit prologus in epistola ad galathas.* Galathe sunt greci. Hii uerbum ueritatis primum ab apostolo . . . scribens eis ab epheso. [Stegmüller 707]; f. 398v Galatians; f. 400 *Incipit prologus in epistola ad ephesos.* Ephesii sunt asiani. Hii accepto uerbo ueritatis . . . per thithicum [*sic*] dyaconem. [Stegmüller 715]; f. 400 Ephesians; f. 401v *Prologus in epistola ad philippenses.* Philippenses sunt macedones. Hii accepto uerbo ueritatis . . . de carcere per epafroditum. [Stegmüller 728]; f. 401v Philippians; f. 402v *Incipit prologus in epistola ad colosenses.* Colosenses et hii sicut laodicences [*corr.*[2]: laodisenses] sunt asiani . . . et oneseyum [*sic*] acolitum. [Stegmüller 736]; f. 402v Colossians; f. 403v *Incipit prologus in epistola ad thessalonicenses.* Thessalonicenses sunt macedones in christo . . . scribens eis ab athenis per tythicum [*corr.*[2] *add.* diaconem] et onesium [*corr.*[2]: onesim; *add.* acolitum]. [Stegmüller 747]; f. 403v 1 Thessalonians; f. 404v *Incipit prologus in epistola secunda ad thessaloncenses* [*sic*]. Ad thessalonisenses [*sic*] secundam scribit epistolam . . . et onesium [*sic*] acolitum. [Stegmüller 752]; f. 404v 2 Thessalonians; f. 405 *Incipit prologus in epistola prima ad thimotheum.* Thimotheum instruit et docet . . . ei a laodicia [*sic*]. [Stegmüller 765]; f. 405 1 Timothy; f. 406 *Incipit prologus secunde epistole ad thimotheum.* Item thimotheo scribit de exhoratione . . . et omnis regule// [Stegmüller 772, ending imperfectly; completed in another hand in the margin]; f. 406 2 Timothy; f. 407 *Prologus ad tytum.* Titum commonefacit et instruit . . . scribens ei a nichopoli. [Stegmüller 780]; f. 407 Titus; f. 407v *Incipit prologus in epistola ad philemonem.* Philemoni familiares litteras . . . ab urbe roma de carcere per supradictum [*sic*] honesim. [Stegmüller 783]; f. 407v Philemon; f. 407v *Incipit prologus in epistola ad ebreos.* In primis dicendum est cur apostolus . . . [Stegmüller 793]; f. 407v Hebrews; f. 411 [added in bottom margin by main scribe:] *Prologus in actus* [*sic*] *apostolorum.* Actus apostolorum nudam quidem sonare uidentur . . . [Stegmüller 631]; *Alius prologus.* Lucas antiochensis nacione syrus cuius laus in euangelio canitur . . . eius proficeret medicina. [Stegmüller 640]; f. 411 Acts; f. 422v *Incipit prologus vii epistolarum canonicarum Ieronimi presbyteri.* Non ita est ordo apud grecos . . . [Stegmüller 809]; f. 422v James; f. 424 1 Peter; f. 425 2 Peter; f. 425v 1 John; f. 426v 2 John; f. 427 3 John; f. 427 Jude; f. 427v [rubric omitted] Omnes qui pie uolunt uiuere . . . [Stegmüller 839]; f. 428 Apocalypse [ends mid column b, f. 433]; f. 433v [additional prologues, hand of main scribe] *Incipit prologus in apocalipsi. Rubrica.* Iohannes apostolus et euuangelista a domino christo electus . . . [Stegmüller 834]; *Alius prologus.* Apocalipsis Iohannis tot habet sacramenta quot uerba . . . [Stegmüller 829].

4. ff. 434–469v *Hic sunt interpretaciones hebraicorum nominum incipiencium per a litteram.* Aaz apprehendens uel apprehensio . . . Zuzim consiliantes eos uel consiliatores eorum, etc. *Hic est finis interpretacionum. Gratiarum.* [Followed by a later note; see discussion of provenance, below; f. 470rv blank.]

   Stephen Langton, *Interpretation of Hebrew Names*; Stegmüller 7709.

(Articles 2–4) Carefully corrected throughout in a contemporary, formal hand, usually supplying omissions in the margin, decoratively boxed in red and blue (cf. ff. 41, 67v, 94, 251v), marking superfluous words within the text (cf. ff. 25, and 432) and, rarely, noting variant readings (cf. f. 280v, Jeremiah 51:54: "Vox clamantis [margin: uel clamoris] de babilone et contricio magna de terra chaldeorum. . . . ," and f. 289, Ezechiel 12:23: ". . . et loquere ad eos, quia [margin: uel quod] appropinquauerunt [*sic*] dies et sermo omnis uisionis."). Quires 8, 33 and 36 (ff. 81v, 392v, and 428v) signed by a corrector, bottom, outer margin, verso of last leaf.

Formal marginal and interlinear glosses and other material added throughout in an Italian hand, s. XIV, likely that of Andreus

Justus Cennis de Vulterris (his ex libris note, f. 469), who also added the foliation and the table of liturgical readings at the beginning of the Bible (art. 1). In the Old Testament, Genesis, Exodus, 1 Kings, and Daniel are most fully glossed; the marginal notes in the New Testament consist mostly of additional prologues, and f. 403v, bottom margin, the Epistle to the Laodiceans (Stegmüller 233). First gloss, f. 1 (commenting on the general prologue, Stegmüller 284): "Paulinus presbiter romanus fuit elegantis ingenii ut patet in secunda epistola Ieronimi ad eiusdem qui renuntiare uolens . . . [some similarites to Guilelmus Brito's commentary on this prologue; Stegmüller 2824]." Examples of the general introductory glosses include: f. 19v, bottom margin, Exodus: "Historia exodi non alia quidem a predictis sed eadem continuata sed propter fastidium tollendum non secundum tempus sed secundum historiam in quinque partitiones distincta sunt . . . [cf. Petrus Comestor, *Historia scholastica*; Stegmüller 6545]," and f. 74v, bottom margin, Judges: "Liber iudicum hebraice sothim [*sic*] dicitur qui iudices describit usque ad hely sacerdotem quod ab hoc dicitur . . . [beginning agrees with Petrus Comestor, *Historia scholastica*; Stegmüller 6550]."

The following prologues are marginal additions in this hand: f. 185v, Job, "In terra quidem habitasse . . . [Stegmüller 349]"; ff. 214v–215, Proverbs, "Tribus nominibus uocatum fuisse . . . [Stegmüller 456]"; f. 304v, Daniel, "Daniel interpretatur iudicium . . . [Stegmüller 495]"; f. 317v, Obadiah, "Abdias qui interpretatur seruus domini . . . [Stegmüller 516]"; f. 319, Micah, "Micheas de morasti . . . [Stegmüller 525]"; f. 320v, Nahum, "Naum qui consolator . . . [Stegmüller 527]"; f. 321v, Habakkuk, "Abacuc propheta amplexans . . . [Stegmüller 530]," and "Abacuc luctator fortis . . . [Stegmüller 529]"; f. 322v, Zephaniah, "Sophonias speculator . . . [Stegmüller 532]"; f. 323v, Haggai, "Aggaeus festiuus . . . [Stegmüller 535]"; f. 324, Zachariah, "Zacharias memor domini . . . [Stegmüller 540]"; f. 328v, 1 Maccabees, "Machabeorum liber licet non habeantur in canone hebreorum . . . [Stegmüller 552]"; f. 346v, Matthew, "Plures fuisse qui euangelia scripserunt . . . quod ecclesiasticis uiuis canendas. [Stegmüller 596, here lacking Stegmüller 600 and ending as in de Bruyne, *Préfaces*, 155–56]," and f. 347, "Beatissimo pape damaso Ieronimus. Nouum opus me cogitis facere . . . [Stegmüller 595]"; f. 357v, Mark, "Petrus apostolus cum secundum historie . . . [Stegmüller 611, partly excised]"; ff. 386v–387, Romans, "Primum queritur quare post euangelia . . . [Stegmüller 670]," "Romani sunt in partes italie. Hii fidem habentes . . . [Stegmüller 676]," and "Romanos nondum uiderat apostolus . . . [Stegmüller 679]"; f. 391v, 1 Corinthians, "Corinthus metropolis Achaye ciuitas perhibetur . . . [Stegmüller 689]"; and f. 401v, Philippians, "In actibus apostolorum legimus . . . [Stegmüller 726]."

Infrequent notes in other hands including, f. 85v, a citation from Jerome in a French hand, s. XIV, pointing hands (cf. ff. 42, 289, etc.) and trefoil readers' marks in the margins.

Parchment, ff. iv (paper) + 463 (incorrectly foliated 1–470 as follows: with three unnumbered folios added before f. 1; medieval foliation, cited, in roman numerals, brown ink, upper, outside corner, recto, 1–434, with the following errors: f. 61 bis, f. 149 followed by f. 160, and f. 377 followed by f. 379; ff. 3, 97, 128, 173, 222 now excised; concludes with modern foliation, bottom, inside corner, ff. 435–470; f. 470 is a blank leaf added to the last quire, possibly contemporary with the unnumbered folios before f. 1) + iv (paper), 375 x 235 (252–247 x 157–150) mm. 2 columns, 52 lines. Ruled in lead, with top and bottom horizontal lines usually full across, and with an extra set of narrow double rules in the upper margin for running titles (lacking in art. 4) and occasionally in the bottom margins; double full-length vertical bounding lines, used for the opening majuscule of each line of text in art. 4. Prickings in top and bottom margins. Article 1 (3 unnumbered folios before f. 1): written space (258–256 x 197–192) mm. 2 columns, 65–67 lines. Ruled very faintly in lead, with top and bottom horizontal lines full across; columns are widely spaced and apparently bounded by full-length double vertical bounding lines, used for the first majuscule of each entry.

1^{4} (–1, cancelled, with no loss of text) 2^{12} (–3, f. 3, excised, with loss of text) 3^{12} 4^{10} $5–9^{12}$ 10^{12} (–4, f. 97, excised, with loss of text) 11^{12} 12^{12} (–11, f. 128, excised, with loss of text) $13–14^{12}$ 15^{12} (–10, f. 173, excised, with loss of text) $16–18^{12}$ 19^{12} (–11, f. 222, excised, with loss of text) $20–36^{12}$ 37^{4} (+5, f. 433, a singleton) $38–39^{12}$ 40^{12} (10 and 12, ff. 467 and 469, singletons; +13, f. 470, a singleton added at the end of quire). Scribe 1 (ff. 1–271v; quires 2–23, excised in quires 2–7, 14, and 22): horizontal catchwords, bottom, inside margin, undecorated except in quires 20 and 21, where they are boxed in red; scribe 2 (ff. 272–469v; quires 24–40, excised in quires 24, 26, 33–35 and 37): horizontal catchwords, bottom, inside margin, decoratively boxed, and usually with flourishes on all sides in brown or brown and red.

Leaf and quire signatures in a number of different hands, possibly remnants of series added at different times, including small minuscule letters in brown ink, bottom margin, recto, designating the order of the leaves (cf. quire 5, f. 36, in the center, with a mark designating the quire, and quire 6, f. 48, outer margin, leaf signature only); larger minuscule letters, middle, bottom margin, recto (cf. quires 7 and 8, ff. 59, 70, 74, and 75, with a mark designating the quire, and quire 13, f. 130, without the mark); small neat roman numerals in brown ink, bottom, outer margin, marking the order of the leaves only (cf. quire 11, f. 111); large, roman numerals in another hand, light brown ink, very bottom, middle margin, marking the order of the leaves only (cf. quire 12, ff. 122 and 123); large, hastily written roman numerals in faint ink or lead, bottom, outer margin, marking the order of the leaves only (cf. quires 14, 15, and 17, beginning on ff. 142, 164 and 188); small neat minuscule letters in blue lead, center to outer bottom margin, recto, designating the order of the leaves, with a mark designating the order of the quires (cf. quires 17–19, and 21–25, beginning on ff. 188, 200, 212, 236, 248, 260, 272, and 284); small red roman numerals, slashed with blue, very bottom, outer margin (quire 20, beginning on f. 224); and small red roman numerals, bottom, outer margin, designating the order of the leaf, with a letter designating the quire (cf. quire 23, beginning on f. 260).

Written below the top line in a formal gothic bookhand by two scribes; the second scribe beginning on f. 272.

Seventy-four historiated initials of very high quality (initials on ff. 3, 97, 128, 173, 222, 317v, and 357v excised) by the Master of the Bible Historiale of Jean de Papeleu, Paris, Bibliothèque de l'Arsenal, MS 5059; likely executed early in his career, c. 1300 in Paris (we thank Joan Diamond Udovitch for this information; Joan Diamond [Udovitch], "Manufacture and Market in Parisian Book Illumination around 1300," *Europäische Kunst um 1300*, eds. G. Schmidt and E. Liskar. Akten des XXV. Internationaler Kongress für Kunstgeschicte 6 (Vienna 1986) 101–10, listing this manuscript

p. 110). Initials are 10- to 5-line (except the letter "I," 15- to 21-line) in blue or pink with white highlights, on grounds of maroon, pink or blue, infilled with diapered backgrounds in contrasting colors; with cusped terminals and bar borders in dark blue, gray, and gold with touches of orange and green, terminating in naturalistic leaves and grotesques. Subjects include: f. 1 (general prologue) Jerome writing; [f. 3 (Genesis) excised]; f. 19v (Exodus) Moses, holding the tablets and rod, speaking to the Israelites; f. 33 (Leviticus) sacrifice of a lamb; f. 42v (Numbers) God, appearing in the clouds, speaking to Moses; f. 55v (Deuteronomy) Moses and Aaron placing the tablets in the tabernacle; f. 66v (Joshua) God, appearing in the clouds, speaking to Joshua; f. 74v (Judges) God, appearing in the clouds, speaking to two kneeling men; f. 83 (Ruth) Elimelech, with stick and bundle, on his journey; f. 85 (1 Kings) Elcana and Anna praying at an altar; [f.97 (2 Kings) excised]; f. 106v (3 Kings) attendant bringing Abishag to David; f. 117v (4 Kings) Ahaziah falling from the tower; [f. 128 (1 Chronicles) excised]; f. 138 (2 Chronicles) Solomon sacrificing a lamb at an altar, with God in the clouds above; f. 160v (1 Ezra) Ezra with scroll, standing and pointing; f. 163v (Nehemiah) Nehemiah presenting the gold cup to Artaxerxes; f. 168 (2 Ezra) asperging the altar; [f. 173 (Tobit) excised]; f. 176v (Judith) Judith beheading Holofernes; f. 181 (Esther) Esther kneeling before Ahasuerus, who is holding a sceptre; f. 185v (Job) Job on the dunghill with his wife and two other figures; f. 194 (Psalm 1) David playing the harp; f. 197 (Psalm 26) David as a young boy being annointed; f. 199 (Psalm 38) David pointing to his tongue, with God in the clouds above; f. 201 (Psalm 52) the fool, holding a club and round object; f. 203 (Psalm 68) 2-compartment letter with God above, and David below, waist deep in water; f. 205v (Psalm 80) David playing the bells; f. 207v (Psalm 97) two clerics singing; f. 210 (Psalm 109) Trinity, shown as the Father and the Son seated on a bench with the dove between them; f. 215 (Proverbs) Solomon instructing Rehoboam; [f. 222 (Ecclesisastes) excised]; f. 224v (Song of Songs) Virgin and Child; f. 226 (Wisdom) soldier kneeling before Solomon and offering him a sword; f. 231 (Ecclesiasticus) Ecclesia enthroned holding a chalice and banner with a cross; f. 244v (Isaiah) Isaiah being sawn in two; f. 261 (Jeremiah) the stoning of Jeremiah; f. 283 (Baruch) Baruch, seated, writing on a scroll; f. 286 (Ezechiel) 2-compartment letter with the heads of the tetramorph above, and Ezechiel, reclining, below; f. 304v (Daniel) Daniel in the lions' den; f. 312 (Hosea) Hosea and Gomer embracing; f. 314v (Joel) Joel seated, holding a scroll and pointing; f. 315v (Amos) God in the clouds speaking to Amos, shown with a sheep and dog; f. 317v (Obadiah) excised; f. 318 (Jonah) 2-compartment letter with Nineveh, above, and Jonah emerging from the whale's mouth, below; f. 319 (Micah) Micah seated with a scroll; f. 320v (Nahum) Nahum standing before Nineveh while its walls crumble; f. 321v (Habakkuk) God in the clouds, reaching down to a figure carrying a jug; f. 322v (Zephaniah) Zephaniah seated with a scroll; f. 323v (Haggai) Haggai standing and pointing to his scroll; f. 324 (Zachariah) Zachariah standing and pointing to his scroll; f. 327 (Malachai) Malachai seated, holding a scroll and pointing upwards; f. 328v (1 Maccabees) beheading of an idolatrous Jew; f. 339v (2 Maccabees) delivery of the letter; f. 347 (Matthew) Matthew seated and writing on a scroll with an Angel above; f. 357v (Mark) excised; f. 365 (Luke) Luke kneeling before an altar, with an Angel standing behind; f. 376v (John) John standing and holding a book, with a dove above; ff. 387, 391v, 395v, 398v (Romans—Galatians) Paul, seated and holding a sword and book; f. 400 (Ephesians) Paul giving a scroll to a man; f. 401v (Philippians) Paul standing with a scroll and sword; f. 402v (Colossians) Paul standing with a sword; f. 403v (1 Thessalonians) Paul standing with scroll and sword; f. 404v (2 Thessalonians) Paul seated with book and sword; f. 405 (1 Timothy) Paul seated with scroll and sword; f. 406 (2 Timothy) Paul seated with sword; f. 407 (Titus) Paul seated with book and sword; f. 407v (Philemon) Paul in prison giving a scroll to a man; f. 407v (Hebrews) Paul with a sword and a disciple; f. 411 (Acts) seated apostles with Peter in the middle; f. 422v (James) James standing with scroll; f. 424 (1 Peter) Peter seated with scroll; f. 425 (2 Peter) Peter standing with keys; f. 425v (1 John) John seated, writing on a scroll; f. 426v (2 John) John seated and teaching; f. 427 (3 John) John standing with scroll; f. 427 (Jude) Jude standing with scroll; f. 428 (Apocalypse) John writing with the seven churches behind him.

The first prologue to each book, Psalm 51 (f. 201), and Lamentations (f. 281) begin with similar 7- to 4-line (except "I," up to 19 lines) rinceaux initials with grotesques and naturalistic leaves. Chapters and remaining prologues begin with 2-line initials, alternating red and blue, set into the text space, with pen flourishes in the other color, extending into full column borders of red and blue superimposed 'J's. Chapters numbered in red and blue roman numerals placed within the text space; running titles in red and blue. Red rubrics; majuscules in text stroked with red. In art. 4, the *Interpretation of Hebrew Names*, the opening initial, f. 434, and the letter 'B', f. 440v, begin with 6- to 5-line rinceaux initials; remaining letters of alphabet, and sporadically, the first entry with a new second letter begin with 2- to 1-line alternating red and blue initials with short pen flourishes in the other color; each entry begins with a 1-line alternating red and blue initial; running titles lacking. Very faint preliminary sketches for historiated initials in the margins, ff. 42v, 328v, 427; notes for the rubricator throughout, usually erased, but visible on ff. 142, 148, 162v, 194v. 271v; notes in lead for running titles often visible, top margin.

Bound in brown blind- and gold-tooled russia leather, s. XIX, possibly in the United States, as suggested by De Ricci; title in gold on spine; marbled pastedowns and endpapers; spine partially detached.

Written in Paris, c. 1300, where it was illuminated by the Master of the Bible of Jean Papeleu (active c. 1295–1334). In Italy by s. XIV, when it was owned by Andreas Justus Cennis of Volterra (Volterra, prov. Pisa), who purchased the Bible from Simon Boccelle of Lucca (note, f. 469v: "Andree Justi Cennis de Vulterris quam emi f[lorentiis] xxxiiii ab heredibus quondam Simonis Boccelle de Luca."), and added the foliation, the table of liturgical readings at the beginning of the Bible (art. 1) and numerous marginal and interlinear glosses. Unidentified shelf mark (?), f. 1, in ink, in early arabic numerals, s. XIV–XV (?), "7.7.1"; unidentified book sellers' or owners' notes, first folio of art. 1, in ink: "0.77 (?)," and, s. XIX (?), "164." Date and source of acquisition by Harvard unknown; former Harvard shelf marks: ARg 1.2; Dr. 69.

secundo folio: [article 1] Dominica prima. Omne quod
[Bible] quod uiros doceant

Bibliography: De Ricci, 979.

MS Lat 37 Northeastern Italy s. $XV^{2/4}$
Ps. Cicero, Rhetorica ad Herennium Pl. 37

ff. 1–104v //quo [*om.* modo] has causas tractari conueniat ostendemus. Oportet igitur esse in oratore Inuentionem, Dispositionem, Elocutionem . . . Haec omnia adipiscemur si rationes praeceptionibus [*sic*] diligentia consequamur exercitationis. *Amen.* [F. 105 blank, ruled leaf from another manuscript with ex libris note: "Retorica nuoua de Miser Zusto (=Giusto) Venier, 1440."]

Fridericus Marx, ed., *Incerti auctoris de ratione dicendi ad C. Herennium libri IV,* reissued with addenda by W. Trillitzsch (Leipzig 1964). Text begins at Book 1.2 (Marx, ed., p. 2, line 19). Divided into four books; books 2–4 beginning on ff. 13, 37v, and 57v. Marginal corrections by the scribe throughout. Infrequent annotations by three later hands, Italy, s. XV–XVI, usually supplying omissions or citing alternate readings (cf. ff. 50v, 69v; ff. 65rv, 67v; f. 68).

Parchment, ff. ii (paper) + 104 + i (=f. 105, blank, ruled leaf from another manuscript, serving as flyleaf) + ii (paper), 235 x 159 (154–145 x 97–90) mm. 23–21 long lines. Ruled in hard point on the hair side; top and bottom horizontal lines full across; single full-length vertical bounding lines. Prickings in outer, bottom, and occasionally top margins. F. 105, blank leaf from another manuscript serving as a flyleaf, ruled in ink.

1^{10} (–1, with loss of text) 2–9^{10} 10^{10} (now +11, f. 100, from quire 11, inserted by a modern binder) 11^{6} (–1, f. 100, now inserted in quire 10; –6, cancelled; +6, f. 105). Vertical catchwords, lower margin, written on the inner bounding line, reading from bottom to top rather than top to bottom as is usual. First leaf in each quire numbered in pencil by two modern binders on the recto, top inside and bottom outside corners; added after first leaf was lost, since the present f. 1 is included in both series. F. 100, the first leaf of quire 11, now a single leaf at the end of quire 10, is numbered "11" in the bottom outside corner only; f. 101, numbered "11" in the top inside and bottom outside corners, the latter cancelled with a diagonal stroke.

Written below the top line by one scribe; through f. 29v (end of quire 3) in a stilted humanistic script with frequent letter unions, and thereafter in a free humanistic script, with a slight slant and usually with long 's' and 'f' below the line, but retaining minuscule 'a'. The scribe's transition between the two scripts is reflected in the first eight lines, f. 30.

Books begin with blank spaces for 2- to 3-line initials (except book 2, f. 13, blank space for 6-line "I"; folio with beginning of book 1 excised); the second letter of each a 1-line capital, brown ink. Ff. 1–7, blank spaces for 2-line initials at the beginning of sections within each book; ff. 68v to end, with red 1-line initials, within the line of text or in the margin if the beginning of a section coincides with the beginning of a line, and marginal headings in hand of main scribe in pale red. Throughout, majuscules at the beginning of sentences which begin on a new line are written in the margin next to the vertical bounding line. Guide letters for initials. Rubrics for books 2 and 3, and marginal headings, ff. 1–7 and 38–51, in a cursive humanistic script in pale red by a later hand.

Bound in red half morocco, June 16, 1906, after its purchase by Harvard.

Written in Northeastern Italy (we thank Professor A. C. de la Mare for this information; July, 1986) in the second quarter of the fifteenth century, probably before 1440; ex libris note, f. 105v, a blank ruled leaf from another manuscript, appended to the last quire: "Retorica nuoua de Miser Zusto [=Giusto] Venier, 1440," evidently a member of the prominent Venetian family, three of whom served as doge between 1382 and 1578. Likely the same as lot 291, dated 1440, in the Phillipps sale, London, Sotheby's, 1896, bought by Henry White; his sale, London, Sotheby's, April 21–May 2, 1902, no. 521, bought by Quaritch. Purchased by Harvard, March 8, 1906 (Salisbury fund; bookplate front pastedown; library stamp, f. 1) from O. Harrassowitz, catalogue 291, no. 1220; original Harvard shelf mark: Lc 66.5.

secundo folio: (now f. 1) quo has causas
(present f. 2) aut id defendimus

Bibliography: De Ricci, 979; De Ricci, "Handlist," 101; [G. H. Thompson], "Description of a Harvard Manuscript of the Rhetorica ad Herenium [*sic*]," (typescript, [Cambridge, 1928]) now Houghton bMS Lat 315(27).

fMS Lat 38 **Spain s. XIII$^{4/4}$–XIV$^{1/4}$**
Aristotle, Logical Treatises in Latin Translation **Pl. 61**

1. pp. 1–7 [Porphyry, *Isagoge*; rubric omitted] Cum sit neccessarium [*sic*] grisarori et ad eam que est apud aristotelem predicamentorum a [later expunged] doctrinam nosse quid sit genus . . . Sunt quidem etiam alie communitates uel proprietates eorum que dicta sunt sed sufficiunt etiam hec ad descriptiones [*sic*] eorum communitatisque [*om.* traditionem]. *Explicit liber porphilii* [*sic*].

   Latin translation by Boethius, without his commentary; *Aristoteles latinus. Codices*, 43 and 114, no. 2; Lorenzo Minio-Paluello and Bernard G. Dod., eds., Categoriarum supplementa; Porphyrii Isagoge translatio Boethii et anonymi fragmentum vulgo vocatum "Liber sex principiorum."

   Aristoteles latinus I.6–7 (Bruges-Paris 1966) 5–31, citing this manuscript p. xvii.

2. pp. 7–20 [Aristotle, *Categories* or *Predicamenta*] *Incipit liber predicamentorum aristotilis*. Equiuoca dicuntur qvorum solum nomen commune est [added: secundum uero nomen] ratio substantie diuersa . . . Forte tamen et alii quidem apparebunt modi in eo quod est habere. Sed qui consueuerunt dici pene omnes enumati [*sic*] sunt.

   Translatio communis or *editio composita*; *Aristoteles latinus. Codices*, 44 and 117–18, no. 6; L. Minio-Paluello, ed., *Categoriae vel praedicamenta; translatio Boethii, editio composita, translatio Guillelmi de Moerbeka*. . . . Aristoteles latinus I.1–5 (Bruges-Paris 1961) 47–79, citing this manuscript, p. xxv.

3. pp. 20–26 [Aristotle, *Periermenias* or *De interpretatione*] Primum oportet constituere quid sit nomen et quid uerbum . . . Manifestum est quoniam est affirmationi contraria quidem est negatio circa idem uniuersale [*corr.*[1]: universalis] ut ei que est quoniam omne bonum bonum est uel quoniam omnis//

   Latin translation by Boethius; *Aristoteles latinus. Codices*, 44–45 and 118–19, no. 7; L. Minio-Paluello and Gerard Verbeke, eds., *De interpretatione vel periermenias; translatio Boethii, specimina translationum recentiorum, translatio Guillelmi de Moerbeka.* Aristoteles latinus II.1–2 (Bruges-Paris 1965) 5–38, citing this manuscript,

p. xiv. Text now ends imperfectly in chapter 14 (ed., p. 38, line 1); it was completed by another scribe in the bottom margin (ed., p. 38, lines 1–7), ending "... non contingit inesse contraria."

4. pp. 27–31 [*Liber sex principiorum*] Forma est compositioni continges [*sic*] simplici et inuariabili essentia consistens ... est autem quod inest secundum naturam mo[ueri ut iginis: completed in a contemporary hand].

   Liber sex principiorum, by an anonymous twelfth-century author, perhaps Gilbert de la Porrée; *Aristoteles latinus. Codices*, 95 and 198, no. viii; L. Minio-Paluello and Bernard G. Dod, eds., *Categoriarum supplementa; Porphyrii Isagoge translatio Boethii et anonymi fragmentum vulgo vocatum "Liber sex principiorum"*. ... Aristoteles latinus I.6–7 (Bruges-Paris 1966) 33–59, citing this manuscript, p. lvi.

   Text ends abruptly, p. 30: "Sedere [later expunged: autem hic explorat difficentem] et iacere//" (VI:60, ed., p. 48, line 17), and resumes imperfectly, p. 31: "//licet quodammodo [*sic*] et in superlatiuis est albissimus et nigermius [corrected later: nigerramus (*sic*)] et huius sine amplius et minus dicitur ..." (VIII:91, ed., p. 57, line 12).

5. pp. 31–61 [Aristotle, *Analytica posteriora*] Omnis doctrina et omnis disciplina [added: intellectiua] ex preexistenti fit cogntitione. Manifestum est enim [*sic*] speculantibus in omnes ... et principium principiis. Hoc autem omne similiter se habet ad omne reruo [*sic*].

   Versio communis, translated by Jacobus Veneticus; *Aristoteles latinus. Codices*, 47 and 122–24, no. 11; L. Minio-Paluello and Bernard G. Dod, eds., *Analytica posteriora; translationes Iacobi, anonymi sive 'Ioannis', Gerardi et recensio Guillelmi de Moerbeka.* Aristoteles latinus IV.1–4 (Bruges-Paris 1968) 5–107, citing this manuscript, p. xxi.

6. pp. 61–79 [Aristotle, *Sophistici elenchi*] *Sophisticorum elencorum a*[*ristotilis*] *liber i. incipit.* De sophisticis autem elincis [*sic*] et de hiis qui uidentur quidem elenchi, sunt autem paralogismi sed non elinchi [*sic*] ... Reliqum [*sic*] erit omnium uestrum uel eorum qui audierint opus omissis quidem artis indultionem inuentis autem multis [*sic*] habere grates.

Versio communis; *Aristoteles latinus. Codices*, 47, 120–1, 787, and 791–2, no. 9, and *Supplementa altera*, 20, 29–30, no. 9; Bernard G. Dod, ed., *De sophisticis elenchis; translatio Boethii, fragmenta translationis Iacobi et recensio Guillelmi de Moerbeke.* Aristoteles latinus 6.1–3 (Leiden 1975) 5–60, citing this manuscript, p. xvii.

7. pp. 80–90 [Aristotle, *Analytica priora*] Primum dicere est quidem et de quo est intentio, quoniam circa demonstrationem et disciplina demonstrancia ... In conclusione autem contingere eodem modo accipiendum est quo in prioribus eius autem quod est ex necessitate non in [expunged later: erit] esse erit sillogismus. Set non ex necessitate inesse, aliud enim est non ex necessitate inesse//

   "*Recensio Florentina*"; translation by Boethius; *Aristoteles latinus. Codices*, 47 and 121–2, no. 10, and *Supplementa altera*, 20 and 31–34, no. 10; L. Minio-Paluello, ed., *Analytica priora. Translatio Boethii (recensiones duae), translatio anonyma....* Aristoteles latinus III.1–4 (Bruges-Paris 1962) 5–139, citing this manuscript, p. xxv. Text now ends imperfectly at I.16 (ed., p. 36, line 22).

   This manuscript listed in *Aristoteles latinus. Codices*, 240, no. 8. Copious marginal notes in a number of hands, s. XIV–XVI, mostly from southern Europe, but including notes in an early English hand, s. XIV (cf. p. 3, top margin). The amount of marginal annotation varies. Arts. 4 (*Liber sex principiorum*) and 6 (*Sophistici elenchi*) virtually without annotation; art. 1 (*Isagoge*) with a moderate amount; the remaining articles heavily annotated, especially art. 5 (*Analytica posteriora*), with extensive marginal and interlinear glosses.

Parchment (prepared in the manner of southern Europe), ff. ii (modern paper) + 45 (paginated, every other page, in a modern hand, pp. 1–90) + ii (modern paper), 339 x 234 (230–221 x 146–143) mm.; trimmed, although generous margins remain, with the loss of some marginal comments. 2 columns, 48–46 lines; ruled lightly in lead or brown crayon. Ruling varies (variation does not coincide with quire structure) with single or double full-length vertical bounding lines at the outside of the columns, and occasionally with an additional single bounding line in the inner margin. No prickings.

1^{12} 2^{12} (–4, following p. 30, with loss of text; all singletons glued together, except 1,12, pp. 25–26 and pp. 45–46, and 6,7, pp. 33–34 and 35–36, conjugate pairs) 3^{12} 4^{12} (beginning p. 71; –11 and 12, following p. 90, with loss of text). Horizontal catchwords, quires 1 (boxed in brown ink) and 3 (pp. 24 and 70). Later quire and leaf signatures, bottom margin, recto, with a letter designating the quire and a number the leaf, in quires 1 and 2, numbering each leaf, and in the remaining quires numbering the leaves in the first half of the quire.

Written by at least two scribes with a broad nib in a formal round gothic bookhand; ink varies from chestnut to dark brown. The first scribe copied pp. 1–26; the second scribe completed the manuscript.

Six- to 2-line (with extensions of up to 8–lines) well-executed red and blue parted initials set into the text column, with pen flourishes, beading and straight tendrils in red and greenish blue used at the beginning of each work (except arts. 4 and 6, pp. 28 and 61, which begin with 3- to 2-line blue initials). Similar 3-line parted initials, pp. 22 and 52, indicating internal divisions. Two-line red and blue initials, imperfectly alternating, partially set into the text column, with pen flourishes in the other color, mark smaller divisions in arts. 1, 2, 3, 6 and 7. Initials in art. 4 are set outside the text column. Art. 5 copied with only two divisions, pp. 52 and 60. Rubrics completed in some articles only. Red paragraph marks, pp. 1–8 and 27–29; often added elsewhere in ink by later hands. No running titles.

Page 1 badly rubbed and partially illegible; part of opening initial is missing. Pages 29–30 and 89–90 trimmed; no loss of text.

Bound, s. XIX, in half-roan with cardboard boards covered in brown marbled paper.

Written in Spain in the last quarter of the thirteenth or the first quarter of the fourteenth century. As the condition of the manuscript and the copious marginal annotations indicate, it was in frequent use from the time it was written through the sixteenth century; marginal annotations indicate that it remained in southern Europe, probably in Spain, through the sixteenth century, although one early user was likely English. Erased inscription, p. 1 (partially visible under ultraviolet, but indecipherable). Given to Harvard by Charles Deane (1813–89) January 2, 1863 (bookplate, inside front cover, and pencil note, front flyleaf, f. ii^{v}); original Harvard shelf mark: Ga 112.499.

secundo folio: infinita sunt

Bibliography: De Ricci, 980; Wilbur High Royster, "A Paleographic Treatise, Part I. A Description of a Ms. of Boethius in the Harvard College Library, Ga 112.499," unpublished manuscript (Cambridge, 1912) now Houghton bMS Lat 315(25); Kristeller, *Iter* 5:226.

fMS Lat 39 **France s. XIV[1]**
Aristotle, Politica, Rhetorica et Magna Moralia in Latin Translation **Pls. 26, 66**

1. ff. 1–92v [Aristotle, *Politica*] Quoniam omnem ciuitatem uidemus communitatem quandam existentem et omnem communitatem boni alicuius gratia institutam eius enim quod uisus boni gratia omnia operantur omnes. Manifestum quod omnes bonum ... palam quia tres has faciendum ad disciplinam quod medium et quod possibile et quod decens. *Reliqua huius operis in greco nondum inueni. Amen.*

   Latin translation by Guillelmus de Moerbeka; *Aristoteles latinus. Codices*, 75 and 163–65, no. 55. Franciscus Susemihl, ed., *Aristotelis Politicorum libri octo cum vetusta translatione Guilelmi de Moerbeka* (Leipzig 1872).

2. ff. 92v–150 [Aristotle, *Rhetorica*] Retorica assecutiua dialetice [*sic*] est [expunged by scribe or near contemporary: omnibus] ambe enim de talibus quibusdam sunt que communiter quodam modo [*sic*] omnium est cognoscere ... Finis autem locucionis congruit inconiuctis [*sic*] quatinus epylogus, sed non oratio sit, 'Dixi, audistis, habete, iudicate.' *Explicit rethorica aristotilis* [*sic*] *translata a greco in latinum. Amen.*

   Latin translation by Guillelmus de Moerbeka; *Aristoteles latinus. Codices*, 77–78 and 167–68, no. 59; Bernhardus Schneider, ed., *Rhetorica; translatio anonyma sive vetus et translatio Guillelmi de Moerbeka.* Aristoteles latinus XXXI.1–2 (Leiden 1978) 159–321, listing this manuscript p. xxxiv, no. 20.

3. ff. 150v–176v [Aristotle, *Magna Moralia*] Quoniam eligimus dicere de moralibus. Primum utique erit considerandum mores cuius sunt pars ut breuiter quidem [*corr.*[2] *add.*: igitur] dicere uidebuntur ...

Quare scrutandum utique erit qualiter oportet uti amico in amicicia que est in equalibus amicis. *Explicit liber magnorum ethicorum aristotilis* [*sic*] *stragerite.*

Latin translation by Bartholomaeus de Messina; *Aristoteles latinus. Codices,* 71–72 and 159–60, no. 49; no printed edition of this translation, but see Christine Pannier, "La traduction latine médiévale des *Magna moralia.* Une étude critique de la tradition manuscrite," *La production du livre universitaire au Moyen Age. Exemplar et pecia,* Louis Bataillon, Bertrand Guyot, and Richard Rouse, eds. (Paris 1988) 165–204, listing 56 manuscripts including this one on p. 166 as '*hd.*'

This manuscript listed in *Aristoteles latinus. Codices,* 240, no. 9. Corrections throughout, usually supplying omissions, sometimes boxed in red or blue, by the scribe or close contemporary. Many later nota marks in lead or ink.

Parchment (poor quality), ff. i (unnumbered parchment) + 177 (incorrectly foliated, in ink, every ten folios only, with eleven folios between ff. 50 and 60, so that f. 60 is actually f. 61; continuous modern foliation in pencil [cited] follows the older foliation: ff. 1–59, *59bis, 60–176), 326 x 232 (210–200 x 135–130) mm. 2 columns, 55–57 ruled lines, written on every other line. Ruled in lead; single full-length vertical bounding lines, with narrow double rulings framing the page in the outer margins (inner rulings not always visible). Prickings top and bottom margins only.

$1–14^{12}$ 15^{12} (–10, 11, 12; possibly with loss of text; see provenance discussion, below). Horizontal catchwords lower, inside margin; some leaf and quire signatures in very faint lead with letters designating the leaf and a mark, the quire.

Written below the top line on every other ruled line by a number of scribes in a quick gothic bookhand (*littera parisiensis*).

Five- to 9-line red and blue parted initials with red and blue cascades of superimposed 'J's extending up to the full length of the column, and on f. 1, across the top of the page as well, with pen flourishes and beading in red and blue, used at the beginning of each work, book 4 of the *Politica,* and books 2 and 3 of *Rhetorica.* 4- to 5-line initials in red or blue with short cascades and pen flourishes in the other color begin the remaining books. 4- to 5-line initials, alternating red and blue with pen flourishes in the other color, placed within the text column at the beginning of chapters; done by at least three, and possibly four hands: cf. for example, ff. 2, 4v, etc., with very quick flourishes consisting primarily of up and down strokes (similar to Destrez, plate 2); ff. 28, 28v, etc., more carefully executed, with beading and corkscrews (similar to Destrez, plate 4); and ff. 158v, 159v, etc., very quickly executed up and down strokes. The initials of the type on ff. 16v and 53 possibly by another hand. Initials, ff. 168–176v, done in the Italian manner with interior harping (similar to Destrez, plate 21), were likely added after the manuscript was completed. Running titles in red and blue designating the work and the number of the book; red and blue majuscules and roman numerals in the same style indicating the number of the book found at the beginning of many books in the lines left blank for the rubrics. Red and blue paragraph marks throughout. Guide notes for the rubrics and running titles, and letters for the initials, sometimes visible.

Many signs of damage from water or dampness, and general wear, without damage to the text.

Bound in Italy, s. XVI (?), in limp vellum over thin pasteboard. Resewn on four leather bands. Title in ink on spine: "Aristotelis Politica, Rethorica, Magna Moralia" with "XIV" at top, and remains of paper label pasted at the bottom: "V/H/<?>/."

Written in France in the first half of the fourteenth century (we thank Professor R. H. Rouse for his assistance, February 1988). The quality of the parchment, script and decoration of this workmanlike manuscript suggest that it was made for the use of a university student, although marginal notes and other annotations by readers are surprisingly scarce. The manuscript was likely brought to Italy shortly after it was written, where the pen initials on ff. 168–176v were added. Belonged to the Dominican house in Florence of Santa Maria Novella, s. XIV–XV (?)–s. XVII–XVIII (?); ex libris note front flyleaf, f. i^{v}, s. XIV–XV: "Iste liber est fratrum predicatorum conventus sancte marie nouelle de florentia"; cf. the later inscriptions, f. 1, top, and f. 176v, bottom, s. XV–XVI: "Conventus Sancte Marie Novelle De Florentia ordinis predicatorum," and round library stamp, s. XVII–XVIII (?), f. 1. List of contents, front flyleaf, f. i^{v}, in the same hand as the ex libris note on that page, indicates that the manuscript also once included the *Propositions* of Proclus; this text not listed on the spine or in the later contents note, f. i^{v}. Listed as MS 321 in the fourth "banco" in the 1489 inventory of the library of Santa Maria Novella, with the *Propositions* of Proclus (see Stefano Orlandi, *La Biblioteca di S. Maria Novella in Firenze dal sec. XIV al sec. XIX* [Florence 1952] 42).

In the sixteenth century, the noted scholar and translator of Aristotle, Pier Vettori (1499–1585) consulted these translations, and possibly this manuscript, according to a note, front flyleaf, f. i^{v}, by his nephew, Francesco Vettori:

> Hic est liber ille veteris translationis non nullorum librorum Aristotelis cuius saepe mentionem fecit Petrus Victorius; praecipue autem in epistola ad studiosos artis dicendi, in commentarios suos in tres libros Aristotelis de arte dicendi affirmat huius auxilio se usum fuisse, in corrigendis libris illis temporum ac librariorum iniuria deformatis; cum enim haec translatio multis antea seculis confecta fuerit, quo tempore libri Aristotelis integriores emendatioresque erant, auctorque ipsius, quicumque ille fuerit, negotium cum multa fide administraverit, ac ne verborum quidem ordinem variaverit, inde se cognovisse. Victorius narrat quam scripturam in suo exemplari ille habuerit. Hoc autem cum in librum inciderim, adnotandum hic censui ego Franciscus Victorius Petri Nepos, ut hoc etiam nomine liber custodi bibliothecae et iis qui illum legent commendatus sit, sententiamque meam laudaturos studiosus bonarum artium speravi, cum vir maximi ingenii atque admirabilis doctrinae, frater Vincentius Civitella, illa approbaverit.

It has been suggested that the notes in Greek and Latin on ff. 1v, 14v, 15 and 93v, may be in Pier Vettori's hand (see F. H. Fobes, "Report for Classical Philology 49 on Harvard MS Ga 112.503," [typescript, 1912] now Houghton, bMS Lat 315[3] p. 8). Acquired in Florence, ca. 1819, by Edward Everett (1794–1865), Eliot Professor of Greek literature at Harvard and statesman (see E. Everett, "An account of some Greek Manuscripts, procured at Constantinople in 1819, and now belonging to the Library of the University at Cambridge," *Memoirs of the American Academy of the Arts and Sciences* IV, part 2 [1821] 409–15, especially 414–15); his gift to Harvard before 1821; original Harvard shelf mark: Ga 112.503.

secundo folio: ad alia animalia

Bibliography: De Ricci, 980; Norman LeRoy Willey, "The Harvard Manuscript of Morbeka's translation of Aristotle's Politica, Rhetorica, and Magna Moralia," [typescript, n.d., given to the library in 1910] now Houghton, fMS Lat 05.39.5; Kristeller, *Iter* 5:226; R. J. Tarrant, "An Aristotelian Excursion," *The Marks in the Fields. Essays in the Uses of Manuscripts,* ed. R. G. Dennis with E. Falsey (Cambridge, Massachusetts 1992) no. 3, 21–28, with plate of f. 92v on p. 20; Rodney Dennis, "Notes Concerning *Le Pliage,*" *Scriptorium* 47 (1993) 167.

MS Lat 40 — Italy (Bologna) 1462
Juvenal, Saturae — Pl. 8

ff. 1–77 *Iunii Iuuenalis Aquinatis Poete Satyrici atque morum magistri et Censoris Liber primus incipit. Satyra prima que ad alias uicem prohemii obtinet feliciter.* Semper ego auditor tantum numquam ne reponam?/ Vexatus tociens rauci theseyde Chodri?/ . . . [Satire 16]. . . Vt leti faleris omnes ac torquibus omnes./ *Iunii Iuuenalis Aquinatis Poetae Satyrici atque morum magistri et Censoris finit Liber. Laus altissimo. Bononie 1462, 23 Iullii. VMA* [*monogram?*]. *Mille tales Iuuenales non referrent certe/ Que uenales curiales comittunt apperte.* [F. 77v blank, but ruled.]

W. V. Clausen, ed., *A. Persi Flacci et D. Iuni Iuvenalis Saturae.* OCT (Oxford 1959) 35–175. Four folios with Satire 1, verse 139–Satire 2, verse 157 (ed., pp. 41–48) missing after f. 3v. Text not divided into the five books found in some manuscripts. Greek written in pale red by the scribe: f. 21v, Satire 6, verse 195; f. 43, Satire 9, verse 37; and f. 53v, Satire 11, verse 27.

With contemporary glosses throughout, not listed in *CTC* 1: 175–238 or in the addenda (2:425–26 and 3:432–45) and apparently unrelated to those described, written between the lines and in unruled space in the outer margin (we thank Marc Laureys for allowing us to consult his unpublished notes on these glosses, October, 1987). First gloss, upper margin, f. 1: "*Satyrici. Lucilius.* qui stans uno pede ut dicitur scribebat mille uersus. *Oratius.* qui preclara composuit. *Persius.* admodum asper. Iuuenalis post istos uenit qui non fuit ita asper, et fuerunt contemporanei isti tres

Statius, Quintilianus et ipse Iuuenalis." Bottom margin: "[Life of Juvenal] Fuit Iuuenalis tempore Domitiani Imperatoris romanorum qui indignatus propter quosdam uersus quos Iunius scripsit ... Erat enim medie etatis trans quadragesimum annum.; *Genera poetarum.* Comedia, Tragedia, Carmen heroicum.... Dithirambicum poetrarum genus erat quod solum in laude deorum uersabatur....; Quinque sunt partes satyre [*sic*]. Laudatiua, deprecatativa, hortatiua, derisoria, reprehensoria...." Satire 1.1–1.3, interlinear glosses: "*semper:* omni etate; *auditor:* scilicet ero; *rauci:* indocti et insulsi; *theseyde chodri:* id est fabula tragica de theseo; *impune:* sine reprehensione; *ille:* aliquis." Marginal gloss, Satire 1.4: "*hic helegos:* Helegi leues uersus miserias amores luctus suspiria et lamentationes continentes." Concluding glosses; f. 76v marginal gloss on Satire 16.42–45: "Antiqui habebant annum Iubileum sicut nos habemus, et in quinquaginta annis sicut nos tamen illi agebant ... Et dictus est Iubileus a Iubilando nam omnes christiani debent Iubilare."; f. 77 Satire 16.60, interlinear gloss: "*ut leti faleris:* ornamentis equorum."

Parchment, ff. ii (paper) + 77 + ii (paper), 201 x 145 (130–132 x 80–75) mm. 24 lines of verse. Horizontal lines ruled in ink, often turning slightly downwards at the end of the line; single full-length vertical bounding lines ruled in brown crayon, with an extra bounding line on the left, length of written space only, forming a column used for the first majuscule of each line. Single pricking, far outer margin, above top horizontal ruled line.

1^{10} (–4, 5, 6, 7, two conjugate pairs after f. 3, with loss of text) 2–8^{10} 9^{1} (one leaf, originally the first of the next quire, now glued to quire 8; presumably with loss of text, see provenance, below). Vertical catchwords, bottom margin, written along the inner bounding line, usually with the opening letter brushed with yellow. Quire and leaf signatures, bottom outer margin, recto, in pale red with a letter designating the quire and an arabic numeral, the leaf, in the first half of the quire; first leaf in second half marked with a cross; mostly cut away, but cf. quires 2 (ff. 9–11); 4 (ff. 27–32), and 5 (f. 42).

Written above the top line by one scribe in a quick running humanistic script. Interlinear and marginal glosses, by the same scribe or a contemporary (opening letters sometimes daubed with yellow, as are the majuscules in the text) in a minute, more cursive humanistic script; on f. 1, a few glosses in red. Nota marks, scalloped lines in outer margin, and pointing hands throughout in pale red, likely by the scribe.

One 4-line initial, f. 1, with white vinestem decoration extending into the margin on a ground of green, pink and blue with yellow and white dots, surrounded by blue which follows the shape of the vine (reproduced in Wieck, fig. 116). Remaining Satires (except Satire 2, beginning now missing) begin with undecorated 2-line initials, alternating red and blue (ff. 4, 11, 14, 17v, 31v, 36v, 42, 45v, 53, 57, 60, 65, 72, 75v). Opening word of each Satire completed in capitals in brown ink, shadowed in pale yellow, sometimes of the type described by Stanley Morison as "Byzantine" (cf. *Byzantine Elements*, and *Politics and Script*, 277–86; see esp. ff. 36v, 57, 65). Decorative capitals in brown ink shadowed or infilled with yellow used at the beginning of each line of verse, written between the bounding lines. Opening rubric and colophon in pale red; blanks for remaining rubrics. Guide letters visible within some initials (for example ff. 17v, 36v).

Ink flaked and/or very faded on many folios, but still legible.

Bound in England in brown calf, s. XIX; rebacked; the label from the spine with the title in gilt ("Juvenalis. Satyrae") is laid down.

Written in Bologna, July 23, 1462 (colophon, f. 77); the formal glosses on the text suggest that it was made for a student or scholar. The manuscript once included another text, most likely Persius, *Saturae*; f. 77v with the reversed images of a vinestem initial at the top, and an undecorated 'O' in the middle; this text was missing by 1836 (contents listed in the Thorpe catalogue as Juvenal). Belonged to Jean Bondieu of Salins, s. XVII; ex libris note, f. 77v: "Joannes Bondieu Salinensia" (possibly the brother of Hughes de Salins [1632–1710]; see *Biographie universelle*, 14:164–65); ff. 45, 51, added in top margin, possibly in the hand of this ex libris note: "Ama deum." Possibly belonged to the Labbey de Billy of Besançon (d. 1825); round library stamp, f. 1, with arms, saltire, and motto "sine lab[or?]e" of the "Bibliotheca Billiana"; but not identified in his sale, Besançon, 1 May 1826 (unavailable for consultation; cf. De Ricci, 980). Sold by Thorpe, London, 1836, no. 735 ("735" in pencil, followed by illegible initials, front flyleaf, f. i^{v}), to Sir Thomas Phillipps (*Phillipps Cat.*, p. 145, MS 9174; "9174" in black ink, front flyleaf, f. ii^{v}); Phillipps sale, London, Sotheby's, 1896, no. 786 to

Quaritch; Quaritch Cat. 164, London, 1896, no. 104. Unidentified booksellers' marks in pencil, front flyleaves, f. i^v: "6245 64," and f. ii^v: "5864 56." Purchased from Quaritch, January 2, 1897 (Charles Minot Fund; library stamp, front flyleaf, f. i^v; bookplate, inside front cover). Front flyleaf, f. i^v, copy of a note signed by Harvard College Librarian, Justin Winsor, authorizing use of the manuscript by the Classics Department (for information about this purchase, cf. Dennis, "Collecting," 287–90). Original Harvard shelf mark: Li 13.105.

secundo folio: Accipiat s[a]ne

Bibliography: De Ricci, 980; De Ricci, "Handlist," 104; Wieck, p. 108, fig. 116 (reproducing f. 1).

MS Lat 41 — Northeastern Italy s. XV[2]
Cornelius Nepos, Vitae

1. pp. 1–2 [Pg. 1, blank, with later notes; pg. 2 table of contents in a cursive humanistic script, s. XV.] Vita Miltiadis, prima; Themistoclis, Secunda; . . . Hanibalis, Vigesima Secunda.

   Probably added, but contemporary with the remainder of the manuscript; listing 22 lives instead of the 23 in the manuscript, since "Graecorum ducum," found on pp. 176–79 (Marshall, ed., 76–78, as "Reges") was originally omitted from the list.

2. pp. 3–196 [Cornelius Nepos, *Liber de excellentibus ducibus exterarum gentium*; prologue] //Sed haec plura persequi . . . et [*om.* in] hoc exponemus [*corr.*[2] *add.*: libro] de uita excellentium imperatorum. [p. 3 text] *Milciadis uita feliciter incipit.* Milciades cymonis filius atheniensis quom et claritate generis et gloria maiorum et sua modestia unus omnium maxime floreret. . . . Atque hoc sosillo hannibal litterarum grae//

   P. K. Marshall, ed., *Cornelii Vitae cum fragmentis* (Leipzig 1977); *idem.*, *The Manuscript Tradition of Cornelius Nepos.* Institute of Classical Studies; Bulletin Supplement 37 (London 1977) listing this manuscript p. 66. Text begins imperfectly in section 8 of the Prologue (Marshall, ed., p. 2, line 7), and breaks off incomplete in the Life of Hannibal, 13.13 (ed., p. 86, line 32).

Carefully corrected throughout in a contemporary hand in a rounded humanistic script; for example, adding omitted words (pp. 3, 72, 40, etc.), or passages (pp. 6, 7, 29, 41, 73, etc.), and noting variant readings (pp. 5, 23, 46, 118, etc.). Back flyleaf, recto, with unidentified notes in Latin in a hasty cursive script, s. XVI (?); on the verso, unidentified notes in Greek.

Parchment (poor quality), ff. ii (paper) + 97 (paginated 1–196; pp. 1–2, original parchment endleaf) + i (original parchment endleaf) + ii (paper), 194 x 134 (120–117 x 79–77) mm. 21 long lines, except quires 10–11 (pp. 181–96) 27–26 lines. Horizontal rules in ink; single vertical bounding lines ruled in brown crayon. With a single pricking, very outer margin, above the top ruled line (see pp. 3–10).

Bound too tightly for accurate collation; catchwords indicate: 1^{10} (–1, with loss of text) $2–9^{10}$ 10^{6} 11^{3} (–3, following p. 196, with loss of text; structure uncertain). Vertical catchwords, lower margin, written on the inner bounding lines. Quire and leaf signatures in ink, very bottom outer corner, recto, with a letter designating the quire and an arabic numeral, the leaf; many trimmed, but cf. quires 2 and 6 (pp. 25, 27, 29, and 107).

Written below the top line in an upright, angular, artificial humanistic script, with adjacent round letters touching, majuscule 'r' often used in a minuscule position, and functionless decorative marks; 'e-cedilla' used incorrectly with 'ae' (for example p. 87, line 8, "aęque").

Four- to 2-line plain capitals, alternating red and blue, at the beginning of each Life (opening initial now missing; blank spaces remain for 2-line initials, pp. 47 and 74). Pale red rubrics in the script of the text (omitted pp. 14, 30, 93; blank spaces remain). The first letter, and occasionally the first word, following an initial usually a capital in brown ink. When the beginning of a sentence coincides with the beginning of a line, the opening majuscule sometimes written in the outer margin next to the bounding line. Running titles added in the top margin, brown ink, pp. 14–27.

Damage from dampness throughout; no loss of text.

Bound in English russia leather, s. XIX (dated by De Ricci, ca. 1850); gilt edges; rebacked with spine laid down.

Written in Northeastern Italy, likely in the Veneto, in the second half of the fifteenth century (we thank Professor A. C. de la Mare for this information; July, 1986). The manuscript now ends imperfectly four lines before the end of the Life of Hannibal. Since the compressed layout of quires 10 and 11 indicates that the scribe was attempting to save space, it is possible that the manuscript once contained the Lives of Cato, Atticus and the Cornelia fragment. Unidentified notation, p. 1, in black ink, now partially effaced, possibly a shelf mark, s. XVII–XVIII: "L I [or L J] I 8," with note on contents. Belonged to Sir Edward Dering (1598–1644); his sale, London, Puttick and Simpson, June 8, 1858, no. 1603, to Boone for Sir Thomas Phillipps (*Phillipps Cat.*, p. 281, MS 14948; "14948" in black ink, p. 1). Phillipps sale, London, Sotheby's, 1896, no. 890, to Quaritch; Quaritch Cat. 164, 1896, no. 51. Unidentified booksellers' notes in pencil, front flyleaf, f. i^{v}: "MHC," "14948 Ph," and "163"; front flyleaf, f. ii^{v}: "5864 57"; p. 1: "LC" (written diagonally). Purchased from Quaritch, January 2, 1897 (Charles Minot Fund; library stamp, front flyleaf, f. ii^{v}; bookplate, front pastedown). Front flyleaf, f. i, copy of a note signed by Harvard College Librarian, Justin Winsor, authorizing use of the manuscript by the Classics Department (for information about this purchase, cf. Dennis, "Collecting," 287–90). Original Harvard shelf mark: Ln 4.110; a brief note about the manuscript, signed M. Grand, glued to the front flyleaf, f. ii.

secundo folio: (now p. 3) Sed haec

Bibliography: De Ricci, 980; De Ricci, "Handlist," 103.

fMS Lat 42 — Northern Italy (Verona) s. XV$^{3/4}$
Ovid, Works — Pl. 15

1. ff. 1–56 [Ovid, *Heroides*] *Codex epistolarum per nasonem editus et ipse elegantissimus, ubi plurimum artis, plurimaque rerum copia cum ornatu summo conspicitur.* [f. 1 Epistle 1] *Penelope ad ulyxem.* Hanc tua penelope lento tibi mittit ulixe./ Nil mihi rescribas, attamen ipse ueni./ . . . Protinus ut redeas, facta uibebor anus./ . . . [f. 56 Epistle 21] *Cydippe Acontio.* Pertimui scriptumque tuum sine murmure legi,/ Iuraret ne quos inscia lingua deos./ . . . At melius uirgo fauisset virginis annis,/ Quos uereor paucos ne uelit esse mihi.

Epistles 1–14, 16–20, and 21.1–12 (does not include letter of Sappho to Phaonis; see art. 7, below); Henricus Dörrie, ed., *P. Ovidii Nasonis Epistulae Heroidum.* Texte und Kommentare; eine Altertumswissenschaftliche Reihe 6, eds. O. Gigon, F. Heinimann, and O. Luschnat (Berlin and New York 1971) 45–275; lacks lines 16.39–144 (ed., pp. 193–215); blank line remains, f. 48, where line 202 of letter 17 (ed., p. 242) was omitted.

2. ff. 56v–94 [Ovid, *Ars amatoria*] *Liber de arte amandi elegantissimus nasonis poetae copiosissimus.* Si quis in hoc artem populo non nouit amandi,/ Me legat et lecto carmine doctus amet./ . . . Vt quondam iuuenes, ita nunc mea turba puellae/ Inscribant foliis naso magister erat.

   E. J. Kenney, ed., *P. Ovidi Nasonis Amores, Medicamina Faciei femineae, Ars amatoria, Remedia amoris.* OCT (Oxford 1961) 113–200; divided into the usual three books, with the second and third beginning on ff. 69 and 81; secondary initials and rubrics, ff. 57 and 60v, book 1, lines 35 and 263.

3. ff. 94–107 [Ovid, *Remedia amoris*] *Initium libri nasonis de remedio amoris* [*added: que*] *ut paruus* [*added: est*] *corpore ita secretus grauissimus, quem non oportet in margine notare, quia totus est aureus et memoriae commendandus.* Legerat huius amor titulum nomenque libelli./ Bella mihi uideo, bella parantur ait./ . . . Post modo reddetis sacro pia uota poetae/ Carmine sanati foemina uirque meo.

   Kenney, ed. (1961) 205–37. Divided into two books, with the second beginning on f. 100v at line 397 (ed., p. 220); secondary divisions, f. 94v at line 41 (ed., p. 206) and f. 96 at line 139 (ed., p. 210).

4. ff. 107–190 [Ovid, *Fasti*] *Pii ouidi nasonis sulmonensis primus fastorum liber incipit.* Tempora cum causis latium digesta per annum./ Lapsaque sub terras, oratque signa canam./ . . . Sic cecinit Clio, cunctae assenere sorores./ Annuit alcides. Increpuitque lyra [*sic*]. [ff. 187v–190 Calendar, January–June].

   E. H. Alton, D. E. W. Wormell, and E. Courtney, eds., *P. Ovidi Nasonis Fastorum Libri Sex* (Leipzig 1978) 1–164. Divided into six books, with books 2–6 beginning on ff. 119, 132v, 147, 162v, and 174; secondary division, f. 107v, 1.27 (ed., p. 2).

5. ff. 190v–248 [Ovid, *Tristia*] *Liber elegantissimus ouidii de tristia.* Parue nec inuideo sine me liber ibis in urbem./ Hei mihi, quod domino non licet ire tuo./ . . . Qui monet ut facias, quod tu facis, ille monendo/ Laudat, et hortanti comprobat acta suo.

   Jacques André, ed. and tr., Ovid, *Tristes.* l'Association Guillaume Budé (Paris 1968) 2–162; Marvin L. Colker, "A Harvard Manuscript Containing Ovid's *Tristia,*" *Harvard Library Bulletin* 4 (1950) 110–11, classifying it among the *deteriores* and noting that it shares readings with the *editio princeps*, Bologna, 1471; and George Luck, "Textprobleme der Tristien," *Philologus; Zeitschrift für das klassische Altertum* 103 (1959) 100–13, esp. 104–5, and note 2, suggesting that this was one of the manuscripts used by the editor of the *editio princeps*, Bologna, 1471. Divided into the usual five books, with books 2–4 beginning on ff. 202v, 211v, 224v, and 235v; secondary divisions agree with the edition, except that 1:4, beginning f. 146, is copied continuously with 1:3; 3:2, beginning f. 213, line 15, is copied contiuously with 3:1; 3:4b, beginning f. 215v, line 26 (ed. p. 73) is copied continuously with 3:4; 4:6, beginning f. 231, line 8, is copied continuously with 4:5; and 4:8, beginning f. 232, line 21, is copied continuously with 4:7.

6. ff. 248–300 [Ovid, *Epistulae ex Ponto*] *Incipit liber nasonis que de ponto dicitur idem clarissimus et elegantissimus.* Naso thomitanae iam non nouus incola terrae/ Hoc tibi de getico litore mittit opus./ . . . Quid iuuat extinctos ferrum dimmitere [above the line, in another hand: *al.* de-] in artus?/ Non habet in nobis iam noua plaga locum.

   J. André, ed. and tr., Ovide, *Pontiques.* l'Association Guillaume Budé (Paris 1977) 2–157. Divided into four books, with books 2–4 beginning on ff. 260v, 273, and 284v.

7. ff. 300–303v [*Epistula Sapphus, Heroides* 15; rubric lacking] Nunquid ubi aspecta est studiosae littera dextrae/ Protinus est oculis cognita nostra tuis? . . . O saltem miserae crudelis epistola dicat,/ Vt mihi leucadiae fata petantur aquae.

   Dörrie, ed., 314–26; not included in Dörrie's list of manuscripts, pp. 297–304, as noted in M. D. Reeve, "Heinsius's Manuscripts of Ovid: A Supplement," *Rheinisches Museum für Philologie* NF 119 (1976) 66.

8. ff. 303v–304v [Ps. Ovid, *De cuculo,* or *Conflictus veris et hiemis*; rubric lacking] Conueniunt cuncti subito de montibus altis/ Pastores pecudum uernali luce sub umbra/ . . . Omnia te expectant, pelagus tellusque polusque./ Salue dulce decus cucule [*sic*] et per saecula salue.

   Alexander Riese, ed., *Anthologia latina sive poesis latinae supplementum. I. Carmina in codicibus scripta* (Leipzig 1870) fasc. 2, pp. 145–88, no. 687; Walther, *Initia* 3288; cf. Walther, *Initia* 3285.

   (Articles 1–8). Art. 1 (ff. 1–56), marginal notes by the scribe or a contemporary in pale red ink, ff. 1–26. Longer contemporary notes in a quick noting hand, brown ink, ff. 1–19v (cf. f. 2v, includes Greek; very long notes in this hand, ff. 6v, 7v, 9, 13, 14v and 16v), which seem to have been added before the notes in pale red (cf. f. 11, marginal note partially cancelled in pale red). Art. 2 (ff. 56v–94), throughout, contemporary marginal notes in pale red ink, including names occurring in the text and sources, and longer glosses in brown ink (for example, ff. 63, 66, 78v, etc.). Art. 3 (ff. 94–107), occasional marginal notes in a small, neat hand (note, f. 100, includes Greek words with Latin definitions); notes in pale red ink, f. 105v, only. Art. 4 (ff. 107–190), throughout, brief marginal notes in pale red ink; a few marginal and interlinear glosses, brown ink, f. 107rv. Arts. 5 and 6 (ff. 190v–300) brief marginal notes in pale red ink. Arts. 7, 8, and 9 (ff. 300–314v) no marginalia. It has been suggested that one of the annotating hands, arts. 1–6, may be identified with the scribe of art. 10 (Reeves, "The Tradition of *Consolatio ad Liviam*," [cited below, art. 10], 86 and note 1).

9. ff. 305–314v [Ovid, *Ibis*; rubric lacking] Tempus ad hoc lustris bis iam mihi quinque peractis/ Omne fuit musae tempus inerme meae/ . . . Et pede quo debent acria bella geri.

   Antonio La Penna, ed., *Publi Ovidi Nasonis Ibis.* Biblioteca di studi superiori 34 (Florence 1957) 3–172; citing this manuscript as 'H_2', pp. cxxxvii–cxxxix, and cliii.

10. ff. 314v–321v [Ps. Ovid, *Ad Liviam Augustam Consolatio*] *Consolatoria ouidii ad ad* [*sic*] *liuiam de morte drasi neronis eius filii.* Visa diu foelix mater modo dicta neronum/ Iam tibi dimidium nominis huius abest./ . . . Est coniux tutula hominum, quo sospite uestram/

Liuia funestam dedecet esse domum. [Ff. 321v–322v blank but ruled.]

Fridericus W. Lenz, ed., *P. Ovidii Nasonis Halieutica Fragmenta, Nux, Incerti Consolatio ad Liviam.* Corpus Scriptorum Latinorum Paravianum (Turin 1956) 177–210, listing this manuscript as 'H', pp. 164–65; M. D. Reeves, "The Tradition of 'Consolatio ad Liviam,'" *Revue d'histoire des textes* 6 (1976) 79–98, listing this manuscript, p. 80, as 'H', and noting its relationship to two manuscripts copied by Bartolomeo Sanvito (cf. pp. 84–86 and 92). As noted by Reeves (p. 86, note 1), there is a long marginal note invoking Thucydides on f. 316 (*Consolatio ad Liviam*, line 106).

Paper and parchment (inner and outer bifolia of most quires parchment; palimpsest from at least two different manuscripts, s. XIV–XV, with underlying texts in a current script; watermark, Piccard Drache II.513, Ferrara 1438, or II.516, Ferrara and Parma, 1438–40, usually obscured by text), ff. ii (modern paper) + ii (paper) + 322 (incorrect modern foliation in pencil, top outer corner, as follows: 1–278, 277 bis, 278 bis, 279–319 + 1 unnumbered leaf; corrected in pencil, top, outer corner, 1–321 + 1 unnumbered leaf [cited]) + ii (modern paper), 330 x 230 mm. Layout varies. Arts. 1–8 (ff. 1–304v), written space (227–226 x 113–75) mm. 32–30 lines of verse; copied with one fewer line so the last ruled line is left blank. Ruled in dry point with the top 2 and bottom 2 horizontal rules full across; double full-length vertical bounding lines used for the first majuscule of each line of verse; the horizontal rules do not cross the vertical bounding lines. Art. 9 (ff. 305–314v), written space (242 x 90–70) mm. 33 lines of verse. Ruled in dry point with the top 2 and bottom 2 horizontal rules full across; double vertical bounding lines. Art. 10 (ff. 314v–321), written space, (252–240 x 100–73) mm. Horizontal lines ruled very lightly in dry point; double full-length vertical bounding lines ruled in lead on the left-hand side only, used for the first majuscule of each line. Ruling in dry point that was not used by the scribe visible on ff. 320–321.

1^{12} (–1 through 4, probably cancelled, with no loss of text; 6 and 7, ff. 2 and 3, conjugate pair; remaining leaves, single; 6, 7 and 12 are parchment, remainder paper; now resewn as two quires of 4, beginning f. 1) $3–21^{12}$ 22^{10} (beginning f. 237; outer bifolium, parchment) 23–26^{12} 27^{10} (beginning f. 295; outer bifolium, parchment) 28^{12} 29^{6} (beginning f. 317; 3 and 4, single; 3, parchment). Flourished vertical catchwords, beginning f. 8v, copied between the bounding lines; a few leaves signed in arabic numerals in ink, bottom outside corner (cf. ff. 36, 130, 132, and 155). In regular quires of 12, outer and center bifolia are parchment; remaining leaves, paper.

Arts. 1–8, ff. 1–304v, written in a running humanistic script using long 's' extending below the line by one or more scribes; the letter forms are similar throughout, but show signs of being written at various speeds. Art. 9, ff. 305–314v, was written on the top line in a formal upright running humanistic script by another scribe; every other line begins with a majuscule copied between the left-hand bounding lines. The manuscript was completed (art. 10, ff. 314v–321) by another scribe in a quick informal humanistic noting hand; since this scribe also annotated arts. 1–6, he may have been the owner of the manuscript or have supervised its copying (cf. Reeves, "The Tradition of *Consolatio ad Liviam*," [cited above, art. 10] 86 and note 1).

Three 5- to 3-line major initials, arts. 1, 2 and 6 (ff. 1, 56v, and 248); initials are sketched in brown (outline only), with white vinestem decoration extending half the length of the inner margin and into the upper margin; the vines are unshaded, infilled with olive green and pale red, edged in blue which follows the shape of the vine and end with orange and blue acanthus or other leaves and rayed balls. Similar secondary 3-line initials mark divisions within art. 2, and the beginning of art. 3 (ff. 69, 81, 94). Three 6- to 3-line red initials, arts. 4, 5, and 8 (ff. 107, 190v, and 303v), with the beginning of vinestem decoration in pencil; two 5- to 4-line plain red initials, ff. 300 and 305 (arts. 7 and 9); 1-line red initial with yellow highlights, f. 314v (art. 10). 3- to 1-line red initials within each text (art. 1 only, alternating red and blue); pale red rubrics (lacking in arts. 7–9).

Bound in Italy, s. XV, in dark brown leather over heavy wooden boards blind-tooled with a rope interlace center ornament surrounded by two borders; in very poor condition with the decoration badly worn and with pieces cut or torn away. Four metal corner ornaments, upper and lower boards, stamped with "ihesus" monograms set in sun-bursts; once fastened back to front [*sic*] (only marks from clasps remain, lower board; brass catches, extant, upper board). Rebacked with a new spine.

Written in Northern Italy in the third quarter of the fifteenth century, probably before 1471, when it was one of the manuscripts used by the editor of the *editio princeps* of the *Tristia*, Bologna, 1471 (art. 5, above). The style of the initials suggests an origin in Northern Italy, possibly Verona (we thank Professor de la Mare, October, 1987). No. 272 in a catalogue, dated by De Ricci, ca. 1825 (modern front flyleaf, f. i, in pencil, "No 272 £<ei?>e"). Belonged to Richard Heber (1773–1833); his sale, London, Evans, February 10, 1836, part XI, no. 1175 to Thorpe; Thorpe Cat. 1836, no. 929 (inside front cover, "929" in pencil). Sold by Thorpe to Sir Thomas Phillipps (*Phillipps Cat.*, p. 143, MS 9045; inside front cover, in pencil, "Ph MS," and, in ink, "Phillipps Ms. 9045"). Phillipps Sale, London, Sotheby's, June 10, 1896, no. 938 to Quaritch (Cat. 164, 1896, no. 128, for £26.5.0). Purchased from Quaritch, January 2, 1897 (Charles Minot Fund; bookplate, inside front cover; library stamp, medieval flyleaf, f. i; cataloguing notes and copy of a description on a library card, medieval flyleaf, f. ii^{v}). Modern front flyleaf, f. i, copy of a note signed by Harvard College Librarian, Justin Winsor, authorizing use of the manuscript by the Classics Department (for information about this purchase, cf. Dennis, "Collecting," 287–90). Original Harvard shelf mark: Lo 10.100.

secundo folio: quam que tibi

Bibliography: De Ricci, 981; De Ricci, "Handlist," 105; Wieck, p. 108, fig. 111 (reproducing f. 56v).

MS Lat 43 — Italy (Florence) s. $XV^{3/4}$
Plautus, Comoediae VIII — Pl. 54

1. ff. 1–22v [Plautus, *Amphitruo*; Argument 1] *Nobilissimi Plavti Poetae Comici Prima Comedia Amphitrio Foeliciter Incipit. Et Primo Argumen-tum.* In faciem uersus [*corr.*[2]: uorsus] amphitrionis iuppi-ter/ ... [f. 1] *Aliud Argumentum.* Amore captus almenas [*corr.*[1]: alcumenas] iuppiter/ ... [f. 1] *Prologus. Mercvrius.* Vt uos in uostris uoltis mercimoniis/ ... [f. 4 Act 1] *Sosia, Mercvrius. So.* Qui me alter est audacior homo aut qui confidentior,/ ... Nunc spectatores iouis summi causa clare plaudite. *Nobilissimi Plauti Comici Comediarum Scriptoris Ex Octo Vna Amphitrio Comedia Foeliciter Explicit.* τελως [*corr.*[2]: τελος.]

G. Goetz and F. Schoell, eds., *T. Macci Plauti Comoediae* (Leipzig 1892–5) fasc. 1, pp. 1–60.

2. ff. 23–40v [*Asinaria*; Prologue; rubric omitted] Hoc agite si uoltis [*corr.*[2]: sultis] spectatores nunciam/ . . . [f. 23] *Argumentum.* Amanti argento filio auxiliarier/ . . . [f. 23 Act 1] *Libanvs Servvs, Demenetus Senex. Li.* Sicut tuum [*sic*] uis unicum gnatum tue/ . . . Remur impetrari [*corr.*[2]: depetrari] posse si plausum sic clarum datis. *Plauti Poete Comici Clarissimi Asinaria Explicit.*

   Goetz and Schoell, eds., fasc. 1, pp. 61–112.

3. ff. 40v–60 [*Captivi*] *Eiusdem Tertia Captivi Dvo Comedia Foeliciter Incipit.* [f. 41] *Argumentum.* Captus est [*sic*] in pugna hegionis filius/ . . . [f. 41] *Prologus.* Vos [*sic*] quos uidetis stare hic captiuos duos/ . . . [f. 42v Act 1] *Parasitvs.* Iuuentus nomen indidit scorto mihi/ . . . Qui pudicitie esse uoltis premium plausum date. *Clarissimi Plavti Poetae Comici Captivi Dvo Inscripta Comedia Explicit Tertia.*

   Goetz and Schoell, eds., fasc. 2, pp. 59–109.

4. ff. 60–73v [*Curculio*] *Eivsdem Incipit Quarta Inscripta Cvrgulio Foeliciter. Prologus Vel Argumentum.* Cvrgvlio missus Phedromi et [*corr.*[2]: it] Cariam/ . . . [f. 60 Act 1] *Palinurus seruus, Phedromus adulescens. Pa.* Qvo te [*sic*] hac noctis dicam proficisci foras/ . . . *M.* Que res bene uortant [*sic*] mihi et uobis. *hy.* Spectatores plaudite. *Plauti poete comici clarissimi curgulio explicit.*

   Goetz and Schoell, eds., fasc. 3, pp. 43–83.

5. ff. 73v–89 [*Casina*] *Eiusdem quinta comedia casina incipit foeliciter. Prologus.* Salvere iubeo spectatores optumos, fidem qui factis maxumi/ . . . [f. 75] *Argumentum.* Conseruam uxorem duo serui expetunt/ . . . [f. 75v Act 1] *Calinus, Olimpio, duo serui. Ca.* Non mihi licere meam rem me solum ut uolo loqui atque cogitare/ . . . Ei pro scorto supponetur hyrcus unctus nausea [*sic*]. *Plauti poete comici clarissimi casina explicit.*

   Goetz and Schoell, eds., fasc. 2, pp. 111–61.

6. ff. 89–98v [*Cistellaria*] *Incipit eiusdem sexta comedia cistellaria foeliciter. Argumentum.* Comprimit adolescens lemnius liconia [*sic*]/ . . .

[f. 89v Act 1] *Meretrices due, Silenium, lena et gimnasium. Si.* Cvm antehac te amaui et mihi amicam esse creui/ . . . More maiorum date plausum postrema in comedia. *Plauti poete comici clarissimi cistellaria explicit.*

Goetz and Schoell, eds., fasc. 3, pp. 1–42.

7. ff. 98v–112 [*Epidicus*] *Incipit eiusdem vii comedia epidicus. Argumentum.* Emit fiducinam filiam credens senex/ . . . [f. 98v Act 1] *Epidicus, Thesprio, serui duo. E.* Heus adolescens. *T.* Quis properantem me prehendit pallio/ . . . Plaudite [*om.* et] ualete lumbos surgite atque extollite. *Plauti comici poete clarissimi epidicus explicit.*

Goetz and Schoell, eds., fasc. 3, pp. 85–130.

8. ff. 112–127v [*Aulularia*; argument 1, incorrectly listed as prologue] *Gurgula* [*corr.*[1]*: Aulularia*] *feliciter incipit. Prologus.* Senex auarus uix sibi/ . . . [f. 112v] *Argumentum.* Avlam repertam auri plenam heuclio/ . . . [f. 112v prologue; rubric omitted] Ne quis miretur qui sum [*sic*] paucis eloquar/ . . . [f. 113v Act 1] *Heuclio senex et Staphila anus. H.* Dixi [*sic*] inquam age exi exeundum hercle tibi hinc est foras/ . . . Vel hercle eneca nunquam feres hinc a me. *Plauti comici poete clarissimi aulularia feliciter explicit. Finis.* [two blank lines, followed by colophon] *Hoc opus o lector transcripsit petrus auorum/ cuius cennina est nomine dicta domus./ Error si quis inest exemplar semina seuit./ Si secus esse putas inuidiosus abi.*

Goetz and Schoell, eds., fasc. 1, pp. 113–58.

(Arts. 1–8) The same eight plays, arranged in an identical order, are often found in fifteenth-century Italian copies of Plautus; for example: Vatican, Biblioteca Apostolica Vaticana, MS Chigi H.VI.200 (Pellegrin, 1:346–47); MS Chigi H.VI.201 (Pellegrin, 1:347–48); MS Pal. lat. 1619 (Pellegrin, 2.2:260–61); MS Ross. 926 (XI, 76) (Pellegrin, 2.2:483); and MS Ross. 960 (XI, 110) (Pellegrin, 2.2:496).

Marginal notes and interlinear glosses in a number of hands, including: nota marks, a majuscule "N" with extensions indicating the "T" and "A," sometimes decorated with flourishes (cf. ff. 2, 2v, 27, 114v [in red]), and corrections (cf. f. 2v, supplying an omission, f. 3, etc.) by the scribe; ff. 74–92, a contemporary hand, possibly the scribe, has written key words from the text in the margin, occasionally with explanations; sparse interlinear glosses through f. 59 (*Captivi*) in a contemporary small, spiky cursive script, for example, on f. 11, commenting on grammatical structure and noting variants, and f. 12, adding simple explanations; occasional later nota marks and comments (cf. ff. 35, 66v–67).

9. ff. 128–129 *Interpretationes personarum quae in his comoediis inducuntur. In Amphitrone.* Amphitrio circumspiciens. Sosia saluus. . . . *In Aulularia.* Euclio bene claudens siue serenus. . . . Megadorus Magna donans.

List of names of the characters in the eight plays included in this manuscript, and in the same order, with explanations of their significance.

f. 129 (arts. 10–14): extracts concerning Plautus, following the previous article without a break:

10. f. 129 *Avlvs Gellivs Noctivm Atticae vii.* Plautus uerborum latinorum elegantissimus.

Aulus Gellius, *Noctes atticae* I:7.17; P. K. Marshall, ed., OCT (Oxford 1968) 1:54; printed in Goetz and Schoell, eds., fasc. 1, pp. xxx–xxxi, no. LXXII.

11. f. 129 *Cicero De Oratore.* Plautus antiquitatem retinet nec est imitandus.

Unidentified; perhaps a paraphrase of Cicero, *De Oratore* 3:12.44–46; K. F. Kumaniecki, ed. (Leipzig 1969) 279; printed in Goetz and Schoell, eds., fasc. 1, p. xxxviii, no. LX.

12. f. 129 *Eusebius De Temporibus.* Plautus ex umbria Sarsinas Romae moritur . . . et uendere solicitus consueuerat.

Jerome, *Chronicon Eusebii* (extr. Vita Plauti); R. Helm, ed., *Die Chronik des Hieronymus.* Die Griechischen Christlichen Schriftsteller der Ersten Jahrhunderte; Eusebius Werke 7 (Berlin 1956) 135–36; printed in Goetz and Schoell, eds., fasc. 1, p. xx, no. XXII. Also found with the Plautine plays in Houghton, MS Lat 271 (Italy, s. $XV^{3/4}$); Vatican, Biblioteca Apostolica Vaticana, MS Ottob. lat. 1745 (Italy, s. XV; Pellegrin, 1:664–65); and MS Pal. lat. 1618 (Italy or Germany, s. XV; Pellegrin, 2.2:259–60).

13. f. 129 *Avli Gellii Epigramma In Plavtum.* Postquam est morte captus plautus comoedia luget./ . . . [*om.* Et] Numeri innumeri simul omnes conlacrimarunt [*corr.*[2]: collacrimarunt].

A. Gellius, *Noctes Atticae* I:24.3 (Epitaphium Plauti); P. K. Marshall, ed., 1:81; printed in Goetz and Schoell, eds., fasc. 1, p. xxvi, no. LIII. Often circulated with Plautus.

14. ff. 129–130 [f. 129] *Nigidius.* Plautus ex umbria fuit Sarsinas qui ex comicis poetis secundus extitit. [Ff. 129v–130 blank, but ruled.]

Extract from unidentified source, with some relationship to Aulus Gellius, *Noctes atticae* XV:24; P. K. Marshall, eds., OCT (Oxford 1968) 2:468.

Paper (watermarks, obscured in gutter, but possibly Briquet Lettre "N" 8431, Geneva 1414 and 1415, Clermont-Ferand 1416, Forez 1419, and Toulouse 1420; and an unidentified chariot), ff. ii (paper) + 130 + ii (paper), 218 x 149 (146–145 x 97–70) mm., ruled space: 147 x 97 mm. 27 long lines. Ruled in hard point; double full-length vertical bounding lines, used for the first majuscule of each line of verse.

$1–14^{12}$ 15^{10} (10, f. 130, a blank leaf). Horizontal catchwords, center, lower margin, decorated on all sides with dots and s-shaped flourishes (f. 84v, quire 7, with red dots); quire and leaf signatures in ink, bottom outside margin, recto, with letter designating the quire and arabic numeral, the leaf, usually numbering the first seven leaves in the quire; many trimmed, but visible in quires 4, and 6–8 (beginning ff. 37, 61, 73, and 85). In quire 4, bottom outside corner, last folio (f. 48) there is a "d" in red, possibly a quire signature (?). Quires reinforced with paper or parchment strips around the outer and in the center bifolia.

Written below the top line by the Florentine scribe Piero Cennini (ca. 1445–84; colophon, f. 127v) in a quick cursive humanistic script.

One 3-line gold initial, f. 1, with white vinestem decoration of mediocre quality, extending into a short border, infilled with pink, green, and blue, outlined in blue with silver dots that follow the shape of the vine, terminating in clusters of gold rayed disks and simple leaves in pink, red or green (reproduced in Wieck, fig. 119). 2- to 3-line gold initials infilled with pink and/or green, on square blue grounds with silver or white flourishes and dots used at the beginning of the remaining plays, and at some divisions within each play; remaining divisions begin with 2-line blue initials. Rubrics, some decorated with dots and other flourishes that serve as line extenders, and running titles, in red, occasionally faded, in a cursive humanistic script or capitals. Red abbreviations in the outer margins or internally, used throughout to indicate the character speaking. Plays and divisions within the plays usually begin with the first word in capitals (or the first line, as f. 60), occasionally in red (cf. f. 13); first majuscule of each line of verse written between the outer bounding lines. Guide letters for initials within the initials (cf. f. 98v) or in the margin in red (cf. ff. 40v, 67) or brown ink (cf. f. 41).

Bound in Italy, s. XVIII, in decorative floral paper over pasteboard; handwritten title in ink and unidentified shelf mark "F.VI.32," on spine.

Written, most likely in Florence, by Piero Cennini (colophon, 127v; *Colophons*, no. 15414); see de la Mare, "New Research," 445, and Appendix 1, no. 60, 526–29, listing this manuscript p. 527, no. 14; Klara Csapodi–Gardonyi, "Les Manuscrits copiés par Petrus Cenninius: Liste revue et augmentée," in *Miscellanea codicologica F. Masai dicata*, eds. P. Cockshaw, M.-C. Garand, P. Jodogne. Les Publications de Scriptorium 8 (Gand 1979) 2:413–16, listing this manuscript p. 415, no. 30; B. L. Ullman, *The Origin and Development of Humanistic Script* (Rome 1960) 123–25, listing this manuscript p. 125, no. 14; Jose Ruysschaert, "Dix-huit manuscrits copiés par le florentin Pietro Cennini," *La Bibliofilia* 59 (1957) 108–12, listing this manuscript, p. 111, [no. 15].

Ullman (*Humanistic Script*, 125) suggested that this manuscript may be dated between 1462–67, since the same colophon appears in the following manuscripts: Paris, Bibliothèque nationale, MS n.a.lat 1705, Servius on Vergil, dated July 1, 1462 (Ullman no. 1, fig. 69; de la Mare no. 24; and Cspaodi–Gardonyi no. 2, listing the date as December 1, 1462); Cesena, Biblioteca Malatestiana, MS S.I.6, Martial, dated August 24, 1463 (Ullman no. 2; de la Mare no. 3; Csapodi–Gardonyi no. 3; Ruysschaert, p.108, [no. 1]; *Colophons* no. 15416); Krakow, Biblioteka Muzeum Narodowego w Krakowie (Czartoryski Library), MS 1514, Frontinus, *Strategematica*, dated June 13, 1467 (Ullman no. 5; de la Mare no. 15; Csapodi–Gardonyi no. 9, and pl. 58b, reproducing colophon, which, contrary to Ullman's statement, differs from that in this manuscript slightly; Ruysschaert p. 109 [no. 7]). The colophon in Lucca, Biblioteca statale, MS 1444, Maffeo Vegio, *De verborum significatione,* etc. dated 1464 (Ullman no. 15; de la Mare no. 19; Csapodi–Gardonyi no. 4; Ruysschaert p. 108 [no. 2]) differs significantly from that in this manuscript, although Ullman cites it as somewhat similar (cf. *Colophons* no. 15417). Additional manuscripts with the same colophon include: Florence, Biblioteca nazionale centrale, MS Magliab. XXVIII.51, dated 1464 (de la Mare no. 9; *Colophons* no. 15418), and Florence, Biblioteca Medicea Laurenzaina, MS Plut. 34,34, Juvenal and Persius (de la Mare no. 5, incorrectly listed as MS Plut 24,34; Csapodi–Gardonyi no. 26; Ruysschaert p. 111 [no. 13]; *Colophons* no. 15415). The colophon in Florence, MS Plut 33,21, Ps. Acron on Horace (de la Mare no. 4; Ullman no. 17; Csapodi–Gardonyi no. 21; Ruysschaert p. 111 [no. 17]) does not agree with this manuscript (cf. incorrect listing in *Colophons* no. 15415, and transcription in Ruysschaert, p. 112). Professor A. C. de la Mare noted that a date in the third-quarter of the fifteenth century, early in Cennini's career is supported by similarities to the script found in the Paris, Bibliothèque nationale, MS n.a.lat 1705, Servius, dated 1462; the catchwords and nota marks are also characteristic of his early manuscripts (we thank Professor de la Mare for this information; in correspondence, 1970; library visit, 1987).

Ms. F.VI.32 in an unidentified Italian library, s. XVIII (paper label on spine; see above). Unidentified booksellers' notes in pencil, inside front cover: "180"; f. 1: "1318"; inside back cover: "n/og" (or "n/oy"[?], very faint). Belonged to Frederick North, fifth Earl of Guilford (1766–1827); his collection sold by Cochran, London, 1829, no. 349, to Sir Thomas Phillipps (*Phillipps Cat.*, p. 94, MS 6332; "6332" in black ink, f. 1). Phillipps sale, London, Sotheby's, June 10, 1896, no. 135. Bought by Quaritch, Cat. no. 164, London, 1896, no. 135. Purchased by Harvard from Quaritch, January 2, 1897 (Charles Minot Fund; bookplate, inside front cover). Front flyleaf, f. i^{v}, copy of a note signed by Harvard College Librarian, Justin Winsor, authorizing use of the manuscript by the Classics Department (for information about this purchase, cf. Dennis, "Collecting," 287–90). Original Harvard shelf mark: Lp 26.227.

secundo folio: Contagione meae

Bibliography: De Ricci, 981; De Ricci, "Handlist," 106; Franklin W. Jones, "MS Lat 43. Plauti, *Comoediae octo*," (typescript, 1928) now Houghton, bMS Lat 315(11); Walters Art Gallery, *Calligraphy*, p. 60, no. 42, with plate of f. 60; Wieck, p. 108, fig. 119 (reproducing f. 1); Kristeller, *Iter* 5:226.

MS Lat 44 — France s. XII$^{2/4}$
Priscian, Institutiones grammaticae — Pl. 23

ff. 1–213v [Dedicatory epistle] //esse inuentionibus posse sua quoque industria ad communem litteratoriae professionis utilitatem congrua rationis proporcione uel addere uel mutare tractantes . . . [f. 1] *Titvli Librorum.* Primus liber continet de uoce et eius speciebus . . . Septimusdecimus et Octavusdecimus de constructione siue ordinatione parcium orationis interse [*sic*]. [f. 1v Text] *Incipit Prisciani Ars Gramatici Caesariensis. I. De Uoce.* Philosophi definiunt uocem esse aerem tenuissimum ictum . . . His accensa super iactatos equore toto et in xi ecce super mesti magna diomedis ab urbe. Legati//

M. Hertz, ed., *Prisciani grammatici Caesariensis institutionum grammaticarum libri XVIII.* Grammatici latini, H. Keil, ed., 2–3 (Leipzig 1855 and 1859; reprint Hildesheim 1961); now ending imperfectly at 14.52 (ed., 3:55, line 21), but likely originally with books 1–16, the *Priscianus major* (ed., through 3:105), although the summary of the contents, f. 1, lists books 1–18. See Margaret Gibson, "Priscian, 'Instiutiones Grammaticae': A Handlist of Manuscripts," *Scriptorium* 26 (1972) 105–124, with a list of 527 manuscripts including this one, p. 108. Briefly described in: Marina Passalacqua, *I codici di Prisciano.* Sussidi Eruditi 29 (Rome 1978) 44, no. *94; Guglielmo Ballaira, *Per il catalogo dei codici di Prisciano* (Turin 1982) 227, no. *94; G. L. Bursill-Hall, *A Census of Medieval Latin Grammatical Manuscripts.* Grammatica Speculativa 4 (Stuttgart-Bad Cannstatt 1981) 93, no. 116.1.

First quire now lacking the first and last leaves, so that text begins imperfectly in the dedicatory epistle [ed., 2:2, line 14], continuing with no breaks through f. 6v: ". . . In mediis inter utrumque supra dictorum locum. Quod facile dinoscitur// [book 1.26, ed., 2:20, line 16]." Resumes on f. 7: "//eiusdem speciei ut in uocalibus breues et longae. Et in consonantibus simplices et duplices ... [book 1.31, ed., 2:23, line 21]"; continuing with no breaks through f. 211v: "... Inuenitur etiam sine casu in quo// [book 14.32, ed., 3:40, line 18]." Last quire missing all but the middle bifolium, so that text resumes on f. 212: "//et stulticiae tuae proauus. Sed hoc quidam ab aduerbio procul compositum affirmant ... [book 14.45, ed., 3:49, line 10]"; and continues through f. 213v [book 14.52, ed., 3:55, line 21], ending imperfectly. Quire 14, ff. 103–108v, beginning with no break in the text: "usus huiuscemodi concisionis Virgilius in ix altaque certant [*sic*] ... [book 7.26, ed. 2:308, line 5]," and ending: "... nemo emat suam quisque partem piscium poscant sibi ducant [*sic*] [bk 7.55, ed. 2:332, line 5]," is an added quire, s. XII^2, replacing the original quire, or supplying omitted text. Divided into 14 books, beginning on ff. 1v, 13v, 29v, 41v, 52v, 69, 95, 120v, 151v, 165v, 179v, 189, 198 and 206.

With marginal and interlinear glosses throughout in a number of hands; in quires 1 and 2, the glosses are tied to the text with letters or symbols, and sometimes include identifications of the authors cited. These glosses have never been the subject of a detailed study. Their potential importance was first discovered in 1947 by Professor Raymond Klibansky, who noted that a few of the glosses in the first two quires are marked *L* and suggested that they may be by Lanfranc of Bec (see Margaret Gibson, *Lanfranc of Bec* [Oxford 1978] 47, discussing this possibility and mentioning our manuscript; cf. also R. W. Hunt, "The Introductions to the 'Artes' in the 12th Century," *Studia mediaevalia in honorem admodum Reverendi Patris Raymundi Josephi Martin* [Bruges 1948] 92, mentioning Dr. Klibansky in connection with William of Conches' gloss on Priscian, but not mentioning any manuscripts). Margaret Gibson noted in a visit to the library, April, 1989, that the glosses were not from the commentary assembled in the eleventh century known as the *Glosulae*. She suggested that they may be related to the commentary of the twelfth-century master William of Conches, or to the commentary of another master from the school of Chartres.

F. 1v, book 1, first marginal gloss: "Aerem eius[?] emissione et contractione spirando uiuit atque subsistit animal intellige, qui ab anima prolatus atque in ore per linguam per ouiss[imus?]. Hoc testante uocatur uox . . ."; f. 29v, book 3, first marginal gloss: "Participem positiui sensus demonstrat ipsa ordinatio comparatiuorum colata uel cum omnibus suis positiuis uel cum omnibus que sunt in loco positiuorum qui est <word expunged> uel prepositio ultra uel intra uel uerbum dentis. Ista omnia sunt participantia positiui sensus. [Continued in another hand:] Et ideo dicuntur participes positiui sensus quia ut comparatio in nomine sepe a positiuo nascitur, sic sepe a uerbis et aduerbiis."; f. 41v, book 4, first marginal gloss: "Hic liber nominatur asilum pro collectione diuersarum specialiter in sua proprietate partium diuisarum que in hoc libro quasi sub uno uinculo coadunatae et constrictae . . ."

Includes glosses in the first person, for example, f. 1 (commenting on: "Huius tantum operis te hortatorem sortitus iudicem quoque facio iuliane consul ac patricie . . ."): "Scio q<uod?> non est iustum usus inter homines ut aliquis sit iudex eius rei quam rogabit fieri et quamuis hoc sit t<antum?>."; and citations from Lanfranc, for example, f. 5: "Lanfrancus dicit reuce capellas secundum eum non ponitur hic pro celeumaticus. Et est <etiam?> contrarius libro qui in hac eadem pagina dicit nulla consonans potest geminata iungi in eadem sillaba . . ." Greek is in the hand of the main scribe, ff. 1–14v (quires 1 and 2); otherwise added by a contemporary.

Parchment (varying types; notably thick, stiff and velvety, quires 3, ff. 15–22v and 5, ff. 31–38v), ff. ii (paper) + 213 + ii (paper), 220 x 121 (text: 170–5 x 80–75; text and gloss: 203–186 x 126–105) mm.; amount of gloss varies, often adding in outer margin c.25–30 mm. to the width of the written space; trimmed so that part of the gloss in the outer margins is now often missing. 35–33 long lines of text, with gloss in unruled space in the outer margin, and occasionally interlinearily and in all four margins. Ruled in dry point (except quire 5, ff. 31–38v, in lead; cf. esp. f. 33); sometimes with top and bottom, or top 2 and bottom 2, horizontal lines full across; double full-length vertical bounding lines. Prickings in the three outer margins, most folios.

Quire 14, ff. 103–108v, is a later addition, s. XII^{2}: written space (176–172 x 80–71) mm. 35 long lines. Ruled in lead, with the top 2 and bottom 2 horizontal lines full across; double full-length vertical bounding lines. Neat slash-type prickings, three outer margins.

1^8 (–1 and 8, following f. 6, with loss of text) 2–13^8 14^6 15–18^8 19^8 (3, f. 143, and 6, f. 146, are single) 20–22^8 23^8 (–2, after f. 173, with no loss of text) 24–27^8 28^8 (–1, 2, 3, and 6, 7, 8, before and after ff. 212–213, a conjugate pair, with loss of text). Quires signed with small roman numerals in ink, verso of last leaf, lower margin, left of center, except quires 3 and 4 (ff. 22v and 30v) signed in the center, last leaf, and quires 21–23 and 25 (ff. 157, 165, 173, and 188) signed on the first leaf, recto, lower margin, left of center; signatures lacking in quires 1, 8, 14, 28 (beginning on ff. 1, 55, 103, and 212). Quires numbered in ink in a modern hand, top right corner, recto, of the first leaf of each quire.

Written above the top line in a neat twelfth-century minuscule with early features ('ae' usually written e-cedilla; amperand used internally for 'et') by as many as three scribes, as follows: 1) ff. 1–14v, quire 1; 2) ff. 15–102v and ff. 109–156v; 3) ff. 157–end (possibly hand 1). Quire 14, ff. 103–108v, added later, s. XII^2, is written above the top line in a neat, upright, twelfth-century minuscule.

Books begin with various types of initials: book 3, f. 29v, 5-line parted orange-red initial, set within the text space; book 5, f. 52v, similar 2-line initial (not parted); book 4, f. 41v, crude 4-line parted initial, brown ink, set within text space; books 1 and 2, ff. 1v and 13v, 2-line initials, brown ink, set partly within text space; book 13, f. 198, 2-line initial, brown ink, set within text space; books 10, 11, 12, and 14, ff. 165v, 180 (initial, rubric, f. 179v), 189v (initial, rubric, f. 189) and 206, 2-line brown ink initials, alongside text in the margin. Blanks remain for 3- to 2-line initials, books 6, 7, 8, and 9, ff. 69, 95, 120v, and 151v. Sections within each book variously indicated by 2- to 1-line initials placed in the margins alongside the text or 1-line initials within the line of text; angular paragraph marks throughout (possibly added). Rubrics in display capitals, brown ink; omitted in books 4–9 and 13; opening words of text in similar capitals, books 3, 4, 6–8, 13 and 14.

Bound in France, s. XIX (dated by De Ricci, ca. 1820) in purple morocco, with gold diamond-shaped center ornament and frame, blind-tooled with 4 corner oranments and border; spine with 6 triple bands, with author and title in Latin in gilt ("Prisciani Ars Grammatica. Script. in Membr. Saec. XI"); speckled edges.

Written in northern France in the second quarter of the twelfth century. Cautionary note added bottom margin, f. 207, s. XIII^{2}–XIV: "Hos qui hic lege letus uel ex diab[olo] iste liber saeuerit uero peterent laudare liber explicit iste." Formerly in a Benedictine monastery; remains of an inscription, s. XVII–XVIII, top margin, f. 1: "Ben[e]dictinorum <erased; illegible under ultraviolet>." Unidentified owners' or booksellers' notes, front flyleaf, f. i^{v}: in pencil, "160"; in another hand, "P." Belonged to Sir Thomas Phillipps (*Phillipps Cat.*, 33, MS 2974; front flyleaf, f. ii, his stamp and "2974"), who acquired it from a "Bibliotheca Parisiensis" (listed as the source, *Phillipps Cat.*, 33; cf. Munby, *Phillipps Studies* 3:150), possibly Royez (pencil note, front flyleaf, f. i^{v}: "From Royez 2974 Mss Ph"). Phillipps sale, London, Sotheby's, June 10, 1896, no. 975, for £7 (as reported by Munby, *Phillipps Studies* 5:59) to Quaritch (Quaritch Cat. 164 [1896] no. 139, £12.12.0). Purchased from Quaritch, January 2, 1897, Charles Minot Fund (library stamp, front flyleaf, f. i^{v}; bookplate, inside front cover). Copy of a note signed by Harvard College librarian, Justin Winsor, authorizing use of the manuscript by the Classics Department, front flyleaf, f. i (for information concerning this purchase, see Dennis, "Collecting," 287–89). Cataloguing notes by Morris Hickey Morgan (1859–1918) and M. Grand (pocket, back flyleaf, f. ii; see Dennis, "Collecting," 289). Former Harvard shelf mark: Lp 41.17.

secundo folio: (now f. 1) esse inuentionibus

Bibliography: De Ricci, 981; De Ricci, "Handlist," 106; Light, *Bible in the Twelfth Century*, 81–82, no. 30.

MS Lat 45 — Germany s. XV^{2}

Terence, Comoediae

1. f. 1v [f. 1 blank with later notes] Nota utilitas huius libri . . . Nota pro titulo poeta scilicet[?] et inuentor dicuntur sic propter excellenciam . . . Item poete sattarici [*sic*] tractatur satturas in orationes uicia. . . .

   Introductory notes on the plays.

2. f. 2 [Epitaph for Terence] Natus in excelsis tectis cartaginis alte/ . . . Hec quicumque leget sic puto cautus erit.

Alexander Riese, ed., *Anthologia latina sive poesis latinae supplementum. I, Carmina in codicibus scripta* (Leipzig 1894–1906) 487c; Walther, *Initia* 11627.

3. ff. 2–35 [Terence, *Andria*] *Argumentum in andria.* Sororem falso creditam meretricule/ ... Hanc pamphilo dat aliam carino coniugem. [f. 1v] *Prologus in andria.* Poeta cum primum animum ad scribendum appulit/ ... Spectande an exigende sint uobis prius. [f. 3 rubric; f. 3v text] *Simo sosya prima zena.* Vos istec intro aufferte abite. Sosia/ ... Intus transietur si quid [*sic*] est quod restat/ Vos valete et plaudite calioppius recensui. [added in another hand: *Terency afri eunchus explicit. Andria incipit*].

   Robert Kauer and W. M. Lindsay, eds., *P. Terenti Afri Comoediae.* OCT (Oxford 1926; reprinted with additions 1958) [1–154].

4. ff. 35v–69 [Terence, *Eunuchus*] Meretrix adolescentem cuius mutuo amore/ Tenebatur exclusit eique reouocato/ ... f. 35v *Prologus eunchyi.* Si quisquam est qui placere studeat bonis/ ... Quid sibi enuchus uelit ut pernoscatis. [f. 36v] *Argumentum enuchy.* Sororem falso dictam thaydis id ipsum ignorans miles/ ... Sed athicus ciuis in primis repertus frater collocat viciatam ephedo [*sic*]. [f. 37 text] *Phedra adolescens parmeno seruus.* Quid igitur ad eam [expunged: ad] eam [*sic*] an ne nunc quidem./ Cum accersor vltro an pocius ita me conparem/ ... Vos ualete et plaudite incensui. [Followed by seven blank lines.]

   Kauer and Lindsay, eds., [111–69].

5. ff. 69–101v [Terence, *Heautontimorumenos*; rubric omitted; argument] [I]n miliciam proficisci gnatum cliniam amantem/ ... hanc clinia aliam[?] clitipho uxorem accipit. [f. 69v] *Prologus heautuntumerominis* [*sic*]. Ce [*corr.*: ne] cui vestrum sit mirum cur partes seni poeta dederit/ ... Ut adolescentuli vobis placere studeant postquam [*corr.*: pocius quam] sibi. [f. 70v text] *Menedemus cremes senex duo.* Quamquam inter nos nuper noticia admodo est inde a deo/ ... *Cre.* Fiet./ Vos ualete et plaudite caliopius recensui. [Ends mid f. 101v; remainder blank.]

   Kauer and Lindsay, eds., [55–110].

6. ff. 102–133v [Terence, *Adelphoe*; rubric omitted; argument] Uvos

[*corr.*: Dvos] cum haberet demea adolescentulos/ . . . Ex orato suo patre duro demea. [f. 102] *Prologus adophi* [*sic*]. Postquam poeta sensit scripturam suam/ . . . Poetae ad scribundam [*sic*] ageat industriam. [f. 103 text] *Micio senex solus.* Tsorax [*sic*] non rediit hac nocte ad cena esthinus/ Neque seruolorum quisquam adforsum [*sic*] igerant . . . *De.* Sino/ habeat in istac finem faciat. *He.* Istuc recte. Uos ualete et plaudite caliopius recensui.

Kauer and Lindsay, eds., [273–323].

7. ff. 134–160v [Terence, *Hecyra*; rubric omitted; argument] Uxorem duxit pamphilus pililomenam [*sic*]/ . . . Uxorem recipit pamphilus cum pamphilus [*sic*] filo [*sic*]. [f. 134] *Prologus echire.* Echira est huic nomen fabule. Haec autem data est./ . . . Alias cognostis eius queso hanc noscite./ [f. 134v second prologue, copied as part of the first prologue] Orator ad uos uenio ornatu prologi/ . . . Nouas expediat post hac precio emptas meo. [f. 136 text] *Philotis <meretrix?> syra lena.* Per pol quam pacos [*sic*] reperias meritricibus [*sic*]/ . . . *Par.* Sequor/ Equidem plus boni feci hodie inprudens/ Quam sciens ante hunc diem unquam/ Vos ualete et plaudite coliapius incensui.

Kauer and Lindsay, eds., [227–72].

8. ff. 161–190v [Terence, *Phormio*; rubric omitted; argument] Chremetis frater aberat peregre Demipho [added in margin: relicto athenis]/ . . . Retinet antipho ad patruo agnitam. [f. 161] *Prologus phormionis.* Postquam poeta uetus poetam non poete retrahere/ . . . Bonitasque vostra adiutans atque equanimitas. [f. 162 text] *Panus suus solus.* Amicus meus et pupularis [*sic*]/ . . . *Na.* Fiat sed ubist phedria/ Iudex noster. *Ph.* Iam faxo hic aderit/ Vos ualete et plaudite caliopius recensui.

Kauer and Lindsay, eds., [171–226].

(Arts. 2–8) Throughout, text accompanied by a marginal commentary, usually short paragraphs at the beginning of each play and scenes within the plays, and interlinear glosses written in a cramped, contemporary hand.

9. ff. 190v–191 [*Didascaliae*] Acta ludis romanis lucio postomio albino lucio [added: cornelio] merula . . . marco ualerio consulibus; Acta ludis megalensibus lucio postomio albino lucio cornelia

merula ... fannio consulibus; Acta ludis megalensibus a lucio cornelio lentulo a lucio ualerio flacto edilibus ... sembronio consulibus; Acta laudis [*corr.*: ludis] funebribus quinto fabio maximo et publico ... ancio marco cornelio consulibus; Acta ludis romanis sexto iulio cesare ... edilibus.

Didascaliae of *Phormio*, *Eunuchus*, *Heautontimorumenos*, *Adelphoe*, and *Hecyra*.

10. ff. 191v–192v Notes on the characters in the plays, and other notes.

Paper (watermarks, similar to Piccard Ochsenkopf XIII.611, Thron, 1441 and 1442, and XIII.621, Schweinfurt, 1448; and similar to Piccard Turm II.491, Augsburg, 1467), ff. ii (paper) + i (parchment, fragment of an earlier manuscript, once used as a pastedown) + 192 + i (parchment from an earlier manuscript) + ii (paper), 307 x 207 (233–230 x 150–92) mm.; ruled space, 246–241 x 135–129 mm. 17 lines of verse, widely spaced to allow for interlinear glosses. Frame ruled in ink, all single and full-length, with an extra single rule, outer margin (trimmed on some folios). With crooked lines of prickings along the outer bounding lines, roughly corresponding to the lines of text, some with ink dots, others with holes only.

$1–16^{12}$. Horizontal catchwords, bottom, inside margin; partially trimmed in most quires.

Written below the top line in a quick cursive gothic bookhand, using long 's' below the line, and some loops; glosses in a smaller cursive script.

Crude 5-line blue initial, f. 2 (Epitaph), clumsily boxed with double red border, infilled with brown touched with blue; surrounded by a pattern of beads with red highlights. Remaining major divisions marked by various types of initials: f. 35v (*Eunuchus*), outline of 2-line red initial; f. 69 (*Heautontimorumenos*) frame in brown ink for 3-line initial (initial lacking); f. 102 (*Adelphoe*) 3-line plain red initial; f. 134 (*Hecyra*) bold 4-line initial, infilled with brown with red highlights; and f. 161 (*Phormio*) 3-line red initial, outlined in brown (unfinished) with brown infilling. Divisions within the plays begin with 3- to 1-line initials, red or outlined in brown and then filled with red, some with simple pen decorations or grotesques (f. 2, argument, infilled with brown beads and a crude sketch of a woman). Red rubrics; each line of text begins with a red slash-mark. Guide notes for rubricator often remain written in the outer margin at right angles to the text.

Bound for Harvard in a half-leather binding; marbled boards; "Terentius Comoediae. Manuscript" and "Harvard University Library" on spine. Parchment flyleaves (pastedowns from an earlier binding) are leaves from a manuscript, Germany, s. XIV^2 (?) of a grammatical text, copied in a gothic bookhand: back flyleaf, bifolium, roughly 306 x 165–161 mm., with the text reading vertically to the main text, trimmed with loss of text at the top, left, and bottom; width of written space about 134 mm. 22 long lines; lifted pastedown, with paper adhering to the recto; text on verso: "Quarta declinacio quot litteras terminales habet duas quas B et U . . ."; front flyleaf, two fragments from the same manuscript, roughly set in with modern tape so the text reads in the same direction as the text in the main manuscript, with 29–lines of text remaining, trimmed top and outside.

Written in Germany in the second half of the fifteenth century. Notes in various fifteenth-century hands, mostly pen-trials, f. 1, and on parchment flyleaves. In pencil, f. 1v, "728." Purchased May 9, 1906 from Liebisch in Leipzig (Salisbury Fund; library note, inside front cover; library stamp with date, f. 1v). Previous Harvard shelf mark: Lt 6.95.

secundo folio: [f. 3] Dissimili oratione

Bibliography: De Ricci, 981; Stephen Bleeker Luce, "Description of a MS of Terence (Lt 6.95) owned by Harvard College Library," (typescript, Cambridge, February, 1912) now Houghton bMS Lat 315(13); De Ricci, "Handlist," 107.

MS Lat 46 — Italy (Florence) s. XV^{med}
Tibullus, Carmina; Ovid, Epistula Sapphus, etc. — Pl. 50

1. ff. 1–41 [Tibullus, *Carmina*] *Albii Tibvlli Poetae Illvstris Prohemium. Quod Spretis Militia Atque Divitiis Deliam Amat Et Amori Vacare Prorsvs Velit.* Divitias alivs fulvo sibi congerat avro/ Et tenneat [*sic*] cvlti ivgera magna soli./ . . . Crimina non hec sunt nostro sine facta

dolore/ Quid miserum torques rumor acerbe tace. τέλος. [f. 41 Domitus Marsus, Epitaph; four verses] *Epitaphivm Ipsivs Tibvlli.* Me [*sic*] quoque Virgilio comitem non aequa Tibvlle/ . . . Aut caneret forti regia bella pede. [f. 41 Life of Tibullus; rubric omitted] Albivs Tibvllvs eques regalis insignis forma cultuque corporis observabilis . . . Obiit adolescens ut eius epitaphio accepimus. *Finis.* [F. 41v blank, but ruled.]

F. W. Lenz and G. C. Galinsky, eds., *Albii Tibulli aliorumque carminum libri tres*, 3rd. ed. (Leiden 1971) 51–170 (text), 171 (epitaph), 171–72 (life of Tibullus). Divided into three books, beginning ff. 1, 17v, 26v; poems begin with red rubrics, not identical to those printed by Lenz; for example f. 2v (book 1.2) "Queritur de ianua clausa et loquitur blande ad Amasiam"; f. 4v (book 1.3) "Queritur quod aegrotat Messala laudatque primam aetatem." Book 2.5 divided into two poems, the second beginning at verse 39, with the rubric, f. 23v: "De euea et urbe habet Sibille uaticinium pernostica future urbis et festa palilia et commendationem sui ad Nemesim"; book 3.6 similarly divided, the second poem beginning at verse 33, with the rubric, f. 32: "Habet conquestionem amatoris uariam et amicitiae solatium."

2. ff. 42–46v [*Epistula Sapphus*] *Epistola Saphos Doctissime Mvlieris Incipit.* Nvnquid vbi aspecta est stvdiosae littera dextrae/ Protinus est oculis cognita nostra tuis/ . . . O saltem misere crudelis epistola dicat/ Vt tibi leucadie fata petantur aquae. τέλος.. *Saphos Doctissime Poetae* [*corr.*[1]*: Poetae Doctissime*] *Mulieris Epistola Explicit Foeliciter. Finis.*

Henricus Dörrie, ed., *P. Ovidii Nasonis Epistulae Heroidum.* Texte und Kommentare: Eine Altertumswissenschaftliche Reihe 6, eds. O. Gigon, F. Heinimann, and O. Luschnat (Berlin and N.Y. 1971) 312–26, listing this manuscript p. 302, no. 107, and grouping the manuscript in family "c" on the basis of two errors (see p. 293); the first error (lines 9–10 following line 12) is not present in our manuscript; the second, lines 129–30 following line 132 (cf. f. 44v), is in our manuscript (we thank William T. Loomis for bringing this to our attention).

3. ff. 47–48 *Ovidii Versus de morte Tibulli.* Memona [*corr.*[1]: memnoa *sic*] si mater, mater plorauit Achillem/ et tangunt magnas impia

facta [*sic*] deas/ . . . Ossa quieta precor tuta requiescite in urna/ Et sit humus cineri non honerosa tuo. *Finis.* [F. 48v blank, but ruled.]

Ovid, *Amores* 3.9 (8); E. J. Kenney, ed., *P. Ovidi Nasonis Amores, Medicamina Faciei Femineae, Ars Amatoria, Remedia Amoris.* OCT (Oxford 1961) 88–90.

Parchment (white and smooth), ff. ii (parchment; conjugate pair, ruled in ink; i, a pastedown) + 48 + ii (parchment; conjugate pair, ruled in ink; ii, pastedown), 185 x 115 (123–121 x 86–67) mm., ruled space: 124 x 74 mm. 25 lines of verse. Ruled in dry point on the hair side, with the top 2 and bottom 2 horizontal lines full across; full-length double vertical bounding lines used for the first majuscule of every other line of verse (except ff. 32v–37, every line). Prickings in outer and bottom margins (some trimmed).

$1–4^{10}$ 5^{8}. Vertical catchwords, lower margin, written along the inner bounding line, flourished and decoratively boxed in brown and red. Remains of leaf and quire signatures in brown ink, bottom, outside corner, recto: quire 1, arabic numerals only (cf. ff. 1, 4, 5); quire 3, arabic numerals with a vertical line (cf. ff. 22, 24).

Written by one scribe in a skilled humanistic cursive script using long 'f' and 's' extending below the line. Marginal annotations in red, ff. 1–19 and in particular ff. 1–6, including key words from the text, usually names, and nota marks (majuscule 'N', with extensions denoting 'T' and 'A' and scalloped lines alongside text). Occasional corrections in brown by the scribe (cf. ff. 11v and 12v, supplying omitted words; f. 43v, altering a reading).

The manuscript is skillfully decorated, possibly by Antonio di Niccolo di Lorenzo (1445–1527), early in his career (we thank Professor A. C. de la Mare for this information, October, 1987); in general, see Mirella Levi d'Ancona, *Miniatura e miniatori a firenze dal XIV al XVI secolo . . .* (Florence 1962) 19–22 and plate 2, and Garzelli, "Le immagini," 249–53 and plates 621–43. One 3-line gold initial, f. 1, with white vinestem decoration extending into the top and outer margins, infilled with green, blue and salmon pink, interspersed with yellow and white dots and terminating in gold rayed disks with pen flourishes; edged in blue which follows the shape of the vine; bottom margin, a green laurel wreath enclosing a coat of arms supported by two putti, set into a similar vinestem border; now partially effaced and difficult to interpret, but possibly the arms of the Capponi family of Florence (we thank Professor A. C. de la Mare for this suggestion, August, 1987): per bend argent[?], with traces of red; bottom painted over in brown (cf. Rietstap vol. 2, pl. XXII). Three 3- to 2-line gold initials at the beginnings of books 2 and 3 in article 1, and article 2 (ff. 17v, 26v, 42) on square grounds of green or pink, infilled with pink with gold highlights or blue with white highlights, respectively. Remaining poems in article 1 and article 3 begin with plain 2-line blue initials. Rubrics in red or red and brown, using a variety of scripts: opening rubrics of article 1 and 2 (ff. 1 and 42) in red square capitals, with the opening lines of text copied using red and brown alternately for each letter; "explicit" at end of books 1 and 2, article 1 (ff. 17v, 26v), also in red and brown square capitals. Opening rubrics of each poem in article 1 copied in a cursive minuscule in red, with the opening words in red and brown. Rubrics copied in red capitals, and text in capitals with alternate letters in red and brown, or in a cursive minuscule with alternate words in red and brown, respectively, in the Epitaph and Life of Tibullus, article 1 (f. 41). Last folio of each article carefully laid out to fill the available space. Opening majuscule of every other line of verse (except ff. 32v–37, every line) written between the outer bounding lines.

Bound in Italy, s. XV, in dark brown leather over wooden boards, blind-tooled with four sets of parallel lines forming a rectangular central panel, with clubbed saltires in a diagonal lattice pattern, separated by small round stamps, a middle pilaster border of foliage separated by horizontal bands with three small round stamps, and an outer border with diagonal rows of small round stamps at each corner. Original sewing on three broad, split bands. Originally fastened front to back with two clasp-and-catch fastenings (holes remain, upper and lower boards). In poor condition; both boards badly rubbed. Described, Quaritch catalogue 166, June 1897, no. 316 as Venetian, ca. 1460–65; binding was then described as rebacked; spine now bare except for traces of leather with remnants of title in gilt.

Written in Florence in the middle of the fifteenth century, most likely in the 1460s, by a scribe who also copied Manchester, John Rylands Library, MS Ital 53, S. Anthony of Florence, *Somma de septe peccati*, and London, British Library, MS Royal 6 A. XV, L. Caelius Firmianus Lactantius, *Opera* (we thank Professor A. C. de la Mare for this information; in correspondence, October, 1978). Coat of arms of the original owner, f. 1 (described above), possibly those of the Capponi family of Florence. Front flyleaf, f. i, ex libris note, s. XV–XVI, treated by reagent and now mostly illegible: "Questo libro e di Gin<o?> <Ca?>pp<oni?> e di <. . .> ligino[?] di<. . .> capi[?] digeri[?] e <. .>pp<. . .>i"; below, an early modern note, possibly a shelf mark in another hand: "C Z[?] 5," and flourished pen trials, s. XVI–XVII; back flyleaf, f. i^v, s. XV–XVI: "E tu che con epso trita[?] stugli, guarda lo dalla lucerna e da famigli"; in another hand: "E tu che come prete titr<?>." Unidentified booksellers' notes: front pastedown, in brown ink, "w/e/ric"; front flyleaf, f. i^v, in pencil, "48." Bought by the Reverend Henry Drury (1778–1841) in 1821 (his signature with date, front flyleaf, f. i); his sale, London, Evans, February 19, 1827, no. 4294 (inside front cover, in pencil: "4294") to Thorpe for Sir Thomas Phillipps (*Phillipps Cat.*, p. 39, MS 3385; front flyleaf, f. i, in black ink: "Phillipps Ms. 3385"). Phillipps sale, London, Sotheby's, June 10, 1896, no. 1247 to Quaritch (Cats. 164, 1896, no. 168, and 166, 1897, no. 316). Purchased from Quaritch, January 2, 1897 (Charles Minot Fund; library stamp, front flyleaf, f. i^v; bookplate, front pastedown). Front flyleaf, f. i, copy of a note signed by Harvard College Librarian, Justin Winsor, authorizing use of the manuscript by the Classics Department (for information about this purchase, cf. Dennis, "Collecting," 287–90). Original Harvard shelf mark: Lt 11.110; cataloguing notes in three hands, including that of M. Grand, glued to back flyleaf, f. i.

secundo folio: Quam iuuat

Bibliography: De Ricci, 981; De Ricci, "Handlist," 107; A. F. Manspeaker, "Description of Manuscript Lat. 46, Tibullus," (manuscript, [Cambridge 1928]) now Houghton bMS Lat 315(15); Wieck, p. 108 and fig. 105 (reproducing f. 1).

MS Lat 47 | Italy (Northeast?) 1432
Seneca, Tragoediae | Pl. 3

1. ff. 1–25v [heading, followed by five blank lines] *L. Annaeus Senecae Tragoediae.* [*Hercules Furens*; rubric omitted] Soror tonan[ti]s hoc enim solum mihi/ Nomen relictum est semper alienum iouem./ ... Facere innocentes terra quae superos solet.

   Otto Zwierlein, ed., *L. Annaei Senecae Tragoediae* (Oxford 1986) 1–50.

2. ff. 26–46v [added, top margin: *Thieste.*] *Tantalus. Megera./ Tantalus.* [Q]uis me furor sede abinfausta [*sic*] extrahit/ Auido fugaces ore captantem cibos./ ... Te puniendum liberis trado tuis./ *Amen.*

   Zwierlein, ed., 293–333.

3. ff. 46v–59 [*Phoenissae*; rubric omitted] *Edipus.* [C]eci parentis regimen ac fessi unicum/ Patris leuamen nata [*corr.*^{2} *add.*: quam] tanti est mihi/ ... *Atreus.* Imperia precio quolibet constant bene.

   Zwierlein, ed., 97–122.

4. ff. 59–83 [*Phaedra*; rubric omitted] *Ipolitus.* [I]te umbrosas cingite siluias [*sic*]/ Summaque montis iuga cecropii./ ... Grauis que [*sic*] tellus impio capiti incubet.

   Zwierlein, ed., 163–210.

5. ff. 83–103 [*Oedipus*; rubric omitted] *Edipus.* [I]am nocte pulsa dubius efulsit dies/ Et nube mestum squalida exoritur iubar/ ... Mecum ite mecum ducibus his uti libet.

   Zwierlein, ed., 211–52.

6. ff. 103–125 [*Troades*; rubric omitted] *Hecuba.* [Q]uicumque regno fidit et magna potens/ Dominatur aula nec leues metuit deos/ ... Iam uella pupis laxat et classis mouet.

   Zwierlein, ed., 51–95.

7. ff. 125v–144v [*Medea*; rubric omitted] *Medea.* [D]ii coniugales tuque genialis thori/ Lucina custos queque domitorem freti/ ... Testare nullos esse qua ueheris deos.

   Zwierlein, ed., 123–61.

8. ff. 144v–163v [*Agamemnon*; rubric omitted] *Thiestes.* [O]paca linquens ditis inferni loca/ Adsum profundo tartari emissus specu/ . . . *Clitemestra.* Furibunda morere. *Cassandra.* Veniet et nobis [*sic*] furor.

   Zwierlein, ed., 253–92.

9. ff. 163v–182 [Ps. Seneca, *Octavia*; rubric omitted] [I]am uaga caelo sidera fulgens/ Aurora fugat surgit titam [*sic*]/ . . . Ciuis gaudet roma cruore.

   Zwierlein, ed., 415–52.

10. ff. 182–219 [Ps. Seneca, *Hercules Oetaeus*] *Hercules.* [S]ator deorum cuius excussum manu/ Utraeque phebi sentiunt fulmen domus/ . . . Fulmina mittes./ *Finis. Anno Domini MCCCC XXXII.* [Ff. 219v–220v blank, but ruled.]

    Zwierlein, ed., 335–414.

(Arts. 1–10) Alexander P. MacGregor, "The Manuscripts of Seneca's Tragedies: A Handlist," *Aufstieg und Niedergang der römischen Welt*, H. Temporini and W. Haase, eds. Principat 32.2 (Berlin and N.Y. 1985) 1134–1241, listing 397 manuscripts; this manuscript listed: p. 1173, no. 432; p. 1206, identifying the watermarks as Briquet 2466, Verona 1442 (not confirmed by our study of the manuscript), and Zonghi 1093, Fabriano 1441 (Aurelio Zonghi, Augusto Zonghi, and A. Gasparinetti, *Zonghi's Watermarks.* Monumenta chartae papyraceae. Historiam illustrantia 3 [Hilversum 1953]); and p. 1229, grouping this manuscript with Italian $_s$-MSS ("defined as MSS with more than 25% E-variants" which were "restricted to the Veneto, centering on Padua"); MacGregor, "L'Abbazia di Pomposa, centro originario della tradizione 'E' delle tragedie di Seneca," *Libri manoscritti e a Stampa da Pomposa all'Umanesimo,* ed. Luigi Balsamo (Florence 1985) 73–87, especially pp. 76 and 86, no. 28.

On the manuscript tradition of Seneca's *Tragedies,* see also (not listing this manuscript): Otto Zwierlein, *Prolegomena zu einer kritischen Ausgabe der Tragödien Senecas.* Akademie der Wissenschaften und der Literatur; Abhandlungen der Geistes- und Sozialwissenschaftlichen Klasse, 1983, no. 3 (Wiesbanden 1984); and R. J. Tarrant, ed., Seneca, *Agamemnon* (Cambridge 1976), especially 84–86, discussing AE manuscripts.

Marginal and interlinear glosses throughout in a number of hands: *Hercules Furens*, short, infrequent glosses in a later slanted hand, s. XVI (?) (for example, f. 2v, line 81, "tellus gigante doris [siculo] . . ."); *Thyestes*, especially ff. 30v–35v, frequent explanatory interlinear glosses in a contemporary hand, and f. 34, another hand, s. XV, citing Cicero in a marginal note; *Phoenissae*, f. 48, lines 70–71, omitted by the scribe, were supplied by a contemporary; *Phaedra*, very few glosses, but f. 70, lines 574–77, omitted by the scribe, were supplied by a contemporary; *Oedipus* and *Troades*, no glosses; *Medea*, frequent interlinear glosses in a neat, contemporary gothic hand, cf. ff. 129–144v, and longer glosses in a similar hand, ff. 136, 137, 139 and 143; *Agamemnon*, interlinear and fairly frequent marginal glosses (first gloss, f. 145, "Hic dicit tiestes quod potius uallet hic poenam uisionis quam colere mundum . . ."); Ps. Seneca, *Octavia*, frequent interlinear glosses, possibly in another hand; Ps. Seneca, *Hercules Oetaeus*, marginal and interlinear glosses in two hands through f. 208.

Throughout there are at least two types of nota marks (cf. f. 5v and ff. 37 and 43v); characters within the plays are identified in pale red ink in the margin or within the line of text (cf. f. 6v); and some passages are marked "comparatio" (cf. ff. 21, 35–36v, 54v, 67, and 78v).

11. f. 221 [added in a contemporary hand; Seneca, *Hercules Furens*, verses 105–10, ending imperfectly] Concutite pectus acrior mentem exquoquat/ . . . Inasaniendum est iuno cur nundum [*sic*] furis./ Me me sorores// [Ff. 221v–222 blank, but ruled.]

Zwierlein, ed., 6–7; text differs slightly from that on f. 3, but lacks important variants.

Paper (watermarks, tête de boeuf, Briquet 14649, Udine 1425 [cf. f. 7]; balance dans un cercle, à plateaux rectangulaire, Zonghi 1093, Fabriano 1441 [cf. ff. 11 and 221]; unidentified bell [cf. ff. 10 and 193]; fleur, Briquet 6391, Utrecht 1426, and Sienna 1433–34; and unidentified wagon with two wheels [cf. f. 86]), ff. ii (paper) + 222 + ii (paper), 279 x 200 (164–158 x 88–50) mm.; ruled space: 167–164 x 108–106 mm. 27 lines of verse. Horizontal lines ruled in ink; full-length vertical bounding lines in lead or ink, double on the left, used for the first majuscule of each line of text.

1–22^{10} 23^{2} (singletons; original structure uncertain). Horizontal catchwords, inner, lower margin, decorated with an s-shaped flourish on each side in brown ink, except quires 2 and 20 (ff. 20v and 200v) decorated in red; quires 3 and 6 (ff. 30v and 60v), undecorated; quires 4, 5, 7, 8, and 9, (ff. 40v, 50v, 70v, 80v, 90v), decorated with numerous s-shaped flourishes on four sides in brown, or as in quire 21, f. 210v, in red and black. First recto of each quire numbered in pencil in a modern hand, bottom margin, gutter, with quire 4 numbered as 6, and then in correct sequence; single leaves of quire 23 (ff. 221–222) numbered as 24 and 25.

Written below the top line in well-spaced gothic bookhands influenced by humanistic script by at least four scribes, as follows: ff. 1–10v (quire 1); ff. 11–127v; ff. 128–191v; and ff. 192 to the end.

One 6-line plain red initial, f. 1; initials at the beginning of the remaining plays are omitted, 8- to 5-line blank spaces remain. Sections within the plays begin with 4- to 2-line plain red initials (some omitted). F. 1, title in poorly formed red and black capitals; remaining titles omitted. 8- to 5-line spaces left blank at the beginning of the plays for introductory arguments. Rubrics identifying sections within the plays in pale red ink (often omitted). Each line begins with a decorative majuscule, written between the outer bounding lines, stroked with red on ff. 43 and 87. Guide notes for the rubrics and letters for the initials remain (for example ff. 12v, 14, and 33v–34). Arabic numerals numbering the plays added by a later hand in the top outer margin, recto, in dark brown ink, ff. 27–49; title, art. 2, f. 26, added in the top margin.

Bound in England by Charles Lewis (1786–1836) for the Reverend Henry Drury (note in Drury's hand, front flyleaf, f. i: "H. Drury. comp: C. Lewis"), in smooth brown calf, with narrow gilt frames on the front and back covers; spine with raised bands, with title lettered in gilt: "Senecae Tragoediae, Codex Chartaceus MCCCCXXXII"; gilt edges. Front cover now detached. Small printed paper label pasted on spine with the Phillipps number, "9463."

Written in Italy in 1432 (dated colophon, f. 219), probably in Northeastern Italy (we thank Professor A. C. de la Mare, August, 1987). Latin fables added in a very informal noting hand, s. XV–XVI, f. 222v, including a fable about a dog, "de formica et columba," a fable about a man, and "De avo [*sic*] et venatoribus"; followed by miscellaneous notes in two additional Italian hands. Belonged to the Reverend Henry Drury (1778–1841), who had the manuscript bound by Charles Lewis (see above); his sale, London, Evans, February 19, 1827, no. 4060 to Butler, possibly Samuel Butler, Bishop of Lichfeld (1774–1839) as suggested by De Ricci, for £3.18.0. Belonged to Richard Heber (1773–1833); his sale, London, Evans, 1836, no. 1510 to Thorpe. Sold by Thorpe, London, 1836, no. 1153 ("1153" in pencil, inside front cover) to Sir Thomas Phillipps (*Phillipps Cat.*, p. 150, MS 9463; paper label pasted on spine with "9463"; front flyleaf, f. i, in black ink: "Phillips MS 9463"). Phillipps Sale, London, Sotheby's, 1896, no. 1064 to Quaritch; Quaritch Cat. 164, London 1896, no. 158. Unidentified booksellers' or owners' notes: front flyleaf, f. i^{v}, in pencil: "£5.5.0"; front flyleaf, f. i^{v}, in pencil: "9463 Ms Ph," and "*a 32.530*"; back flyleaf, f. i, in pencil, in two hands: "20" and "^{c}v"; back flyleaf, f. ii, "N/K R/-." Purchased from Quaritch, January 2, 1897 (Charles Minot Fund; library stamp, front flyleaf, f. i^{v}; bookplate, inside back cover). Front flyleaf, f. i, copy of a note signed by Harvard College Librarian, Justin Winsor, authorizing use of the manuscript by the Classics Department (for information about this purchase, cf. Dennis, "Collecting," 287–90); Harvard cataloguing notes, front flyleaf, f. ii^{v}. Original Harvard shelf mark: Ls 19.100.

secundo folio: Leone et idra

Bibliography: De Ricci, 982; Roy Merle Peterson, "A Description of a manuscript of Seneca in the Harvard College Library," unpublished manuscript (Cambridge 1912) now Houghton, bMS Lat 315(20); De Ricci, "Handlist," 107.

MS Lat 48 — Central Italy s. XIV$^{2/4}$

Valerius Maximus, Factorum et dictorum memorabilium libri — Pl. 41

ff. 1–124v [f. 1 chapter list, book one] De Religione, 1; De neglecta religione, 2; . . . De miraculis, 6. [f. 1 prologue] *Incipit liber primus valerii maximi factorum et dictorum memorabilium ad tyberium imperatorem prologus.* Urbis Rome exterarumque [*corr.*^{2}: externarumque] gentium facta simul ac dicta memoratu digna . . . [f. 1 text] *De religione. capitulum primum.* Maiores statas solempnesque cerimonias pontificum scientia ... dementere [*sic*] imperio iminens iusto impendi supplicio coegit. *Explicit liber nonus maximi valerii factorum et dictorum memorabilium romanorum et quorumdam aliorum externorum et per consequens explicit totus liber.* [f. 123v chapter list, with references to column numbers in arabic numerals] *Capitula totius libri. Incipiunt capitula libri primi.* De Religione, capitulum primum, 2; De Neglecta religione, secundum, 8; ... [Book 9] ... De hiis qui infimo loco nati mendacio se clarissimis familiis inserere conati sunt, XVI^m^, 489. *Expliciunt capitula omnia totius valerii maximi.*

Carolus Kempf, ed. *Valerii maximi factorum et dictorum memorabilium libri novem*, 2nd ed. (Leipzig 1888) 1–472; Dorothy M. Schullian, "A Revised List of Manuscripts of Valerius Maximus," in *Miscellanea Augusto Campana*, 2. Medioevo e Umanesimo 45 (Padua 1981) 695–728, citing this manuscript, 700.

The manuscript includes a sophisticated apparatus to aid the reader in finding his place in the text. Running titles in red, with the columns numbered consecutively throughout the manuscript in early arabics, beginning on ff. 1 (columns 1 and 2) and continuing through f. 123v (columns 491 and 492). The letters 'a'-'f' are written between the columns of each opening, dividing each column into three sections of approximately equal size. Each book is prefaced by a numbered chapter list. Cumulative chapter list follows the text, ff. 123v–124v, listing chapter titles, numbered in black roman numerals, and column numbers in red arabics.

Manuscript is distinguished by copious marginal annotations in a number of hands: throughout, the scribe or contemporary has corrected the text and added variant readings in a formal hand; formal marginal comments probably copied by the scribe (note change of hand, f. 49), including cross references and explanations of the text, with frequent citations of other authors (for example, f. 24v, Augustine; ff. 82 and 84v, Cicero, and ff. 83v–84, Livy); nota marks of various types, some of which seem to be by the scribe, and pointing hands; throughout, notes in a number of later hands, including f. 70, citing Bocaccio, ff. 3v and 4, brief comments in a very minute script, and ff. 1, 1v, and 5, in a small noting script.

2. f. 124v Nota quod urbs secundum quosdam dicitur recta et gubernata per septem maneries regiminum. Primo quidem per reges et

hii fuerunt vii et fuerunt anni ccxliii . . . Secundo fuerunt consules . . .

Short paragraph discussing the seven kinds of rulers in Ancient Rome.

Parchment (moderate quality; prepared in the manner of southern Europe), ff. ii (paper; f. ii, possibly from an earlier binding) + 124 + ii (paper; f. i, possibly from an earlier binding), 214 x 155 (144–142 x 105–104) mm. 2 columns, 33 lines. Ruled in lead; single full-length vertical bounding lines. Prickings, top, and on some folios, bottom margins.

$1–10^{12}$ 11^{8} (–5,6,7,8, probably cancelled with no loss of text). Horizontal catchwords, center, lower margin: quire 1, f. 11v, boxed in brown ink; quires 2–6, ff. 24v, 36v, 48v, 60v, and 72v, boxed in brown ink and decorated with red angle brackets; quires 7–10, ff. 84v, 96v, 108v, and 120v, boxed in brown ink with short extensions ending in dots at each corner and decorated in red. The first folio of quires 3–7 (cf. ff. 25, 37, 49, 61, and 73) are signed in the bottom, outer corner, with a letter, 'c'-'g', in ink, probably in a later hand (s. XV–XVI?).

Written above the top line by at least two scribes; the first scribe copied ff. 1–48v in a quick, rounded gothic bookhand; the second scribe copied ff. 49–end in a distinctive gothic bookhand using broken minims.

Major divisions marked by 4- to 3-line plain red initials set within the text space; similar 2-line secondary initials. Smaller divisions marked with red paragraph marks; red rubrics and running titles. Majuscules within the text stroked with red. Guide notes for the rubricator written in an informal noting script, together with the numbers for the running titles; ff. 73–end, in the bottom margin; earlier in the manuscript, in the top margin (often erased; visible ff. 4v–39). Guide letters for the initials and chapter numbers visible in the inside margin or between the columns.

Ink faded and/or flaked with some loss of legibility especially on ff. 86–87v, 96v–97, 100v–101, 106v–108, 116v–117, 123 and 124v.

Bound in England in the nineteenth century (dated by De Ricci, ca. 1825) in smooth orange-brown calf; flat spine with title in gold; traces of small rectangular paper label visible at the bottom of the spine and a larger label at the top. In very poor condition with the spine and both covers detached.

Written in Central Italy in the second quarter of the fourteenth century (we thank Professor Giuseppe Billanovich for his assistance; visit to the library, October 1986; correspondence, November 10, 1986). Layout and marginal notes indicate that it was used for study. It was once suggested that this manuscript belonged to Petrarch (1304–74) and included notes in Petrarch's hand; see Raymond Klibansky, "Report on the Progress of the Corpus Platonicum Medii Aevi," University of London, *The Warburg Institute Annual Report* (1946–47) 12; *Renaissance News* 1 (1948) 42; and A. N. L. Munby, *The Dispersal of the Phillipps Library*. Phillipps Studies 5 (Cambridge 1960) 62. Professor Klibansky informs us that he no longer believes that the notes are in Petrarch's hand, although he still maintains that the manuscript may have some connection with Petrarch and he plans to publish a study of the manuscript (in correspondence, November 14, 1986 and October 29, 1987). Other scholars have concluded that the manuscript has no connection with Petrarch; see Giuseppe Billanovich, "Il Petrarca e i classici," *Studi petrarcheschi* 7 (1961) 27, n. 18 (= *Atti del Congresso dell'Associazione Internazionale per gli studi di lingua e letteratura italiana* [31 March–5 April 1959]); B. L. Ullman, *Petrarch Manuscripts in the United States* (Padua 1964) 25, n. 1 (=*Italia medioevale e umanistica* 5 [1962] 467, n. 1); and Dennis Dutschke, *Census of Petrarch Manuscripts in the United States* (Padua 1986), tacitly rejecting the connection with Petrarch and therefore not including this manuscript.

Belonged to the Jesuit College at Agen, France (maintained by the Jesuits from 1591–1762); f. 1, top margin, in ink, s. XVII: "Collegii Agen[nensis] Societ[atis] Jesu Catal[ogo] Inscr[iptus]"; Houghton, MSS Lat 179 and possibly Lat 150 were also owned by the Agen Jesuits. Number of columns and folios recorded on the back flyleaf, f. i, in ink, s. XVIII[?]. Owned in 1778 by Marie-François Duchesne de Beaumanoir (ex libris note in ink, f. 1: "Ex Bibliotheca Marie francisci Duchesne in S. Aquitaniae Senat[us] Consuli patroni. 1778"), who also owned a copy of André Theuet, *Cosmographie de levant* (Lyon 1554), Houghton Library, Typ 515.54.831, also with his ex libris. No. 749 in an unidentified English sale according to a note in ink, f. 1; remains of circular paper label, front flyleaf, with number in ink, mostly erased: "<. .>9," probably no. 749. Unidentified price code, inside front cover, in pencil: "w/tr"; and note in pen, s. XIX[?], front flyleaf, f. i: "Light Cf." Sold ca. 1825 by Thorpe to Sir Thomas Phillipps (*Phillipps Cat.*, p. 32, MS 2714); in pencil, front flyleaf, f. ii: "Thorpe MS"; Phillipps' stamp with crest and manuscript number, in ink, front flyleaf f. ii, and later note in ink, f. 1, "MSS Phillipps 2174." Phillipps Sale, London, Sotheby's, April 27, 1903, no. 1149 to Dobell for £2 15s (cf. Munby, Phillipps Studies 5:62). Purchased August 28, 1909, Henry Lillie Pierce Fund (round library stamp, f. 1; bookplate, inside front cover; Harvard library catalogue slip glued to front flyleaf, f. i). Original Harvard shelf mark: *Lv 7.7.

secundo folio: diis recte dicari

Bibliography: De Ricci, 982; De Ricci, "Handlist," 108; Henry Phillips, "A Description of a Harvard MS. of Valerius Maximus," (typescript, May, 1931), now Houghton, bMS Lat 315(21).

MS Lat 49 — Northeastern Italy s. XV$^{2/4\text{–med}}$
Ps. Plutarch, De liberis educandis — Pl. 49

ff. 1–25v [dedicatory epistle] *Magni Oratoris Guarini ueronensis in plutarchum de liberis educandis proemium incipit feliciter ad Angelum corbinellum Florentinum.* Maiores nostros angele mi suauissime non admirari et maximis prosequi laudibus non possum . . . Sed de his alias plutarchum ipsum audiamus. *Explicit proemium.* [f. 2v text] *Incipit plutarchus de liberis educandis.* Quod de ingenuorum educatione liberorum dicere quispiam posset . . . At humano effici posse constat ingenio. *Explicit plutarchus de liberis educandis feliciter.* [F. 26 blank.]

Translation by Guarinus Veronensis (1374–1460). Printed, s. XV (Hain 13146–13148), and in *Plutarchi Chaeronei Philosophi, historicique clarissimi opuscula moralia* (Lyon 1542) 241–67 (without the dedicatory epistle). Dedicatory epistle edited in R. Sabbadini, *Epistolario di Guarino Veronese.* Miscellanea di Storia Veneta ser. 3, v. 8 (Venice 1915) 1:15–16, no. 5.

Marginal notes on contents (ff. 3v, 4, 14) and scalloped lines alongside text (ff. 10v–11) in brown ink in a contemporary hand, likely that of the scribe(s). Marginal annotations, ff. 3–4v, including short notes in another contemporary hand, and names of authors cited in a later Italian hand (ff. 3v, 4v); paragraph marks added in brown ink. Occasional pointing hands added by a later reader (ff. 3, 5, 7, 7v).

Parchment (quire 1, ff. 1–8v) and paper (ff. 9–26; watermark, obscured in gutter but similar to Briquet Cerf 3296, Ferrara 1406; with similar marks, Siena 1400, Reggio Emilia 1407, Ferrara 1407–20, Bologna 1409–30, Pistoia 1411–17, Lucca 1415, and Rome 1418), ff. ii (paper) + 26 (modern foliation 1–25 + 1 blank leaf) + ii (paper), 178 x 120 (107–100 x 62–60) mm.; ruled space, quire 1: 105 x 71–59 mm. 23–25 long lines (except ff. 1–2v and 7rv, 22–21 lines). Quire 1, ff. 1–8v, ruled very faintly in dry point on the hair side; double full-length vertical bounding lines; ff. 9 to end, frame ruled in dry point on the verso, with the top and bottom horizontal rules extending beyond the written space; full-length single vertical bounding lines. Some prickings in outer margin, quire 1 only, and in the top and bottom margins, throughout.

$1\text{–}2^{8}$ 3^{10} (10 blank, unnumbered). Horizontal catchwords, center lower margin; in quire 2 (f. 16v), flourished on four sides. Leaves in quire 1 signed with arabic numerals in ink, bottom, outer corner recto (leaf 5 marked 'X').

Written above the top line by two scribes, or possibly by one scribe in two different scripts: ff. 1–8v (parchment quire), in a humanistic script with ff. 4–8v evidently copied more quickly, with an increasing number of ligatures; ff. 9–end, in a cursive bookhand, varying from a quickly written script to a neat, controlled script (cf. ff. 9 and 25v); incipits and explicit, ff. 1, 2v, 25v, copied by one scribe in a neat humanistic script; this hand is very similar to that of the opening folios, and possibly suggests one scribe copied the entire manuscript. F. 1, top margin: "Ihesus" in a contemporary hand, most likely the scribe.

Four-line violet initial, f. 1, on a gold ground, infilled with deep blue and green with white highlights, now smudged with red, edged in black, with simple green, pink, and blue flowers with centers of gold or white and green leaves in the outer margin (badly rubbed). 4-line red initial, f. 2v, with quick pen flourishes in blue. Rubrics, ff. 1, 2v, 25v, in brown; red paragraph mark, f. 1.

Bound in blue half morocco after its acquisition by Harvard in 1908; title in gilt on spine.

Written in northeastern Italy in the second quarter to middle of the fifteenth century (we thank Professor A. C. de la Mare for her assistance, August, 1987). F. 1, top margin: "Ant[oni]o <G?>u<e?>rr^{o} [possibly Giurr^{o}, Gucirr^{o}, Cuerr^{o}, or Ciurr^{o}]," s. XVI. Unidentified booksellers' notes in pencil, f. 1: "A5367"; f. 1v: "1741/5." Belonged to Richard Ashhurst Bowie of Philadelphia; his library given to Harvard by Mary Bryant Brandegee, widow of E. D. Brandegee (A. B. Harvard, 1881) in memory of her grandfather, W. F. Weld, November 9, 1908 (bookplate front pastedown; library stamp, f. 1; not included in "Catalogue of the Library of Richard Ashhurst Bowie Presented by E. D. Brandegee" [typescript n.d.], now in the Houghton Library). Original Harvard shelf mark: Gp 86.350.

secundo folio: [ludi]bria sunt

Bibliography: De Ricci, 982; Allen R. Hyde, "Guarino's Translation of the *De Liberis Educandis* falsely ascribed to Plutarch; A Description of MS Lat 49 in the Harvard Library," (typescript, 1938) now Houghton bMS Lat 315(8); Kristeller, *Iter* 5:226.

MS Lat 50 — **Southern Germany s. $XV^{3/4}$**

Bible, part — **Pl. 37**

Partial Bible, now arranged as follows: [part 1] 1 Maccabees, 2 Maccabees, Acts, Catholic Epistles, Apocalypse, *prologue to Romans, *capitula* lists to the following books: Pauline Epistles in the usual order, Acts, Catholic Epistles, and the Apocalypse, biblical text resumes with Pauline Epistles, with Colossians following, rather than preceding 1 and 2 Thessalonians, and with Laodiceans following Colossians (Romans, 1 Corinthians, 2 Corinthians, Galatians, Ephesians, Philippians, *1 Thessalonians, *2 Thessalonians, *Colossians, *Laodiceans, 1 Timothy, 2 Timothy, Titus, Philemon, Hebrews); [part 2] Ecclesiastes, beginning imperfectly, Job, Tobit, Judith, Esther, Ezra 1–3 and 5, and prologues to Maccabees.

Section 1 concludes, f. 169v, with a blank folio which is darkened and stained, perhaps from a chain or binding. It is most likely that the manuscript is now misbound, and part 2 (now incomplete) once preceded part 1. Notes in the rubrics imply that this Bible was copied from an exemplar with the Old Testament books in a more usual order, i.e., Chronicles, Ezra, Nehemiah, Tobit, Judith, Esther, Job, Maccabees (cf. ff. 217 and 237v). Jerome's Epistle 22 to Eustochium, a text not usually found in Bibles, is here copied at the end of part one, following Hebrews.

Prologues as follows: [part one] Stegmüller 640 (Acts), Stegmüller 809 and 807 (Catholic Epistles), Stegmüller 806 (James), Stegmüller 812 (1 Peter), Stegmüller 818 (2 Peter), Stegmüller 822 (1 John), Stegmüller 823 (2 John), Stegmüller 824 (3 John), Stegmüller 825 (Jude), Stegmüller 835 and 839 (Apocalypse), Stegmüller 651, 670 and 674 (Romans), [series of *capitula* lists], Stegmüller 677 (Romans), Stegmüller 690 and 685 (1 Corinthians), Stegmüller 699 and 697 (2 Corinthians), Stegmüller 707 (Galatians), Stegmüller 715 (Ephesians), Stegmüller 728 (Philippians), Stegmüller 747 and 749 (1 Thessalonians), Stegmüller 752 and 753 (part only) (2 Thessalonians), Stegmüller 736 (Colossians), Stegmüller 765 and 760 (1 Timothy), Stegmüller 772 and 770 (2 Timothy), Stegmüller 780 (Titus), Stegmüller 783 (Philemon), Stegmüller 793 (Hebrews), Stegmüller 674 (Romans); [part 2] Stegmüller 344, 357 and 349 (Job), Stegmüller 332 (Tobit), Stegmüller 335 (Judith), Stegmüller 330 (Ezra), Stegmüller 551 and 552 (Maccabees). Extensive notes throughout comment on the choice of prologues and the phrasing of the rubrics.

1. ff. 1–169: f. 1 1 Maccabees [Ends mid f. 24; f. 24v blank, but ruled.]; f. 25 2 Maccabees; f. 43v *Incipit prologus hieronimi super actus apostolorum.* Lucas antiocensis naratione [*corr.*[2]: natione] syrus cuius laus in ewangelio canitur . . . [Stegmüller 640; followed by rubric, f. 43v, *Sequitur alter prologus scilicet dauid psalmista etc. non reperimur* (referring to Stegmüller 633?)]; f. 44 Acts; f. 72v *Sequitur prologus hieronimi super vii epistolas canonicas etc.* Non ita ordo est apud grecos . . . [Stegmüller 809]; f. 73 *Alius prologus in canonicas.* Jacobus petrus iohannes iudas septem epistolam [*corr.*[2]: epistolas] ediderunt . . . [Stegmüller 807, copied in a smaller script and underlined in red]; f. 73 *Prologus in epistolam iacobi.* Iacobus apostolus sanctum instruit [*sic*] . . . [Stegmüller 806]; f. 73 James; f. 76 *Incipit argumentum epistole prime petri apostoli sedis.* Discipulus saluatoris in uictus toto orbe diffusus et peregrinus in hoc seculo

monstrat . . . [Stegmüller 812, here ending imperfectly: ". . . cum sollicitudine exhortatur//"; completed by the scribe or contemporary in a smaller script immediately after the rubric: "//symon petrus iohannis filius provincie galilee vice bethsaida frater andree."; this line repeated below as rubric to 1 Peter]; f. 76 *Incipit cononica* [*sic*] *prima petri. Incipit epistola prima petri. Symon petrus filius iohannis provincie galilee inuico bethsaida frater andree apostoli.* 1 Peter; f. 78v *Incipit argumentum ii epistole* [*corr.*[2]*: Incipit prologus petri in secunda*]. Per fidem huic mundo sapientes mortuos essem declarat . . . [Stegmüller 818]; f. 78v 2 Peter; f. 80 *Incipit argumentum epistole iohannis apostoli.* [*corr.*[2]*: prologus in canonica iohannis*]. Racionem uerbi quod deus ipse sit caritas manifestat . . . [Stegmüller 822]; f. 80v 1 John; f. 83 *Explicit argumentum in epistola secundam* [*corr.*[2]*: Sequitur prologus in secundam*]. Usque adeo ad sanctam feminam scribit . . . [Stegmüller 823]; f. 83 2 John; f. 83 *Argumentum in epistola iohannes* [*sic*] *apostoli.* [*corr.*[2]*: Sequitur prologus in terciam*]. Gaium pietatis causa extollit . . . [Stegmüller 824]; f. 83 3 John; f. 83v *Incipit argumentum epistole iude apostoli.* [*corr.*[2]*: Incipit prologus in epistolam iude apostoli*]. Iudas apostolus fratres iacobi de corruptoribus vie veritatis informat [*sic*] . . . [Stegmüller 825]; f. 83v Jude; f. 84v [underlined in red] *Prologus in apocalipsi, apocalipsi* [*sic*] *tot habet sacramenta etc.* [*Stegmüller 829*] *primus prologus, Gilberti in apocalipsi, omnes qui pie uolunt uiuere etc.* [*Stegmüller 839*] *secundus, Johannes apostolus et ewangelica* [*corr.*[2]*: ewangelista*] *etc.* [*Stegmüller 835*] *ut infra.* [*continues in red:*] *Explicit prologus primus hieronimi super apocalipsm.* f. 84v *Incipit secundus.* Iohannes apostolus et ewangelista a domino christo electus atque dilectus in tanto amore dilectionis ab eo est . . . [Stegmüller 835]; f. 84 bis [half-sheet copied in a different hand] *Incipit prologus primus in apokalipsim.* Omnes qui pie volunt vivere . . . [Stegmüller 839]; f. 84 bis[v] *Incipit secundus.* Iohannes apostolus et ewangelista. etc. [cue only; Stegmüller 835]; f. 84v Apocalypse; f. 97 *Incipit prefacio sancti hieronimi presbiteri de corpore beati pauli apostoli.* Epistole pauli ad romanos causa hec est . . . [Stegmüller 651; version 'DIRW' as printed in de Bruyne, *Préfaces*, 217–18]; f. 97v *Item aliud eiusdem.* Primum queritur quare post ewangelia que supplementum legis sunt . . . Quod si inconueniens absurdumque est ipsius magis esse credenda est que tanto doctrine// [Stegmüller 670; printed Wordsworth 2:1–5, here ending imperfectly at p. 3, line 1]; f. 98 [prologue, rubric lacking] //ipse se venisse testatus est dicens non veni nisi ad oues que perierunt [*sic*] ... eos humilians ad pacem et concordiam cohortatur. [Stegmüller 674; printed Wordsworth 2:35–38, here beginning imperfectly, p. 36, line 7]; f. 98 *Incipit capitula in epistola ad romanos.* i. De natiuitate domini secundum carnen [*sic*] ... li. De mysterio dei ante passionem in silencio habito post passionem vero ipsius reuelatio. [series AKMOVZ, Wordsworth 2:44–60]; f. 99 *Incipit argumentum in epistola ad romanos.* Romani sunt in partibus italie. Hi preventi sunt ... scribens eis a corintho. [Stegmüller 677]; f. 99v *Incipiunt capitula in epistola ad corinthios.* i. Obsecro itaque uos fratres ... xxv. Obsecro autem vos fratres. [series BV, Wordsworth 2:157–73]; f. 99v *Incipiunt capitula in epistola secunda ad corintheos* [*sic*]. i. Benedictus deus et pater domini nostri ihesu christi ... xx. Predixi et predico vt presens. [series V, Wordsworth 2:283–91]; f. 100 *Incipiunt capitula in epistola ad galatas.* i. Miror quod sic tam cito transferimini ... xii. Videre [*sic*] qualibus litteris scripsi uobis. [series BV, Wordsworth 2:359–65]; f. 100 *Incipiunt capitulam* [*sic*] *in epistola ad epheseos.* i. De sanctis quod ante constitucionem mundi in domino electi sunt ... xxxii. De fidelitate et ministerio tichici [*sic*]. [series ABFKMOSVZ, Wordsworth 2:408–14]; f. 100v *Incipiunt capitula in epistola ad philippenses.* i. Gracias ago deo meo ... viii. Gauisus sum autem in domino. [series BV, Wordsworth 2:459–61]; f. 100v *Incipiunt capitula in epistola ad colosenses.* i. Gracias agimus deo ... x. Mulieres subdite estote viris. [series BV, Wordsworth 2:492–94]; f. 101 *Incipiunt capitula in epistola ad thelonicenses* [*sic*]. i. Gracias agimus deo ... x. Ipse autem deus pacis. [series V, Wordsworth 2:526–30]; f. 101 *Incipiunt capitula in epistola ii ad thesalonicenses.* i. Gracias agere debemus deo semper pro uobis ... vi. Vobis autem fratres nolite deficere. [series V, Wordsworth 2:556]; f. 101 *Incipiunt capitula in epistola ad timotheum.* i. Sicut rogaui te ut remaneres ... x [*sic* for xii]. Diuitibus huius seculi. [series V, Wordsworth 2:576–80]; f. 101 *Incipiunt capitula in epistola ii ad timotheum.* i. Gratias ago deo meo. ii. Scis hoc quia auersi sunt a me ... vii. Festina ad me venire cito. [series V, Wordsworth 2:618–20]; f. 101 *Incipiunt capitula in epistola ad titum.* i. Huius rei gracia ... vi. Fidelis sermo est. [series V, Wordsworth 2:648–50]; f. 101 *Incipiunt capitula in epistola ad philemonem.* i. Gracias ago deo meo semper ... iii. Ego paulus scripsi mea manu. [series S. Petri A.I, Wordsworth 2:671]; f. 101 *Incipiunt capitula in epistola ad hebreos.* i. Multifarie multisque modis . . . xiiii. [*sic* for xxiv]. Deus autem pacis qui eduxit de mortuis pastorem. [series V, Wordsworth 2:682–88]; f. 101v *Incipiunt capitula in libro actuum apostolorum.* i.Vbi precepit ihesus discipulis ab hierusalem ne discederent . . . lxviiii. Vbi post menses tres in nauim [*sic*] alexandrinam que [*corr.*[1] *add.*: in] insula hiemauerat nauigauerunt. [series BFΘKRSU, Wordsworth 3:6–32]; f. 102v *Incipiunt capi-tula in epistola sancti Iacobi etc.* i. De inimicorum insecucionibus risui deputandis . . . xx. De virtutibus sanctorum et conuersoribus [*sic*] eorum qui fuerint peccatis astricti. [series ABFIKU, Wordsworth 3:234–36]; f. 103 *Incipiunt capitula in epistola sancti petri.* i. De generacionibus [*sic*] in uicta potencia . . . xx. De deo qui optimum opus iniciantes ad consummationem perducit. [series ABFIKU, Wordsworth 3:268–70]; f. 103v *Incipiunt capitula in epistola ii sancti petri.* i. De sanctis quos in hoc mundo ut interfectos alloquitur . . . xi. De epistolis apostoli pauli. [series BFΘIK, Wordsworth 3:311–12]; f. 103v *Incipiunt capitula in epistola sancti iohannis prima.* i. De verbo vite quod erat antequam mundi machina principium sortiretur . . . xx. De mundo qui est in maligno positus et simulacorum [*corr*[1]: simularorum] fugienda cultura. [series BFΘIKU, Wordsworth 3:335–37]; f. 104 *Incipiunt capitula in epistola sancti iohannis ii.* i. De diligendis cultoribus veritatis . . . v. De sua presencia [*sic*] narrandi [*sic*] omnia seruauit. [series BFΘIKU, Wordsworth 3:381]; f. 104 *Incipiunt capitula in epistola sancti iohannis iii.* i. De filiis apostoli rigorem tenentibus veritatis . . . iiii. [*sic* for v]. De multiplici sacramento. [series BFΘIKU, Wordsworth 3:388]; f. 104 *Incipiunt capitula in epistola sancti iude.* i. De falsis doctoribus negatoribus scilicet christi inpudicis . . . vii. De inenarrabili gloria saluatoris et epistole fine. [series CT, Wordsworth 3:395–96]; f. 104 *Incipiunt capitula in apocalipsi iohannis apostoli.* i. De ecclesiis septem et saluatoris aduentu . . . xlvi. De perfectione bonorum atque malorum. [series I, Wordsworth 3:410–18]; f. 104v [added by the scribe in bottom margin following the chapter list] Quere ante 4' folio. Post quatuor ewangelia sequitur prologus in epistolam ad romanos scilicet, epistole pauli ad romanos causa hec est ecclesiam duobus etc. [Stegmüller 651; cf. f. 97]. Secundus prologus, primum queritur quare post ewangelia etc. [Stegmüller 670; cf. f. 97v] quere 3° prologus [*corr.*[1]: folio] pro alteracione sunt bis rationis etc. Deinde sequitur argumentum in epistolam ad romanos scilicet, romani sunt qui ex iudeis gentibusque etc. [Stegmüller 674; cf. f. 98]. Queritur 3° folio ante finem libri cum <habet?> signo •I•. Deinde sequitur aliud argumentum scilicet, Romani qui in urbe roma in christum ihesum crediderant ita a falsis apostolis deprauati erant . . . et ewangelicam fidem scribens ab athenis [Stegmüller 675; another hand indicates that this prologue should be omitted]. Sequitur primum capitulum.; f. 105 [prologue; rubric omitted] Romani sunt in partibus italie. Hy preuenti sunt a falsis apostolis . . . [Stegmüller 677]; ff. 105–124 Romans; f. 123 bis [half-sheet with added prologue] *Incipit prologus primus in epistolam primam ad corinthios.* Epistola prima ad corinthyos multas causas diuersas que [*sic*] complectitur . . . [Stegmüller 690]; f. 124 *Incipit argumentum* [*corr.*^{2}*: secundus prologus*] *epistole prime ad corinthios.* Corinthy sunt achaici. Et hy similiter ab apostolo . . . per timotheum discipulum suum. [Stegmüller 685]; f. 124v [top margin, copied in a smaller script; underlined in red] Prologus in epistolam primam ad corinthios, Epistola prima ad corinthios multas causas etc. [Stegmüller 690]. Deinde sequitur argumentum scilicet, corinthy sunt achay [*sic*] et hii similiter etc. [Stegmüller 685] vt infra.; ff. 124v–133 1 Corinthians; f. 133 *Sequitur prologus in secundam epistolam scilicet in secunda ad corinthios epistola etc. Deinde sequitur argumentum scilicet post actam penitenciam etc. ut infra.* [cf. additional note, bottom margin: *Incipiunt prologi in epistolam secundam. Primus prologus. Post actam.*] Post actam penitenciam consolatoriam . . . emendatos ostendens. [Stegmüller 699]; f. 133 *Sequitur* [*expunged: epistolam ad corinthios*] *secundus prologus.* In secunda. *Vide in cedula.*; f. 132 bis^{rv} [half-sheet with added prologue] *Secundus prologus.* In secunda ad corintheos [*sic*] epistole quasi in parte superiori post tribulacionum suarum relaciones reddit . . . [Stegmüller 697]; f. 133v 2 Corinthians; f. 139 [bottom margin] *Prologus in epistolam ad galatas.* [*expunged: scilicet galatas post suscepcionem etc. (Stegmüller 709)*] *Deinde sequitur argumentum, ut infra.*; f. 139 *Incipit argumentum* [*added above, corr.*^{2}*: uel prologus*] *ad Galatas.* Galathe sunt greci. Hy uerbum viritatis [*sic*] ab epistolo [*sic*] primum . . . scribens eis ab epheso. [Stegmüller 707]; f. 139 Galatians; f. 142 [bottom margin; with red line drawn through text] *Sequitur prologus scilicet ephesy sunt asiani etc.*; f. 142 *Incipit* [*added above, corr.*^{2}*: prologus in epistolam*] *argumentum ad ephesys* [*corr.*[2]*: ephesyos*]. Ephesy sunt asiani. Hy accepto verbo veritatis . . . per tichicum [*corr.*[2]: tithytum] dyaconem [expunged: diaconem]. [Stegmüller 715]; f. 142 Ephesians; f. 145 *Incipit* [*added above, corr.*[2]*: prologus in epistolam*] *argumentum* [*expunged: eodem*] *ad philippenses.* Philippenses sunt macedones. Hy accepto verbo veritatis . . . de carcere per epafroditum. [Stegmüller 728]; f. 145 [bottom margin, boxed in red] Prologus in epistolam ad philippenses, Philippis [*sic*] macedonie ciuitatis est etc. [Stegmüller 733]. Deinde sequitur argumentum illud sequuntur.; f. 145v Philippians; f. 147v *Sequitur prologus in epistolam ad colosenses scilicet* [*expunged: prima apocolypsos etc.; added above the line, brown ink: Colosenses et hy sicut et habetur post tertia folia*]. *Deinde sequitur* [*expunged: argumentum scilicet; added above the line, brown ink: capitula ad*] *colosenses et habet* [*corr.*[2]*: habetur*] *etc. post quartus* [*corr.*[2]*: tertia*] *folio* [most likely referring to Stegmüller 741, "Prima apud colossenses epaphrae . . ." and Stegmüller 736, "Colossenses et hi sicut laodicenses . . ."]; f. 147v *Incipit argumentum ad thessalonicenses* [*corr.*[2]*: Incipit prologus in epistolam ad thessalonicenses*]. Thessalonicenses sunt macedones qui accepto verbo veritatis perstiterunt . . . ab athenis per timotheum dyaconum [*corr.*[2] *add.*: per ticicum et onesimum; in another hand, added after "ab athenis": "et honesimum accolitum. Non solum illi in omnibus perfecti erant, sed alii eorum verbo perfecuntur [*sic*] et exemplo. Laudando ergo illos apostolus ad maiora prouocat et invitat."; Stegmüller 747 (original scribe) + Stegmüller 749 (added; in form printed in de Bruyne, *Préfaces*, 246, no. 8)]; f. 148 1 Thessalonians; f. 150 [top margin] Prologus secunda in epistolam ad thessalonicense scilicet seruatur in secunda epistola, etc. [Stegmüller 759]. Deinde sequitur quod hic ponitur.; f. 150 *Incipit* [*added above the line: prologus*] *argumentum* [*added above the line: in secundam epistolam*] *ad thesalonicenses.* Ad thessalonicenses secundam scribit epistolam . . . et onesimum acolitum [Stegmüller 752, with passage from Stegmüller 753 added in another hand after "de aduersarii deiectione": "laudans eos gratias agendo [*sic*] pro eis quod pacientur sustinuerunt . . . ut perseuerent."]; f. 150 2 Thessalonians [ends with rubric, f. 151 *Sequitur argumentum tymotheum etc., quere post tria*[*?*] *folia.*]; f. 151 *Incipit prologus in epistolam ad colocenses.* Colosenses et hy sunt [*corr.*[1]: sicut] laodicenses sunt asiani . . . et onesimum acolitum. [Stegmüller 736]; f. 151 Colossians; f. 153 *Sequitur prologus* *in primam epistolam ad thesalonicenses scilicet gaude* [*sic*] *fidei etc.* [*Stegmüller 743*]. *Deinde sequitur argumentum thessalonicenses sunt. Quere ante sex folio.* f. 153 Laodiceans [Stegmüller 233]; f. 153v *Incipit argumentum* [*corr.*^{2} *in red: prologus in epistolam primam ad*] *ad* [*sic*] *timotheum.* Timotheum instruit et docet . . . scribens ei a [*sic*] laodicia. [Stegmüller 765]; f. 153v [added, bottom margin] Hic episcopus fuit discipulus pauli huic per litteras . . . esse vitandos. *Sequitur capitulum primum.* [Stegmüller 760]; f. 153v 1 Timothy; f. 156 *Sequitur prologus in secundam epistolam scilicet, inter initia episcopatus, etc.* [*Stegmüller 771*]. *Deinde sequitur falsa scientia est, etc. Deinde argumentum ad timotheum* [*expunged: primam*]. *Incipit prologus in secundam.* Item timotheo scribit de exhortacione . . . ab urbe romana [*sic*]. [Stegmüller 772]; f. 156 [added in another hand, bottom margin] Cum esset rome in vinculis constitutus scribit thimotheo . . . predicant magis quam veritatem. *Sequitur capitulum primum.* [Stegmüller 770]; f. 156v 2 Timothy; f. 158 [added: *Incipit*] *prologus hieronimi in epistolam ad titum scilicet numero etc.* [*possibly Stegmüller 775*]. *Deinde argumentum. Incipit argumentum epistole ad titum.* Titum commonefacit et instruit . . . scribens [*corr.*^{2} *add.*: ei] anicopli [*corr.*^{2}: anthopoli (*sic*)]. [Stegmüller 780]; f. 158 Titus; f. 159 *Incipit argumentum* [*corr.*^{2}*: prologus*] *epistole ad pilemenem* [*sic*]. Philemoni familiares litteras facit . . . per eundem onesimum acolitum. [Stegmüller 783]; f. 159 Philemon; f. 159v *Incipit eodem ad eodem* [*corr.*^{2}*: argumentum ieronimi in epistolam hebreos*]. f. 159 [marginal note, boxed in red] Illum prologum quere post octo folio circa signum a □□. Et incipitur, in primis dicendum est cur apostolus [Stegmüller 793; similar note, bottom margin]; f. 159v Hebrews; f. 167 [top margin] Sequitur prologus in actus apostolorum, scilicet lucas antiocensis, etc. [Stegmüller 637]. Quere tercia medium; f. 167 *Incipit argumentum Ieronimi epistola ad hebreos.* In primis dicendum est cur apostolus . . . [Stegmüller 793; □□ appears in inner margin]; f. 167 *Incipit controuersia gentibus primo iudeorum.* Romani sunt qui ex iudeis gentibus que crediderunt . . . [Stegmüller 674; □□ appears in inner margin]; f. 168 *Sequitur secundum argumentum. Explicit controuersia. Incipit liber sancti hieronimi ad ewstochium uirginem.* Audi filia et uide et inclina aurem tuam . . . quas michi preteritorum recordacio peccatorum eximis visceribus exuebat, etc. *Deo gracias.* [Excerpts from Jerome, Epistula XXII ad Eustochium, ed. Isidorus Hilberg, Corpus scriptorum ecclesiasticorum latinorum (Vienna and Leipzig 1910; reprint N.Y. and London 1970) 54:143–211; here ending imperfectly p. 189, line 16; Bernard Lambert, *Bibliotheca Hieronymiana manuscripta.* Instrumenta patristica 4 (Steenbruge 1969) 1:8–10, not listing this manuscript (cf. 1:450–60)]; f. 169v blank.

2. ff. 170–268v: f. 170 Ecclesiastes, beginning imperfectly at 19:20: "//[in]sipiens qui minuitur sapientia m<elior est homo qui> deficit . . .; f. 193v *Incipit prologus compositus a hierinimo* [*sic*] *presbytero in librum Iob. Incipt secundus interpretacionem ewseby prologus hieronimi super iob etc.* Cogor per singulos scripture libros . . . [Stegmüller 344]; f. 193v Ibi est paruus defectus respice in cedula primus interea quidem ☞. Sequitur alius prologus, scilicet si autem fiscellam iunco etc. [Stegmüller 357]. Vide in cedula F̸. f. 194 bis [added quarter-sheet; F̸ in margin] *Sequitur alius prologus beati Jeronimi presbiteri in librum Iob.* Si autem [*sic*] fiscellam iunco teperem [*sic*] aut palmarum . . . [Stegmüller 357]; f. 194 bis^{v} [☞ in margin] In terra quidem hys habitasse iob auxitiden in finibus ydumee et arabie dicitur et erat . . . [Stegmüller 349]; f. 195 Job [ending, f. 217, with note, underlined in red] *Explicit liber iob. Sequitur prologus in librum machabeorum primum qui in* [*sic*] *incipit domino excellentissimo et in cultu christiane religionis strenuosissimo ludewico etc.* [*Stegmüller 547*]. *Deinde alius qui incipit machabeorum duo libri etc.* [*Stegmüller 551*]. *Deinde sequitur primum capitulum scilicet, et factum est postquam etc. Quod quere post 44 folia.* [continues, same hand, not underlined] Hic inter pretatur de siriaco libro iob quidem in terra habitasse austidi in finibus idumee et arabissa . . . Sophar minerorum princeps.; f. 217 *Prologus hieronimi super tobiam. Iste prologus sequitur secundam librum Esdre in mediate. Incipit prologus conpositus ab hieronimo presbitero in libro Thobie.* Chromatio et heliodoro episcopis hieronimus presbyter in domino salutem. Mirari non desino . . . [Stegmüller 332 with salutation]; f. 217v Tobit; f. 222v *Incipit* [*expunged: explicit*] *prologus hieronimi super Iudith. Sequitur apud he* [*sic*]. Apud hebreos liber Iudith inter agiographa legitur . . . [Stegmüller 335]; f. 230 Esther [beginning with note] *Prologum* [*sic*] *super librum hester quere <in-pu.?>* [*expunged: libri*] *<. . us?> post quatuor folia.* [Esther concludes with marginal note] Nunc sequitur prologus in Iob quam quere ante hoc folio 44; f. 237v *Iste prologus sequitur secundum librum*

paralipomenon in mediate. Incipit prologus hieronimi super esdram etc. Utrum difficimus [*sic*; *corr.*[2]: difficile] sit facere quod poscitis an negare ... [Stegmüller 330]; f. 238v 1 Ezra; f. 244v Nehemiah; f. 253v 2 Ezra [= 3 Ezra; Stegmüller 94,1; concludes with note, f. 263v] *Amen. <W?> Re. quadri duo par. Es. pri. nee. esdre secundus. Et sic est finis in biblia monastery <huius?> secundi esdre.*; f. 264 5 Ezra [Stegmüller 96], ending imperfectly, f. 266, at 3:31: "... nichil nemini quodmodo debeat derelinqui."; f. 266v–267v blank; f. 268 *Incipit prologus in libro primo machabeorum.* Machabeorum libri duo prenotant prelia ... [Stegmüller 551]; f. 268 Machabeorum libri licet non habeantur ... [Stegmüller 552; ending mid-folio; remainder blank]; f. 268v *Incipit liber machabeorum. Et primo prologus venerabilis Bede.* [rubric only; remainder blank; 1 Maccabees now begins f. 1].

Modern chapters throughout; Maccabees 1–2 through Ecclesiasticus, and Ezra, Nehemiah and 2 Ezra also divided into shorter unnumbered chapters; stichometry indicated in concluding rubrics for 2 Maccabees and Acts, ff. 43v and 72v.

Throughout, the scribe and a corrector have added extensive notes about the order of the books, the choice of prologues, and the wording of the rubrics; additional prologues were copied on half- and quarter-sheets, which were then added in after ff. 84, 123, 132, and 194. Corrected througout in a contemporary hand, supplying omissions (for example ff. 8v, 9); deleting repetitions (for example ff. 14 and 15), and adding omitted chapter divisions (f. 44v).

Paper (watermark, similar to Piccard Waage V.265–66, Vienna, 1459, 1456, V.290–91, Innsbruck and Nuremberg, 1458, and V.292, Nuremberg, 1460), ff. iii (paper) + 262 (incorrectly foliated, 1–268, top outer corner in pencil, every ten folios only, and continuously, bottom inside margin, with f. 109 followed by f. 120, and with unnumbered half- or quarter-sheets following ff. 84, 123, 132, and 194) + iii, 278 x 209 mm. Layout varies; ff. 1–217, and ff. 253v–end, written space (206–202 x 143–137) mm. 35–30 long lines (2 column format sometimes used for chapter lists, ff. 98–104v); ff. 217v–253, written space (199–197 x 140–135) mm. 42–37 long lines. Lightly frame ruled in lead with all four bounding lines full length.

1–2^{12} 3^{10} 4–7^{12} 8^{12} (+1, f. 84bis, half-sheet added after 2) 9^{12} (–4, following f. 97, with loss of text) 10^{12} (+1, f. 123bis, quarter-sheet added after 8) 11^{12} (+1, f. 132bis, quarter-sheet added after 5) 12–13^{12} 14^{6} (beginning f. 164, structure uncertain) 15^{9} (beginning f. 170, structure uncertain) 16^{12} 17^{12} (+1, f. 194bis, half-sheet added after 4) 18–22^{12} 23^{6}. Horizontal catchwords beginning with a red slash, lower inside margin: visible, quires 15–18 (ff. 178v, 190v, 202v, 214v); traces remain, quires 2–4, 6–7, 9, 12, 19, and 21–22; trimmed, quires 1, 5, 8, 10, 11, 13–14, and 20.

Written below the top line probably by a number of scribes in a vigorous gothic *cursiva formata* script, with some loops; the hands are precise and controlled, with changes of hand very difficult to discern, although layout and size of script varies.

Books begin with 5- to 2-line red initials set within the text space; prologues begin with similar 4- to 2-line initials. Chapters begin with 2- to 1-line red initials. Red rubrics; majuscules within the text slashed with red. Guide letters within the initials and notes to rubricators remain.

Bound in black half morocco, s. XIX; marbled end papers; speckled edges.

Written in southern Germany in the third quarter of the fifteenth century for a monastic house (cf. rubric, f. 263v; we thank Dr. Paul Needham for his assistance; March, 1991). The Bible is bound out of order, and the beginning is now missing (text on f. 1 once followed f. 268v; f. 169v is darkened and stained with marks from a chain or binding, and was likely the end of the volume). Unidentified bookseller's or owner's note, f. 1, in pencil, "n c." Purchased February 11, 1868, by John Harvey Treat (1839–1908), historiographer, M. A. Harvard 1862 (bookplate, inside front cover, with date in ink, and price code, "γδ∈"); this date repeated in pencil, f. 1, with "A L L"; his gift to Harvard, April 25, 1888 (bookplate, inside front cover; library note and stamp, front flyleaf, f. iii^{v}). Original Harvard shelf mark, III.4696.

secundo folio: holocausta et

Bibliography: De Ricci, 982.

MS Lat 51 **Germany s. XIV[1]**
Boethius; Ps. Dionysius the Areopagite

1. ff. 1–8v [Excerpts from Boethius, *Philosophiae consolatio*] *Incipit notabilia boecii de consolatione. Liber primus.* Mors hominum felix que se non [*sic*] dulcibus annis/ Inserit et mestis sepe uocata uenit [book 1, M I.13]/ . . . [f. 1] Philosophia est uelud mulier reuerendi admodum vultus oculis ardentibus et vltra communem hominum valentiam perspicatibus [book 1, 1.1] . . . Magna uobis est indicta neccesitas probitatis cum ante oculos agamus iudicis vniuersa cernentis. *Explicit.*

   Ludovicus Bieler, ed. CC 94 (Turnholt 1957); *CPL* 878.

   Three folios missing following f. 7v, so that f. 7v ends in book 4, ". . . Segnis ac stupidus asinum viuit. Leuis atque inconstans nichil differt ab auibus. Deditus libidine// [cf. book 4, 3.19–20]"; f. 8 begins imperfectly in book 5, "Sensus et ymaginatio quorum notio corporales figuras non valet excedere . . . [cf. book 5, 5.7]."

2. ff. 8v–11v [Excerpts from Ps. Dionysius the Areopagite, *De caelesti hierarchia*] *Excerpta ex libro dyonisii de angelica ierarchia.* Omnis apparitio luminis ad uos bonitatis dono ueniens rursus ut vnifica uirtus nos ad implet et conuertit . . . et super nos occultum silentio veneramur. *Explicit.*

   Latin versions printed in Phillipe Chevalier, *et al.*, eds., *Dionysiaca: Recueil donnant l'ensemble des traductions latines des ouvrages attribués au Denys de l'Aréopage* . . . (Paris and Bruges 1937–50) 2:727–1039, and *PL* 122:1037–70.

3. ff. 11v–17 [Excerpts from Ps. Dionysius the Areopagite, *De ecclesiastica hierarchia*] *Incipit ecclesiastica ierarchia.* Nostra ierarchia est habitus in deo manentis sancte et diuine operationis et deifice perfectionis . . . et communicatricem ipsorum in profectibus sanctis. *Expliciunt exserpta* [*sic*] *ecclesiastice ierarchie.*

   Latin versions printed in Chevalier, *et al.*, eds., *Dionysiaca* 2:1071–1476 and *PL* 122:1069–1112.

4. ff. 17–22v [Excerpts from Ps. Dionysius the Areopagite, *De divinis nominibus*] *Incipiunt de diuinis nominibus.* Theologi virtute spiritus sancti ineffabilibus et ignotis ineffabiliter et ignote coniunguntur

secundum vnitionem meliorem nostra rationali . . . vnum et omnium causa et <nl. . .?> ex<. . .?> participat[?] . . . <followed by six lines, bottom margin, copied in a cramped script, now erased and mostly illegible under ultraviolet, ending *Explicat.*>

Latin versions printed in Chevalier, *et al.*, eds., *Dionysiaca* 1:5–561 and *PL* 122:1111–72. F. 22, col. b and f. 22v copied in a progressively smaller script with an increasing number of lines; this compression and dirt, water stains, and abrasion sometimes render f. 22v illegible.

Parchment, ff. i (paper) + 22 + i (paper), 227 x 162 (195–181 x 134–131) mm. 2 columns, 38–36 lines (f. 22, col. b, 38 ruled lines, but 48 lines of text; f. 22v, 55 lines of text). Ruled in ink with the top and bottom horizontal lines full across; single full-length vertical bounding lines. Prickings in 3 outer margins (double prickings for top and bottom lines, outer margin).

1^2 2^4 3^8 (–2 through 4, following f. 7, with loss of text) 4^8 5^3 (structure uncertain).

Written by three scribes; the first scribe copied ff. 1–11v, column a, and f. 15v, line 19–f. 17, in an upright conservative gothic bookhand, below the top line, except ff. 3–11v, which begin above the top line; the second scribe copied ff. 11v, column b–15v, top, and ff. 17, column b–21 in an upright, well-spaced gothic bookhand with sharper letter forms, below the top line; the third scribe copied ff. 21–22v in a less formal gothic script, which becomes progressively smaller and more cramped.

Two-line plain red initials at the beginnings of books and chapters; 1-line initials within the text; red rubrics. Guide letters for the rubricator, between the columns (for example, f. 11v) or in the outer margins (for example, ff. 12–15v and ff. 17v–18); another set of very similar tiny marginal letters (possibly for indexing?) are visible on some folios; cf. ff. 16rv and f. 17, between the columns, and ff. 17v–18, inner margins.

Bound, s. XIX (?), possibly in England, in brown half-morocco with marbled paper boards; spine lettered in gilt.

Ff. 1 and 22v stained; f. 22v, very dirty and rubbed with loss of legibility.

Written in Germany in the first half of the fourteenth century. Unidentified notes from dealers and owners include, back flyleaf, f. 1, in pencil: "202 [circled]," price code, "£ a/-/-," "<..?> 16/6 <..3> [partly erased]," and "If5."; front flyleaf, f. i, "Cat 17, £3." Purchased March 15, 1917 (Constantius Fund; bookplate inside front cover); De Ricci records that it was purchased from Davis and Orioli (not identified in their catalogues or verified in library records).

secundo folio: ueritatis sentenciis

Bibliography: De Ricci, 982; Kristeller, *Iter* 5:226.

MS Lat 111 — France s. XVI^{1} (after 1515)
Carthusian Breviary for Terce, Sext and None — Pls. 18, 64

1. ff. 2–19v [f. 1 ruled flyleaf, blank except for ex libris note; see discussion of provenance, below] Calendar in red and black, with feasts graded three lessons, commemoration, Mass, twelve lessons, chapter, sermon, solemnity, and with candles; July is copied out of order; the scribe added an 'A', top of f. 12, a 'B', top f. 11v, and tie marks at the end of ff. 11v and the top of 12v to indicate the correct order (ff. 11, 12, 11v, 12v); among the feasts included are Thomas Aquinas (7 March), Hugh of Grenoble (in red, 12 lessons, 1 April), Visitation (in red, with candles, 2 July), Processus and Martinianus (commemoration, 2 July), octave of Visitation (in red, 12 lessons, 9 July), Mary Magdalene (in red, with candles and sermon, 22 July), Anne (Mass, 26 July), the dedication of a church (in red, solemnity, 1 October), Bruno (in red, solemnity, sermon, 6 October), Fides (commemoration, 6 October), octave of Bruno (Mass, added by later hand, 13 October), the relics (in red, with candles, 8 November), "commemoratio fratrum nostrorum defunctorum" (in red, Mass, 9 November), Hugh of Lincoln (in red, with candles and sermon, 19 November), Columbanus (commemoration, 21 November), and the Presentation of the Virgin (in red, with candles, 21 November).

2. ff. 20–46v Offices for the week at terce, sext and none.

3. ff. 46v–71 Temporale from the first Sunday in Advent through Corpus Christi ("*De sacramentis altaris*") with antiphons, capitula,

verses and some prayers for terce, sext and none, including the feast of the Compassion of the Virgin (f. 62).

4. ff. 71v–86 Sanctorale from Andrew (30 November) through Catherine of Alexandria (25 November) with antiphons, capitula and verses for terce, sext and none; directions for the Presentation of the Virgin (21 November) copied following the office for Catherine, with a mark indicating the error; includes the feasts of the Conception of the Virgin (8 December), Hugh of Grenoble (1 April; rubric only, directing the reader to the common of the saints), the Visitation (2 July), "*in dedicatione huius ecclesie*" (1 October), Bruno (6 October), "*in festo reliquarum*" (8 November), and Hugh of Lincoln (17 November).

5. ff. 86–99 Common of the saints, with antiphons, capitula, verses and usually with prayers for terce, sext and none; with concluding rubric, "*Et sic est finis. Deo gratias.*"

6. ff. 99v–102 Petitions, beginning "*Sequuntur preces pro pace postulanda inter principes*"; concluding with prayers: "Deus qui corda fidelium sancti spiritus illustratione docuisti . . . [Bruylants, *Oraisons* 2: no. 349; printed *Sarum Breviary* 1:ix]"; "Concede nos famulos tuos quesumus domine deus perpetua . . . [Bruylants, *Oraisons* 2: no. 122; printed *HE*, 44 and 51]"; "Deus a quo sancta desideria recta consilia et iusta sunt opera . . . [Bruylants, *Oraisons* 2: no. 201; printed *Brev. O.P.*, lxxxiv]"; "Domine sancte pater omnipotens eterne deus te deprecamur per unicum filium tuum dominum nostrum iesum christum . . ." [Ff. 102v–103v blank, but ruled.]

(Articles 1–6) Occasional contemporary corrections, altering punctuation (cf. ff. 55 and 71), word order (cf. f. 81) or supplying omissions (cf. f. 63). Additions (s. XVI) include: f. 56, bottom margin, antiphon, capitula and verse for the Feast of the Holy Name of Jesus, celebrated by the Carthusians, 1597; f. 70v, capitula at terce for Trinity Sunday, celebrated with a proper office by the Carthusians, 1582; f. 78v, bottom margin, antiphon and capitula for the Feast of the Transfiguration, celebrated by the Carthusians, 1582. Later additions: f. 78, capitula for Mary Magdalene; f. 78v, top margin, capitula at terce for Anne.

Parchment (sturdy), ff. ii (parchment) + i (ruled medieval parchment, numbered f. 1) + 103 (incorrect modern foliation in pencil, 1–102, bottom outer corner recto, including f. 1, a flyleaf, with unnumbered folios following ff. 14, 16, and 36, and with f. 71 followed immediately by f. 73) + ii (blank ruled medieval parchment; ii = pastedown), 165 x 115 (95–92 x 70–66) mm. 12 long lines. Ruled lightly in lead with the top two and bottom two horizontal rules full across; single full-length vertical bounding lines. Calendar, ff. 2–19v, ruled space: 97–96 x 67–66 mm.; ruled with 3 narrow columns and a wide column for main entry, 12 lines. No prickings.

1^8 (beginning f. 2) $2–12^8$ 13^8 (–8, stub remains, cancelled with no loss of text).

Written in a formal gothic bookhand in two sizes depending on liturgical function. Punctuation includes the *punctus flexus*.

Ten 3-line parted red and blue initials, infilled and with pen decoration in brown and sepia: f. 20 (art. 2, offices for the week); f. 47 Advent; f. 51 Christmas; f. 55 Epiphany; f. 63v Easter; f. 72v Andrew; f. 79 Assumption of the Virgin; f. 82 Michael Archangel; f. 84v All Saints; f. 88 common of the saints. Secondary initials, 2-line, alternately red and blue, placed at the beginning of a new line within the text space; similar 'KL'-monograms. 1-line initials, alternately red and blue, within the text. Red and blue line fillers; red rubrics, often prefaced by blue paragraph marks for emphasis. Majuscules within text infilled with red. Small guide letters usually visible within 1-line, and in the margin next to 2-line initials.

Bound in England in the late eighteenth century in light-brown morocco with narrow blind-tooled borders on both covers; spine with three raised bands and title "Horae diurne in usum Carthusianorum" in gold; rebacked with spine laid down; spine cracked and fragile.

Written in the early sixteenth century in Northeastern France, probably at the Carthusian house of Val-Saint-Esprit of Gosnay, Bethune, Pas-de-Calais, France (founded 1320, suppressed 1791; Gruys, *Cartusiana* 2:286–7), where it was MS AA6<?> in their library; ex libris note, f. 1v, in a contemporary hand: "Liber carthusianorum vallis sancti spiritus in pago gosnay secus bethuniam in arthesia. AA6<?>." Liturgical evidence suggests a date after 1515 (calendar includes Fides, 6 October, celebrated with a commemoration, and Bruno, 6 October; both feasts were observed from 1515; and other feasts reflecting the Carthusian liturgy in the later fifteenth century; for example, temporale includes the feast of the Compassion of the Virgin, permitted 1477, and obligatory 1486), and before 1545 (octave of Bruno, with Mass, added, observed 1545; lacks many sixteenth-century feasts, for example Joseph, 19 March, observed 1567–8 and Thomas Aquinas, 7 March, here with three lessons, raised to commemoration in 1568; cf. Hourlier and du Moustier, "Le Calendrier Cartusien"). Belonged, s. XVIII to F. Bishop, of Dunkirk, France; f. 1, in ink, "F. Bishop presbyter [?], Dunkercq"; and then to W. Wollaston of Finborough, Suffolk; his armorial bookplate, pasted inside front cover, with motto "Ne Quid Falsi," signed by the engraver, George Bickham, Jr. (1706?–1771; cf. Walter Hamilton, *Dated Book-Plates* [London 1895] 89). Sale of a clergyman, London, Sotheby's, 8 March, 1911, no. 45 to Ellis. Ellis Cat. 138, November 1911, no. 38 for £8.8.0, described as "Horae diurnae"; Ellis' note, in pencil, inside front cover: "Horae" written diagonally, and price, £8.8.0. Purchased from Ellis, 22 November 1911 (John Harvey Treat Fund; library stamp with note in pencil, f. 1; bookplate, inside back cover). Original Harvard shelf mark: C 9343.6*.

secundo folio: [text, f. 21] Da mihi

Bibliography: De Ricci, 983.

MS Lat 112 — England 1366
Charter

Charter, August 17, 1366, in which a plot of land at Hardenasse owned by Matilda, widow of Johannes de Lustote is ceded to her daughter Matilda and Thomas Vela. [Verso, blank.]

Trimmed at the bottom, and lacking signatures or marks of the four witnesses.

Parchment, rough rectangle, folded at the bottom, with seal attached, 140–137 x 226–216 mm. 15 long lines.

Written in an anglicana script.

Written in England, August 17, 1366. Later medieval note, in pen, verso, written vertically to the bottom edge: "<J>antmonti." Bought, May 1904, by George Dunn (1865–1912; in pencil, recto, price code, and "G.D. May 1904"); possibly part of lot 3033 in his sale, London, Sotheby's, November 23, 1917. Purchased, August 19, 1918 (Kittredge Fund; library stamp, verso) from F. C. Carter, Cat. 59, no. 921 (as noted by De Ricci; unverified in manuscript or library files).

Bibliography: De Ricci, 983.

MS Lat 115 — Germany s. XIII^2
Dominican Portable Breviary — Pl. 13

1. ff. 1–69v Psalter and canticles; psalter in biblical order, with antiphons, versicles, responses and prayers, beginning imperfectly in Psalm 27:3: "//proximo suo mala autem in cordibus eorum . . ."; major divisions at Psalms 38, 51, 52, 68, 80, 97, 101, 109, and 137 (ff. 7, 13v, 14, 20, 28, 35v, 37, 44, and 58); Psalm 118, ff. 46v–52, divided into sections, with the "Quicumque vult" between verses 32 and 33; Psalm 120, f. 53v, followed by rubrics for vespers; Psalms 148–150, ff. 62v–63v, written as one psalm without divisions; f. 63v canticles for the days of the week, some with antiphons, and New Testament canticles (Benedictus, Pater noster, Credo in deum, Magnificat, Nunc dimittis and Te deum).

2. ff. 69v–72v Litany, following the preceding article without a break, including Pantaleon, Christopher, Denis, Maurice, Thomas of Canterbury, and Peter martyr among the martyrs, Dominic, Francis and Bernard among the confessors, and Elizabeth (of Thuringia?), Agatha, Agnes, Catherine of Alexandria, Christina, Walburga, Bridget, Tecla, Clare, Odilia, Sophia and Ursula among the virgins; concludes with prayers: "Concede quesumus omnipotens deus ut intercessio nos sancte dei genitricis . . ."; "Ineffabilem misericordiam tuam quesumus domine ostende . . . [Bruylants, *Oraisons* 2: no. 648; printed *Brev. O.P.*, lxxxiv]"; "Deus qui caritatem dona per gratiam sancti spiritus . . ."; "Pro domine ut famula tua N. ut deus omnipotens per honorem quincque wlnerum tuorum per passionem et crucem tuam . . ."; "Domine deus omnipotens tibi commendo animam et corpus famuli tui . . ."; "Pater sancte serua eum in nomine tuo et da ei benedictione [*sic*] in seculum seculi. . . ."

3. f. 72v Prayers added in contemporary or slightly later hands at the

end of the preceding article: "Deus qui ecclesiam tuam beati Dominici confessoris tui illuminare dignatus es meritis et doctrinis, concede ut eius intercessione temporalibus non destituatur . . ."; "Quoniam ex precepto regule iubemur . . ."; [in another hand:] "[E]cclesiam tuam domine beati antonii confessoris tui sollempnitas uotiua letificet. . . ."

4. ff. 73–116v Temporale, very abbreviated; no lessons; cues only for the psalms; hymns are not noted; begins imperfectly with the antiphon for the Magnificat ("Ne timeas maria inuenisti gratiam apud dominum. . .") at vespers, the first Sunday in Advent, and continues through the twenty-fifth Sunday after Pentecost, concluding with the dedication of a church; includes Trinity Sunday, but Sundays are counted after Pentecost; lacks Corpus Christi.

5. ff. 116v–154v Sanctorale from the Vigil of Andrew (29 November) through Saturninus, usually very brief; fuller offices, but without lessons, for Stephen, Conversion of Peter and Paul, Purification, Annunciation, Alexander, Eventius and Theodolus, Feast of the Crown of Our Lord, John, Peter and Paul, Paul, Mary Magdalene, Dominic, Lawrence, Assumption, Augustine, Nativity of the Virgin, Michael Archangel, All Saints, and Catherine of Alexandria; office for Peter martyr (ff. 127v–130) with three lessons at lauds, written out in full; saints included conform to those in Humbert's Calendar printed in William R. Bonniwell, *A History of the Dominican Liturgy* (N.Y. 1944) 100–101.

6. ff. 154v–180v Common of the saints; ff. 154v–156 vesper prayers for one or many apostles, a martyr and bishop, many martyrs, a confessor and bishop, a confessor and doctor, a confessor not a bishop, a confessor and abbot, a virgin martyr, and a virgin not a martyr; ff. 156–160v brief offices for one apostle, one evangelist, a martyr, many martyrs, a confessor, a virgin whether martyr or not; f. 160v invitatory and antiphon for feasts with three lessons for one martyr, many martyrs, a confessor, and a virgin; f. 161 commemorations of many confessors and many virgins; ff. 161–162 office of Vincent of Saragossa (22 January) with lessons; ff. 162–163 short office of the Virgin; ff. 163–165v short office of the Trinity, with rubric in German, f. 165v: "Dis dv eirste nocturne di lis hie"; ff. 165v–168v short office of the dedication of a church; ff. 168v–169

versicles, antiphons and invitatories during Eastertide for one apostle, one or many evangelists, a martyr, and many martyrs; ff. 169–180 offices (outside of Eastertide?) for apostles, a martyr, many martyrs, a confessor and bishop, an abbot, and a virgin, each of which has nine lessons written out in full; concludes, f. 180rv, with invitatory and antiphon for the common of the saints with three lessons (same text as on f. 160rv).

7. ff. 180v–181v [possibly added] Gradual psalms by cue, each set of five with prayers; benedictions for the first nocturn at matins; John 1:1–3; prayer, "Quoniam ex precepto regule iubemur habere. . . ."

8. f. 181v Added prayers, s. XV; ink is very faded: "Nos cum prole pia benedicat virgo maria. Amen. [cue only]"; "Dulce nomen domini nostri ihesu christi . . ."

9. ff. 182–228v Noted hymnal (notation occasionally not completed; blank staves, ff. 217–218v, 219v–220, 221rv and 222v) including the major feasts of the temporale, ff. 182–201, from Advent through Trinity Sunday, concluding with the dedication of a church, the sanctorale, ff. 201–217, from the Holy Innocents (28 December) through Catherine of Alexandria (25 November), including Peter martyr and Dominic, and the common of the saints, ff. 217–225, with variations for feasts of different ranks (simplex, semi–duplex, duplex, and totum duplex); ff. 225–227v notation for the eight tones; f. 228rv the Magnificat and Benedictus in two settings.

10. ff. 229–231v Office for matins of the first Sunday after the Octave of Epiphany, here beginning abruptly with the reading for the first nocturn (Romans l:l), with lessons given in full; followed immediately, f. 231rv, with matins for the first Sunday in August, responses and versicles only.

11. f. 232rv Two suffrages of Dominican saints, added after 1461 (canonization of Catherine of Siena) on otherwise blank leaf; the first with 8–line verse antiphon: "O quam felix gloria/ semper est sanctorum/ quam preclara merita/ sunt praedicatorum/. . ."; versicle: "Exultabunt sancti in gloria . . . ," and prayer: "Concede quesumus omnipotens deus ut ad meliorem uitam sanctorum tuorum petri thome uincencii et katherine exempla. . . ."; the

second with a 4-line verse antiphon, "Cristi pia gratia sanctos sublimauit/ quos patris dominici ordo[?] propagavit/ . . ." and a versicle, "Sapientiam sanctorum narrantur populi . . .", but lacking the final prayer.

12. ff. 233–237 Service for the dead beginning defectively, "//ut a cunctis reatibus absoluti tecum sine fine letentur . . ."; the service includes directions for a "cantor," "fratres," and "sacerdos"; f. 233 Office of the Dead, Dominican use; vespers concludes with prayers, f. 233rv: "Deus uenie largitor et humane salutis . . . [printed *HE*, 111]"; "Omnipotens sempiterne deus cui numquam sine spe misericordie supplicatur . . . [printed *HE*, 101]"; "Inclina domine aurem tuam ad preces nostras . . . ut animam famule tue . . . [printed *HE*, 101]"; "Deus qui nos patrem et matrem honorare precepisti . . .[printed *HE*, 111]"; "Deus indulgentiarum domine da famule tue . . ."; "Fidelium deus omnium conditor et redemptor animabus. . . . [Bruylants, *Oraisons* 2: no. 567; printed *HE*, 30 and 98]."

13. ff. 237–256v Offices, following the preceding article without a break, for matins on Easter, Ascension, Pentecost, and John the Baptist, ending imperfectly at the beginning of the third nocturn, f. 241v, Assumption of the Virgin, beginning imperfectly, f. 242, at the end of the first lesson, Nativity of the Virgin, Invention of the Cross, the Crown of Our Lord, Exaltation of the Cross, Michael Archangel, Dominic and Augustine; lessons given in full.

14. f. 256v Short homily in German, added later: "Sancte iohannes ewang gewan nahe vns vrowvn . . ."; prayer to Dominic, in Latin, added in another hand (now faded and almost illegible).

Parchment (very thin), ff. ii (paper) + 256 (modern foliation in pencil, bottom, inside margin, recto [cited]; early modern pagination in black ink, upper outside corner, recto and verso, as follows: 9–75, *78–137, 137 bis and ter, 138–152, *155–157, 156 bis, 157 bis, 158–163, 162 bis, 163 bis, 164–247, 246 bis, 247 bis, 248–249, 248 bis, 249 bis, 250–333, *336–516) + ii (paper), 121 x 84 (93–88 x 60–58) mm. 25 long lines, except ff. 1–24v, 26 lines, and hymnal, ff. 182–228v, with the equivalent of 20–18 lines of text, but with text and 4-line staves interspersed. Ruled lightly in dark brown ink, with the top

2 and occasionally bottom 1 horizontal rules full across; single full-length vertical bounding lines. Some prickings, outer margin; ff. 230–231, with double rows of prickings.

Original first quire is lacking (manuscript begins imperfectly). 1–6^{12} 7^{12} (–1, before f. 73) 8–15^{12} 16^{13} (2, f. 181, loose singleton) 17–19^{12} 20^{4} (ff. 229–232v; singletons; original structure uncertain) 21^{8} 22^{16}. Last folio of quire 18, third quire of the hymnal, art. 10, signed "iii," middle, bottom margin (partly cut away).

Written below the top line in a gothic bookhand by at least three scribes; the hymnal copied by two different scribes, (ff. 182–225 and ff. 225v–228v).

Three 11- to 9-line historiated initials; ff. 13v and 37, orange initials, heavily outlined and decorated in black, with traces of gold highlights on square polished gold grounds, edged with orange; f. 128, pink initial decorated in white and black and outlined in black on a similar ground; subjects as follows: f. 13v (Psalm 51) the Ascension of Christ, with Christ shown half-length, from the waist down; scalloped green clouds at the top, and Mary and the apostles at the bottom; holes for a protective flap, now missing, at the top; f. 37 (Psalm 101) the Apostles, possibly at Pentecost (top now damaged); f. 128 (sanctorale) Peter martyr with crude pen and wash drawing of 2 small seated figures in the upper margin. 4- to 3-line red and blue parted initials at the major divisions of the psalms, art. 1, with pen decoration in red, blue or both colors; some infilled with yellow wash (ff. 7, 14, 20, 28, 35v, 44, and 58). Some of the remaining psalms begin with 2-line alternately red and blue initials with pen decoration in the other color, sometimes highlighted with yellow wash. Minor initials, 2- to 1-line alternately red and blue, undecorated. Pen and ink drawing of acrobats in the margin, f. 1, probably added, s. XIX.

Bound, s. XIX, in France in quarter mottled calf and green and black paper; printed endpapers imitating marbled paper; spine with four raised bands, with a blank orange label between the first and the second; front cover loose.

Written in Germany in the second half of the thirteenth century, after the canonization of Peter martyr in 1254, and before 1318, since Corpus Christi is lacking in the temporale. Possibly to be used by Dominican nuns, since Dominican saints are emphasized, feminine forms are used in prayers, and the litany includes many female saints.

Language (rubrics and prayers in German) and saints indicate Germany, probably southern Germany (litany includes Walburga, Odilia, Sophia, and Ursula). The manuscript bears signs of long use including heavily soiled corners, torn and worn lower margins, numerous missing sections, and additions in a number of hands through the fifteenth century (cf. art. 4, 8, 9, and 12). Given to Harvard by Morton Davis Mitchell, class of 1887, September 14, 1918 (bookplate, inside front cover; library stamp, front flyleaf, f. ii^{v}).

Bibliography: De Ricci, 984; listed in William R. Bonniwell, *A History of the Dominican Liturgy* (New York 1944) 359, where it is dated fourteenth century.

MS Lat 116 England s. XIV^{2}; s. XV
Ranulf Higden, Polychronicon

1. ff. 1–150v //nonennis quondam iurauerat patri suo ad aras deorum quod quam cito posset bellum romanis inferret ... [f. 15 book 4] In principio igitur quadragesimi secundi anni ... [f. 43 book 5] Marcianus copulata sibi ... [f. 81 book 6] Alruedus [added in another hand: domine alfredus secundum alios] quartus natu ... [f. 109 book 7] Willelmus igitur londoniam ueniens ... mare tranquillitatem ecclesia libertatem.

C. Babington and J. R. Lumby, eds., *Polychronicon Ranulphi Higden monachi cestrensis*. Rolls Series 41 in 9 volumes (London 1865–86; Kraus reprint 1964). For a list of manuscripts, see John Taylor, *The Universal Chronicle of Ranulf Higden* (Oxford 1966) Appendix I, listing this manuscript p. 152. Text begins imperfectly in book 3, chapter 33 (ed., 4:52, line 5); this hand continues through 1327, ending f. 150v, 5 lines from the bottom, in book 7, chapter 44 (ed., 8:324, line 7).

Folio missing between ff. 24v–25, so that f. 24v ends, "... Nero vna et eadem die// [book 4, chapter 9; ed., 4:412, line 11]," and f. 25 begins, "//paleis repletos ictibus opponens plagam delusam emollit ... [book 4, chapter 10; ed., 4:428, line 9]." Two folios missing between ff. 34v–35, so that f. 34v ends, "... quia quamuis dioclitianus [*sic*] et Maximianus tertio huius persecutionis// [book 4, chapter 25; ed., 5:110, line 9]," and f. 35 begins, "//scriptis cartulis adversum se querimonias coram Augusto attulerunt ... [book 4, chapter 26; ed., 5:140, line 16]." Folio missing betwen ff. 105–106, so that f. 105v ends, "... Cuius dum vixit circum-// [book 6, chapter 26; ed., 7:198, line 19]," and f. 106 begins, "//-tionem quam propinqui sic deriderent latrunculi ... [book 6, chapter 27; ed., 7:212, line 13]."

Throughout, the dates of the calendar and the regnal year are recorded in the outer margin; marginal notes include contemporary corrections (for example ff. 19 and 21), and short comments on contents in a number of hands, s. XV–XVI. Contemporary running headlines with the book and chapter number.

2. ff. 150v–160v [Continuation of the Chronicle from 1327–1376, added in a later hand.] Tertio nonas aprilis translatus est rex antiquus de Kenelworth [*sic*] usque castrum de berkeleya ... sub pena capitis [added above: et careis (*sic*)] interdixit. [f. 152v book 7, chapter 45] Hoc anno nonis iunii natus est regi Edwardus Edmundus apud langeley ex philippa regina ... Erat namque inter illos de comitate quidam miles sapiens verax et facundus nomine petrus de lamarus in cuius ore summa[?] omnium dependebatur. Hic.//

This version of the continuation has been classified as (C); see Taylor, *The Universal Chronicle*, 114, 116 (noting textual similarities with Eton, Eton College MS 213), and appendix IV, 179; and John Taylor, "The Development of the Polychronicon Continuation," *English Historical Review* 76 (1961) 25–27, and 35. Through f. 152v, the end of book 7, chapter 44, the text follows the edition (ending 8:338, bottom of page). The remainder of this continuation has not been printed, and here ends imperfectly.

Calendar year noted, outer margin, through f. 155v; throughout, frequent notes on contents by the scribe in the outer margin. No running headlines.

3. ff.161v–170v [Alphabetical index] Abraham, book 2, chapter 10; Abdon dux israel, book 2, chapter 15; Abessa, dux israel, book 2, chapter 24 ... Vastoma terra, book 1, chapter 18; Varro marcus, book 3, chapter 37; Uasepanus [*sic*] imperator, book 4, chapter 23//

Contemporary with art. 1; references are to book and chapter number; index ends imperfectly with the entries beginning with 'V'.

Parchment, ff. ii (stiff modern parchment) + 170 + ii, 270 x 200, trimmed, text in top margin partly lost on some folios (205–200 x 143–140) mm. 31 long lines. Ruled in lead, usually with the top two and bottom two horizontal rules full across, with full-length vertical bounding lines re-traced in thick red pen; single in the inner margin, and triple in the outer forming two narrow columns used to record the calendar and regnal year. Prickings in three outer margins (some trimmed). Chapter list, ff. 161–170v, (210 x 160–155) mm. 2 columns, 31 lines. Ruled in brown crayon, with the top two and bottom two horizontal rules full across; full-length vertical bounding lines, with two additional bounding lines inside and out, and four between the columns, forming narrow columns for the opening majuscules of each entry, and the numbers of the books and chapters.

Article 2, ff. 150v–160v (later hand): ff. 150v, 5 lines from bottom–152v, the quire was completed following the layout of the earlier scribe (see above); added quire, ff. 153–160v, (207–202 x 140–135) mm. 45–42 long lines. Ruled very lightly in lead (?); apparently frame ruled since only the top and bottom horizontal rules (full across) are visible; full-length vertical bounding lines, single in the inner margin, double in the outer; with an additional single bounding line in the far outer margin forming a column for the marginal comments.

Tightly bound, making accurate collation difficult: $1–2^{12}$ 3^{12} (–1, before f. 25, and –12, following f. 34, both with loss of text) 4^{12} (–1, before f. 35, with loss of text) $5–9^{12}$ 10^{12} (–1, before f. 106, with loss of text) $11–13^{12}$ 14^{12} (ff. 153–160v, added quire; structure uncertain; –9 through 12, following f. 160) 15^{10} (structure uncertain; ends imperfectly). Horizontal catchwords, bottom inside corner, in quires 1–7, boxed in red.

Written below the top line in a careful bastard anglicana script by numerous scribes; for example, changes of hand may be noted, mid f. 66, top f. 98, top f. 106v, f. 122, line 2, f. 126v, line 7 (previous hand then resumes), f. 141v, four from bottom, and mid f. 142. The continuation, ff. 150v–160v copied later in a cursive gothic bookhand.

Books and chapters begin with 2-line blue initials with red infilling and pen flourishes. Red rubrics and paragraph marks; chapter numbers boxed in red; majuscules within text stroked in red. Running titles in brown with the number of the book and chapter (boxed in red) on each opening. In the added quire, ff. 153–160v, chapters begin with blank spaces for 2-line initials; guide letters visible in the blank spaces.

Bound in England in 1904 by Douglas Cockerell (binder's monogram and date, inside back cover) in uncovered wood boards (front cracked) with a calf back, decoratively tooled. Title on spine in gilt, "Polychronicon, sec. 14–15." Two braided leather clasps, fastening back to front.

Written in England in the late fourteenth century; text continued and quire added, s. XV. Belonged, s. XV, to Thomas Baker and John Jalkyn<s?>: bottom margin, f. 169v, "I be the <ba..s?> be time Thomas baker and john jalkyn<s?>." Purchased from C. Howes, St. Leonards-on-Sea, England (*Catalogue of Ancient and Modern Books* no. 187; cf. bookseller's notations in pencil, front flyleaf, f. i verso) for £25, June 9, 1923 (Child Memorial Library; library stamp, front flyleaf, f. ii verso; bookplate, inside front cover).

secundo folio: [can]tilenis et gestibus (book 3, chapter 33; ed. 4:66, line 16)

Bibliography: De Ricci, 984; Phyllis W. Goodhart, "A Manuscript of the Polychronicon. Harvard: Widener Library MS Lat 116, saec. XIV, XV. Child Memorial Library," unpublished typescript, housed in library files.

MS Lat 117 — France s. XIV^{2}
Evangelium Nicodemi

1. ff. 1–22 *Hystoria nichodemi de passione christi.* [Prologue, copied as part of the main text] Factum est autem in anno nonagesimo imperii tiberii cesaris imperatoris romanorum . . . Theodosius autem magnus imperator fecit ea transferri de hebreo in latinum. [f. 1 text, part one, chapters 1–16] Annas et Cayphas, Symeon et datan, Gamaliel et Iudas, leui et neptalim, alexander et Iairus et reliqui iudeorum uenerunt ad pilatum . . . et illi tres uiri testificati sunt quod biderunt [*sic*] eum cum discipulis suis in montem olitueti et ascendentem in celum. [f. 13v, line 12 part 2, chapters 17–28] Exurgens autem Ioseph dixit principibus sacerdotum anne et cayphe vere bene admiramini quia audistis quod uisus est . . . posuitque omnia miracula hec in codicibus publicis pretorii sui. [f. 21 chapter 28] Post hec ingressus pilatus templum iudeorum

congregauit . . . A transmigratione babilonis usque ad incarnationem Ihesu christi anni quadringenti. Et fiunt simul anni quinquemilia et semis. [F. 22v blank, but ruled.]

Stegmüller 179,11 and 179,12 (*Evangelium Nicodemi* or *Gesta Pilati*, part 1, chapters 1–16), followed immediately by Stegmüller 179,18 (*Evangelium Nicodemi*, part 2, ch. 17–28, or *Descensus christi ad inferos*, ch. 1–12). Printed in Johannes Albertus Fabricius, *Codex Apocryphus Novi Testamenti, collectus, castigatus testimoniisque, censuris et animadversionibus illustratus*, 2nd ed. (Hamburg 1719) 1:238–298; in Johannes Carolus Thilo, *Codex Apocryphus novi testamenti. . . .* (Leipzig 1832) 1:495–795; and in H. C. Kim, ed., *The Gospel of Nicodemus. Gesta Salvatoris. Edited from the Codex Einsidlensis. Einsiedeln, Stiftsbibliothek MS 326.* Toronto Medieval Latin Texts 2 (Toronto 1973) 13–49; cf. also Constantinus Tischendorf, ed., *Evangelia Apocrypha* . . . (Leipzig 1853; 2nd. ed. 1876). This manuscript listed in Zbigniew Izydorczyk, *Manuscripts of the 'Evangelium Nicodemi': A Census.* Subsidia Mediaevalia 21 (Toronto 1993) 42, no. 62. Textual tradition, focussing on the early versions, discussed in: G. C. O'Cealliaigh, "Dating the Commentaries of Nicodemus," *The Harvard Theological Review* 56 (1963) 21–58.

F. 17 is a blank leaf, inserted later; text is continuous from ff. 16v–18.

In common with the late Latin recension found in Einsiedeln, Stiftsbibliothek, MS 326 (H. C. Kim, ed.; designated 'D' by O'Cealliaigh), our manuscript lacks the first half of the prologue found in earlier versions ("Ego Emaus [*sic*] Hebraeus qui eram legis doctor . . . Pax sit ista legentibus sanitas audientibus"; cf. Thilo, ed., 1:491–495). Unlike the Codex Einsidlensis, our manuscript lacks Pilate's letter to Claudius (Kim, ed., 49–50, as chapter 28), and includes a long chapter following chapter 27 (printed as chapter 28 in Thilo, ed. 1:789–795 and in Fabricius, ed., 1:295–298, incorrectly numbered as ch. 27 bis). Textually, our manuscript differs significantly from that printed by Kim, Thilo and Fabricius; for example: in chapter 5, following f. 5v, line 14, "Et nunc dimittite hominem istum non enim est dignum morte (Thilo ed, p. 555)," there is an interpolation, not found in the printed editons: "Forsitan iste ihesus venit missus a deo propheta sicut nobis dixit moyses patribus nostris prophetam . . ." (continuing through f. 5v, line 24); wording in chapter 7, beginning f. 6, line 13, differs significantly from the printed editions, and the woman with hemorrhage, identified as Veronica in most versions, is here unnamed; order of the Crucifixion narrative in chapter 10 (beginning f. 7v) differs from that of the printed editions, although the same names are used for the thieves in our manuscript and the Codex Einsidlensis, and in both manuscripts Longinus pierces Christ's side before He dies.

Professor Zbigniew Izydorczyk has kindly informed us that our manuscript contains the same version as the following manuscripts: Berlin, Deutsche Staatsbibliothek, MSS lat. theol. fol. 688 and 690; Cambridge, Corpus Christi College, MS 500; Cambridge, Trinity College, MS 1422; Hannover, Niedersächsische Landesbibliothek, MS 247; Poitiers, Bibliothèque Municipale, MS 425; and Troyes, Bibiliothèque Municipale, MS 1636. All of these manuscripts date the Passion "anno nonagesimo," and include the sentence, "Theodosius autem magnus imperator fecit ea transferri de hebreo in latinum" (cf. f. 1, line 12).

Parchment (moderate quality), ff. ii (paper) + 22 (modern foliation in pencil, top, outer corner) + ii (paper), 201 x 127 (161–60 x 90–84) mm. 30–29 long lines. Quickly ruled in lead with all horizontal rules full across; single full-length vertical bounding lines. Prickings in three outer margins.

$1\text{–}2^{8}$ 3^{6} (–6, cancelled, with no loss of text; + 1, f. 17, blank singleton inserted later before 1).

Written in a quick cursive bookhand, with looped 'h', 'd' and 'l', long 's' and 'f' extending below the line, and simple single-looped 'a'.

Text begins with 4-line plain red initial placed within the written space. Text copied without chapter divisions except for 2-line red initials, ff. 20, 20v and 21 (Thilo, ed., p. 781, chapter 27; p. 787, line 7; and p. 789, chapter 28). Red rubric, upper margin, f. 1.

Bound in smooth brown calf, s. XIX (ca. 1840?) in England for Walter Sneyd; front and back covers with Sneyd's monogram blind-stamped within a center ornament, and with simple blind-tooled rules; flat spine with "Evangelium Nicodemi MS Saec. XV" stamped in gold gothic letters; gilt edges; marbled end papers.

Written in France in the second half of the fourteenth century. This is a small-format, unpretentious copy of the text; leaves are dirty, but there are no readers' notes or other marginalia. Belonged to Michelet, s. XV; ex libris, ca. 1500, bottom margin, f. 1: "Ex-libris patris mei Michelet"; and later, s. XVIII to D'Azincourt (signature, bottom margin, f. 1). Belonged to the Reverend Walter Sneyd (1810?–1888; round bookplate, inside front cover, with his ex libris and coat of arms); Sneyd sale, London, Sotheby's, December 16, 1903, no. 546 to Maggs. Belonged to Hubert Greville Palmer (bookplate with his coat of arms, front flyleaf, f. i). Front flyleaf, f. i^{v}, printed description from an unidentified catalogue; below, erased note (a price?): "3/0/-," and in another hand: "Sol 12"; f. 1, in pencil: "104"; front flyleaf, f. ii^{v}: "Mcoblemus[?]". Purchased February 16, 1924 from R. Atkinson (Stephen Salisbury fund; bookplate, inside front cover; library stamp, f. ii^{v}). Modern marginal notes in pencil throughout, marking divisions into books and adding line numbers which do not correspond to any of the editions cited above.

secundo folio: saluator. Igitur

Bibliography: De Ricci, 984.

fMS Lat 119 — England s. XIII^{2}
Aristotle, Physica in Latin Translation, fragment

ff. 1–4v //esse et adhuc cuius recepcio est ut si uini uinum. . . . uacuum autem cum non sit aliquid et priuatio//

Two conjugate bifolia from Aristotle, *Physica*, book 4, chapters 5–11; probably in the "new" translation by Guillelmus de Moerbeka; on this translation, see *Aristoteles latinus. Codices*, 52 and 126–27, no. 17. Printed in the fifteenth century (*GKW* 2440–2443) and thereafter. Text continues from f. 1 through f. 4v with no breaks; cf. *Expositio Diui Thome Aquinatis Doctoris Angelici super octo libros Physicorum aristotelis cum duplici translatione Antiqua videlicet et Joannis Argiropyli* . . . (Venice 1535) beginning in this edition f. 43v, col. b, line 3 and ending f. 50v, col. a, 4 lines from the bottom (the text of this manuscript close to the text printed here as the "antiqua translatio"). This manuscript listed in *Aristoteles latinus. Codices*, 241, no. 10 and *Supplementa altera*, 48, no. 10.

Contemporary corrections in a script similar to the text script, usually supplying omitted words, or occasionally, omitted lines (cf. f. 3); marginal notes, usually brief corrections, in an anglicana script, ff. 1 and 2; longer notes in a pointed cursive script, cf. ff. 3 and 4v.

Parchment, 4 ff. removed from a binding, and stored flat as two separate bifolia, 226–207 x 162–147 mm., unevenly trimmed, (177–160 x 105–102) mm. 33–31 long lines. Ruled in lead; single full-length vertical bounding lines, and with an extra set of double rules, full across the top margin for running titles, left blank, except ff. 1 and 2, added in a later hand.

Written below the top line in a mature gothic bookhand.

Blank spaces for 2-line initials; guide letters in the margins.

Two bifolia from a manuscript written in England in the second half of the thirteenth century, which were used as the pastedowns in Harvard University, Houghton, Inc 5067, Aegidius Columna, *In Aristotelis De sophisticis elenchis commentum* and Iohannes Duns Scotus, *Quaestiones in Aristotelis Metaphysica* (Venice 1497) (see James Walsh, *A Catalogue of the Fifteenth-Century Printed Books in the Harvard University Library* [Binghamton, New York 1993] 2:396, no. 2330). Inscriptions, s. XV (?), ff. 1v and 2: "Johannes brissett," and ff. 1v and 4, "F. <K?>alkey"; other early inscriptions are erased and illegible, cf. ff. 1v and 4. Unidentified bookseller's note in pencil, f. 4: "1779/32007." Purchased May 27, 1926 from Davis and Orioli (Jackson Fund; library stamp, f. 3v).

Bibliography: De Ricci, 984; Kristeller, *Iter* 5:226.

MS Lat 120 — Italy (Northeast?) s. XV^{med}

Prosdocimo de' Beldomandi, Canones de motibus corporum supercoelestium

1. ff. i^{rv} and iv^{rv} Leaf from an Italian manuscript, s. XIV, of Alexander de Villa Dei, *Doctrinale*; ed. Dietrich Reichling, *Das Doctrinale des Alexander de Villa-Dei. Kritisch-Exegetische Ausgabe.* Monumenta Germaniae Paedagogica 12 (Berlin 1893); recto: f. i verso, with lines 878–89 and f. iv, with lines 891–98 (ed. pp. 59–60); verso

(quite faded, rubbed, and only partially legible): f. i, with lines 901–911, and f. iv verso, with lines 915–924 (ed., pp. 60–61; we thank Paul Meyvaert and Jan Ziolkowski for their help in identifying this text).

2. ff. ii–iii^v [Table of contents, added, s. XV^ex; f. ii, blank but ruled; f. ii^v, list of topics] Prologus in Tabulis ex Alphonso extractis, f. 41; Modum inueniendi Medius motus, f. 42, T. 2; . . . Quota feria intrat unusquisque mensis, f. 61, T. 40; [f. iii List of tables] Tabula Mediorum motuum in annis christi collectis per 28, f. 2; . . . Tabula feriarum mensium totius anni, f. 40. [F. iii^v blank.]

   References are to folio numbers that were also supplied in this hand.

3. ff. 1–39v [f. 1 blank, with later notes; f. 1v] *Tabula mediorum motuum. In annis christi Collectis per 28*; [ff.1v–2] *Tabula mediorum motuum. In annis christi expansis ab vnitate usque ad 28*; . . . *Tabula feriarum mensium totius anni.* [F. 40rv blank but ruled.]

   Prosdocimo de' Beldomandi, *Tabulae mediorum motuum, equationum, stationum et latitudinum planetarum, elevationis signorum, diuersitatis aspectus lunae, mediarum coniunctionum et oppositionum lunarium, feriarum, latitudinum climatum, longitudinum, et latitudinum ciuitatum*; Thorndike and Kibre, 1552; Antonio Favaro, "Intorno alla vita ed alle opere di Prosdocimo de' Beldomandi matematico padovano del secolo XV," *Bulletino di bibliografia e di storia delle scienze matematiche e fisiche publicato da B. Boncompagni* 12 (1879) 1–74; 115–251; listing seven manuscripts of this text, 206–208, including this manuscript, p. 207, when it was owned by Baldassarre Boncompagni. See also C. Vasoli, "Prosdocimo de Beldemandis," *DBI* 7:554 (not listing this manuscript).

   Calculations are for Padua (cf. f. 22v *Tabula mediarum coniunctionum luniarium ad annos collectos per 76 ad meridianum padue*) with corrections for Venice and Mantua (see f. 1v). On f. 26, the headings for a "Tabula equationis Solis" for the years 1494–1532 were added in the same hand as art. 2 and the foliation; the table itself was not completed.

4. ff. 41–60v [Title added in a later hand: *Prologus iacobi de dondis Paduani in Tabulis ex Alphonso Extractis.*] Facta et ordinata sunt

quam plura et varia tabularum ad celestes motus et de hiis quas vidi alique imperfecte sunt ... [f. 41v text] *Modum inveniendi medius motus.* Quemlibet medium motum per tabulam sibi appropriatam invenire. Queras primo annos perfectos in linea numeri annorum collectorum ... [f. 60v] *Qvota feria intrat vnusquisque mensis invenire.* Feria idem est quod dies ... Ianuarii usque ad locum bisexti scilicet usque ad festum mathei apostoli et secunda littera deseruit pro littera dominicali per totum annum siue per totum residuum anni. [Ends mid f. 60v; remainder blank.]

Prosdocimo de' Beldomandi, *Canones de motibus corporum supercoelestium*; Thorndike and Kibre, 549; Favaro, "Intorno alla vita ed alle opere di Prosdocimo de' Beldomandi," 187–206, listing eight manuscripts, 187–196, including our manuscript, pp. 194–96, when it was owned by B. Boncompagni. See also Vasoli, "Prosdocimo," *DBI* 7:553 (not listing this manuscript). Prologue printed in Enrico Narducci, *Catalogo di manoscritti ora posseduti da D. Baldassare Boncompagni, notabilmente accresciuta, contenente una descrizione di 249 manoscritti non indicati nella prima* ... (Rome 1892) 253–54, no. 415.

Prosdocimo mentions in his prologue that he used the tables of the earlier astronomer Jacopo Dondi (s. XIII), explaining the added heading which apparently ascribes this text to Jacopo in our manuscript; cf. Prague, Universitni Knihovna, MS 2436 (XIV.B.3) with the rubric, f. 2, *M. Prosdocimi de Peldemando* [*sic*] *Paduani Canones tabularum astronomicarum Jacobi de Dondis Paduani.* The year 1436 is mentioned in the prologue of our manuscript, f. 41, "Sit tempus in quo volo verificare locum alicuius planete anni christi 1436 ..."; cf. Lynn Thorndike, *A History of Magic and Experimental Science* (New York 1934) 4:79, note 49, noting that in the Prague manuscript, which was copied in 1454, the text is dated 1426.

Although there is no sign that this manuscript is itself imperfect, the text is incomplete; see Favaro, p. 196, note, comparing our text with the text in Bologna, Biblioteca Universitaria, MS 2284.

Parchment (prepared in the manner of southern Europe), ff. ii (modern paper, contemporary with binding) + i (early modern paper) + iv (earlier flyleaves, foliated i–iv; i, iv, parchment leaves from another manuscript, possibly once pastedowns; ii–iii, smaller format paper leaves) + 60 (fifteenth-century foliation in arabic numerals, top, outer corner) + ii (modern paper), 179 x 125 mm. Layout varies. Tables, ff. 1v–39v, written space (146–136 x 110–101) mm. Some tables are arranged horizontally, using the width of a two-page opening; others are arranged vertically on a single page. Ruled in red and black ink, with the top (occasionally top 2) and bottom rules full across; single vertical bounding lines, with the outer bounding line usually full length. Each page was first ruled in a grid pattern in light brown ink with 44–43 horizontal lines, and 32–31 vertical lines; the scribe then used dark brown and red ink to create the columns he needed for each table. Prickings remain, top, bottom, and occasionally outer margin (cf. ff. 21–26). Text, ff. 41–60v, written space (114–111 x 82–80) mm. 34–31 long lines. Ruled in dry point (?) very lightly; no ruling visible on most folios, but cf. ff. 52v–53, apparently frame ruled with all bounding lines full-length. Prickings, ff. 42v, 47 and 48, top and bottom outer margins (for vertical bounding lines).

$1–6^{10}$. First leaves of quires two and four numbered in early arabic numerals, bottom outer corner (see ff. 11 and 31).

Written in a cursive gothic bookhand influenced by humanistic script, probably on the top line; opening lines of each section copied in a larger script; tables copied in arabic numerals.

Two-line red initials at the beginning of sections within the text; majuscules at the beginning of sentences dotted or slashed with red; some use of red paragraph marks; red rubrics. Five-line black initial, f. 41, and paragraph marks in dark brown ink, added.

Bound in brown calf, s. XX, probably in the United States for Robert Willson. Front flyleaves, ff. i and iv, likely from an earlier binding: leaf from an Italian manuscript, s. XIV, folded and positioned so the text now runs vertically to the main text; f. i, 175 x 108–105, f. iv, 175 x 123; original dimensions approximately 228–225 x 175 mm. (top margin, now outer margin, f. i, trimmed), written space approximately (168 [90 + 78] x 90–85) mm. 22 lines of verse (originally with 23 lines). Written in a rounded gothic bookhand, with notes in an informal running script.

Written in Italy, likely in Northeastern Italy, in the middle of the fifteenth century (date suggested in Bond and Faye is incorrect, since the table, f. 26, is a later addition). Note, s. XV (?), f. 1: "Quidam tabule astrologia, 43"; early modern notes in Italian, in pen, f. iv. Belonged to Baldassarre Boncompagni (1821–1894); see Narducci, *Catalogo* (Rome 1892) 253–54, no. 415 (cited above, art. 4) and Favaro, 194–196, note 1, and 207; the manuscript has been rebound and refoliated since it was described by Favaro (the last five front flyleaves were once foliated I–V; a back flyleaf, once foliated f. 61, is now missing; the first two front flyleaves and two back flyleaves are additions that are contemporary with the present binding). Boncompagni sale, February 12, 1898; see *Catalogo della Biblioteca Boncompagni, parte prima contenente Manoscritti, Facsimili, Edizioni del Secolo XV* ... (Rome 1898), no. 371. Unidentified dealer's note, front flyleaf, in pencil, written diagonally, f. iii^{v}: "5864/59." Belonged to Robert Wheeler Willson (1853–1922), Harvard professor of astronomy; presented to Harvard, January 12, 1927 (library book plate, inside front cover; library stamp, front flyleaf, preceding f. i).

secundo folio: [text, f. 42] scribe sub

Bibliography: Bond and Faye, 236; Kristeller, *Iter* 5:227.

fMS Lat 121 — Austria 1433; s. XV^{1}

Miscellany — Pls. 4, 5

I. Speculum humanae saluationis — Austria 1433

1. ff. 1–56 [f. 1 Summary of chapters] *Incipit speculum humane saluationis.* Incipit prohemium cuiusdam noue compilacionis cuius nomen et titulus est speculum humane saluacionis. Expediens videtur et vtile quod primo in hoc prohemio ponatur de quibus materiis et hystoriis in quolibet capitulo dicatur ... In capitulo primo agitur de casus luciferi et suorum seciorum ... si sciunt hystorias possunt de ipso prohemio predicare. *Explicit prohemium* [*corr.*^{1}*: prothema*]. [f. 4 prologue] *Sequitur prohemium.* Ad iustitiam erudiunt multos/ ... [f. 4] Abbatia quedam quercum valde magnum in se stantem/ ... Proximos edificet et gratos [*sic*] tibi faciat. [f. 5 text] *De casu luciferi de formacione ade et eue et de dignitate eorum.* Incipt speculum humane saluacionis de [*sic*] quo patet casus hominis et modus reparacionis/ ... Quod nobis omnibus prestare dignetur dominus ihesus christus/ Qui cum patre et spiritu sancto

est in perpetuum benedictus. Amen. *Et sic est finis. Deo gratias. Explicit speculum humane saluacionis sub anno domini 1433 in sancti iohannis baptiste.* [Text ends mid col. a; remainder blank; ff. 56v–60v blank, but ruled.]

J. Lutz and P. Perdrizet, eds., *Speculum humanae salvationis* (Mulhouse and Leipzig 1907) 1:2–99, not printing the chapter summary, and listing 200 Latin manuscripts pp. lx–xvii, not including this one; Evelyn Silber, *The Early Iconography of the "Speculum Humanae Salvationis"; the Italian Connection in the Fourteenth Century*, unpublished Ph.D. dissertation, Cambridge University (1982) listing this manuscript, p. 98 (Appendix, no. 364); cf. also Adrian Wilson and Joyce Lancaster Wilson, *A Medieval Mirror. Speculum humanae salvationis 1324–1500* (Berkeley, Los Angeles and London 1984) 42–43, and figs. II-16–II-18, discussing Houghton, MS Typ 50, incorrectly identified as Houghton, MS Lat 121.

Divided into numerous unnumbered chapters and smaller sections, each beginning with subject headings in red. Although this is a text in verse, it is here copied continuously in two columns in the manner of a prose text with the beginning letter of each verse stroked in red.

II. Was ist Adel — Austria s. XV^{1}

2. ff. 61–65 *Was ist Adel.* Adel ist stëte gotleiche vnd Bruderleiche lieb. Adel ist volkomne tugent in aller gesthesst gotes micht allain in den menschen ... Auch ritter machn wye wol sy nicht. Ritter sein ist[?] <?>. [Ff. 65v–71v blank but ruled.]

Alphons Lhotsky, *Quellenkunde zur mittelalterlichen Geschichte Österreichs.* Mitteilungen des Instituts für Österreichische Geschichtsforschung, Ergänzungsband 19 (Graz and Cologne 1963) 352, listing this manuscript as MS Seitenstetten 31; printed in Franz Krones, *Kleine Beiträge zur mittelalterlichen Quellenkunde.* Mitteilungen des Instituts für Österreichische Geschichtsforschung 7 (1886) 260 sq. (not available for consultation). Divided into 17 unnumbered chapters.

III. The Golden Bull and other texts — Austria s. XV^{1}

3. ff. 71 bis–87v *Aurea bulla.* In nomine sancte et indiuidue trinitatis feliciter amen. Karulus [*sic*] quartus diuina fauente clementia

romanorum imperator semper augustus et bohemie rex, ad perpetuam rei memoriam. Omne regnum in se diuisum desolabitur. . . . et tunc demum ad premissa procedat seu quodlibet premissorum. [f. 83v] *Alie constitucionum.* Infra scripte leges promulgate sunt in curia Mentensi [*sic*] per dominum karolum quatum [*corr.*[2]: quartum] romanorum imperatorum et bohemie regem augustum. Anno domini millesimo trecentesimo quinqagesimo sexto omnibus sibi assistentibus sacri imperii romani electoribus . . . quorum conuersacione pariter et doctrina in linguis ualeant erudiri. *Explicit aurea bulla. Hic est finis auree bulle.*

Wolfgang D. Fritz, ed., *Bulla aurea Karoli IV Imperatoris anno MCCCLVI promulgata.* Fontes iuris germanici antiqui in usum scholarum ex monumentis germaniae historicis separatim editi (Weimar 1972) 44–79 ("Die Nürnberger Gesetzbuch vom 10. Januar 1356") and 80–90 ("Die Metzer Gesetze vom 25. Dezember 1356"); this manuscript not listed.

Divided into unnumbered sections, each beginning with a rubric; divisions and rubrics do not always correspond to those in this edition; for example: f. 71v Qualis debeat conductus electorum a quibus (ed., p. 46, ch. 1); f. 72 De electione regis romanorum (ed. p. 47, section 3, line 23, no division); f. 74v De iuramento electorum (ed., p. 53, ch. 2 "De electione Romanorum regis"); f. 75 De sessionibus electorum spiritualium (ed. p. 56, ch. 3 "De sessione Treverensis, Coloniensis et Maguntinensis archiepiscoporum"); f. 75v De principibus electoribus et aliis in communi (ed. p. 57, ch. 4); divisions and headings generally agree thereafter, until the end of the Golden Bull (f. 83v), but note, f. 77v "De regis bohemie et regnicularum eius priuilegio libertatis" (ed. p. 62, ch. 8 "de regis Boemie et regnicularum eius immunitate"); f. 78v "de libertate principum electorum et suorum regnicularum" (ed., p. 66, ch. 11, "de immunitate principum electorum"); and f. 83, col. a, line 25, no division (cf. ed., p. 77, ch. 21). The interpolation in chapter 11 (ed. p. 67, lines 18–29), is found in this manuscript (see f. 79v, col. a, lines 9–33). The divisions and rubrics, ff. 83v–87v, often do not correspond to those in this edition.

4. ff. 87v–96v *De ordine et forma coronacionis et vnccione regis et regine Romanorum.* Ad consecrandum seu coronandum Regem alemanie hoc modo procedat primo in ecclesia Aquensi sit indutus plenis

pontificalibus dominus archiepiscopus Coloniensii . . . [*De unctione regine*] . . . vnde tibi in perpetuum placere valeat in regione uiuorum. [f. 91v written in the margin, *Prophecia*] Lectio ysaie prophete surge illuminare ierusalem quia uenit lucem tuum et gloria domini sumpte <no?>ta est . . . Omnis de salia veniet aurum et thus deferentes et laude domino anuncciantem [*sic*]. [f. 91v rubric lacking] Collacio facta per dominum theodericum de monasteriis sacre theologie doctorem coram serenissimo principe dominus [*sic*] <S?> Romanum et ungarie etc. Rege in magna aula regali Colonie . . . xix die Nouembris Anno etc. Quadrigencesimo XIIII . . . et in terra deus omnium dominus in secula benedictus. [f. 93v rubric lacking] O rex sit tue maiestati semper <re?>commendata uniuersitas studii Coloniensii . . . Amen. Et regia maiestas michi paupercule clerico de hac in culto multiloquio. [f. 94] *Sequitur alia collacio.* Collacio facta per dominum Johannem de nouo lapide legum doctorem in coronatione illustrissimi principis domini Sigismundi Romanii Regis celebrata Aquensi[?] Anno ad XIIII [in the margin: 1414] mensis nouembris die octaua. Ad honorem et laudem dei omnipotentis eterni regis cuius prouidencia sacrum imperium gubernata bella iusta per aguntur . . . que est rex regum dominus dominancium deus super omnia benedictus. Amen. [f. 96v] *Sequitur Rubrica Capituly primum. Qualis debet esse conductus electorum et a quibus.* De elecione regis romani . . . De benedictoribus archiepiscoporum.

Divided into sections including: De iuramento regis; De vnccione regis; De tradicione gladii; De armilo [*sic*] regali; De corona regali; De professione regis romanorum; De coronatione regine; and De unctione regine.

5. ff. 96v–97 [rubric lacking; introduction; *Iuramento cessionis Iohannis pape xxii*] Cardinalis florensium [*sic*] legit illam cedulari. In nomine domini nostri ihesu christi amen. Sanctissiums dominus noster papa hic presens quamquam nullis notis. Iuramentis et promissionibus ab infra scripta . . . cuius tenor per omnia sequitur in hec verba. [f. 97] *Iuramento cessionis Iohannis pape.* Ego Iohannes papa xxii propter quidem populi christiani profiteor . . . et uniuersitates Parisiensii Orliensi Ammonencii Oxoniensii et Montispessalencii.

6. f. 97 *Sequentes articulos obtuli frater Johannes Valkenberg ordinis*

predicatorum magister in sacra pagina. De polonia <domine?> Rege Romanorum et Vngarie; Nec gregorium <amice?> suo nec benedictum suo si quod alter eorum ad papatum habent . . .; . . . deuoti existant. *Et sic est finis.* [Ff. 97v column b–100v, blank.]

Short list of fourteen articles.

IV. Historia de preliis alexandri magni (recension J^2) Austria 1433

7. ff. 101–148v *Incipit hystoria magni Alexandri Regis Macedonie viri dilectissimi ac potentissimi.* Sapientissimi namque egipcii scrutantes mensuram terre atque vndas maris denumerantes . . . defunctus est secunda die stante mensis martii. Fabricauit ciuitates xii que actenus habitantur. Igitur magnus Allexander [*sic*] trementem sub se mundum ferro pressit. Principes vero eius post mortem ipsius infra xiiii annos dilaniaverunt et uelud optimam predam magno leone prostratam rapaces discerpere catuli id est se ipsos inuicem mutatos in rixam prede emulatione fregerunt, etc. Et sic est finis. *Explicit hystoria magni Alexandri Imperatoris sub anno domini 1433 in uigilia ascensionis.*

Alfons Hilka, ed., prepared for the press by Hans-Josef Bergmeister, *Historia Alexandri Magni (Historia de Preliis) Rezension J^2 (Orosius-Rezension).* Beiträge zur klassischen Philologie 79 and 89 (Meisenheim am Glan 1976, 1977) two volumes, here ending vol. 2, p. 200, sec. 130, line 9 (p. 200, lines 9–15 omitted), and ending with nine lines not included in the edition; listing this manuscript, vol. 1, p. 15* and vol. 2, p. XV, as no. 33, 'S(H)' (using older incorrect foliation, ff. 103–150v).

Text divided into sections; ff. 101–103, introduced by long subject headings in red; blank spaces left for rubrics thereafter; divisions and headings do not correspond to those used in the Hilka and Bergmeister ed., but they are included in the critical apparatus of the text printed in Oswald Zingerle, *Die Quellen zum Alexander des Rudolf von Ems. Im Anhange: Die Historia de preliis.* Germanistische Abhandlungen 4 (Breslau 1885; reprint Hildesheim and New York 1977) 129–265, listing this manuscript, p. 20, as 'S', Codex Seitenstettensis XXXI (ff. 103 sq.).

Occasional contemporary readers' notes in the margin, for example, f. 8: "nota tactus," "amor," "nota pietas," etc. Most of col. b, f. 114v, was left blank where the ink from the recto bled through; the scribe noted: "Propter defluxum papiri dimisi locum hunc vaccuum. Sed nullus defectus hic est."

See also, Hermann-Josef Bergmeister, *Die Historia de preliis Alexandri Magni (Der lateinische Alexanderroman des Mittelalters); Synoptische Edition der Rezensionen des Leo Archipresbyter und der interpolierten Fassungen* J^1, J^2, J^3, *Buch 1 and 2.* Beiträge zur klassischen Philologie 65 (Meisenheim am Glan 1975), listing this manuscript as 'S', p. XIIIb (ff. 103–150v); Francis Peabody Magoun, Jr., *The Gests of King Alexander of Macedon* (Cambridge, Mass. 1929) 56–59, esp. p. 57, note 4, and p. 63, note 3; A. Hilka and F. P. Magoun, "A List of Manuscripts Containing Texts of the *Historia de preliis Alexandri Magni*, Recensions I^1, I^2, I^3," *Speculum* 9 (1934) 84–86, listing this manuscript, p. 85, as 'S(H)' (ff. 103–150v); Alfons Hilka, ed., *Der Altfranzösische Prosa-Alexanderroman nach der Berliner Bilderhandschrift nebst dem Lateinischen Original der Historia de preliis (Rezension* J^2*)* (Halle 1920; reprint Geneva 1974) listing this manuscript p. xxiv, no. 8, as 'S' (Seitenstetten, Stiftsbibl. XXXI, f. 103 sq.). This recension also discussed (but this manuscript not listed) in Fr. Pfister, "Die Historia de preliis und das Alexanderepos de Quilichinus," *Münchener Museum für Philologie des Mittelalters und der Renaissance* 1 (1912) 251–252, and David J. A. Ross, *Alexander Historiatus. A Guide to Medieval Illustrated Alexander Literature.* Beiträge zur klassischen Philologie 186 (Franfurt am Main 1988) 53–54.

A composite manuscript, assembled from four parts: paper (watermarks listed below), ff. i (paper, marbled on recto) + i (unnumbered early modern [?] paper, with watermark, scissors) + 149 (modern foliation, in pencil, bottom, inside margin, with f. 71 bis [cited]; earlier foliation, top, outer corner, verso, in ink in early arabic numerals, as follows: 13–72 [= ff. 1–60; ff. 61–65, unfoliated], 73–102 [= ff. 71 bis–100], 103–150 [= ff. 101–148]) + i (early modern [?] paper) + i (paper, marbled on verso), 286 x 205 mm.

I. 1–5^{12} (through f. 60v) II. 6^{12} (–9, following f. 68, cancelled with no loss of text; through f. 71) III. 7–8^{12} 9^{6} (through 100v) IV. 10–13^{12} (ff. 101–148v). Quires 1–5 reinforced in the middle with parchment strips from an earlier manuscript; quires 8 and 10–12, reinforced with blank parchment strips around the outer bifolia.

I. ff. 1–60v: paper (watermark, similar to Piccard Ochsenkopf XII.210–211, Heidelberg, Munich and Kassel, 1432–33), written space, (210 x 155–147) mm., ruled space, 213–206 x 148–147 mm. Frame ruled in dark-brown ink, with all rules full length. 2 columns, 39–37 lines.

$1–5^{12}$. Horizontal catchwords in the first 4 quires, bottom inside margin, extending into the gutter; reinforced with parchment strips in the center.

Written in a gothic bookhand approaching hybrida script, with two forms of 'd', with and without loops, long straight 's' and 'f' extending below the line, without loops, and simple tear-drop 'a'; words continued on the next line are marked "2" in the margin, possibly by a corrector.

Thirteen-line dull-orange initial, f. 1, placed outside the text space, with red and blue pen decoration including simple floral motifs, with a profile of a face sketched in red at the bottom of the initial; plain 4-line dull-orange initial, f. 4 (beginning prologue). Remaining initials, 3- to 2-line, placed within the text space (except 'I', up to 13 lines) alternating red or dull-orange and blue, often extending into decorative terminals; initials are plain, or with simple pen and wash decoration in the other color. Red rubrics; majuscules within the text slashed with red. Guide letters visible within the initials.

II. ff. 61–71v: paper (watermark, similar to Briquet Monts 11876, Palermo, 1437), written space, (185 x 135–133) mm. 27 long lines. Frame ruled very lightly in lead, probably several pages at once, leaving lead on the top sheet, and impressions on the remaining sheets, with the rules extending past the text space, but not to the outer edge.

One quire of 12 ($=6^{12}$), with the ninth leaf cancelled, with no loss of text.

Written in a slanting cursive gothic bookhand, with 'd' and 'h' written with and without loops, looped 'b' and 'l', simple tear-drop 'a', and long 'f' and 's' extending below the line.

Six- to 3-line red initials, decoratively shaped, a few parted red and brown, all set within the text space. Red rubrics; majuscules within the text stroked with red. Guide letter visible, f. 61, alongside the initial.

III. ff. 71 bis–100v: paper (watermark, similar to Piccard Ochsenkopf XII.313, Redsyn and Thorn, 1429–1433, and XII.314, Nuremberg, 1409), written space, (215–212 x 145–143) mm. 2 columns, 37–36 lines. Frame ruled in ink, with all rules full-length.

Three quires ($7–8^{12}\ 9^{6}$).

Written below the top line by one scribe in a flowing cursive gothic bookhand, with loops.

Four- to 3-line red initials, decoratively shaped; opening initial, f. 71 bis, with amateur pen decoration in red and brown. Red rubrics; majuscules within text slashed with red.

IV. ff. 101–148: paper (watermark, unidentified Bell), written space, (224–218 x 147–145) mm. 2 columns, 39–37 lines. Frame ruled in dark-brown ink, with all rules full-length.

Four quires of 12 ($10–13^{12}$).

Written in a cursive gothic bookhand; 'd' written with and without loops; looped 'h', 'b' and 'l', simple tear-drop 'a', and long 's' and 'f' extending below the line.

Five-line red initial, f. 101, drawn in outline, with decorative motifs within the body of the initial; sections within the text begin with 3- to 1-line red initials (except 'I', up to 7 lines) decoratively shaped, within the text space; a few 1-line red initials within the line of text. Red rubrics, ff. 101–103; blank spaces for rubrics thereafter. Capitals within the text stroked with red.

Bound in Austria, s. XVIII, in mottled calf; spine with six raised bands, gilt ornaments and title, "Speculum Humanae Salutis [*sic*]; Aurla [*sic*] Bulla; Vita Alexandri Magni."

A composite manuscript, made up of four manuscripts copied in Austria, s. XV^{1} (parts I and IV are dated, 1433; see ff. 60v and 148v; part III must date after 1414, since it includes a sermon from that year; see f. 97), and brought together at an early date. Early foliation in ink, top outer corner, verso, indicates that the first text may have once been preceded by another text, since it begins with f. 13; this foliation also omits the present ff. 61–65, although this text seems to have been included in the manuscript from an early date. F. 1, top margin, "facultatis philosophica vienna, 1686." Later owned by the Benedictine monastery at Seitenstetten (founded 1109; O.S.B. 1116; diocese of Passau), where it was MS 31 in their library (cf. list of contents, s. XVIII, glued on the front flyleaf, f. ii). Acquired by E. P. Goldschmidt from Seitenstetten (Goldschmidt Cats. XI, no. 355 and XIII [1928], no. 90; not available for consultation); letter from Goldschmidt to A. C. Potter, librarian, Harvard College, February 22, 1928, glued on front flyleaf, f. ii, states that Goldschmidt acquired the manuscript from "an agent who does a great deal of buying in Austrian monasteries," and assuring Potter that the export of the manuscript was legal. Dealers' annotations in pencil include, f. 56, "#9125"; f. 65v, "#9127"; f. 97v, "#9126"; and f. 148, "#9128"; in another hand, in pencil, top margin, f. 101: "RE 1/RE-," and front flyleaf, f. ii^r: "£27.10/RE/RE/-," and in another hand (?) "A4 X1/ 355"; and back flyleaf, recto, in pencil: "2402/RNW-, 2403/RNW-, and 2404/RNW-." Purchased, February 8, 1928 from Goldschmidt (Child Memorial Library; library bookplate, inside front cover).

secundo folio: I. (f. 2) capitulo agitur; II. (f. 62) Adel und; III. (f. 72) cum personis; IV. (f. 102) Interea phylippus

Bibliography: De Ricci, 984.

MS Lat 122 — Germany s. XV

Extracts from Historia de preliis Alexandri Magni (recension J^2), and Godefridus de Viterbo, Pantheon

1. ff. 1–6 Legitur in hystoria magni alexandri regis quod Alexander subiugata sydone castra metatus est ibi super ciuitatem tyrum . . . Nota Alexander fecit cornu eneum artificio mirali [*sic*] fabricatum quo ex lx. miliaris suum [*sic*] exercitum connouerit . . . Et ego credo quod multa metallorum resonantium genera in eius conponere concurrebant. *Hec pauca ex hystoria magni Alexandri collecta sufficiant.*

   Extracts from the *Historia de preliis Alexandri Magni* (J^2 recension); Alfons Hilka, ed., prepared for the press by H.-J. Bergmeister and Rüdiger Grossmann, *Historia Alexandri Magni (Historia de preliis) Rezension J^2 (Orosius - Rezension)*. Beiträge zur klassischen Philologie 79, 89 (Meisenheim am Glan 1976, 1977), listing this manuscript 1:17* and 2:XVII, no. 40, as 'h'.

   Text as follows: [f. 1–f. 1v, line 12] ed. 1:78, line 4–1:86, line 24; [f. 1v, line 13] Et hic nota uersus magistri galtheri quos ponit in libro alexandreidos libro i^o c. vlt. 'At si me tibi forte vides occurrere talem./ Parce meis inquam superasque evasit in auras./

Discedensque domum miro perfudit odore' [Marvin Colker, ed., *Galteri de Castellione, Alexandreis*, ed. Marvin Colker. Thesaurus mundi. Bibliotheca scriptorum latinorum mediae et recentioris aetatis 17 (Padua 1978) 34, lines 534–536]; [f. 1v, lines 16–29] ed. 1:86, line 25–1:88, line 38; [f. 1v, line 30–f. 2, line 23] 1:216, line 11–ed. 2:6, line 24; ed. 2:8, lines 25–26; ed. 2:8, lines 36–37; ed. 2:8, line 40–2:10, line 41; [f. 2, line 24–f. 3, line 10] ed. 2:112, sec. 104, line 1–2:122, line 51; [f. 3, lines 11–23] ed. 2:148, sec. 113, line 1–2:150, sec. 113, line 5; ed. 2:150, sec. 113, lines 13–18; [f. 3, lines 24–29] ed. 2:150, sec. 114, line 1–2:152, sec. 114, line 2; ed. 2:152, sec. 115, lines 1–3; [f. 3, line 30–f. 4, line 17] ed. 2:156, sec. 115, line 24–2:168, sec. 119, line 23; [f. 4, lines 18–26] ed. 2:168, sec. 120, lines 1–9; [f. 4, line 26 – f. 4v, line 14] ed. 1:40, sec. 14, line 1–1:46, sec. 16, line 3; [f. 4v, lines 15–22] ed. 2:168, sec. 119, lines 25–26; ed. 2:170, sec. 122, lines 1–5; [f. 4v, line 23–f. 5, bottom line] ed. 2:36, sec. 85, lines 1–9; ed. 2:38, sec. 86, lines 13–14; ed. 2:40, sec. 86, lines 27–29; "Milites vero eius alii lingebant ferrum alii bibebant oleum alii ad talem necessitatem veniebant quod vrinam bibebant [unidentified]."; ed. 2:40, sec. 87, lines 1–2; ed. 2:42, sec. 87, line 6–2:48, sec. 87, line 42; [f. 5v, lines 1–7] ed. 2:50, sec. 89, lines 1–2; ed. 2:52, line 19; ed. 2:54, lines 31–2; [f. 5v, lines 8–20] ed. 2:54, sec. 91, line 11–ed. 2:56, sec. 91, line 21; ed. 2:56, sec. 92, lines 3–8; [f. 5v, line 21–bottom line] ed. 2:60, sec. 94, lines 1–7; ed. 2:60, sec. 95, lines 1–13; "Predictam ab illa parte supra. Nunciatum est alexandro quod habetur in folio precedenti ordina supra ante illud in 2° folio ad tale signum⊙—In yndia autem rex alexander etc. [cf. f. 2]"; [f. 6, line 1] ed. 2:168, sec. 119, lines 25–26; ed. 2:170, sec. 122, lines 1–5; ed. 2:170, sec. 123, lines 1–3; ed. 2:172, sec. 123, lines 6–11; [f. 6, line 12] cf. ed. 2:198, sec. 130, lines 1–6; [f. 6, line 13 to end] unidentified.

On the J^2 recension, see also H.-J. Bergmeister, *Die Historia de preliis Alexandri Magni (Der lateinische Alexanderroman des Mittelalters). Synoptische Edition der Rezension des Leo Archipresbyter und der interlopierten Fassungen J^1, J^2, J^3 (Buch 1 and 2)*. Beiträge zur klassischen Philologie 65 (Meisenheim am Glan 1975) viii.b–x.a; Francis Peabody Magoun, Jr., *The Gests of King Alexander of Macedon. Two Middle-English Alliterative Fragments Alexander A and Alexander B* ... (Cambridge, Massachusetts 1929) 56–59, this manuscript mentioned p. 57, note 3; A. Hilka and F. P. Magoun, "A List of Manuscripts Containing Texts of the *Historia de preliis Alexandri Magni*, Recensions I^1, I^2, I^3," *Speculum* 9 (1934) 84–86 (not listing this manuscript); Alfons Hilka, ed., *Der Altfranzösische Prosa-Alexanderroman nach der Berliner Bilderhandschrift nebst dem lateinischen Original der Historia de preliis (Rezension J^2)* (Halle 1920; reprint, Geneva 1974); Fr. Pfister, "Die Historia de preliis und das Alexanderepos des Quilichinus," *Münchener Museum für Philologie des Mittelalters und der Renaissance* 1 (1912) 251–2; and David J. A. Ross, *Alexander Historiatus. A Guide to Medieval Illustrated Alexander Literature.* Beiträge zur klassischen Philologie 186 (Franfurt am Main 1988) 53–54 (this manuscript mentioned in passing, p. 54).

2. ff. 6–8v [f. 6rv first extract] *Nota uersus de libro pantheorum* [*sic*] *magistrum Godefridus viterbiensis.* [R]ex erat yndorum sub eodem tempore porus/ Climata regnorum tenuit 30 duorum/ . . . Et reliqui libri dent potiora tibi [Ends near the bottom, f. 6v; remainder blank] . . . [f. 7v fourth extract] *De sibillis.* [S]ibille generaliter omnes femine dicuntur prophetantes que ob diuinam voluntantem hominibus interpretari . . . In aliis uero regionibus tribulationes multe erunt et prelia. Tunc exurget//

Extracts from Godfrey of Viterbo, *Pantheon de universo veteri et novo testamento*; Stegmüller 2610; Georgius Waitz, ed., *Gotifredi Viterbiensis Opera.* Monumenta Germaniae Historica. Scriptores 22 (Hanover 1872; reprint, Stuttgart and New York 1963) 107–307 and Ioannes Pistorius, *Germanicorum scriptorum qui rerum a germanis per multas aetates gestarvm historias vel annales posteris reliquerunt* (Frankfurt 1584) tomus alter: 5–580.

Text as follows: text begins Pistorius ed., chronica, pars xi, col. 227, line 30–col. 229, line 4; cf. MGH ed., p. 147; this section not printed; [f. 7 second extract] Iulianus imperator et apostata regnauit anno domini 365 [sic]. Hic <ciore?> mortis Constancii patris sui. Primus monachus factus aquadam . . . Igitur imperator factus christianos grauiter afflixit [some relationship to MGH ed., part xxii, p. 179, lines 8–28; and to Pistorius ed., part 16, col. 390–1]. Item secundum pictagoram dicebat in se spiritum magni alexandri requieuisse . . . kathedram sibi ad imperium romanorum parari, etc. [MGH ed., part xxii, p. 179, lines 30–51; Pistorius, ed., pt.

16, 391–2]; [f. 7, last four lines, third extract; continuing in the same hand, smaller script] Iste Iulianus priscianum grammaticum a fide christi peruertens. Sed secundum donatum peruertens non ualens patrem et matrem illius occidit. Iste donatus episcopus libellum conposuit quem pueri legunt in scolis que uiuis et mortuis miraculis multis corsicans martiro coronatus est. 7° Idus Augusti [unidentified]; [f. 7v fourth extract] text ends abruptly, Pistorius ed., pars x, col. 214–18, line 40; cf. MGH ed., p. 145; this section not printed.

Paper (rough, pronounced chain lines, unidentified watermark hidden in gutter and obscured by script), ff. 8 (modern foliation, in pencil, upper, outside corner), 211 x 143 (165–160 x 120–114) mm., margins trimmed with some loss of marginalia; script often extends past ruled lines so lines may measure up to 120 mm. Ruled in ink, with single full-length vertical bounding lines only. 40–35 long lines, except art. 2 in two columns, with additional double vertical bounding lines between the columns. No prickings.

Single quire of eight, with 8, f. 8, detached. Reinforced with parchment strip from another manuscript in the center; remains of narrow strip of paper and glue around the outer leaves, inner margin.

Written by one scribe in a current gothic text hand, with long 's' extending below the line, and with loops.

Sections within art. 1 begin with informal 1-line initials in brown ink, presumably by the scribe; otherwise blank-spaces remain for 2- to 1-line initials; guide letters for initials, inner margins.

Last leaf detached; fragile and cracking along parchment reinforcement; some pages with water damage (ff. 1v, 2, 2v).

Now unbound; described by De Ricci as bound in modern white vellum; earlier described as bound in boards (Goldschmidt Cat. 15).

Written in Germany in the fifteenth century. Presumably once part of a longer manuscript since the text ends abruptly. No dealers' notes or other marks of ownership. Purchased September 15, 1928 (Child Memorial Library) from E. P. Goldschmidt (Cat. 15, 1928, no. 2).

secundo folio: partibus orientis

Bibliography: De Ricci, 985.

MS Lat 124 Italy (Florence) s. XV$^{2/4}$; s. XV$^{3/4}$
Humanist Anthology: Translations and Other Texts Pls. 47, 48

1. f. 4v [table of contents; ff. 1–4 blank] In hoc volumine continetur Decreta Atheniensium Nonnulla; Epistola Eschinis Ad Atheniensis; . . . Ovidii Epistola Noviter Reperta; Philippi Regis Epistola Ad Athenienses.

   Copied in Roman capitals; entries are unnumbered and arranged continuously on the page; contents listed out of order (arts. 2, *4–15, *3) since the scribe omitted art. 3 and then added it at the end.

2. ff. 5–18 [Rinuccio Aretino da Castiglione, *De decretis Atheniensium*; prologue] *Rynucius Poggio suo Oratori Eximio felicitatem.* Ille rem optimam et sibi salutarem facere dicendus iure uidetur suauissime mi Poggi . . . inter que epistola quedam iisdem de rebus sigillatim non de nihilo inserui. [f. 7 text] *Decretum Demostenis.* Mnesiphilo preside, Aprilis prima intrantis trybu paridionide prerogatiuam sortitia, Demostenes Demostenis peanieus dixit . . . At in vita nemini datur effugere fatum. *Finis.* [F. 18v blank.]

   Prologue and opening and closing sections of the text ed. in Dean P. Lockwood, "De Rinucio Aretino graecarum litterarum interprete," *Harvard Studies in Classical Philology* 24 (1913) 84–86, this manuscript listed as 'H', Harvard 25. Bertalot 9309 and 12189, listing this manuscript. The text is dedicated to Poggio Bracciolini, and this may be the dedicatory copy.

   Infrequent marginal notes in another formal hand (proper names ocurring in the text), ff. 6, 8v, 14.

3. ff. 19–24 [Anaximenes of Lampsacus, (Ps. Philip of Macedon), *Epistola ad Athenienses,* tr. Leonardo Bruni Aretino] *Rex Macedonum Philippus Atheniensium Senatui plebique Salutem, traducta per leonardum aretinum.* Quoniam persepe iam legatos misi . . . et diis testibus inuocatis pro rebus meis pugnabo.

   No printed edition; see Baron, *Leonardo Bruni Aretino,* 171, no. 8, and 178, listing three manuscripts, not including this one.

4. ff. 24–26v [Aeschines, *Epistola senatui populoque Atheniensi,* tr. Leonardo Bruni Artetino] *Eschines atromiti senatui populoque athe-*

niensi salutem. Ego me ad rem publicam contuli . . . magis quam Menalopo contra nos roganti annuere.

No printed edition; see Baron, *Leonardo Bruni Aretino,* 171, no. 6, and 178, listing four manuscripts, not including this one; Bertalot 5666, listing this manuscript.

5. ff. 26v–32 [Suetonius (or Donatus), *Vita Virgilii*] *Leonardi aretini in vitam virgilii excerptam ex comentariis Seruii gramatici* [*sic*]. Virgilius Maro Mantuanus parentibus modicis fuit . . . ut omnia ad societatem maliuolorum cederent.

Karl Bayer, ed., *Vergil-Viten* in *Vergil Landleben,* eds. Johannes and Maria Götte (Würzburg 1970) 214–241, here ending 228, line 200; the text is also ascribed to Leonardo Bruni in Vatican, Biblioteca Apostolica Vaticana, MS Ottob. lat. 1455 (ending where our manuscript does) and Florence, Biblioteca Medicea Laurenziana, MS Strozz. 114 (cf. Bayer, 661); see also Baron, *Leonardo Bruni Aretino,* 185, noting and rejecting the attribution to Leonardo Bruni.

Arts. 6,7,8, and 9: four excerpts from the *Continuatio medievalis* of Curtius Rufus' *Historia Alexandri* that circulated independently; see Hankins, "Bruni Manuscripts," 67, no. 9, citing Edmé R. Smits, "A Medieval Supplement to the Beginning of Curtius Rufus's Historia Alexandri: An Edition with Introduction," *Viator* 18 (1987) 89–124, esp. 101; and Ludwig Bertalot, "Forschungen über Leonardo Bruni Aretino," in Bertalot, *Studien zum italienischen und deutschen Humanismus,* ed. Paul O. Kristeller. *Storia e Letteratura* 130 (Rome 1975) 2:393. The attribution of the translation from the Greek to Leonardo Bruni is incorrect.

Pietro Marcello has also been suggested as the author; cf. Remigio Sabbadini, "Antonio da Romagno e Pietro Marcello," *Nuovo Archivio Veneto* NS 30 (1915) 207–46, esp. 221–24; see also Ludwig Bertalot, "Uno zibaldone umanistico latino del Quattrocento a Parma," *La Bibliofilia* 38 (1936) 77–78; and José Ruysschaert, *Codices vaticani latini: codices 11414–11709* (Vatican City 1959) 286–87.

6. f. 32rv [Ps. Aeschines (Pietro Marcello?)] *Eschinis oratoris ad Athenienses oratio.* Reminiscor athenienses Alexandrum hac in nostra urbe liberalibus studiis instructum . . . si nos obsequentes sibi supplicesque inuenerit.

Printed in Remigio Sabbadini, "Antonio da Romagno e Pietro Marcello," 241; and in Vittorio De Falco, *Demade Oratore; Testimonianze e frammenti.* Collana di Studi Greci 25 (Naples 1955) 52.

7. ff. 32v–33 [Ps. Demades (Pietro Marcello?)] *Demadis oratoris ad Athenienses contio.* Admirans uehementer admiror athenienses . . . et consiliis uacuam facilius diripiat.

   Printed in Sabbadini, "Antonio da Romagno e Pietro Marcello," 241–42; and in De Falco, *Demade Oratore*, 52–53; translation once attributed to Leonardo Bruni; see also Baron, *Leonardo Bruni Aretino*, 178, listing four manuscripts, not including this one; Bertalot 771.

8. f. 33rv [Ps. Demosthenes (Pietro Marcello?)] *Demosthenis oratoris ad Athenienses contio.* Apud uos in questione uerti uideo . . . Alexandro qui seruiuimus Philippo ne similes simus Thebanis.

   Printed in Sabbadini, "Antonio da Romagno e Pietro Marcello," 242; and De Falco, *Demade Oratore*, 53–54; Bertalot 1411.

9. ff. 33v–35v [Ps. Demosthenes (Pietro Marcello?)] *Demosthenis ad Alexandrum macedonie regem epistola.* Nihil habet rex Alexander uel fortuna tua maius quam ut possis . . . nullam de laudebus [*sic*] tuis ampliorem fore, quam eam que hodierno die cum hec feceris consecuturus es. Vale.

   Printed in Sabbadini, "Antonio da Romagno e Pietro Marcello," 243–44; discussed in De Falco, *Demade Oratore*, 54; translation once attributed to Leonardo Bruni; see Baron, *Leonardo Bruni Aretino*, 179, listing five manuscripts not including this one.

10. ff. 36–55 [Tacitus, *De origine et situ Germanorum liber*] *Cornelii Taciti Equitis Romani De Origine Et Situ Germanie Liber Incipit Feliciter.* Germania omnis a gallis rhetiisque et pannoniis rheno et danuuio fluminibus a sarmatis dacisque mutuo meatu aut montibus separatur . . . quod ego ut incompertum in medium [*sic*] relinquam.

    Rodney Potter Robinson, ed., *The Germania of Tacitus: A Critical Edition.* Philological Monographs 5 (Middletown, Connecticut 1935) 271–326, this manuscript listed as "e"; cf. pp. 81, 232, 349; see also Edward K. Rand, "A Harvard Manuscript of Ovid, Palladius and Tacitus," *American Journal of Philology* 26 (1905) 300–29, discussing the text of this manuscript in some detail; and Clarence W. Mendell, "Discovery of the Minor Works of Tacitus," *The American Journal of Philology* 56 (1935) 113–30, esp. 128.

11. ff. 55v–69v [St. Basil the Great, *Oratio ad adolescentes*, tr. Leonardo Bruni Aretino; prologue] *Basilii oratio de studiis secularibus traducta per Leonardum aretinum ad colucium salutatum.* Ego tibi hunc librum Colucci ex media ut aiunt ... in quo animaduerte quaeso quanta grauitas sit. [f. 56v text] *Basilii oratio incipit traducta a leonardo aretino ad Colucium Salutatum uirum clarissimum.* Multa sunt filiique hortantur ... Quod uos non patiamini nunc recta consilia aspernantes.

    Printed in Basilio di Cesarea, *Discorso ai Giovani; Oratio ad adolescentes con la versione latina di Leonardo Bruni*, ed. Mario Naldini (Florence 1984) 231–48; see also Baron, *Leonardo Bruni Aretino,* 160–61, and 99–100 (printing the prologue); Luzi Schucan, *Das Nachleben von Basilius Magnus 'Ad adolescentes': ein Beitrag zur Geschichte des christlichen Humanismus* (Geneva 1973) listing this manuscript p. 240, no. 284; Bertalot 5718 and 12348.

12. ff. 69v–86v [Xenophon, *Libellus de tyranno,* tr. Leonardo Bruni Aretino; preface] *Incipit prohemium Xenophontis phylosophy de uita tyrannica traducti a Leonardo aretino ad Nicolaum niccolum uirum doctissimum.* Xenophontis phylosophi quemdam libellum quem ego exercendi ingenii gratia e greco sermone in latinum conuerti ... ac pulcherrima in his primitiis studiorum nostrorum nullo modo ausi sumus attingere. [f. 71 text] *Xenophontis de tyramnica* [*sic*] *uita liber incipit.* Cvm Ad Hyeronem Tirannvm Symonides poeta aliquando uenisset ... felix enim cum sis nemo tibi inuidebit.

    Preface printed in Baron, *Leonardo Bruni Aretino,* 100–101; cf. also p. 161; text printed s. XV (cf. Hain 15983–*15987, and 16225–16226); Bertolot 2909, listing this manuscript.

13. ff. 86v–108v [Ps. Petrarch (Benvenuto Rambaldi da Imola), *Liber Augustalis*; preface] *Commentaria imperatorum romanorum a Iulio caesare edita per Franciscum Petrarcham usque ad tempora sua.* [O]ptas clarissime marchio heroicarum cultor uirtutum posse faciliter et cito internoscere ... quia non aliud quam ueritatem

tradere posteris [*sic*] curauerunt. [f. 87 text] *Iulius cesar i imperauit anno iii mensibus vi.* Primus igitur qui romanorum arripuit . . . nunc pro dolor nichil possideat nisi modicum occidentis.

Printed in *Francisci Petrarchae Florentini . . . Opera quae extant omnia. . .* (Basel 1554) 1:575–90.

14. ff. 108v–113 [Palladius, *De insitione liber*; prologue] *Palladii carmina de arte insitionis.* [H]abes aliud indulte fiducie testimonium . . . quia nescio quomodo note quedam sunt maximarum personarum minuta compendia. [f. 109 text; rubric omitted] Pasiphile ornatus fidei cui iure fatemur/ Siquid in arcano pectoris umbra tegit./ . . . Carmina tu duros inter formata bidentes./ Aspera sed miti rusticitate lege. *Finis.*

Palladius, *Opus agriculturae, De veterinaria medicina, De insitione,* ed. Robert H. Rodgers (Leipzig 1975) 292–301, listing this manuscript as 'p', pp. xx–xi; see also Rand, "A Harvard Manuscript of Ovid, Palladius, and Tacitus," 295–300, discussing the text of this manuscript; R. H. Rodgers, "The Manuscript Tradition of Palladius' *Carmen de insitione,*" *University of London, Institute of Classical Studies, Bulletin* 16 (1969) 55–62, esp. 55–56; Josef Svennung, *Untersuchungen zu Palladius und zur lateinischen Fach- und Volkssprache* (Uppsala 1935) 94–102, esp. 95; "Palladius," in *Texts and Transmission: A Survey of the Latin Classics,* ed. L. D. Reynolds (Oxford 1983) 288, listing this manuscript.

15. ff. 113v–116v [Ovid, *Heroides,* 21:1–144] *Cedippe Acontio Heroidvm Ovidii Vltima Epistola.* Pertimui scriptumque tuum sine murmure legi/ Iuraret nequos inscia lingua deos./ . . . Non ego iuraui, legi iurantia uerba./ Vir mihi non isto more legendus eras.

H. Dörrie, ed, *P. Ovidii Nasonis Epistulae Heroidum.* Texte und Kommentare: Eine Altertumswissenschaftliche Reihe 6, eds. O Gigon, F. Heinimann, and O. Luschnat (Berlin 1971) 275–80; cf. also E. K. Rand, "Notes on Ovid," *Transactions and Proceedings of the American Philological Association* 35 (1904) 128–36, discussing the text of this manuscript.

Heinrich Dörrie has argued that this manuscript is one of a small group of manuscripts containing *Heroides* 21.13–144 and Palladius, *De insitione* that were copied from the printed edition, Rome 1471 (see "Untersuchungen zur Überlieferungsgeschichte von Ovids Epistulae Heroidum, part III" *Nachrichten der Adademie der Wissenschaften in Göttingen. I. Philologisch-Historische Klasse* 6 (1972) 282–283; cf. part II, 7 (1960) 375, discussing three related manuscripts). His conclusions were accepted by R. H. Rodgers, "The Manuscript Tradition of Palladius' *Carmen de insitione* [cited above, art. 14]," 56; cf. also M. D. Reeve, "The Tradition of *Consolatio ad Liviam*," *Revue d'histoire des textes* 6 (1976) 87–88.

(Arts. 3–15) Arts. 3 and 4, no marginalia; art. 5, heavily annotated with marginal notes summarizing the events of the text; arts. 6–9, very few annotations except nota marks (majuscule 'N' in a half-circle); art. 10, a few variant readings in the margin (for example ff. 36, 36v and 39v); art. 11, fairly frequent annotations, usually summarizing the text (f. 62, supplying an omitted line) and nota marks; arts. 12–15, no annotations.

Manuscript contains two sections of independent origins: part I., ff. 5–18, was added to part II, ff. 19–116; the table of contents, f. 4v, is in the hand of the second scribe, and includes both parts.

Parchment, ff. i (original parchment flyleaf, now trimmed and glued to the paper flyleaf) + ii (modern paper, included in the foliation as ff. 1–2) + 114 (incorrect modern foliation in pencil, upper, outside margin, recto, ff. 3–116) + ii (modern paper), 200 x 130 mm.

1^{2} (conjugate pair, numbered ff. 3-4) 2^{14} $3\text{–}11^{10}$ 12^{10} (–9, 10, following f. 116, cancelled with no loss of text).

Part I. ff. 5–18 (art. 2): copied on parchment ruled for another purpose; traces of dry point rulings and prickings remain; written space (118–117 x 66–62) mm. 22 long lines. Ruled lightly in brown crayon or lead, with the top and bottom horizontal rules extending full across on some folios; double full-length vertical bounding lines.

Written on the top line by one scribe in a humanist script; ink on the flesh side of some folios badly flaking (for example, ff. 8v–9, 10v–11, etc.).

One 3-line initial, f. 5, blue with purple pen flourishes extending the length of the text; secondary divisions indicated by plain 3- to 2-line alternating red and blue initials. Vivid red rubrics. Guide letters within initials or in the margin.

Part II. ff. 4v and 19–116: copied on parchment ruled for another purpose; traces of dry point ruling remain (for example, ff. 39–51) and at least ff. 51–88 are palimpsest with an unidentified Latin text in an early fifteenth-century humanistic script; written space (130–122 x 65–63) mm. 24–23 long lines or lines of verse. Ruled in ink with double vertical bounding lines; horizontal rules do not extend across vertical bounding lines. Ff. 89–104v and 113–115 with a single pricking, below the last horizontal rule, and outside the outer bounding line (cf. also ff. 19–20). Ff. 3–4, bifolium added at the beginning with table of contents, f. 4v, ruled in dry point, 25 lines, copied every other line.

Written above the top line by Jacopo di Poggio Bracciolini in a cursive humanistic script (de la Mare, "New Research," 507, no. 37).

Plain 2-line blue initials at the beginning of each article. Rubrics in brownish-red, ff. 19–88v, and variously in reddish-brown or bright red, ff. 89–116.

Bound in Italy, s. XV, in dark brown leather over wooden boards, blind-tooled with five sets of triple or quadruple rules forming a center panel and borders filled with small stamps, including clubbed saltires, a continuous heart-shaped leaf pattern, and small floral stamps in lozenges; five brass bosses on front and back; remains of four clasps, fastening front to back; gilt edges.

Two sections of independent origins (we thank Susan Shroff for her research on this manuscript). Article 2, ff. 5–18v, was copied in Florence in the second quarter of the fifteenth century; the text, of which this may be the dedicatory copy, is dedicated to Poggio Bracciolini, and may be dated before 1453 when Poggio left Rome, and possibly as early as 1425. The remainder of the manuscript, arts. 3–15, and the table of contents, f. 4v, which includes art. 2, was written in Florence by Jacopo di Poggio Bracciolini (1442–1478; de la Mare, "New Research," 448, and 507, no. 37). It must date after ca. 1455 when Pier Candido Decembrio saw a manuscript of Tacitus including the *Germania* (art. 10, above), and almost certainly dates after 1471, because it includes Ovid, *Heroides* 21:13–144, copied from the printed edition, Rome, 1471, and before 1478, the year of Jacopo's death.

Note on paper describing the contents of the manuscript, s. XIX, tipped in before f. 3. Sold by Payne and Foss, Cat. 1826, no. 646 (according to De Ricci; not available for consultation) to Sir Thomas Phillipps (*Phillipps Cat.*, 100, MS 6748; inside front cover, "Phillipps MS 6748"). Phillipps Sale, London, Sotheby's, 1896, no. 1235 to Quaritch. Quaritch Cats. 164 (1896) no. 165, 186 (1899) no. 9, and 211 (1902) no. 132. Dealers' notes include: in pencil, inside front cover, "6748 Ph./a20.1475"; and in pencil, front flyleaf, f. i: "Tacitus tr 210." Purchased from Quaritch, February 10, 1902 (Henry Lillie Pierce Fund; bookplate, inside front cover; library stamp, f. 3, which lists the date of purchase as February 19, although other library records list February 10; printed library catalogue description, front flyleaf, f. i). Former Harvard shelf mark: *L25.

secundo folio: [now f. 5] *Rynucius Poggio*
[now f. 6] uero ut opes

Bibliography: De Ricci, 985; De Ricci, "Handlist," 107 (listed as MS L. 25); Berthold L. Ullman, "Petrarch Manuscripts in the United States," *Italia Medioevale e Umanistica* 5 (1962) 448, no. 13; Dennis Dutschke, *Census of Petrarch Manuscripts in the United States.* Censimento dei Codici Petrarcheschi 9 (Padua 1986) 83–85, no. 21; Kristeller, *Iter* 5:226; Hankins, "Bruni Manuscripts, 67, no. 9.

MS Lat 125 — England s. XIII^{ex}–XIV^{in}
Thomas of Cantimpré, Liber de natura rerum

1. ff. 1–14v [f. 1 darkened and almost illegible] *De//* [outer third of leaf excised] //Ossa etiam eius precipue sunt <?> de maioul aliorum ossibus animalium. *De elep//* . . . [f. 14v] *De symea* [*sic*]. Facies symie est similis faiei hominis . . . Solus enim homo facie eleuatur ad celos.

   Extracts from Thomas of Cantimpré, *Liber de natura rerum,* book 4, with *De silamandra* from book 8, and with additional chapters from an unidentified source or sources; H. Boese, ed., *Thomas Cantimpratensis Liber de natura rerum. Editio princeps secundum codices manuscriptos. Teil I: Text* (Berlin and New York 1973). The following extracts have not been identified in Thomas' text: f. 4, "*De cartomorionte.* Caritomorionte [*sic*] bestia est orientis cuius magnitudo ut magnitudo leonis animalis est . . . et uenatur homines et eos deuorans manducat"; f. 5, *De benchire*; f. 6, *De obicibus, De Musco,* f. 6v, *De arica, De naab,* f. 7, *De cartara, De rolli,* f. 8, *De lora, De ylione, de equo flu*[*men*]*is,* f. 8v, *De animalibus,* f. 9v, *De uattis,* and f. 11v, *De porcis.*

   As the analysis of the entry *De elephante* demonstrates, the text of this manuscript is shorter than the usual text of Thomas' work: [f. 1–3v] *De elep//* [followed by 6 lines, virtually illegible, parchment darkened, text worn] [f. 1v] //[red]dit ori suo et per ipsam bibit . . . et cum [ipsa h]omines capiunt suis partibus adversantes [ed. 4.33, p. 126, lines 9–16; outer margin trimmed with consegent loss of text]. Cum ge[neratur] elephas subito cum cogenerant [*sic*] dentes ap[parent] . . . [datur cum] succo plantaginis [ed., 4.33, p. 127, lines 29–34]. Et hec venacio elephantum [ed., 4.33, p. 127, line 44]. [Homin]es uenatores domesticos elephantes inequitate [*sic*] querunt . . . Unde bene accipit [*sic*] instrucionem [ed., 4.33, pp. 127–28, lines 57–66]. Demum [*sic*] oculos uel aures petunt eo quod hec loca non defendantur promuscide [ed., 4.33, p. 128, lines 89–90]. Prosternit enim elephas cum suis culmis magnos parietes et magnas arbores cum sua fronte prosternit [ed., 4.33, p. 128, lines 98–100]. In coitu elephantis femina incurvatur . . . Mas etiam elephas mamillas habet ut hec sed non irriguas [ed. 4.33, p. 129, lines 114–125]. Elephas sedet super renes aliquantulum sed tamen pedes poteriores non flectit . . . flectere quatuor pedes propter pondus corporis [ed. 4.33, pp. 129–30, lines 145–149]. Sed tamen digitos iunctura latenti . . . uel thauri ambulare post ipsum [ed. 4.33, p. 130, lines 168–72]. Et notandum quod contra omnia animalia terre intestina eius disposita et formata sunt . . . mergit se in aqua usque ad additamentum [ed., 4.33, pp. 130–31, lines 173–98]. Super faciem aque est et inspirat per ipsum. Et non potest multum durare natando propter sui corporis// [ed. 4.33, p. 131, lines 199–200; ending imperfectly; bottom of f. 3v torn away with loss of text].

2. f. 14v–19 *Incipiunt capitula diuersarum edicionum seu libro de naturis rerum. De bestiis orientalibus,* De homine, De menstruosis [*sic*] hominibus, De leonibus, De elephante, De unicornio, . . . *De monstris marinis*, De cocodrillis [*sic*], . . . *De animalibus qui communiter*[*?*] *per orbem habentur,* De asino, . . . *De arboribus aromaticis*, De thure, . . . De artemesia.

   Chapter list for art. 3 with 309 headings; original scribe made no distinction between titles of books and chapters; later hands drew a line through the titles of books or rewrote them for emphasis.

3. ff. 19–112v [Summary of contents] *Incipit ordo edicionum in libro de*

naturis rerum. Liber primus de bestiis orientis. Liber secundus de monstris marinis. Liber tercius de animalibus qui communia per orbem habentur. Liber quartus de auibus. Liber quintus de piscibus. Liber sextus de serpentibus. Liber septimus de uermibus. Liber octauus de arboribus aromaticis. Liber decimus de aromaticis [*sic*]. Liber vndecimus de lapidibus preciosis. Liber duodecimus de fluminibus et fontibus. [f. 19v Text] *Liber primus de bestiis orientis. Capitulo primo de homine.* Deus omnipotens qui in principio plenum bonis omnibus uisibilium ... [f. 20] *De proprietatibus humani corporis.* Corpus autem humanum quod ex ossibus et carnibus constat ... [f. 105v] *Incipit liber de herbis aromaticis et uirtutibus. De nardo.* Nardus herba est spicosa ... [f. 112v] *De artemesia.* Artemesia herba est calida et sicca folia eius uerida ... muscate confectis cum siroto simplici.

Extracts from Thomas of Cantimpré, *Liber de natura rerum*; analysis of the text suggests the extracts were taken from books 4–9, 11 and 12; Boese, ed. (cited, art. 1, above); G. J. J. Walstra, "Thomas de Cantimpré, *De naturis rerum*. Etat de la question," *Vivarium* 5 (1967) 146–71, and 6 (1968) 46–61, listing this manuscript pp. 50–51 as no. 20 (contents noted as books 4, 5, 8, and 10); Lynn Thorndike, "More Manuscripts of Thomas of Cantimpré, *De naturis rerum*," *Isis* 54 (1963) 269–77, listing this manuscript, p. 273 (as Harvard University 125; contents noted as books 4, 8 and 10). See also Stephanus G. Axters, O.P., *Bibliotheca dominicana neerlandica manuscripta, 1224–1500.* Bibliothèque de la revue d'histoire ecclésiastique 49 (Louvain 1970) 84 (this manuscript listed as Harvard College Library MS 125).

In the list of books (ff. 19–19v) book nine is omitted, and books eleven and twelve are included, although the text and chapter list (art. 2) end with book ten. In general, the text in art. 1 (extracts from Thomas de Cantimpré and an unidentified source or sources) is not repeated in art. 3; the choice of topics is different in both, and where the same topics are copied, different sections of the text are selected. For example, both arts. 1 and 3 include abbreviated versions of "de hyena" and "de elephante," but the text they include does not overlap. Names of authorities cited in the text are written in red in the margin.

Parchment (poor quality, uneven in size, holes and sewings), ff. 112 (modern foliation in pencil, upper outer corner), 104 x 135 mm. Layout varies. Art. 1 (ff. 1–14v), written space, (91–87 x 66–65) mm. 18 long lines. Ruled in lead with the top 1 or 2 and bottom 1 or 2 horizontal rules full across on some folios; single full-length vertical bounding lines. Slash prickings in three outer margins. Chapter list, art. 2, (ff. 14–19), written space (93–90 x 60–55) mm. 2 columns, 18 lines. Art 3 (ff. 19–112v), written space, (103–100 x 66–65) mm. 23–22 long lines. Ff. 14–112v, ruled in lead with the top 2 and bottom 2 horizontal rules full across; single full-length vertical bounding lines. Slash prickings, outer edge (often cut away), and a row of small round prickings, outer margin (cf. ff. 19–20 and ff. 73–96v, two rows of prickings remain); round or slash prickings, top and bottom margins.

$1–9^{12}$ 10^{4}. Horizontal catchwords, bottom, inside margin, boxed in brown ink in quires 1, 5, and 9 (ff. 11v, 60v, and 108v).

Written below the top line in brown ink in a gothic bookhand.

Two- to 1-line red initials; guide letters visible within the initials. Majuscules within the text stroked with red; red rubrics. Some notes to the rubricator remain (cf. ff. 74–76v, and f. 111, etc.).

Front and back covers missing, and first quire detached. Vellum(?) spine, darkened and in poor condition, with rough stitches, top, bottom and middle. Housed in a modern slip case.

Written in England at the end of the thirteenth century or the beginning of the fourteenth century. Notes in later hands, mostly expunged and difficult to read, ff. 1 and 112v. Dealers' notes include: f. 2, in pencil, "/R1 1–1"; and inside slip case, in pencil, "£42.-.-/Ro/-.-," below, "L3," and "Cat 23/327 [from Goldschmidt, see below]." Purchased November 25, 1930 (Degrand Fund; library note, in pencil, f. 2) from E. P. Goldschmidt (Goldschmidt Cat. 23, no. 327).

secundo folio: [ine]quitate [*sic*] querunt

Bibliography: De Ricci, 985–86.

MS Lat 126 Italy s. XV
Commentary on Boethius, Philosophiae consolatio Pl. 43

ff. 1–78 *Carmina qui quondam studio florente peregi* [book 1, M I.1], Ego boethius *flebilis* ploragibilis, qui *quondam*, id est in preterito, *peregi*, id est complevi, *carmina studio florente. Heu cogor inire* [book 1, M I.2], id est incipere, *mestos modos*, id est tristos versus . . . *Magna necessitas probitatis* [book 5, 6.48], id est bonitatis. Enim pro certe inest ipso *indicta*, si ita *uobis* tunc cum in quoniam uos *agitis*, id est facitis. *Ante oculos iudicis*, id est dei, *cernentis*, id est iudicantis. *Cuncta si uos non uultis disimulare*, id est infingere etc. *Amen. Deo gratias amen. Explicit liber boetii de consolatione philosofica. Amen.* [F. 78^{v} blank with later note.]

Commentary on Boethius, *De philosophiae consolatio*; for Boethius' text, see Ludovicus Bieler, ed. CC 94 (Turnholt 1957); *CPL* 878; see also Kottler, "The Vulgate Tradition," 209–214 (not mentioning this manuscript). Commentaries on this text are surveyed in Pierre Courcelle, *La consolation de philosophie dans la tradition littéraire* (Paris 1967). The commentary on Book 3, M IX, begins on f. 43v, as follows: "*O qui perpetua mundum ratione.* Cum ipse pulcerrimus gerens, id est faciens mundum pulcrum menteque pro et formam ipsum mundum cum simili imagine . . ."

Divided into the usual five books, as follows: ff. 1, 14v, 33, 51 and 66v. Within each book, text is divided into sections, each beginning with a short passage from Boethius' text, copied in a larger and more formal script, followed by the commentary, copied in a smaller hand in a cursive script. Divisions correspond to the beginning of new sections of prose and verse within Boethius' text. Manuscript includes a few contemporary marginal annotations (cf. for example, ff. 2, 4, and 8v).

Parchment (palimpsest of Italian legal documents, s. XIV; see below, provenance), ff. ii (paper) + 78 + iii (paper), 226 x 146 (126–123 x 79–71) mm. 38–34 long lines. Crudely frame ruled in lead with all four rules sometimes full across and with an extra horizontal rule, bottom margin (for example, ff. 37v–38, and ff. 57v–end). Prickings, three outer margins on most folios.

$1–4^{12}$ 5^{8} 6^{12} 7^{10}. Horizontal catchwords, bottom margin; position varies from the center of the page to below the last words of the text.

Written on the top line; passages from Boethius' text which begin each new section vary in the formality and size of the script; cf. ff. 1–14, written in the same color ink as the commentary in an informal gothic bookhand, slightly larger than the commentary; ff. 14v–end, generally written in a darker ink, in a larger, more formal rounded southern gothic bookhand; commentary is copied in a quick gothic cursive script, with loops.

One well-executed 5-line red historiated initial, f. 1, with a monochrome sketch of Boethius at his desk in shades of brown; remaining books begin with 8- to 6-line one color parted red initials (with "I" extending to 12-lines). Divisions within the books are indicated by 3-line red initials, usually plain (but cf. ff. 23v and 32v, with harping, and f. 1, with pen tendrils in very light brown ink). Red paragraph marks. Crude roman numerals added in brown ink through f. 59, top, outer corner, recto, indicating the division into books.

Bound in Italy, s. XV (?), in white tawed skin over bevelled boards, cut flush with the book-block; sewn on three split bands; spine with three raised bands; in poor condition with the plain head- and tailbands broken where they enter the boards; once fastened front to back (remains of strap for a clasp, front board, and impression of diamond-shaped clasp, back board). Rebacked, with remains of original spine laid down; early modern paper label on spine: "Boetius."

Written in Italy in the fifteenth century, on previously used parchment from Italian legal documents (cf. f. 37v, date, February 11, 1388, visible). Contemporary hand, possibly the scribe, f. 78v: "cartas lxxx habet." Annotations by early owners, s. XV, suggest that the book was owned by a Dominican friar; annotations include in ink, front flyleaf, f. i^v: "Commentarius boetii florentius[?]"; and "f<rater?> domenicus[?]"; the same name appears, front flyleaf, f. ii, and back flyleaf, f. iii: "Frater domenicus da <romanum?>"; back flyleaf, f. ii^v: "pro de<functi?> de f<. . .>"; and back flyleaf, f. iii, partially torn away, "<. .>CCCC XXX iii emi a sartici [*sic*] no[?] fratri." Unidentified booksellers' or owners' notes in pencil, inside front cover: "Manuscripts/ Boethius/ 15 guineas"; and "763/sw/m a/-." No. 290 or 300 in an English catalogue, possibly Tregaskis, according to De Ricci (unverified; unnumbered clipping from an English catalogue, inside front cover). Purchased from Tregaskis, June 9, 1919

(Constantius fund; library bookplate, inside front cover; library stamp, front flyleaf, f. ii^{v}). Former Harvard shelf mark: MS Lat 51.3*.

secundo folio: et ipsi

Bibliography: De Ricci, 986; Bond and Faye, 236–37; Wieck, 108, and fig. 84 (reproducing f. 1).

MS Lat 127 — **England s. XII$^{4/4}$**
Boethius, Philosophiae consolatio — **Pl. 20**

1. ff. 1–51v Carmina qui quondam studio florente peregi/ flebilis heu mestos cogor inire modos./ . . . Magna uobis est [*corr.*[2] *add.*: si] dissimulare non uultis neccessitas [*sic*] indicta probitatis, cum ante oculos agitis iudicis cuncta cernentis. [Added in a contemporary hand: *Explicit liber boetii deo gratias. Sine defectu.*]

Ludovicus Bieler, ed., *CC* 94 (Turnholt 1957); *CPL* 878. Greek in hand of main scribe (for example: f. 2v, line 15, book 1 1.4, ed. p. 2; f. 4, lines 26–7, book 1 4.1, ed. pp. 6–7; f. 21, lines 21–22, book 3 6.1, ed., p. 45; f. 41v, lines 3–4, book 4 6.38, ed., p. 82; f. 42, lines 9–10, book 4, 6.53, ed., p. 83; and f. 45, line 2, book 5, M II.1, ed., p. 91). Greek passages usually rewritten in Latin between the lines by the scribe or in a later hand. Glosses throughout in many hands including simple summaries of the text (cf. ff. 7–12; ceases f. 25v), long outlines and corrections, throughout (especially after f. 45) in a current English hand, and copious notes throughout in a very small, quickly written script (for example, ff. 1, 23v, 24).

Only the prose and poetic sections were originally distinguished in the text; apparatus was added to the text to facilitate reference in England, s. XIII–XIV (?): division into five books not indicated by original scribe, but running titles with the number of the book added sporadically later (books begin ff. 1, 9v, 19, 32, and 44); each prose and verse section numbered in the margin in early arabics (many now trimmed), beginning again at one at each new book; letters were added, possibly for reference: cf. f. 3, line 7; f. 33v, outer margin; f. 34, lines 15 and 18; and especially f. 46v, outer margin ('A', 'B'); f. 47 ('C', 'D'); and f. 48v, inner margin ('A', 'B', 'C').

2. f. 51v [Unidentified *accessus* to Boethius, added in another hand] Primus liber continet expelli musas querulas et ipsum boetius[?] paulisper[?] resipiscere per quasdam interrogationes philosophie et suas responsiones ... ab alio et iusto iudicio dei bonis premia eterna, mal<lis?> suplicia sempiterna dispensari. [Concluding in another hand] Quod uobis prestare dignetur qui uiuit et regnat per omnia secula seculorum. Amen.

3. f. 52r Diagram of a tree of knowledge: Sciencia, divided into two branches, Philosophia sive sapientia (poetica, teorica; etica [*sic*], economica, politica, teologia [*sic*], matematica, phisica, astronomia, geometria, musica; metrica, instrumentalis), and eloquentia (grammatica, dialectica, rhetorica). [F. 52v blank, with later notes, erased.]

Parchment (moderate to poor quality), ff. i (parchment) + 52 + i (parchment) + vi (modern note paper, sewn together and glued between the back flyleaf and the endpaper, with a transcription of the opening of the *Consolatio*), 192 x 124–120 (134–130 x 80–77) mm. 27 long lines, with verse sections interspersed as required by the text copied in one to three columns. Ruling usually indiscernible. Prickings in three outer margins on many folios.

$1–6^8\ 7^4$.

Written in a stiff late twelfth-century minuscule; all minims finish with upward strokes, no letter unions, 'ae' written 'e'. Majuscules that coincide with the beginning of a new line are written outside the written space; first majuscule of each line of verse written to the left of the bounding line.

Each new section of prose or verse begins with a 3- to 2-line initial, alternately red and green, with extensions into the margins of up to three more lines, most decorated with two circular shapes at the curves of the initials; some with other simple decorative motifs such as void spaces within the body of the initial. Guide letters for the initials in the margins.

Bound in France, s. XVIII, in green vellum; spine with five raised bands forming six compartments with "Boetius" in gilt, and five gilt lions rampant.

Written in England in the fourth quarter of the twelfth century, as indicated by the early glosses in English hands (we thank Professor R.H. Rouse, visit to the library, April 27, 1987). F. 52v includes various medieval notes, now erased. "No. 2031," in ink, inside front cover (identified by De Ricci as French, s. XVIII). Other owners' and dealers' notes include: inside back cover, in pencil, price code: "Lj/Vz"; inside front cover, remains of a printed label, with "56" in ink; and front flyleaf, f. i, "F/N," in ink (possibly in Dredge's hand, see below). Belonged to John Ingle Dredge of Halybridge, April, 1849 (in ink, front flyleaf, f. i), and to G. Sumner of Woodmanson, 1855, his "MS Case B/BI" (in ink, front flyleaf, f. i). Purchased July 22, 1920 from Dobell (Salisbury Fund; bookplate, inside front cover, and library stamp, front flyleaf, f. i; Houghton plate, inside back cover, with date, May 5, 1922). Previous Harvard shelf mark: MS Lat 51.4.

secundo folio: fructuosis affectuum

Bibliography: De Ricci, 986; Light, *Bible in the Twelfth Century*, 107 (checklist).

pfMS Lat 128 — **Italy s. XVI**
Gradual — **Pl. 59**

1. ff. 1–62 Sanctorale from the vigil of Andrew (29 November) to Didacus (12 November); among the feasts included are the Feast of the Holy Name of Jesus (the Sunday between 1 and 6 January), Berard and companions (16 January), Joachim (between 12 and 21 March), Joseph (between 25 March and 25 April), "in translatione beati patris nostri francisci" (25 May), Anthony of Padua (13 June), Transfiguration (6 August), Donatus, bishop of Arrezo (7 August), Lawrence (10 August) with octave, Louis of Toulouse (19 August), Stigmata of Francis (17 September), and Francis (4 October).

2. ff. 62–121v and f. 124rv Common of the saints from the vigil of one apostle to the dedication of a church.

   Office of the dedication of a church is now interrupted by art. 3, ff. 122–123v, added later, so the text ends imperfectly, f. 121v, and then resumes, with no breaks, f. 124rv.

(Arts. 1 and 2): fragment of a parchment leaf, s. XVII–XVIII (?), glued inside back cover with a table of the "Introiti," "Versetti," "Offertorii," and "Comunioni" in the manuscript, listed alphabetically within these categories with page references.

3. ff. 122–123v [added] *Missa Patrociny sancti Ioseph*, with the introit: "Adiutor et protector noster est dominus in eo laetabitur . . ."

Later addition, s. XVIII–XVIII (?); cf. bottom margin, f. 124v, in an artificial script, s. XVII–XVIII (?): "Iste liber comperit loco sancti iosephi sexti calendarium."

Parchment, ff. 124 (medieval foliation in red roman numerals on the left-hand side of each double-page opening, middle outer margin), 600 x 427 (470–467 x 304) mm. Ruled in lead with 35–36 long lines; red 4-line staves for music, and text written between four ruled lines; single full-length vertical bounding lines. Small round prickings, top and bottom margins at the intersection of the horizontal and vertical rules on some folios. Added leaves, ff. 122–123v, written space (480 x 334) mm. 35 long lines. Ruled in lead, with single vertical bounding lines, length of text only.

1–20^6 21^2 (ff. 121 and 124) 22^2 (ff. 122–123, later leaves, inserted after 1, f. 121, in quire 21). All leaves are single, and joined together to form "bifolia."

Written in a bold artificial liturgical gothic bookhand. Rubrics copied in a round gothic bookhand with decorative majuscules. Added leaves, ff. 122–123v, copied in a liturgical gothic bookhand by a less practiced scribe.

Three major 5-line initials (equivalent to 4-line staff and one line of text); initials, f. 1, vigil of Andrew, and f. 56v, Francis, are pink with lush multi-colored acanthus leaves (green, blue and yellow) on brushed gold grounds, infilled with bold flowers and gold balls on black edged in lighter pink, with heavy acanthus leaves extending from the corners of the initial to form full- to 1/2-length borders in the outer margin in green, pink, purple, blue and gold with touches of yellow and orange, terminating in spiky flowers and gold balls set in ink-scrolls; initial, f. 44v, Assumption, is gold on a blue ground, infilled with flowers and leaves with ink tendrils on bright yellow with large pink and orange leaves extending from the corners to form a border. Numerous 5-line (equivalent to 4-line staff and one line of text) initials in art. 1 (sanctorale), usually pink, but sometimes blue or green, on notched gold or yellow grounds edged in black (gold has sometimes worn away); initials are shaded to resemble overlapping petals or infilled with blue flowers on a black ground, sometimes with acanthus leaves extending from the upper corners (a few initials vary in style; cf. f. 25v Invention of the Cross, infilled with a cross; f. 31v Nativity of John, pink initial on a blue ground infilled with a flower on bright orange, and f. 52v Stigmata of Francis, blue initial on a gold ground infilled with jewels on black, with gold balls on an ink vine sprouting from the initial; initials, ff. 18v, 33v, and 60, Annunciation, vigil of Peter and Paul, and Didacus, infilled with thin flowers and vines on rubbed gold grounds, with gold balls set in an ink vine sprouting from the intials. Five-line initials in art. 2 (common of the saints) are similar in style but simpler, on alternating gold, yellow and silver grounds. One-line alternating red and bright blue initials within the text; red staves and rubrics. Parted blue and purple 5-line initial, f. 122 (added later), decorated with tulips.

Bound in original heavy wooden boards and red-brown leather; upper and lower boards and spine with hammered metal borders that wrap around the edges of the board, and which are fixed with numerous small bosses; lower board with large metal center ornament in the shape of a sun-burst with "ihs" stamps, surrounded by four large bosses, and title, "Graduale festivem" in a metal frame.

Written in Italy in the sixteenth century, probably after 1588 (canonization of Didacus; also included are the Transfiguration, O.F.M. 1467, Berard, 1481, and Feast of the Holy Name of Jesus, O.F.M. 1530) for use by Franciscans (numerous Franciscan feasts included). No. 885 in an American sale (clipping glued inside front cover, describing this manuscript as an Antiphonal, s. XV; cf. pencil note, inside front cover, "885"). Inside front cover, in pencil, "44, 56, 78" written in a vertical column. John S. Lawrence Collection, Grand Rapids, Michigan; given in his memory, August 8, 1924, by his sister, Mary Loomis Lawrence (library stamp with date, and bookplate, inside front cover; G. Mattingly, "The Lawrence Bequest," *Harvard Library Notes* 14 [1925] 30).

secundo folio: O inuenimus

Bibliography: De Ricci, 986; Wieck, 108, and fig. 80, reproducing f. 44v.

MS Lat 129 Germany 1474–1477
Breviary Pl. 11

1. f. 1 [Short invocation] Ach vnica spes. Iaia [*sic*; as exclamation?] culmine celsior omni. [F. 1v blank, with traces of paper (possibly from a printed bookplate once glued in).]

2. ff. 2–88v Temporale from the first Sunday in Advent to Holy Saturday; monastic use (12 lessons read at matins on Sundays and major feasts); text is preceded by nine lines of verse as scribal invocation: "Consurge pietate nitens tege ardua culmen/ . . . Rege igitur servulum demet ne libri arator," and concludes with four lines of verse at the end of the Office for Holy Saturday, f. 87: "Ach spes pretiosa reis via portus. Ihesu redemptis/ . . . Et collaudet omnibus te pro donis, spiritus unus et omnis"; lessons for Maundy Thursday from Lamentations, ff. 87v–88v, ending with a scribal colophon, f. 88v: "O vera merces omnium ihesu memor esto laborum/ Huius scriptoris sisque merces ipse laboris." [F. 89rv blank.]

3. ff. 90–193 Temporale, continued, from Easter through the twenty-fourth Sunday after Trinity Sunday, here called *Dominica ultima ante aduentum domini*; prefaced by seven lines of verse as scribal invocation: "O jhesu pietas altissima, o laude potestas colenda/ . . . Utque semper bibam latices, celesti sede manantes [*sic*, for "emanentes"?]."; f. 191, six lines of verse following the office for the last Sunday before Advent: "Nunc o alma potestas rerum, tibi gloria laus et in evum/ . . . Ach obuia in pelago, lux rerum, ihesu fons et origo."; concludes, ff. 191–93, with canticles for Lent and Easter; ending with a scribal colophon, f. 193: "Sicut portus oportunus est nauigantibus/ Ita scriptori versus vltimus pax omnibus legentibus/ Scriptorique scabiles [*sic*], fundat lux aurea menses."

4. ff. 193v–331v [f. 193v blank, except for drawing on paper glued in] Sanctorale, preceded by five lines of verse: "O Ihesu princeps alme, astringam regis que aulam/ . . . Venerit, hoc promat carmine leta fides. Amen."; from the feast of Andrew (30 November) through Catherine of Alexandria (25 November), concluding with the dedication of a church; among the feasts included are Scholas-

tica (10 February), *In natali sanctissimi patris nostri Benedicti* (21 March), Boniface (5 June), Denis (26 June), Visitation (2 July) with octave, *In commemoracione sanctissimi patris nostri benedicti* (11 July), Aegidius (1 September), Aurelius (bishop? 13 September; here between Exaltation of the Cross, 14 September and Octave of Nativity of Mary, 15 September), Denis (9 October), Gallus (16 October), Eustachius (3 November), Elizabeth of Thuringia (19 November), and Placidius and companions (5 October?; added after Catherine of Alexandria); internal to the sanctorale, ff. 246–249, is the common of the saints for Eastertide, preceded on f. 245v by the scribe's verses: "Desuper irradia scribenti gloria dya[?]/ sis dux sis socia mera lux et vera sophia."

5. ff. 332–376 [short invocation, upper margin] Assis [*sic*] christe, daque clementer valete; *Incipit lectionarius trium lectionum*, readings for feasts with three lessons from All Saints to Maundy Thursday, and, ff. 374–376, canticles for Advent and Christmas, with note that the canticles for Lent and Easter are found at the end of the temporale (see above, art. 3); concludes, f. 376, *Anno 1474, Urbani episcopi. Laude grata* [*sic*] *deum, celebret uox* [*added above the line: pia*] *lectorum/ Scriptor robur fidei, licet aura tactus* <*n. . .i?*>/ *Firmiter optinuit, constancia quem stabiliuit/ Hinc labor inde quies, decursos scriptor agnens* [*sic, for agens?*]/ *Sumat in eternum, dic christo dominante triumphum.*

6. ff. 376v–377 [in another hand:] *Rabanus de sancta cruce.* O uere bona et uere sancta crux et passio christi quis te rite enarrare potest . . .; *Sermo beate uirginis.* Cum aliquid dilectissimi in amore creatoris in creatura eius dignis laudibus predicat . . . Sub cuius defensione proteguntur regna terrarum cum ipso uirgo maria fugit in egiptum. Qui est benedictus in secula. Tu autem. *Uale o vnica spes Maria. Scriptoremque regendo comendare christo numquam cessa.*

7. f. 377v [invocation] O maria[?] spes humana/ pro me[?] ventris fluctus [*sic*] plana [*sic*]/ Corporis christi Anno et cetera lxxvii.

Parchment (velvety), ff. 378 (incorrectly foliated 1–250, 250 bis, 251–377), 110 x 83 (73–74 x 55–54) mm. 29–27 long lines. Ruled lightly in lead with the top 2 and bottom 2 horizontal rules full across; single full-length vertical bounding lines. Prickings in three outer margins (some trimmed).

1–45[8] 46[10] (–1, before f. 360, cancelled with no loss of text) 47[8] (+9, f. 377, added singleton). Horizontal catchwords, inside, bottom edge, bracketed and sometimes underlined in red (lacking in quire 11, f. 88v, where a blank leaf follows; trimmed in quires 17 and 40, ff. 136v and 319v; partly trimmed in other quires).

Written on the top line in a hybrida script by an accomplished scribe, in two sizes depending on liturgical function; tall, flourished majuscules, top and/or bottom lines on many folios.

Three miniatures in pen and ink with red, blue and green wash on paper, pasted in; carefully drawn with attention to detail; inside front cover: Christ in majesty (fragmentary, with evidence of inscription in outer margin); f. 193v (sanctorale) St. John, holding a chalice from which a serpent emerges, with a kneeling monk; around the outer, top, and inner margins, a legend reads: "Totus catholico resplendet flore Johannes. Totus habet grauium certissima dicta virorum"; banderole with legend from the monk reads: "Ich Johannes pater alme, leuamen lapso porige [*sic*] et <disto?> cum omne corrige"; and legend in the bottom margin: "Oratio super amore potens"; f. 377v the Virgin, crowned and holding a sceptre, with a kneeling monk from whose praying hands a red line runs to two lines of virtually illegible text on a narrow strip of paper along the gutter. F. 184v 15-line "I" decoratively extending into the bottom margin, with green foliage and terminating in a grotesque mask, drawn in pen. Two initials, apparently with heraldic devices; f. 147v, three horizontal rows of horseshoes (?) facing diagonally to the upper right corner, surmounted by a helmet and hunting horn; and f. 185, an animal skull(?) with two red horns(?), the tips cut off, surmounted by a helmet and the same red horns(?).

Major initials, 11- to 7-line, blue or red, infilled and on grounds of void-design acanthus or other motifs against a cross-hatched background, some with grotesques and decorative beading; in the case of blue initials these designs were first executed in brown pen, and the initials were then added on top of them: f. 2 (first Sunday in Advent); f. 20 (Christmas), f. 90 (Easter), f. 105v (Ascension), f. 119 (Corpus Christi), f. 123 (Sunday within the octave of Corpus Christi), f. 124v (octave of Corpus Christi), f. 126v (first Sunday after Trinity Sunday), f. 195 (Andrew), f. 199 (Conception of the Virgin), f. 207v

(John the Evangelist), f. 214v (Agnes), f. 218v (conversion of Paul), f. 221v (Purification), f. 236 (Benedict), f. 243 (Ambrose), f. 246 (saints during Eastertide), f. 260v (John the Baptist), f. 306v (Nativity of Mary). Secondary initials, 6- to 4-line red or blue, with pen decoration or grotesques of type described above, or with simpler pen decoration in brown or red. 2- to 1-line red initials and red paragraph marks (blue used rarely). Red rubrics; majuscules within the text slashed with red; red underlining used for emphasis, particularly for sacred names (for example, "deus," "dominus," "christus").

Bound in Germany in brown leather, s. XV, over beech boards that are square at the corners, but otherwise bevelled, blind-tooled with rules forming an outer rectangular border, within which are intersecting diagonal rules, and with single diamond stamps above the central boss, front and back (now rubbed and indecipherable); with decorative brass central bosses, four corner ornaments, and fastening with catch on upper board (one corner ornament, central boss, and catch remain, upper board; three corner ornaments and part of fastening remain, lower board). Sewn on three double cords, with head- and tailbands wound in decorative red, white and green thread. Condition poor; front cover detached and broken, with the top outer corner, and bottom third of the board now missing; remnants only of spine remain.

Written in Germany in 1474–1477 (ff. 376 and 377v); intended for use in a Benedictine monastery (feasts in sanctorale refer to Benedict as "sanctissimus pater noster") belonging to one of the reformed Benedictine congregations (office for the dedication of a church with liturgical direction, f. 331v: "Nota si in aliquo monasterio nostre vnionis dedicacio ecclesie inter diem pasce et pentecostis euenerit. . ."); sanctorale includes Aurelius, probably Bishop Aurelius, who was patron of Hirsau, and it is possible that the manuscript was made for Hirsau or one of its foundations (Hirsau joined the Bursfeld congregation in 1458). Colophon, f. 376, includes the name "Urbanus episcopus" following the year, 1474; an Urban was Bishop of Sirmium in Yugoslavia between the Danube and Sava rivers, between 1460 and 1473, but since it seems unlikely that this is our manuscript's Urban the reference may be to a saint's feast, such as Urban I (May 25). Note on paper scrap, glued to f. 1: "Bought in Paris in 1858 by W. F. Olis and given to S. E [probably Samuel Eliot (1821–

1898), historian, educator, and grandfather of Samuel Eliot Morison]." Obtained, 12 June 1926 from the American historian, Professor Samuel Eliot Morison (1887–1976; pencil note, f. 1v, and Harvard College Library stamp). Original Harvard shelf mark: 9290.15.

secundo folio: Regionem uestram

Bibliography: De Ricci, 986; Wieck, 108–9 and fig. 131 (reproducing f. 193v).

fMS Lat 130 — Southern Italy s. XII^2
Fragment of a Noted Breviary

One leaf [recto; beginning imperfectly in the response] //sed maiora tibi debentur pro fide christi certamina. [*V.*] Nos quasi senex leuioris pugne cursum recepimus ... [Lesson] Erant <two lines, almost expunged ...> nomine lucillus, qui plorando <. .m?> amiserit[?] occulorum. Cui ait beatus laurentius, crede in filium dei dominum ihsesum christum ... expectabat uerba eorum. [*R.*] O yppolite si credas in dominum iesum christum ... [*V.*] Si dicta inquid factis conpenses faciam ... tuum michi tantum modo prebe cossensum [*sic*]. Et//; [verso; beginning imperfectly in the Lesson] //[T]unc beatus laurentius catecizauit eum ... ponebat manum super eorum occulos et illuminabantur. [*R.*] Stridebantur [*sic*] corporis membra posita super craticula [*sic*] subicientibus prunas insultat ... [*V.*] Carus es uero urgentes ministrabantur ... [Lesson] Videns autem hec yppolitus dixit ... O yppolite si credas in deum patrem et in filium eius//

One leaf with matins for the feast of Lawrence (August 10); noted responses and versicles; the text of the lessons (first two lines, recto, illegible) is equivalent to the Passion of Lawrence printed in Boninus Mombritius, novam editionem curaverunt duo monachi Solesmenses, *Sanctuarium seu vitae sanctorum* (Paris 1910; reprint Hildesheim and N.Y. 1978) 2:92, line 42–93, line 14, although the wording of the two versions is not the same.

Parchment, one leaf, 326 x 230–224, unevenly trimmed (244–243 x 164–160) mm. 2 columns, 28 lines, but copied with 26 lines, leaving two empty ruled lines below the text. Ruled in dry point with double vertical outer bounding lines, single between the columns.

Written on the top ruled line in a Beneventan script; staffless neumes written above the appropriate text in ruled space equivalent to one line of text.

Two 1-line orange-red initials, partially filled with pale yellow. Majuscules within the text infilled with orange-red and bright yellow. Red rubrics.

Written in southern Italy in the second half of the twelfth century. Possibly used as a cover for a binding; once folded on all edges, leaving only the turned in edges on the recto clean, while the remainder is stained, especially the middle which probably covered the spine; remains of title (?) in ink, early modern hand: "Regi[?] Casscell[?]"; verso is fairly clean and undamaged except in the middle. Given to Harvard September 27, 1927 by a friend of the library (identified by De Ricci as Professor Walter Ashburner, Oxford; unconfirmed in manuscript or library files). Original Harvard shelf mark: 9290.20.

Bibliography: De Ricci, 986; Elias A. Lowe, "A New List of Beneventan Manuscripts," *Collectanea Vaticana in honorem Anselmi M. Card. Albareda*. Studi e testi 220 (Vatican City 1962) 218; E. A. Loew [=Lowe], rev. ed. by Virginia Brown, *The Beneventan Script. A History of the South Italian Minuscule. 2. Hand List of Beneventan Manuscripts*. Sussidi Eruditi 34 (Rome 1980) 2:28.

MS Lat 132 — **Flanders s. XV$^{2/4}$**
Book of Hours, use of Rome — **Pl. 21**

1. ff. Eight folios, labelled 'A'–'H' [f. 'A', blank.] Calendar, rather empty, with major feasts in red including Amand and Vedast (6 February), Basil the Great (14 June), translation of Eligius (25 June), Visitation (2 July), Aegidius (1 September), Remigius and Bavo (1 October), Donatianus (14 October), Martin of Tours (11 November), Eligius (1 December) and Nicasius (14 December); among the remaining feasts in black are Bathildis (30 January), Bridget (1 February), Blasius (3 February), David, bishop (1

March), Adrian (4 March), "resurrexio domini" (27 March), Valeric (1 April), Medard (8 June), Vitus and Modestus (15 June), Gervasius (19 June), Mildred (13 July), Bertin (5 September), Lambert (17 September), Quentin (31 October), and Maclovius (15 November). Added feasts include, in a closely contemporary hand, ordination and translation of Martin (July 4) and Victor (21 July); in another hand, probably later, "Sauueur" (Salvius?, 10 July), "Toren[?]" (24 August), Sulpice, archbishop of Bourges (27 August), Fiacre (30 August), and "Denis" added next to the Latin, Dionysius (9 October); and in a formal bâtarde hand in French, the seven brothers (10 July), King Louis (25 August), Lupus, bishop of Sens (1 September), Firminus, bishop of Amiens (? here 1 September; usually 25 September), apparition of Michael on Mons Tumbae (16 October), and translation of Lucianus, patron of Beauvais (also 16 October). [F. 'H', blank.]

2. ff. 1–46v Hours of the Virgin, use of Rome; matins (ff. 1–8v) followed by the Hours of the Cross, short form (ff. 9–11v) and the Hours of the Holy Spirit, short form (ff. 12–14v); lauds through compline conclude with the prayers usual for use of Rome, as follows, lauds: "Deus qui de beate marie uirginis utero . . . [Bruylants, *Oraisons* 2: no. 230]"; "Protege domine populum tuum et apostolorum tuorum . . ."; "Omnes sancti tui quesumus domine nos . . ."; "Et pacem tuam nostris concede . . ."; prime: "Que est ista que progreditur quasi aurora . . ."; "Deus qui virginalem aulam beate marie . . ."; "Exaudi nos deus salutaris . . ."; "Omnes sancti tui quesumus domine nos . . ."; "Et pacem tuam nostris concede . . ."; terce: "Deus qui salutis eterne beate marie virgine . . . [Bruylants, *Oraisons* 2: no. 440]"; "Protege domine populum tuum et apostolorum tuorum . . ."; "Omnes sancti tui quesumus domine nos . . ."; "Et pacem tuam nostris concede . . ."; sext: "Concede quesumus misericors deus fragilitati nostre . . ."; "Exaudi nos deus salutaris . . ."; "Omnes sancti tui quesumus domine nos . . ."; "Et pacem tuam nostris concede . . ."; none: "Famulorum tuorum quesumus domine delictis ignosce . . ."; "Presta quesumus omnipotens deus ut familia per uiam salutis intercedat . . . [Bruylants, *Oraisons* 2: no. 856]"; "Omnes sancti tui quesumus domine nos . . ."; "Et pacem tuam nostris concede . . ."; vespers: "Concede nos famulos tuos quesumus domine deus perpetua mentis . . . [Bruy-

lants, *Oraisons* 2: no. 122; printed *HE,* 44 and 51]"; "Protege domine populum tuum . . ."; "Omnes sancti tui quesumus domine nos . . ."; "Et pacem tuam nostris concede . . ."; compline: "Beate et gloriose semperque virginis . . ."; "Exaudi nos deus salutaris . . ."; "Omnes sancti tui quesumus domine nos . . ."; "Et pacem tuam nostris concede . . ."; "Salue regina misericordie uita. . . . [*RH* 18150]"; "Omnipotens sempiterne deus qui gloriose uirginis et matris marie . . . [printed *HE,* 63]." Two additional prayers follow compline: *deuote orison a la uierge marie.* Sancta maria mater domini nostri ihesu christi in manus tuas . . .; and *Orison a son bon angele.* Angele qui meus es custos pietate superna me . . . deffende guberna. Amen [Wilmart, 556; here with 2 lines of verse only].

3. ff. 47–52v Suffrages of Michael, John the Baptist, Peter, Christopher, Sebastian, Anthony, Francis, Nicholas, Mary Magdalene, Catherine of Alexandria, Margaret and Barbara.

4. ff. 53–57v *Item oracio ad uirginem mariam.* Obsecro te domina sancta maria . . . Et michi famulo tuo . . . [Leroquais, *LH* 2:346]; [f. 55v] *Alia oracio ad uirginem mariam.* O intemerata . . . orbis terrarum. Inclina mater misericordie aures tue pietatis . . . esto michi miserrimo peccatori pia . . . [Wilmart, 488–90].

5. ff. 57v–60 Gospel pericopes, John 1:1–14 and Luke 1:26–38 only; followed by prayers: f. 59v *Tous contris confez et repentans qui diront deuotement ceste orison entre le eleuation nostre seigneur et le tiers agnus dei ueullent acquerir ii mille ans de uray pardon.* Domine ihesu christe qui hanc sacratissimam carnem et preciosissimum sanguinem tuum . . . [Wilmart, 377–78, note 1, no. 10; printed *HE,* 72]; f. 60 *Orison quont on entre en leglize.* Deus propicius esto michi peccatori [cue only; printed *HE,* 125]; O mater dei memento mei [cue only]. [F. 60v blank, but ruled.]

6. ff. 61–72v Penitential psalms and litany, including Silvester, Gregory, Ambrose, Jerome and Augustine as the "holy doctors," Leonard, Bernard, Francis, Eligius, and Dominic among the confessors, Clare, Amelberga, Genevieve, Adelgundis, Juliana, Elizabeth, and Ursula among the virgins; concludes with prayers: "Deus cui proprium est misereri semper et parcere suscipe deprecacionem nostram . . . [printed *HE,* 97]"; "Deus qui nos patrem et matrem honorare precepisti miserere clementer animabus paren-

tum meorum ... [printed *HE*, 111]"; "Fidelium deus omnium conditor et redemptor ... [Bruylants, *Oraisons* 2: no. 567; printed *HE*, 30 and 98]"; "Anime omnium fidelium defunctorum per misericordiam dei ..."

7. ff. 73–88v Office of the Dead; matins with one nocturn of three lessons: Parce michi domine..., [*R.*] Credo quod redemptor meus ...; Tedet animam meam vite mee ..., [*R.*] Qui lasarum resuscitasti ...; Manus tue domine..., [*R.*] Domine quando ueneris iudicare ...; vespers concludes with prayers: "*Oratio.* Deus qui nos patrem et matrem honorare precepisti ... [printed *HE*, 111]"; "Quesumus domine pro tua pietate miserere anime famule tue ... [printed *HE*, 113]"; "Fidelium deus omnium conditor et redemptor ... [Bruylants, *Oraisons* 2: no. 567; printed *HE*, 30 and 98]"; lauds concludes with prayers: "Partem beate resurrectionis optineat uitam que eternam habere ..."; "Fidelium deus omnium conditor et redemptor ... [as above]." [Ff. 89–92v blank, but ruled.]

Parchment, ff. 100 (foliated 'A'–'H' + 1–92; ff. 'A' and 'H', blank, possibly modern parchment), 195 x 140 (119–118 x 78–76) mm. 18 long lines. Ruled in pale red ink with top and bottom horizontal rules extending full across the inner margins only, leaving the outer margin empty; single full-length vertical bounding lines. Calendar, ff. 'B'–'G': ruled space, 127 x 78–77 mm. 4 columns (3 narrow, and 1 wider column for main entry), 33 lines. Ruled in red ink with top and bottom horizontal rules extending full across the inner margins only, as above; vertical bounding lines, single between columns 1 and 2, and 2 and 3, and double between columns 3 and 4; full-length at the far inside and outside; remaining, length of ruled space only.

1^6 (+1 and 8, ff. 'A' and 'H', possibly added conjugate pair) 2^8 3^6 $4–6^8$ 7^6 8^2 (through f. 46v) 9^6 $10–14^8$.

Written below the top line in a formal gothic script by two scribes; the first scribe copied the calendar.

Twelve large miniatures painted in the style of the School of the Masters of the Gold Scrolls (Wieck, 109; Dogaer, *Flemish Miniature Painting*, 27–31, this manuscript listed p. 31); predominate colors are deep blue, orange, shades of green, pink-beige, and blue-gray; generally lacking in depth or convincing perspective; drapery carefully modelled with dark folds; simple faces with features lightly sketched in shades of brown; set in interiors with diapered backgrounds (for example, f. 1), in landscapes with blue skies (for example, f. 24) or against deep beige backgrounds decorated with brushed-gold scrolls (ff. 9, 12, 37; similar background in smaller miniatures, ff. 48, 50v, 51v, and 52). Quality of the miniatures varies; the crucifixion miniature, f. 9, skillfully executed, possibly by another hand; smaller miniatures for the suffrages quickly and clumsily painted. Miniatures are placed above five lines of text and fully enclosed by narrow pink and polished gold arched frames, edged in black and cusped on the arch; text framed by narrow L-shaped red, blue, and polished gold bars extending from the initial; with full borders, rather empty in the inner margins, of black ink sprays with gold motifs and thin multi–colored acanthus leaves, flowers and occasional strawberries. Subjects as follows: f. 1 (Hours of the Virgin, matins) Annunciation, set in an interior; at the top, the heavens depicted with the face of God in blue; f. 9 (Hours of the Cross) Crucifixion with Mary and John; f. 12 (Hours of the Holy Spirit) Pentecost with the dove descending from the sky; Mary with an open book in the center, surrounded by the apostles; f. 15 (Hours of the Virgin; lauds) Visitation, set in a landscape; f. 24 (prime) Nativity with Mary kneeling before the Child and Joseph with a lighted candle; f. 28 (terce) Annunciation to the shepherds; an angel with scroll above; f. 31 (sext) Adoration of the Magi; f. 34 (none) Presentation in the Temple, set in the interior of a gothic church; Simeon with a cloth covering his hands, accepts the Child from Mary; Joseph, an attendant with the basket of birds and the prophetess Anna, look on; f. 37 (vespers) Flight into Egypt; f. 42 (compline) Coronation of the Virgin; an angel blows a trumpet in the background; f. 61 (Penitential psalms) Last Judgement; Christ with stigmata, seated on an orb, flanked by angels blowing trumpets; the heads of the dead emerge from the ground below; f. 73 (Office of the Dead) Funeral set inside a church with two vested clerics before the coffin and three mourners, dressed in hooded black robes, behind.

Twelve suffrages, ff. 47–52, copied one per page, with smaller 6-line miniatures, surrounded by text in the outer and bottom margins, with narrow gold frames edged in black; short angle borders with black vine spray, flowers, strawberries and gold motifs: f. 47 Michael slaying the devil; f. 47v John the Baptist holding the lamb; f. 48 Peter holding book and keys; f. 48v Christopher carrying the Christ child across a river; f. 49 Martyrdom of Sebastian; f. 49v Anthony abbot with staff and two pigs; f. 50 Francis with stigmata; f. 50v Nicholas with the three boys in the tub; f. 51 Mary Magdalene with ointment jar; f. 51v Catherine of Alexandria with wheel and sword, and with the Emperor Maxentius behind; f. 52 Margaret emerging from the dragon, with God the Father in the clouds; f. 52v Barbara holding book and a palm, next to her tower.

Major initials on pages with miniatures, 4-line white-patterned blue or pink, imperfectly alternating, on cusped grounds of the other color and gold, or gold alone (cf. ff. 11, 59 and 67), infilled with colored trilobe leaves against a burnished gold ground. Similar 3-line white-patterned pink initial on a blue patterned ground edged in gold, art. 4 (f. 53), with an angle border similar to those used for the Suffrages, but including acanthus leaves. 2-line gold initials edged in black against white-patterned cusped grounds in pink with touches of blue, or blue, with infilling of the other color; similar "KL" monograms. 1-line initials alternating blue and gold with quickly executed pen decoration in red and black respectively. Red and blue line fillers with gold dots; red rubrics. Majuscules within the text stroked with red.

Bound in France, s. XVI[2] (dated by De Ricci, ca. 1570), in dark brown calf, gold-tooled with center and four cornerpiece ornaments; inner panel stamped with dots; outer border bounded by narrow rules filled with arabesque ornament; rebacked; gilt edges.

Written in Flanders in the second quarter of the fifteenth century, probably for use in Bruges as indicated by the saints included in the calendar (Basil the Great, 14 June; Remigius and Bavo, 1 October; and Donatianus, 14 October; all in red). In France by the sixteenth century when the book was bound and a number of saints were added to the calendar. Belonged to the family of Diogo de Mello; his armorial bookplate, s. XVIII, inside front cover, with the engraver's: "Carmona fecit" (gules six roundels or 2, 2 and 2; cf. dexter side of the shield for Mello e Castro in Rietstap, vol. 4, pl. 183: gules a double traverse cross or and six roundels argent 2, 2, and 2; but note that the verbal description of this shield specifies gold roundels); earlier engraving of the same coat of arms pasted on f. 'A', with a contemporary note in Portuguese describing the contents, above. Belonged to Fernando Palha (d. 1897); bookplate inside front cover, with shelf mark (?) added: "N°. Meza Gab [?] n° 2,"; *Catalogue de la bibliothèque de M. Fernando Palha* (Lisbon 1896) 1:11–12, no. 28. Presented on December 3, 1928 by John Batterson Stetson, Jr. (1884–1952), A. B. Harvard 1906, who was curator and then honorary curator of Portuguese literature, Harvard College Library, 1923–43 (library stamp, front flyleaf, f. 'A'v). Former Harvard shelf mark: 9290.25.

Bibliography: De Ricci, 987; Wieck, p. 109 and fig. 28 (reproducing f. 9).

MS Lat 133 — Northern France s. $XV^{4/4}$
Horae, use of Rouen — Pl. 29

1. ff. 1–12v Calendar in French, rather empty, with major feasts in red, including Simeon Stylites (5 January), Lucianus, patron of Beauvais (8 January), William of Bourges (10 January), Maurus (15 January), Launomar (19 January), Vincent (in red, 22 January), Julianus (16 February), Honorina (27 February), Denis of Corinth (8 April), Opportuna (22 April), Germanus, bishop of Paris (28 May), Landericus, bishop of Paris (10 June), Leufroy (21 June), Arnulph, bishop of Tours (18 July), Anne (in red, 26 July, and in black, 28 July), Dominic (4 August), Justinus (7 August), King Louis (24 August; usually 25 August), Fiacre (29 August), Francis (4 October), Denis, bishop of Paris (in red, 9 October), Mellonius, bishop of Rouen (22 October), Magloire (24 October), Marcellus, bishop of Paris (3 November), Lazarus (17 December), and Thomas of Canterbury (in red, 28 December).

2. ff. 13–71v Hours of the Virgin, use of Rouen; matins (ff. 13–32v) with nine psalms and three lessons, but without rubrics; f. 27v is blank, but ruled; the text continues in a new hand, f. 28, with no break; lauds, prime, terce, and vespers conclude with prayers: "Concede nos famulos tuos quesumus domine deus perpetua mentis ... [Bruylants, *Oraisons* 2: no. 122; printed *HE*, 44 and 51]," and "Deus qui corda fidelium sancti spiritus illustratione docuisti ... [Bruylants, *Oraisons* 2: no. 349; printed *Sarum Breviary*, 1:ix]"; sext and none conclude with "Concede nos famulos tuos ... [as above]" only; compline concludes with "Graciam tuam quesumus domine mentibus nostris infunde ... [printed *HE*, 61]."

3. ff. 72–75v Hours of the Cross, short form.

4. ff. 76–78v Hours of the Holy Spirit, short form.

5. ff. 78v–95v [Prayers] f. 78v Doulce dama [*sic*] de misericorde me [*sic*] de pitie ffontaine de tous biens ... [The Fifteen Joys of the Virgin; Sonet 458; printed Leroquais, *LH* 2:310–11, no. 5; incorrectly copied with the ninth (ending abruptly) and the tenth stanzas after the seventh on f. 81rv, followed by the eighth, then resuming correctly with the eleventh and twelfth on f. 82; the ninth then copied again, in full, on f. 82v, followed by the "Ave maria," in full; f. 83 begins with a fragment from the end of the fifteenth stanza: "//que ce soit a son saint non et au sauuemen de mon ame. Ave."; text then resumes correctly, ff. 83–84, with the thirteenth, fourteenth and fifteenth stanzas, the last ending imperfectly: "et pour les trespasses que il aient merci et pardon//"]; f. 84 [prologue] Quiconques ueult estre bien conseilles ... [text] Doulx dieu doulx pere sanite [*sic*] trinite ung dieu ... [The Seven Requests; Sonet 1760 (prologue) and 504; printed Leroquais *LH*, 2:309–10, no. 4]; f. 87v Obsecro te domina sancta maria ... Et michi famulo [*om* tuo] ... [Leroquais, *LH* 2:346]; f. 91 Gaude flore uirginali, honoreque spirituiali [*sic*] transcendens splendiferium [*sic*] ... [seven stanzas; printed *HE*, 64–65]; f. 92v Aue domine ihesu christe uerbum patris et filius uirginis ... [printed Wilmart, 412–3, no. III, here with the first, second ("... laus angelorum ...") and seventh verses ("... uia dulcis ... pax dulcedo retines uera uita perhempnis. amen.") only]; f. 93 Domine ihesu christe qui septem uerba die ultimo uite tue in cruce pendens dixisti ut semper illa sacratissima uerba in memoriam haberemus ... et conmorari per infinita seculorum secula. amen. [*Lyell Cat.*, 379, no. 159]; f. 95 Per tuum uirgo filium per patrem per paraclitum affinis presens ad obitum meumque muni spiritum. . . .

6. ff. 96–107 Passion according to John; text is misbound: f. 96rv (John 18:1–6), should be followed by ff. 103–104v (John 18:6–23); text continues with no breaks, ff. 97–101v (John 18:23–19:24); f. 102rv repeats the text on f. 101rv, ending two lines sooner, and then continues, with no breaks on ff. 105–107 (John 19:24–19:42); followed by "Aue regina celorum, aue domina angelorum salue radix sancta ... [*RH* 2070]," and "Regina celi letare allelulia ... [*RH* 17170]." [F. 107v blank, but ruled.]

7. ff. 108–126v Penitential psalms and litany, including Denis, Maurice, Nicasius, Eustachius, Marcellinus, Albinus, Quentin and Leodegar among the martyrs, Vedast, Germanus, Leonard and Romanus among the confessors and Juliana among the virgins; the scribe mistakenly added a second group of martyrs (Silvester, Gregory, Hilary, Martin and Ambrose) following Leodegar; these same saints are listed again as the first confessors; followed by the prayer, "Deus cui proprium est misereri semper et parcere ... [printed *HE*, 97]."

8. ff. 127–151v Office of the Dead; vespers ending imperfectly, f. 131v, at the end of the Magnificat; when copying matins (beginning f. 132), the scribe began f. 149 with text already copied on f. 148v; the text then continues correctly, and ends imperfectly on f. 151v with psalm 41:6 ("Quare tristis es anima mea et quare contrbas [*sic*] me//") of the third nocturn; lessons and responses in the first two nocturns agree with the Use of Paris; lauds lacking.

9. ff. 152–153 [added in a contemporary hand] John 1–1:14. [Ff. 153v–157v blank, but ruled.]

Parchment (calendar copied on thicker and glossier parchment), ff. iii (paper) + iv (parchment) + 157 + iii (paper; preceded by stub of earlier parchment flyleaf), 175 x 127 (84 x 59–56) mm. 14 long lines. Ruled lightly in brown ink with the top 2, and bottom 1 horizontal rules full across; single full-length vertical bounding lines. Prickings, top margin only. Calendar (ff. 1–12v): written space (88–87 x 61) mm. 4 columns (1 wider column for main entry and 3 narrow columns; the third column is empty), 17 lines. Ruled in red ink, with the top and bottom horizontal rules full across; single vertical bounding lines, full-length on the far inside and outside, and otherwise, length of the written space only. No prickings. Quire 4 (ff. 28–35v): written space (86–85 x 59) mm. 14 long lines. Ruled lightly in pale red ink, with the top and bottom horizontal rules full across; single full-length vertical bounding lines. No prickings.

1^{12} 2^{8} 3^{8} (–8, following f. 27, cancelled with no loss of text) 4^{8} (through f. 35v) 5–6^{8} 7^{6} (through f. 57v) 8^{8} 9^{10} (through f. 75v) 10^{6} 11^{10} 12^{12} (–6,7, after f. 96, conjugate pair misbound in quire 13 as ff. 103–104) 13^{4} (+ two leaves after 1, ff. 103–104, from quire 12) 14–15^{8} 16^{8} (originally with nine leaves; now –9, after f. 131v, with loss of text) 17^8 18^8 (+9, f. 148, singleton) 19^{12} (–4, with loss of text after f. 151v; –8, 9, following f. 154, with no loss of text). Horizontal catchwords in ink, not copied by the main scribes: quire 2 (f. 20v), lower, inside margin, and, in another hand, quire 4 (f. 35v), center, bottom margin. Each quire numbered by a modern hand in pencil on the first folio, recto, lower, very inside margin.

Written below the top line in mature gothic bookhands in two sizes depending on liturgical function, by at least five scribes: 1. calendar (ff. 1–12v), possibly same scribe as 2; 2. ff. 13–27, leaving f. 27v blank, and 36–82v; 3. quire 4, ff. 28–35v, added; 4. ff. 83–107, leaving 107v blank; 5. ff. 108–end. Ff. 152–153 added by a close contemporary.

Thirteen large miniatures by a follower of Mâitre François, who also decorated a book of hours, Dôle, Bibliothèque municipale, MS 43 around 1480 (see E. Spencer, "The Mâitre François and His Atelier" Unpublished Ph.D. dissertation [Harvard University 1931] 146, 166–67; cf. Wieck, p. 30, no. 14, attributing this manuscript and Houghton, MS Lat 159 to Mâitre François); predominant colors are blue, dark rose, light pink, and brown, with occasional use of bright yellow; draperies and other details often highlighted in gold; interiors, usually with small arched windows and checkered floors in shades of green, are framed by pink columns, meeting at the top in a traceried arch. Miniatures are placed above four lines of text, fully enclosed by narrow gold arched frames (now mostly effaced), edged in black and cusped on the arch, touching the outer bounding line at the top (miniatures, ff. 44, 63, 108 lack black ink frames, but faint traces of gold remain); text and miniatures bordered by narrow red, blue and gold U-shaped frames, edged in black; well-executed full outer borders, empty at the top of the arch, completely bounded on the outside by red ink rules, of black ink sprays with gold ivy leaves and other motifs, blue and beige acanthus, naturalistic flower sprays and strawberries. Miniature, f. 32v (quire 4), probably by another artist working in a very similar style, is set above five lines of text, framed in gold as above, with a broad U-shaped frame of trilobe leaves and vines on gold, edged on the inside with narrow bands of red and blue extending from the initial around the text and miniature; similar full outer border with a monkey, fly, rooster and beetle, bounded on the outside by a narrow gold rule. Subjects as follows: f. 13 (Hours of the Virgin, matins) Annunciation in a vaulted interior, with Mary kneeling in front of a lectern, and an angel with scroll above; the dove descends on gold rays; f. 32v (lauds) Visitation set outside a town gate; probably by another artist, see above; f. 44 (prime) Nativity in an open thatched shed, with Mary and Joseph kneeling on either side of Christ; a wattle and daub fence in the background; f. 50 (terce) Annunciation to the shepherds, with river in the foreground, and an angel with banner above; f. 54 (sext) Adoration of the Magi in the same setting as the Nativity; f. 57v (none) Presentation in the Temple, with Mary's and Simeon's hands covered by a cloth; an attendant with basket of birds and candle (?) stands behind Mary; f. 61 (vespers) Flight into Egypt, with the miracle of the reaper in the background; f. 67v (compline) Coronation of the Virgin; an angel places a crown on Mary's head from above, with another angel standing behind; choir of angels in dark red and orange forms the background; f. 72 (Hours of the Cross) Crucifixion, with Mary and John on the left, and soldiers, holding a standard with an eagle, on the right, the sun and moon above, and a town in the background; f. 76 (Hours of the Holy Spirit) Pentecost, set in a gothic interior, with Mary kneeling at an altar with an open book, the apostles grouped on three sides, and a dove descending on rays of gold; f. 96 (Passion according to John) Betrayal of Christ, with Judas kissing Christ; Peter with drawn sword; Christ reaches down to restore Malchus' ear, who is shown kneeling with a lantern in the foreground; f. 108 (Penitential psalms) David, wearing his crown, kneeling in an interior before an altar, his harp behind him; f. 127 (Office of the Dead) burial in a church yard, with a priest reading the service, and an acolyte holding bucket and staff, while the shrouded body is lowered into the grave.

Major initials on folios with miniatures, except in quire 4 (see below) begin with 4-line (f. 96, 2–line) white-patterned blue initials on rectangular gold grounds, edged in black, infilled with orange and blue trilobe leaves on gold. Prayers, ff. 78v and 84v, begin with similar 4- to 3-line initials; text and initial framed by narrow red, blue and gold bars in the outer margin, with blue and gold acanthus and other flowers at the top and bottom; outer borders on three sides (lacking on the inside) in the same style as the full borders. 2- to 1-line (except ff. 73–75, 3-line) polished gold initials on grounds of white-patterned blue or pink-red, often with touches of the other color, infilled with the other color; similar 2-line "KL"-monograms; red and blue white-patterned bar line fillers, with gold dots. Guide letters for the initials often visible in the margins. Blank spaces remain for rubrics.

Decoration in quire 4, ff. 28–35v, differs from that in the remainder of the manuscript (miniature, f. 32v, described above). 2-line white-patterned blue initials, on square gold grounds, infilled with blue and orange trilobe leaves on gold; with short borders extending from the initials in the inner margins, now incomplete and including only gold motifs edged in black. Every text page with incomplete panel borders in the outer margins, with gold motifs, edged in black, set into a vine sketched in very faint lead or ink. 1-line initials and line fillers as in the remainder of the manuscript. Red rubrics; majuscules skillfully highlighted in pale yellow.

Bound in England (?) in modern gold-tooled dark green morocco; spine with four raised bands, framing elaborately tooled compartments, with title in Latin, and "1429" at the bottom; red morocco doublure; endleaves lined with silk; edges gauffered in a floral pattern, and gilt; front cover and spine damaged.

Written in the last quarter of the fifteenth century, probably in Northern France, where it was illuminated by a follower of the Mâitre François, possibly for use in the diocese of Rouen, as indicated by the use of the Hours of the Virgin; the Office of the Dead, now incomplete, is likely Paris use. The calendar, which is copied on parchment that is thicker and glossier than the parchment of the remainder of the manuscripts, lacks the usual Rouen saints, but includes a number of saints venerated in Paris and Northern France: Marcellus, bishop of Paris, 3 November, Honorina, 27 February, Opportuna, 22 April, Denis, bishop of Paris, in red, 9 October; some other common Parisian feasts are lacking. Unidentified shelf mark in pencil, front flyleaf, f. i^v: "Shelf 7/722"; bookseller's note, f. 1, written diagonally in pencil: "M[?]/d/." Belonged to George Robert White (bookplate, front flyleaf, f. ii). Bequeathed by Mrs. H. J. Bradbury, June 26, 1930 (library records). Former Harvard shelf mark: 9290.26; changed in 1931 at the request of De Ricci to Lat 133. Typed description by E. P. Spencer, dated July 1930, pasted between the front flyleaves.

Bibliography: De Ricci, 987; E. P. Spencer, "The Mâitre François and His Atelier" unpublished Ph.D. dissertation (Harvard University 1931) 146, 166–67, referring to this manuscript as Widener Library, the Bradbury Hours; Roger S. Wieck, "French Illuminated Manuscripts in the Houghton Library: Recent Discoveries and Attributions," *Harvard Library Bulletin* 31 (1983) 192; Wieck, p. 109 and fig. 8 (reproducing f. 13).

MS Lat 134 **Southern Germany s. XIV²**
Prayers for Exorcism, Benedictions, etc. **Pls. 35, 67**

1. ff. 1–25 [f. 1] Deus angelorum deus archangelorum deus prophetarum deus apostolorum deus martyrorum [*sic*] deus confessorum deus uirginum deus pater domini nostri ihesu christi. Inuoco nomen sanctum tuum ac preclare maiestatis tue clemenciam ... [Aldoph Franz, *Die kirchlichen Benediktionen im Mittelalter* (Freiburg im Breisgau 1909) 2:596–7, III.1; 2:601, IV.4; and 2:608, V.14]; [f. 1v] Domine sancte pater omnipotens eterne deus Osanna in excelsis pater domini nostri ihesu christi qui illum refugam tyrannum gehenne deputasti ... [Franz 2:597–9, III.3; 2:601, IV.6; and 2:604, V.5]; [f. 4] Omnipotens sempiterne deus pater domini nostri ihesu christi te suppliciter deprecamur impera dyabolo qui hunc famulum tuum N. detinet ... [Franz 2:571, note 4]; [f. 4] Recede ergo a capite a capillis a lingua a sublingua a brachio ... [Franz 2:602, IV.9, here beginning with line 10]; [f. 4v] Signo caput tuum sicut signavit dominus omnipotens [*sic*] infirmos in chana galylee ... [Franz 2:602–3, IV.10]; [f. 5] Repelle domine ab hoc famulo tuo N. omnem infestacionem inimici ... [Franz 2:601, IV.3]; [f. 5] Coniuro te et contestor dyabole per nomen domini nostri ihesu christi et imperium eius et per uirtutem sancte trinitatis et omnipotentie [*sic*] eius ut exeas sathana et omnis dyabolica potestas de homine isto ... [Franz 2:605–8, V.8]; [f. 8] Deus conditor et defensor generis humani qui hominem ad ymaginem et similitudinem tuam formasti ... [Franz 2:597, III.2; 2:601, IV.5; and 2:608, V.15]; [f. 8v] Adiuro te per deum altissimum maledicte sathanas ne famulum suum artibus tuis temptare nitaris ...; [f. 9] Obsecro te domine ihesu christe ut eicias omnes languores ab omnibus membris hominis istius a capite a capillis a cerebro ...; [f. 9v] Exorcizo te maledicte et immunde spiritus draco basilisce serpens noxie per uerbum ueritatis ... [Franz 2:590, II.3]; [f. 10]

Exorcizo te auctor dyabolice potestatis inuentor malicie cum satellitibus tuis precipiens . . . [Franz 2:596, II.12]; f. 10v Exorcizo te spiritus inmunde per deus patrem omnipotentem qui fecit celum et terram mare et omnia que in eis sunt. Pro inde omnis uirtus aduersarii omnis exercitus dyaboli omnis inimici et omnne fantasma sathane eradicare . . . [f. 10v] Non ego tibi impero neque peccata mea inmundissime spiritus sed imperet . . . [Franz 2:594, II.10, here ending line 10; 2:602, IV.9, here ending line 10; and 2:608, V.17]; [f. 11] Nec te latheat sathanans imminere tibi penas imminere tormenta diem iudicii diem supplicii sempiterni diem qui uenturus est . . .; [f. 12v] Domine sancte pater omnipotens eterne deus qui peccatorum non uis animas perire sed culpas conteri . . .; [f. 12v] Adiuro te per deum uiuum et per deum omnipotentem inmundissime spiritus qui es inueterator malicie . . .; [f. 14] *Alie oratio.* Omnipotens domine uerbum dei patris ihesu christe deus et dominus uniuerse creature qui sanctis apostolis tuis dedisti potestatem calcandi serpentes et scorpiones . . . [Franz 2:599–601, IV.1, here omitting lines 5–11]; [f. 16] Domine sancte pater eterne deus pater domini nostri ihesu christi in tuo nomine et in tua uirtute confidens diuinam potenciam inuocans . . .; [f. 17v] Omnipotens sempiterne deus salus eterna credencium exaudi nos pro famulo tuo, da ei ueram humilitatem, ueram pacienciam . . . [Van Dijk, *SMRL* 2:321]; [f. 18] Domine sancte pater omnipotens semper deus expelle dyabolum ab homine isto N. de capite de capillis . . . ut operetur in eo uirtus christi ihesu filii dei altissimi. Qui regnat in secula seculorum. Amen. [Franz 2:601–2, IV.7; and 2:608, V.11]; [f. 18v] Quesumus omnipotens deus ut mittere digneris sanctos angelos tuos qui defendant . . .; [f. 19] Deus abraham deus ysaac deus iacob deus qui moysi famulo tuo in monte synai apparuisti et filios israel de terra egypti eduxisti . . .; [f. 19] Exorcizo te omnis occursus sathane et omne fantasma ut recedas . . .; [f. 19v] Domine deus omnipotens qui omnia proprio dispensas arbitrio. Tuo pater clemens tu pius propiciator tu mestorum [*sic*] consolator . . .; [f. 20] Sanet te deus pater omnipotens qui te creauit. Sanet te deus filius qui pro te passus est in cruce . . .; [f. 20] Sanet te deus pater sanet te deus filius sanet te spiritus sanctus sanent te omnes sancti angeli et archangeli . . .; [f. 20v] Sanet te deus pater omnipotens sanet te ihesus christus filius dei sanet te spiritus sanctus. Sanet te fides tua que te liberauit . . .; [f. 21]

Sancta trinitas sit tecum omnibus diebus uite tue. Benedicat te dominus custodiat te christus ostendatque dominus faciem suam . . .; [f. 21v] Benedicat te dominus et custodiat te. Illuminet dominus ihesus faciem suam super te . . .; [f. 21v] Benedicere digneris et sanctificare domine famulum tuum istum celesti benedictione . . .; [f. 21v] Domine ihesus christus aput [*sic*] te sit ut te defendat intra te sit ut te reficiat . . .; f. 22 Benedicat te deus pater, sanet te dei [*sic*] filius illuminet te spiritus sanctus corpus tuum custodiat animam tuam . . .; [f. 22] Benedicat te deus celi adiuuet te christus filius dei corpus tuum in suo seruicio custodiri . . .; [f. 23v] Benedicat te deus pater qui in principio cuncta creauit . . .; [f. 23v] Benedicat te deus pater custodiat te ihesus christus illuminet te spiritus sanctus cunctis diebus uite tue . . .; [f. 23v] Benedicat te pater et filius et spiritus sanctus unitas natura trinitatis et perfecta persona [unitas . . . persona: later expunged] . . .; [f. 24] Benedicat te deus pater qui te creauit, benedicat te deus filius pro te passus est, benedicat te [later expunged: deus] spiritus sanctus qui in te filius est . . .; [f. 24] Lumen splendoris tui quesumus domine luceat in cordibus nostris et lumine tuo nos protege . . .; [f. 24] Spiritus te benedicat et animam tuam uiuificet et cor tuum illuminet . . .; [f. 24] Domine sancte pater omnipotens sempiterne deus qui es uia ueritas et uita. Exaudi et conserua hunc famulum tuum N . . .; [f. 24] Partem merearis cum sanctis et electis tuis habere perseuerare te christus filius dei . . .; [f. 24v] Benedictio dei patris et filii et spiritus sancti descendat et maneat super te semper amen. Benedicat te dominus benedictione perpetua . . .; [f. 25] Sancta trinitas et inseperabili unitas te benedicat . . .; [f. 25] Benedicat te deus pater et filius et spiritus sanctus ut habeas uitam eternam . . . et uiuas in secula seculorum. Amen.

Feminine forms superscript throughout (for example, see ff. 2, 4, 5, 8v, 17v and 21v).

2. f. 25rv [Added in red in another hand] Ach mala centum pastoksica seksica/ Syn r Evalk scaras olvpchinque <sin?> arrag/ Edypel edulpea mala uaf fanus affanus/ Hec caput edentis <sac?>, Hec in uertice mentis. [F. 25v blank, but ruled.]

Possibly a charm.

Parchment (soft and fuzzy), ff. i (parchment pastedown) + 25 + i (parchment pastedown), 156 x 110 (116–114 x 84–80) mm. 20 long lines. Ruled in ink with the top and bottom horizontal rules full across; single full-length vertical bounding lines. Neat slash-type prickings three outer margins (some trimmed, top and bottom).

1^{10} 2^{8} 3^{8} (8, unnumbered pastedown, conjoint with 1). Horizontal catchword, bottom, inside margin, quire 1; leaves signed in ink, arabic numerals, bottom, outer corner in the first half of each quire.

Written below the top line in an angular, clumsy, gothic bookhand.

Two-line plain red initials, set within the text space. Initials within the text stroked with red; crude red wavy line fillers.

Bound in Germany, s. XIV (?), in thick wooden boards cut flush with the book-block, covered with light-colored leather, now darkened, decorated with simple diagonal lines; original sewing on three cords; head- and tailbands are broken; upper and lower boards once with corner and center ornaments (some nails and center studs remain; rust holes and marks, front and back pastedowns and ff. 1–3, 23–25); lower board once with two brass fasteners and straps (part of brass fastener remains), which fastened to pins set in the center, upper board (one pin remains).

Written in Southern Germany in the second half of the fourteenth century. Belonged, s. XVI, to the Benedictine monastery at Alpirsbach (1095–1554; diocese Konstanz; Krämer, *Handschriftenerbe* 1:8); front pastedown, s. XVI: "Forma exorcisandi daemoni qua vtebantur in monasterio Alpirspach <hercinie?>," and in the same hand, "Fundatum est hoc monasterium Anno domini 1094 [*sic*]. Imperatore Henrico quarto, papa pascali. Obiit pius coenobii externus abbas Huldrichus Ham[m]an Anno 1545 die 19 octobris friburgi Brisgoiae ibidemque sepulcrus Huldricho duce Wi<nchu?>bergense patri<?> re<?>." Belonged to Severus of the parish of Alpirsbach; inside front cover, "Seuero Bersthyre parocho alp<irsbach>"; and back pastedown: "Seuerus me possidet." Given to the library by Alice L. Cushing, April 24, 1931 (library note, f. 1^{v}). Previous Harvard shelf mark: MS 9290.24.

secundo folio: hominem ad ymaginem

Bibliography: De Ricci, 987.

MS Lat 135 **Northern Italy s. XV²**
Juvenal; Persius **Pl. 53**

1. ff. 1–98 [Juvenal, *Saturae*] *Decimi Iunii Iuvenalis Aquinatis Satirici Libri Feliciter Incipit.* Semper ego auditor tantum numquamne reponam/ Vexatus totiens rauci theseide codri?/ . . . [Satire 16] . . . Vt leti faleris omnes et torquibus omnes. [Ends line 16, f. 98; ff. 98v–101v blank, but ruled.]

   W. V. Clausen, ed., *A. Persi Flacci et D. Iuni Iuvenalis Saturae.* OCT (Oxford 1959) 35–175. Not divided into the five books found in some manuscripts. Greek added in another hand: f. 31, Satire 6, verse 195; f. 56v, Satire 9, verse 37; f. 69v, Satire 11, verse 27.

2. ff. 102–118v [Persius, *Saturae;* Prologue] *Persius Flaccvs.* Nec fonte labra prolui cabballino [*sic*]/ . . . [f. 102v Satire 1] O cvras hominum, o quantum est in rebus inane/ . . . [Satire 6] . . . Inuentus chrysippe tui finitor acerui. [Ff. 119–120 blank, but ruled; f. 120v with miscellaneous notes and pen trials, s. XV–XVII.]

   Clausen, ed., 1–28; listed as no. 78 in Scarcia Piacentini. In Satire 3, f. 108, verse 12 was left incomplete, and verses 13 and 14 omitted; supplied by a later hand.

Parchment, ff. ii (parchment; i, pastedown) + 120 + i (parchment pastedown), 170 x 105 mm. Copied by two scribes, using two different layouts. Scribe 1, ff. 2–22v (quires 1 and 2): written space (107 x 62–65) mm.; ruled space, 110 x 63–53 mm. 20 lines of verse; ruled in light brown ink with the top 2 and single bottom horizontal lines full across; double full-length vertical bounding lines, used for the first majuscule of each line of verse. Prickings in the top, bottom, and outside margins. Written below the top line in a humanistic script by a practiced scribe.

Scribe 2, ff. 23–118v: written space (113–115 x 60–67) mm.; ruled space, 112 x 62–50 mm. 20 lines of verse; horizontal lines ruled in ink; double full-length vertical bounding lines, used for the first majuscule of each line of verse, ruled very faintly in lead. Single prickings, outside margin, slightly above the top horizontal ruled line (some trimmed), and occasionally, in the top and bottom margins.

Written on the top line in an uneven humanistic script. F. 1, replacing an excised leaf, written in an upright mannered humanistic script, s. XVI–XVII (?).

1^{12} (–1, now replaced with single leaf glued to 2) 2–9^{10} 10^{10} (–10, after f. 101, cancelled) 11^{10} 12^{10} (10, unnumbered pastedown). Vertical catchword, quire 11 (f. 111v) only, written on the bounding line. Quires 1–9 signed with a series of small majuscule letters, beginning with 'A', written between the inside vertical bounding lines, bottom margin, verso of last leaf (cut away in quire 3, 4, 6, and 8; partially visible in quires 7 and 9); leaves in the first half of quires 1, 2 and 5 signed with very small letters that designate the quire, bottom right corner, recto ("a," "b" and "e" respectively).

Twelve 4- to 5-line gold initials used to begin each of Juvenal's satires (initials for satires 1, 5, 7 and 11 cut out); set on tricolor square grounds of blue, bright pink and green, with white (possibly silver) or gold highlights, embellished with a fine tracery of vine stems, leaves and other flourishes in brown pen with gold balls, some with details in red (cf. ff. 5v, 9v, and 26). Prologue to Persius (f. 102) begins with a 5-line gold initial with white vinestem decoration in the style of Jacopo da Verona (we thank Professor A. C. de la Mare, October, 1987), extending the full length of the outside margin, on a ground of dark blue, infilled with deep red and green; with naked male figure holding a book seated at the top of the initial, sheltering under a leaf-motif ending in gold balls edged in black; and with a face, surrounded by leaves, decorated with bells and gold balls, at the bottom (reproduced in Wieck, fig. 112). Top margin, lightly sketched in pencil, a roundel with an incomplete coat of arms (unidentified motif, perhaps a tower or rook with a rounded top?), surrounded by vines; top margin, f. 104, vine with flowers, also in pencil. Both possibly added by a later hand. Six 3- to 4-line undecorated initials before each satire of Persius; all red, except f. 112, greenish-gold. In quires 1–4 sections within each satire delineated by large 1-line plain initials in red, blue, or occasionally, gold. Throughout, each line begins with a small majuscule in brown ink written between the bounding lines. Guide letters visible in interior of initials in art. 2. Rubrics throughout; running titles in red only through f. 18, possibly added.

The manuscript has been extensively damaged and repaired; f. 1, and gaps in the text left by cutting out the initials on ff. 21v, 42v, and

68v, rewritten, s. XVI–XVII (?), with crudely drawn initials in red and brown; many minor initials also excised.

Bound in Italy, s. XV, in wooden boards covered with brown leather, blind-tooled with three sets of triple rules; the inner set forming a large rectangular center panel with small floral and round stamps in a cruciform-shape; between the first and second set, a narrow band of chevrons interspersed with small round stamps; corners joined with scored diagonal lines between the second and third set. Spine scored with intersecting lines. Original sewing on three thongs which enter the boards by means of slanted channels. Two brass catches, lower board, with initial 'S'; straps with clasps (now missing) were fastened to the upper board by two brass rosettes. Remains of red and white paper label, upper board.

Written in Northern Italy in the second half of the fifteenth century (we thank Professor A. C. de la Mare for this information; August, 1987). Numerous miscellaneous notes, pen trials, etc., on the front and back pastedowns and facing flyleaves, including: names of early owners or readers, front flyleaf, f. i, "peiero [*sic*] es pergiurone et[?] falso," s. XVI, and note signed "S. Gras[?]," s. XVII; front flyleaf, f. i^{v}: "al sempo[?] di Traiano," s. XVI (?) (read under ultra-violet); f. 120v and back pastedown, translations into Italian of some Latin words occurring in Persius and Juvenal, s. XVI (we thank Dr. Consuelo Dutschke for this information). Possibly belonged to the Mannucci of Florence; front flyleaf, f. i^{v}, crudely painted coat of arms, s. XVII–XVIII (azure between two chevrons or a six-pointed estoile of the second; Rietstap, v. IV, pl. cxxxv). F. 118v, bottom margin, erased modern oval book stamp, now illegible. Given by Daniel B. Fearing (1859–1918) to Morris Hickey Morgan (1859–1910) in 1904 in Rome (note in Morgan's hand, front flyleaf, f. 1). Gift of Morgan to Harvard, January 1, 1910 (bookplate, front pastedown; library stamp, f. 1v); original Harvard shelf mark: Lp 15.2.4.

secundo folio: Quod superest

Bibliography: De Ricci, 987; De Ricci, "Handlist," 104 (listed as Lp 15.2.4); J. F. Chatterton Richards, "A description of a manuscript of Juvenal and Persius in Harvard College Library; MS Lp 15.2.4," (typescript, 1931) now Houghton bMS Lat 315(24); Wieck, p. 109, fig. 112 (reproducing f. 102).

MS Lat 136 Italy (Northeast?) 1471
Juvenal; Persius Pl. 10

1. ff. 1–81 [Guarinus Veronensis, 1–line argument] *Materiam et causas Satyrarum hac inspice prima.* [Juvenal, *Saturae*] *Iunii Iuuenalis Aquinatis Satyricorum poetarum facetissimi et grauissimi libri Satyrarum principium foeliciter.* Semper ego auditor tantum numquam ne reponam/ Vexatus totiens rauci theseide codri/ ... [Satire 16] ... Vt laeti faleris omnes et torquibus omnes. *Iunii Iuuenalis Aquinatis Satyricorum poetarum facetissimi libri Satyrarum finis MCCCCLXXI quarto octobris. Deo gloria laus et honor.*

   W. V. Clausen, ed., *A. Persi Flacci et D. Iuni Iuvenalis Saturae.* OCT (Oxford 1959) 35–175. Not divided into the five books found in some manuscripts. Greek in the hand of the main scribe: f. 25v, Satire 6, verse 195; f. 57v, Satire 11, verse 27; clumsily written in red, possibly added: f. 47, Satire 9, verse 37. Each satire introduced by the argument of Guarinus Veronensis (1374–1460) in red; S. Endlicher, ed., *Catalogus codicum philologicorum latinorum Bibliothecae Palatinae Vindobonensis* (Vienna 1836) 116.

2. f. 81 [Added in the blank ruled space at the end of article 1 by a contemporary hand; unidentified line of verse] Nec pietas opes nec missa minuit iter. [Followed by Ovid, *Remedia amoris,* verses 91–2] Principiis obsta sero medicina paratur/ Cum mala per longas conualuere moras. [F. 81v blank, with notes in a later hand, s. XVI–XVII.]

   E. J. Kenney, ed., *P. Ovidi Nasonis Amores, Medicamina Faciei Femineae, Ars Amatoria, Remedia Amoris.* OCT (Oxford 1961) 208.

3. ff. 82–96 [Persius, *Saturae;* Prologue] *A persii volaterrani Satyrarum Libelli initium.* Nec fonte labra prolui caballino/ ... [f. 82 Satire 1] *Satyra prima de peruersis exercitationibus poetarum.* O curas hominum. o quantum est [*corr.*[2]: *add.* in] rebus inane/ ... [Satire 6] ... Inuentus chrysippe tui finitor acerui. *A persii volaterrani Satyrarum Libelli finis foeliciter vi octobris MCCCCLXXI. Laus deo honor et gloria. Amen.* [Ends top f. 96; f. 96v blank, but ruled.]

   Clausen, ed., 1–28; listed as no. 79 in Scarcia Piacentini. Each satire begins with an explanatory argument in red, also found in

Houghton, MS Lat 138 (Northeastern Italy, s. XV$^{3/4}$): satire 1, see above; f. 85 "Satyra secunda de falsis uotis"; f. 86v "Satyra tertia de incerta iuuenum et humana desidia"; f. 89 "Satyra quarta contra ambitiosos ciues"; f. 90 "Satyra quinta ad cornutum philosophum et poetam preceptorem suum de rebus uariis precipue de laudibus preceptoris et uera liberalitate"; f. 94 "Satyra vi ad bassum <et?> illos qui nimium cupidi rerum et habentibus multa inuidentes misere uiuunt, cum etiam nimiam habeant herendum [?] considerationem."

(Articles 1–3) Marginal annotations and corrections found infrequently in Juvenal, often in Persius, including: infrequent corrections, throughout, in an Italian hand, s. XV–XVI (cf. f. 83, supplying the omitted verse 46 of Persius, satire 1); f. 88v, verse 94 of Persius, satire 3, rewritten, a better reading supplied, and verses 95 and 96, omitted by the scribe, then added in another hand, s. XV; frequent annotations added throughout in later hands, s. XVI–XVII, including a long note ending in Greek, f. 81v, at times citing other authors including Horace, and often commenting on the text as on f. 40v, where verse 7 of Juvenal, satire 8, omitted by the scribe, is added, with a note beginning, "Inscribatur in libro vester . . ."; in another hand, s. XVIII, frequent explanatory and textual comments on Persius, usually in red ink, some in Greek, often citing the readings of the "Codex Pinellianus" (see provenance, below).

Parchment, ff. i (paper) + i (parchment) + 96 + i (parchment) + i (paper), 180 x 112 (115–110 x 72–65) mm. 24 lines of verse. Ruled in light brown ink and lead; left margin with double full-length vertical bounding lines used for the first majuscule of each line; right margin with single full-length vertical bounding lines; top horizontal line sometimes full across.

1–9^{10} 10^{8} (–7, 8, cancelled). Horizontal catchwords throughout, center, bottom margin. First recto of each quire numbered in pencil in a modern hand, inside bottom margin.

Written below the top line by one scribe in a quick current humanistic script.

Eighteen 4- to 2-line gold initials used at the beginning of each satire in Juvenal, and in Persius, prologue and satire 1; f. 1, boxed in red with a gold border and crude decorations in red; f. 4v, boxed in gold; f. 8, boxed in brown ink; remaining initials plain or embellished with simple decoration. Blank spaces left for the initials to Persius, satires 2–6. Arguments of Guarinus and introductory rubrics to Persius copied in a very pale red, at times written in the unruled space in the upper margin (cf. ff. 1, 49v). First majuscule of each line written between double bounding lines. Some very small guide letters next to the initials, and in the blank space intended for initials. A few satires numbered in the margins in small roman numerals in ink, possibly by a later hand (cf. ff. 49v, 61).

Bound in England by Charles Lewis (1786–1836) for the Reverend Henry Drury in 1822 (see note, front flyleaf, f. i, cited below) in orange morocco with narrow gold borders, front and back covers; gold tooling on spine with title; gilt edges.

Written in Italy, possibly in the Northeast (we thank Professor A. C. de la Mare for this information; July, 1986) in 1471; dated by the scribe, ff. 81 and 96. Since the scribe specifies that the Satires of Juvenal were completed on October 4, and those of Persius on October 6, the entire manuscript presumably could have been completed in as little as fifteen to sixteen days; see C. H. Jones, Jr., "A quickly written manuscript," *Speculum* 7 (1932) 94–95. Marginal additions and corrections indicate that the book was used for study through the eighteenth century. Probably in Venice, s. XVIII, when notes were added to Persius comparing the readings in this manuscript with those in a manuscript from the library of Maffeo Pinelli (1736–85), referred to as the "Codex Pinellianus"; possibly MS 7942 in Jacobo Morelli, *Bibliotheca Maphaei Pinelli Veneti*. . . (Venice 1787) 3:359, copied in 1457 by Leonardus filius Saraceni de Sancto Iohanne Civis Vincentinus, as suggested by A. Palmieri in a typed description dated 1916, included in the manuscript between the front endleaves, ff. i–ii. Belonged to Abate Luigi Celotti (c.1768–c.1846); his sale, London, Sotheby's, February 26, 1821, no. 235, to the Reverend Henry Drury (1778–1841); note in Drury's hand, front endleaf, f. i: "H. Drury. adornante C. Lewis. 1822." Drury sale, London, Evans, February 19–March 12, 1827, no. 2124, to Thorpe. Belonged to Edward Craven Hawtrey, headmaster and provost of Eton; his sale, London, Sotheby's, July 1, 1853, I, no. 838, to Molini. Belonged to Ambroise Firmin-Didot (1790–1876; bookplate with date, 1850, inside front cover); his sale, *Catalogue des livres précieux, manuscrits et imprimés* . . . (Paris, June 9–15, 1881) vol. 3, no. 8, to Claudin. Description from an unidentified sale catalogue in French glued on the front flyleaf, f. i^{v}. Gustav von Emick sale, London, June 20, 1900, no. 72, to Gardener. Unidentified initials in pencil, partially erased, inside back cover: "H. K." Given in 1901 by Daniel B. Fearing (1859–1918) to Morris H. Morgan (1859–1910) as a Christmas present (note in Fearing's hand, front endleaf, f. i; Morgan's bookplate, inside front cover). Gift of Morgan to Harvard, January 1, 1910 (library stamp, f. 1v, bookplate, inside back cover); original Harvard shelf mark: Lp 15.2.3.

secundo folio: Quid referam

Bibliography: De Ricci, 988; De Ricci, "Handlist," 104 (listed as Lp 15.2.3); Carroll H. Jones, Jr., "A manuscript of Juvenal and Persius belonging to the XV century in the Library of Harvard College," (in manuscript, May, 1931) now Houghton bMS Lat 315(9).

MS Lat 137 — Italy (Florence?) s. $XV^{1/4}$
Persius, Saturae; Commentarius in Persii — Pl. 44

1. ff. 1–16 [Persius, *Saturae*; Prologue] Nec fonte labra prolui caballino/ . . . [f. 1 Satire 1] O Curas hominum o quantum est in rebus inane/ . . . [Satire 6] . . . Inuentus crisippe tui finitor acerui. *Laus deo et virgini.* [F. 16v blank, but ruled.]

   W. V. Clausen, ed., *A. Persi Flacci et D. Iuni Iuvenalis Saturae.* OCT (Oxford 1959) 1–28; listed as no. 80 in Scarcia Piacentini. On f. 11v, Satire 5, verse 79 was incorrectly copied as "Marcus dama pape marco sub iudice palles" (cf. verse 80); correct reading supplied by the scribe or a contemporary corrector in the margin.

   (Articles 2–6) ff. 17–89 A version of the Vulgate Commentary on Persius, *Saturae*, grouped by Robothan and Cranz (*CTC* 3: 201–312) with fifteenth-century manuscripts of tradition A (see esp. p. 219), but with interpolations from tradition B, and with introductory material reflecting a number of traditions.

2. ff. 17–18, line 12 [*Vita* of Persius] A Perseus Flaccus natus est

pridie nonas decembris . . . ne hoc in se Nero dictum arbitraretur.

The usual Life of Persius, often attributed in the manuscripts, most likely incorrectly, to Valerius Probus (cf. Robothan and Cranz, 204); Clausen, ed., 31–34.

3. f. 18, lines 12–21 [Biographical fragment, following article 2 without a break] Perseus hic [*om.* diu] dubitans utrum militie an poetriae incumberet . . . Solarium non est unius diei prebenda.

   Found in manuscripts of tradition D; cf. Robothan and Cranz, 229–231.

4. f. 18–18v, line 7 [Discussion of Satire] Satyra genus clarni [*sic*] est uel lancis multis. . . . quod personis factisque saciata habundare uidetur [*sic*]. Satyra igitur a saturitate quod plena sit conuiuiis et reprehensionibus hominum.

   Found in manuscripts of tradition B; cf. Robothan and Cranz, 221.

5. f. 18v, line 20–f. 20 [Commentary, prologue, following article 4 without a break] Quod Esiodus dicit. Dicitur enim[?] pegasus errando ad eliconem peruenisse ibique siti oppressus cum ungula fodisse terram . . . *pegaseum* id est dulce carmen.

   Similar to the text in manuscripts of tradition A, with the opening lemma omitted; cf. Robothan and Cranz, 216–20, esp. 219.

6. ff. 20–89 [Commentary, satires 1–6] *O curas hominum.* semet ipsum arguit quod sciat neminem esse qui tam robuste uelit studere . . . Vt que eius auariti<e> finem uoluerit ponere facile uideatur etiam Silogismum Crysippi diffinire. *Laus deo et Virgini matri. Amen.* [Ff. 89v–92v blank, but ruled.]

   Basically tradition A, as indicated by Robothan and Cranz, 219, listing this manuscript, but with material from tradition B. For example, in the commentary on Satire 1, f. 20rv: "Multi sic exponunt *o curas hominum* yronice dictum sit. hominum cogitationes. Alii uero admiratione dicunt dictum . . ." (cf. Robothan and Cranz, 221). A similar commentary printed in Otto Iahn, ed., *Auli Persii Flacci Satirarum Liber* (Leipzig 1843) 233–350; the introductory materials are not identical, and the text in MS Lat 137 is usually fuller. Ff. 48v–49, part of a bifolium inserted into quire 6, are blank; no break in the text. Throughout, blanks left for Greek; cf. f. 20, line 22.

Paper (unidentified watermark, scales in a circle, obscured in gutter), ff. i (early modern paper, with unidentified large heraldic watermark with ecclesiastical hat and tassels, mostly cut away; cf. Churchill, no. 480, pl. ccclvii, for a similar type) + 94 (incorrectly foliated 1–93, with two unnumbered, blank, ruled leaves before f. 1, and with f. 93, an endleaf) + i (early modern paper; f. 93), 210 x 142 mm. Layout varies; ff. 1–16 (article 1): written space (130–129 x 77–70) mm. 22 lines of verse (quire 2, ff. 1–8, ruled for 23 lines, with the last line left blank); ff. 17 to end: written space (130–129 x 80–83) mm. 25 long lines. Ruled lightly in lead or brown crayon throughout; single full-length vertical bounding lines. Prickings top and bottom margins.

1^{2} (unnumbered conjugate pair, blank) 2^{8} (beginning with f. 1) 3^{8} $4–6^{10}$ 7^{8} (+ conjugate pair, ff. 48–9, after 1) $8–10^{10}$ 11^{4} 12^{2} (ff. 91, 92, blank, ruled leaves). Horizontal catchwords, bottom inside margin, mostly cut away; leaf and quire signatures, bottom, outside margin, recto, with arabic numerals designating the leaves, and letters, the quires; text of the commentary (beginning f. 17) treated as the beginning of a new series with quire 4 labelled as 'a' (signature now trimmed; cf. f. 29, quire 5: 'b'). Quires reinforced around the outer and in the center bifolia with narrow strips of parchment from a noted liturgical manuscript (too small for identification or description).

Written below the top line in a fere-humanistica script; gothic letter forms, especially round 'd', and straight 's' and 'f' extending below the line, more frequent in the commentary, which was evidently hastily copied. Lemmata copied in a slightly larger script. Some corrections in a contemporary hand; cf. f. 37, quire 5, where the last line of f. 36v is repeated, although the catchword is correct, now marked "vacat."

Satires, article 1, and sections in the commentary, begin with plain 2-line initials, alternating red and blue. Lemmata in the commentary underlined in brown ink. Blank lines for rubrics throughout.

Bound in Italy, s. XV, in brown leather over wooden boards, stamped with four sets of double rules; the inner set forming a center panel with rope interlace in the shape of three diamonds, interspersed with small round stamps; between the first and second set, a narrow band of twisted rope; between the second and third set, a wider border of heart-shapes, enclosing fleur-de-lis; between the third and fourth set, small round stamps; traces of gilt remaining on the front cover. Spine scored with intersecting lines. Original sewing on three thongs; headband missing. Four bosses, upper and lower boards, and clasp, upper board, now missing. In poor condition; spine partly recovered in calf, with added title in gilt.

Written in Italy, possibly in Florence, in the first quarter of the fifteenth century (we thank Professor A. C. de la Mare for this information; July, 1986). Sold by Thorpe, London, 1836, no. 991 ("991" in pencil, front endleaves, ff. ii and iii) to Sir Thomas Phillipps (*Phillipps Cat.*, p. 153, MS 9618; "9618" in black ink, inside front cover and endleaf, f. iii^{v}); Phillipps sale, London, Sotheby's, May 1, 1903, no. 907 (clipping, inside front cover), to Maggs. Unidentified bookseller's note, front endleaf, f. ii: "N^{c} 234 0"; inside front cover, shelf mark (?), in pencil: "B11.385"; inside back cover: "201" in pencil. Given by Daniel B. Fearing (1859–1918) to Morris Hickey Morgan (1859–1910), Christmas, 1904 (note in Fearing's hand, front flyleaf, f. i; bookplate, inside front cover). Gift of Morgan to Harvard, January 1, 1910 (library stamp, f. 1v; bookplate, inside back cover); original Harvard shelf mark: Lp 15.2.2. Typed description by A. Palmieri, 1916, glued between the front endleaves.

secundo folio: Romulide saturi

Bibliography: De Ricci, 988; De Ricci, "Handlist," 106 (listed as Lp 15.2.2).

MS Lat 138 — Northeastern Italy s. XV$^{3/4}$
Persius, Saturae

ff. 1–15v [Prologue] *Auli persii uulterani uel arentini* [*sic*] *secundum aliquos. Satyrarum liber incipit.* Nec fonte labra prolui Cabalino/ . . . [f. 1 Satire 1] *Satyra de parueris* [*sic; for "peruersis"*] *exercitationibus poetarum.* O curas hominum, o quantum est rebus inane/ . . . [Satire 6] . . . Inuentus crysippe tui finitor aceruі./ *Persius satyrus explicit foeliciter.* [F. 16 blank, but ruled; f. 17 blank.]

W. V. Clausen, ed., *A. Persi Flacci et D. Iuni Iuuenalis Saturae.* OCT (Oxford 1959) 1–28; listed as no. 81 in Scarcia Piacentini. Satire 1 with interlinear glosses in the hand of the main scribe, explaining difficult words (see esp. f. 3rv); marginal comments in the same hand, f. 8 (Satire 3, verse 98), comparing the passage with Juvenal, Satire 1, and f. 8v (Satire 4, verse 6) citing Lucan. Each satire begins with an explanatory argument, in red: satire 1, see above; f. 4 (satire 2) "Satyra tercia [*sic*] de falsis uotis"; f. 5v (satire 3) "Satyra de inertia [*sic*; a confusion of "tertia" and "incerta"] iuuenum"; f. 8 (satire 4) "Satyra contra ambitiosos Ciues"; f. 9v (satire 5) "Ad cornutum philosophum de illecebris[?] Satyra vi [*sic*]"; f. 14 (satire 6) "Satyra ad bassum musicum. vii [*sic*]." A more accurate copy of these same rubrics found in Houghton, MS Lat 136 (Italy [Northeast?], 1471).

Paper (unidentified watermark, possibly a bull's head in a circle, obscured in gutter), ff. 17, 205 x 153 (134–132 x 85–68) mm.; ruled space: 132 x 90 mm. 24–21 lines of verse. Frame ruled in lead, with a single horizontal bounding line, full across, at the top only, and full-length vertical bounding lines, double on the left, used for the first majuscule of each line of verse.

1^8 2^8 (+1, f. 9, before 1). Vertical catchword, quire 1, lower margin, written along the inner bounding line.

Written on the top line in a quick cursive humanistic script by one scribe.

Three-line red initial at the beginning of the prologue, f. 1. Satires begin with similar 2-line initials (omitted, Satire 5, f. 9v). Rubrics in red. Guide letter visible alongside the initial, f. 1. Each line of verse begins with a majuscule written between the outer bounding lines.

Rubrics, f. 1, faded and almost illegible; red used for initials has bled, especially f. 1.

Bound in a modern library binding after its acquisition by Harvard; previously unbound, but in a vellum wrapper, retained in the present binding.

Written in Northeastern Italy in the third quarter of the fifteenth century (we thank Professor A. C. de la Mare for this information; July, 1986). Belonged to Morris H. Morgan (1859–1910); his gift to Harvard, January 1, 1910 (library stamp, f. 1v; bookplate, inside front cover). Original Harvard shelf mark: Lp 15.2.1. Typed description by A. Palmieri, dated June, 1916, glued to f. 1.

secundo folio: Nic [*sic*] aliquis

Bibliography: De Ricci, 988.

fMS Lat 139 **France s. XV**^{2}
Persius, Saturae

ff. 1–14v [Prologue] Nec labra fonte prolui caballino/ . . . [f. 1 Satire 1] *Satira prima.* O Curas hominum, o quantum est in rebus inane/ . . . [Satire 6] . . . Inuentus crisipe tui finitor acerui./ *Explicit persius satiricus null* [*sic*] *parcende deo gracias amen.*

W. V. Clausen, ed., *A. Persi Flacci et D. Iuni Iuvenalis Saturae.* OCT (Oxford 1959) 1–28; listed as no. 82 in Scarcia Piacentini.

With the following portions of the text out of order: Satire 1, verse 49 (f. 2, line 14), followed by verse 114 through the end; Satire 2, verse 40 (f. 3v, line 6) followed by Satire 1, verses 50–113, and then on f. 4v, line 22, with Satire 3, verses 31–95; Satire 2 resumes with verse 41 on f. 6, line 15. In Satire 3 (f. 7v, line 6) verses 31–95 are omitted.

Prologue and Satires 1–3, ff. 1–6v, with marginal and interlinear glosses written in a minute, formal hand.

Paper (watermark, similar to Briquet Ancre 384, Vesoul 1461), ff. i (modern paper) + 14 (modern foliation, 1–14; previously foliated, in ink, 82–95) + i (paper), 300 x 222 (text and gloss: 200–195 x 188–186; text: 195–193 x 100–95) mm. 24 lines of verse. Ruled in ink with one narrow column of text with space for glosses between the lines and in two narrow, unruled columns in the inner and outer margins; top and bottom two horizontal lines full across; double full-length vertical bounding lines on each side of the text, and single full-length outer vertical bounding lines. Prickings in top, bottom and outside margins (top pricking partially trimmed).

1^{12} (+2, ff. 13, 14, singletons glued to 12).

Written by one scribe below the top line in a running bâtarde script; gloss carefully written by a contemporary, perhaps the main scribe, in a very small, running script. A few glosses added in a different hand, contemporary or slightly later (cf. ff. 1, 2v, 4v).

One 3-line parted red initial, f. 1 (prologue); similar large 1-line initial, f. 7 (Satire 3). Two large 1-line red initials, f. 1 (Satire 1) and f. 7v (Satire 1, verse 61); blanks for remaining initials. Majuscules stroked in red, ff. 1, 2, 6v, and 7 only. Marginal glosses, f. 1, begin with red paragraph marks. Some guide letters for the initials.

Outer margin of f. 1 repaired; no apparent loss of text, although some of the gloss may have been lost.

Bound in paper boards, s. XIX–XX, half covered with leaves from a printed missal; vellum spine with title in ink.

Written in France in the second half of the fifteenth century as indicated by the script. Formerly ff. 82–95 in a larger codex (foliated in a modern hand). Unidentified German bookseller's mark, inside front cover, in pencil: "L.B. 1028." Typed description in German of unknown origin laid in, designating the manuscript as "fMS Fol. 16146." Purchased, August 12, 1926 (Salisbury fund; library stamp, front flyleaf, f. i; bookplate, inside front cover); original Harvard shelf mark: Lp 15.2.8F.

secundo folio: Elicat et tenero

Bibliography: De Ricci, 988.

MS Lat 143 — England s. XVI
Fragment of a letter

One leaf [recto] Occupationibus est factum meis et subita tua profectione ne tecum coram de hac gerem quam ob causam vereor ne absentia mea leuior sit . . . A Cesare petii ut Septime Elodium restinet . . . [line 6] Si tu conssesses [*sic*] quo magis laboro, ut tua volu// [verso blank].

Six line fragment, apparently of a letter; text ends abruptly.

One rectangular piece of parchment, 170 x 94 (105–102 x 36) mm. Six long lines. No ruling.

Written in a set hand, court of common pleas, using the characteristic double-looped 'a', two-compartment 'g', and circular reverse 'e' (cf. Anthony Petti, *English Literary Hands from Chaucer to Dryden* [London 1977] 21, fig. 29 for an example of a similar script).

Bounded top and bottom by three heavy horizontal bars, brown ink, probably added later.

Written in England in the sixteenth century. Two letters, dated 1815 and [18]48, now housed with the manuscript, explain that the fragment was found in a stone coffin in the Parish churchyard in Southstocke near Bath, and call the fragment a funeral vow, or "Passport to St. Peter," deposited with the dead. Although there is no evidence that supports this explanation of the origin of the fragment and the circumstance of its discovery, it is repeated in all subsequent descriptions including De Ricci's. Handwritten transcription, s. XIX, said to be a copy of a transcription by the medievalist and Oxford professor, Paul Vinogradoff (1854–1925), also housed with the manuscript. Belonged to Frederick Hendriks. Listed in a James Tregaskis catalogue (date uncertain), no. 501, for 8 guineas, which dates the fragment s. XIII (followed by De Ricci), and suggests that it was fraudulently passed off as a plenary indulgence, and therefore buried with some unsuspecting layman. Letter dated July 1, 1911 from Charles Taylor (?) of the Boston Globe to P. K. Foley, Beacon Street, Boston, expressing interest in acquiring the fragment (housed with the manuscript). Obtained in 1934 from the journalist and Harvard graduate, Charles H. Taylor (1867–1941).

Bibliography: De Ricci, 2302.

MS Lat 144 — **Italy (Venice?) s. XV$^{1/4}$**
Franciscus Barbarus, De re uxoria — **Pl. 45**

ff. 1–50v [Dedicatory preface to Lorenzo dei Medici (1395–1440)] *Francisci Barbaro Veneti ad Laurentium de Medicis Florentinum civem. De Re Vxoria Liber incipit.* Maiores nostri laurenti carissine [*sic*] benivolentia uel necessitudine sibi coniunctos in nupciis suis donare consueuerunt . . . in hisce nupciis tuis suscipies. [f. 2 text] *Incipit tractatus Libri de Re uxoria in quo diffinit quid sit coniugium in principio.* Antequam de delectu vxoris et officio dicere incipiam, de ipso coniugio prius pauca mihi dicenda sunt . . . Uel quod ab optima fide ac animo certe tibi deditissimo proficiscitur. *Laus deo. Uiri Patricii et Oratoris Insignis Francisci Barbari Veneti De Re Uxoria Liber Feliciter Finit.* [Ff. 51–57v blank, but ruled.]

Attilo Gnesotto, ed., in *Atti e Memorie della R. Accademia di Scienze Lettere ed Arti in Padova* n.s. 32 (1916) 23–100.

Paper (unidentified watermark, obscured in gutter, similar in design to Briquet Fleur 6382–6390, but without a cross), ff. i (paper) + 57 + i (paper), 193 x 140 (122 x 90–88) mm. 22 long lines. Horizontal rules in ink; single vertical bounding lines in very faint lead.

1^{11} (structure uncertain) $2–4^{12}$ 5^{12} (–4, 5, blank folios after f. 50). Horizontal catchwords in decorative boxes, center, lower margin.

Written above the top line by one scribe in a humanistic script, using simple teardrop 'a', and idiosyncratic majuscules. A few marginal annotations in Latin, s. XVI–XVII (cf. ff. 7, 25).

One 9-line decorated pen initial, f. 1, outlined in brown ink and with decorative shading and an intertwined vine terminating in large acanthus leaves, also in brown ink, on quartered red and blue ground with white outlining and dots. Chapters begin with 2- to 3-line initials, alternating red and blue with pen flourishes in light brown or red respectively. Red rubrics copied in a fere-humanistica script, ff. 1 and 2 only; thereafter blank spaces for rubrics. Opening line of each chapter (opening two lines, f. 1) in large decorative capitals in brown ink, of the type described by Stanley Morison as "Byzantine" (cf. *Byzantine Elements,* and *Politics and Script,* 277–86).

Water damage (no loss of text) most folios; initials, ff. 22v and 32v to end, smudged or effaced.

Bound in England in green morocco with gold tooling, s. XIX; gilt edges.

Written in Italy, probably in Venice, in the first quarter of the fifteenth century, shortly after the treatise was composed for Lorenzo dei Medici's marriage in 1415 (we thank Professor A. C. de la Mare for this information; October, 1987). Possibly once circulated together with Ps. Plutarch, *De liberis educandis,* translated by Guarinus Veronensis; cf. f. 57v, offset red rubric, in a contemporary hand: "Guarini Veronese ex Plutarco de liberis educandis incipit." In Italy until s. XVIII, as indicated by note added at the end of the text, f.

50v: "Francisco Barbaro fioriva nel 1435, vedi Foscarini[?] Letteratura Italiana." Belonged to Joseph Barrois (1780–1855). Purchased in 1849 by Bertram, fourth Earl of Ashburnham (1797–1878); MS 401 in a *Catalogue of the Manuscripts at Ashburnham Palace; Part the Second comprising a Collection Formed by Mons. J. Barrois* (London, n.d.); his sale, London, Sotheby's, 10 June and 4 following days, 1901, no. 46, to Leighton. Clipping from unidentified sales catalogue in English, front flyleaf, f. i; price, £2.15.10, in ink, inside front cover. Unidentified booksellers' notes: front flyleaf, f. i: "401/⊙÷/"(Sotheby's, 1901?); inside back cover: "d/ib/." (?). Collection of Murray Anthony Potter (1871–1915), assistant professor of Romance Languages, Harvard (bookplate, inside front cover); obtained from his collection, June 18, 1935.

secundo folio: plerisque cibis

Bibliography: De Ricci, 2302; Kristeller, *Iter* 5:226.

MS Lat 145 — Northeastern Italy s. $XV^{3/4}$
Juvenal; Persius; Batrachomyomachia — Pl. 55

1. ff. 1–62 [Juvenal, *Saturae*; rubric omitted] Semper ego auditor tantum nunquam ne reponam/ Vexatus totiens rauci theseide codri/ . . . [Satire 16] . . . Vt laeti faleris omnes et torquibus omnes. [possibly added:] τέλος.

   W. V. Clausen, ed., *A. Persi Flacci et D. Iuni Iuvenalis Saturae.* OCT (Oxford 1959) 35–175. Not divided into the five books found in some manuscripts. Greek included, hand of main scribe, f. 20, Satire 6, verse 195; omitted, f. 36v, Satire 9, verse 37. Satire 11, verse 27, f. 43v, reads "scito te ipsum" in hand of main scribe, in place of Greek. Satire 6, verse 268, f. 21, omitted; supplied by a later hand. Leaf following f. 39, containing Satire 10, verses 89–150, missing.

2. ff. 62–73 [Persius, *Saturae*; Prologue] *Aulii Persii volaterani liber primus foeliciter incipit./ Musarum ambicio pugnat proposse poeta/ Ne trahat hiantem sed raptos carpit inique/* Nec fonte labra prolui caballino/ . . . Cantare credas per pegaseum melos/ *Qui prece uel precio falsam acquirere famam/ Nec doctos gemma dici nunc ueste poetas/* [f. 62v

Satire 1] O curas hominum [*om.* O] quantum est in rebus inane/ . . . [Satire 6] . . . Inuentus chrisippe cui [*sic*] finitor acerui. *Finis.*

Clausen, ed., 1–28; listed as no. 83 in Scarcia Piacentini. The introductory argument in verse also found in Bergamo, Biblioteca Civica, MS Delta.6.7 (Bergamo, 1471) f. 8 (cf. Scarcia Piacentini, no. 21).

3. f. 73 [Added in a contemporary bookhand following the Satires; Quintilian, *Institutio oratoria*, bk. 10.1, line 94] Multum et uerae gloriare [*sic*] quamuis uno libro Persius meruit. [Followed immediately by six hexameters on Persius, also found in Vatican, Biblioteca Apostolica Vaticana, MS Reg. lat. 1701, Italy, s. XV, f. 130v; here beginning with a verse not in the Vatican manuscript; cf. Pellegrin, 2.1: 367–70] Persius in mondo [*sic*] foelix fuit orbe secondo [*sic*]/ Dogmate romanus sed tusco stemate natus/ . . . Omnia non moesta sed fronte legantur aperta./ [One blank line, followed by two additional hexameters] Persi si poteris totum percipere sensum/ Facilius reliquis dabitur uia crede loquenti.

4. ff. 73v–78v [*Batrachomyomachia*] *Vatroconlomiamachia* [*sic*] *ranarum murumque prelia.* Ranarum murumque simul crudelia bella/ Queque super genibus descripsi carmina nuper/ . . . Phebus cum tanti cessit discordia belli./ *Finis.* [added in a later hand] *Finis.* [F. 79r blank; f. 79v with later notes and miscellaneous pen trials in Latin and Italian.]

Verse translation of the ps-homeric *Batrachomyomachia* by Carolus Marsuppinus Aretinus (ca. 1399–1453); Hain 8783–86; [Michael Mattaire, ed.], *Batrachomyomachia graece ad veterum exemplarium fidem recusa: glossa graeca, variantibus lectionibus, versionibus latinis* . . . (London 1721) unpaginated, following the Greek text, with the epistle of Carolus Marsuppinus to Marassius, not included in this manuscript; *La Batracomiomachia di Omero, greca, latina e italiana* (Venice 1744) [xix]–xxxvi.

Parchment, ff. i (modern paper) + 79 (f. 79, a lifted pastedown; two sets of modern foliation: correctly foliated, lower inside margin [cited]; incorrectly foliated, upper right margin, with an unnumbered leaf between ff. 5 and 6) + i (modern paper), 210 x 123 (145–143 x 76–70) mm. 31 lines of verse. Horizontal lines ruled in ink; vertical bounding lines ruled in hard point. Full-length vertical bounding lines, double on the left, used for the first majuscule of each line of text, and single on the right. Prickings, top and bottom margin (pricked for double vertical bounding lines, inside and outside), and with a single prick-mark in the upper, outside margin.

1–3^{10} 4^{10} (–10, after f. 39, with loss of text) 5–8^{10} (10, f. 79, lifted pastedown). Vertical catchwords written on the inner bounding lines, quires 1–6 (lacking in quire 4); quire 7, f. 69v, horizontal catchword with flourishes on all sides.

Written by two scribes: 1) ff. 1–62 (article 1), written below the top line in a humanistic script, using round 'r' and trailing round 's' finally; 2) ff. 62–end, written in a skilled, upright fere-humanistica script, also below the top line. A few corrections and variant readings added by an Italian hand, s. XV (cf. ff. 2, 3, 12, etc.); marginal pen drawings of abstract shapes in the margins, ff. 33, 33v, 34, 38, 40v, perhaps nota marks of an early reader; some later nota marks in trefoil shape and pointing hands.

Two 5-line gold initials (ff. 1 and 62) with white vinestem decoration, infilled and on square grounds of blue, green and red with small white dots; edged in black. Top margin, f. 1, fleshy acanthus leaf in reddish pink with white highlights, not connected to the initial. F. 72v, one plain 3-line red initial at the beginning of the *Batrachomyomachia*. Satires in articles 1 and 2 begin with 2-line initials, alternating red and blue. Rubrics at the beginnings of article 2 and 3 only. Throughout, each verse begins with a majuscule letter written between the double bounding lines; ff. 73v–79, occasionally stroked in red. Some guide letters for the initials (cf. ff. 62v, 64v, 67v).

F. 1, bottom margin and part of the last line of text cut away; repaired and rewritten. Some water damage throughout in the bottom margins; no loss of text.

Bound in Italy, s. XV, in undecorated red-brown leather over wooden boards with five bosses on each board (four now missing). Original sewing on three split bands. Now with one brass catch with Agnus Dei motif, lower board, fastening front to back. In poor condition, with missing headband, and broken corners; rebacked in brown leather.

Written in Northeastern Italy, probably in Venice or Padua, in the third quarter of the fifteenth century (we thank Professor A. C. de la

Mare for this information; October, 1987). Unidentified early modern shelf mark, f. 79: "M VI." Pen trials in Latin and Italian, s. XVII (?), f. 79v (verso of lifted pastedown), including the opening lines of the Satires of Juvenal and Persius, and a name, possibly an owner or user of the manuscript: "D. Gieorgius <di or da?> Fievi [or Trevi?]" (we thank Dr. G. N. Knauer for his assistance in interpreting this note, May, 1987). Purchased from Davis and Orioli, February 26, 1935 (Norton Fund; bookplate, inside front cover; pencil note, front endleaf, f. i^v).

secundo folio: Cum fas esse

Bibliography: De Ricci, 2302; Edward Loomis Bassett, "A Description of MS Lat 145 in the Harvard College Library," (in manuscript, May 31, 1938) now Houghton, bMS Lat 315(1); Wieck, p. 109, and fig. 122 (reproducing f. 62); Kristeller, *Iter* 5:227.

MS Lat 146 — Bohemia (Prague?) s. XV[1]
Poetry

1. ff. 1–7 [*Asinarius*] [R]ex erat ignote quondam regionis et urbis/ Sed nomine regis fabula nulla docet/ . . . Idem preterea sortitur patris honorem/ Sicque regit regum rex regna duum. *Explicit asinarius per manus alicuius, et cetera.*

   Walther, *Initia* 16719 and 16728; Karl Langosch, ed., *Asinarius und Rapularius.* Sammlung mittellateinischer Texte, ed. Alfons Hilka 10 (Heidelberg 1929) 15–45; Karl Langosch, "Neue Überlieferung des 'Asinarius,'" *Orbis Mediaevalis. Festgabe für Anton Blaschka zum 75. Geburstag am 7. Oktober 1967,* eds. Horst Gericke, Manfred Lemmer, and Walter Zöllner (Weimar 1970) 123–44, listing this manuscript p. 126.

   A few scribal or later corrections, adding omitted words and noting variant readings.

2. ff. 7v–15 [*Apocalypsis goliae*] [T]auro torrida lampade cinthii/ fundente iacula feruendis [*sic*] radii/ . . . mentis uestigia feisse [*sic*] lubrica/ [continuing with 4 addititional lines] Qui raptus fueram celum ad tercium/ . . . Satis apperuit cuique mortalium/ *Explicit apocalipsis Alany per manus.*

Walther, *Initia* 91, listing this manuscript; Karl Strecker, ed., *Die Apokalypse des Golias.* Texte zur Kulturgeschichte des Mittelalters 5 (Leipzig 1928) 16–37 and 39, printing the four concluding lines found in this manuscript, found in manuscripts of the β group; also edited in Wright, ed., *Walter Mapes*, 1–20 (lacking the last four lines).

3. ff. 15–20v [*De mundi miseria*] *Incipiunt carmina disputationis de corpore et anima edita per reuerendum patrem domini magistrum Rudbertum grossicapitis Episcopum lynconiensem.* [E]cce mundus moritur viciis sepultus/ Ordo rerum vertitur cessat christi cultus/ . . . [f. 16] Que dat unicuique prout operatur/ [continuing with 16 additional lines] Adamantes dominum summum genitorem/ Et eiusdem filium christum saluatorem/ . . . Pro rigore spiritus et carnis seuere/ Huic morbo domine rex regum medere. [f. 16, line 18 *Dialogus inter corpus et animam*, following immediately with no break; begins with 8 lines not found in all manuscripts] Vir quidam extiterat dudum heremita/ Philibertus francigena cuius erat vita/ . . . Visio sibimet apparebat talis./ Noctis sub silencio tempore brumali/ . . . Et me totum manibus christi commendaui. Amen.

Two poems which circulated independently, but which are also found together, copied as one poem with no breaks, as in this manuscript; in general, see H. Walther, *Das Streitgedicht in der lateinischen Literatur des Mittelalters.* Quellen und Untersuchungen zur lateinischen Philologie des Mittelalters 5.2 (Munich 1920) 63–75, and 211–214 (listing 132 manuscripts not including this one).

De mundi miseria, ff. 15–16: Walther, *Initia* 5114; Wright, ed., *Walter Mapes*, 149–51; our manuscript lacks the last four lines printed by Wright, but includes 16 additional lines, printed in A. Gabrielli, "Il Codice 'Mss. Varia 4' della Biblioteca Nazionale di Roma," *Archivio della R. Società Romana di Storia Patria* 9 (1886) 229–71, esp. p. 233.

Dialogus inter corpus et animam, f. 16, line 18–f. 20v: Walther, *Initia* 20421 and 11894; Wright, ed., *Walter Mapes*, 95–106, printing the first 8 lines of our manuscript in a note; also edited by Th. G. von Karajan, *Frühlingsgabe für freunde Älterer Literatur* (Vienna 1839) 85–98, with the first 8 lines. The attribution to Robert Grosseteste is unlikely; see S. Harrison Thomson, *The Writings of Robert Grossesteste, Bishop of Lincoln 1235–1253* (Cambridge 1940) 247–48, no. 16.

4. f. 20v *Item alia metra.* Post hominis mortem querunt auide tria sortem/ Wlt vernis carnem sathay umbram posteritas rem.

   Two lines; Walther, *Initia* 14318

5. f. 20v *Item alia.* Lancea crux claui mors spine que tolleraui./ Otstendunt qua vi <peccancium?> crimina laui.

   Two lines; Walther, *Initia* 10100; printed in Francesco Novati, ed., *Carmina medii aevi.* Operette inedite o rare della libreria Dante 4 (Florence 1883) 43.

6. f. 20v *Item alia domini Cancellarius episcopi Olumucensis.* Aspice qui transis quod tu michi causa doloris/ ... Ut vinas morior non est dileccio maior.

   Six lines; Walther, *Initia* 1598; Cancellarius Johannes Noviforensis or Jean de Neumarkt (Novo Foro) (b. 1310), Bishop of Olmütz (1364–1380).

7. ff. 20v–22v *Item alia carmina de vine et ydolis edita per venerabilem domini Wlachiconem prothonotario Romanorum et Boemie Regis semper Augusti.* [E]x fideli ueterum scriptura cognoui/ ... Nec passum inspicere hunc uiso iocundo.

   Walther, *Initia* 5984.

8. f. 23rv [17-line prose introduction] Scio equidem scio domine Nicole amice carissime qui quamuis theotonicali pro cesseritis ... quam ominis participio <p...tur>. [f. 23 poem] *Praga civitas apostrophat in theonicos* [*sic*] *qui eam multis affecerunt* [*sic*] *molestiis sicut clarebit in sequentibus. Idcirco hortatur ut per suos filios velud lese maiestatis obnoxii a suis limitibus perpetue profligentur.* Usque modo tacui non admissa loqui/ Consternata iacui sed attendant O qui/ ... Assumunt iacta uicia quod nomine preclarum// [F. 24rv blank.]

   57 lines; ending imperfectly; see Paul Meyvaert, "'Rainaldus est malus scriptor Francigenus' — Voicing National Antipathy in the Middle Ages," *Speculum* 66 (1991) 761, note 63.

Paper (watermarks, in gutter, unidentified bow and arrow[?] and bell), ff. i (paper) + 24 (modern foliation in pencil, bottom, inside corner [cited], and medieval foliation through f. 23, partly trimmed, in ink in roman numerals, top, outer corner, 207–228, with 215 bis) + i (paper), 195 x 140, ruled space, arts. 1–2, 158–157 x 81–80 mm; arts. 3–8, ruled space, 153 x 86–78 mm. Frame ruled in ink, with all bounding lines full-length; number of lines per page varies: art. 1, ff. 1–7, 32–30 lines of verse; art. 2, ff. 7v–15, 31–27 lines of verse; arts. 3–7, mid f. 15–f. 22v, 37–35 lines of verse; art. 8, f. 23rv, 37 long lines, written outside the text frame to the bottom of the page.

Written by at least three scribes. The first scribe copied ff. 1–7 below the top line in an upright cursive gothic script; the second scribe copied ff. 7v–15 (art. 2) in a quicker, less formal, rounded gothic cursive script; the last scribe completed the manuscript in a small, quick, angular gothic cursive script.

Blank spaces left for 3-line initials, ff. 15 and 20v (arts. 3 and 7).

1^{12} 2^{12} (12, f. 24, added singleton, glued to 1; original 12 cancelled, with no loss of text).

Bound in modern white vellum over stiff pasteboard.

Written in the first half of the fifteenth century in Bohemia, probably by a student at the University of Prague (see art. 8, above). Once part of a longer codex (cf. medieval foliation). Top margin, f. 1, in ink, large ".M.," (s. XVIII?) partially trimmed. Dealers' and owners' notes include, inside front cover: "L 48," "A4," and "KIC 60"; front flyleaf, f. i, in purple pencil, "H[?] 753"; and inside back cover, "#15163." E. P. Goldschmidt, *List No. 12 of Mediaeval Literature*, pp. 1–2, no. 1; purchased from Goldschmidt, January 23, 1935 (with funds from an anonymous gift for the humanities; bookplate, inside front cover; library note, front flyleaf, f. i^v).

secundo folio: An vestis

Bibliography: De Ricci, 2302–3.

MS Lat 150 — Southern Europe s. $XII^{2/4}$
Augustinus, Confessiones — Pl. 60

ff. 1–111 *In nomine domini, Incipiunt Libri Confessionvm Avrelii Augustini.* Magnus es domine et laudabilis ualde et magna uirtus tua et sapientie tue non est numerus et laudare te uult homo . . . A te petatur, in te queratur, ad te pulsetur, sic, sic accipetur, sic inuenietur, sic aperietur. *Expliciunt Libri confessionvm Aurelii Augustini deo gratias. Amen.* [F. 111v blank.]

Martinus Skutella, ed. (Leipzig 1934), revised by H. Juergens and W. Schaub (Stuttgart 1969); *CPL* 251; see also A. Wilmart, "La tradition des grands ouvrages de Saint Augustin," *Miscellanea Agostiniana. Testi e Studi Pubblicati a Cura Dell'Ordine Eremitano di S. Agostino nel XV Centenario dalla Morte del Santo Dottore* (Rome 1931) 2:259–66, listing this manuscript, p. 262, no. 46, as Cheltenham, Phillipps MS 9460.

Divided into the usual 13 books, beginning on ff. 1, 8, 12, 17v, 24v, 31v, 39, 47, 55v, 64v, 81v, 90 and 100.

Marginal notes throughout, including brief notes on the contents, for example: s. XII, f. 24 "Nota mirabile ingenium augustini"; s. XIII^{1}, f. 5v "troie equus ligneus," f. 51 "Exempla de antonio et aliis," and "Exemplum de contempnendo mundum," and f. 74 "De continentia et contra pollutiones quere usque ad sequentem rubricam"; another hand, s. XIII, f. 15 "contricio;" s. XV, f. 48 "in impressis, populi asiam mali" and "platonici"; another hand, s. XV, f. 28 "de scolasticis." Infrequent marginal corrections, s. XIII–XIV^{in}, for example, f. 7v, changing "hominis" to "homines." Throughout, nota marks in a number of different hands, s. XII^{ex}–XV.

Parchment, ff. 111 + i (unnumbered paper), 243 x 185 (200–197 x 146–140) mm. 29–28 long lines. Ruled lightly in hardpoint on the hair side, with the top 3 and bottom 4 horizontal rules full across on some folios; full-length double vertical bounding lines. Prickings in outer and bottom margins.

1–2^{8} 3^{8} (3, f. 19, and 6, f. 22, are single) 4^{8} 5^{8} (3, f. 35, and 6, f. 38, are single) 6–10^{8} 11^{8} (3, f. 83, and 6, f. 86, are single) 12–13^{8} 14^{8} (–8, following f. 111, cancelled with no loss of text).

Written on the top line in an upright twelfth-century minuscule; round uncial 'd' used; 'ae' written 'e'; the scribe avoids carrying words over two pages by finishing words below the written space, under the last word on a page.

Each book begins with a 8- to 4-line initial, drawn in outline in brown ink with acanthus motifs used to form the initial or entwined around it, infilled or outlined in red-orange; book 10, f. 64v, begins with a "C" in the form of a wolf. Headings for each book in freely-formed red rustic capitals, highlighted in a pale yellow wash; yellow lines drawn through the rubrics for highlighting; explicit and opening words of most books in similar rustics in black daubed with red. Majuscules in the text on the first page of each book, or on the double-paged opening with an initial, daubed with red. Red used sporadically throughout to fill in spaces left by the scribe because of defects in the parchment (for example, f. 95rv), and to indicate that the scribe has completed a word at the beginning of a new line, or above or below the line (majuscules in the text on such pages are usually also daubed in red).

Inside, bottom margin, ff. 1–16, partly worn or chewed away, with some minor loss of text.

Bound in marbled calf, s. XVIII, probably in France; spine with five raised bands, forming panels stamped with gilt ornaments; title on red label between the first and third: "S. August. Confessi. MS 1381."

Written in Southern Europe in the second quarter of the twelfth century, probably in Italy or Spain. De Ricci recorded that the manuscript was traditionally said to have belonged to the Jesuit College at Agen, France (maintained by the Jesuits from 1591–1762; cf. Phillipps Sale, London, Sotheby's, June 15–18, 1908) but this manuscript lacks their ex libris found in Houghton, MSS Lat 48 and 179; possibly in their sale, London, Stewart, Wheatley, and Adlard, June 27, 1831 (not available for consultation). Number of folios recorded in ink, inside back cover, "111 f"; inscription in brown pen, s. XIX, likely copied from the binding, f. 1: "Sancti augustini confessiones MS MCCCLXXXI." Sold by Thorpe, London, 1836, no. 75, where 1381 is incorrectly accepted as the date of the manuscript, to Sir Thomas Phillipps (*Phillipps Cat.* p. 150, MS 9460; "Phillipps MS 9460" in black ink, f. 1, bottom margin). Phillipps Sale, London, Sotheby's, 1908, no. 44 to Maggs. Placed by J. Martini in a sale by Anderson (December 14, 1909, no. 408) and purchased by John Batterson Stetson (1884–1952; bookplate, inside front cover). Unidentified price code in pencil, inside back cover, "ioseo." Stetson's gift to the library, December 11, 1935 (library stamp, bottom margin, f. 1v; bookplate, inside back cover).

secundo folio: hanc et apprehendam

Bibliography: De Ricci, 2303; Light, *Bible in the Twelfth Century*, 47–50, no. 17 (no plate).

MS Lat 154 **Italy s. XIV**
Geoffrey of Vinsauf, Poetria nova **Pl. 40**

ff. 1–38v [Dedicatory preface to Pope Innocent III (1198–1216)] *Incipit poetria nouella gaufredi anglici.* Papa stupor mundi si dixero papa nocenti/ Acephalum nomen tribuam tibi, si caput addam./ . . . Hoc opus exiguum, breue corpore uiribus amplum/ [f. 1v text] *Incipit de prima parte rethorice scilicet de inuentione.* Si quis habet fundare domum, non currit ad actum/ Impetuosa manus: intrinseca linea cordis/ . . . Quam fine [*sic*] premissis recitatio facta uenuste./ *Explicit de quinque partibus rethorice, finis operis et commendatio libri et sui ipsius domino pape.* [f. 37v Epilogue] Iam mare transcurri gades in littore fixi/ . . . Plene sed res est longe facundior ore./ [f. 37v] *Commendatio sui libri domino G. episcopo cardinali* [William, bishop of London (1199–1221?)] Quod pape scripsi munus speciale libelli/ . . . Crescere non poteris quantum de iure mereris/ [f. 38 rubric omitted] Imperialis apex cui seruit poplite flexo/ . . . Flexilis et sit ei melius ratione potentis. *Explicit liber poetrie nouelle Gaufredi Anglici deo Gratias. Amen.*

Edited in Edmond Faral, *Les arts poétiques du XIIe et XIIIe siècle* (Paris 1958) 197–262, listing forty-two manuscripts, pp. 27–28, not including this one, and in Ernest Gallo, *The 'Poetria Nova' and its Sources in early Rhetorical Doctrine.* De Proprietatibus litterarum, ed. C. H. Van Schooneveld, Series Maior 10 (The Hague and Paris 1971) 14–129, with English translation and some emendation of Faral's text. Epilogue, ff. 37v–38v (Faral, ed., pp. 261–62) is not in the order of the edition, but as follows: lines 2066–80, 2099–2116, 2081–98. Text is well-organized and carefully presented; divided into numerous clearly delineated short chapters; many chapters include subject headings copied by the scribe in the margin.

See also Margaret F. Nims, tr., *Poetria Nova of Geoffrey of Vinsauf* (Toronto 1967) and W. B. Sedgewick, "Notes and Emendations on Faral's *Les arts poétiques du XIIe et du XIIIe siècle,"* *Speculum* 2 (1927) 331–43, especially 336–40.

Parchment (prepared in the manner of southern Europe), ff. iii (unnumbered paper) + 38 (modern foliation, upper, outside corner in pencil) + iii (unnumbered paper), 265 x 195 (178–77 x 94–71) mm; ruled space: 180 x 104 mm. 30 lines of verse. Ruled lightly in lead; full-length vertical bounding lines, double on the left, used for the first majuscule of each line of verse. Prickings top and bottom margins.

1–4^{8} 5^{8} (–7,8, cancelled with no loss of text; stubs remain). Horizontal catchwords, middle bottom margin, below the last line of text; flourished on four sides.

Written below the top line by one scribe in a rounded southern gothic bookhand.

Seven-line crude zoomorphic initial ('P' with a dragon forming the upper loop), f. 1, in muddy shades of green, orange and brushed gold, continuing to form a border, top and inside margins, of orange and light green acanthus on a brushed gold bar, with gold balls heavily edged in black with four dots; initial is rubbed and in poor condition. Two-line alternately red and blue initials set within the text space with simple pen decoration and infilling in the other color. Paragraph marks, alternately red and blue, with touches of the other color; opening majuscule of each line of verse copied between the left-hand bounding lines and highlighted with a red diagonal stroke. Red rubrics and marginal headings.

Bound in modern (s. XIX–XX?) half calf and marbled paper; spine with author and title in gilt.

Written in Italy in the fourteenth century. The quality of the parchment, script and secondary decoration, and the care with which the manuscript was laid out, contrasts with the very crude decoration of the first page, which may be added (we thank Professor Lilian Armstrong for her assistance; January 1989). Sold by Thorpe, London, 1836, no. 495, to Sir Thomas Phillipps (*Phillipps Cat.*, p. 147, MS 9292; "Phillipps MS 9292" in pen, f. 1). Phillipps Sale, London, Sotheby's, April 24–28, 1911, no. 430 to J. Rosenthal. Unidentified booksellers' notes, front flyleaf, f. i^{v}, in pencil: "06047"; and in another hand: "a 29.460"; back flyleaf, f. iii, erased price code (?), and in pencil, "H 10681." Acquired March 2, 1936 (Norton Fund; bookplate, inside front cover; library note in pencil, front flyleaf, f. ii^{v}), perhaps from the estate of W. M. Voynich as recorded by De Ricci (no confirming evidence now in manuscript or library files). Unidentified typed description from a dealer pasted to the front flyleaf, f. i.

secundo folio: Figat. Opus totum

Bibliography: De Ricci, 2303; Kristeller, *Iter* 5:226.

MS Lat 155 — Northern Italy (Venice?) s. XV^{ex}
Persius, Saturae — Pl. 58

ff. 1–22 *Auli Flacci Persii. Poete Satyrarum Opus.* [Prologue] Nec fonte labra prolui caballino/ . . . [f. 1v] *Satyra Prima.* O cvras hominum o quantum in rebus inane est/ . . . [Satire 6] . . . Inuentus chrysippe tui finitor acerui./ *Finis Persii.* [F. 22v blank, but ruled.]

W. V. Clausen, ed., *A. Persi Flacci et D. Iuni Iuvenalis Saturae.* OCT (Oxford 1959) 1–28; listed as no. 84 in Scarcia Piacentini. No notes in later hands or other marginalia.

Parchment, ff. 24 (foliated 1–22; the unnumbered, blank, ruled leaves serving as endleaves before f. 1 and after f. 22, are part of the first and last quires, respectively), 158 x 106 (115–113 x 77–72) mm. 16 lines of verse. Ruled very lightly in brown ink or crayon; single full-length vertical bounding lines. Prickings, bottom margin, on a few leaves; throughout, a single pricking, outer margin, above the top ruled line.

1^{10} (1, blank, unnumbered endleaf; –10, cancelled) 2^{8} 3^{8} (–1, cancelled; 8, blank, unnumbered endleaf). Vertical catchwords written on the inner bounding line. Ff. 1–4 numbered in the lower outside margin, recto, on the bounding lines, possibly by the scribe.

Written on the top line by one scribe in a well formed italic script.

One 2-line gold initial, f. 1, on a square ground of dark blue, flanked by dark red and green rectangles, with highlights in white, silver and gold, with classical motifs (derived from urns or candelabras) in red, blue and green with gold highlights extending from the initial; bottom margin, a dark green wreath, enclosing a coat of arms, now almost entirely effaced in the bottom half (possibly sable [?], a lion rampant or overall a fess azure, in chief 3 fleurs-de-lis; cf. Wieck, fig. 60). The style of the initial is reminiscent of the Bentivoglio Hours copied by Pierantonio Sallando in Bologna, ca. 1500, London, Victoria and Albert Museum, Reid MS 64 (see Joyce I. Whalley and Vera Kaden, *The Universal Penman* [London 1980] 36, no. 61). Two-line gold initials begin each satire (initial for satire 4, f. 11v, excised) infilled with blue or green, set on rectangular grounds of dark red and green or red and blue, edged in black, with delicate highlights in white and gold, and very skilled pen decoration in purple or olive green, some with classical motifs, some with fine loops, beading, leaves and birds, and some with a combination; the style of the pen decoration is similar to Houghton, fMS Typ 217, Pontifical, Venice (?), after 1485; see Wieck, 74–5, no. 36, and in general, Susy Marcon, "Ornati di penna e di pennello: appunti su scribi-illuminatori nella Venezia del maturo umanesimo," *La bibliofilia* 89 (1987) 121–43, esp. 134–5 (we thank Professor Lilian Armstrong for these suggestions, and for her assistance in interpreting the coat of arms; January, 1989). Rubrics throughout in very pale red, now almost brown; f. 1 (prologue), the first 1–3 lines of each satire, and the first letters in lines 4, 5, and 6 of Satire 1, f. 1v, copied in the same red. Opening words or word of each satire in majuscules.

Bound in Italy, s. XV, in wooden boards covered with brown blind-tooled morocco; panelled sides with interlace border, surrounding a diaper-pattern panel with diamond center ornament. Original sewing on three thongs; head- and tailbands no longer enter boards, which are broken at these points. Two brass catches, lower board; stubs of straps remain on upper.

Initial, f. 11v, excised with consequent loss of text on f. 11.

Written in northern Italy at the end of the fifteenth century, most likely in Venice, as indicated by the style of the pen decoration. Unidentified coat of arms of original owner, mostly effaced, f. 1 (described above). Belonged to Sir Francis Sharp Powell, Bart., of Horton Hall, Bradford, Yorkshire; his sale, London, Sotheby's, December 16, 1929, no. 783. Unidentified booksellers' marks in pencil, front flyleaf, f. i: "25/EN"; "41/47"; "L4"; and back flyleaf, verso: "11308." Purchased with funds from the Friends of the Library, November 23, 1936 (pencil note, front flyleaf, f. i^{v}; bookplate, inside front cover).

secundo folio: Et natalitia

Bibliography: De Ricci, 2303; Wieck, p. 109, fig. 60 (reproducing f. 1).

fMS Lat 156 — Austria (Salzburg) s. IX^{in}

Sacramentary, fragment ("The Arno-Sacramentary") — Pl. 33

ff. 1–2v [Fragment of a bifolium; f. 1 rubric lacking; *Post communionem*] //Sollemnis nobis intercessio beati laurentii martyris quesumus domine prestet ... ecclesiae tuae recensita laetitia. Per domninum nostrum.// [f. 1v *Preface*] *V + D.* Qui ecclesiam tuam sempiterna pietate non deserens per apostolos tuos iugiter eam et erudis et protegis. et ideo. *Post communionem.* Sumpsimus domine pignus salutis aeternae celebrantes.// [f. 2 *Preface*; initial and opening words cut away] //uirtutem quos diuersis terrarum partibus gregis sacros diuino pane pascentes, una fide eademque die pari nominis tui confessione coronasti. Per christum. *Post communionem.* Sacro munere uegitatos sanctorum martyrum// [f. 2v *Preface*; top line partially cut away] *V + D.* Qui ecclesiam tuam in tuis fidelibus pollentem apostolicis facis constare doctrinis presta quesumus ut per quos initium diuinae cognitionis accepit, per eos usque in finem secule capiat. Regni caelesti augmentum per. *Post communionem.//*

Fragments of a bifolium from the Arno-Sacramentary; Sieghild Rehle and Klaus Gamber, eds., *Sacramentarium Arnonis. Die Fragmente des Salzburger Exemplars.* Textus patristici et liturgici 8 (Regensburg 1970); this Sacramentary, which survives as fragments in Munich (Bayerische Staatsbibliothek, Clm 29164 I/Ia) and North America (six manuscripts listed, ed., p. 13, including our fragment) has been reconstructed by the editors; the text in our manuscript consists of 4 discontinuous sections from ff. 4–5 of this reconstruction as follows: p. 35, no. 30 (octave of Lawrence), p. 36, nos. 37 and 38 (Bartholomew), p. 37, nos. 40–41 (Cornelius and Cyprian), and p. 38, no. 48 (Matthew).

See also Klaus Gamber, *Codices liturgici latini antiquiores,* 2nd ed. (Freiburg 1968) 2:374–75, no. 806; *idem.*, "Das Salzburger Arno-Sakramentar," *Scriptorium* 14 (1960) 106–8 and plate 15 (of Munich, Bayerische Staatsbibliothek, Clm 29164; our fragment not mentioned); *idem.*, *Sakramentartypen. Versuch einer Gruppierung der Handschriften und Fragmente bis zur Jahrtausendwende.* Texte und Arbeiten herausgegeben durch die Erzabtei Beuron 49–50 (Beuron 1958) 106–7, our fragment not mentioned.

Parchment (3 strips, removed from the gutter of a binding, where they served to reinforce the sewing, reassembled to form portions of a bifolium), 53–51 x 365, trimmed on all sides, each folio approximately 53–51 x 183 (33–31 x 125–115) mm. 4 long lines, with part of a fifth, mostly cut-away, visible at the top. Ruling obscured by impressions from binding-strings.

Written in an early caroline minuscule; ascenders slightly clubbed; ligatures include 'st', 'rt' and 'sti'.

Two–line initials and 'V–D' monograms, drawn in outline; possibly filled with pale yellow.

Written in Salzburg for Bishop Arno (785–821) probably in the first ten years of the ninth century (Rehle and Gamber, eds., p. 22). This fragment, as well as others, survived in a binding, probably of an incunable, purchased by Erik von Scherling of Leyden; probably no. 49 in a von Scherling catalogue (no date, 1936?), where it is described as Swiss, 9th century. Purchased from von Scherling, January 18, 1937 (Treat Fund).

Bibliography: Bond and Faye, 237; Gerard Austin, "Liturgical Manuscripts in the United States and Canada," *Scriptorium* 28 (1974) 96.

fMS Lat 157 **Southern Italy s. XII^2**
Fragment of a Noted Breviary

One leaf [recto, column a; beginning imperfectly with the response and versicle after the first lesson] //deus meus. [*V.*] <In die tribulationis mee> clamaui ad te . . ." [ending imperfectly in the second lesson; Jerome, *Commentary on Matthew,* eds. D. Hurst and M. Adriaen. *CC* 77 (Turnholt 1969) 245, lines 973–78, book 4, chapter 26.2] Porro quod ait: 'Post biduum pascha fiet,' simplici . . . dicitur phase <mostly torn away: non a passione> ut pler<ique arbitrantur sed a> transitu// [recto, column b; beginning imperfectly in the third lesson; ed., p. 245, lines 989–94] //<parie>tes pauimenta <uerrere uasa> mundare et sec<undum ritum leg>is purificare ut <esu agni> digni fierent . . . ne auxilio populo [*sic*] de suis manibus tolleretur. [*R.*] Adtende [*sic*] domi<ne> ad me et aud<i voces aduersari>orum meorum// [verso, column a; beginning imperfectly in the fourth lesson; ed., p. 246, lines 1001–3] //<vir>tus curantis appareat. <Nam> et in catalogo apo<stolorum cum> pristino uitio et officio Matheus caruerit publicanus appellatur qui cer<te> publicanus esse desierat. [*R.*] Conclusit uias meas inimicus insidiatur . . . repleuit et ineb<riauit me> amaritudine dedux<erunt in lacum> mortis// [verso, column b; beginning imperfectly in the sixth lesson; ed., p. 246, lines 1013–17] //hil t<ale scriptum est.> Nec enim poterat statim cap<ite> domini meretrix digna fieri . . . ut fidem ecclesie [*om.* et] gentium demonstraret. [*R.*] Noli esse michi domine alienus pa<rce mihi in die> mala confundan<tur omnes qui me perseq>uuntur. Et non//

Middle part of a leaf (text missing from top and bottom) with matins for Palm Sunday; noted responses and versicles; lessons from Jerome's *Commentary on Matthew*, book 4, chapter 26.

Parchment, irregularly-shaped fragment from the bottom of a leaf, possibly removed from a binding (holes in the outer margin may be sewing holes) roughly rectangular at top, but with holes, and with large gaps at bottom; approximately 194–100 x 291–248 (ca. 130 x ca. 208–202) mm. 2 columns, 14 lines. Ruled in dry point on the hair side; probably with double vertical bounding lines, outer margin.

Written in a Beneventan script; staffless neumes written above the appropriate text in ruled space equivalent to 1–line of text.

Two- to 1-line brown initials, with simple red infilling and pen-flourishes.

Top three to four lines of the fragment are so stained that most of the text is virtually expunged.

Written in Italy in the second half of the twelfth century. Another fragment of the same manuscript is now Chicago, Newberry Library, Frag 49 (B-12) (see Lowe, "New List" 220 and *Beneventan Script*, 34, cited below; and M. Masi, "Newberry Mss Fragments, s. XII–s. XV," *Medieval Studies* 34 [1972] 108). Probably no. 69 in an Erik von Scherling catalogue (no date, 1936?), where it is ascribed to Monte Cassino and dated c. 1200; purchased, January 18, 1937 from von Scherling (Treat fund).

Bibliography: Bond and Faye, 237; Elias A. Lowe, "A New List of Beneventan Manuscripts," *Collectanea Vaticana in honorem Anselmi M. Card. Albareda.* Studi e testi 220 (Vatican City 1962) 218–19; Virginia Brown, "A Second New List of Beneventan Manuscripts (1)," *Medieval Studies* 40 (1978) 289, correcting M. Huglo, "Liste complémentaire de manuscrits bénéventains," *Scriptorium* 18 (1964) 91, who misleadingly listed the location of this fragment as Washington; E. A. Loew [=Lowe], rev. ed. by Virginia Brown, *The Beneventan Script: A History of the South Italian minuscule.* Sussidi Eruditi 34 (Rome 1980) 2:29; Light, *Bible in the 12th Century,* 107 (checklist).

MS Lat 158 — Germany s. $XII^{3/4}$

Remigius of Auxerre, Expositio missae

ff. 1–8v //streque martirium duxit, instituit ut hymnus angelicus diceretur hoc est gloria in excelsis deo ante sacrificium . . . [f. 1, line 4] Postea dicit sacerdos dominus uobiscum salutans populum et orans . . . iuxta quod ipse dicit, "Sancti estote quoniam sanctus sum dominus deus uester [1 Peter 1:16]." Primum fuit deus omnipotens//

Printed as chapter 40 of Ps. Alcuin, *Liber de divinis officiis* in *PL* 101:1246–71, here beginning and ending imperfectly, col. 1248C–1265D. For a discussion of the author and sources of this work, see Jean-Paul Bouhot, "Les sources de l'*Expositio missae* de Remi d'Auxerre," *Revue des Etudes augustiniennes* 26 (1980) 118–69 (printing two treatises which were used by Remigius). Although our manuscript generally seems to agree with the printed text, the wording of the opening section discussing the hymn, "Gloria in excelsis," differs significantly.

Parchment, ff. i (paper) + 8 + i (paper), 222–219 x 142–137, unevenly trimmed (183–181 x 108–105) mm.; ruled space: 182 x 115–106 mm. 41 long lines. Ruled in dry point with the horizontal rules extending irregularly past the vertical bounding lines, with some full across; double full-length vertical bounding lines. Prickings three outer margins (trimmed on some folios).

One quire of 8; originally the third quire of a longer manuscript: signed "III," f. 1, bottom margin, right of center, in a hand other than the main scribe.

Written on the top line by one scribe in an informal twelfth-century minuscule, influenced by chancery practice; using uncial round 'd', and round 's' occasionally, and 'e' for 'ae'. "Qui" is abbreviated in the Italian manner, but the hand exhibits no other Italian characteristics. Punctuation is confined to the *punctus*, used medially and finally. Marginal notes are rare, but include a few near contemporary corrections and later nota marks (cf. f. 2).

Divided into short sections beginning with a 2- to 1-line simple initial, brown ink, presumably in the hand of the main scribe, placed within the written space; decoration confined to dots on the initial and elaboration of the letter form, for example, "S" is elongated and copied on its side. Majuscules within the text stroked with red, ff. 1 and 8v.

Bound in modern white vellum over pasteboard.

Written in the third quarter of the twelfth century, possibly in Germany, as indicated by the script (we thank Professor Richard H. Rouse for his assistance, April 27, 1987). No. 1 in an Erik von Scherling catalogue (no date, 1936?) for £5.5.0 (clipping, inside front cover). Purchased January 18, 1937 from von Scherling (Treat Fund; bookplate, inside front cover; library note in pencil, front flyleaf, f. i^v).

secundo folio: [huius]modi uoce laudacionis

Bibliography: Bond and Faye, 237; Light, *Bible in the 12th Century,* 45–47, no. 16 (no plate).

MS Lat 159 **Northern France (Paris?) s. $XV^{3/4}$**
Book of Hours, use of Paris **Pl. 28**

1. ff. 1–12v Full calendar in French, with major entries in gold, the others alternating red and blue; March–December are generally similar to the type printed by Perdrizet, including Lubin (13 March; usually 14 March), Pope Felix I (30 May), Anne (in gold, 28 July), Felix, bishop, falsely called Pope Felix II (29 July), King Louis (in gold, 25 August), Denis (in gold, 9 October), and Mellon (22 October). January and February, ff. 1 and 2, likely added from another source; feasts include: Genevieve (in gold, 3 January), Lucianus (8 January), Salvius, bishop of Amiens (10 January; usually 11 January), Souplice, bishop of Bourges (17 January), Severus, bishop of Avranches (1 February), Ansbert, archbishop of Rouen (9 February), and Austreberta (12 February; usually 10 February).

2. ff. 13–19 Gospel pericopes; John 1:1–14 followed, ff. 14v–15, by the antiphon: "Te inuocamus te adoramus. . . ," versicle, response and prayer: "Protector in te sperantium. . . . [Perdrizet, 25]."

3. ff. 19–28 [Prayers, following the preceding article immediately] *Oratio devota.* Obsecro te domina sancta maria . . . et michi famulo tuo . . . [Leroquais, *LH* 2:346]; f. 23 *Alia oratio deuota.* O intemerata . . . orbis terrarum. De te enim . . . Et esto michi miserrimo peccatori . . . [Wilmart, 494–5]; f. 27 *Prosa.* Inuiolata integra et casta es maria/ Que es effecta fulgida celi porta . . . [*RH* 9094], with versicle, Post partum uirgo inuiolata . . .; f. 28 Concede nos famulos tuos quesumus domine deus . . . [Bruylants, *Oraisons* 2: no. 122; printed *HE,* 44 and 51]; f. 28 *Ant.* Aue regina celorum . . . [*RH* 2070]. [F. 28v blank, but ruled.]

4. ff. 29–92v Hours of the Virgin, use of Paris; matins (ff. 29–52; f. 52v blank, but ruled) with rubrics indicating the division into three nocturns, each with three psalms and three lessons; compline (ff.

90–92v), beginning imperfectly at Psalm 42:5: "//Spera in deo quoniam adhuc confitebor illi . . ."; lauds through compline conclude with the usual prayers for use of Paris (listed in full for MS Lat 17).

5. ff. 93–110v Penitential psalms and litany, including Denis and Arnulph among the martyrs, Marcellus, Francis, Dominic, Louis, Bernard and Maurus among the confessors, and Genevieve and Gertrude among the virgins; followed by prayers: "Deus cui proprium est misereri semper et parcere . . . [printed *HE*, 97]," and "Fidelium deus omnium conditor et redemptor. . . . [Bruylants, *Oraisons* 2: no. 567; printed *HE*, 30 and 98]."

6. ff. 111–113v Hours of the Cross, short form, beginning imperfectly, "//Domine exaudi. Et clamor. *Oratio.* Domine ihesu christe fili dei uiui pone passionem crucem. . . ."

7. ff. 114–117v Hours of the Holy Spirit, short form.

8. ff. 118–162v Office of the Dead, use of Paris; leaf excised after f. 128v, with Psalm 7:2–10, in the first nocturn of matins; vespers and lauds conclude with prayers: "Inclina domine aurem tuam ad preces nostras . . . [printed *HE*, 101]," "Deus uenie largitor et humane salutis amator . . . [printed *HE*, 111]," and "Fidelium deus omnium conditor et redemptor . . . [Bruylants, *Oraisons* 2: no. 567; printed *HE*, 30 and 98]."

9. ff. 162v–171 [f. 162v rubric] *Les quinze ioyes de nostre dame* [text, f. 163, beginning imperfectly] //de uostre cher filz en terre. Ave maria./ E tres doulce dame pour ycelle grant ioye que uous eustes, quant le saint archange gabriel . . . [Sonet 458; printed Leroquais, *LH* 2:310–11, no. 5]; f. 167v *Les sept requestes a nostre seigneur.* Doulx dieu doulx pere saincte trinite et ung dieu . . . [Sonet 504, here lacking the prologue, Sonet 1760; printed Leroquais, *LH* 2:309–10]; f. 171 Saincte uraye croix aouree. Qui du corps dieu fus aournee . . . [Sonet 1876].

10. ff. 171–183 Suffrages of Michael, John the Baptist, Peter and Paul, Andrew, James, Sebastian, Denis, Anthony, Nicholas, Mary Magdalene, Catherine of Alexandria and Genevieve; followed by prayers: f. 179 "*Quant on lieue nostre seigneur.* Aue domine ihesu christe uerbum patris, filius uirginis, agnus dei . . . Aue domine

ihesu christe uia dulcis . . . pax dulcedo [*sic*], requies nostra, uita perhennis. [five verses; printed in Wilmart, 412–13, no. III, here lacking the last two lines]," f. 179v "*Ad sanguinem.* Sanguis domini nostri ihesu christi . . . [a similar prayer printed in *HE*, 71]," f. 179v [rubric lacking] "Anima christi sanctifica me. Corpus christi salua me . . . [*RH* 1090; printed *HE*, 127]," f. 180 "*Sequitur oratio deuota.* Domine ihesu christe qui hanc sacratissimam carnem de gloriose uirginis utero assumpsisti . . . [printed *HE*, 72; cf. Wilmart, 377, note I, no. 10]," f. 180v "*Oratio.* O benignissime domine ihesu christe respice super me oculos [*sic*] misericordie tue . . . Concede michi peccatrice . . . [prayer asking for the graces of Peter and Mary Magdalene]," f. 181 "*Ad uirginem mariam.* Saluto te sancta uirgo maria regina celorum et domina [*om.* angelorum] ea salutatione qua salutauit te gabriel . . . [similar to *Lyell Cat.*, 394, no. 387]," f. 181v "*Les vii vers sainct bernart.* Illumina oculos meos ne unquam obdormiam in morte, . . . [Leroquais, *LH* 1: p. xxx]," and f. 182v "*Oratio.* Omnipotens sempiterne deus qui ezechie regi iude . . . concede mihi indigne famule tue N." . . . [F. 183v blank, but ruled.]

Parchment (very thin; miniatures usually on thicker parchment), ff. iii (paper) + 183 + iii (paper), 164 x 120 (85–83 x 60–56) mm. 15 long lines. Ruled in pale red ink, with the top and bottom horizontal rules full across; single full-length vertical bounding lines. Calendar (ff. 1–12v): written space (90–89 x 55–54) mm. 4 columns (1 wide column for main entry and 3 narrow columns), 17 lines. Ruled in red ink, with the top and bottom horizontal rules full across; single full-length vertical bounding lines at the far inside and outside; remaining bounding lines run length of the written space only, and are double between the third and fourth columns.

1^{12} (1, 2, 11, and 12 are single; 1 and 2, possibly added from another manuscript) $2–7^{8}$ 8^{8} (+1 leaf with miniature, f. 64, after 3) 9^{8} (+1 leaf with miniature, f. 75, after 5) 10^{8} 11^{6} (originally with leaf after 3; now excised following f. 89 with loss of text and miniature) $12–13^{8}$ 14^{6} (–3, after f. 110, with loss of text and miniature) 15^{8} 16^{8} (–8, after f. 128, with loss of text) $17–20^{8}$ 21^{8} (–3, following f. 162, with loss of text and miniature) $22–23^{8}$.

Written below the top line by one scribe in a formal gothic bookhand; ff. 1 and 2 (calendar), leaves added from another manuscript, written in a similar but less even script.

Thirteen large miniatures by the Mâitre François (see Wieck, 30–31, no. 14, with plate of f. 79); cf. the Annunciation in Baltimore, Walters Art Gallery, MS W.252, f. 30, also attributed to the Mâitre François (reproduced in E. P. Spencer, "Dom Louis de Busco's Psalter," *Gatherings in Honor of Dorothy Miner,* Ursula E. McCracken, Lilian Randall, and Richard Randall, Jr. eds. [Baltimore 1974] 234 and fig. 30), and the very similar Adoration of the Magi in Oxford, Bodleian Library, MS Rawl. liturg. f.26 (reproduced in Otto Pächt and J.J.G. Alexander, *Illuminated Manuscripts in the Bodleian Library Oxford* [Oxford 1966] 1:56, no. 713, plate LIV). The composition and general style of the miniatures are very similar to those in Houghton, MS Lat 133, attributed to a follower of Mâitre François; the miniatures in MS Lat 159, however, are in general more carefully executed, with greater attention to detail, more carefully modelled drapery, and a different palette. Miniatures are set in landscapes with turreted towns in soft blues, and often with gold rays in the sky, or in interiors, often with gray-pink gothic traceried arches, supported by columns which frame the miniature; predominant colors are blue, soft green, rose, gray, soft violet, with occasional use of bright yellow and orange; draperies often highlighted in gold. Miniatures are placed above three lines of text (except f. 13, above four), fully enclosed by narrow gold arched frames, edged in black and cusped on the arch; with U-shaped frames around the text and miniatures extending from the initials, with narrow gold, blue and red strips in the inner margins, some with blue and gold acanthus leaves or other leaves or flowers sprouting from the top, and wider gold bands with trilobe leaves or berries and flowers on the other two sides; full outer borders, edged with pink rules, of black ink sprays, gold motifs, flowers and berries, with gold and blue acanthus, usually symmetrical, placed at the corners. Subjects as follows: f. 13 (Gospel pericopes) John, seated on a clearly indicated island, writing on a scroll, with an eagle holding his ink; f. 29 (Hours of the Virgin; matins) Annunciation, with Mary kneeling, her hands crossed on her breast, and Gabriel holding a scepter; f. 53 (lauds) Visitation, set outside a town gate; f. 64 (prime) Nativity, with Mary kneeling before the child, and Joseph holding a candle; f. 70 (terce) Annunciation to the shepherds, with a river in the foreground and an angel with banner above; f. 75 (sext) Adoration of the Magi, with the first king kissing Christ's foot; f. 79 (none) Presentation in the Temple, with Simeon's and Mary's hands covered by cloths, and a serving woman handing a basket of birds to an attendant; f. 83 (vespers) Flight into Egypt, with Mary offering the Child fruit, and an idol falling off a column in the foreground; [following f. 89, miniature for compline excised]; f. 93 (Penitential psalms) David kneeling in prayer before an altar with his harp beside him; God the Father, half-length, in upper left; [following f. 110, miniature for the Hours of the Cross excised]; f. 114 (Hours of the Holy Spirit) Pentecost, with Mary kneeling at a prie-dieu, surrounded by the apostles; tongues of fire enter through a window at the back; f. 118 (Office of the dead) burial service in a church yard; two tonsured and vested clerics read the service, while the shrouded body is lowered into the grave by two workmen; [following f. 162, miniature for the prayer, the Fifteen Joys, excised]; f. 169 (the Seven Requests) the Trinity, with God the Father and Christ enthroned with a dove between them, surrounded by a choir of angels in shades of dark blue.

Seven 8-line miniatures before some of the suffrages, in narrow rectangular gold frames, edged in black; text and miniatures bordered in the outer margins by red, blue and gold bars, which sprout acanthus leaves; 3/4-borders of the same type as the full borders. Subjects as follows: f. 171v Michael slaying the dragon; f. 172 John the Baptist in a forest, holding a book; a lamb rests on the book; f. 173 Paul with a drawn sword, and Peter with keys, both with open books; f. 174 James with staff and open book; f. 175 martyrdom of Sebastian; f. 176v Anthony abbot with pig, staff and open book; f. 177v Mary Magdalene with ointment jar and open book. Two 5-line white-traceried red initials on rectangular gold grounds, edged in black, infilled with scrolls on gold, f. 19 ("Obsecro te") and f. 23 ("O intermerata") with similar 3/4-borders. Each text page with traced panel borders of black vine sprays with gold motifs, blue and gold acanthus and flowers, in the outer margin. Major initials on folios with large miniatures, and before the gospel pericopes which lack miniatures, 4- to 3-line, white-patterned red or blue on cusped gold grounds, edged in black, infilled with trilobe leaves on gold. Similar 2-line initials throughout, and "KL" monograms in the calendar, on rectangular grounds. 1-line gold initials, infilled with dark red or blue, on white-patterned grounds of the other color; bar line fillers in white-patterned red and blue, with gold; flowers occasionally used as smaller line fillers. Dark red rubrics. Calendar with main entries, names of months and numbers, in gold; remaining entries, alternating red and blue. Majuscules in text outlined in pale yellow.

Bound in France, s. XVI, in red morocco; gold-tooled with two rows of double rules, joined at the corners with diagonal lines, framing a Patriarchal Cross and instruments of the Passion, encircled by a laurel wreath; spine tooled with two rows of double rules; marbled endpapers.

Written in Northern France, probably in Paris, in the third quarter of the fifteenth century, where it was illuminated by the Mâitre François, for use in the diocese of Paris (use of the Hours of the Virgin and the Office of the Dead). The two leaves of the calendar with January and February (ff. 1–2), are singletons, and probably from another manuscript; although their layout is identical to the remaining leaves, they are executed in different colors, and include a number of saints which indicate connections with Rouen (note especially Severus on February 1, Ansbert on February 9, and Austreberta, here on February 12). Ex libris note, s. XV–XVI, end of last prayer, f. 183: "Ysabel de bellrisseau." Initials in red ink, possibly stamped, inside front cover: "BM." Clipping from unidentified sales catalogue in English glued to front flyleaf, f. i^{v}. Bookseller's note in pencil, front flyleaf, f. ii^{v}: "YM/-." Belonged to Arthur H. Lea; given by his wife, Caroline T. Lea, June 20, 1938 (bookplate inside front cover; library note, front flyleaf, f. ii^{v}).

Bibliography: Bond and Faye, 237; Roger S. Wieck, "French Illuminated Manuscripts in the Houghton Library: Recent Discoveries and Attributions," *Harvard Library Bulletin* 31 (1983) 192 and fig. 6 (reproducing f. 75); Wieck, pp. 30–31, no. 14 (reproducing f. 79).

MS Lat 160 — Northern France (Paris?) s. XVI$^{1/4}$
Book of Hours, use of Paris — Pl. 32

1. ff. 1–12v Full calendar in French with alternate entries in red and blue and major feasts in gold; among the feasts in gold are Vincent of Saragossa (22 January), the subventio against the Danes of Martin (13 March; usually 13 May), translation of Nicholas (9 May), Lawrence (9 August; usually 10 August), Lupus and Aegi-

dius (1 September), Michael (29 September), Denis (9 October), Martin (11 November), Nicholas (6 December), and the Conception of the Virgin (8 December); among the remaining saints are Genevieve (3 January), Ansbert of Rouen (9 February), Severinus (11 February), Eleutherius (20 February), Gencian (21 February), Aubert[?] (27 February), Euphemia (twice, 12 and 13 April), Ferreolus (16 June), Medard (8 August; usually 8 June), King Louis (25 August), Maircille (Maurilus, bishop of Angers?; 13 September), Lambert (18 September; usually 17 September), Macarius (11 October; usually 16 October), Venantius (15 October; usually 13 October), Mellonius (22 October), Romanus (23 October), Marcellus, bishop of Paris (3 November), and Ursinus (30 December).

2. ff. 13–18v Gospel pericopes.

3. ff. 18v–25 *Oratio de beata maria.* Obsecro te domina sancta maria . . . et michi famulo tuo . . . [Leroquais, *LH* 2:346]; [f. 22v] *Oratio de beata maria.* O intemerata . . . orbis terrarum. Inclina mater misercordie aures tue pietatis . . . et esto michi miserrimo peccatori pia . . . [Wilmart, 488–90]. [F. 25v blank, but ruled; f. 26 blank.]

4. ff. 26v–96v Hours of the Virgin, use of Paris; matins (ff. 26v–48) with three nocturns of three psalms and three lessons, without rubrics; lauds through compline conclude with the usual prayers for use of Paris (listed in full for MS Lat 17); the short Hours of the Cross and Holy Spirit worked in following lauds through compline; the concluding prayer, f. 96v is complete, but the last leaf of quire 13 is lacking and it may have been followed by additional prayers.

5. ff. 97–113v Penitential psalms and litany, beginning imperfectly at Psalm 6:7, "//Laboraui in gemitu meo lauabo per singulas noctes . . ."; litany, ff. 108–113v, including Denis, Maurice, Eustace, George and Eutropius among the 14 martyrs, Nicasius, Remigius, Marcellus, Lubin, Sulpicius and Leonard among the 17 confessors, and Agnes and Genevieve among the 13 virgins; concludes with prayers: "Deus cui proprium est misereri semper et parcere . . . [printed *HE*, 97]," "Inclina domine aurem tuam ad preces nostras . . . [printed *HE*, 101]," and "Fidelium deus omnium conditor et redemptor . . . [Bruylants, *Oraisons* 2: no. 567; printed *HE*, 30 and 98]."

6. ff. 114–154v Office of the Dead, unidentified use, with lessons and responses as follows: Parce michi . . . , [*R.*] Qui lazarum . . .; Tedet animam . . . , [*R.*] Heu michi . . .; Manus tue . . . , [*R.*] Domine quando ueneris . . .; Quantas habeo iniquitates . . . , [*R.*] Ne recorderis . . .; Homo natus . . . , [*R.*] Domine quando ueneris . . .; Quis michi hoc tribuat . . . , [*R.*] Peccantem me quotidie . . .; Spiritus meus . . . , [*R.*] Peccantem me quotidie . . .; Pelli mee consumptis . . . , [*R.*] Domine secundum actum . . .; Quare de uulua eduxisti . . . , [*R.*] Libera me domine de morte eterna . . .; vespers concludes with prayers, ff. 120–121: "Inclina domine aurem tuam . . . [printed *HE*, 101]," "Deus uenie largitor et humane salutis amator . . . [printed *HE*, 111]," and "Fidelium deus omnium conditor et redemptor . . . [Bruylants, *Oraisons* 2: no. 567; printed *HE*, 30 and 98]"; lauds concludes, ff. 153v–154v, with the same prayers.

7. ff. 155–165v Suffrages of the Trinity, Michael, John the Baptist, John the Evangelist, Peter and Paul, James, Lawrence, Sebastian, Nicholas, Anthony, Anne, Mary Magdalene, Catherine of Alexandria, Margaret, Genevieve, Barbara and Roch.

Parchment, ff. ii (paper) + 165 + ii (paper), 182 x 121 (94–93 x 60–59) mm. 17 long lines. Ruled in red ink with top and bottom horizontal rules full across; single full-length vertical bounding lines. Calendar (ff. 1–12v): ruled space, 108 x 64–62 mm. 3 columns (2 narrow columns and 1 wide column for main entry), 18 lines; vertical bounding lines, length of written space, all single, except between columns 2 and 3, where they are double.

$1–2^6$ 3^8 4^8 (+1 leaf, f. 26, singleton with miniature on verso, after 5) $5–10^8$ 11^6 12^8 13^6 (–6, after f. 96, apparently with no loss of text) 14^8 (–1, leaf with miniature, before f. 97, with loss of text) $15–21^8$ 22^6. F. 29v, quire 4, possibly with remains of horizontal catchword, bottom, inside edge. Name of each month written in a very minute cursive script, bottom outer corner, recto, ff. 1–12, possibly added.

Written by at least four scribes in a mature gothic bookhand; new scribes begin on ff. 14v, 97, and 152.

This is a very fine, carefully planned and skillfully decorated manuscript, although not the work of artists of the top rank. The predominant colors are blue and gold, emphasized in the miniatures, the borders, the initials, and the rubrics. One full page miniature by the artist who also painted the calendar miniatures, f. 26v (Hours of the Virgin, matins) of Anne and Joachim at the Golden Gate, enclosed in a heavy renaissance architectural frame. A second artist painted twelve large miniatures set in landscapes with rocky outcrops and distant backgrounds in shades of blue, or in interiors which include renaissance details such as marble floors, pilasters, etc. Figures have large and rounded noses, red-orange cheeks and lips; quickly excecuted drapery with dark shadows. Predominant colors are blue and dull red, with touches of dull purple and brown and green wash, with lavish use of gold for highlights. Miniatures are set above 4 to 3 lines of text enclosed in narrow gold arched frames, bounded on both sides in black ink and cusped on the arch, touching the outer bounding line at the top; text and miniatures bordered by U-shaped red or black ink rules; with full outer borders divided into compartments with naturalistic flowers and strawberries on liquid gold grounds, strewn with black ink flecks, alternating with blue and gold acanthus on grounds of natural parchment with black flecks and gold dots; f. 62, gold compartments alternate with areas of blue and white acanthus on blue grounds, flecked with gold dots, and gold acanthus on red; ff. 27 and 59, without compartments, but with similar motifs on liquid gold grounds; most borders with a realistic bird or grotesque. Borders are bounded by black or red ink rules, some with gold highlights, and on ff. 27, 48v, 59 and 60v, also include U-shaped outer frames of brown and gold branches and a band of green grass at the bottom of the miniatures (f. 13 with similar band of green, bounded by gold, but without the outer frame of branches). Subjects as follows: f. 13 (Gospel pericopes) John on Patmos with his eagle holding the inkwell; set on a clearly depicted island with a townscape in the distant background; f. 27 (Hours of the Virgin, matins) Annunciation set in a renaissance loggia, with Mary kneeling at a lectern, Gabriel holding a wand or sceptre, and God the Father in the upper right sending down the dove; f. 48v (lauds) Visitation, with Joseph standing behind Mary; f. 59 (Hours of the Cross) Crucifixion, with Mary and John on the left, Joseph of Arimathea and soldiers on the right, and a skull at the foot of the cross; f. 60v (Hours of the Holy Spirit) Pentecost with Mary kneeling under a canopy at a lectern with an open book; the Apostles grouped behind her; f. 62 (Hours of the Virgin, prime) Nativity; f. 69 (terce) Annunciation to the shepherds, with a large gold angel dominating the sky;

f. 74 (sext) Adoration of the Magi, with Mary enthroned against a brocade background, holding the Child, and flanked by two kings, while the third king offers Christ the cup; f. 79 (none) Presentation in the Temple, with Simeon, his hands covered by a cloth, handing the child back to the kneeling Mary, while Joseph, holding a lighted candle, presents the basket of birds to an attendant; f. 84 (vespers) Flight into Egypt, set on a wooded slope; f. 91 (compline) Coronation of the Virgin, with God enthroned, placing the crown of Mary's head; two kneeling angels behind; a band of clouds across the bottom; [miniature at the beginning of the Penitential psalms excised before f. 97]; f. 114 (Office of the Dead) Raising of Lazarus, set in a renaissance loggia.

Twenty-two 9- to 7-line rectangular miniatures, simply framed in gold, some with gold tracery at the top of the miniature, and with 3/4-compartment borders which leave the inner margin empty similar in style to the full outer borders: f. 14v (Gospel pericopes) Luke, seated and writing on a scroll, with his ox; f. 16 Matthew, against a blue brocade background, seated and pointing towards his book, held by an angel; f. 17v Mark, against a red brocade background, seated, with a book open on his lap, holding his pen at eye level; his lion beside him; f. 19 ("Obsecro te") Virgin and Child, who gestures with outstretched arms, flanked by angels; f. 22v ("O intemerata") Pietà, with a town in the distant background; f. 155 (Suffrages) Gnadenstuhl; f. 155v Michael, in armor, slaying the dragon; f. 156 John the Baptist, holding the Paschal lamb; f. 156v John the Evangelist, holding the chalice with snakes; f. 157 Peter with keys and Paul with sword; f. 157v James, seated, with pouch, staff, and hat with shells; f. 158v Lawrence with an open book and gridiron; f. 159 martyrdom of Sebastian; f. 159v Nicholas with the two boys in the tub; f. 160 Anthony abbot, seated, holding a book, with a staff and pig; f. 161 Anne teaching the Virgin to read; f. 161v Mary Magdalene with her ointment jar; f. 162 Catherine of Alexandria, holding a sword and open book; a broken wheel beside her; f. 162v Margaret emerging from the dragon; f. 163v Genevieve holding an open book and a candle lit by an angel; f. 164 Barbara, holding a palm branch, standing next to a tower; f. 164v Roch with staff, pouch and dog, and an angel tending his sores.

Each page of the calendar with three small rectangular miniatures illustrating saints or major feasts found on that page in the outer margin, decorated with gold tracery at the top, and framed in brushed gold, and a miniature in the bottom margin of the labor of the month on the recto, and the sign of the zodiac on the verso, framed in brushed gold, top and bottom, separated from the bottom saint by a short renaissance pillar; pages bounded by pillars in the inner margin, and by architectural friezes in blue or dull red with gold highlights on the top; style similar to that of the miniatures in the remainder of the manuscript, but the faces are darkly shadowed and with coarser features; San Marino, California, Huntington Library, MS HM 1088, a book of hours, use of Rome, copied in France just before 1513, also includes a calendar with miniatures of the saints, although the layout is different. Subjects as follows (saints listed from top to bottom): January, f. 1 martyrdom of Stephen (octave, 2 January), Adoration of the Magi (Epiphany), Maurus with staff and book (15 January), man feasting by the fire, while a servant brings in another plate, and f. 1v Anthony abbot, with pig (17 January), Vincent of Saragossa holding a palm frond (22 January), Paul with sword (25 January), man drawing water from a river in a large cask for Aquarius; February, f. 2 Presentation in the Temple (Purification of the Virgin), Apollonia with tongs and tooth (9 February, but not included in calendar), bishop with wolf, couple warming their hands by a fire, and f. 2v bishop, Peter with keys (22 February), Matthew and his angel (error for Matthias, 24 February?), river with four large fish for Pisces; March, f. 3 Benedictine saint, Adrianus with anvil and lion[?] (4 March), Martin dividing his cloak (in calendar 13 March, usually 13 May), man pruning vines, and f. 3v Benedict (21 March), Annunciation, bishop holding a trowel[?], the ram for Aries; April, f. 4 Mary of Egypt (2 April), Helen, with the Cross (in calendar 5 April), Leo I (11 April), two women in a garden, and f. 4v Peter martyr (here 17 April, as well as the usual 29 April), Opportuna (22 April), Mark (25 April), the bull for Taurus; May, f. 5 James the greater (1 May), a bare Cross (the Finding of the Cross, 3 May), Nicholas with the boys in the tub (9 May), King hunting, and f. 5v Ambrose at a lectern, with his books on a shelf above him (17 May), abbot with Gnadenstuhl, bishop with staff, twins, as a naked couple, half-length, standing in a leafy thicket for Gemini; June, f. 6 priest exorcising, Paul with sword (7 June, Paul I, bishop of Constantinople, but Apostle Paul depicted), Barnabas (11 June), man in a hay field sharpening his scythe, and f. 6v bishop in a boat with an angel, John the Baptist with Paschal lamb (24 June), Peter and Paul (29 June), the crab on the shore of a lake for Cancer; July, f. 7 Hubert and the stag with the crucifix in its antlers (in calendar 1 July, usually 3 November), male saint with lance[?], bishop, man reaping, and f. 7v Mary Magdalene (22 July), James the greater (25 July), Germanus with staff (31 July), the lion for Leo; August, f. 8 Peter with key (1 August), Lawrence with gridiron (10 August), Assumption of the Virgin (15 August), man winnowing, and f. 8v King Louis (in calendar, 19 August, Louis of Toulouse, and 25 August, King Louis, depicted), Bartholomew (24 August), decollation of John the Baptist (29 August), a young woman in a landscape for Virgo; September, f. 9 Lupus of Sens and Aegidius in one picture (1 September), Anne in bed, and a servant bathing the infant Mary (Nativity of Mary; 8 September), bare Cross (Exaltation of the Cross; 14 September), man treading on grapes in a wine cellar, while another man carries a load, and f. 9v bishop with staff, Matthew, an angel holding his book (21 September), Michael, in armor, holding a staff and scales (29 September), woman holding scales for Libra; October, f. 10 Remigius (1 October), Francis receiving the stigmata (4 October), Denis, holding his head (9 October), man sowing, and f. 10v Luke (18 October), the 11,000 Virgins (21 October), Simon and Jude (28 October), the scorpion on the banks of a river for Scorpio; November, f. 11 crowd with a virgin, bishop and martyr in front (All Saints, 1 November), two angels supporting a group of naked souls above the flames (All Souls, 2 November), Martin dividing his cloak (11 November), man thrashing for acorns, f. 11v bishop with an anchor, Catherine of Alexandria holding a sword (25 November), Andrew (30 November), the archer as a bearded centaur for Sagittarius; December, f. 12 Eligius with staff and hammer (1 December), Nicholas with the boys in the tub (6 December), Anne and Joachim at the Golden Gate (Conception of the Virgin, 8 December), man roasting a boar, f. 12v Thomas with spear (21 December), the Nativity (Christmas), martyrdom of Stephen (26 December), the goat emerging from a sea shell for Capricorn.

Each text page with compartment panel borders, length of the written space, edged inside and out by red ink lines, some with red and gold, of the same type as the full borders; occasionally, natural parchment compartments are replaced by blue and dull beige compartments with modelled white acanthus and gold flecks (for example, ff. 20rv and 51rv). Initials on pages with large miniatures are 4- to 3-line white-patterned blue on cusped polished gold grounds, edged with black, infilled with trilobe leaves on polished gold; similar 2-line initials throughout, on ff. 62v–127, alternating imperfectly with 2-line white-patterned blue initials on polished gold grounds, infilled with a delicate naturalistic flower on brushed gold; initials, ff. 152–end, executed by a different hand, using bright orange in the infilling, and heavier black outlines. 1-line polished gold initials, alternately infilled with dark red and blue with white highlights, on square grounds of the other color; similar bar line fillers; circles in these colors also used as line fillers. All rubrics in blue; some majuscules in the text carefully infilled with pale yellow. Calendar with 2-line white-patterned blue "KL"-monograms on cusped brushed gold grounds, infilled with brushed gold with small blue and orange circles; names of the months, golden numbers, and major feasts in gold; remaining feasts alternately in red and blue; dominical letters in brown ink.

Bound in France, s. XVIII (dated by De Ricci ca. 1700) in green morocco, gold-tooled with narrow borders of triple rules with small floral stamps in each corner, front and back covers; spine with five raised bands, gold-tooled with delicate floral and small round stamps and title: "Heures en latin, M$^{ss.}$ sur velin en miniatu"; gilt edges; marbled endpapers.

Written in Northern France in the first quarter of the sixteenth century, probably in Paris as indicated by the use of the Hours of the Virgin and the saints venerated in the litany (especially Denis, Eustace, Marcellus, Agnes) and the inclusion of Roch at the end of the suffrages; the evidence of the calendar, which includes saints venerated in Rouen as well as in Paris is inconclusive. The inclusion of a full page miniature of Anne and Joachim at the Golden Gate may indicate that the original owner was particularly devoted to the Feast of the Conception of the Virgin. Unidentified armorial bookplate, inside front cover (argent, a chevron gules between 3 molets gules, on a chief 3 bucks' heads cabossed), with an erased inscription below it, and in another hand in brown ink, the date, "December 14, 1771" and a price code: "S = S = o." Belonged to R. A. Godwin-Austen; clipping from an unidentified exhibition catalogue which indicates that the manuscript was from his collection glued on front flyleaf, f.

ii. No. 73 in an unidentified English sales catalogue, glued on front endleaf, f. ii, listing the price, £50, and suggesting that the binding may be by Padeloup. Belonged to Arthur A. Lea; gift of his wife, Caroline T. Lea, June 20, 1938 (pencil note, front flyleaf, f. i^v); bookplate, inside back cover.

Bibliography: Bond and Faye, 237; Wieck, pp. 40–41, no. 19 (with plate of f. 13).

MS Lat 161 — **Flanders (Bruges?) s. $XV^{3/4}$**
Book of Hours, use of Rome — **Pl. 22**

1. ff. 1–6v Calendar, rather empty, with major feasts in red including Nicasius, bishop of Reims (14 December). Among the remaining feasts are Julianus (9 January), Macarius (23 January), Adelgundis of Maubeuge (30 January), Amandus (6 February), Stephen, bishop of Lyons (13 February), Victor (20 February), Julianus (27 February), Poche[?] bishop (6 March), Wulfram, bishop of Sens (20 March), Felicis, bishop of Trier (26 March), Timothy (8 April), Maximus (15 April), Timothy (15 May), Maximinus, bishop of Trier (29 May), Rufinus (19 July), Julianus (21 August), Marcellus, bishop of Trier (4 September), Winnoc (6 November), and Brictius (13 November).

2. ff. 7–10v Gospel pericopes.

3. ff. 11–14 Hours of the Cross, short form.

4. ff. 14v–17 Hours of the Holy Spirit, short form.

5. ff. 17v–20v Mass of the Virgin.

6. ff. 21–23 *Oracio de domina nostra.* Obsecro te domina sancta maria . . . Et michi famulo tuo . . . [Leroquais, *LH* 2:346].

7. ff. 23v–24v *Oracio de sancta maria et de sancto iohanne ewangelista.* O intemerata . . . orbis uiuit terrarum, inclina aurem [*sic*] tue pietatis . . . [an abbreviated form of the text printed in Wilmart, 488–90].

8. ff. 25–32v Suffrages of John the Baptist, Peter, Paul, John, Andrew,

James, Stephen, Lawrence, Vincent, Victor, Martin, Agatha, Barbara, Margaret, Mary Magdalene, and Anne.

9. ff. 33–75 Hours of the Virgin, use of Rome; matins with nine psalms with rubrics indicating variations for the days of the week set into the text before the three lessons; folio missing after f. 53 so that terce now begins imperfectly at Psalm 119:7; Advent Office begins f. 70v; lauds through compline conclude with the usual prayers for use of Rome (listed in full for MS Lat 132).

10. ff. 75v–87 Penitential psalms and litany including Blasius, Quentin, Livin and Gereon among the martyrs; Amandus, Vedast, Eligius, Aegidius, Audomar, Bertin, King Louis, Winnoc, Bavo, Francis, Dominic, and Leonard among the confessors; and Barbara, Amalberga, Walburga, Dympna, Genevieve, and Adelgundis among the virgins and widows. Concludes, ff. 86v–87, with prayers: "Deus cui proprium est misereri semper et parcere suscipe deprecacionem nostram . . . [printed *HE*, 97]," "Exaudi nos quesumus domine supplicum preces confitencium tibi . . . ," "Ineffabilem nobis domine misericordiam tuam clementer ostende . . . [Bruylants, *Oraisons* 2: no. 648; printed *Brev. O.P.*, lxxxiv]," "Deus qui culpa offenderis penitencia placaris preces populi tui . . . ," and "Fidelium deus omnium conditor et redemptor . . . [Bruylants, *Oraisons* 2: no. 567; printed *HE*, 30 and 98]."

11. ff. 87v–111v Office of the Dead, use of Rome; vespers concludes with prayers, ff. 91v–92: "Deus qui inter apostolicos sacerdotes famulos tuos . . . ," "Fidelium deus omnium conditor et redemptor . . . [Bruylants, *Oraisons* 2: no. 567; printed *HE*, 30 and 98]," and "Deus venie largitor et humane salutis amator . . . [printed *HE*, 111]"; lauds concludes with prayer, f. 111v: "Partem beate resurrectionis optineant. . . ."

Parchment, ff. iii (parchment) + 111 + iii (parchment), 196 x 132 (106–104 x 70) mm. 20 long lines. Ruled lightly in red or violet ink; single vertical bounding lines. Calendar, ff. 1–6v, ruled space, 113–108 x 71 mm. 3 columns (2 narrow columns and a wide column for main entry), 34 lines. Ruled lightly in red or violet ink; full-length vertical bounding lines, double between columns 2 and 3; remaining single. Prickings occasionally remain in top (ff. 1–6v only) and bottom margins (throughout).

1^6 $2–6^8$ 7^8 (–8, following f. 53, with loss of text) $8–14^8$ 15^2 (conjugate pair). Sporadic remains of quire and leaf signatures, bottom outside corner, recto: quire 3, f. 18, signed in pencil with a letter designating the quire and an arabic numeral the leaf; quires 9 and 10, ff. 63 and 79, leaves signed with letters in ink.

Written in a liturgical gothic bookhand; the calendar copied in a smaller script.

Nineteen large miniatures skillfully painted in the style of the School of Willem Vrelant (Wieck, 46; Dogaer, *Flemish Miniature Painting*, 99–105, listing this manuscript, 103; and in general, J. D. Farquhar, *Creation and Limitation. The work of a Fifteenth Century Manuscript Illuminator* [Fort Lauderdale, Florida 1976]); predominate colors are shades of deep blue and red; set in green and blue landscapes or in interiors opening on to landscapes; figures with stiff, simple faces; draperies with crisp, dark shadows and white folds. Miniatures are placed above three to four lines of text and fully enclosed by narrow red and gold arched frames; text and miniature bordered by similar U-shaped frames; full outer borders bounded on the outside with red ink rules, of black ink sprays and red and gold motifs with blue, green and red acanthus leaves, flowers, and strawberries. Miniatures, ff. 62 and 87v, heavily repainted; ff. 7, 11, 44, 59, 67, 70v, and border, f.86, with some repainting. Subjects as follows: f. 7 (Gospel pericopes) John, seated, reading; f. 8 Luke, writing, with ox; f. 9 Matthew, reading, with an angel supporting his book; f. 10 Mark, reading, with lion; f. 11 (Hours of the Cross) Crucifixion with John, Mary, Joseph of Arimathaea and a soldier; f. 14v (Hours of the Holy Spirit) Pentecost, set in an interior; f. 17v (Mass of the Virgin) Virgin enthroned, holding the Child to whom she offers a flower, flanked by kneeling angels; f. 21 (Prayer, "Obsecro te") Pietà; f. 23v (Prayer, "O intemerata") Virgin, standing, holding the Child, blessing, with John the Evangelist holding a chalice; f. 33 (Hours of the Virgin, matins) Annunciation, Mary kneeling with a book in an open room with arcades, angel with a scroll, a vase of lilies, and God the Father looking on from the clouds; f. 44 (lauds) Visitation; f. 51 (prime) Nativity in an open shed; [miniature for Terce removed after f. 53v]; f. 56 (sext) Adoration of the Magi; f. 59 (none) Presentation in the Temple, Simeon with his hands covered by a cloth; f. 62 (vespers) Massacre of the Innocents; f. 67 (compline) Flight into Egypt; f. 70v (Advent Office)

Coronation of the Virgin, with God enthroned, holding a crown and orb, and an angel with harp behind, set against a diapered background with scalloped blue clouds at the top; badly rubbed, but possibly by another hand; f. 75v (Penitential psalms) King David kneeling in prayer beside his harp, with God the Father looking on from the clouds; f. 87v (Office of the Dead) funeral service in a church, with three women seated in foreground, a robed priest, and two figures with halos behind.

Sixteen suffrages, ff. 25–32v, copied one per page, each with smaller, 9-line miniatures in narrow gold and black frames; bordered in outer margin only with narrow gold and colored strips and with C-shaped floral borders in the same style as the full borders, but lacking the acanthus motif: f. 25 John the Baptist in hair shirt and the lamb with banner and staff, but depicted as a real lamb standing next to John; f. 25v Peter with book and keys; f. 26 Paul with book and sword; f. 26v John the Evangelist with chalice; f. 27 Andrew with cross; f. 27v James with staff, book, and a shell on his mitre; f. 28 lapidation of Stephen; f. 28v Lawrence with book and gridiron; f. 29 Vincent with book; f. 29v Victor in armor with sword; a windmill behind; f. 30 Martin with staff giving alms to a beggar; f. 30v Agatha with book and tongs; f. 31 Barbara with tower; f. 31v Margaret emerging from the dragon as the dove descends from the clouds; f. 32 Mary Magdalene with ointment jar; f. 32v Anne teaching the Virgin to read.

Each text page and the calendar pages with panel borders in the outer margins, length of the written space, usually with red ink rules bordering all sides except the side alongside the text, in the same style as the full borders, but again lacking the acanthus motif. Major initials on pages with illumination, 4- to 3-line, white-patterned blue or red on square grounds of the other color with a narrow, cusped gold frame (some initials on grounds of gold only) edged in black, infilled and with extensions of crude trilobe leaves on gold. 3- to 1-line gold initials within the text, infilled with blue or red on grounds of the other color with white highlights; 1-line initials of this type used at the beginning of each verse of the psalms and the litany. Red and blue rectangular line fillers with gold. Red rubrics; majuscules in text stroked with red.

Bound in England (?) in green velvet over wooden boards, s. XIX–XX, with ornamental corners; gauffered and gilt edges; silk pastedowns and end papers.

Written in the third quarter of the fifteenth century, most likely in Bruges, where it was illuminated in the style of the the School of Willem Vrelant; possibly for use in Northeastern France or Flanders; the calendar includes a number of saints venerated in Northeastern France, but lacks saints associated with Flanders in general, and especially Ghent and Bruges (lacks Bavo, 10 May; Basil, 14 June; Amalberga, 10 July; Aegidius, 1 September; Remigius and Bavo, 1 October; Livin, 12 November; Eligius, 1 December); the litany, however, includes saints especially venerated in Ghent (Livin, and possibly, Amalberga and Adelgundis; note the Adelgundis of Maubeuge in the calendar on 30 January is not the saint venerated at Ghent, 20 June). No. 277 in an English catalogue; clipping glued to front flyleaf, f. ii. Unidentified booksellers' notes: front flyleaf, f. i^{v}: in pencil, "XVième Siècle"; in pencil, identifying the manuscript and listing the number of pages and miniatures in English; in pencil, partially erased, "Glass/13" circled; front flyleaf, f. ii, top, outer corner in pencil, partially erased: "16<?>/15"; in orange crayon, "96," circled; back flyleaf, f. iii, bottom outer corner in pencil, partially erased, but including "74" over an "x". Belonged to Arthur H. Lea; presented by his wife, Caroline T. Lea, June 20, 1938 (library note, f. ii^{v}; bookplate, inside front cover).

Bibliography: Bond and Faye, 237; Wieck, pp. 46–47, and fig. 22 (reproducing f. 21).

MS Lat 162 — Austria (Vienna) s. XV$^{2/4\text{–med}}$
University of Vienna, Theological Disputations

1. ff. 1–5 [ff. 174–178] *In nomine sancte et indiuidue trinitatis. Amen. Anno domini 1426 disputata fuit hec questio in aula ducali collegii wiennensis* [*continues in the margin: et respondit ad eam reverendus magister Johannes de Gmund, baccalaureus formatus in theologia et canonicus ecclesie sancti stephani Wiennensis* . . .] Utrum sacramentum nove legis efficatoria sit immediate a christi passione derivata etc. . . . et hec sunt sacramentum noue legis de quo laus deo trino et vno. M. p. p. etc.

2. ff. 5–7 [ff. 178–180] *Secunda Questio disputata anno domini etc. 26* [*1426*] *et ad hanc ipsam respondit magister Johannes Himmel, bacca-*

laureus formatus in theologia, etc. [*Johannes Himmel von Weits or Johannes Coeli (d. 1450).*] Utrum possibile sit unam personam sine alia mentem rationalem sanctificative inhabitare ... et ille est nouus modus habendi deum. M. p. de p. s. th. d.

3. ff. 7v–10 [ff. 180v–183] Utrum quodlibet peccatum mortale requirat plenum rationis consensum etc....

4. ff. 10–12 [ff. 183–185] [In the margin: *Magister Narcissus, baccalaureus in theologia formatus* [*Narcissus Herz von Berching (d. 1442)*] *ad hanc respondit. Questio quarta.* Utrum omne mortale peccatum sit aliquo pracepto decalogi prohibitum, etc. Conclusio prima licet omnia precepta decalogi in lege naturale sint ...

5. ff. 12–13v [ff. 185–186v] Utrum angelus intelligat deum et creaturam per sensum acquisitum vel innatam ... [In the margin: Fridericus de nurimberga (Friderich Schön von Nürnberg)].

6. ff. 14–17 [ff. 186 bis-189] De fraterna correctione est questio subscripta. Utrum quelibet omissio fraterne correctionis constitutat omittentem reum peccati mortalis.... [In the margin: Questio 7 ad quam respondit magister Johannes Geysz (Johannes Gouss von Teining [d. 1440]) immediate post festum assumptionis gloriose virginis marie.]

   The text records this as *Quaestio* 7, although it is actually the sixth.

7. ff. 17–19v [ff. 189v–191v] *Questio 8.* Utrum ad deletionem [*sic*] cuiuslibet peccati actualis requiratur attritio et contritio specialis ... [f. 19v (f. 191v)] Magister Paulus de Giengen ad hanc responsit. [Ends mid f. 19v (f. 191v); remainder blank.]

8. ff. 20–24v [ff. 192–196v] *Questio nona.* Utrum virtutes dona et beatitudines sint ydem habitus in anima... [f. 22v (f. 194v)] Magister Michael de hungaria ... [f. 24 (f. 196)] *De modo amandi deum...* Modus vero amandi deum conditor deut. xxx....

9. ff. 25–29v [ff. 197–201v] Utrum eodem habitu caritatis quo diligitur deus, sit etiam propiquus diligendus ... m. p. p. non habet. [A note following this *quaestio* ends, “Magister Nicolaus de Gretz stirensis baccalaureus pro tempore formatus in theologia (Nikolaus von Grätz)”].

10. ff. 30–32v [ff. 202–204v] Utrum sicut omne mendacium sic et omne periurium sit mortale peccatum . . . Magister Urbanus de epella [Urban von Melk]

11. ff. 32v–33v [ff. 204v–205v] Utrum persone divine consubstantiales sint in potentia equales . . . [f. 33v (f. 205v)] Exodi xx. Hec sunt decem precepte que dominus deus dedit Moysi scripta in tabulis duabus lapideis . . . Non concupistes rem.

12. ff. 34–36v [ff. 206–208v] Utrum vi consecrationis in eukaristie sacramento fiat substantie panis in corpus et vini in sangwinem christi vera transsubstantiatio [*sic*] . . . [f. 36 (f. 208)] Magister Jodocus de Haylprunna [Jodocus Weiler von Heilbronn].

Text was copied out of order, so that f. 35v [f. 207v] is followed by f. 36v [f. 208v], and then concludes on f. 36 [f. 208]; cf. marginal directions on the correct order supplied by the scribe, f. 35v [f. 207v]; note on f. 36v [f. 208v]: "Magister Stephanus de Egenburga respondit ad hanc questionem."

13. ff. 37–40v [ff. 209–212v] Utrum in deo summe simplici sit aliqua pluralitas siue distinctio perfectionum attributalium preueniens actualiter omnem operationem intellectuum. . . . [Ff. 41–44v (ff. 213–216v) blank.]

14. ff. 45–46 [ff. 217–218] Questio utrum quelibet creatura rationalis videns divinam essentiam. . . . [F. 46v (f. 218v) blank.]

15. ff. 47–48v [ff. 219–220v] Utrum agens contra conscientiam nimis strictam grauius peccet quam agens secundum conscientiam nimis largam. . . . [Ends, top f. 48v (f. 220v); remainder blank.]

16. ff. 49–50 [ff. 221–222] Utrum reuelatione prophetica veraciter cognoscantur diuine prouidentie fata. . . . [F. 50v (f. 222v) Later notes, written with the sheet reversed so they now read upside down.]

Arts. 1–16 (ff. 1–50) A series of sixteen theological *quaestiones* from the University of Vienna; the first two are dated 1426. Note that the manuscript records the sixth *quaestio* as the seventh (see art. 6 above). We owe special thanks to Dr. H. G. Senger, University of Cologne, for his description of this manuscript and identification of many of the masters mentioned (in correspondence, November

29, 1972). Simple marginal notes indicate the structure of the disputations. "M. p. p." or "Habet m. p. de p" [magister p. de p.?] often noted at the bottom of pages or at the end of sections of the text. Numerous marginal additions, ff. 1–27, amplify the argument in the main text by adding comments from other masters; thereafter there are few marginal additions (except f. 29v).

17. ff. 51–56 [ff. 223–228] [*Carta visitationis monasterii Gotwicensis.*] 1451. In nomine domini amen. Nos fratres Stephanus Mellicensis [Stephan Spanberg von Melk] Martinus scotorum uienne et laurentius Celle Marie monachorum abbates ibidem patri Benedicti patris diocesis visitatores . . . constitutorum per reuerendissimum in christo patrem et dominum nicolam tituli et petrus ad vincula. . . . *In monasterio Gotwicensi, anno 1451, in die ss. nazarii et celsi* [*July 28*]. [Short additional note on the visitation, top f. 56 (f. 228); remainder, and f. 56v (f. 228v) blank.]

Paper (unidentified watermarks, usually obscured by text or in gutter; cf. ff. 44v and 50, scales (?) and f. 56, flower with six petals), ff. iv (paper) + 56 (modern foliation, bottom, inside corner [cited]; original foliation, top outer corner, ff. 174–228, with f. 186 bis [cited in square brackets]) + iv, 216 x 154 mm. Layout varies. Quires 1–3 (ff. 1–36v), written space, (166–162 x 109–105) mm. 35–32 long lines (except quire 3, ff. 25–36v, written space, [158–155 x 105] mm., 35–32 long lines); frame ruled in ink, with all rules full-length; prickings, three outer margins. Quire 4, ff. 37–44v, written space, (170 x 115) mm.; 36 long lines; frame ruled in lead, with all rules full-length. Quire 5 (ff. 45–50v), outer dimensions vary; creases indicate that the quire was once folded in half; written space, (170 x 105) mm.; 36 long lines; frame ruled in dry point, with all rules full-length. Quire 6 (ff. 51–56v), written space, (166–164 x 99–96) mm. 42–39 long lines; ruling indiscernible.

$1–3^{12}$ 4^{8} $5–6^{6}$. Catchword, quire one only, alongside the last word of text; quires 2 and 5 reinforced with strips from another manuscript.

Written by many scribes; the first three quires (through f. 36v) copied in cursive gothic bookhands by many scribes; each *quaestio* appears to have been copied independently (change in ink color visible), and possibly each by a separate scribe; more certain changes of hand visible at ff. 14, 25, 27, 32v, and 36 (?). Quire 4 copied by at least two scribes: ff. 37–40, copied in a small, neat, hybrida script; ff. 45–50v, copied in a cursive gothic bookhand, with possible changes of hand at ff. 47 and 49. Quire 5 (ff. 51–56) copied in a very small, cramped, cursive gothic bookhand. Thoughout, the opening lines of each *quaestio* are copied in larger, more formal scripts.

No initials or rubrics.

Bound in modern marbled boards; brown morocco spine.

Written in Austria, probably at the University of Vienna in the second quarter to the middle of the fifteenth century; includes University disputations from 1426, which were probably copied shortly after they were given, and the *Carta visitationis* for the Benedictine monastery at Göttweig (founded 1094; diocese Passau) from the year 1451. Formerly ff. 174–228 of a longer codex (original foliation). Belonged to the Benedictine monastery of Saints Peter and Paul at Melk (founded 1089; diocese Passau), where it was part of Codex Melk 862 [843/ P 33]; library stamps, Melk, Bibliothek des Stiftes, ff. 227v and 228v. Dealers' annotations include, inside back cover, in pencil, "19093"; and inside front cover, in pencil, "£25.-.-/LB/Z/A." Bought June 27, 1938 from E. P. Goldschmidt (Jackson Fund; library note in pencil, front flyleaf, f. iii^{v}; library bookplate, inside front cover).

secundo folio: peccatis sit dimittentur

Bibliography: Bond and Faye, 237; Kristeller, *Iter* 5:226.

MS Lat 163 — Italy (Florence) s. XV$^{4/4}$
Franciscus Barbarus, De re uxoria — Pl. 56

ff. 1v–91v [f. 1r blank; f. 1v frontispiece] *In Hoc Codice Continetur Francisci Barbari De Re Vxoria Ad Laurentivm Medicem. Liber I.* [f. 2 dedicatory preface to Lorenzo dei Medici (1395–1440)] *Francisci Barbari Veneti Ad Laurentivm Medicem De Re Vxoria Liber Incipit.* Maiores nostri laurenti carissime uel beniuolentia uel necessitudine sibi coniunctos a [*sic*] nuptiis donare consueuerunt ... in hisce nuptiis tuis suscipies. *Explicit Prohemium.* [f. 5v text] *Incipit Narratio.* Antequam de dilectu [*sic*] uxoris et officio dicere incipio, de ipso coniugio prius pauca mihi dicenda sunt.... uel quod ab optima fide ac animo certe tibi deditissimo proficiscitur. *Finis.*

Francisci barbari veneti patricii ac equestris ordinis uiri illustrissimi ad Laurentium medicum ciuem florentinum De re vxoria Liber explicit.

Attilo Gnesotto, ed., in *Atti e Memorie della R. Accademia di Scienze Lettere ed Arti in Padova* n.s. 32 (1916) 23–100. Marginal apparatus in the hand of the main scribe indicating authors cited in the text, and occasionally subjects (cf. f. 26: "Quibus rebus forma contineatur"), with some appreciative remarks (cf. f. 33v: "apta similitudo"; f. 62: "apta comparatio per contrarium").

Parchment (good quality), ff. i (parchment) + 92 (foliated 1–91, with blank unnumbered leaf before f. 1) + i (parchment), 188 x 119 (119–18 x 64–60) mm. 21 long lines. Ruled in dry point on the hair side; top and bottom horizontal lines full across; double full-length vertical bounding lines. Prickings in outer and bottom margins.

1^2 (conjugate pair; 1, unnumbered and blank) 2^{10} (beginning on f. 2) $3–10^{10}$. Vertical catchwords written between the inner bounding lines, lower margin; quire and leaf signatures in ink with a letter designating the quire and an arabic numeral the leaf, very bottom outside corner, recto; leaves in quire 2 are numbered only; alphabetical series begins, quire 3, with "b" (often cut away; visible on ff. 23, 46, 56, 66, etc.).

Written above the top line in a skilled, rounded humanistic script by one scribe, who also copied Vatican, Biblioteca Apostolica Vaticana, MS Urb. lat. 389, *Vitae sanctorum*, for Federico da Montefeltro and Venice, Biblioteca Nazionale Marciana, MS Lat Z.64 (Cod. 1799), Augustine, for Cardinal Bessarion between 1470–72, while working for the Florentine bookseller, Vespasiano da Bisticci (see de la Mare, "New Research," 553, appendix I, no. 104, and appendix III, pp. 572–73).

Well executed initial with full page border and facing frontispiece which probably can be attributed to Francesco di Lorenzo Rosselli of Florence (1445–1513) or to the Master of the Hamilton Xenophon; on Francesco Rosselli, see Avril, "Review," 367; M. L. d'Ancona, "Francesco Rosselli," *Commentari: rivista di critica e storia dell'arte* n.s. 16 (1965) 56–76, and Garzelli, "Le immagini," 173–88, not mentioning this manuscript, cf. especially plate 500 of Vatican, Biblioteca Apostolica Vaticana, MS Vat. lat. 1789, f. 7; on the Master of the Hamilton Xenophon, see Garzelli, "Le immagini," 157–62 (we thank

Professor A. C. de la Mare for this suggestion, October, 1987). F. 2, 7-line gold epigraphic initial infilled with dark blue on a rectangular olive-green ground with gold highlights, enclosing a roundel with a profile bust of a man on a blue background; full page flower-scroll border in pink, blue, and green, interspersed with small gold balls, set on a thin gold trellis, with landscape miniatures (badly rubbed) in the top and outside margins, gold urns with flames, and two pairs of putti: seated, flanking a pedestal, outer margin; standing, lower margin, supporting a green and gold wreath, infilled with bright red and with the coat of arms of the Sforza family of Pesaro: quarterly; 1 and 4 effaced (or, an eagle sable?); 2 (azure, effaced) and 3, azure, a lion rampant or holding a branch with a quince of the same (reproduced in Wieck, fig. 42; Elisabeth Pellegrin, *La Bibliothèque des Visconti et des Sforza, Ducs de Milan; Supplément* [Florence 1969] 61–62). Frontispiece, f. 1v, red and gold wreath enclosing an inscription in blue and gold square capitals; surrounded by round flower-scroll border. Chapters begin with 2- to 3-line plain epigraphic initials, alternating gold and blue. Rubrics in pale red square capitals (except colophon, f. 91v, in minuscules); omitted at beginning of chapters, f. 36v to end, with blank lines remaining. Opening word of each chapter (opening line, f. 2) in square capitals, brown ink; when the beginning of a sentence coincides with beginning of the line, majuscule is written between the outer bounding lines.

Bound in Italy, s. XV, in dark brown morocco over wooden boards; blind-tooled with four sets of parallel lines forming a rectangular center panel with rope interlace interspersed with small round stamps, enclosing a diamond rope interlace center ornament, a narrower middle border of s-shaped scrolls, and a plain outer border; center panel and outer corners joined with diagonal rules; spine scored in a lattice pattern. Original sewing on four bands (endbands no longer attached to boards). Four leaf-shaped brass catches with decorative trefoil cutouts, lower board; for similar catches see T. de Marinis, *La Biblioteca napoletana dei re d'Aragona* (Milan 1957) v. 1, plate 48 B; straps (now missing) were fastened to upper board with pairs of brass rosettes.

Written in Florence in the fourth quarter of the fifteenth century, probably ca. 1470–80, for a member of the Sforza family of Pesaro. Alessandro Sforza (d. 1473) and his son Constanzo are known to have ordered many books from the bookseller Vespasiano da Bisticci (see de la Mare, "New Research," 451). A copy of this work listed in the 1500 inventory of the library of Giovanni Sforza (1466–1515); see A. Vernarecci, "La Libreria di Giovanni Sforza Signore di Pesaro," *Archivio storico per le Marche e per l'Umbria* 3 (1886) 509. Remained in Italy, possibly until s. XIX: notes, s. XVIII, front flyleaf, f. i: "Petrus damiano de f<. . .>," f. 1: "<. . . .> Lorenzo," and f. 53: "Legesi"; miscellaneous pen trials, front flyleaves, and pen sketch of angels, verso back flyleaf and inside back cover, s. XVII–XVIII; s. XIX, note in Italian concerning Franciscus Barbarus now in the library files, but likely once in the manuscript, signed Professor Ales[sandro] de Pazzi. Unidentified bookseller's mark in pencil, front flyleaf, f. i: "443TM" (?); and price, 320. Purchased January 7, 1939 from Hess Antiquariat (Nash Fund; pencil note, front flyleaf, f. i^{v}).

secundo folio: secundissimis rebus

Bibliography: Bond and Faye, 237; Wieck, p. 109, fig. 42 (reproducing f. 2); Kristeller, *Iter* 5:226.

MS Lat 165 — England s. XV^{1}

Speculum humanae salvationis; Richard Rolle, etc.

I. 1. ff. 1–91 [chapter summary; chapter 13] //Et quomodo christus in gula superbia et auaritia superauit . . . [chapter 43] . . . Quibus autem modis christus in portando <c. .tem?> adiuuatur// [f. 5 text] //Potest etiam homo videre quomodo per diaboli fraudem sit dampnatus . . . Quod nobis omnibus prestare dignetur dominus noster ihesus christus/ Qui cum patre et spiritu et sancto est in perpetuum benedictus. Amen. *Explicit tractatus dictus speculum humanae saluationis.* [Text ends mid f. 91; remainder f. 91, and ff. 91v–92v blank.]

J. Lutz and P. Perdrizet, eds., *Speculum humanae salvationis* (Mulhouse and Leipzig 1907) 1:2–99 (not printing the chapter summary); Evelyn Silber, *The Early Iconography of the "Speculum Humanae Salvationis"; the Italian Connection in the Fourteenth Century,* unpublished Ph.D. dissertation, Cambridge University (1982) listing this manuscript, pp. 98–99 (Appendix, no. 365).

Text begins imperfectly in the chapter summary for chapter 13, and continues through f. 4v, ending in the chapter summary for chapter 43; text resumes abruptly, f. 5, with the text, chapter 1, line 5 (ed. p. 4, line 5). Throughout, portions of folios with initials have been cut away, with consequent loss of text; in addition to the folios lost before f. 1, mutilated folios include: ff. 4v (ch. 1), 6v (ch. 2), 12 (ch. 5), 13v (ch. 6), 15v (ch. 7), 17v (ch. 8), 19 (ch. 9), 30 (ch. 15), 33v (ch. 17), 34 (outer half of folio excised, with loss of text in ch. 17), 38v (ch. 20), 40v (ch. 21), 44 (ch. 23), 46 (ch. 24), 47v (ch. 25), 53 (ch. 28), 55 (ch. 29), 63v (ch. 34), 67v (ch. 36), 72v (ch. 39), 74v (ch. 40), and 83v (ch. 44).

Throughout, running headlines with chapter numbers and general headings. Marginal notes by the scribe include identification of scriptural passages and comments on contents.

II. 2. ff. 93–113 [Added in the top margin: *Ihesus. Oleum effusum nomine tuum.*] Expulsus a paradiso pro transgressione diuini precepti in pomo uetito primus parens cum posteriate sua ... per quem saluus fio illabere mihi in tua dulcedine te mecum et meis commendo sine fine. Amen. [Added in a later hand: *Hic finitur tractatus super illo verbo oleum effusum etc. per Ricardum de hampole theorice procedentem* (*sic*).]

Richard Rolle, *Oleum effusum*, part of his *Commentary on the Canticles*; Hope Emily Allen, *Writings Ascribed to Richard Rolle Hermit of Hampole* (New York and London 1927) 62–67, not listing this manuscript.

A few marginal corrections (for example, ff. 93, 94v, 96v) and nota marks, in lead (for example, ff. 98 and 105) and ink (for example, f. 95); longer contemporary note, f. 101, top margin, in a less formal hand, ending "... Nichil ita illuminat ad congnoui. Nichil ita dilatat ad graciarum ... Nichil ita in anima operat uniuersalem sanctificationem sicut medita[tio] dominice passion[is], habet Bonaventuram." Added, top margin, f. 108, "I O" in large red capitals; outer margin, f. 108v, "G <A?>" in large blue capitals.

III. 3. ff. 113v–139v *Deuota meditacio de beneficiis dei de quibus bernardus dicit quod expediret christiano cotidie cogitare cum mora ad excitandum amorem in domini scilicet creacionis nostre incarnacionis et pas-*

sionis eius que uocatur stimulis compassionis. Incipit prologus. Ihesu christi celeri miseracione/ Et marie uirginis intercessione/ . . . Et in corde sepius gemendo tractare./ [f. 114] *Incipit stimulis compassionis.* O homo miserime [*sic*] quid sis memoraris/ . . . Ffac uos uelle que tu uis uolle que odisti/ Nos que salua meritis matris ihesu christi. Amen. [Following text, hand of main scribe] Nota quod in hoc opere habet duo uerba dulcissima ihesu christi sunt prima et nouissima. *Explicit stimulus compassionis.*

Walther, *Initia* 12689. Includes occasional marginal notes on the contents in the hand of the main text, for example: f. 113v, "Nota quod totus hic prologus sit legendus et modus meditandi in eo notatus tenendus ab eo qui optat intime compati," and "Nota Bernardus dicit si accedas ad legendum non queras scienciam set saporem,"; and f. 116, long note ascribed to the "horlogio diuine sapientie."

IV. 4. ff. 140–146 [*Dialogus inter corpus et animam*] *Disputacio inter corpus et animam.* Noctis sub silencio tempore brumali/ Deditus quodammodo sompno speciali,/ . . . Nostre sociaberis de hinc [*sic*] aciei/ Et assimilaberis nostre modo spei. [f. 145 *De mundi miseria*; following the preceding article immediately] *Lamentacio auctoris de miseria mundi.* Ecce mundus omnibus uiciis sepultus/ Error rerum uertitur cessat chrsti cultus/ . . . Non est qui tunc friuolis siue ludis uacet/ Ubi uiget ueritas et fraus omnis tacet. [Ff. 146v–147v blank, but ruled.]

Two poems which sometimes circulated independently, but which are also found together as in this manuscript; in general, see H. Walther, *Das Streitgedicht in der lateinischen Literatur des Mittelalters.* Quellen und Untersuchungen zur lateinischen Philologie des Mittelalters 5.2 (Munich 1920) 63–75 and 211–14 (listing 132 manuscripts, not including this one).

Dialogus inter corpus et animam, ff. 140–145: Walther, *Initia* 11894; Wright, ed., *Walter Mapes*, 95–106, here ending p. 106, line 303; listing 10 manuscripts, p. 95, not including this one; also edited by Th. G. von Karajan, *Frühlingsgabe für freunde Älterer Literatur* (Vienna 1839) p. 85, line 9–p. 97, line 306.

De mundi miseria, ff. 145–146; Walther, *Initia* 5114; Wright, ed., *Walter Mapes*, 149–51, here ending p. 150, line 46.

A composite manuscript, assembled from four parts: ff. ii (paper) + i (medieval parchment; lifted pastedown) + 147 (two sets of modern foliation, inside, bottom margin [cited], and top, outer corner in pencil, 1–92, and then beginning again, 1–47 [through ff. 93–139]) + ii (paper), 230 x 158 mm.

[Part I] 1^8 (–1 through 3, cancelled with loss of text; stubs remain) $2–11^8$ 12^8 (–8, following f. 92, cancelled with no loss of text); [Part II] $13–15^8$ (through f. 116v); [Part III] $16–17^8$ 18^8 (–8, following f. 139, cancelled with no loss of text); [Part IV] 19^8.

I. ff. 1–92v: parchment (poor quality, thin, crisp, hair side yellowed and rough; many folios are almost scraps with irregular bottom margins, etc.), written space (147–142 x 100–65) mm; ruled space, main column, 147–142 x 108–105 mm. 28 lines of verse. Ruled in lead or brown crayon with the top and bottom rules full across, and with an extra one or two horizontal rules full across the upper margin for running headlines; full-length vertical bounding lines, triple in the outer margins forming a narrow column used for the marginal apparatus, and single in the inner margin. Single prickings, outer margin, slightly above the top and bottom ruled lines, and single prickings for the vertical bounding lines, top and bottom margins.

1^8 (–1 through 3, cancelled with loss of text; stubs remain) $2–11^8$ 12^8 (–7, following f. 91, cancelled with no loss of text). Horizontal catchwords, lower, inside margin; quire and leaf signatures in ink, bottom outer corner, recto, with a letter indicating the quire, and roman numerals, the leaf (lacking in quires 1 and 5); in quires 4 and 11, the first leaf is signed with a double letter; cf. f. 22, "dd i" and f. 78, "ll i."

Written below the top line in a formal anglicana script with looped ascenders, and with long 'f', 's' and forked 'r' extending below the line.

Mutilated with many initials cut away; chapters begin with 3- to 1-line blue initials with red infilling and quick red pen flourishes. Running titles copied by the main scribe in brown ink at the top of each page with the chapter number and a heading, beginning with paragraph marks, alternating red and blue. Alternating red and blue paragraph marks used at the beginning of lines within the text and in the marginal apparatus. Red rubrics (omitted ff. 24v, 26 and 28, and ff. 35–91).

II. ff. 93–116v: parchment (similar to type used in section I, but of better quality with all edges even), layout through f. 113, as follows (ff. 113v–116, see section III, below); written space (163–162 x 120–118) mm. 38–37 long lines. Ruled lightly in lead with the top and bottom lines full across; full-length single vertical bounding lines. Most folios with a single pricking, top margin at the vertical bounding line, and two prickings, outer margin at the top and bottom lines.

13–15^{8} (through f. 116v). Horizontal catchwords, lower, inside margin, quires 13–14; catchword, quire 15, added by the scribe of section III (see below); quire and leaf signatures in ink, bottom outer corner recto, with a letter designating the quire, and a roman numeral, the leaf (the first leaf, quire 14, f. 101, "bb i").

Written below the top line in a gothic bookhand.

Well-executed parted red and blue 3-line initial, f. 93, infilled with a leaf, and with skillful blue, red and violet pen flourishes forming a C-shaped frame which extends partially into the outer margin including red and blue stylized cascades, oak leaves, and other decorative motifs. Chapters begin with 2-line blue initials with red pen flourishes, infilled with leaves.

III. ff. 117–139v: parchment (thicker and stiffer, with both sides uniform in color and slightly fuzzy); ff. 113v–116v of section II were originally left blank, and were used by the scribe of art. 3 to begin his text; uniform layout used, ff. 113v–139v; written space (170–163 x 70–65) mm.; ruled space, 198 x 119 mm. 31–30 lines of verse. Ruled in brown crayon with 36 lines; sometimes with the top and bottom horizontal rules full across; single full-length vertical bounding lines; horizontal rules often extend past the vertical bounding lines. Prickings, top margin (at the vertical bounding lines only), outer margin (at the first line) and inner margin (single pricking near the last line of text).

16–17^{8} 18^{8} (–8, following f. 139, cancelled with no loss of text); horizontal catchwords, lower margin, right of center, decoratively boxed (quire 15 also includes a catchword of this type).

Written below the top line in a bastard anglicana script with some loops, and with long 'f', 's', and forked 'r' extending below the line; elongated, decorated ascenders in the top line of script.

Two-line blue initial, f. 113v, with red pen decoration, infilled with a red leaf; sections within the text begin with 2-line blue initials. Copied in 4-line stanzas each beginning with a paragraph mark, alternating red and blue.

IV. ff. 140–147v: parchment (good quality, even, creamy, slightly rough both sides), 230 x 159 (162–161 x 91–70) mm; ruled space, 165–164 x 93–90 mm. 24 lines of verse. Ruled in ink with the top two and bottom two horizontal rules full across; single full-length vertical bounding lines. Prickings, outer margin (complete row for horizontal rules), and top and bottom margins.

One quire of eight: 19^8; once the second quire of a manuscript; quire and leaf signatures, outer corner, recto, below the last line of text, "b i, b ii," etc.

Written below the top line in a formal gothic bookhand, using slightly forked ascenders; decorative capitals at the beginning of each line.

Opening rubric, first line of text, and first line of each 4-line stanza begin with 1-line alternating red and blue initials. Red rubrics introduced by blue paragraph marks. Marginal comments (possibly added?) begin with alternating red and blue paragraph marks. Guide letters visible within the initials.

Bound, s. XVIII (?), in green vellum decorated with lines scored in blind; rebacked with brown calf; spine with three raised bands and stamped ornaments.

A composite manuscript made up of four parts, all English, and dating from the first half of the fifteenth century. Parts I and II have similar physical characteristics; the scribe of art. 3 began his text on leaves left blank at the end of part II; he then completed his text in a section of independent origin; part IV (art. 4) was once the second quire of another manuscript. These parts were brought together as early as s. XV–XVI when the contents were listed on the verso of the parchment leaf, now a front flyleaf, but once a pastedown (glue visible on recto, and marks from a clasp of an earlier binding). Owners' and dealers' marks include, parchment flyleaf, f. i^v: "a/y"; front flyleaf, f. i^v, in pencil: "G1," circled; and "5864/61"; and back paper flyleaf, f. ii, in pencil: "H 4/39"; and "S/00." Clipping from an English sale catalogue, front paper flyleaf, f. i^v. Purchased December

1, 1939 from Maggs (Treat Fund; bookplate, inside front cover; and library note, front paper flyleaf, f. ii^v^).

secundo folio: [manuscript begins imperfectly]; II. (f. 94) diis damnabilem; III. (f. 118) Vt in me; IV. (f. 141) species aromatum

Bibliography: Bond and Faye, 237–8.

MS Lat 167 Belgium or Germany s. XII$^{3/4}$
Gregory the Great, Moralia in Job, books 23–29

ff. 1–119v [Book 23] *Incipit Liber <erasure> in expositione beati iob, Moralia beati Gregorii pape per contemplationem sumpta.* Prefatione hvius operis totiens necessario repeto, quotiens hoc in distinctionem uoluminum locutionis meae pausatione succido . . . [book 29] . . . Cuncta quae pateris tanto tolerare patientius debes, quanto secretorum caelestium ignarus, cur haec pateris nescis.

Marcus Adriaen, ed., CC 143, 143A and 143B (Turnholt 1979–1985); books 23–29 ed. in vol. 143B:1143–1490; this manuscript listed, vol. 143, p. xviii; *CPL* 1708; Stegmüller 2634. Major divisions at the beginning of books, ff. 1, 16v, 31, 43, 67, 87 and 103 (rubric f. 102v). All scribes use point, *punctus elevatus* and *punctus circumflexus*. Early nota marks throughout in a number of hands: cf. ff. 2v, 4v, 9; ff. 10, 10v; and ff. 5v, 10; ff. 12v, 69v, 91. Contemporary corrections include ff. 8, 13, 40 (supplying omitted words) and f. 46v (variant reading); another hand, f. 85v (?); and a later note in lead, f. 7v; bottom margin, f. 97 "B" in pencil (added later).

Parchment (smooth, uniform, medium weight), ff. ii (paper) + 119 + ii (paper), 283 x 194 mm. Layout varies: ff. 1–2 (219–217 x 157–155) mm. 2 columns, 32 lines; ff. 2v–end (237–224 x 159–155) mm. Ruled in 2 columns, 33 lines through f. 102v, and then with 2 columns, 34 lines, f. 103 to the end. Ruled in lead; ff. 1–58v and ff. 103–end, with the top, third, antepenultimate and bottom horizontal rules full across; ff. 59–102v, ruled very lightly, on some folios horizontal rules extend randomly full across, and on others the top 2, middle and bottom 2 horizontal rules are full across; throughout, horizontal rules do not extend across the column except when the rules are full across; full length vertical bounding lines, all single, except ff. 103–end, with triple rules between the columns. Prickings, top and bottom margins, quires 1–3 (ff. 1–24v) and quires 10–13 (ff. 73–102v); prickings, top, bottom, and inside margins quires 4–9 (ff. 25–72v) and 14–16 (ff. 103–119v).

$1–9^{8}$ 10^{6} $11–14^{8}$ 15^{6} 16^{3} (structure uncertain; 1 and 2, conjugate pair; no loss of text). Quires 3–6, 14, and 15 signed in roman numerals, decoratively boxed and flourished in red and brown, lower margin between the two columns, verso of last leaf of the quire.

Written on the top line in a twelfth-century minuscule by several scribes as follows: ff. 1–49v; ff. 50–59v; f. 59v, col. B, line 8–f. 65; ff. 65–67; ff. 67–102v; and ff. 103–end (completed by the first scribe).

Six 11- to 7-line maroon and green parted initials at the beginning of books, ff. 1, 16v, 43, 67, 87, and 103, with "arabesque" pen-decoration in blue, green and orange, highlighted with pale yellow wash ("arabesque" initials defined by J. J. G. Alexander, "Scribes as artists; the arabesque initial in twelfth-century English manuscripts," in *Medieval Scribes, Manuscripts and Libraries; Essays Presented to N. R. Ker*, M. B. Parkes and A. G. Watson, eds. [London 1978] 87–116). 15-line interlace "I" at the beginning of book 25, f. 31, in red outline, with the shaft of the initial filled with blue and green, terminating in an animal head and acanthus leaves in red ink. Biblical quotations begin with 1-line orange-red or green initials within the line of text, or, infrequently, when the beginning of a quotation coincides with the beginning of a line, outside the written space next to the bounding line (lacking ff. 67–102v); quotations also marked in the margins by quotation marks, stroked in red. Opening words following large initials of books 23, 24, 25 and 29, ff. 1, 16v, 31, and 103, copied in display capitals in blue, orange and green. Majuscules in text stroked with red (except f. 16, pale yellow). Ff. 67–102v, majuscules, black ink, coinciding with the beginning of a line placed outside the written space next to the bounding lines. Guide letters for initials and decorative letters in a minute, formal hand, ff. 16v and 31; small guide letters occasionally visible within 1-line initials (for example, ff. 37 and 39v).

Bound in dark purple morocco by James Adams of Dublin in 1834; binder's name and "Bibliotheca Conoviana. Dublini" and date,

1834, stamped inside, front cover; blind-stamped center ornament added on front cover, with coat-of-arms lettered "Iacobvus Elwin Millard, STP"; gilt border, with interlace at the corners surrounding the center ornament; broad gilt outer border; spine with five raised bands and title in gold, "Beati Gregorii Moralia. MS. Perg. Seculi XII"; gilt edges; decorative silk endpapers.

Written in Belgium or Germany in the third quarter of the twelfth century (I owe special thanks to Rodney Dennis and to the students from his codicology seminars for their analysis of the layout and hands found in this manuscript). In ink, bottom margin, f. 1, "N° 46" (s. XVIII?). Unidentified dealers' and owners' notes include, front flyleaf, f. i verso, in pencil: "V/79" and "a 275—"; front flyleaf, f. ii, in pencil: "26" (boxed), and "+CG." Bibliotheca Conoviana, Dublin, 1834 (stamped, inside front cover; see binding, see above). Belonged to James Elwin Millard (1823–94; front cover; see binding, above), and sold in 1890 or 1895. Belonged to Henry White (book plate, inside front cover); his sale, London, Sotheby's, April 21, 1902, lot 980. Belonged to William Inglis Morse, honorary curator of Canadiana (round ex libris stamp, with date, 1946, inside front cover); his gift to Harvard, 1946 (library book plate, inside front cover). Accession record: *46M–28.

secundo folio: unam personam

Bibliography: Bond and Faye, 238; Light, *Bible in the Twelfth Century,* 51–55, no. 20, and plate 13, of f. 16v; [R. Stoddard and A. Anninger], *Centuries of Books and Manuscripts; Collectors and Friends, Scholars and Librarians Build the Harvard College Library* (Cambridge, Mass., 1992) no. 3 (unpaginated).

fMS Lat 168 — Italy (Central or Tuscany) s. $XII^{2/4}$
Hieronymus, Commentariorum in Danielem — Pl. 38

1. ff. 1–32v [prologue] *Incipit prefatio hieronimi presbiteri in expositionis* [*sic*] *danielis prophetae.* [C]ontra prophetam danielem librum scripsit porfirius nolens eum ab ipso cuius scriptus est . . . et aliarum gentium litteris contineri. *Explicit prefatio.* [f. 2 book 1] *Incipit expositionis danielis liber primus.* "[A]nno tertio regni ioachim regis

iudae uenit nabuchodonosor rex babilonis in iherusalem et obsedit eam [Daniel 1:1]." Joachim filius iosiae cuius tertio decimo anno prophetare orsus est ... Tunc querendum est quid ei resondere debeamus. *Explicit expositio.*

Franciscus Glorie, ed., CC 75A (Turnholt 1964) 771–950; Lambert, *Bibliotheca Hieronymiana* 2: no. 215, listing this manuscript, p. 142; Stegmüller 3358 (this manuscript not listed); *CPL* 588.

Divided into only two numbered books, with book 2 beginning on f. 12; book 3 (ed., p. 860), f. 22v, line 7, and the section "De antichristo in danielem" (book 4 in some manuscripts, ed. p. 914), f. 27v, line 16, are copied continuously with book 2; the final section, "De Susanna" (ed., p. 945) begins on f. 30v, and is marked by a red initial.

The text has been abbreviated; for example, f. 24, line 3: ed., p. 865, line 140, followed by p. 886, line 553; f. 27v, line 16: ed., p. 900, line 890, followed by p. 914, line 1 ("De antichristo"); f. 28, line 13: ed., p. 915, line 42, followed by p. 917, line 2; f. 28, line 29: ed., p. 918, line 3, followed by p. 921, line 166; f. 28v, line 3: ed., p. 922, line 2, followed by p. 922, line 193; f. 28v, line 16: ed., p. 923, line 213, followed by p. 924, line 223; f. 28v, line 20: ed., p. 924, line 228, followed by p. 932, line 410; f. 29, line 12: ed., p. 934, line 1, followed by p. 935, line 471; f. 29, line 15: ed., p. 935, line 477, followed by p. 935, line 482, etc.

Contemporary corrections throughout, usually correcting simple scribal errors; Greek in the hand of the main scribe, with occasional Greek words copied using the Latin alphabet (for example, f. 1, line 27 "filomathesathe"; f. 2v, line 19 "catacribian"). Early nota marks ('N' with extensions indicating 't' and 'a') throughout. On many folios minute letters ('a' and 'b') have been added in the outside margin.

2. f. 32v [rubric lacking] Huic testimonium perhibet beatus ieronimus in commentario danielis. In primis in ipsa prefatione cum dicit "contra prophetam danielem librum scripsit porfirus" ... quae qui scire uoluerit in ipsorum libris poterit inuenire.

Brief (15–line) passage dealing with Jerome's commentary.

Parchment (prepared in the manner of southern Europe, white and thin), ff. 32 (modern foliation, top, outer corner, recto), 320 x 220

(233–230 x 135–129) mm. 36 long lines. Ruled in dry point with the top 2, middle 2, and bottom 2 horizontal rules full across, and with the remaining rules extending past the inner bounding line into the margin; single full-length vertical bounding lines, with an additional bounding line near the gutter on some folios. Neat slash-type prickings, outer margin, and on some folios, top and bottom margins.

$1–4^{8}$. Horizontal catchwords, bottom, inside margin.

Written in a clear, rounded, twelfth-century minuscule. Punctuation indicated only by the medial stop. Display scripts used for the rubrics and the first line of each new section (uncial used, ff. 1 and 12). Biblical quotations often marked by quotation marks in the outer margin; simple bracket paragraph marks added by an early hand, possibly the corrector, to indicate the beginning of new sections of the commentary.

Blanks remain for 6- to 5-line initials (ff. 1, 2 and 12); crude initials, black ink, supplied by a later hand, ff. 1 and 2. Two-line plain red initials, ff. 30v and 32, set outside the written space.

Bound in modern half calf; strips from an Italian manuscript, s. XIII (?), used to strengthen the spine.

Written in Central Italy or Tuscany in the second quarter of the twelfth century. Margins, ff. 1 and 2, used for notes in Latin, s. XVII–XVIII (partially washed and/or erased). Unidentified booksellers' notes, in pencil: inside front cover, "S 052" written diagonally; inside back cover, "L.B 27/No. 46/RT2" (from a German dealer, likely Kraus). H. P. Kraus Cat. 19 (New York n.d. [1940?]) no. 57, for $240.00 (typed version of this description in library files, formerly housed with manuscript). Purchased, March 18, 1941 from H. P. Kraus (Treat fund; bookplate, inside front cover; library note, f. 32v). Original Harvard shelf mark: Cl 8147F.

secundo folio: magnitudo lectori

Bibliography: Bond and Faye, 238; Light, *Bible in the Twelfth Century,* 72–73, no. 27 (no plate).

fMS Lat 169 **Germany (Southwest) s. XV²**
Jacobus de Cessolis, De ludo scaccorum

ff. 1–36 [Prologue, rubric lacking] [E]go frater Iacobus de Cessolis multorum fratrum ordinis nostri et diuersorum secularium precibus persuasuui [*sic*] ... Tractatibus autem quatuor opus ipsum lector eius nouerit esse distinctum. [f. 1 chapter list] *Incipit tractatus primus.* Tractatus primus de causa invencionis ludi scacorum [*sic*]. *Capitulum primum.* Sub quo rego inventus sit ludus ... [f. 1v text] *Incipit liber qui intytulatur de moribus et officys viuendi. Incipit capitulum primum, sub quo rege ludus sit inventus. Capitulum primum.* Inter omnia mala signa in homine vnum est precipuum. Quando aliquis non timet deum per culpam ... ut in perpetuum possim [*sic*] cum ipso uiuere et regnare, hunc autem libellum ad honorem et solacium nobilium et maxime ludum sciencium. Ego frater Iacobus de Cesullis [*sic*] ordinis predicatorum conposui et ad hunc finem produxi donante illo a quo descendit omne datum optimum et perfectum cui sit honor et gloria in seculorum secula. *Amen. Explicit liber de moribus hominum et officys nobilium super ludum schachorum etc.* [F. 36v blank, but ruled.]

E. Köpke, ed., *Mittheilungen aus den Handschriften der Ritter-Akademie zu Brandenburg an der Havel, II. Iacobus de Cessolis.* Programm Nr. 59, beigegeben dem XXIII. Jahresbericht der Ritter-Akademie (Brandenburg an der Havel 1879); Kaeppeli, *SOPMA* 2066, listing this manuscript, p. 313; Axters, *Bibliotheca dominicana neerlandica,* 158–60 (this manuscript not listed).

Divided into chapters, usually numbered in the rubrics. Marginal notes throughout in many contemporary hands (generally commenting on the subject discussed in the text).

Paper (watermark, Briquet Coeur 4293, Hirschberg 1474), ff. i (paper) + 36 + i (paper), 295 x 209 (244–38 x 144–42) mm. 2 columns, 42–39 lines. Frame ruled in ink with horizontal rules full across and full-length vertical bounding lines, inside, outside and between the columns.

$1–3^{12}$.

Written below the top line in a cursive gothic bookhand by three scribes; changes of hand at f. 5v and f. 10.

F. 1v, 6-line red initial with decorative extensions; f. 1, blank space for 7-line initial. Red 3– to 2–line initials at the beginning of books and chapters (many left blank) and red rubrics by two hands using different shades of red. Red used within the text, ff. 1–5, to highlight the initials and underline lemmata.

Bound, s. XIX, in England in half sheepskin and marbled paper; flat spine, very worn, with traces of simple gilt tooling and darker leather labels, with "VI" at the top, and "circ. <?>147" at the bottom; small diamond-shaped paper label glued on front cover, with "1080" in ink; edges dyed yellow.

Written in Southwestern Germany in the second half of the fifteenth century. Belonged to George John Warren, fifth Baron Vernon (1803–66; bookplate inside front cover); Lord Vernon sale, London, Sotheby's, June 10, 1918 and 2 following days, no. 135 for £7.15.0 to Merton, probably the noted collector Wilfred Merton (1889–1957), although the manuscript lacks Merton's usual notes and bookplate, and was not included among Merton's books sold after his death by Martin Breslauer (Breslauer Cats. 90 and 92, 1958 and 1960). Unidentified booksellers' notes: inside front cover, written diagonally in pencil: "100–/antt"; front flyleaf, f. i, in pencil "<?>2[?]55"; front flyleaf, f. i^{v}: "1080" (cf. label, front cover). Bequest of Silas W. Howland (1879–1938), A.B. Harvard 1904, L.L.B. 1907, 8 November 1938 (library label, inside front cover). Original Harvard shelf mark: B C1 3174f.

secundo folio: Tante enim iusticie

Bibliography: Bond and Faye, 238.

MS Lat 170 **Northern Italy s. XV$^{med-3/4}$**
(formerly MS Norton 2002) **Pl. 52**
Leonardo Bruni Aretino, De bello italico adversus gothos

ff. 1–57v [dedicatory epistle] *Leonardi de Bello Italico Aduersus Gothos Gesto Libri quarti* [*sic*]. *Incipiunt epistolam* [?] *ad Reuerendissimum Patrem Dominum Julianum Cardinalem Sancti Angeli.* Etsi longe mihi iocundius [*sic*] fuisset italie felicitatem quam clades referre tamen quia tempora sic tulerunt . . . Principium uero narrandi hinc potissimum assumemus. [f. 2 text] [Z]enone romano principe imperante gothi theodorico duce in uadere [*sic*] italiam statuerunt ... Quo facto cumas ac cetera que supererant oppida narses recepit. Finisque fuit anni decimi octaui huius belli. *Deo gracias. Amen.*

Printed, Foligno 1470, and thereafter (GKW 5600–5602); dedicatory epistle to Cardinal Julianus Caesarinus edited in Baron, *Leonardo Bruni Aretino,* 147–49, no. 24; further, see p. 176. Divided into four books, beginning on ff. 2, 18v, 31 (rubric; text begins f. 31v), and 44v. Possibly copied from a defective exemplar, or one the scribe found difficult to read; on f. 55, almost three lines were left blank after "... et transitu aduentuque narsetis ad urbem rauennam intellecto quamquam copie sue fere omnes apud teiam erant tamen ipse//"; the text then continues "Gothi quicumque exprelio [*sic*] aufugerunt padum amnem transgressi ...," omitting "cum Narsete manum conserere statuit sed commissa pugna ab hostibus interfectus est" (cf. ed., Paris 1534, p. 198, lines 17–19).

Occasional notes in later hands, including marginal subject headings in a shaky, humanistic cursive script (cf. ff. 22v, 23, 55, 55v), and brief notes in two other contemporary hands (ff. 35 and 37v); "Yhesus" added in ink, top margin, ff. 28v and 31.

Parchment, ff. iii (paper) + 57 + iii (paper), 232 x 160 (145–141 x 104–101) mm. 31 long lines. Ruled in ink, with the top 3, middle 2, and bottom 3 horizontal lines full across; full-length single vertical bounding lines. Prickings occasionally visible in the top, bottom, and outer (less frequently) margins (cf. f. 57, where slash-type prickings remain).

1^{10} 2^{10} (4, f. 14, and 7, f. 17, singletons) 3^{10} (2, f. 22, and 9, f. 29, singletons) 4^{8} 5^{10} 6^{10} (–10, with no loss of text). Horizontal catchwords, center, lower margin, with quickly-executed flourishes in brown ink on all sides.

Written below the top line by one scribe in an even, round gothic bookhand; the scribe commonly writes between, rather than on, the ruled lines. Rubrics and the opening words of each book copied in decorative majuscules with tall, flourished ascenders.

Ten- to 7-line pink or purple initials, f. 1 and at the beginnings of books 2, 3 and 4 (ff. 18v, 31v, 44v; ff. 1 and 44v, badly rubbed; f. 31v, some damage) on polished gold square grounds, edged in black, infilled with white-patterned dark blue or yellow, edged in green; ff. 18v and 31v, with a large pink flower; with dark borders of heavy purple, blue, green, pink and red acanthus, loosely interwoven and sprouting clusters of gold balls in the outer, and on f. 1, top margins, not attached to the the initials. F. 1, bottom margin, unidentified coat of arms, partly effaced at the bottom (azure a tree-trunk, possibly eradicated, vert), supported by two naked youths. Blank space remains for 2–line initial, f. 2, at the beginning of book 1. Red rubrics (omitted at the beginnings of books 1 and 2); majuscules within the text, f. 1, stroked with red. Guide letter for initial, f. 2, and note for rubricator, f. 50.

Damaged throughout by water or dampness; text partly effaced on some folios (cf. ff. 6, 12v–13, 29).

Bound, s. XIX (dated by De Ricci, ca. 1805) in English russia leather, gold- and blind-tooled with narrow rules and simple garland borders; spine with five raised bands, with the title in gold; gilt edges.

Written in Northern Italy in the middle to the third quarter of the fifteenth century (we thank Professor A. C. de la Mare; August, 1987). Unidentified arms, f. 1, of the original owner (described above). Belonged to William Roscoe (1753–1831); his sale, Liverpool, Winstanley, August 19, 1816, no. 1789 to Ford for £2.3.0 (cf. front flyleaf, f. i^{v}: "Bibl. Rosciana N. 1789," followed by a note discussing the reception of the work by Bruni's contemporaries, possibly in the same hand). Price, £3.8.0, in pencil, front flyleaf, f. i^{v}. Belonged to Charles Eliot Norton (1827–1908). Purchased from Norton, May 4, 1905, with funds from the Friends of the Library (library stamp, front flyleaf, f. iii^{v}; bookplate, inside front cover).

secundo folio: [Z]enone romano principe

Bibliography: De Ricci, 998 (=MS Norton 2002); Bond and Faye, 238; Wieck, p. 110 and fig. 79 (reproducing f. 18v); Kristeller, *Iter* 5:226; Hankins, "Bruni Manuscripts," 67, no. 10.

MS Lat 171 Italy (Florence?) 1465
Franciscan Breviary Pl. 9

1. ff. 1–6v Graded calendar, in brown, with major feasts in red; copied one month per page, with additions in later hands; includes Latin month verses as printed in the calendar in Van Dijk, *SMRL* 2:365–376 (lacking for January, May, October, and December); among the feasts included are Berard, added (in red, duplex maius, 16 January), Purification, possibly added (in red, duplex maius, 2 February), translation of Anthony of Padua, added (in red, 15 February), Gregory (in brown with "duplex minus" added, 12 March), translation of Bonaventure, added (in red, duplex minus, 14 March), Longinus, probably added (in red, 15 March), Patrick, added (17 March), Anselm, added (in red, 18 March), Joseph, in brown (recopied in a later hand in red, with "duplex maius" added, 19 March), Vincent Ferrer (5 April), translation of Bernardinus, added (in red, 17 May), Bernardinus (in red, duplex maius, 20 May), octave of Bernardinus, added (in red, semiduplex), Bonaventure, added (in red, July 14), St. Mary of the Angels of the Portiuncula, added (in red, duplex, 2 August), "Festum nivis" (in red, 5 August), Dominic (in red, 5 August), Transfiguration, possibly added (in red, duplex maius, 6 August), Clare of Assisi (in red, duplex maius, 12 August), octave of Lawrence, originally in brown (duplex added in a later hand, 17 August), Louis of Toulouse (in red, with duplex maius added, 19 August), Bernard (duplex minus added, 20 August), octave of the Assumption (duplex minus added, 22 August), King Louis (26 August), octave of Louis of Toulouse, added (in red, duplex, 27 August), Nicholas of Tolentino (10 September), Eleazar of Sabran, added (27 September), translation of Clare of Assisi, added (in red, duplex minus, 2 October), "Nativitas Beati patri nostri Francisci fundatoris ordinis minorum" (in red, duplex maius, 4 October), octave of Francis, added (in red, duplex minus, 11 October), Ivo of Tréguier, added (27 October), octave of All Saints, added (in red, with duplex minus in another hand, 8 October), Presentation of Mary, added (in red, duplex maius, (21 November), Ansanus (1 December), and the octave of the Conception of Mary, added (in red, duplex, 15 December).

2. ff. 7–163v Temporale, beginning imperfectly in feria five of the third week of Advent ("[*ant.* Convertere Domine, aliquantulum et ne tardes] //venire ad seruos tuos. *Ant.* De sion ueniet qui regnaturus est dominus, Hemanuel magnum nomen eius. . . .") through the 24th Sunday after Pentecost, concluding with Old Testament lessons, antiphons and responses for August through November; matins with nine lessons for major feasts; litany, ff. 58v–60v, to be said in the ferial office during Lent after matins, with Louis of Toulouse among the bishops and confessors, Benedict, Francis, Anthony, Dominic, Bernard and Bernardinus among the monks and hermits, and Clare of Assisi and Elizabeth among the virgins; litany concludes with prayers: "Deus cui proprium est misereri semper et parcere . . . [printed *HE*, 97]," "Exaudi quesumus domini supplicum preces et confitentium tibi . . . ," "Ineffabilem nobis domine misercordiam tuam clementer ostende . . . [Bruylants, *Oraisons* 2: no. 648; printed *Brev. O.P.*, p. lxxxiv]," "Deus qui culpa offenderis . . . ," "Omnes scripture deus miserere famulo tuo . . . ," "Deus a quo sancta desideria recta consilia . . . [Bruylants, *Oraisons* 2: no. 201; printed *Brev. O.P.*, p. lxxxiv]," "Ure igne sancti spiritus . . . [Van Dijk, *Ordinal*, 177]," "Fidelium deus omnium conditor et redemptor . . . [Bruylants, *Oraisons* 2: no. 567; printed *HE*, 30 and 98]," "Actiones nostras quesumus domine aspirando . . . [Van Dijk, *Ordinal*, 177]," and "Omnipotens sempiterne deus qui vivorum dominaris . . . [Bruylants, *Oraisons* 2: no. 802; Van Dijk, *Ordinal*, 177]"; these same ten prayers, with the exception of the fifth, follow the litany in the Roman Breviary.

3. ff. 163v–166 *Incipiunt rubrice generales* . . . , the General Rubrics, printed Van Dijk, *SMRL* 2:114–21.

4. ff. 166–168v General rubrics usually known as the "rubricae novae," as follows: *Incipit tabula de aduentu. In anno illo in quo natiuitas domini in dominica uenerit secundum presentem tabulam procedatur.* . . . [Parisian tables of Ferial antiphons before Christmas, including seven tables for each possible day of the week for Christmas; printed Van Dijk, *SMRL* 2:401–8; see also 1:140–43]; f. 168 [*R*]*ubricha* [*sic*] *qualiter ordinantur et ponuntur ystorie mensis septembris per ebdomadas et dies ut in ferialibus declarantur.* . . . [Parisian table for Scripture readings in September; cf. Van Dijk, *SMRL* 1:168]. [F. 168v, table of absolutions, benedictions, anti-

phons, versicles and responses, obscured by ink bleeding through from the recto.]

5. ff. 169–231 Ferial Psalter, including versicles, responses, antiphons and hymns, beginning imperfectly in Sunday at matins with Psalm 3:8–9 ("[contri]//uisti. Domini est salus et super populum tuum benedictio tua."), concluding, ff. 229–231, with canticles (Benedicite, Benedictus dominus, and Nunc dimittis), Pater noster, Apostles' Creed and Te Deum.

6. ff. 231–239v Hymnal, with the temporale, sanctorale and common of the saints; opening initial and eight lines of the hymn "Conditor alme [*RH* 3734]" trimmed; ending imperfectly, "*In festo confessorum* ... Iste confessor domini sacratus/ ... Membra languentum modo sanitati/ Quolibet morbo [*sic*] fuerint// [*RH* 9136]"; hymns as in Oxford, Keble College, MS 31, Franciscan Breviary, Italy (Venice or Padua), s. XV[1] (see M. B. Parkes, *The Medieval Manuscripts of Keble College Oxford* [London 1979] 109, art. 4) except that the rubric preceding "Vexilla regis [*RH* 21481]" is here *Dominica de passione*, rather than *Sabbato*, and our manuscript lacks hymns for Trinity Sunday, Anthony of Padua, Peter and Paul, the Commemoration of Paul, the Visitation, Peter's Chains, Clare of Assisi, Louis of Toulouse and the Stigmata of Francis, all present in Keble MS 31.

7. ff. 240–399 Sanctorale, beginning imperfectly with the invitatory at matins for the feast of Andrew (30 November), and concluding with Catherine (25 November), as in Van Dijk, *SMRL* 2:121–73, with the following additional feasts: the Conception of Mary, Anthony of Padua (included in Van Dijk, *SMRL* 2:142–43 from MSS A and G), the Visitation, Festum nivis, Clare of Assisi, Louis of Toulouse, King Louis, and the Stigmata of Frances.

8. ff. 399v–420 Common of the saints from the apostles to the dedication of a church.

9. ff. 420v–424 Hours of the Virgin, use of Rome.

10. ff. 424–426v Office of the Dead, use of Rome, ending imperfectly with the liturgical direction printed in Van Dijk, *SMRL* 2:195: "... dicitur ant. 'Dirige' cum suis antiphonis et psalmis, versiculo [*sic*], lectionibus et responsoriis ut supra in primo nocturno//"

11. f. 427 The conclusion of the Office of the Annointing of the Sick [Van Dijk, *SMRL* 2:388–390], here beginning imperfectly in the prayer, "[Domine deus qui per apostolum tuum . . .] //eiusque dimitte peccata atque dolores cunctos cordis . . . . Qui cum patre eodemque spiritu sancto uiuis et regnas in secula seculorum." Concludes with liturgical directions [Van Dijk, *SMRL* 3:390] and a dated colophon, "*Postea stuppa prohiciatur* [*sic*] *in ignem. . . . Excepto quod crux remaneat coram infirmo. Deo gratias. Finis Die xi*[a] *Nouembris 1465.*"

12. ff. 427–442v Offices added in another hand; f. 427 Lessons 7–9 for the Immaculate Conception, and an indulgence conceded by Urban VI (1378–89) to those who pray on the feast of the Visitation for the end of the schism; f. 428 *Incipit officium Inmaculate conceptionis uirginis marie. Edictum per reuerendum patrem dominum leonardum prothonotarium apostolicum artium ac sacre theologie doctorem famosissimum. . . .* [Office by Leonard of Nogarolo; indulgence granted in 1472]; f. 432 translation of Clare of Assisi; f. 433 translation of Louis of Toulouse; f. 434 Transfiguration; f. 437v Clare of Assisi; f. 438 Last Sacraments, with communion, the annointing of the sick, the litany for the commendation of the soul (as Van Dijk, *SMRL* 2:390–92, except with Anthony and Bernardinus among the monks and hermits and Clare of Assisi among the virgins), and the prayers said at the deathbed, f. 441 (*Deinde proximo mortis cum in agone sui exitus anima visa fuerit anxiari hec orationes dicuntur*), ending imperfectly, *Si ansiatur* [*sic*] *adhuc anima, di* [*sic*] *dicantur hiis psalmis scilicet,* Confitemini domine; Beati immaculati *usque* Ad dominum cum tribularer [Van Dijk, *SMRL* 2:392, line 59]//

Parchment (very thin; prepared in the manner of Southern Europe), ff. i (parchment pastedown, blank but ruled) + i (paper) + 442 + i (paper) + i (pastedown, blank but ruled), 144 x 100 (88–85 x 61–60) mm. 2 columns, 35–30 lines. Ruled in ink; single full-length vertical bounding lines. Calendar, ff. 1–6v, ruled space, 93–91 x 61 mm. 3 columns (2 narrow columns and 1 wider column for main entry), 33 lines. Ruled very lightly in ink, with single vertical bounding lines. The golden numbers are copied in a column on the left, outside the written space. Leaves with text in a later hand, ff. 427–

442v, written space (84 x 60–59) mm. 2 columns, 31–30 lines. Ruled in ink; single full-length vertical bounding lines.

1^6, quire missing between 1 and 2, $2–16^{10}$ 17^{12} 18^{10} (–1, before f. 169, with loss of text) 19^8 (through f. 185) $20–24^{10}$ 25^{10} (–5 and 6, conjugate pair, after f. 239, with loss of text) $26–43^{10}$ 44^8 (–4 and 5, conjugate pair, after f. 426, with loss of text) 45^{10} 46^{10} (–4 through 10, after f. 442, with loss of text; stubs for 4 through 9 remain; 10 possibly detached and used as pastedown). Horizontal catchwords, middle, lower margin, flourished on 4 sides. Quire and leaf signatures, lower, outer margin on the rectos, with a letter designating the quire and an arabic numeral, the leaf, in the first half of the quire; the first leaf in the second half signed with an "x"; most signatures are now trimmed; the missing quire following the calendar must have been signed "a," since the present second quire is "b"; quire 8 is signed "h." Quire 19, ff. 178–185v, a quire of 8, is incorrectly signed as if it were a quire of 10 ("t1–t5, x"), although the text is complete.

Written on the top ruled line in a rounded southern gothic bookhand, in two sizes depending on liturgical function. Added offices, ff. 427–442v, in a regular, round gothic bookhand with decorative majuscules within the text.

Now with two skillful historiated initials, one 3/4-border, and fifteen painted initials, but with twenty-seven additional initials excised (painted or historiated). The remaining historiated initials are: f. 28 (Vigil of Epiphany) 9-line initial of the Virgin and Child, seated, with the head of a bearded man kneeling before them (one of the Magi?), against a blue sky, framed in brushed-gold; initial is green with lush curling pink and blue leaves at the corners, on a rectangular polished gold ground, with a short border extending from the top and bottom of the initial of leaves, flowers, yellow fruit (apples?) and gold rayed balls set within a delicate brown ink trellis; and f. 244v (Conception of Mary) 7-line initial of an Angel pointing to St. Anne, both partly cut off by the frame, against a blue ground and framed in brushed gold; initial is pink, with lush green leaves at the corners on a polished gold ground, with short border as above. One 3/4-floral border (leaving the inside margin empty), f. 399v, at the beginning of the common of the saints, with acanthus spirals in blue, green and pink, highlighted with polished gold in the outer and bottom margins, set into a delicate ink trellis with flowers, leaves, yellow fruit and gold-rayed balls, with two long-billed birds and a rabbit in the outer margin; bottom margin, possibly once with a coat-of-arms or roundel with miniature, now partly excised; 9-line initial, also excised.

Fifteen 4- to 9-line initials in pink, blue, or green, or a combination of these colors, at the beginning of major feasts, terminating in curling leaves on gold grounds (polished or brushed), with short pen-tendril borders extending from the initials, with gold balls, and some with flowers, yellow fruit and leaves; infilled in contrasting colors with brushed-gold frames, some with flowers. Borders remain for most of the twenty-seven excised initials. Throughout, 2-line alternately red and blue initials, set within the text space at the beginning of a new line, with pen flourishes in violet or red, respectively; 1-line alternately red or blue plain initials within the line of text. Red rubrics. Some majuscules within the text brushed with pale yellow wash. Ff. 427–442v (added texts), plain 2-line alternately red and blue initials.

F. 282 is torn and the outer half is missing.

Bound in Italy, s. XV, in brown leather over original wooden boards, blind-stamped with three sets of narrow rules, with rope interlace between the second and third, and with the inner set forming a central panel with two rope interlace ornaments in 16-sided polygons inscribed within circles; spine with four raised bands; marks from clasps remain, upper board; once fastened to pins on the lower board (holes remain). In large letters, back cover, black ink[?]: "S 7." Rebound in August 1949 (pencil note, back flyleaf), preserving original boards, with remains of spine and front and back covers laid down.

Written in 1465 (colophon, f. 427), in Italy, possibly in Florence, as indicated by the style of the decoration (we thank Professor A. C. de la Mare for her assistance, August 1987; cf. also the review of Wieck by Avril, "Review," 368, suggesting a Florentine origin, this manuscript incorrectly listed as Lat 179), for Franciscan use as indicated by liturgical forms and the feasts observed. The book was in active use at least through the end of the fifteenth century; latest addition in the calendar is the feast of Bonaventure (July 14; canonized 1482); the additional offices added at the end of the text in another hand (see art. 12) must date after 1472, since they include the Office of the Conception of the Virgin by Louis of Nogarolo. Presented, March 30, 1942 by Mrs. Charles B. Perkins (bookplate, inside front cover). Accession record: *41–3140.

Bibliography: Bond and Faye, 238; Wieck, 110 and fig. 66 (reproducing f. 28).

fMS Lat 172 Northeastern France or Germany s. XIV[1]
Thomas Aquinas, Catena aurea in Mattheum Pl. 27

ff. 1–313 [Dedicatory preface to Pope Urban IV (1261–64)] Sanctissimo ac reuerentissimo patri domino vrbano diuina prouidencia pape quarto . . . Fons sapientie [Ecclesiasticus 1:5] unigenitum dei uerbum presidens in excelsis . . . [f. 1v prologue] *Glossa.* Euangelii prenunciator apertus, ysaias propheta, euangelice doctrine sublimitatem nomen et materiam breuiter comprehendens . . . [f. 3v commentary on Matthew 1:1 "Liber generacionis"] *Ieronimus.* Quia faciem hominis matheus [*sic*] significat quasi de homine exorsus est scribere dicens *Liber generationis* . . . [f. 313] *Leo papa.* Qui enim ascendit in celos non deserit adoptatos . . . Cuius glorie participes nos faciat ipse christus rex glorie qui est deus benedictus in secula. Amen. [F. 313v blank.]

Ed., *Opera omnia* (Parma 1860; reprint N.Y. 1949) 11:1–334; Stegmüller 8044, listing this manuscript, p. 336, when owned by Mrs. Milton E. Getz; this manuscript lisited in Dondaine and Shooner, *Codices* 1:213, no. 559.

Names of authors cited in the commentary are written in red, with the title of the work formally written in red in the margin. Lemmata in the text underlined in red.

Parchment, ff. i (paper) + 313, 315 x 226 (215–214 x 129; except f. 1, 210 x 129) mm. Layout varies, 4 to 2 columns, 47–44 lines. Biblical text written in narrow columns, comprising one fourth of the ruled space, every other line; commentary written on every line surrounding the text or in two wide columns. Ruled in lead; single full-length vertical bounding lines in the inner and outer margins and between the columns. Prickings, top and bottom margins.

$1–6^{12}$ 7^{10} (+1, f. 76, after 3) $8–14^{12}$ 15^{8} 16^{14} $17–18^{12}$ 19^{2} $20–24^{12}$ 25^{10} $26–27^{12}$ 24^{4}. Horizontal catchwords, bottom inside margin, or centered under the middle column (quire 12, f. 143v, underlined in red); leaf and quire signatures in very faint lead, lower right corner, recto, with a letter designating the leaf, and a mark, the quire; leaf signatures in lead, bottom left corner, recto, in some quires numbering the leaves throughout the quire, as follows: p'[rimus], s'[ecundus] . . . duod[ecimus] (for example, see quires 10 and 11, beginning on ff. 108 and 120); remains of leaf signatures, small roman numerals, bottom left corner, recto, visible in quire 12 in red (ff. 133, 138, 139), and in quire 22 in lead (ff. 244, 245, etc.).

Written below the top line (text and commentary) in dark brown to black ink by at least five scribes im similar quick gothic text hands (*littera parisiensis*). Text written in a larger and slightly more formal hand than the commentary. Ink flaked and badly rubbed in places.

Two 8- to 7-line red and blue parted initials, f. 1rv, with full column borders of red and blue superimposed 'Js' and decorative motifs, including beading, crosshatch balls and daisies. Similar 5- to 3-line initials, which do not extend the full length of the column, used at the beginning of Matthew, f. 3v, and for chapters and occasionally other sections of the biblical text. Smaller divisions in text indicated by 3-line, and in commentary, 2- to 1-line alternating red and blue initials with pen flourishes in the other color. Running headlines and marginal chapter numbers in red and blue. Majuscules in text and commentary stroked with red. Chapter numbers added, top right corner of each opening; through f. 57 in brown ink, romans; then in red in romans or arabics through f. 175, then continuing in brown ink.

Bound in Germany, s. XVII, in white blind-stamped pigskin over angled boards; spine with five raised bands; head- and tailbands with green and white chevron stitching; two fore edge clasps crudely repaired with snap fastenings, and catches (now missing) on straps (once fastened front to back); rebacked with spine laid down.

Written in Northeastern France or Germany in the first half of the fourteenth century, probably for a monastery (cf. chain mark, f. 1). Belonged in 1630 to the Benedictines of Weingarten, near Altdorf, diocese Konstanz (see Krämer, *Handschriftenerbe,* 803); erased inscription, f. 1: "Monasterii Weingartensis. 1630." Manuscript B.43.fol. in the catalogue of 1712 as published in Karl Löffler, *Die Handschriften des Klosters Weingarten.* Beiheft zum Zentralblatt für Bibliothekswesen 41 (Leipzig, 1912) 62 (cf. note, s. XVIII, pasted inside front cover, describing the manuscript in terms identical with those of the 1712 catalogue). In the collection at Fulda in 1807, when it was possibly given to the Landgrave of Hesse-Darmstadt by the French general Thiebault (b. 1769; erased inscription, f. 1: "Imperiali bibliothecae Lutetiis, Thiebault, Fuldensis regionis gubernator, 1807," with shelf mark, "B.48.64"; this shelf mark also added to the 1630 ex libris note by a later hand). Since the Weingarten books with this inscription were in the Hofbibliothek at Darmstadt in the later nineteenth century, it is likely that this manuscript was also, although Löffler does not list a Darmstadt shelf mark (Löffler, 62). For a discussion of the probable fate of the books alienated by Thiebault from Fulda, see Löffler, 22–5, and A. Spont, "Les manuscrits de Weingarten" *Bibliothèque de l'école des chartes* 56 (1895) 599–600. Description from unidentified English sales catalogue, pasted inside front cover. Booksellers' and owners' notes (?) in pencil; inside front cover: "6386, NKRKR, 850^{00}," "4476 (written vertically)/ saez," and "ITL"; and front flyleaf, f. i: "Acquinas [*sic*]," "1108^{a} (circled)," and "Ris=." Possibly the same as the manuscript once belonging to J. E. Schulte and sold by Anderson, N.Y., May 1910, no. 367 to E. Dawson, as suggested by De Ricci, although the sale catalogue describes the manuscript as on paper. In the library of Mrs. Milton E. Getz, Beverly Hills, California in 1935, when the manuscript was first described by De Ricci (p. 15, no. 22); her sale, New York, American Art Association, Anderson Galleries, November 24 and 25, 1936, no. 1545. Purchased, February 1942 from C. A. Stonehill, Inc. (Jackson fund; bookplate, front flyleaf); accession record: *41–2663F.

secundo folio: [ap]parendo. *Leo papa.*

Bibliography: De Ricci, p. 15, no. 22 and p. 2240; Bond and Faye, 238.

MS Lat 173 — Germany s. XV^2

Penitential psalms, litanies, etc. for Dominican use — Pls. 16, 17

1. ff. 1–10v Penitential psalms.

2. ff. 10v–19 *Dy letuany,* beginning with the antiphon, "Ne reminiscaris [printed *Sarum Breviary* 2:250]" and Psalm 69 (complete), including Maurice among the martyrs, Dominic (twice), Thomas Aquinas, Vincent Ferrer, Francis, Henry emperor, Louis (of

Toulouse?) and Sebald among the confessors, and Catherine of Siena (twice), Barbara, Ursula, Cunigundis, and Elizabeth (of Thuringia?) among the virgins; concludes with eight prayers, ff. 17v–19: "Protege domine famulos [*om.* tuos] subsidiis pacis et beate marie . . ."; "Concede quesumus omnipotens deus ut peccatorum nostrorum pondere premimur beati dominici confessoris . . ."; "Preces quesumus tibi domine offerimus domine in credente beato petro martire . . ."; "Deus qui ecclesiam tuam mira beati thome confessoris tui erudicione . . ."; "Ineffabilem misericordiam tuam domine nobis clementer ostende . . . [Bruylants, *Oraisons* 2:648]"; "Pretende domine famulis et famulabus tuis dexteram celestis . . ."; "Ecclesie tue domine preces placatus admitte . . . [Bruylants, *Oraisons* 2:517]"; "Deus a quo sancta desideria recta consilia . . . [Bruylants, *Oraisons* 2:201]."

The same eight prayers, with the addition of a prayer to Vincent Ferrer ("Deus qui gencium multitudinem mira beati Vincencii confesoris tui predicacione . . .") after the fourth prayer are also found in Claremont, California, Claremont College, Honnold Library, MSS Crispin 8, and Crispin 9, both Dominican Psalters, s. XV^2; this same series is printed in the modern Dominican breviary (cf. *Brev. O.P.*, lxxxiv, "litaniae sanctorum"), except that the third and fourth prayers and the prayer to Vincent Ferrer are replaced by a prayer to all the saints of the order.

3. ff. 19–26v *Di totem letuany*, litany for the dead; saints identical with those in art. 2, feminine response to the petitions ("libera eas"); concludes with five prayers, ff. 23v–26: "Inclina domine aurem tuam ad preces nostras quibus misericordiam tuam . . . fratrum et sororum ordinis nostri . . . [cf. *HE*, 101]"; "Quesumus domine pro tua pietate miserere animabus famularum tuarum . . . [printed *HE*, 113]"; "Deus uenie largitor et humane salutis actor [*sic*] . . . fratres et sorores familiares et benefactores . . . [printed *HE*, 111]"; "Deus qui nos patrem et matrem honorare precepisti miserere clementer animabus parentum nostrorum . . . [printed *HE*, 111]"; "Fidelium deus omnium conditor et redemptor animabus famulorum famularumque . . . [Bruylants, *Oraisons* 2: no. 567; printed *HE*, 30 and 98]."

4. ff. 26v–31v *Incipit cursus debitam*, Hours of the Virgin, fragment of

the office for matins, ending imperfectly before the first lesson: "Jube damna [*sic*] benedicere. Alma maria uirgo uirginum intercedat//," followed by the catchword: "pro nobis."

(Articles 1–4) The scribe omitted Psalm 95:3–4 between ff. 25v and 27, and later added f. 26, a half-sheet, with the missing text. "Ihesus," decorated with trefoil dots and enclosed in a rough triangle, all in red, added by the scribe, bottom margin, ff. 14v, 24, 26v, 27v. Occasional marginal corrections throughout by the scribe or contemporary, usually supplying omitted words (cf. ff. 2, 3, 5v).

5. [Detached single leaf from another manuscript, numbered by a modern hand as f. 32] Antiphon, versicles and prayers, dated 1494, to be said after compline, *Im sterben der do was 1494 Jar sungen wir nach Complet*, including the prayers: "Ineffabilem [cue only]," and "Deus qui contritorum non despicis gemitum et merencium non spernis affectum . . ."; followed by *So in an procession wolt gen so sungen wir zu vor an kiryel* [*eison; i.e., kyrie eleison?*] *in Kor*, including antiphons, versicles and the two prayers [cues only]: "Deus qui non mortem et cetera," and "Concede nostris et cetera."

Parchment (poor quality; repaired in green and purple thread, ff. 12, 19 and 23), ff. 31 + i (f. 32, detached leaf from another manuscript, described below), leaves unevenly trimmed: 101–95 x 72–67 (74–69 x 48–47) mm. 16–14 long lines. Frame ruled in lead, usually with both sets of bounding lines full across; vertical rules not always visible (present, ff. 11–14v, 17–19r, etc.). Prickings in all margins, most leaves.

$1–2^{10}$ 3^{11} (regular quire of 10, with a half-sheet, f. 26, added between 5 and 6). Horizontal catchwords, bottom, outer margin, including quire 3, since manuscript now ends imperfectly.

Written below the top line in an uneven square gothic bookhand by an unskilled scribe.

Red initials, including 2-line initials at the beginning of Psalms and prayers, large 1-line initials before the saints in the litany, each on a new line, and 1-line initials placed within the line of the text. Red rubrics.

F. 32 (art. 5; leaf from another manuscript): parchment (thin), 92 x 53 (72 x 40–36) mm. 20 long lines. Frame ruled in ink on 3 sides (lacks bottom bounding line), all full across. Written below the top line in a skilled hybrida script. Two-line red initial. Red rubrics.

Bound in a limp vellum wrapper, s. XV–XVI, with the bottom cover intended to overlap the top to form an envelope, once fastened with a tie (three small holes remain, bottom cover). Original sewing in long stitches without bands, joined together in an 'x' shape on the spine.

Written in Germany in the second half of the fifteenth century. The saints in the litany suggest that it was intended for use by Dominicans (Dominic and Catherine of Siena both occur twice, along with other Dominican saints), most likely for Dominican nuns since feminine forms are used in the litany for the dead (art. 3). The inclusion of Vincent Ferrer, added to the Dominican litany in 1456, and Catherine of Siena, added in 1461, indicates a date in the second half of the fifteenth century. The saints cited also suggest a connection with Germany: Maurice (Magdeburg), Sebald (Nuremburg), Henry Emperor and his wife, Cunigundis (venerated especially at Bamberg). This very tiny devotional book, now incomplete, was copied by an inexpert scribe, perhaps its original owner. F. 32 (see article 5), a detatched leaf from an unrelated manuscript, was written in Germany after 1494 (text dated in rubric); there is no evidence to show how long it circulated with this manuscript. Unidentified bookseller's note in pencil, back cover: "15 O." Presented in memory of Abbot Lawrence Rotch (Harvard Professor of Meteorology, 1906–12) and Mary Randolph Rotch, March 22, 1943 (perhaps from their library, cf. bookplate, inside front cover). Accession record *42M–630.

secundo folio: Beati quorum

Bibliography: Bond and Faye, 238.

MSS Lat 174–175 **Italy (Venice?) s. XV[1]**
Ps. Cicero; Ps. Boethius **Pl. 46**

The evidence suggests that these two manuscripts once circulated together; they are described as one manuscript, bound in two volumes.

1. ff. 1–109 [MS Lat 174; Ps. Cicero, *Rhetorica ad Herennium*] Etsi negotiis familiaribus impediti uix satis ocium [*sic*] studio suppeditare possimus . . . Hec omnia [expunged by scribe or later hand: disputem] adipiscemur si rationes preceptionis diligentia consequemur et [*sic*] exercitationis. [Ff. 109v–110v blank, but ruled.]

   Fredericus Marx, ed., *Incerti auctoris de ratione dicendi ad C. Herennium libri IV*, reissued with addenda by W. Trillitzsch (Leipzig 1964). Text divided into four books, beginning on ff. 1, 15, 39v, 60. Blank spaces scattered throughout, usually one or two words in length, possibly indicating that it was copied from a defective exemplar, or one which the scribe found difficult to read; for example, f. 6v, I.8 (ed., p. 9, line 24): "Alterum genus est narrationis [*om.* quod intercurrit] non numquam [*sic*] fidei . . ."; f. 16v, II.3 (ed., p. 27, lines 14–15): ". . . ad quos aliquid emolumenti ex aliqua re peruenerit in suspectionem maleficii [*om.* devocari]."

   Occasional variant readings added in the margin, likely contemporary with hand of main scribe (cf. ff. 1, 3, 5, etc.). Ff. 1–6 with marginal, and occasionally interlinear glosses in a minute gothic noting script, s. XV, mostly explaining words or phrases, for example f. 1 (1.1) "*familiaribus*: id est familie uel amicorum; *ut de ratione*: id est rhetorica; *conscriberemus*: id est tractaremus scribitur." Sporadic interlinear glosses of a similar type added in a later hand, s. XV, ff. 72–93. A few short notes in later hands, throughout, for example: f. 76, top margin: "Ihesus christus noster dominus," s. XV–XVI; and f. 82rv, notes and corrections.

2. ff. 1–27 [MS Lat 175; Ps. Boethius, *De disciplina scolarium*; prologue] Uestra nouit intentio de scolarium disciplina conpendiosum postulare tractatum . . . [f. 1v text] Cvm autem indiscreti et inpotentis septennit [*corr.*[2]: septennis] infancia ducitur ad imbuendum . . . ultima uero saporis alterius inquinamenta permanebunt. *Explicit liber Boetii de Scolarium disciplina. Deo gratias amen.* [f. 25v table of contents] Qvo tempore primo pueri ad literas sunt ponendi.

Qualem debent habere dispositionem corporalem . . . Quam male catoni adulterio. *Explicit tabula Boetii de scolarium disciplina. Deo gratias amen.* [Ff. 27v–28rv blank, but ruled.]

O. Weijers, ed., Studien und Texte zur Geistesgechichte des Mittelalters 12 (Leiden and Cologne 1976), listing this manuscript, p. 69, nos. 19 and 20, as Chicago, C. L. Rickets [*sic*] Library, MSS 190 and 224. Text divided into 21 unnumbered sections of varying lengths which do not correspond to the division into three books and a larger number of short sections listed in the table of contents. As in art. 1, blank spaces left by the scribe; f. 25v, 6.33 (ed, p. 134, line 11): ". . . [*om.* sterquilinio] supponitur transeuntibus expoitus [*sic*] . . .", and frequently in the table of contents.

Lengthy marginal gloss added in a cursive script, s. XV, f. 2: "*In primis.* postquam autor [*sic*] docuit et emouere impedimenta que possunt impedire discipulum ad adiscendum scientiam. . . ."

Paper (watermarks, obscured in gutter, but similar to Briquet Monts 11662, Florence 1432 [both volumes]; and Briquet Lion 10500, Bologna 1420–30, Ferrara 1420–32 [volume 2 only]), ff. i (early modern paper) + 110 (two sets of modern foliation in pencil: bottom, inner margin, cited; and top, outer margin, first folio of each quire only; remnants of earlier foliation in brown ink, top, outer margin, on ff. 1–4 only) + i (early modern paper); + i (early modern paper) + 28 (two sets of modern foliation in pencil as in volume 1: bottom, inner margin, 1–28, cited; top, outer margin, first folio of each quire only, ff. 111–131, followed by 7 unnumbered folios) + i (early modern paper with watermark, unidentified fleur-de-lis), 216 x 147 mm. Layout varies; v. 1 (Lat 174): (120–118 x 63–60) mm. 25–21 long lines; v. 2 (Lat 175): (118–117 x 70) mm. 24–22 long lines. Both volumes frame ruled in lead, with all four bounding lines extending to the outside of the page. Some remains of prickings in bottom (throughout), outer (v. 1), and top (v. 2) margins.

$1–11^{10}$ (through f. 110, v. 1) $12–13^{10}$ 14^{8} (through f. 28, v. 2). Horizontal catchwords, center, lower margin, decorated on all sides with flourishes. Signatures in ink clearly visible in v. 2, lower, outside corner, recto: quire 1, arabic numerals; quire 2, parallel horizontal lines; quire 3: vertical lines; in each case the first leaf in the second half of the quire marked with an 'x'. Quires in both volumes also numbered consecutively, 1–14, in pencil in a modern hand, top, outer corner, recto.

Written by two or three scribes. The first scribe copied v. 1 (MS Lat 174) above the top line in a running gothic bookhand, using long 'f' and 's' extending below the line. Volume 2 (MS Lat 175) was written above the top line, possibly by two scribes, in a rounded running gothic bookhand with straight 'f' and 's' written on the line; scribe 1: ff. 1–2v, line 3; scribe 2: ff. 2v, line 4 to end.

Each volume seems to have been decorated independently, although there is some similarity between the initial, f. 1, in v. 1, and the initials in v. 2. 5-line blue initial with red pen flourishes, f. 1 (v. 1). Remaining initials in this volume are more crudely executed and are possibly added, including 5- to 3-line red initials at the beginning of the remaining books, plain or with simple pen decoration; sections within the books begin with 2-line red initials set into the text column, usually undecorated, exceptionally, as on f. 69v, with simple internal red pen decoration. Rubrics omitted. Opening words of each book in decorative majuscules, brown ink, stroked with red. Guide letters often visible within the initials. A later hand added faces within the initials in brown ink (cf. ff. 73v, 76v, 84v, 90) and pen flourishes of the Italian type, ff. 76v–77. Initials, v. 2, are generally more skillful: f. 1, 5-line parted blue initial with red pen flourishes; text divided into numerous unnumbered sections beginning with 2-line initials, alternating red and blue, with brown or red pen flourishes respectively. Following each colored initial is a decorative majuscule in brown ink.

Bound in two volumes in pasteboard covered with leaves from an antiphonal, stained dark green. Described as unbound when in the collection of C. L. Ricketts (cf. De Ricci, 652); the use of early modern endpapers and the manner of sewing suggest that this may be an earlier binding used again for these manuscripts.

Written in Northeastern Italy, probably in Venice, in the first half of the fifteenth century (we thank Professor A. C. de la Mare for this information; July, 1986). In Florence in 1740 when the Jesuit scholar Girolamo Lagomarsini (1698–1773; cf. Cosenza 3:1894–95) collated the *Rhetorica ad Herennium*, recording the readings as number 33 in his copy of the text; see v. 1, f. 1: "Hic codex a me Hieronymo

Lagomarsino a Societate Jesu cum vulgatis diligenter collatus in mea rhetoricorum Ciceronis operum editione; numero 33 designabitur. Florentie, 21 Octobri 1740."; his shelf mark, "l.33," written below. A copy of the manuscript was made for Lagomarsini by Alexander Politus, professor of theology and later of Greek at Genoa (ca. 1679–1752; cf. Cosenza 4:2897); note in Lagomarsini's hand below the previous note: "Ejus mihi copiam perhumanitate fecit doctissimus atque amicissimus Alexander Politus de Cl. Schol. Piar." Samuel Allen sale, London, Sotheby's, January 30, 1920, no. 11 (cf. Lat 174, f. 110, in pencil: "11") to Quaritch. Listed in the catalogues of Payne and Foss, London, for three years: May, 1825, no. 91; February, 1826, no. 532; and 1827, no. 1408, when the manuscript was described as including both the *Rhetorica ad Herennium* and the *Disciplina ad scolarium*. Unidentified booksellers' notes and prices in pencil, Lat 174, inside front cover: " $35.00"; f. 110: "50.00"; f. 110v: "34"; Lat 175, f. 28v: "34." Belonged to Coella L. Ricketts of Chicago when the manuscript, at that time unbound, was erroneously described twice by De Ricci (p. 646, no. 190, with the *Disciplina ad scolarium* only; and p. 652, no. 224, both texts); the manuscript was subsequently bound in two volumes. Not included in Ricketts' sale, New York, Parke-Bernet, April, 1942. Bought by Harvard from William H. Schab Gallery (cf. v. 1 and 2, inside back cover: "WS 481/RE" and "WS 480/RI" respectively), November 24, 1942 (Salisbury fund; pencil notes, v. 1, f. 110v and v. 2, f. 28v; bookplates, inside front cover). Accession record, MS Lat 174: *42M–274; MS Lat 175: *42M–275.

secundo folio: volume 1 (MS Lat 174): causas tractari
volume 2 (MS Lat 175): uitalibus tandem

Bibliography: De Ricci, p. 646, no. 190 and p. 652, no. 224; Bond and Faye, 238; *Houghton Library Report* (1942–43) 3.

MS Lat 176 (formerly MS Norton 1003) Italy (Florence) s. XV$^{4/4}$
Cicero, Tusculanae disputationes Pl. 57

ff. 1–109v Cum defensionum laboribus senatoriisque muneribus aut omnino aut magna ex parte essem aliquando liberatus, retuli me ... uariisque et undique circunfusis [*sic*] molestiis alia nulla potuit inueniri leuatio. *Laus deo. Marci Tvllii Ciceronis Tvscvlanarum Questionvm Finis. Antonius torrigiani antonii de torrigianis scripsit.* [F. 110rv blank, but ruled.]

M. Pohlenz, ed. (Stuttgart 1957). Four pages (center bifolium, quire 8) missing after f. 84; f. 84v ends "... ut Socrates dicitur, cum in conuentu multa uitia collegisset in//" (book IV:80; ed. 2:96, line 1); f. 85 begins "//antiquissimam qum [*sic*] uideamus nomen tamen confitemur ..." (book V:6; ed. 2:103, line 12).

Greek usually added by another hand (cf. f. 14, line 12, f. 20v, lines 1–2, f. 61, line 4, etc.), but f. 9, lines 22–3, possibly written by the scribe. Infrequent corrections throughout; cf. ff. 21, 50v, possibly by the scribe and ff. 19, 51v, 89v–90, in another early hand. Subject headings and nota marks in a contemporary hand in pale red, ff. 32v, 38. Occasional subject headings and identification of authors cited added in the margins in minute, precise capitals (cf. ff. 25, 98v, etc.).

Parchment, ff. iii (paper, with unidentified fragment of watermark in gutter, possibly a monogram) + 110 + iii (paper), 245 x 155 (157–155 x 84–80) mm., slightly trimmed (cf. f. 1, bottom of border missing). 29 long lines. Ruled in dry point on the hair side; top 2 and bottom 2 horizontal lines full across; double full-length vertical bounding lines. Prickings in outer margins, and very rarely, top and bottom (cf. f. 75).

1–8^{10} 9^{10} (–5, 6, conjugate pair after f. 84, with loss of text) 10–11^{10} 12^{2}. Carefully written horizontal catchwords, lower, inner margin, written between double bounding lines when possible (omitted end of quire 11, f. 108v). Quire and leaf signatures, brown ink, recto, bottom outside corner, with majuscule letter designating the quire, and arabic numeral, the leaf, now mostly trimmed (cf. ff. 13, 15, 23, 54, 65, etc.; none remain in quires 5, 9, 11 and 12); a second set added by a modern binder in pencil, bottom inside margin, recto, throughout.

Written below the top line in a round, even humanistic script by Antonius Torrigiani (colophon, f. 109v).

Five-line gold epigraphic initial, f. 1, edged in black, enclosing a bust portrait of a bearded man, three-quarter view, on a square ground of deep blue with gold highlights (now partially rubbed), edged in black. C-shaped border of spiraling acanthus leaves and flowers in green, blue, red-purple and dark yellow, interspersed with gold balls with thin, delicate stems and rays in brown ink; bottom margin, a green laurel wreath framed in gold, with the coat of arms of the Pugliese of Florence, surrounded by a blue border (or, three bars gules and a demy lion rampant issuant in chief gules; Rietstap, v. 5, pl. CVI); bounded on the inside only with a thin gold bar, looped at the corners and ends (reproduced in Wieck, fig. 50). Three similar 5- to 4-line gold initials at the beginning of books (ff. 30, 46, 66v; beginning of book 5 missing), infilled with red, on dark blue square grounds, both with gold highlights; embellished with similar acanthus and floral motifs extending into the outer margin. Blank spaces for rubrics at the beginning of each book. Opening word of each book (opening line, f. 1) in capitals, brown ink. When the beginning of a sentence coincides with the beginning of a line, majuscule is written between the outer bounding lines.

Small repair, top margin, f. 37; ff. 97 to end, stained (no loss of text); ink flaked on some folios.

Bound, s. XIX, by Hagué according to the 1883 catalogue from the Firmin-Didot sale, but without binder's signature or ticket, in black morocco, blind-stamped with a narrow vine scroll border with aldine leaves around a blank, central rectangular panel; gilt leaves in outer corners, front and back; spine tooled with bands of similar design, separating four gilt leaves.

Written in Florence in the fourth quarter of the fifteenth century as indicated by the decoration, by Antonius Torrigiani (colophon, f. 109v; *Colophons*, no. 1263, listing no other manuscript by this scribe) for the Pugliese of Florence (with their coat of arms, f. 1; see above; we thank Professor A. C. de la Mare for the identification of the arms; in correspondence, March 24, 1983). Erased notation, f. 110, in ink, possibly a shelf mark: "16–4Mip (?)." Belonged to Ambroise Firmin-Didot (1790–1876; bookplate with date, 1850, inside front cover); his sale, *Catalogue des livres précieux, manuscrits et imprimés*

... (Paris, June 11–16, 1883) v. 5, no. 28, to Hénaux. Belonged to Charles Eliot Norton (1827–1908); note in his hand, front endleaf, f. i, dated 1885. Purchased from Norton with funds from the Friends of the Library, May 4, 1905 (library stamp, f. 1v; bookplate, inside back cover).

secundo folio: dicitur. Themistoclesque

Bibliography: De Ricci, 998 (= MS Norton 1003); Bond and Faye, 238; De Ricci, "Handlist," 101; Rudge Nichols, "Ms. Nor. 1003," (typescript, June 1, 1928) now Houghton, bMs Lat 315(8); Wieck, p. 110, fig. 50 (reproducing f. 1).

MS Lat 177 — **Italy (Rome or Florence) s. XV^{med}**
(formerly MS Sumner 69) — **Pl. 51**
Cicero, De officiis

ff. 1–129v *M. T. Ciceronis Officiorvm Ad Marcvm Ciceronem Filivm Liber Primvs Faeliciter* [*sic*] *Incipit.* Qvanqvam te marce fili annum iam audientem Cratippum idque athenis abundare ... sed ad voluptatem vtilitatemque referantur.//

C. Atzert, ed. (4th. ed.; Leipzig 1963) 1–123. Text ends imperfectly at 3.118 (p. 122, line 24). The following portions of the text are now missing: following f. 53v, 1.150 (p. 52, line 6)–1.153 (p. 53, line 6); following f. 111v, 3.61 (p. 104, line 6)–3.65 (p. 104, line 30); following f. 118v, 3.83 (p. 111, line 3)–3.86 (p. 111, line 30); following f. 124v, 3.102 (p. 117, line 7)–3.106 (p. 118, line 13). Divided into the usual three books, which are in turn divided into unnumbered chapters with introductory rubrics, for example: f. 3v "Tractatus Secundus Officiorvm Libri Primi. Capitulum De Divisione Et Diffinitione Officii."; f. 4 "Alia Divisio Officii."; f. 5 "Naturale Esse Omnibus Animantibus Necessaria Vitae Acquirere Capitulum Secundum."

Marginal apparatus in the hand of the main scribe in pale red, indicating authors cited in the text and subjects (cf. f. 2v, "De finibus bonorum et malorum"; f. 6, "Fortitudo et magnanimitas"); also occasional corrections (for example ff. 41, 61, 115, supplying omissions), nota marks (majuscule 'N' with decorative extensions), and admonitions to the reader (cf. f. 2v, "Attende diligenter"; f. 3, "Attende preclare"). Variant reading in black, same hand, f. 107. Throughout, annotations in a humanistic cursive, s. XV–XVI, correcting the text (cf. f. 7 supplying an omission), or adding explanatory comments (cf. f. 21v discussing the battle of Marathon).

Parchment, ff. iii (parchment) + 129 + iii (parchment), 245 x 165 (155 x 82–80) mm., trimmed, with some marginalia partly cut away. 23 long lines. Ruled in hard point; double full-length vertical bounding lines.

$1–6^8$ 7^8 (–6, following f. 53, with loss of text) $8–14^8$ 15^8 (–1, following f. 111, with loss of text) 16^8 (–1, 8, conjugate pair following ff. 118 and 124, with loss of text) 17^6 (–6, following f. 129, with loss of text). Horizontal catchwords, center lower margin, decorated on all four sides with red dots and s-shaped flourishes; quire and leaf signatures in ink, bottom margin, verso, between the outer bounding lines, with a letter designating the quire and an arabic numeral, the leaf (mostly trimmed; cf. ff. 26v, 27v, 33v, 41v, etc.).

Written below the top line in a skilled, rounded humanistic script by one scribe.

Decorated by the German illuminator Gioacchino di Giovanni de Gigantibus (see Avril, "Review," 368); probably executed early in his career in the 1450s in Rome, or possibly in Florence (we thank Professor A. C. de la Mare for this information; in correspondence, October, 1987). F. 1, 7-line polished gold initial infilled and surrounded by white vinestem on a square ground and extending into a full border, infilled with green, blue and red, with white, silver and gold dots, edged on all sides in blue following the shape of the vinestem. In the border are carefully executed animals, including three birds, two with square tails, and a rabbit, a gold bar, double in the bottom and inside margins and interlaced in inside margin, and two putti with coral necklaces flanking a green wreath containing a coat of arms (unidentified; per pale: 1, sable; 2, gules, a lion rampant argent; reproduced in Wieck, fig. 95). The shape of the border and initial, the square tailed birds and the rabbit are virtually identical to those in J. R. Abbey Collection, MS 3212, Giannozzo Manetti, written in Florence, probably in 1453, for Alfonso V of Aragon and I of Naples (see Alexander and de la Mare, *Italian Manuscripts .. of*

Major J. R. Abbey, pp. 36–8, no. 10, pl. XIV, with list of similar manuscripts; for Gioacchino's career, especially at the court of Naples from 1471, see T. de Marinis, *La Biblioteca napoletana dei re d'Aragona* 4 vols. [Milan 1947, 1952] especially I: 149–50). Three similar 10- to 6-line gold initials with white vinestem decoration used at the opening of the prefaces of books 2 and 3 and at the beginning of book 2 (ff. 57, 59v, 91), with extensions at the outer corners terminating in three gold balls. 2- to 3-line gold initials at the divisions within each book, and at the beginning of book 3 (f. 93), on square tripartite grounds of green, pinkish-red, and blue with white highlights (occasionally on red and green parted grounds, cf. ff. 53v, 81, 104v). Rubrics throughout in pale red capitals; red majuscules within the text and between the outer bounding lines when the beginning of a sentence coincides with the beginning of a line; marginal notes and running headlines in red. Opening line of each book in capitals.

Stained in outer margins; no loss of text.

Bound in England in gold-tooled brown morocco by Francis Bedford (1799–1883; binder's signature, inside front cover); gilt edges.

Written in Italy in the middle of the fifteenth century, probably in Rome or possibly Florence, where it was decorated by Gioacchino di Giovanni de Gigantibus; unidentified arms of original owner, f. 1 (described above). In England, s. XIX, when it was sold by Ellis and White, London, Cat. no. 30 (no date), no. 174 (clipping, inside front cover; bookseller's notes, possibly Ellis', inside back cover: "E/C/-" and "10"). Belonged to Charles Sumner (1811–74); likely acquired from Ellis, ca. 1871; cf. Peebles, cited below, 23, and Edward L. Pierce, *Memoir and Letters of Charles Sumner* (Boston 1893) 4:541. Acquired by Harvard, Sumner bequest, April 28, 1874 (bookplate and library label, inside front cover, with "38.122" in pencil, underlined in blue; cf. Winsor, p. 17, col. 2, no. 5). Note by George P. Winship, Assistant Librarian, Harvard, front flyleaf, f. i, recording that S. Cockerell believed the manuscript to be Neapolitan.

secundo folio: qui iam fere

Bibliography: De Ricci, 1018 (=MS Sumner 69); De Ricci, "Hand-list," 102; Bond and Faye, 238; Bernard Mann Peebles, "A Harvard Manuscript of Cicero's *De Officiis,*" (typescript, May 19, 1928) now Houghton, bMS Lat 315(19); Wieck, p. 110, fig. 95 (reproducing f. 1).

MS Lat 178 (formerly MS Norton 1000) Northern Italy s. XV$^{1/4}$
Boethius, Philosophiae consolatio Pl. 42

ff. 1–49v Carmina qui quondam studio florente peregi/ Flebilis heu mestos cogor inire modos./ . . . Magna uobis est si dissimulare non uultis necessitas probitatis indicta, cum ante oculos agitis iudicis cum cuncta cernentis. *Explicit liber anicii seuerini Boecii, viri consolatorii de philosophica* [*sic*] *consolatione. Deo gratias. Amen.*

Ludovicus Bieler, ed. CC 94 (Turnholt 1957); *CPL* 878; Kottler, "The Vulgate Tradition," 209–214, listing this manuscript as MS Norton 1000, p. 210, note 3, with the sigla 'Ch'.

Major initials at the beginning of books 1 and 4, ff. 1 and 30; book 5, f. 41, begins with a slightly more elaborate initial; books 2 and 3, ff. 8 and 16, begin with minor initials; blank lines for rubrics at the beginnings of books 1, 4 and 5; rubrics added in the margin, books 2–5, in a neat, precise hand, brown ink. Greek usually copied by the main scribe (for example f. 3v, line 15, book 1,4.1, ed., pp. 6–7, and ff. 38, bottom line–f. 38v, lines 1–2, book 4,6.38, ed., p. 82); Greek omitted f. 20v, bottom line, book 3,6.1, ed., p. 45. On f. 44, lines 15–16 (book 5, M III.9–10, ed., p. 94) were copied in another hand. Occasional corrections in later hands, usually correcting minor scribal errors.

Parchment (prepared in the manner of Southern Europe), ff. i (paper) + i (parchment) + 49 (modern foliation in pencil, upper, outside corner; f. 49 also incorrectly numbered as f. 46, in ink, top outer corner, in an earlier hand, and as f. 48 in another modern hand, bottom outside corner) + i (parchment) + i (paper), 251 x 190 mm. Layout varies. Ff. 1–16v, written space (177–175 x 135–131) mm.; 30 long lines. Ff. 17–end, written space (190–183 x 139–128) mm.; 32–30 long lines. Throughout, verse sections are copied with 1, 2, or 3 columns, depending on the length of each line. Ruled in brown crayon; single full-length vertical bounding lines. Ff. 1–16v, prickings for vertical bounding lines, top and bottom margins, near the edge of the page (some trimmed); ff. 17–end, prickings at the intersection of the vertical and horizontal rules, or sometimes with the bottom, outside pricking instead at the intersection of the vertical bounding lines and the penultimate horizontal rules (for example, f. 44).

$1–2^{8}$ $3–4^{10}$ 5^{13} (regular quire of 12, + 1, f. 49, after 12). Horizontal catchwords, middle, lower, margin. In quire 1, ff. 1v–3v and 5v–7v, and quire 2, ff. 9v–15v, the opening word of the following page has been written in a small noting script in brown ink on each verso in the lower, inside margin.

Written below the top line in a formal round gothic bookhand by two scribes. The first scribe copied quires 1 and 2 (ff. 1–16v) in a chestnut brown ink; majuscules within the text are brushed with pale yellow. The second scribe used a darker brown ink; majuscules within the text often distinguished by decorative hairlines or other elaborations.

One 8-line historiated initial, f. 1, of Boethius and Philosophy conversing in jail, depicted against a white-traceried blue ground; now somewhat rubbed, but well-executed; initial is pink with white filigree on a polished gold ground, heavily edged in black, with lush acanthus leaves at the corners of the initial, extending into the margins to form a 3/4-border (leaving the inner margin empty) of red, green, pink and blue acanthus leaves and knots, interspersed with gold and brown balls, edged in black and with four circular knobs placed symetrically around the balls. One 17-line illuminated initial, f. 30, at the beginning of book 4; initial is pink with white filigree on a highly polished gold ground edged in black; infilled with a bold foliage spiral in red, blue, green, and dark-brown against a white-traceried blue ground, with acanthus extending from the initial and forming a border on the inside and bottom margins.

Secondary initials at the beginning of the remaining books and each new section of prose and verse are red or blue, imperfectly alternating, with blue-violet and red pen decoration, respectively; ff. 1–26v (quires 1–3), initials are 2-line; ff. 27–end, initials are 5- to 3-line; blue initial, f. 41, at the beginning of book 5, is 5-line, with more elaborate red pen scrolls. Rubrics lacking (added in the margins in brown ink, books 2–5); the number of the book added in brown ink in a small precise hand, top margin, on some folios.

Bound, s. XVIII, in France or the Netherlands (cf. De Ricci) in mottled brown calf; narrow gilt border, front and back boards; spine, tooled delicate flowers and filigree, with five raised bands with a dark green label between the first and second; gilt edges; rebacked with spine laid down. Front board now detached.

Written in Northern Italy in the first quarter of the fifteenth century (we thank Professor Lilian Armstrong for her assistance, January 1989). Belonged to the Reverend Henry Drury (1778–1841); note in pencil, front flyleaf, f. i, possibly in his hand: "Henry Drury, Harrow, a very pretty and tolerably ancient manuscript of Boethius . . ." His sale, London, Evans, February 19 and 11 following days and March 12 and 10 following days, 1827, probably no. 803, which was sold to Henry G. Bohn (1796–1894) for £1.15.0 (cf. inside back cover, "H. Bohn. £9."), possibly through Thorpe, as suggested by De Ricci, as no. 5815 ("5815" in pencil, inside front cover, but not identified in Thorpe's catalogues). Not identified in Bohn's sale, London, Sotheby, parts 1–3, February 10, 1868, May 9, 1870, and July 1, 1872. Belonged to William G. Medlicott (1816–83), collector and scholar of English literature (see J. R. Hall, "William G. Medlicott [1816–83]: An American Book Collector and His Collection," *Harvard Library Bulletin* n.s. 1 [1990] 13–46, especially 23); sold in 1878 to Charles Eliot Norton (1827–1908), professor of history of art, Harvard, for $12.50; see *Catalogue of a Collection of Books formed by William G. Medlicott of Longmeadow, Massachusetts* . . . (Boston 1878) no. 2681. Note in Norton's hand, front flyleaf, f. i: "C. E. Norton, 1878"; quotation from Dante on Boethius copied by Norton in pencil, inside, front cover. Price codes, in pencil, inside back cover in two hands: "G/kl/" and "K[?]L[?]/." Purchased from Norton with funds from the Friends of the Library, May 4, 1905 (library stamp, front flyleaf, f. ii^{v}; bookplate, inside front cover).

secundo folio: [auc]toritatis obstupui

Bibliography: De Ricci, 997 (=MS Norton 1000); Bond and Faye, 238; Paul Robert Murphy, "A Harvard Manuscript of Boethius" (typescript; [Cambridge 1936]) now Houghton, bMS Lat 315(17).

MS Lat 179 **Southern France or Spain s. XIV²**
(formerly MS Norton 1001) **Pl. 62**
Boethius, Philosophiae consolatio

ff. 1–70 *Auctorem primus consolandum miserum dat.* Carmina qui quondam studio florente peregi/ flebilis heu mestos cogor inire modos./ . . . Magna uobis est si dissimulare non uultis necessitas indita [*sic*] probitatis cum ante occulos [*sic*] agitis iudicis cuncta cernentis. *Explicit liber boetii de consolatione/ deo gratias. Amen* [words off-set from the previous page appear between the lines of the explicit]. [F. 70v blank with later notes.]

Ludovicus Bieler, ed. CC 94 (Turnholt 1957); *CPL* 878; Kottler, "The Vulgate Tradition," 209–14, listing this manuscript as MS Norton 1001, p. 210, note 3, with the sigla 'C'.

Divided into the usual 5 books, each beginning with an intoductory rubric: book 2, f. 11 "Tristicie causam liber explicat inde secundus"; book 3, f. 24 "Tertius in rebus mundi non esse curandum"; book 4, f. 42v "Hinc consolatum auctorem denique quartus"; book 5, f. 58v "Quintus perfectum notat hunc et rite refectum." Greek copied by the main scribe, with Latin translation added by later hands (for example, f. 4v, book 1,4.1, ed., pp. 6–7; f. 30v, lines 2–4, book 3,6.1, ed., p. 45; f. 54v, book 4,6.38, ed., p. 82; f. 60v, book 5, M II.1, ed., p. 91). Layout allows for large margins on all sides. Short elementary interlinear glosses in a contemporary noting script; frequent through f. 31, and then sporadically to the end, usually providing simple synonyms, for example, f. 2: *inflamata* "irata"; *inquit* "id est dixit"; *blandicie* "deceptiones"; *achademicis* "id est platonicis." Occasional notes in at least two later hands (cf. ff. 5 and 13), pointing hands, and angle brackets added within the text.

Parchment (moderate quality; prepared in the manner of Southern Europe), ff. ii (paper) + 70 (modern foliation in pencil, upper, outer corner) + ii (paper), 288 x 200 (160–158 x 92–88) mm. 27 long lines of prose; verse copied in long lines or in two columns. Ruled very lightly in lead, with single vertical bounding lines; indiscernible on most folios (cf. ff. 20v–21 and 28v, where vertical bounding lines are visible, and f. 41v, with faint traces of horizontal rules). Few prickings remain; cf. f. 33, two prickings, lower margin, for vertical bounding lines; see also ff. 21 and 22, with a row of very small, closely spaced prickings in the upper margin, running along the vertical bounding line.

$1\text{–}6^{8}\ 7^{10}\ 8^{8}\ 9^{4}$. Horizontal catchwords, center, lower margins, with flourishes (lacking in quire 7, f. 58v).

Written in a formal round southern gothic bookhand.

Nine- to 4-line blue initials at the beginning of each book, with decorative void spaces within the body of the initial, and red pen tendrils; some initials with blue infilling (cf. f. 1, infilled in a red and blue diaper pattern). Remaining divisions within the text begin with 3- to 2-line plain initials, alternately red and blue, placed within the text-space, but extending into the margin. Red rubrics.

Ff. 68v–70, damaged by dampness, leaving the parchment darkened and the ink flaked, so that the text is difficult to read.

Bound in French mottled calf, s. XVIII^{2}–XIX^{1} (dated by De Ricci ca. 1805); flat spine with urns and flowers tooled in gold, red label, “Boetius/ De Cous [*sic*]/ Philos/,” and a green label, “M.S. XIII/S.”; rebacked with spine laid down.

Written in the second half of the fourteenth century in Southern France or Spain. Notes and pen trials in numerous Southern European hands, most completely or partially erased, f. 70v. Belonged to the Jesuit College at Agen, France (maintained by the Jesuits from 1591–1762); f. 1, top margin, s. XVII: “Coll[egii] Agen[nensis] Soc[ietatis] Jesu Catal[ogo] Inscr[iptus].” F. 1, bottom margin, in an eighteenth-century hand, “Opera boetii de consolatione philosophia et aliis, scripta anno 1362” (no evidence in the manuscript supports this date). It is interesting that New Haven, Yale University, Beinecke Library, MS 155, also from the Agen Jesuits, and Houghton, MS Lat 150, which is said to have belonged to the Agen Jesuits, also include notes that seem to record the year the manuscripts were copied, even though the manuscripts themselves are not dated. Number of folios recorded in ink, inside back cover: “70f.” Belonged to Abbé Luigi Celotti (ca. 1768–ca. 1846); his sale, London, Sotheby’s, March 14, 1825, no. 405 (not available for consultation) to Thorpe for Sir Thomas Phillipps (inside front cover, in pencil “gu.<or “qn”?>Celotti,” and in another hand, “Thorpe”). Phillipps MS 1001 (*Phillipps Cat.*, p. 12), then MS 24305 (front flyleaf, f. 1, stamped crest, and ex-libris, “Sir T. P.; Middle Hill” with “1001” in ink; now expunged, and with "24305" added below; inside front cover, and f. 1, bottom margin: "Phillipps MS 24305.") Toronto, Canada, Royal Ontario Museum of Archaeology, MS 951.153, a twelfth-century copy of this text, also from Agen, has also been identified as Phillipps MS 1001 and Celotti Sale, no. 405 (see J. R. O'Donnell, "A Manuscript of the 'De philosophiae consolatione' of Boethius, in the Royal Ontario Museum [No. 951.153]," *Royal Ontario Museum. Bulletin of the Division of Art and Archaeology* 24 [1956] 10–13; we thank Dr. Patricia Stirnemann for bringing this manuscript to our attention; in correspondence, June, 1989). Phillipps sale, London, 1896, no. 130 to Webster, and 1899, no. 223, to Quaritch (not available for consultation). Sold by Sotheby's, London, 17 December 1900, no. 164 to Ridler as reported by De Ricci. Unidentified owners' and booksellers' notes: front flyleaf, f. i (below Phillipps' ex libris): "4<77?>4" and "B8.219," and "MS Boethius," written diagonally in pencil; inside front cover, in pencil, in four hands: "B"; "Uide Boethius"; "£5–5–0"; "a/s[?]/a/." Belonged to Charles Eliot Norton (1827–1908); purchased from Norton with funds from the Friends of the Library, May 4, 1905 (library stamp, front flyleaf, f. i^v; bookplate, inside back cover).

secundo folio: uis inflamata

Bibliography: De Ricci, 997 and 2304 (=MS Norton 1001); Bond and Faye, 239; Edwin A. Quain, S. J. "A Description of Latin Manuscript Norton 1001 of the Harvard College Library Containing the *De Consolatione Philisophiae* of Boethius" (typescript, May 1939) now Houghton, bMS Lat 315(22).

Indices

Numbers in the index entries refer to the manuscript number rather than to the page number.

Index I
Dated Manuscripts

Index II
Other Manuscripts Cited

Index III
Scribes and Artists

SCRIBES:

ARTISTS:

Index IV

Owners: persons and institutions

Index V
Iconography

Index VI
Saints and Liturgical Feasts

Saints' names are usually given in the form found in F. G. Holweck, *A Biographical Dictionary of the Saints* (St. Louis and London 1924; repr. 1969); depictions of saints are entered in the Iconograpy Index.

Index VII
General Incipits

The spelling found in the manuscripts has been retained where possible; some spellings have been normalized in the case of texts appearing in multiple manuscripts, and where necessary to retain alphabetical order. The incipits of the biblical prologues and chapter lists in MSS Lat 6 and 50 are not indexed; these can be found in F. Stegmüller, *Repertorium biblicum medii aevi* (Madrid 1950–61; Supplement 1976–80).

Index VIII
Incipits of Prayers and Liturgical Texts

The spelling found in the manuscripts has been retained where possible; some spellings have been normalized in the case of texts appearing in multiple manuscripts, and where necessary to retain alphabetical order.

Index IX
General Index

PLATES

List of Plates

Plates 1–18 are dated/datable manuscripts.

1. fMS Lat 35, f. 1; Italy (Bologna or Venice?) 1353 (64% of natural size)
2. MS Lat 18, ff. 2v–3; Italy (Florence) 1416 (47% of natural size)
3. MS Lat 47, f. 36; Italy (Northeast?) 1432 (64% of natural size)
4. fMS Lat 121, f. 1; Austria 1433 (59% of natural size)
5. fMS Lat 121, f. 101; Austria 1433 (59% of natural size)
6. fMS Lat 12, f. 54v; Italy (Padua) 1442 (55% of natural size)
7. MS Lat 9, f. 1; Germany (Cologne) 1452 (58% of natural size)
8. MS Lat 40, f. 1; Italy (Bologne) 1462 (88% of natural size)
9. MS Lat 171, f. 399v; Italy (Florence?) 1465 (slightly reduced)
10. MS Lat 136, f. 1; Italy (Northeast?) 1471 (95% of natural size)
11. MS Lat 129, f. 207v; Germany 1474–1477 (natural size)
12. MS Lat 3, ff. 4v–5; Northeastern Italy (Venice or Padua) 1492–1516 (54% of natural size)
13. MS Lat 115, f. 128; Germany s. XIII^{2} (after 1254, before 1318) (natural size)
14. MS Lat 37, f. 30; Northeastern Italy s. XV$^{2/4}$ (before 1440) (79% of natural size)
15. fMS Lat 42, f. 248; Northern Italy (Verona) s. XV$^{3/4}$ (before 1471) (54% of natural size)
16. MS Lat 173, ff. 10v–11; Germany s. XV^{2} (after 1461?) (75% of natural size)
17. MS Lat 173, f. 32; Germany s. XV^{ex} (after 1494) (86% of natural size)
18. MS Lat 111, f. 20; France s. XVI^{1} (after 1515) (slightly reduced)
19. fMS Lat 27, f. 1; England s. XII^{2} (59% of natural size)
20. MS Lat 127, f. 1; England s. XII$^{4/4}$ (95% of natural size)
21. MS Lat 132, f. 12; Flanders s. XV$^{2/4}$ (93% of natural size)

22. MS Lat 161, f. 51; Flanders (Bruges?) s. $XV^{3/4}$ (93% of natural size)
23. MS Lat 44, f. 2; France s. $XII^{2/4}$ (87% of natural size)
24. fMS Lat 6, f. 1; Northeastern France or Flanders s. $XIII^{2/4}$ (47% of natural size)
25. fMS Lat 36, f. 19v; France (Paris) s. XIII/XIV (48% of natural size)
26. fMS Lat 39, f. 1; France s. XIV^{1} (54% of natural size)
27. fMS Lat 172, f. 3v; Northeastern France or Germany s. XIV^{1} (54% of natural size)
28. MS Lat 159, f. 29; Northern France (Paris?) s. $XV^{3/4}$ (92% of natural size)
29. MS Lat 133, f. 32v; Northern France s. $XV^{4/4}$ (95% of natural size)
30. MS Lat 4, f. 1; Northern France s. XV/XVI (96% of natural size)
31. MS Lat 17, f. 84v; Northern France s. XV/XVI (natural size)
32. MS Lat 160, f. 7; Northern France (Paris?) s. $XVI^{1/4}$ (natural size)
33. fMS Lat 156, ff. 1v–2; Austria (Salzburg) s. IX^{in} (50% of natural size)
34. MS Lat 5, f. 2v; Germany s. XIII^{ex}–XIV^{1} (73% of natural size)
35. MS Lat 134, f. 25; Germany s. XIV^{2} (natural size)
36. MS Lat 15, ff. 23v–24; Germany s. XV^{1} (?) (49% of natural size)
37. MS Lat 50, f. 147v; Southern Germany s. $XV^{3/4}$ (57% of natural size)
38. fMS Lat 168, f. 2; Italy (Central or Tuscany) s. $XII^{2/4}$ (55% of natural size)
39. MS Lat 34, f. 1; Italy (Bologna) s. XIII^{ex}–s. XIV^{1} (61% of natural size)
40. MS Lat 154, f. 1; Italy s. XIV (65% of natural size)
41. MS Lat 48, ff. 48v–49; Central Italy s. $XIV^{2/4}$ (49% of natural size)
42. MS Lat 178, f. 1; Northern Italy s. $XV^{1/4}$ (68% of natural size)
43. MS Lat 126, f. 1; Italy s. XV (85% of natural size)
44. MS Lat 137, f. 1; Italy (Florence) s. $XV^{1/4}$ (85% of natural size)
45. MS Lat 144, f. 1; Italy (Venice?) s. $XV^{1/4}$ (87% of natural size)
46. MS Lat 175, f. 1; Italy (Venice?) s. XV^{1} (80% of natural size)
47. MS Lat 124, f. 5; Italy (Florence) s. $XV^{2/4}$ (before 1453) (96% of natural size)

48. MS Lat 124, f. 19; Italy (Florence) s. $XV^{3/4}$ (96% of natural size)
49. MS Lat 49, f. 1; Northeastern Italy s. $XV^{2/4\text{–}med}$ (natural size)
50. MS Lat 46, f. 1; Italy (Florence) s. XV^{med} (natural size)
51. MS Lat 177, f. 57; Italy (Rome or Florence) s. XV^{med} (74% of natural size)
52. MS Lat 170, f. 1; Northern Italy s. $XV^{med\text{–}3/4}$ (75% of natural size)
53. MS Lat 135, f. 9v; Northern Italy s. XV^{2} (natural size)
54. MS Lat 43, f. 60; Italy (Florence) s. $XV^{3/4}$ (84% of natural size)
55. MS Lat 145, f. 1; Northeastern Italy s. $XV^{3/4}$ (90% of natural size)
56. MS Lat 163, f. 2; Italy (Florence) s. $XV^{4/4}$ (natural size)
57. MS Lat 176, f. 30; Italy (Florence) s. $XV^{4/4}$ (78% of natural size)
58. MS Lat 155, f. 5v; Northern Italy (Venice?) s. XV^{ex} (natural size)
59. pfMS Lat 128, f. 1; Italy s. XVI (29% of natural size)
60. MS Lat 150, f. 64v; Southern Europe s. $XII^{2/4}$ (64% of natural size)
61. fMS Lat 38, pg. 7; Spain s. $XIII^{4/4}$–$XIV^{1/4}$ (50% of natural size)
62. MS Lat 179, f. 11; Southern France or Spain s. XIV^{2} (58% of natural size)
63. MS Lat 9, inside front cover
64. MS Lat 111, f. 1v
65. MS Lat 15, f. 1
66. fMS Lat 39, f. i^{v}
67. MS Lat 134, front paste down

PLATE 1

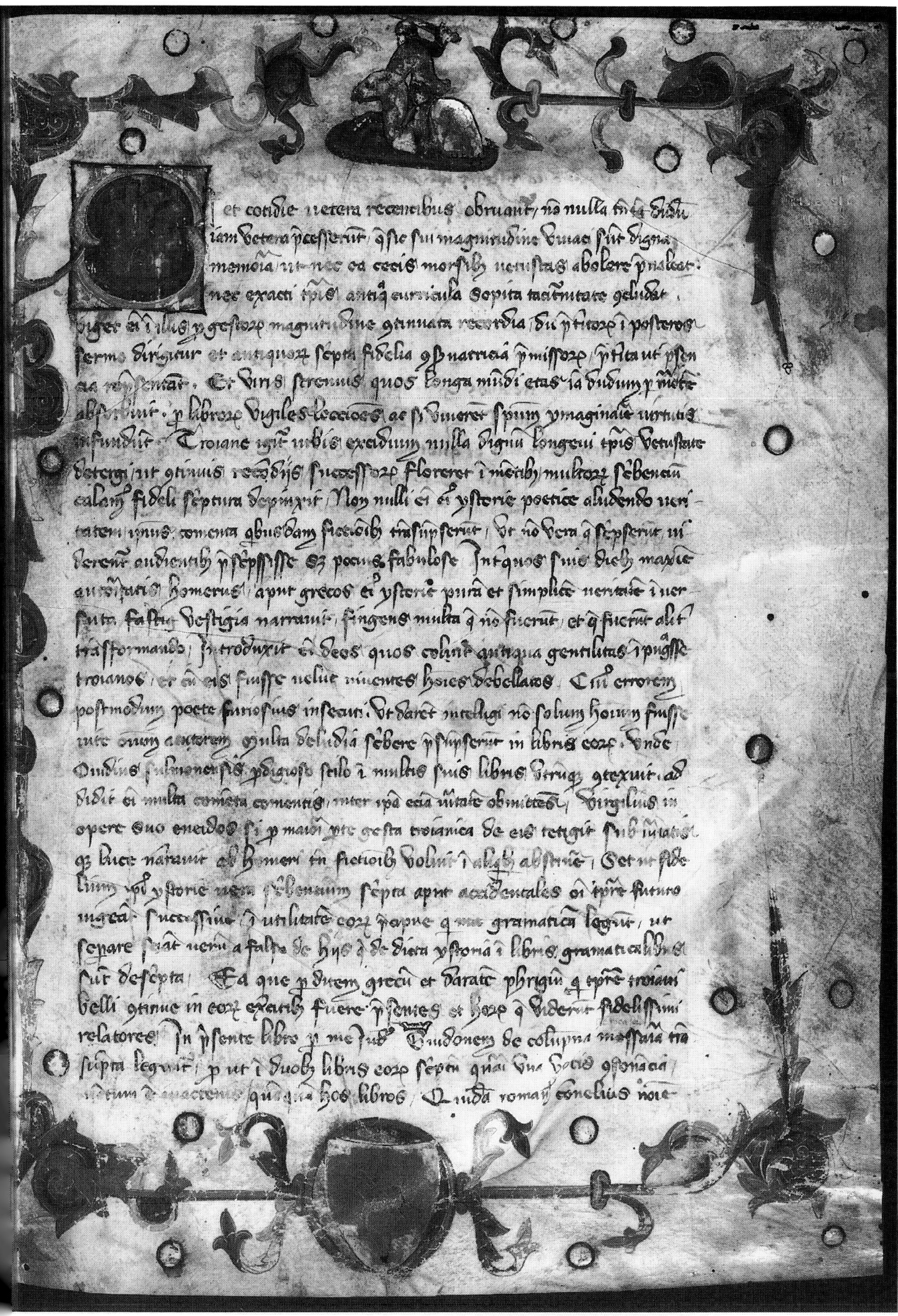

Licet cotidie vetera recentibus obruant, nonnulla tamen iam dudum vetera precesserunt que sui magnitudine vivaci sunt digna
memoria ut nec ea cecis morsibus vetustas abolere prevaleat:
nec exacti temporis antiqua curricula sopita taciturnitate concludat.
Viget enim in illis pro gestorum magnitudine continuata recordatio dum preteritorum in posteros
sermo dirigitur et antiquorum scripta fidelia que narrative premissorum preterita ut presencia representant. Et viris strenuis quos longa mundi etas iam dudum per mortem
absorbuit, per librorum vigiles lectiones ac si viverent spiritum ymaginarie virtutis
infundit. Troiane igitur urbis excidium nulla dignum longevi temporis vetustate
deteri ut continuis recordiis successorum floreret in mentibus multorum sub benenato
calamo fideli scriptura depinxit. Nonnulli et eius ystorie poetice alludendo veritatem ipsius commenta quibusdam fictionibus transumpserunt, ut non vera que scripserunt vi-
derentur audientibus perscripsisse sed potius fabulose. In quos suis diebus maxime
auctoritatis Homerus apud grecos eius ystorie puram et simplicem veritatem in ver-
suta falsitatis vestigia narravit, fingens multa que non fuerunt et que fuerunt aliter
transformando. Introduxit enim deos quos coluit antiqua gentilitas impugnasse
troianos et cum eis fuisse velut viventes homines debellatos. Cuius errorem
postmodum poete furiosius insecuti ut daret intelligi non solum Homerum fuisse
inter omnes ceteros [illegible] deludia scribere persuaserunt in libris eorum. Unde
Ovidius sulmonensis prodigioso stilo in multis suis libris utrumque contexuit, ad-
didit enim multa commenta commentis inter ipsa eciam veritate obmittens. Virgilius in
opere suo eneidos licet per maiori parte gesta troianica de eis tetigit sub veritatis
quodam luce narravit ab Homeri tamen fictionibus voluit in aliquibus abstinere. Set ut fidelium ipsius ystorie vera scribenium scripta apud occidentales eciam tempore futuro
ingrata successiue in utilitate eorum perpetue que [illegible] gramatica leguntur, ut
separare sciant verum a falso de hiis que de dicta ystoria in libris gramatica [illegible]
sunt descripta. Ea que per Ditem grecum et Daretem phrigium qui tempore troiani
belli continue in eorum exercitibus fuere presentes et horum que viderunt fidelissimi
relatores. In presente libro per me iudicem Guidonem de columpna messanam trans-
scripta leguntur, prout in duobus libris eorum scripti quasi una voce concordia
[illegible] [illegible] hos libros. Quidam romanus Cornelius nomine

fMS Lat 35, f. 1; Italy (Bologna or Venice?) 1353.
By permission of the Houghton Library, Harvard University.

PLATE 2

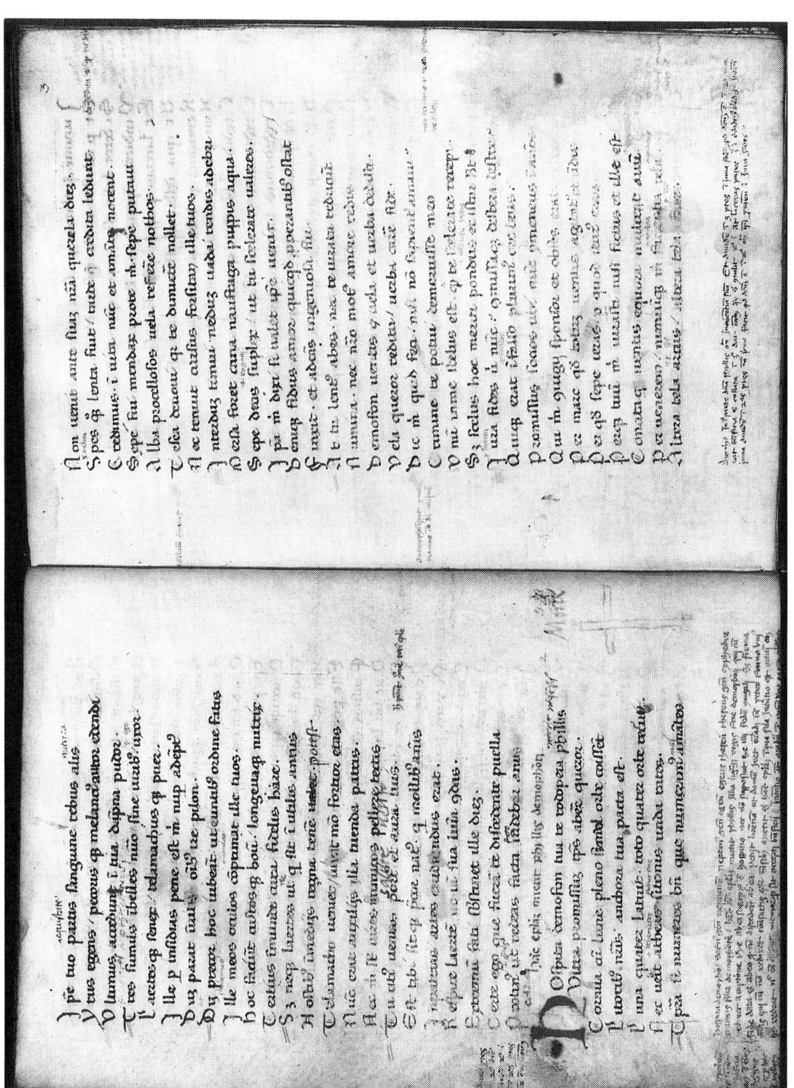

MS Lat 18, ff. 2v–3; Italy (Florence) 1416
By permission of the Houghton Library, Harvard University

PLATE 3

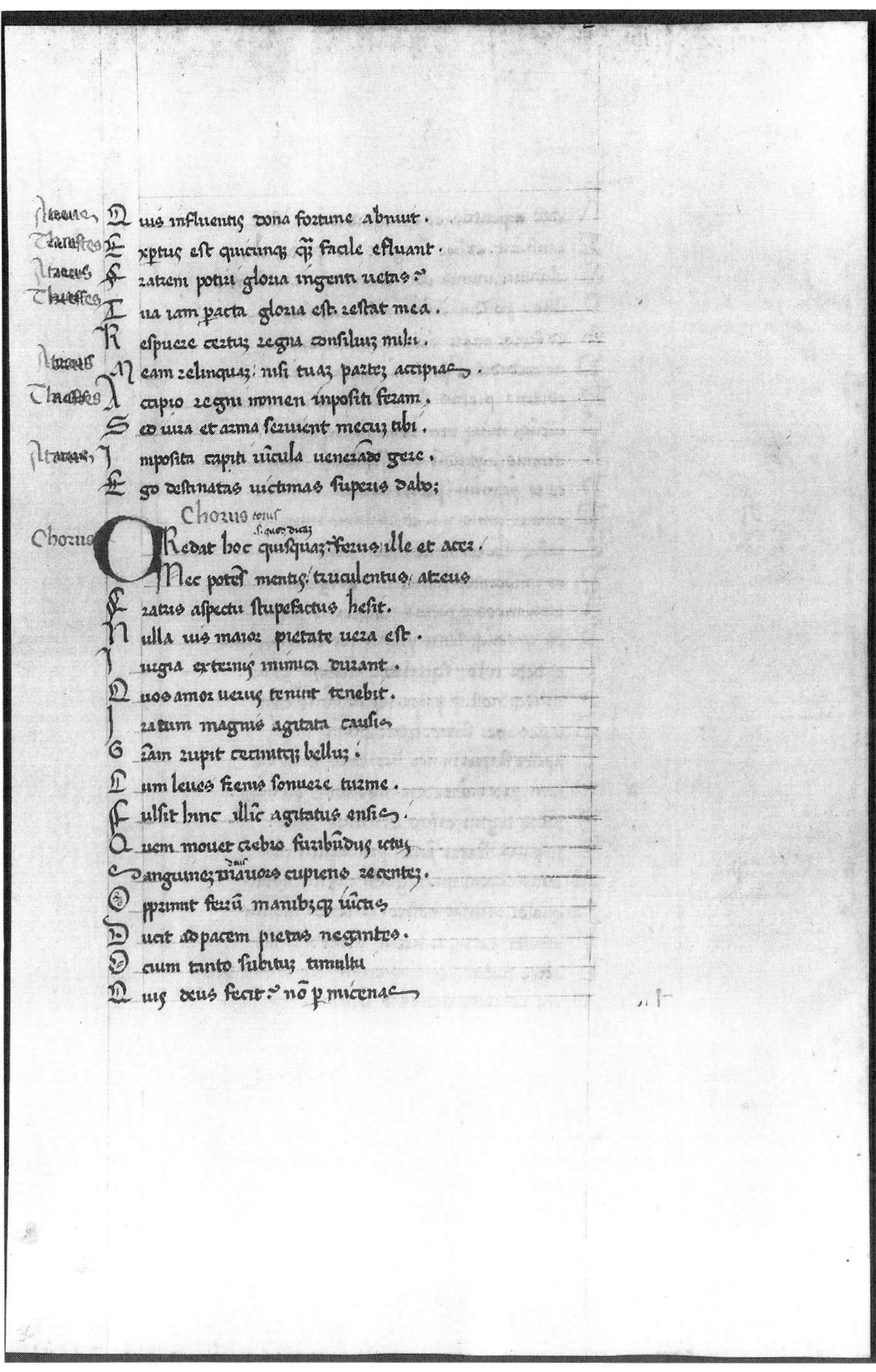

MS Lat 47, f. 36; Italy (Northeast?) 1432

By permission of the Houghton Library, Harvard University

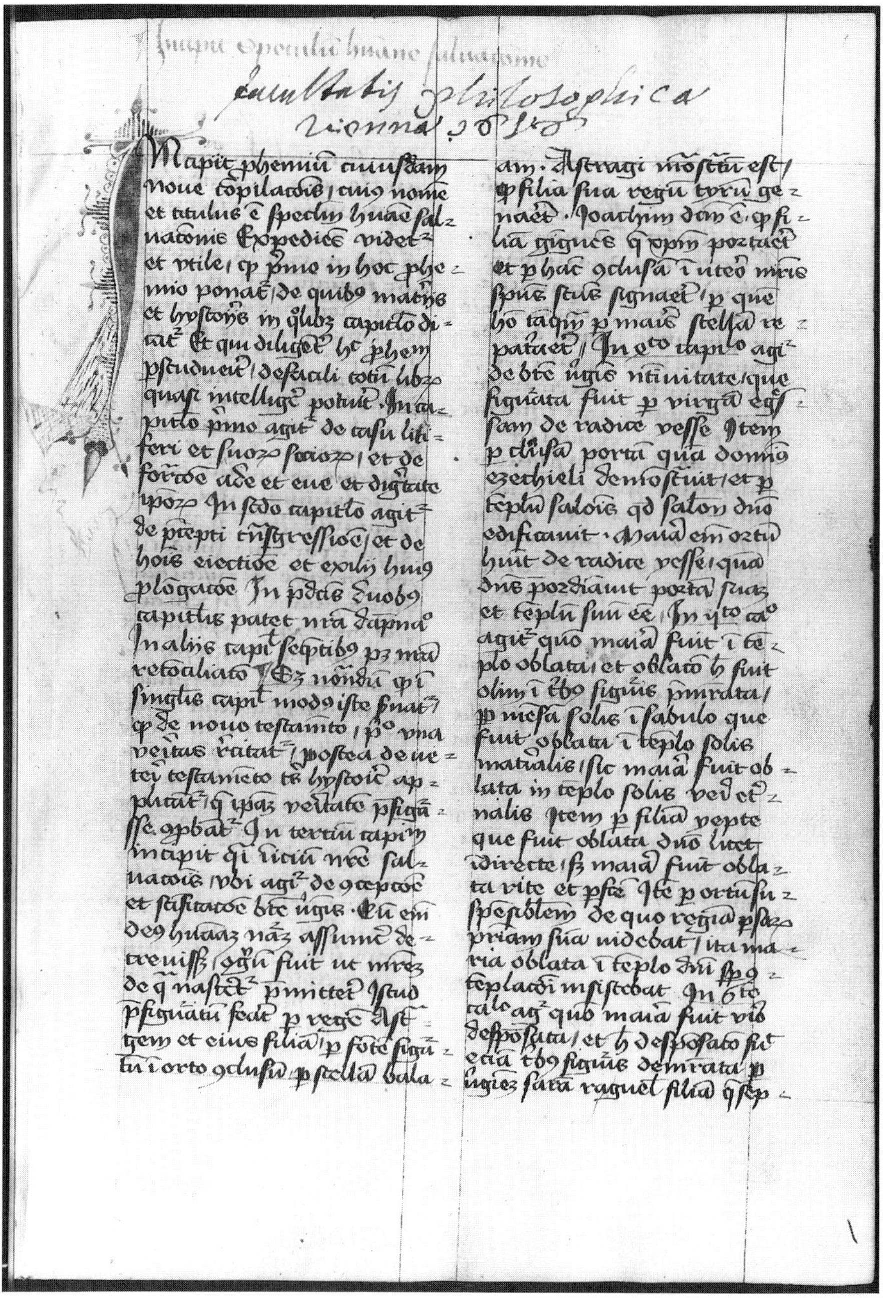

PLATE 4

fMS Lat 121, f. 1; Austria 1433
By permission of the Houghton Library, Harvard University

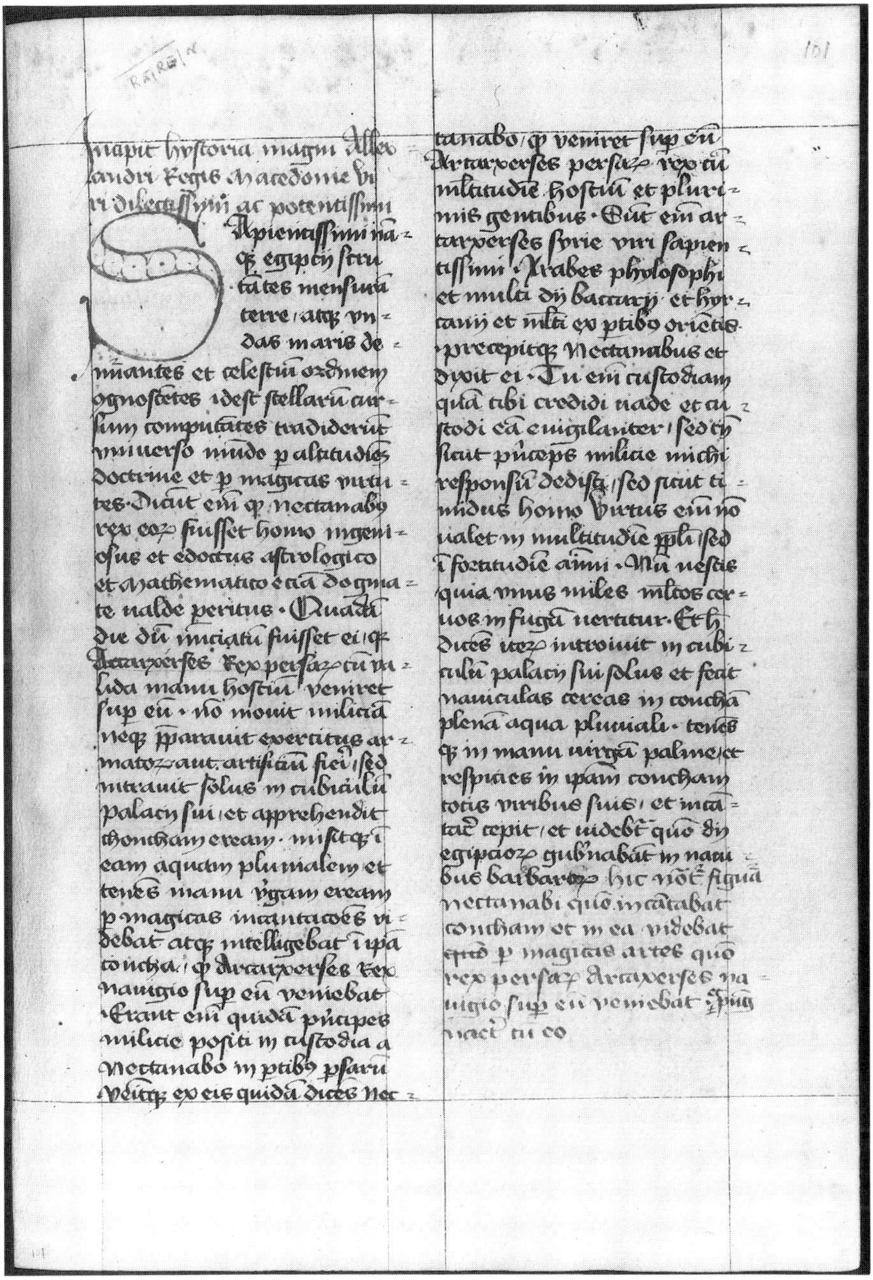

PLATE 5

fMS Lat 121, f. 101; Austria 1433

By permission of the Houghton Library, Harvard University

PLATE 6

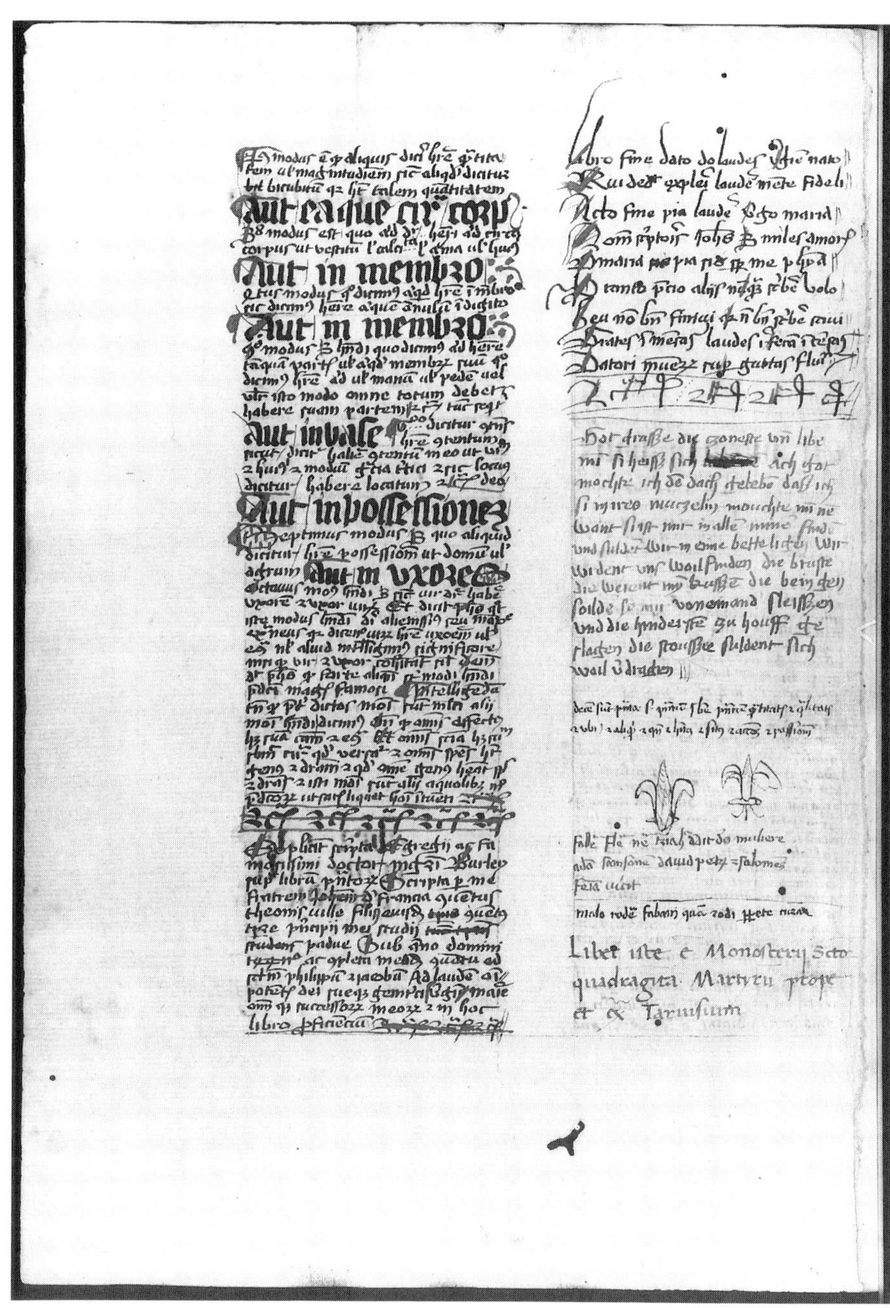

fMS Lat 12, f. 54v; Italy (Padua) 1442
By permission of the Houghton Library, Harvard University

PLATE 7

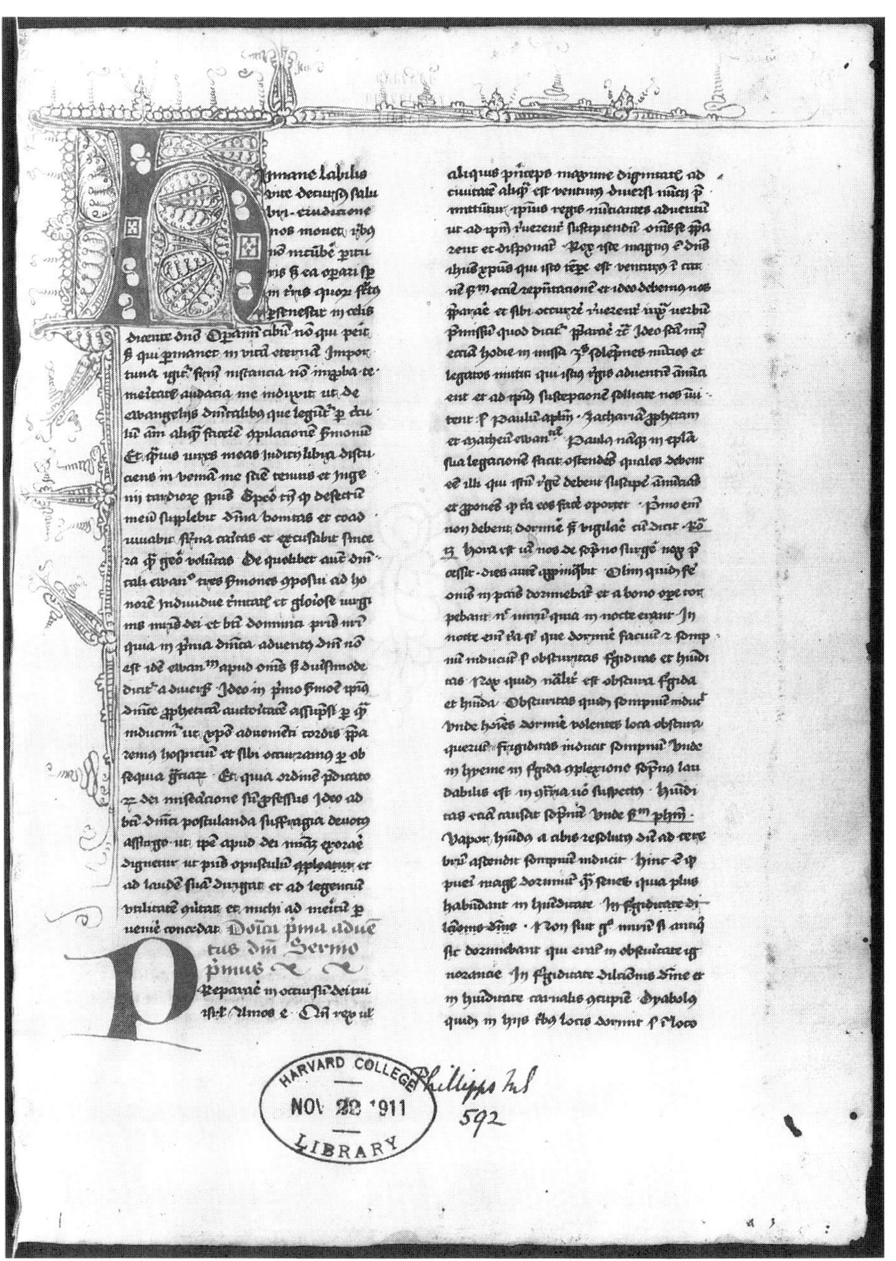

MS Lat 9, f. 1; Germany (Cologne) 1452
By permission of the Houghton Library, Harvard University

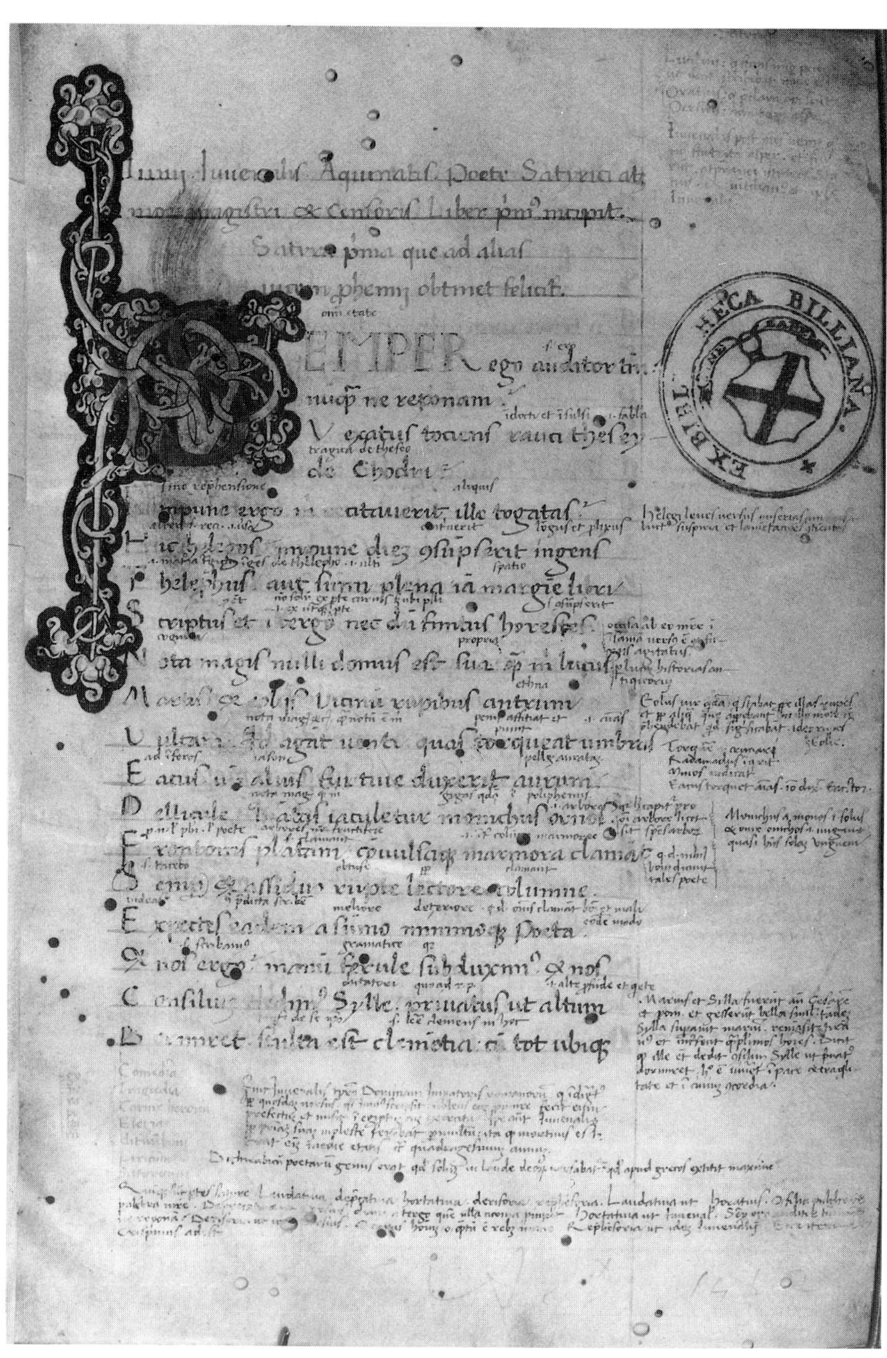

MS Lat 40, f. 1; Italy (Bologne) 1462
By permission of the Houghton Library, Harvard University

MS Lat 171, f. 399v; Italy (Florence?) 1465
By permission of the Houghton Library, Harvard University

PLATE 10

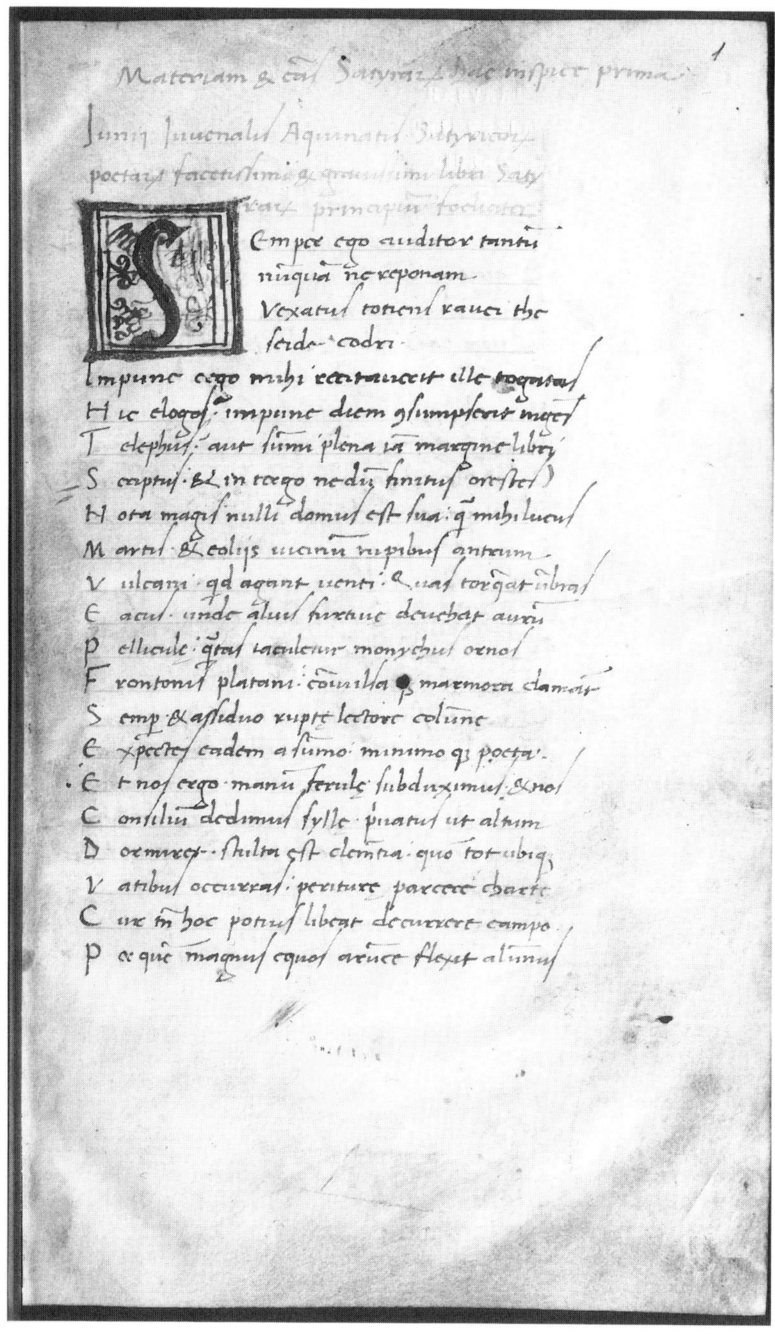

MS Lat 136, f. 1; Italy (Northeast?) 1471
By permission of the Houghton Library, Harvard University

PLATE 11

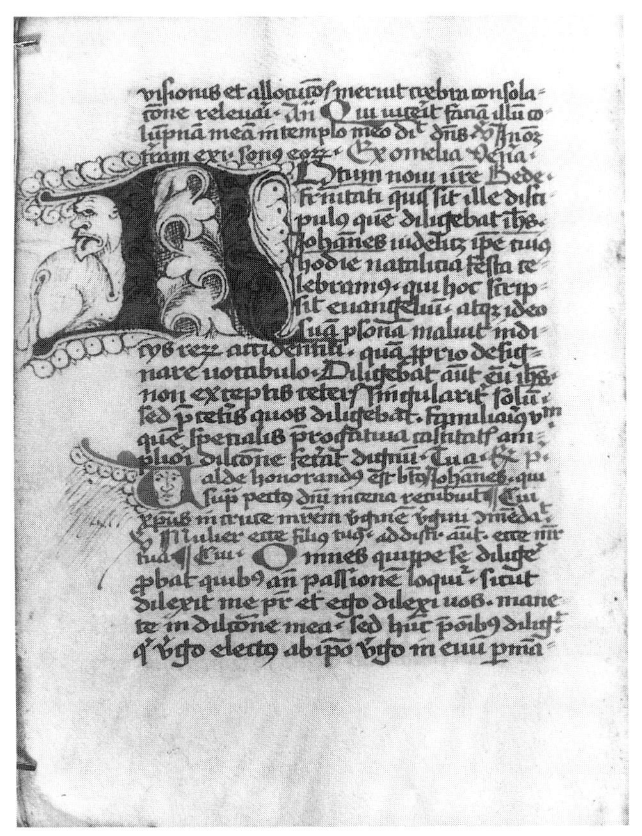

MS Lat 129, f. 207v; Germany 1474–1477

By permission of the Houghton Library, Harvard University

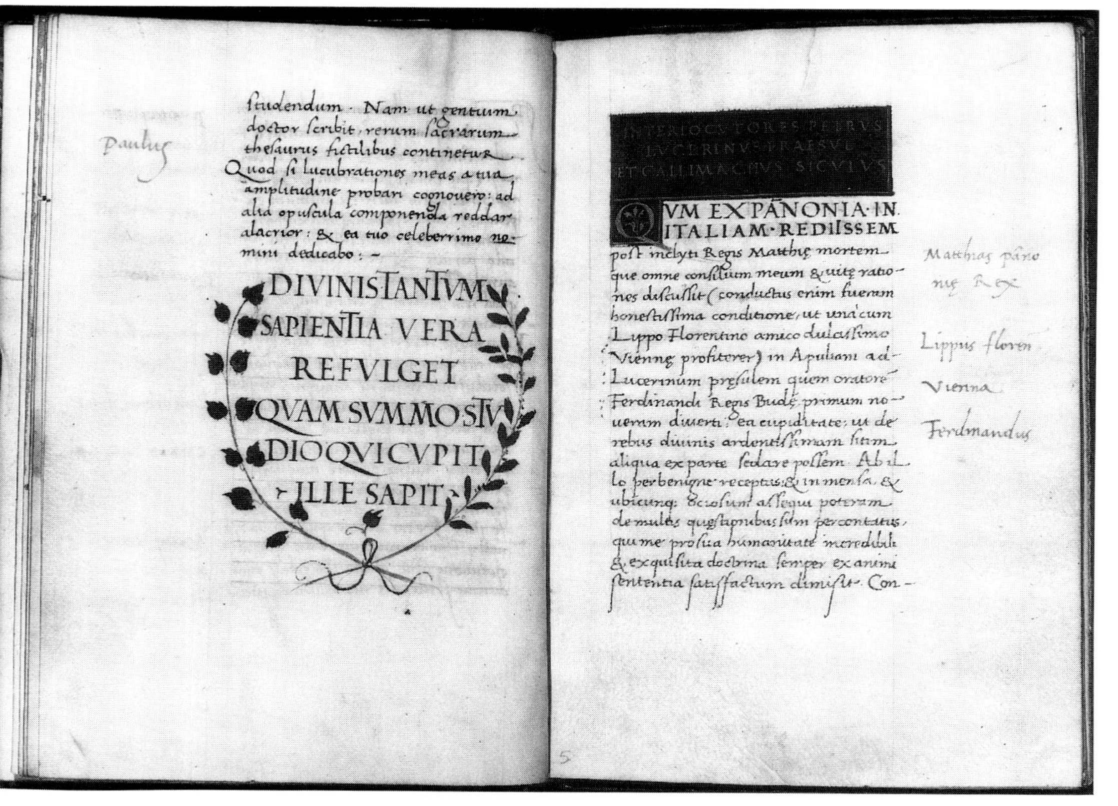

MS Lat 3, ff. 4v–5; Northeastern Italy (Venice or Padua) 1492–1516
By permission of the Houghton Library, Harvard University

PLATE 13

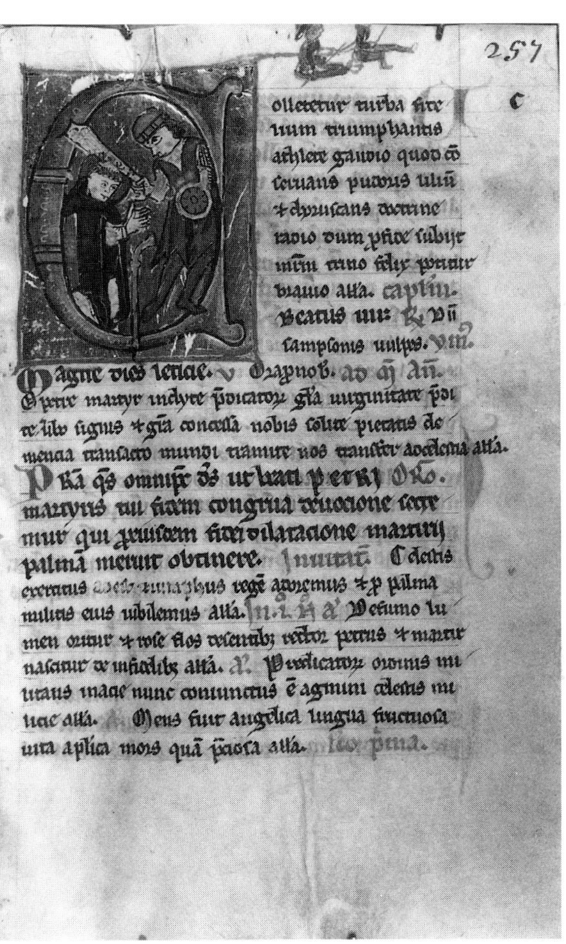

MS Lat 115, f. 128; Germany s. XIII[2] (after 1254, before 1318)
By permission of the Houghton Library, Harvard University

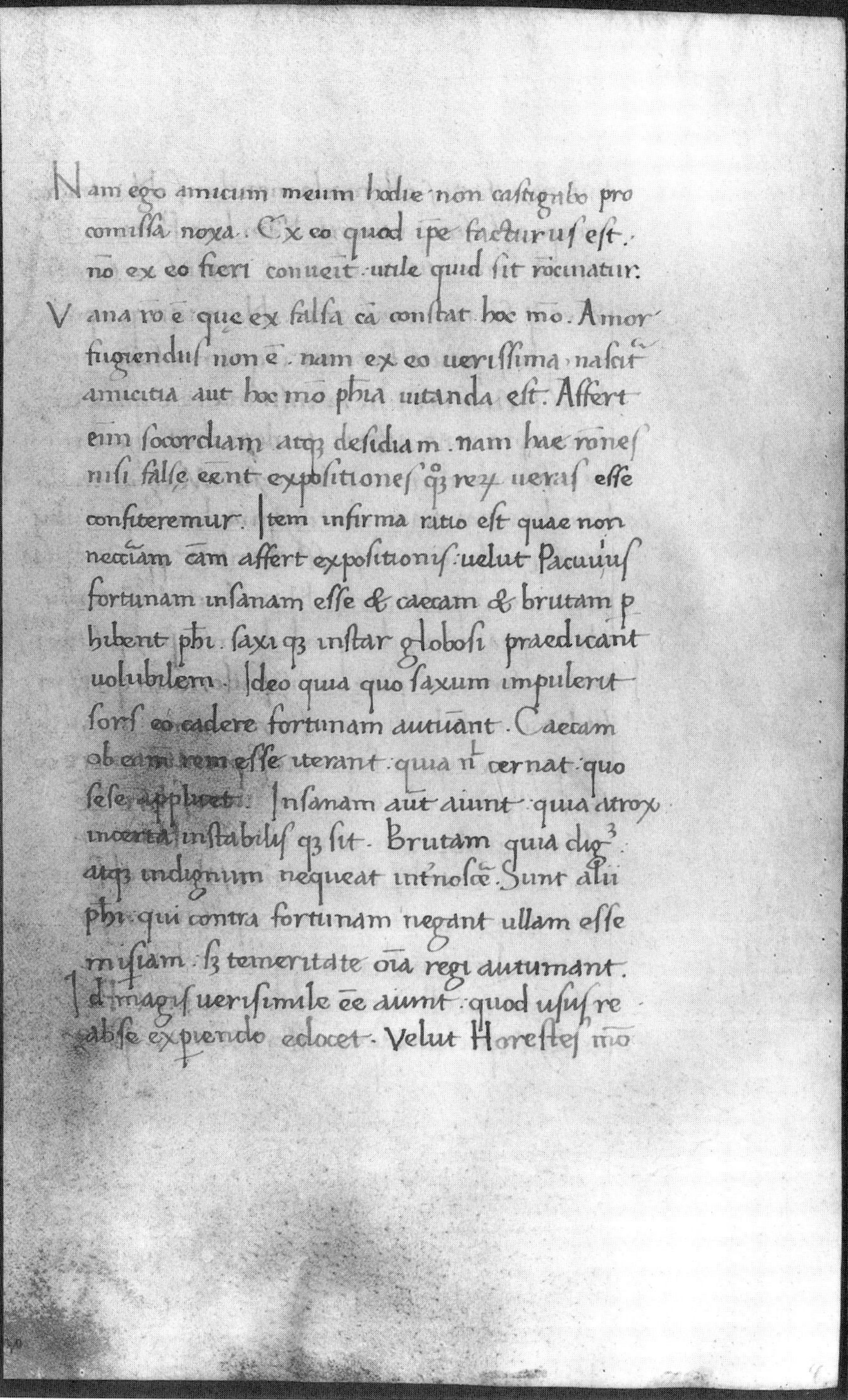

Nam ego amicum meum hodie non castigabo pro
comissa noxa. Ex eo quod ipe facturus est.
no ex eo fieri conueit. utile quid sit rocinatur.
Vana ro e que ex falsa ca constat hoc mo. Amor
fugiendus non e. nam ex eo uerissima nascitur
amicitia aut hoc mo phia uitanda est. Affert
enim socordiam atqz desidiam. nam hae rones
nisi falsae eent expositiones qz rerum ueras esse
confiteremur. Item infirma ratio est quae non
necciam cam affert expositionis: uelut Pacuuius
fortunam insanam esse & caecam & brutam p
hibent phi. saxiqz instar globosi praedicant
uolubilem. Ideo quia quo saxum impulerit
fors eo cadere fortunam autumant. Caecam
ob eam rem esse iterant: quia nl cernat quo
sese applicet. Insanam aut aiunt quia atrox
incerta instabilisqz sit. Brutam quia dig
atqz indignum nequeat internosce. Sunt alii
phi qui contra fortunam negant ullam esse
misiam: sz temeritate oia regi autumant.
Id magis uerisimile ee aiunt: quod usus re
ipsa expiendo edocet. Velut Horestes mo

MS Lat 37, f. 30; Northeastern Italy s. XV$^{2/4}$ (before 1440)
By permission of the Houghton Library, Harvard University

PLATE 15

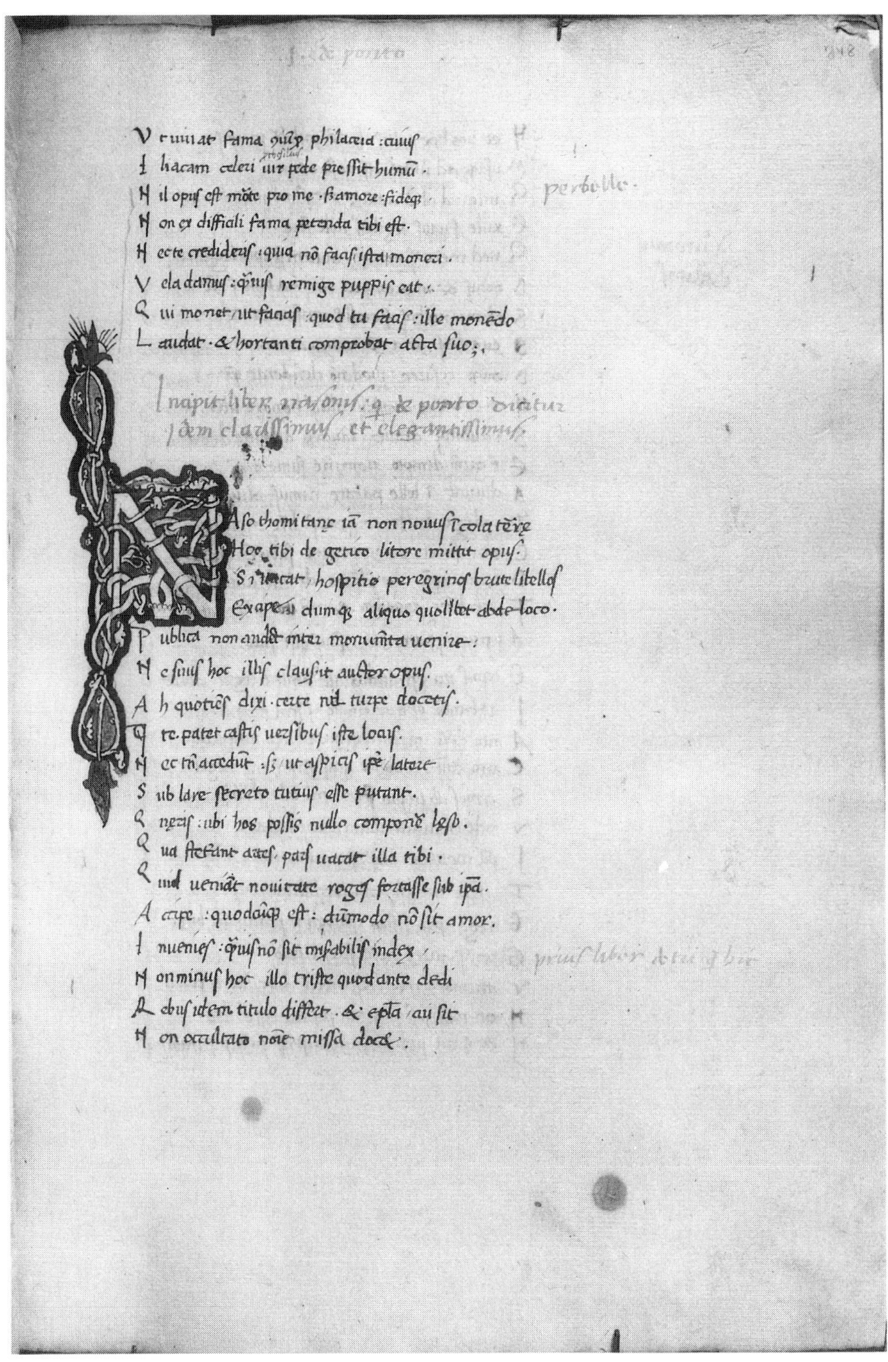

fMS Lat 42, f. 248; Northern Italy (Verona) s. XV$^{3/4}$ (before 1471)
By permission of the Houghton Library, Harvard University

PLATE 16

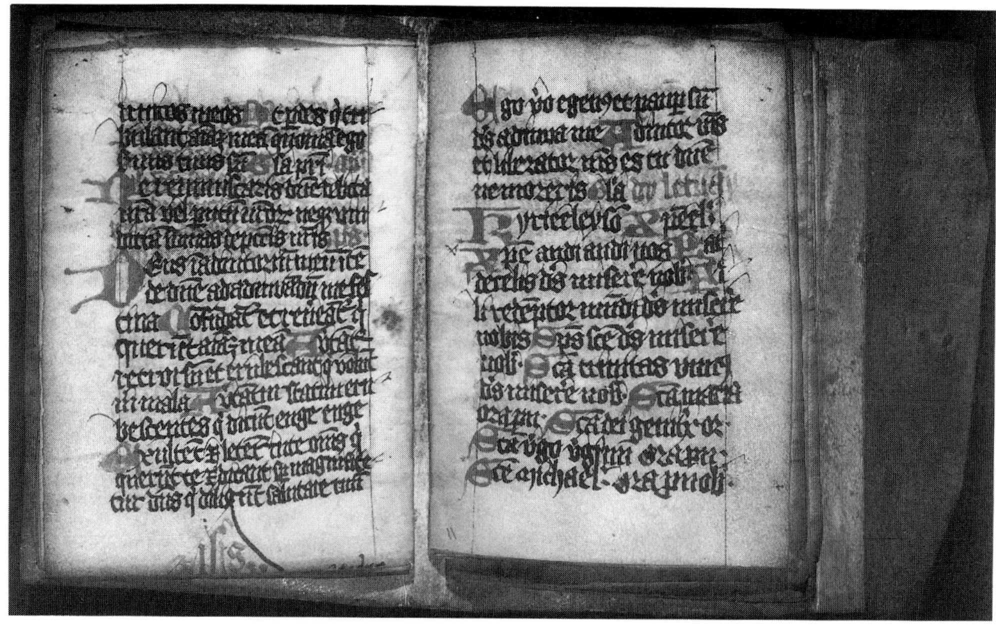

MS Lat 173, ff. 10v–11; Germany s. XV^{2} (after 1461?)
By permission of the Houghton Library, Harvard University

PLATE 17

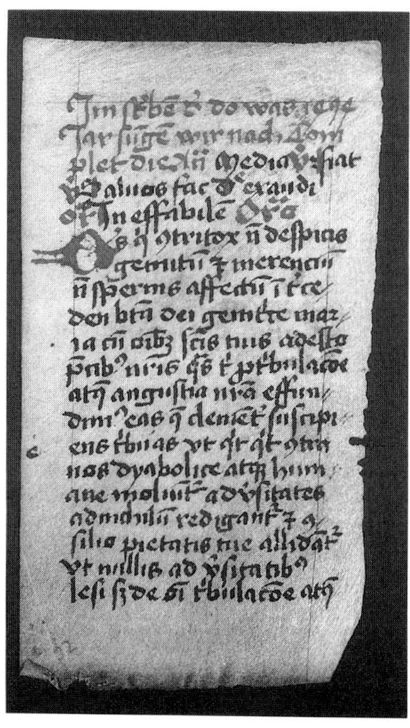

MS Lat 173, f. 32; Germany s. XV^{ex} (after 1494)
By permission of the Houghton Library, Harvard University

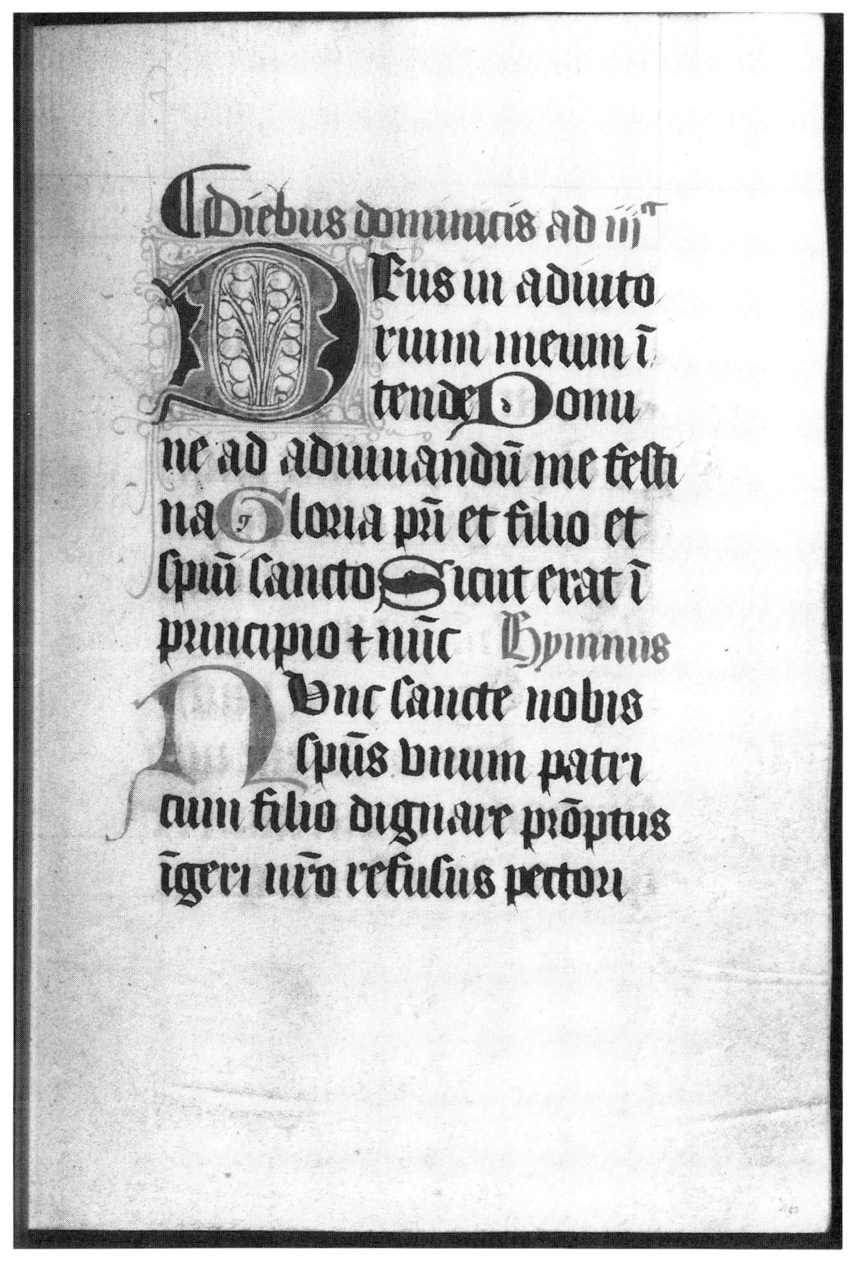

Diebus dominicis ad iii
Deus in adiuto
rium meum ĩ
tende Domi
ne ad adiuuandũ me festi
na Gloria prĩ et filio et
spũi sancto Sicut erat ĩ
principio & nũc Hymnus
Nunc sancte nobis
spũs unum patri
cum filio dignare prõptus
ĩgeri nr̃o refusus pectori

MS Lat 111, f. 20; France s. XVI[1] (after 1515)
By permission of the Houghton Library, Harvard University

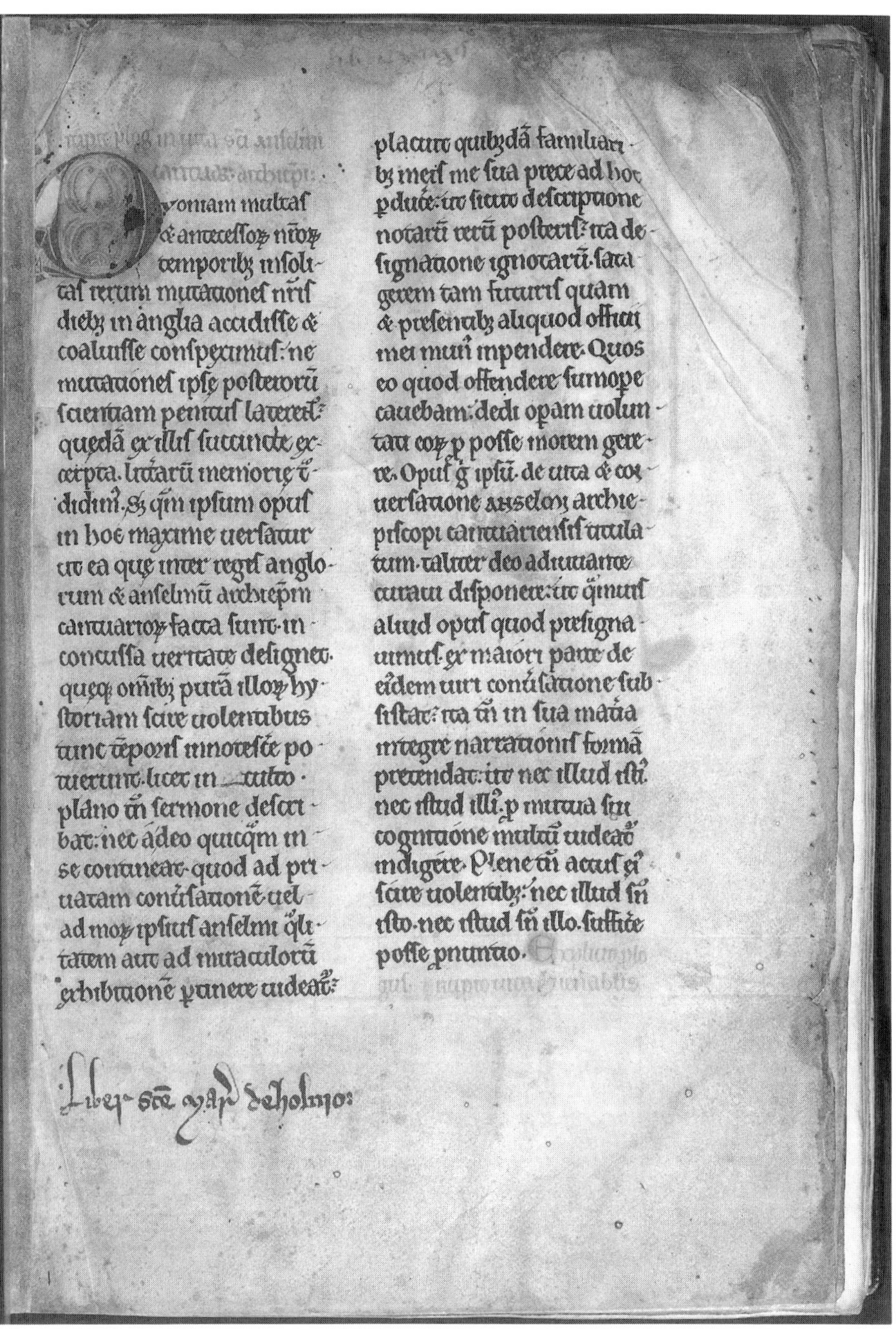

fMS Lat 27, f. 1; England s. XII[2]
By permission of the Houghton Library, Harvard University

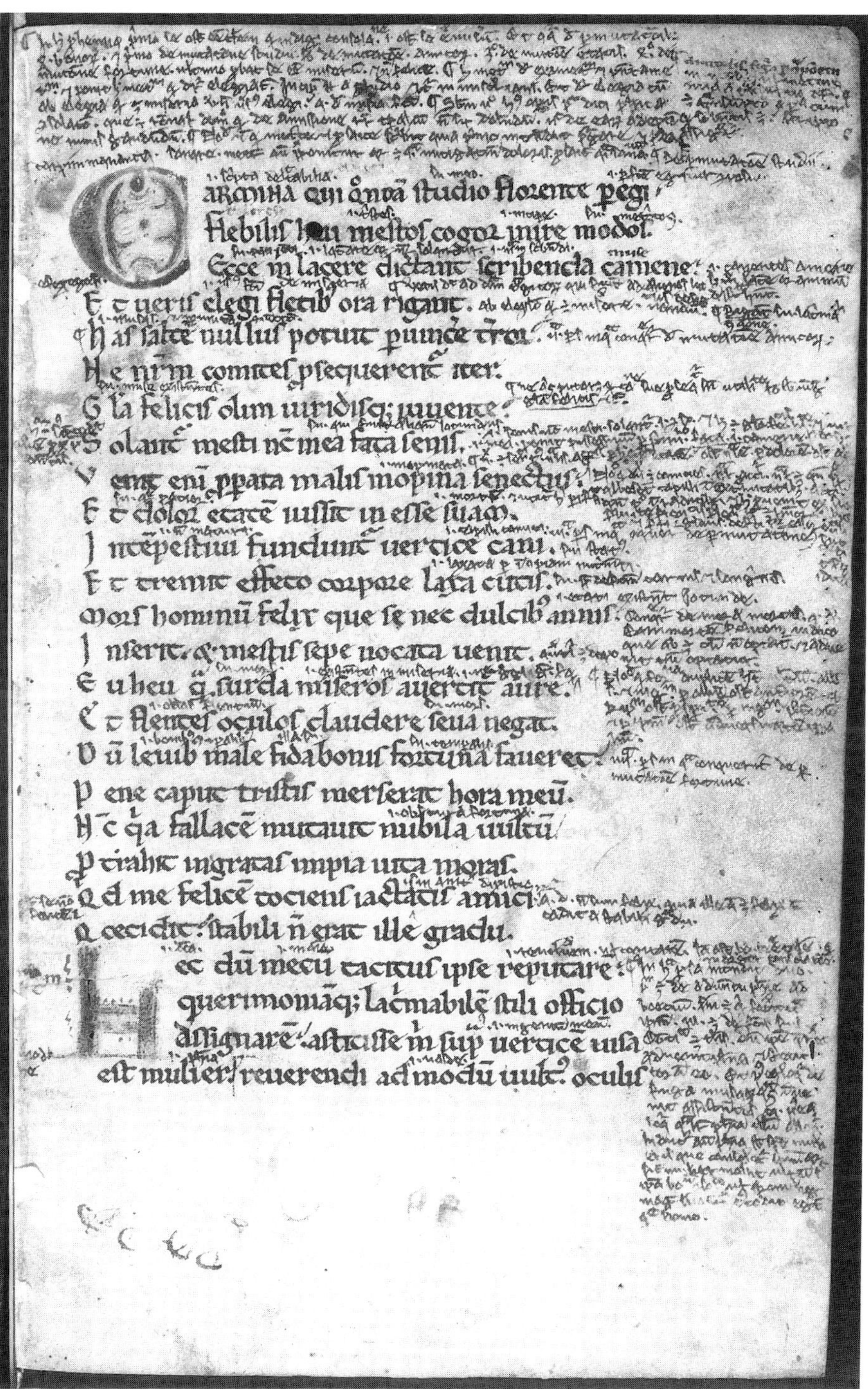

MS Lat 127, f. 1; England s. XII[4/4]
By permission of the Houghton Library, Harvard University

PLATE 21

MS Lat 132, f. 12; Flanders s. $XV^{2/4}$
By permission of the Houghton Library, Harvard University

PLATE 22

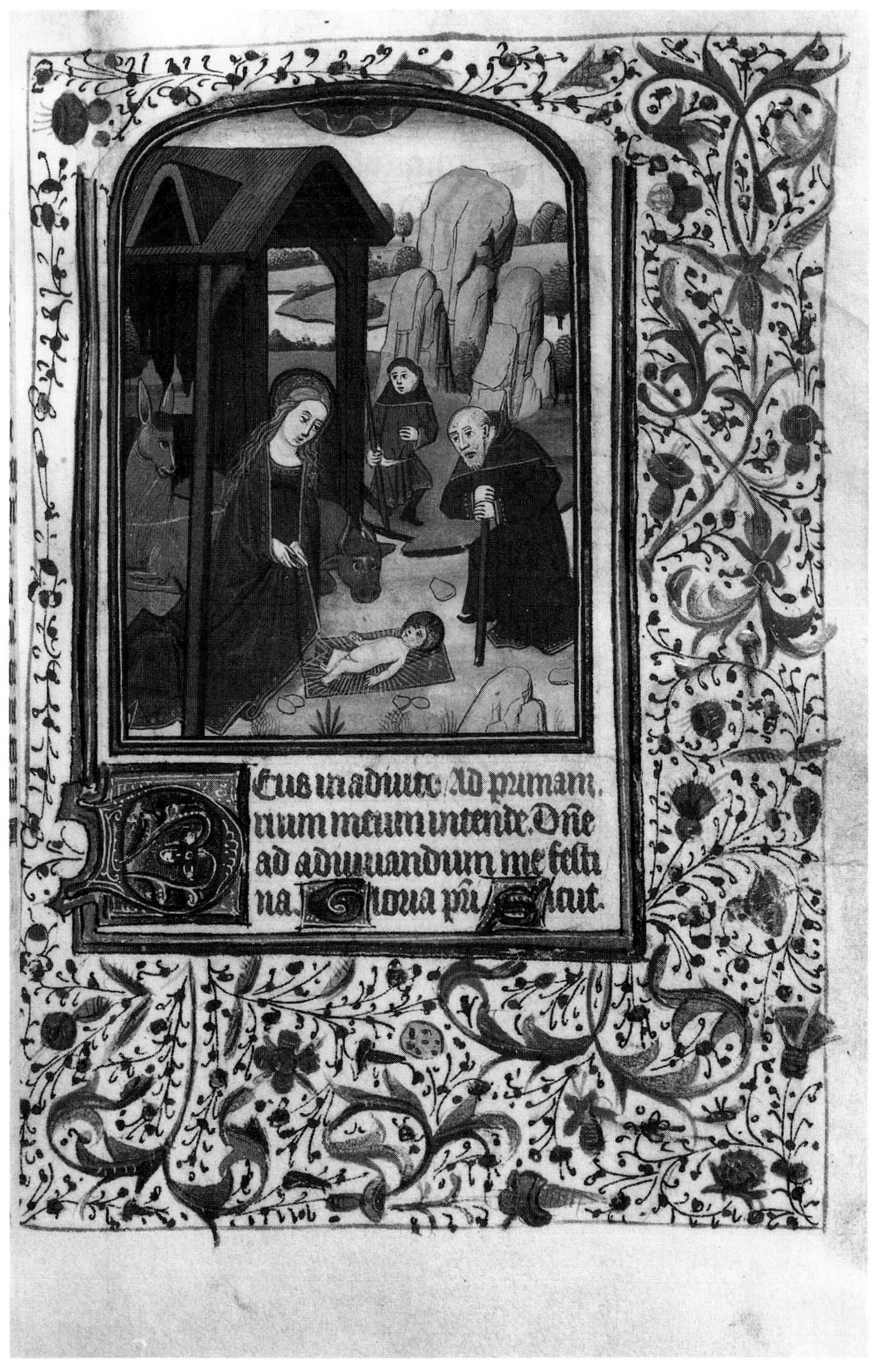

MS Lat 161, f. 51; Flanders (Bruges?) s. XV$^{3/4}$
By permission of the Houghton Library, Harvard University

MS Lat 44, f. 2; France s. XII$^{2/4}$

By permission of the Houghton Library, Harvard University

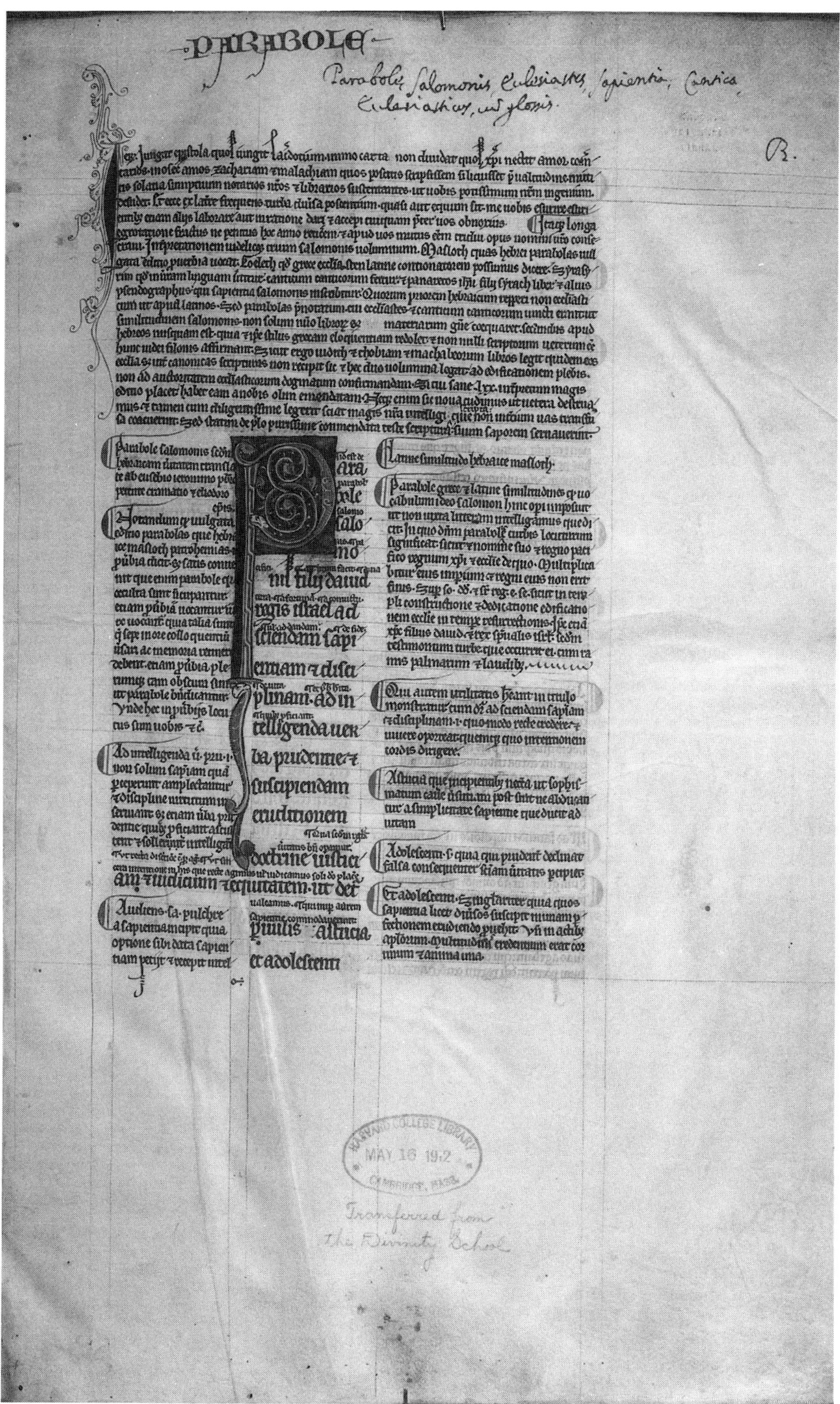

fMS Lat 6, f. 1; Northeastern France or Flanders s. XIII 2/4
By permission of the Houghton Library, Harvard University

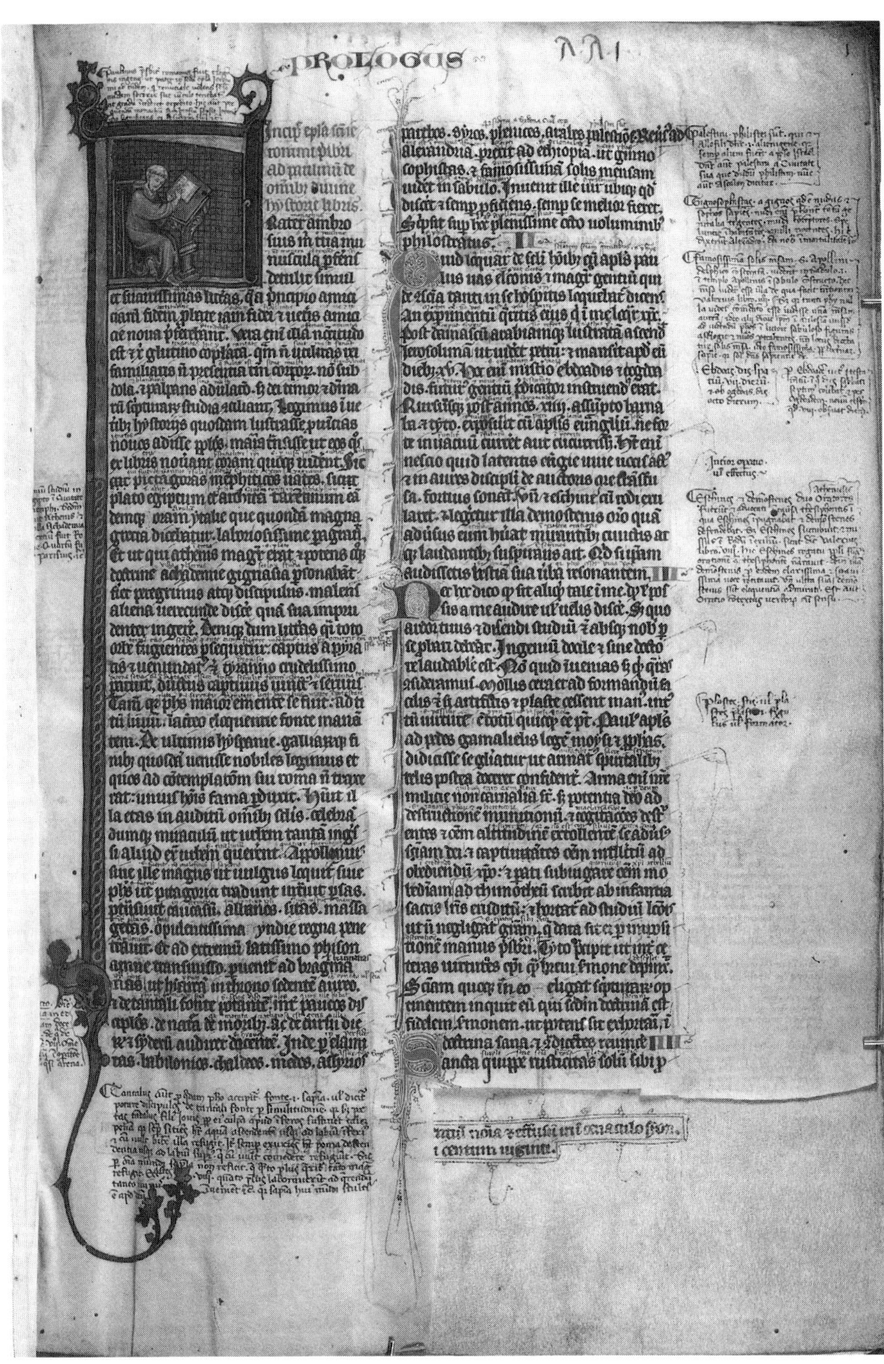

fMS Lat 36, f. 19v; France (Paris) s. XIII/XIV
By permission of the Houghton Library, Harvard University

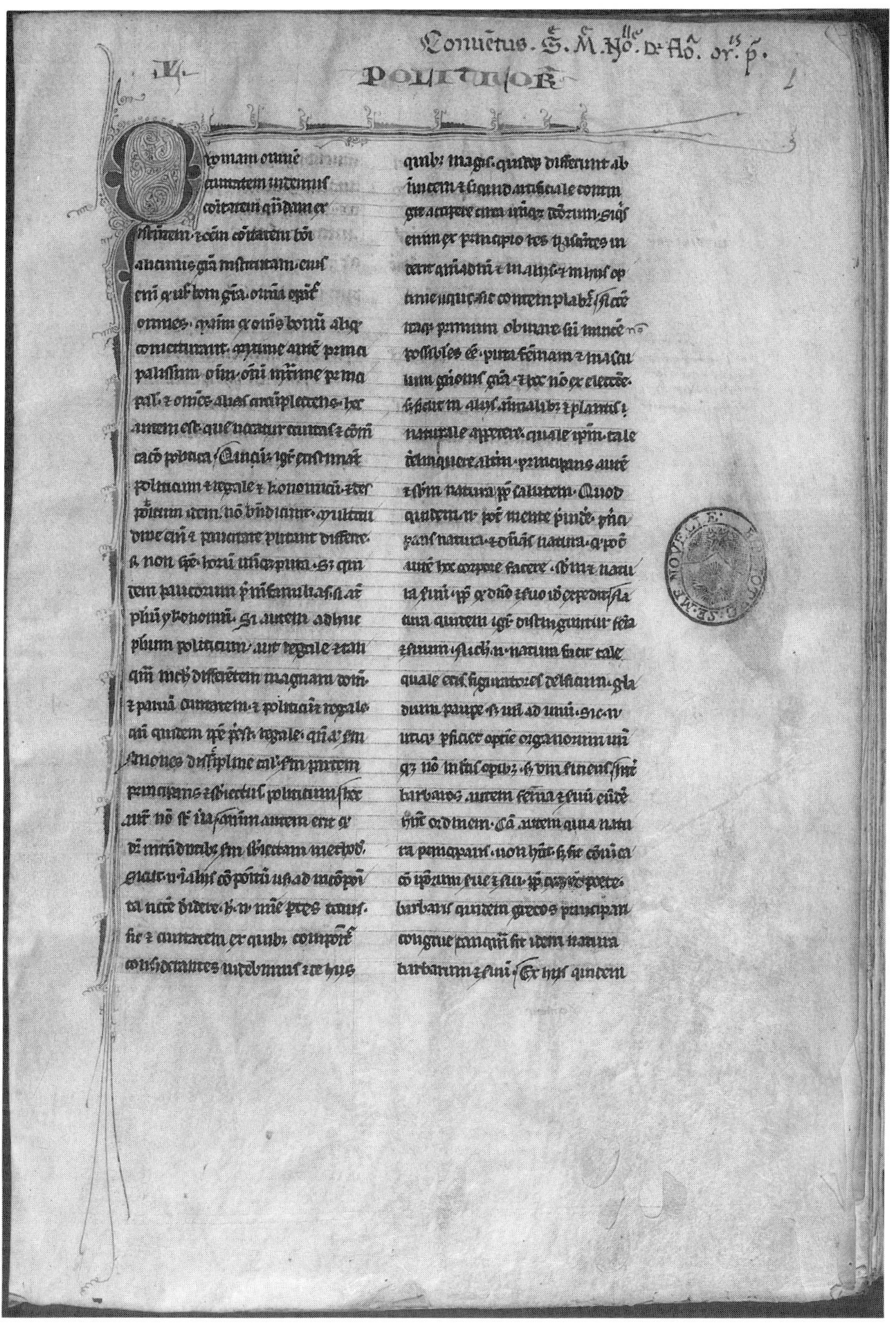

fMS Lat 39, f. 1; France s. XIV[1]
By permission of the Houghton Library, Harvard University

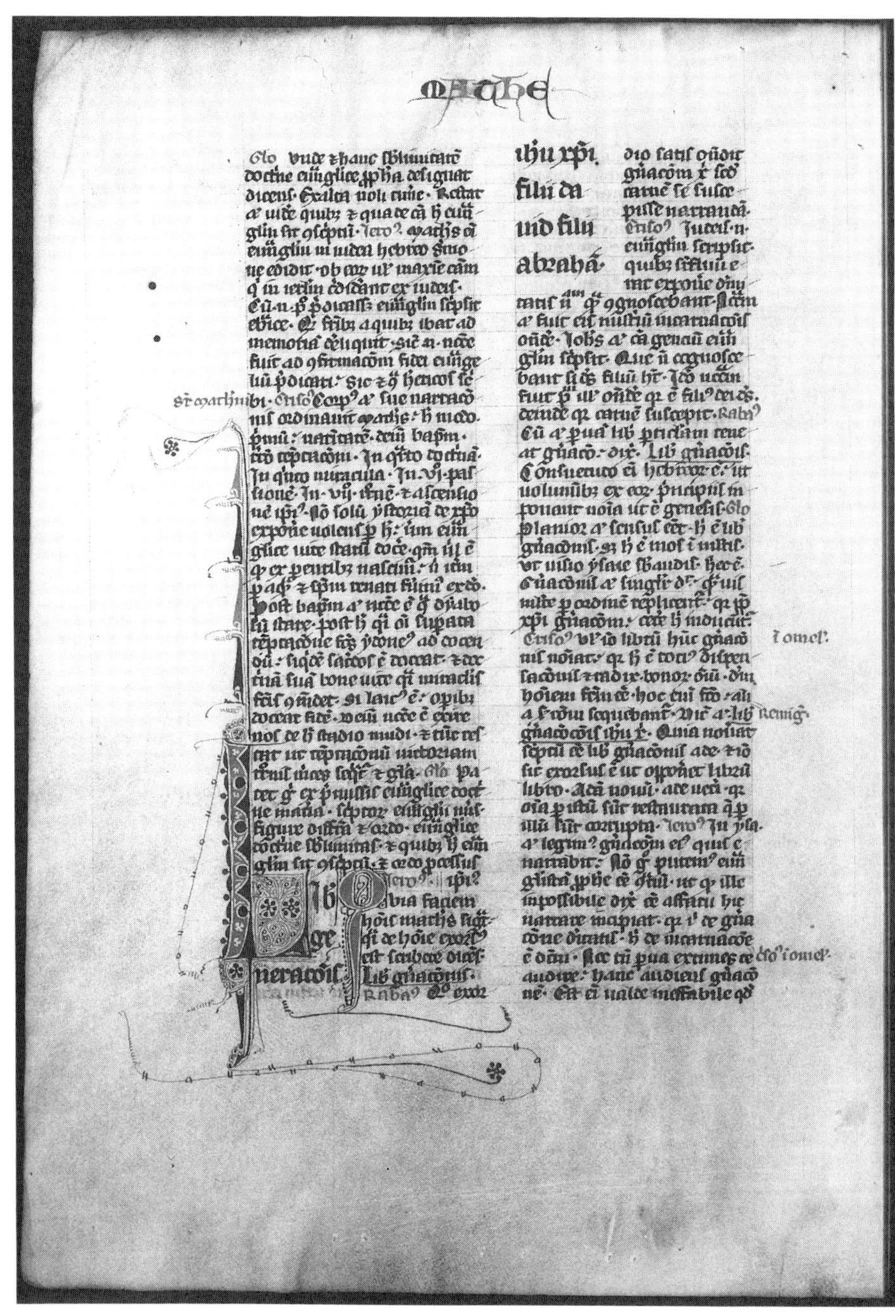

fMS Lat 172, f. 3v; Northeastern France or Germany s. XIV[1]
By permission of the Houghton Library, Harvard University

PLATE 28

MS Lat 159, f. 29; Northern France (Paris?) s. XV$^{3/4}$
By permission of the Houghton Library, Harvard University

PLATE 29

MS Lat 133, f. 32v; Northern France s. $\text{XV}^{4/4}$

By permission of the Houghton Library, Harvard University

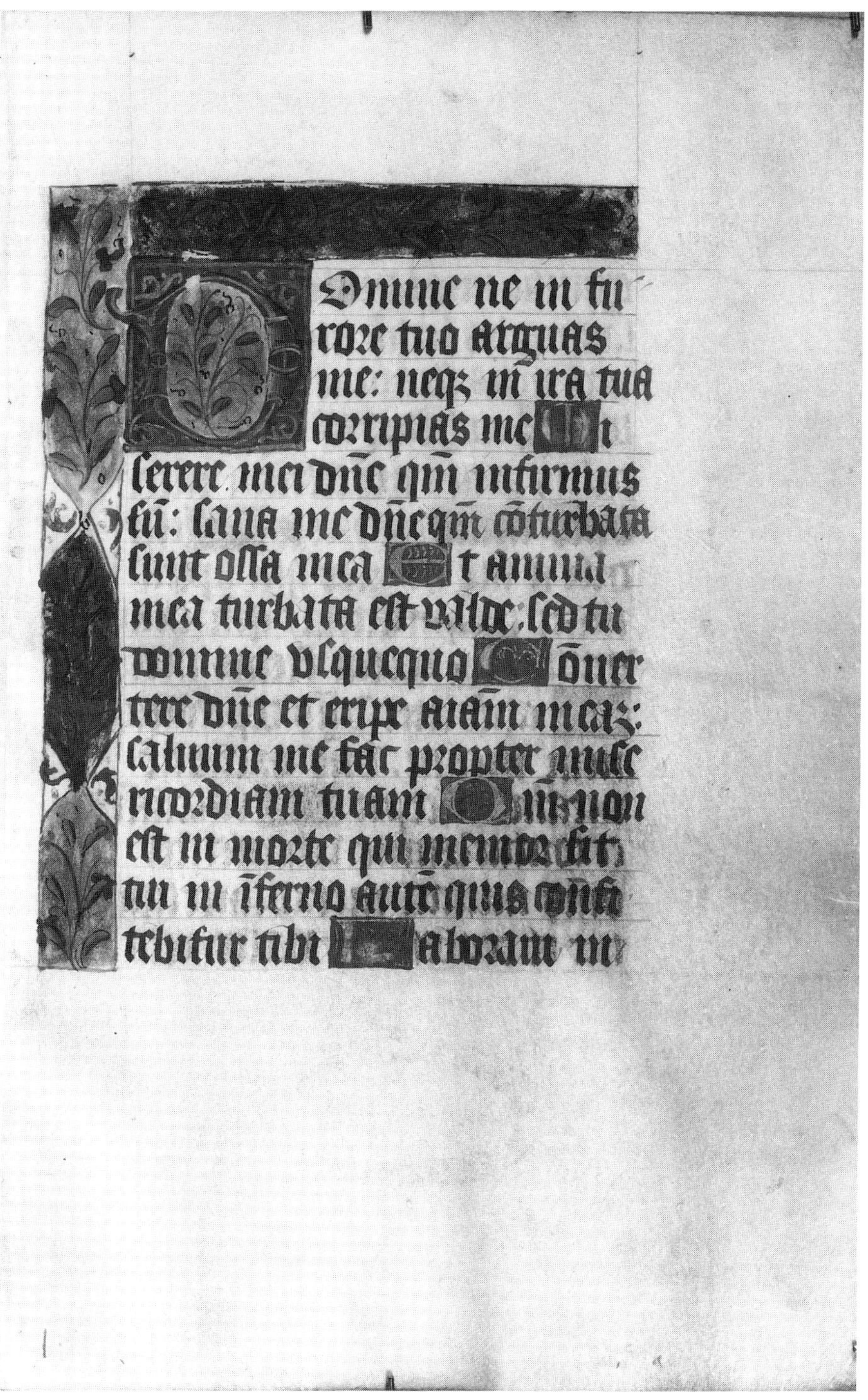

omine ne in fu
rore tuo arguas
me: neqz in ira tua
corripias me i
serere mei dn̄e qm̄ infirmus
sū: sana me dn̄e qm̄ cōturbata
sunt ossa mea t anima
mea turbata est valde. sed tu
domine usquequo onuer
tere dn̄e et eripe aiām meā:
saluum me fac propter mise
ricordiam tuam m̄ non
est in morte qui memor sit
tui in īferno autē quis confi
tebitur tibi aboraui in

MS Lat 4, f. 1; Northern France s. XV/XVI
By permission of the Houghton Library, Harvard University

PLATE 31

MS Lat 17, f. 84v; Northern France s. XV/XVI
By permission of the Houghton Library, Harvard University

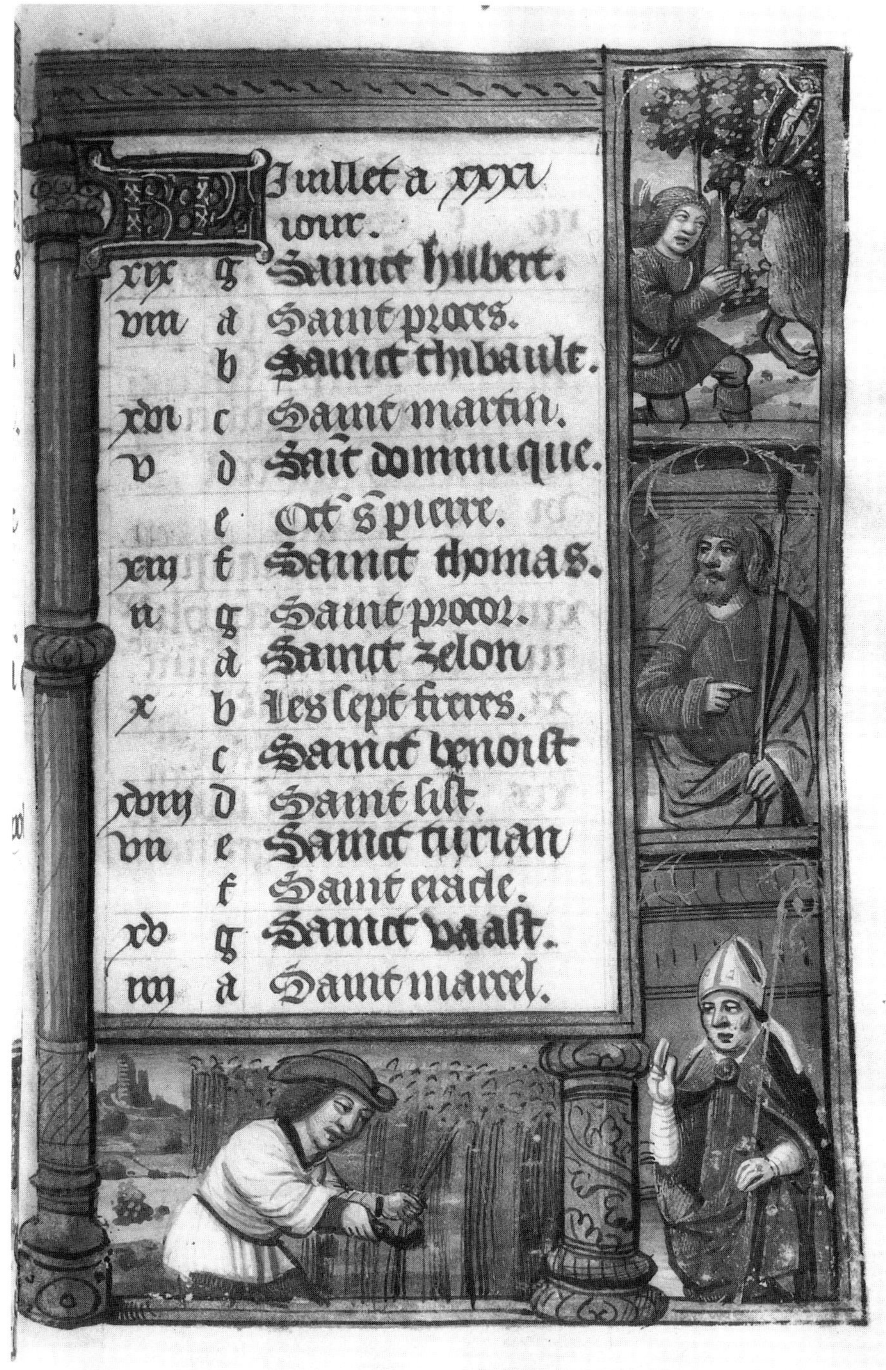

Juillet a xxxi
iour.
xix g Sainct hubert.
viii a Saint proces.
b Sainct thibault.
xvi c Saint martin.
v d Sait dominique.
e Oct' s pierre.
xiii f Sainct thomas.
ii g Saint procop.
a Sainct zelon
x b Les sept freres.
c Sainct benoist
xviii d Saint sixt.
vii e Sainct cirian
f Saint eracle.
xv g Sainct vaast.
iiii a Saint marcel.

MS Lat 160, f. 7; Northern France (Paris?) s. XVI 1/4
By permission of the Houghton Library, Harvard University

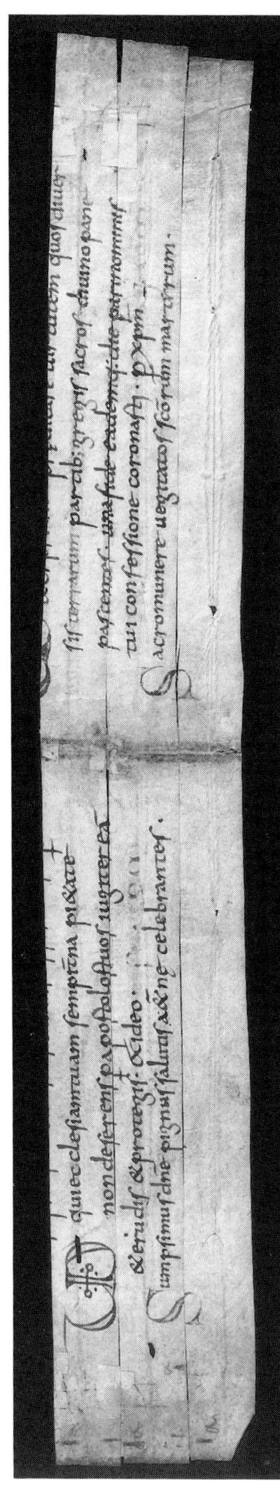

fMS Lat 156, ff. 1v–2; Austria (Salzburg) s. IX^{in}
By permission of the Houghton Library, Harvard University

PLATE 34

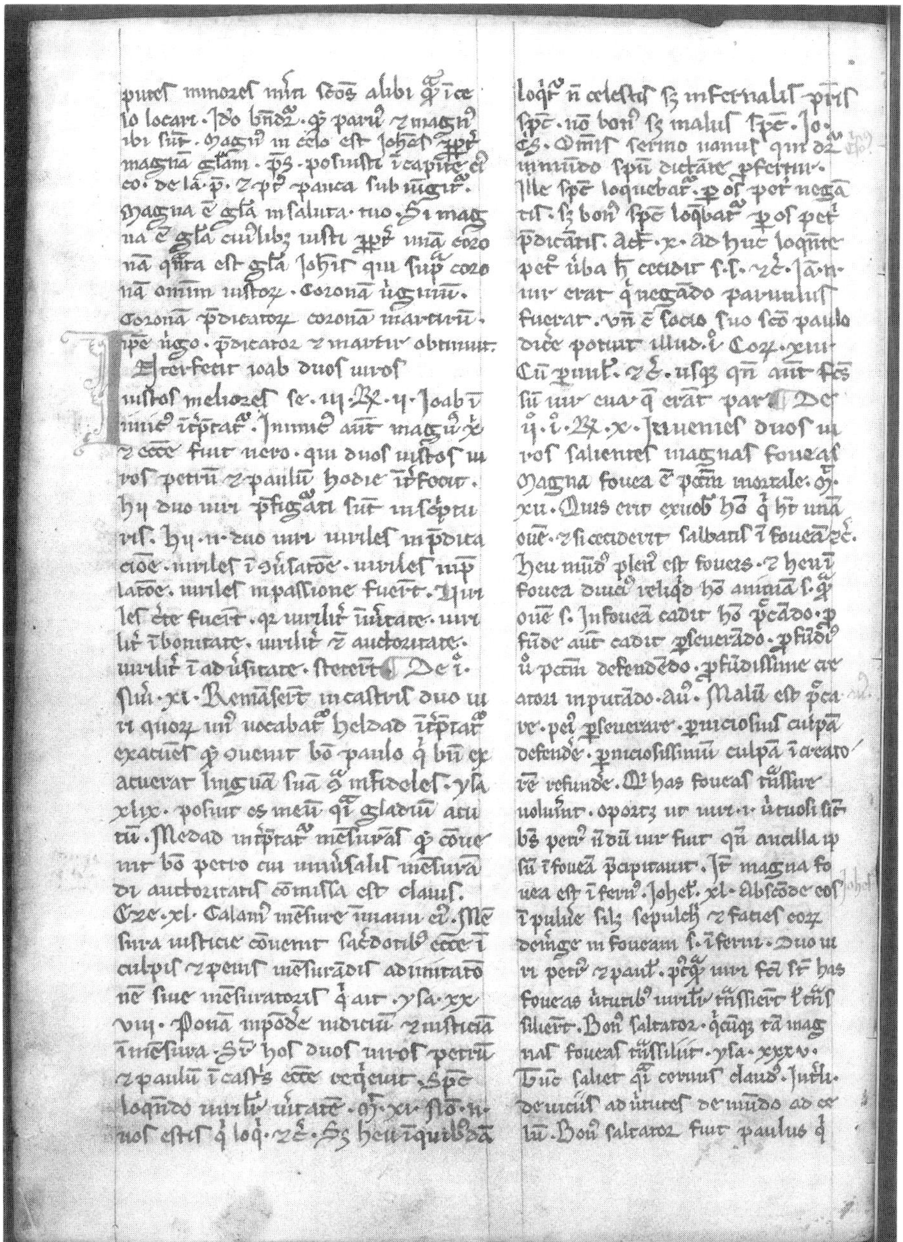

MS Lat 5, f. 2v; Germany s. XIII^{ex}–XIV^{1}
By permission of the Houghton Library, Harvard University

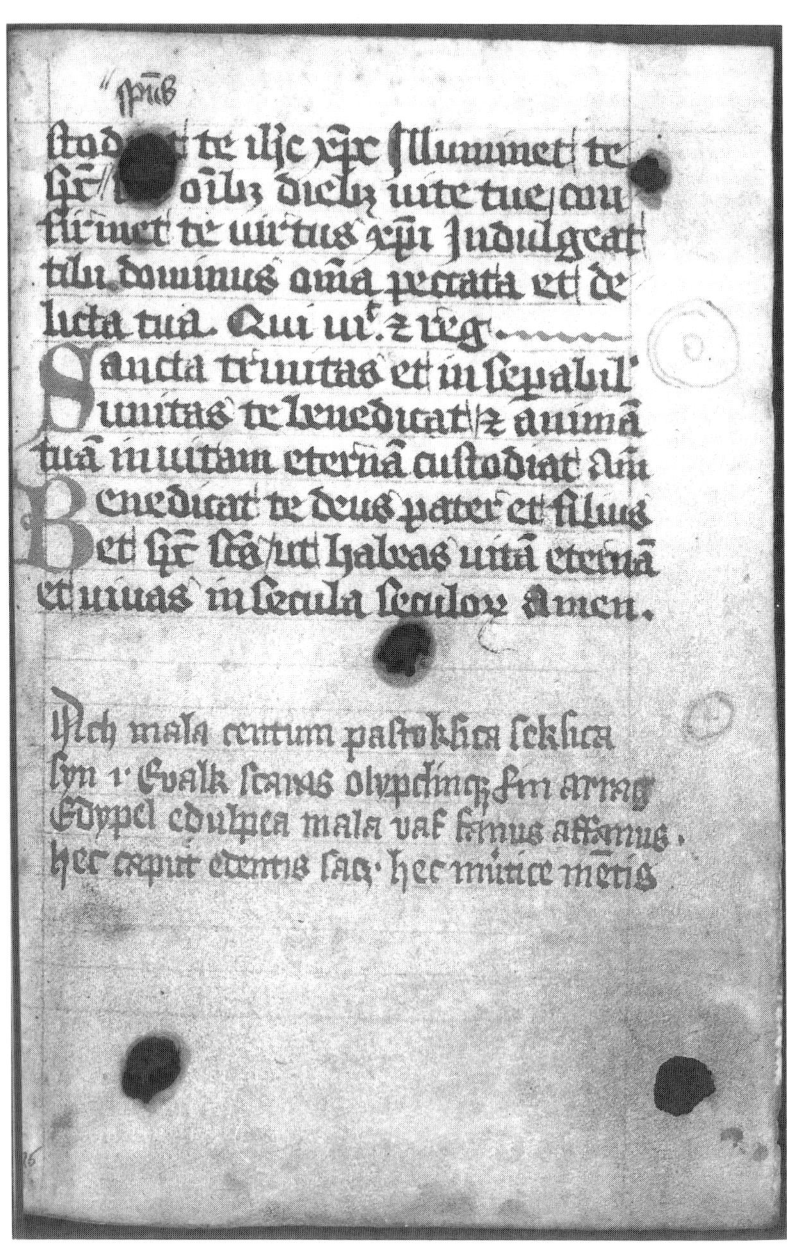

MS Lat 134, f. 25; Germany s. XIV[2]
By permission of the Houghton Library, Harvard University

PLATE 36

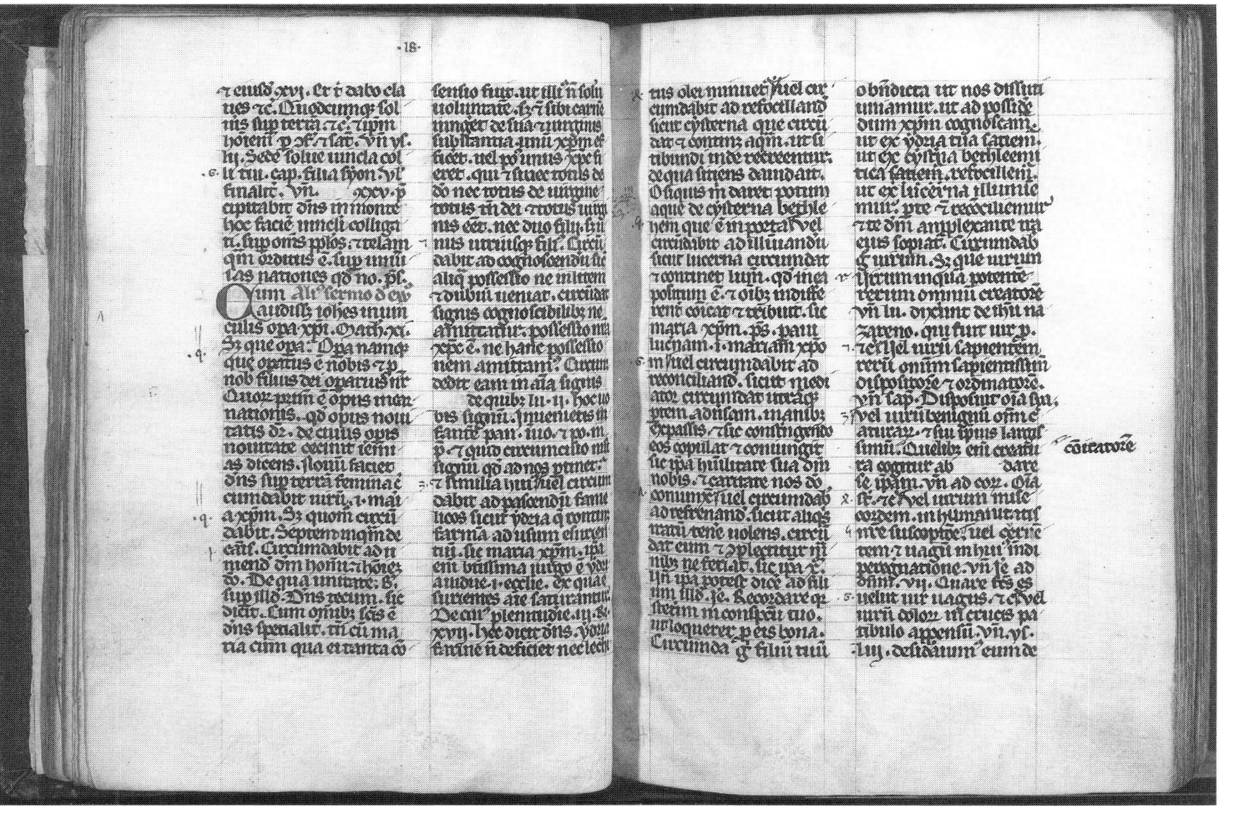

MS Lat 15, ff. 23v–24; Germany s. XV[1] (?)
By permission of the Houghton Library, Harvard University

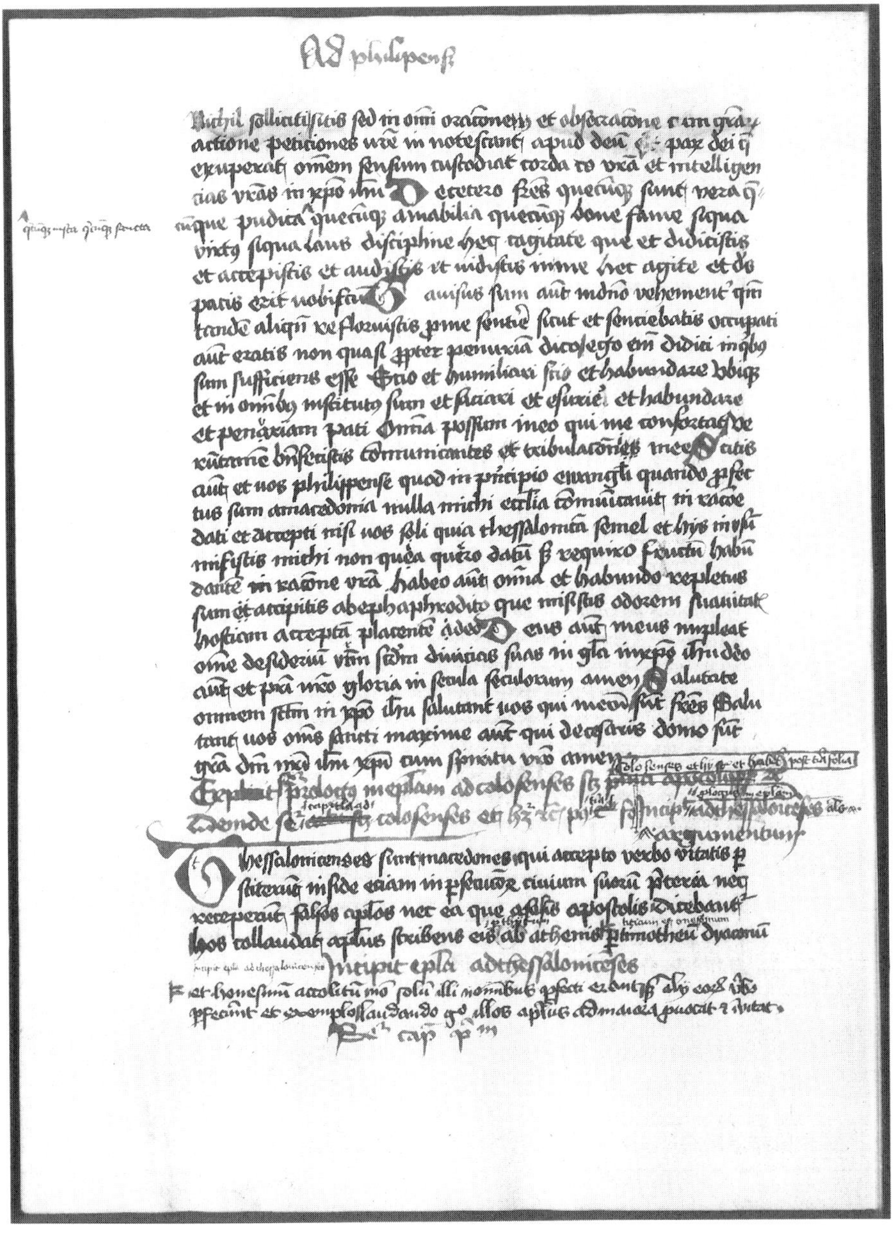

PLATE 37

MS Lat 50, f. 147v; Southern Germany s. XV$^{3/4}$

By permission of the Houghton Library, Harvard University

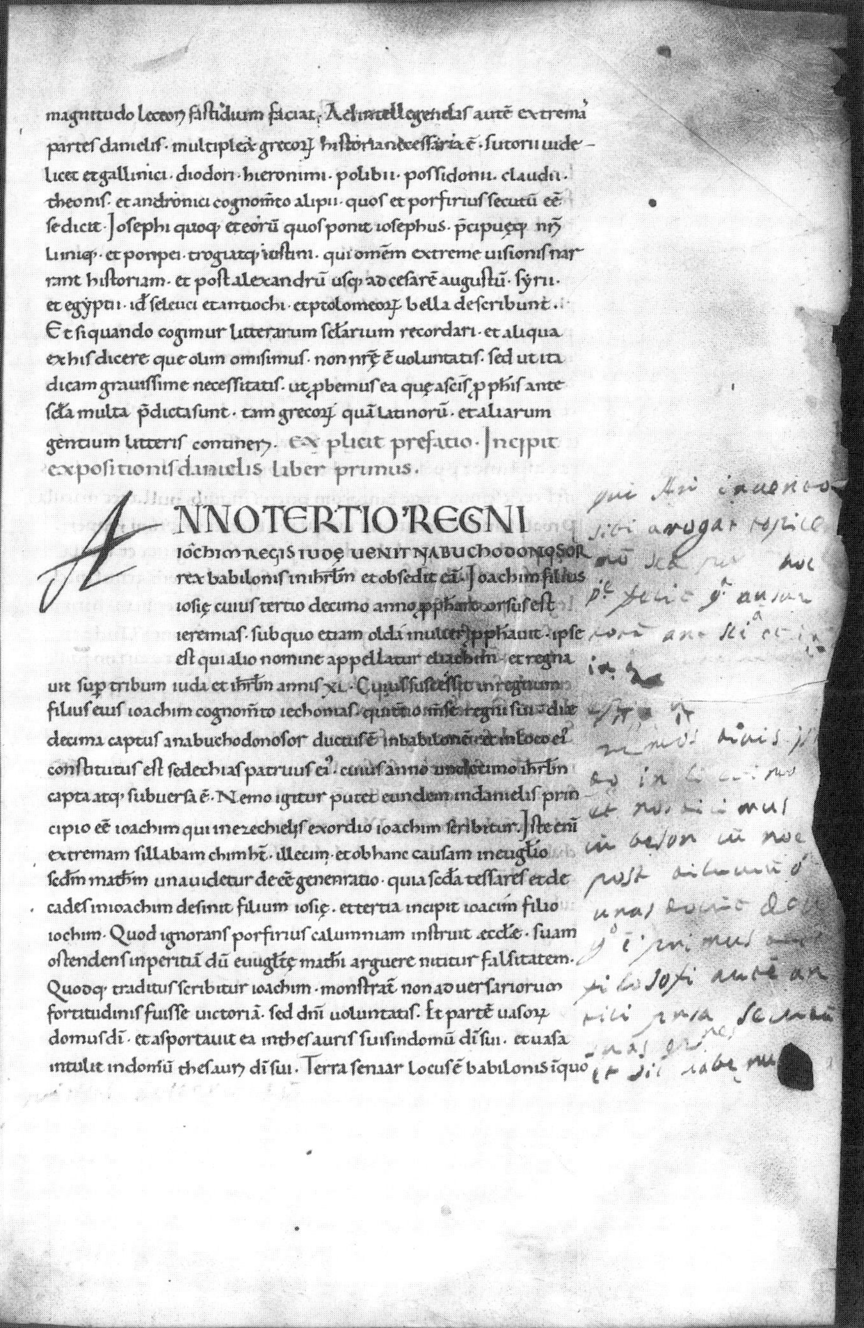

magnitudo lectorum fastidium faciat; Ad intellegendas autē extremā
partes danielis· multiplex grecorum historia necessaria ē· sutorii uidelicet et gallinici· diodori· hieronimi· polibii· possidonii· claudii·
theonis· et andronici cognomto alipii· quos et porfirius secutū eē
se dicit· Josephi quoq; et eorū quos ponit iosephus· pcipueq; nr̄i
liuiiq;· et pompei· trogi atq; iustini· qui omēm extreme uisionis nar
rant historiam· et post alexandrū usq; ad cesarē augustū· syrię·
et egypti· id ē seleuci et antiochi· et ptolomeorum bella describunt·
Et siquando cogimur litterarum secularium recordari· et aliqua
ex his dicere que olim omisimus· non nr̄e ē uoluntatis· sed ut ita
dicam grauissime necessitatis· ut pbemus ea que a sc̄is pphis ante
scła multa pdicta sunt· tam grecorum quā latinorū· et aliarum
gentium litteris contineri. Explicit prefatio· Incipit
expositionis danielis liber primus.

ANNO TERTIO REGNI
iochim regis iude uenit nabuchodonosor
rex babilonis in ihr̄lm et obsedit eā· Joachim filius
iosię cuius tertio decimo anno pphare orsus est
ieremias· sub quo etiam oldā mulier pphauit· ipse
est qui alio nomine appellatur eliachim· et regna
uit sup tribum iuda et ihr̄lm annis xi· Cui successit in regnum
filius eius ioachim cognomto iechonias· qui tertio mense regni sui ·x· die
decima captus a nabuchodonosor ductus ē in babilonē· et in loco ei
constitutus est sedechias patruus ei'· cuius anno undecimo ihr̄lm
capta atq; subuersa ē· Nemo igitur putet eundem in danielis prin
cipio eē ioachim qui in ezechielis exordio ioachin scribitur. Iste eni
extremam sillabam chim hē· ille cim· et ob hanc causam in euglio
scdm matheū una uidetur deeē generatio· quia scd̄a tessartes et de
cades in ioachim desinit filium iosię· et tertia incipit a ioacim filio
iochim· Quod ignorans porfirius calumniam instruit ecclē· suam
ostendens imperitiā dū euuglię mathi arguere nititur falsitatem·
Quodq; traditus scribitur ioachim· monstratē non ad uersariorum
fortitudinis fuisse uictoriā· sed dn̄i uoluntatis· Et partē uasorum
domus dī· et asportauit ea in thesauris suis in domū dī sui· et uasa
intulit in domū thesauri dī sui· Terra sennaar locus ē babilonis in quo

fMS Lat 168, f. 2; Italy (Central or Tuscany) s. XII[2/4]
By permission of the Houghton Library, Harvard University

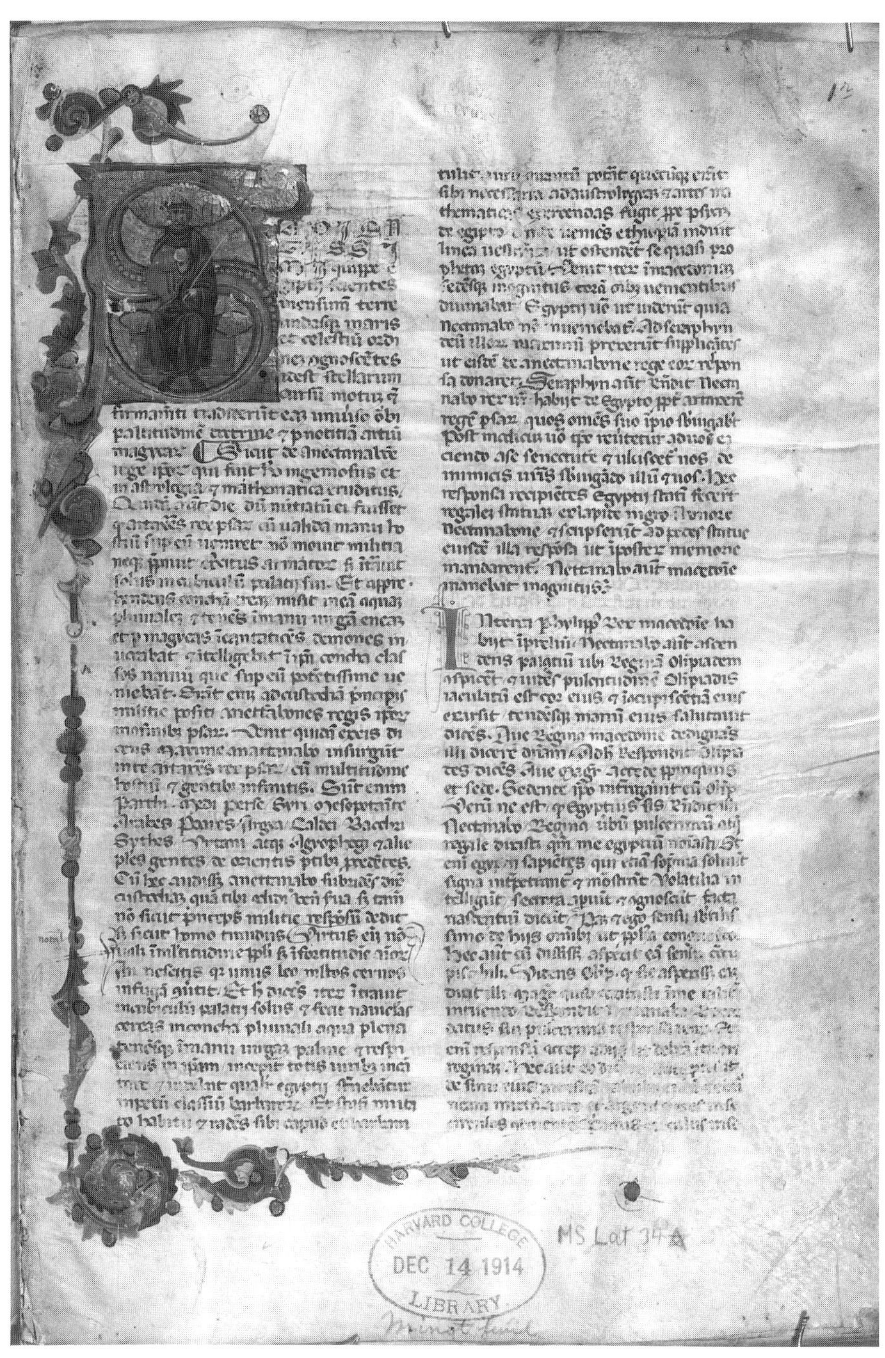

MS Lat 34, f. 1; Italy (Bologna) s. XIII^{ex}–s. XIV^{1}
By permission of the Houghton Library, Harvard University

MS Lat 154, f. 1; Italy s. XIV
By permission of the Houghton Library, Harvard University

PLATE 41

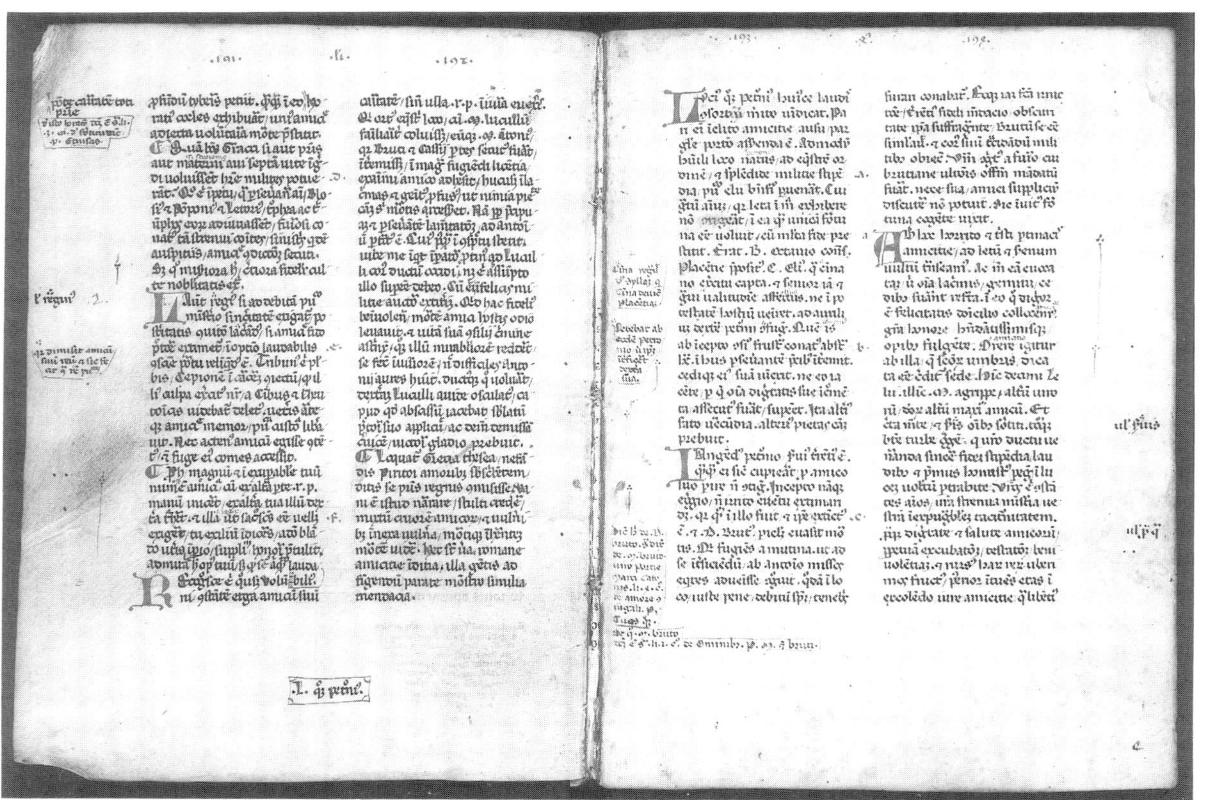

MS Lat 48, ff. 48v–49; Central Italy s. XIV$^{2/4}$

By permission of the Houghton Library, Harvard University

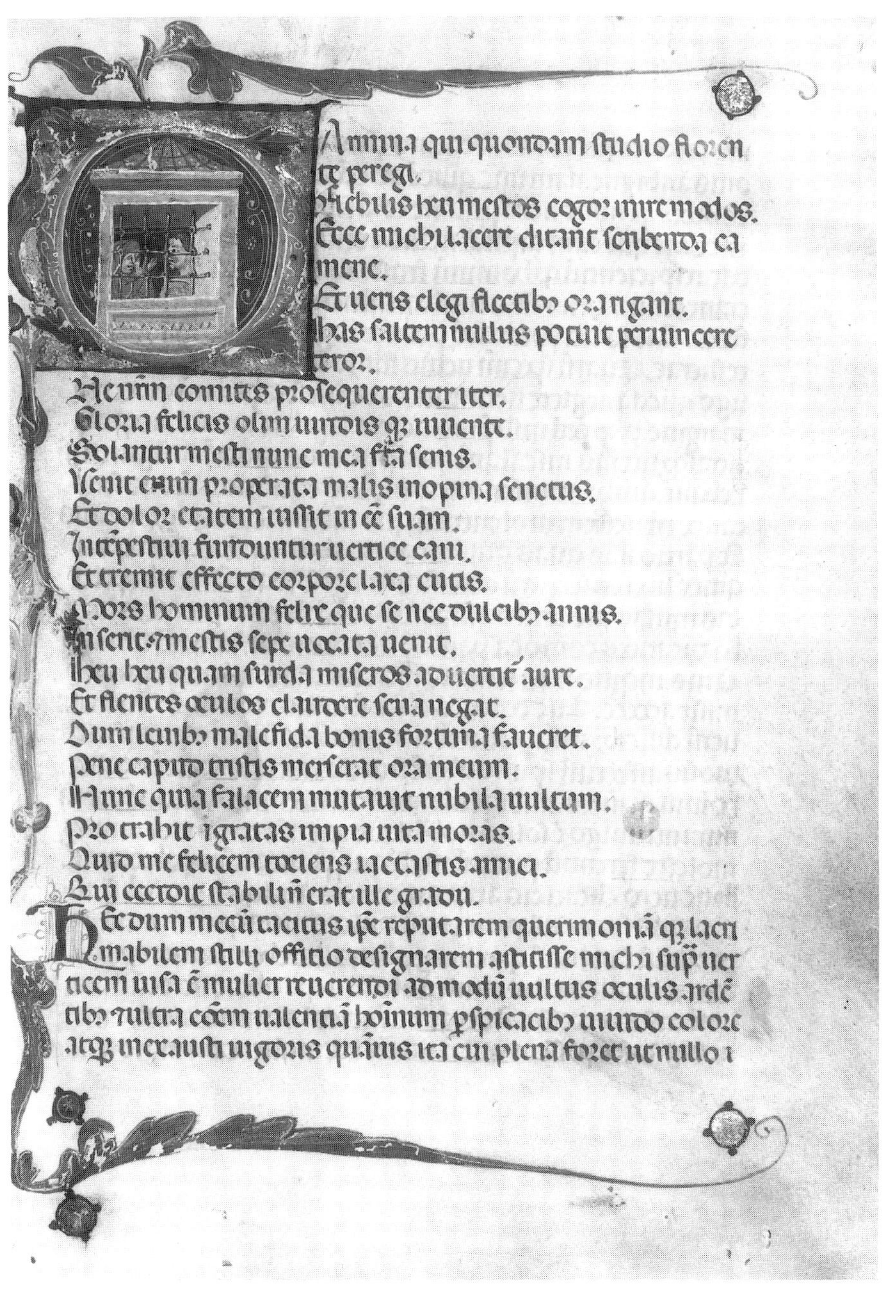

Carmina qui quondam studio floren
te peregi.
Flebilis heu mestos cogor inire modos.
Ecce michi lacere dictant scribenda ca
mene.
Et ueris elegi fletibus ora rigant.
Has saltem nullus potuit peruincere
teror.
Ne nostrum comites prosequerentur iter.
Gloria felicis olim uiridisque iuuente.
Solantur mesti nunc mea fata senis.
Venit enim properata malis inopina senectus.
Et dolor etatem iussit inesse suam.
Intempestiui funduntur uertice cani.
Et tremit effeto corpore laxa cutis.
Mors hominum felix que se nec dulcibus annis.
Inserit et mestis sepe uocata uenit.
Heu heu quam surda miseros auertitur aure.
Et flentes oculos claudere seua negat.
Dum leuibus malefida bonis fortuna faueret.
Pene caput tristis merserat hora meum.
Nunc quia fallacem mutauit nubila uultum.
Protrahit ingratas impia uita moras.
Quid me felicem totiens iactastis amici.
Qui cecidit stabili non erat ille gradu.

Hec dum mecum tacitus ipse reputarem querimoniamque lacri
mabilem stili officio designarem astitisse michi super uer
ticem uisa est mulier reuerendi admodum uultus oculis arden
tibus et ultra communem ualentiam hominum perspicacibus uiuido colore
atque inexausti uigoris quamuis ita eui plena foret ut nullo i

MS Lat 178, f. 1; Northern Italy s. $XV^{1/4}$

By permission of the Houghton Library, Harvard University

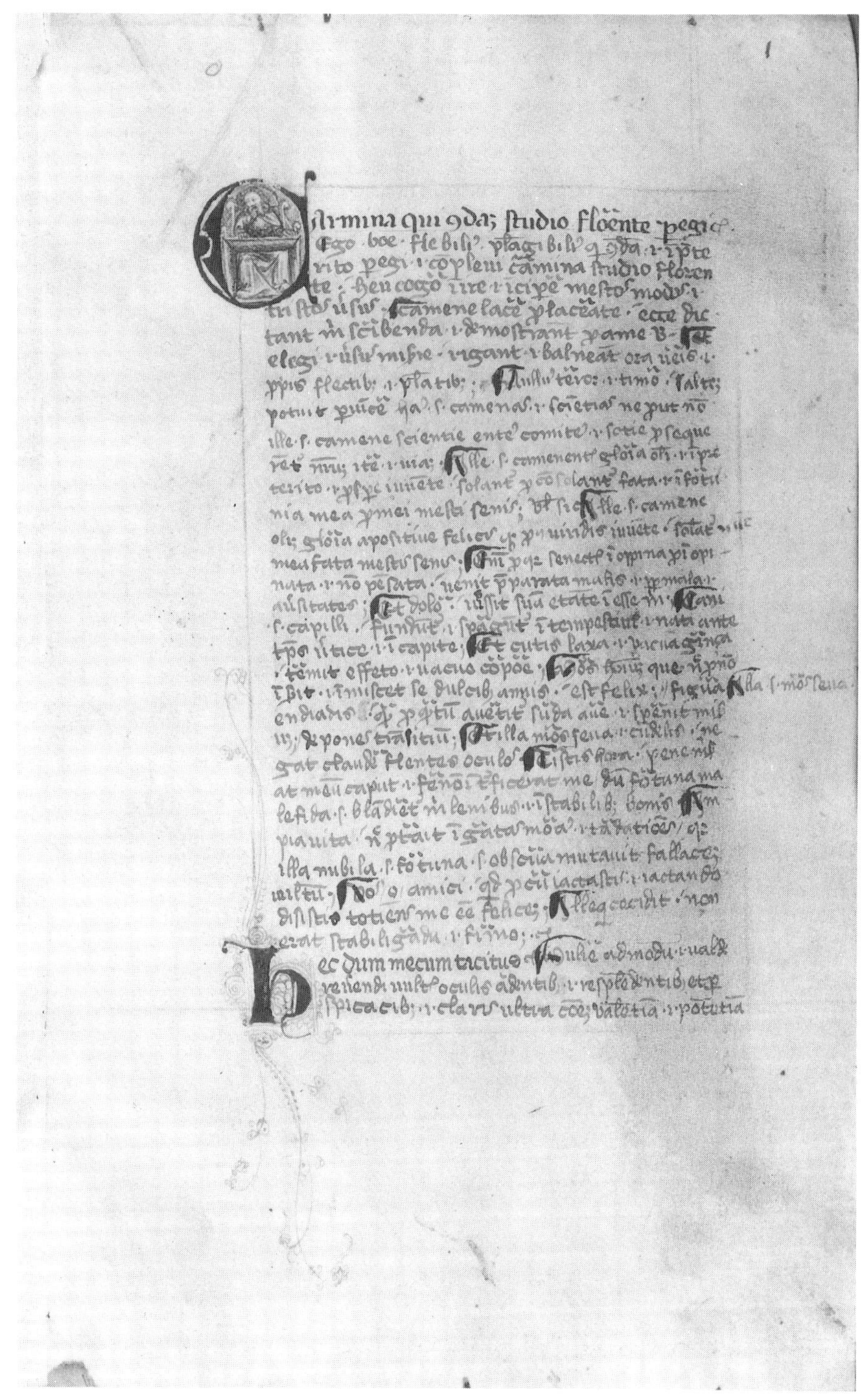

MS Lat 126, f. 1; Italy s. XV
By permission of the Houghton Library, Harvard University

HARVARD
UNIVERSITY
LIBRARY

Nec fonte labra prolui caballino
Nec in bicipiti somniasse parnaso
Memini me: ut repente sic poeta prodirem
Heliconiadas palidamque pirenem
Illis relinquo. quorum imagines lambunt
Hedere sequaces. ipse semipaganus
Ad sacra vatum: carmen affero nostrum
Quis expedivit psitaco suum chere
Picasque docuit nostra verba conari
Magister artis ingeniique largitor
Venter: negatas artifex sequi voces
Quod si dolosi spes refulxerit nummi
Corvos poetas et poetridas picas
Cantare credas pegaseium melos
O Curas hominum o quantum est in rebus inane
Quis leget hec: min tu istud ais: nemo
Vel duo vel nemo. turpe et miserabile quare? hercle. nemo.
Ne mihi polidamas et troadas labeonem
Pretulerint: nuge: non si quid turbida roma
Elevet accedas: examen ne improbum in illa
Castiges trutina. nec te quesiveris extra
Nam rome est quis ac si fas dicere: sed fas

MS Lat 137, f. 1; Italy (Florence) s. XV[1/4]
By permission of the Houghton Library, Harvard University

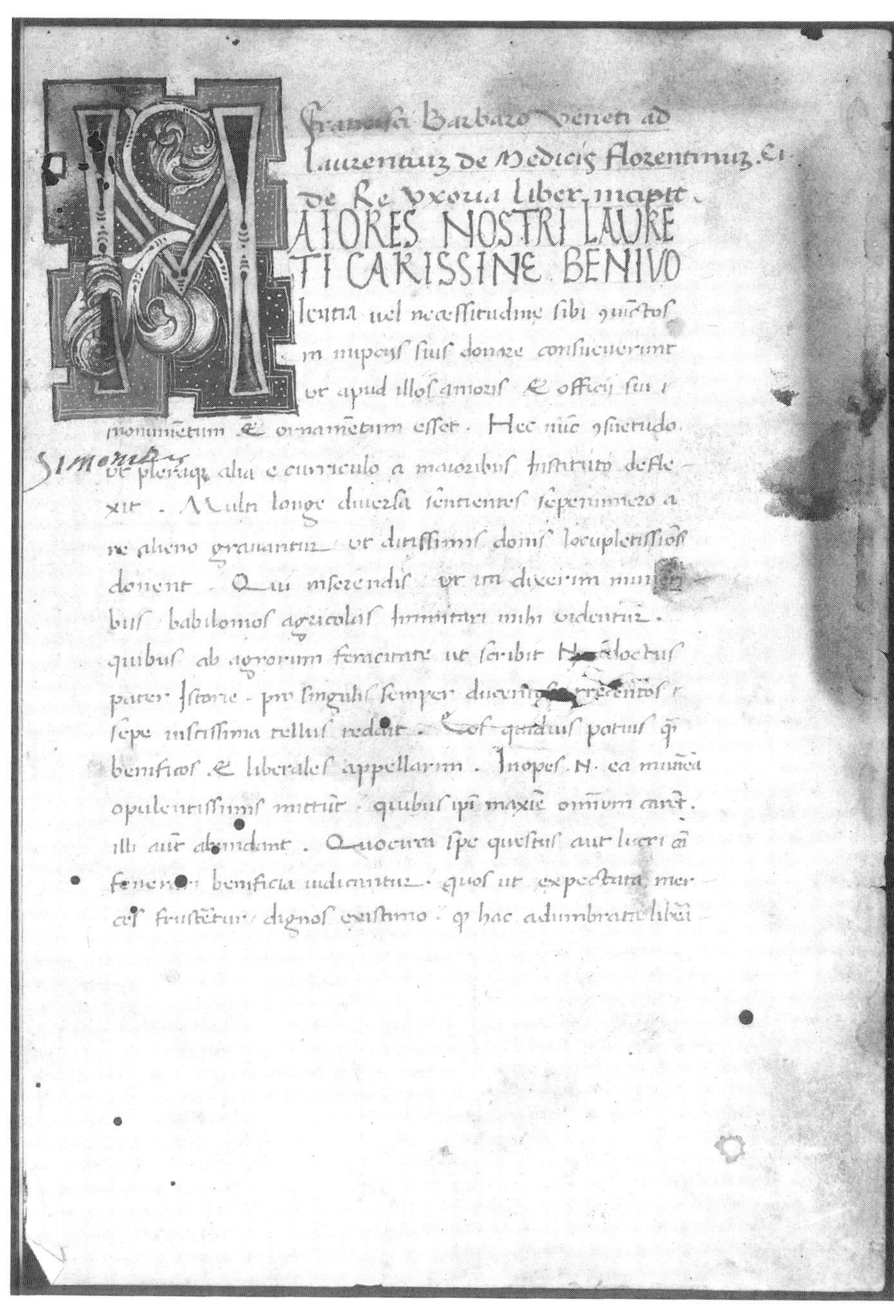

MS Lat 144, f. 1; Italy (Venice?) s. XV[1/4]
By permission of the Houghton Library, Harvard University

PLATE 46

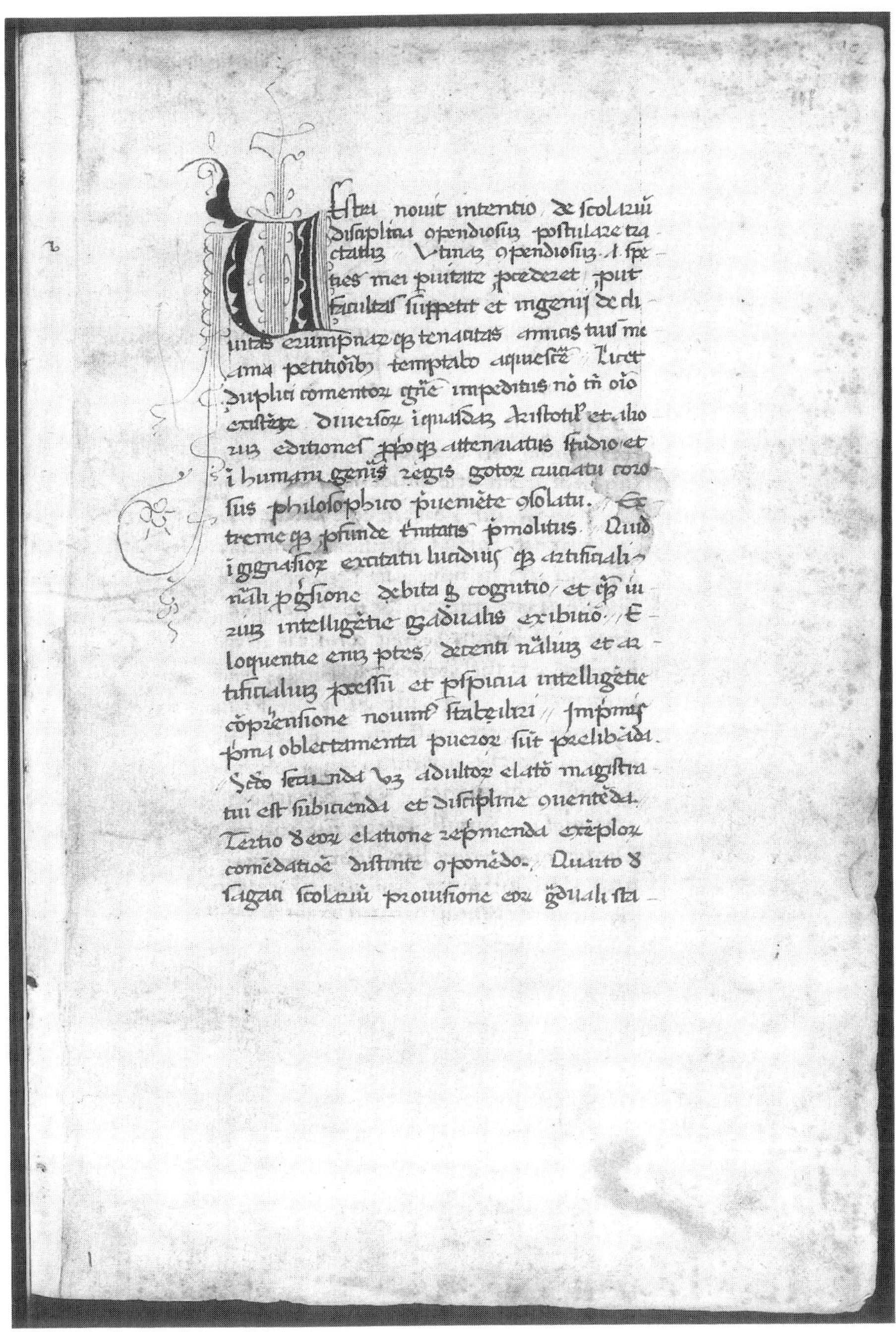

MS Lat 175, f. 1; Italy (Venice?) s. XV[1]
By permission of the Houghton Library, Harvard University

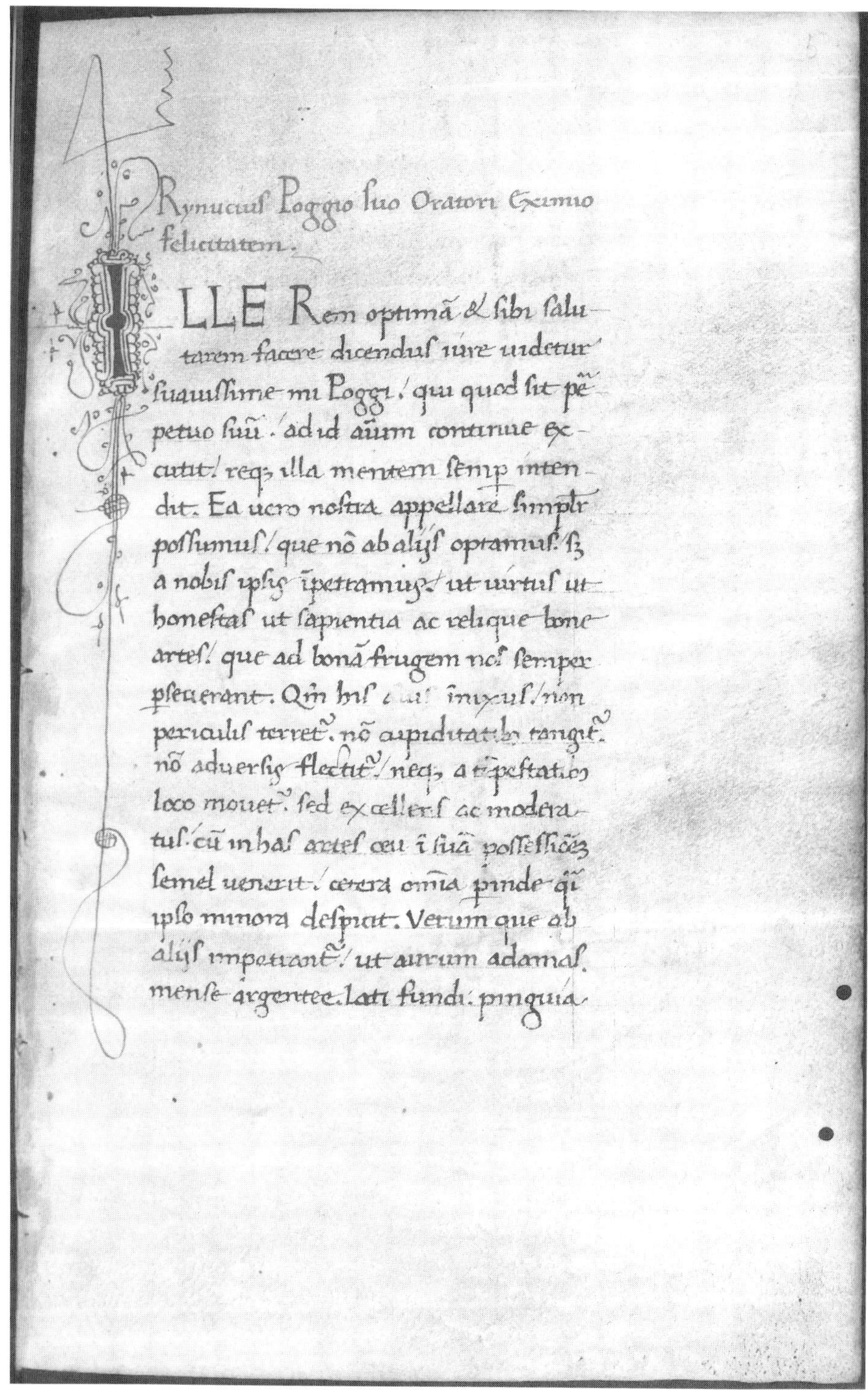

Rynucius Poggio suo Oratori Eximio
felicitatem.
ILLE Rem optimã & sibi salutarem facere dicendus iure uidetur
suauissime mi Poggi. qui quod sit pẽ-
petuo suũ. ad id aĩum continue ex-
citat. neq; illa mentem semp intendit.
dit. Ea uero nostra appellare simplr
possumus. que nõ ab aliis optamus. sʒ
a nobis ipsis ĩpetramus. ut uirtus ut
honestas ut sapientia ac relique bone
artes. que ad bonã frugem nos semper
pserrerant. Qm his [illegible] innixus. non
periculis terret. nõ cupiditatib; tangit.
nõ aduersis flectit. neq; a tẽpestatiõe
loco mouet. sed excellens ac modera-
tus. cũ in has artes ceu ĩ suã possessiõẽ
semel uenerit. cetera omĩa pinde qĩ
ipso minora despicit. Verum que ab
aliis impetrant. ut aurum adamas.
mense argentee. lati fundi. pinguia

MS Lat 124, f. 5; Italy (Florence) s. XV[2/4] (before 1453)
By permission of the Houghton Library, Harvard University

19

Rex Macedonum Philippus Atheniensium
Senatui plebiq; salutem: traducta p. leo. aretinu.
Quoniam persepe iam legatos misi: qui
vobiscum agerent, ut pacta conventio
nesq; servaremus: nec ea res adhuc vos
potuit continere, decrevi scribere ad vos
quibus in rebus iniurias mihi illatas ar
bitror. Ne miremini autem longitudi
nem epistole mee: Nam cum multa sint
crimina necesse habui cuncta simpliciter
exponere. Principio quidem igitur Ni
cea caduceatore ex meo regno per vim
rapto: non eos qui contra legem patra
ti fuerant ulla pena affecistis: sed ipsum
iniurias passum .x. menses in carcere
tenuistis & quas a me ferebat epl(ist)as in
contione legistis. Deinde cum Thasij
Bizantiorum triremes et latrones quos
cumq; reciperent: vos ea fieri omnino
neglexistis: q(uamvis) q(uidem) federa nostra aperte di
cerent eos qui talia fecissent pro hostib(us)
habendos. Per hec eadem tempora Dio
pytes in res nostras impetum fecit: &

MS Lat 124, f. 19; Italy (Florence) s. XV$^{3/4}$
By permission of the Houghton Library, Harvard University

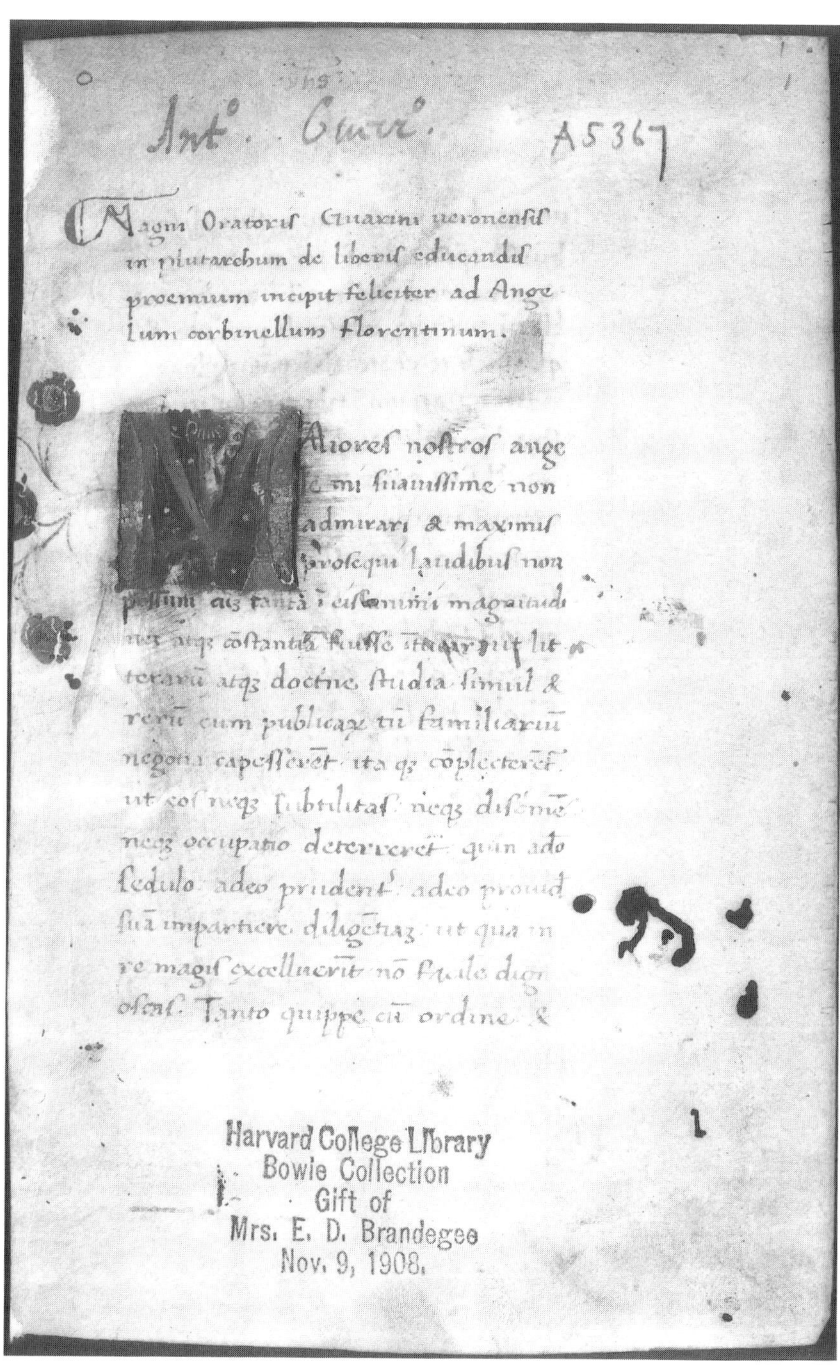

Ant.o Guar.o A5367

Magni Oratoris Guarini veronensis
in plutarchum de liberis educandis
proemium incipit feliciter ad Angelum corbinellum florentinum.

Maiores nostros ange-
le mi suavissime non
admirari & maximis
prosequi laudibus non
possum atque tantam in eis animi magnitudi-
nem atque constantiam fuisse ut quantumvis litterarum atque doctrine studia simul &
rerum cum publicarum tum familiarium
negotia capesserent ita quod complecterentur
ut eos neque subtilitas neque discrimen
neque occupatio deterreret quin adeo
sedulo adeo prudenter adeo provide
suam impartiere diligentiam ut qua in
re magis excelluerint non facile dig-
noscas. Tanto quippe cum ordine &

Harvard College Library
Bowie Collection
Gift of
Mrs. E. D. Brandegee
Nov. 9, 1908.

MS Lat 49, f. 1; Northeastern Italy s. XV$^{2/4\text{–med}}$
By permission of the Houghton Library, Harvard University

PLATE 50

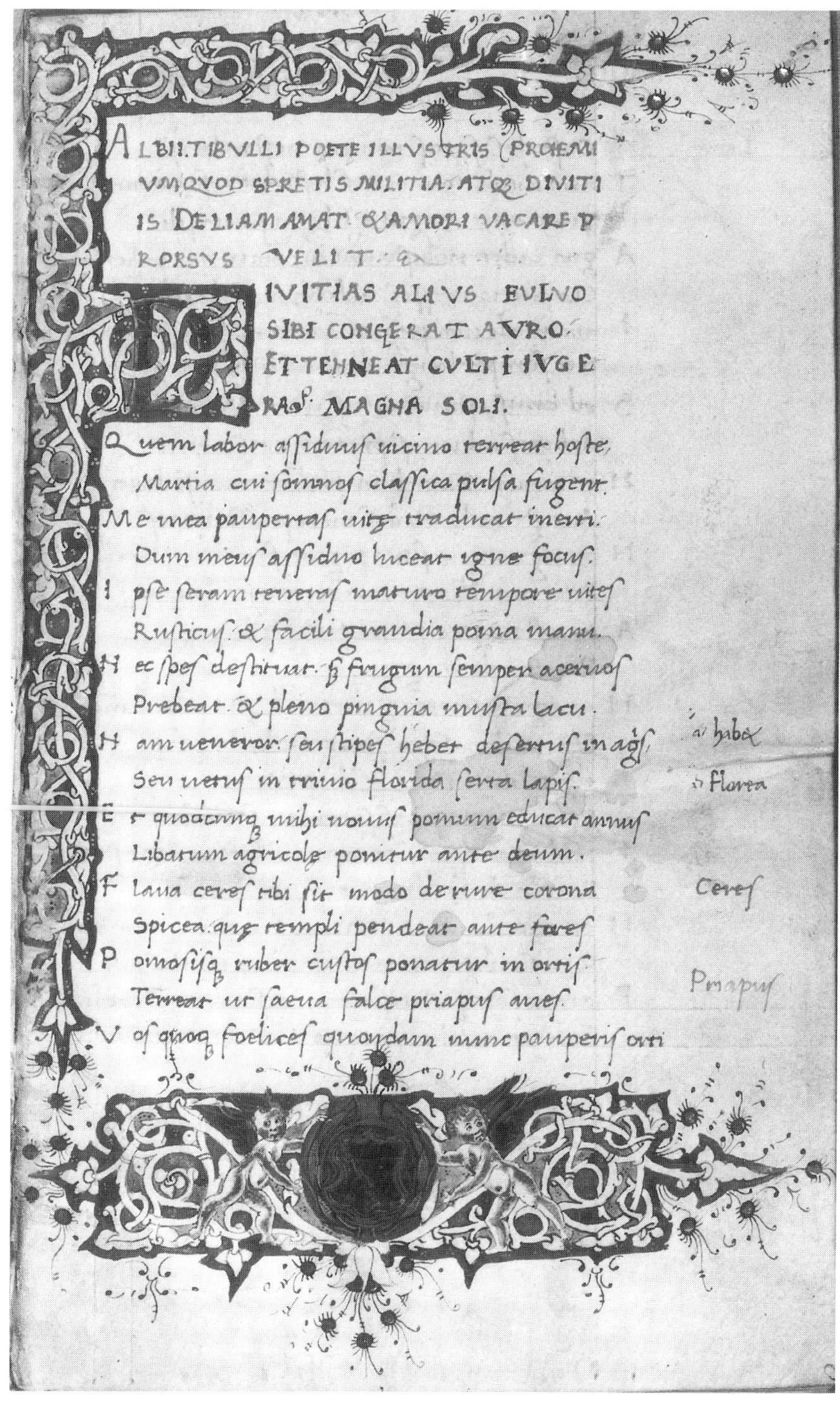

ALBII TIBULLI POETE ILLUSTRIS (PROEMI
VM QUOD SPRETIS MILITIA. ATQ(UE) DIVITI
IS DELIAM AMAT ET AMORI VACARE P
RORSUS VELIT.
DIVITIAS ALIUS FULVO
SIBI CONGERAT AURO.
ET TENEAT CULTI IUGE
RA MAGNA SOLI.

Quem labor assiduus uicino terreat hoste,
Martia cui somnos classica pulsa fugent.
Me mea paupertas uite traducat inerti.
Dum meus assiduo luceat igne focus.
Ipse seram teneras maturo tempore uites
Rusticus. & facili grandia poma manu.
Nec spes destituat. sed frugum semper aceruos
Prebeat. & pleno pinguia musta lacu.
Nam ueneror. seu stipes heber desertus in agris, — a: habet
Seu uetus in triuio florida serta lapis. — a: florea
Et quodcumque mihi nouus pomum educat annus
Libatum agricole ponitur ante deum.
Flaua ceres tibi sit modo de rure corona — Ceres
Spicea que templi pendeat ante fores
Pomosisque ruber custos ponatur in ortis — Priapus
Terreat ut saeua falce priapus aues.
Vos quoque foelices quondam nunc pauperis orti

MS Lat 46, f. 1; Italy (Florence) s. XV[med]
By permission of the Houghton Library, Harvard University

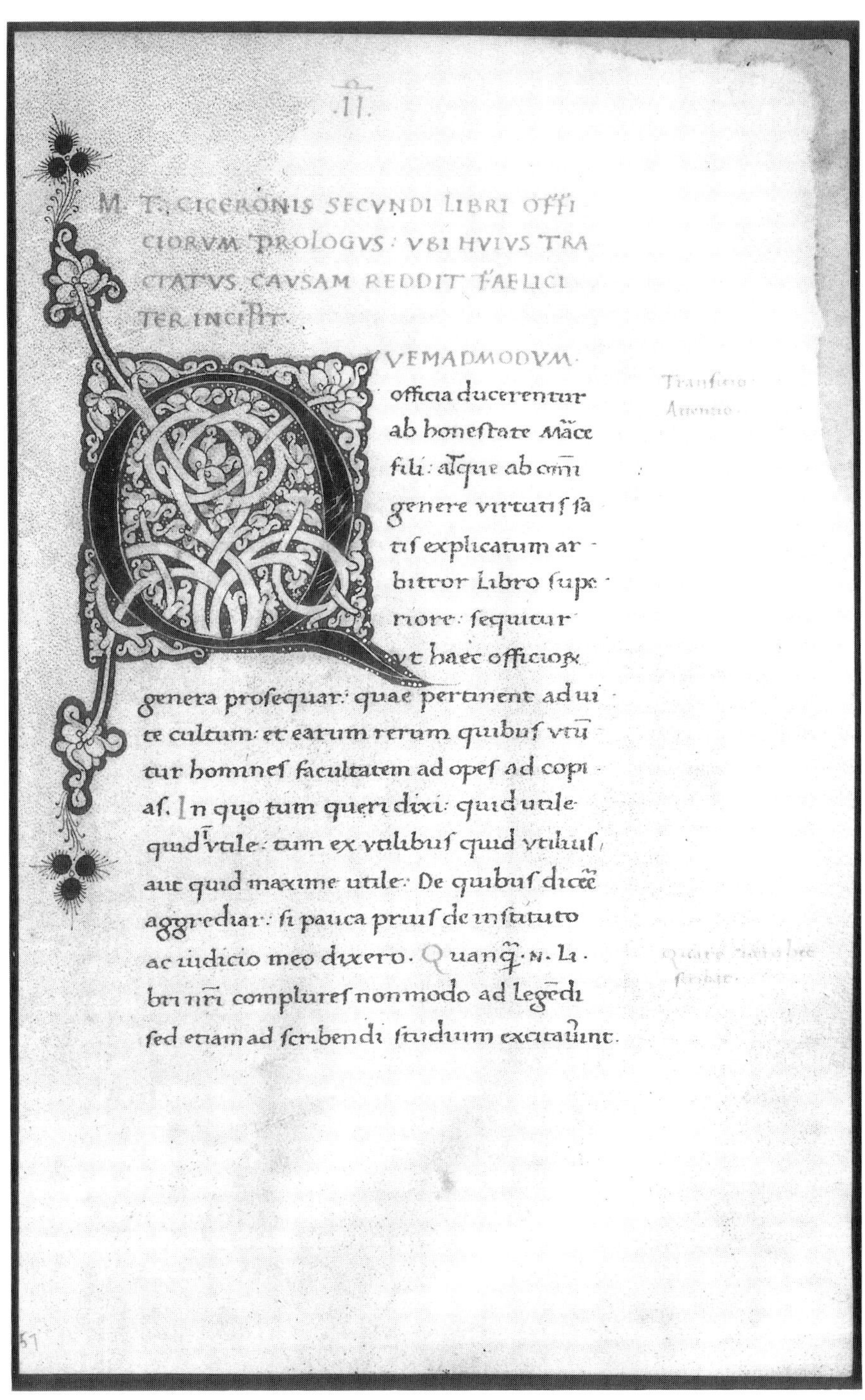

.II.

M. T. CICERONIS SECVNDI LIBRI OFFI
CIORVM PROLOGVS: VBI HVIVS TRA
CTATVS CAVSAM REDDIT FAELICI
TER INCIPIT.

QVEMADMODVM.
officia ducerentur
ab honestate Marce
fili: atque ab omni
genere virtutis sa
tis explicatum ar-
bitror libro supe-
riore: sequitur
ut haec officiorum
genera prosequar: quae pertinent ad vite cultum: et earum rerum quibus utun
tur homines facultatem ad opes ad copi-
as. In quo tum queri dixi: quid utile
quid inutile: tum ex utilibus quid utilius,
aut quid maxime utile: De quibus dicere
aggrediar: si pauca prius de instituto
ac iudicio meo dixero. Quanquam n. libri nostri complures nonmodo ad legendi
sed etiam ad scribendi studium excitaverunt.

MS Lat 177, f. 57; Italy (Rome or Florence) s. XV[med]

By permission of the Houghton Library, Harvard University

PLATE 52

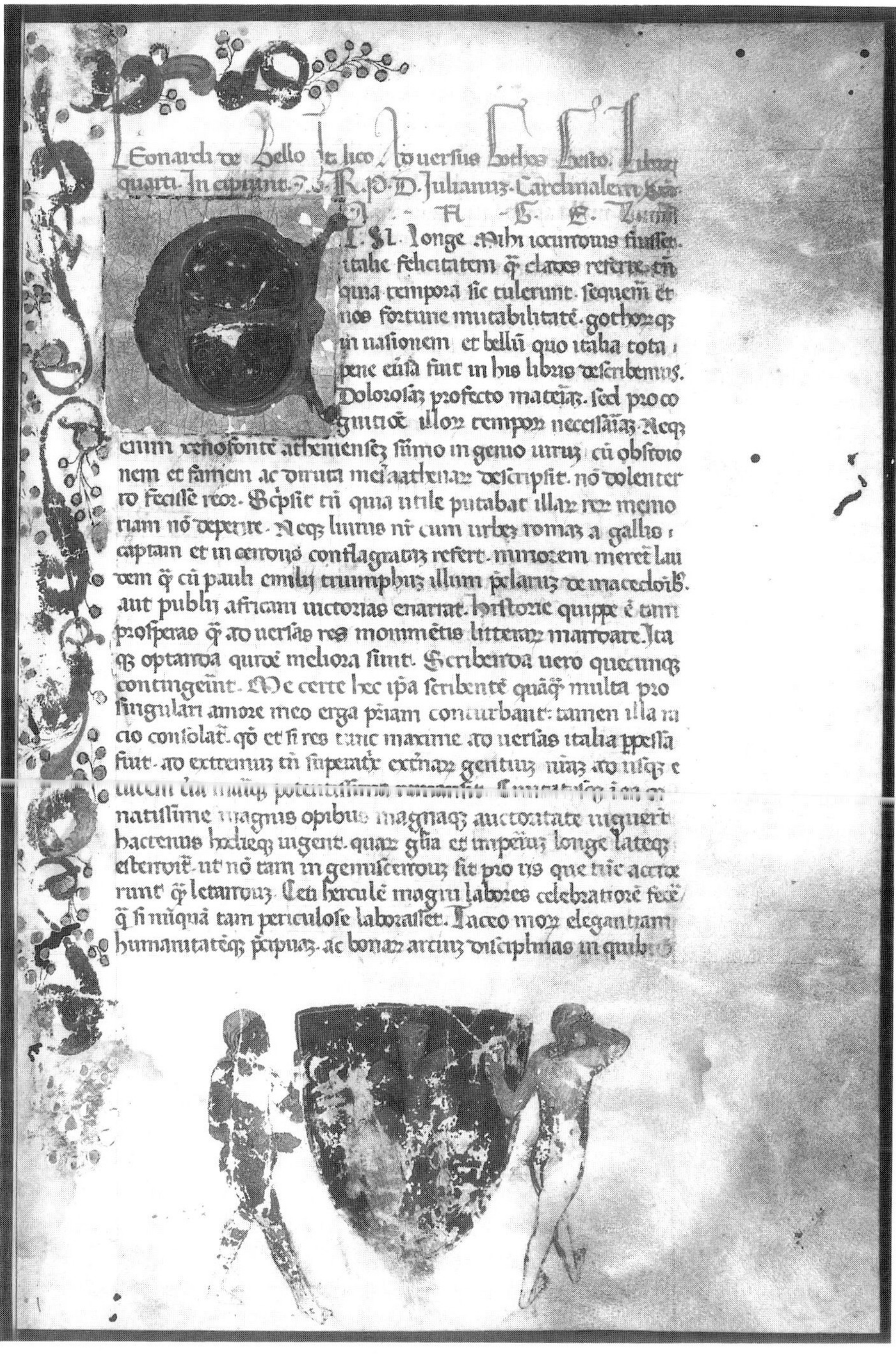

MS Lat 170, f. 1; Northern Italy s. XV$^{med-3/4}$

By permission of the Houghton Library, Harvard University

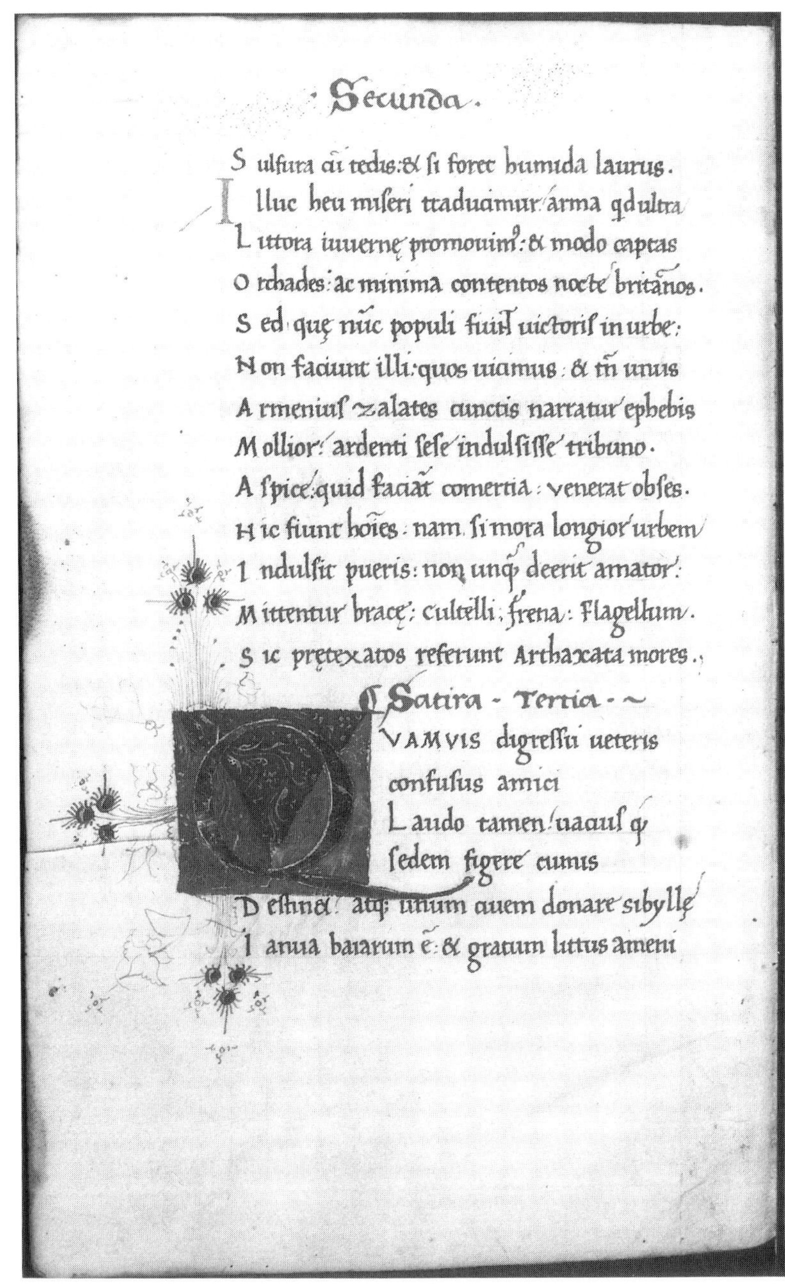

Secunda.

S ulfura cũ tedis: & si foret humida laurus.
I lluc heu miseri traducimur: arma q̄d ultra
L ittora iuuernę promouim⁹: & modo captas
O rchades: ac minima contentos nocte britãnos.
S ed quę nũc populi fiunt uictoris in urbe:
N on faciunt illi: quos uicimus: & tñ unus
A rmenius zalates cunctis narratur ephebis
M ollior: ardenti sese indulsisse tribuno.
A spice: quid faciat comertia: uenerat obses.
H ic fiunt hoĩes. nam si mora longior urbem
I ndulsit pueris: non unq̄ deerit amator:
M ittentur bracę: cultelli. frena: Flagellum.
S ic pretextatos referunt Arthaxata mores.

Satira Tertia

Q VAMVIS digressu ueteris
confusus amici
L audo tamen: uacuis q̄
sedem figere cumis
D estinet: atq; unum ciuem donare sibyllę
I anua baiarum ē: & gratum littus ameni

MS Lat 135, f. 9v; Northern Italy s. XV[2]

By permission of the Houghton Library, Harvard University

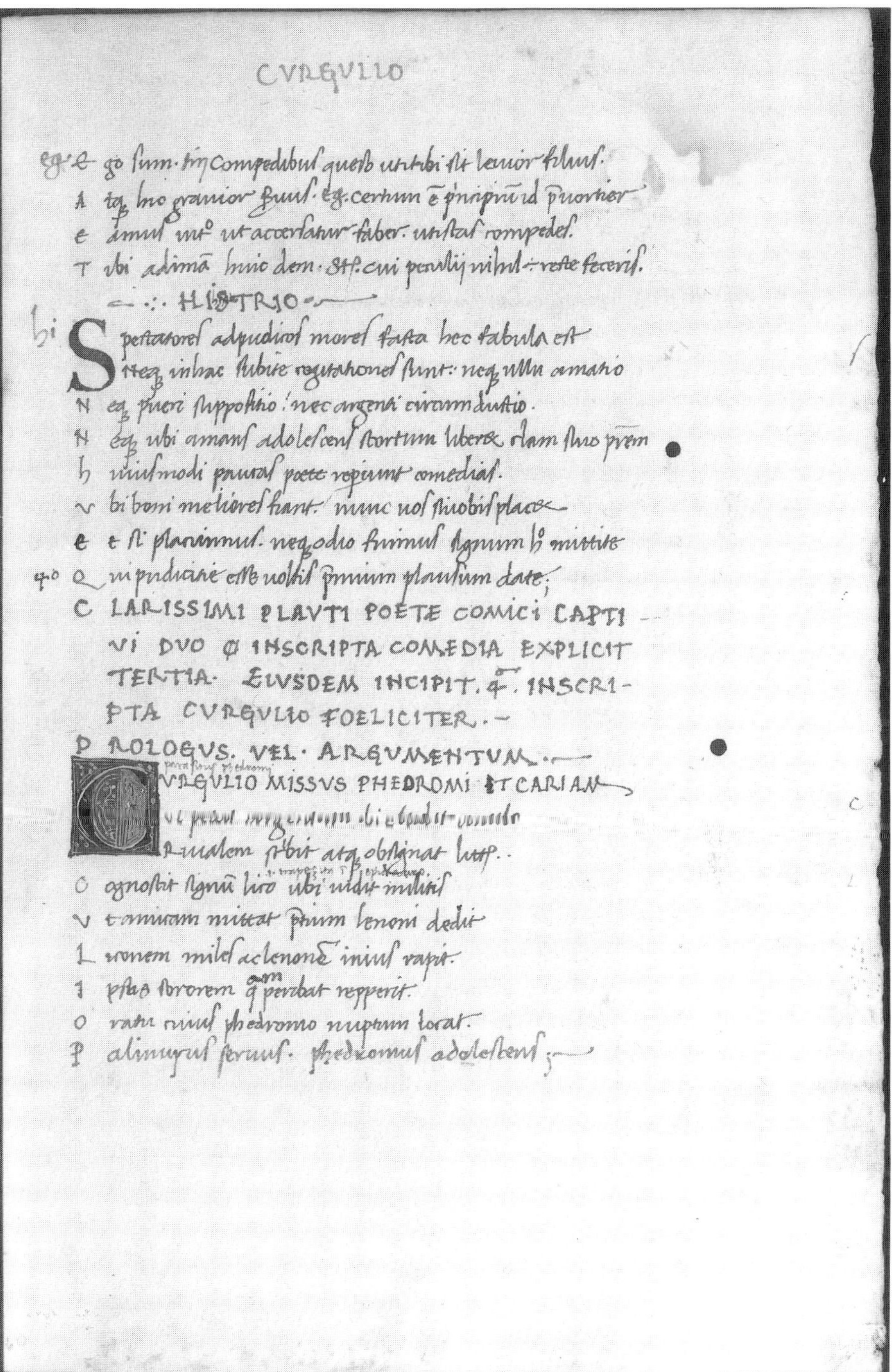

MS Lat 43, f. 60; Italy (Florence) s. $XV^{3/4}$
By permission of the Houghton Library, Harvard University

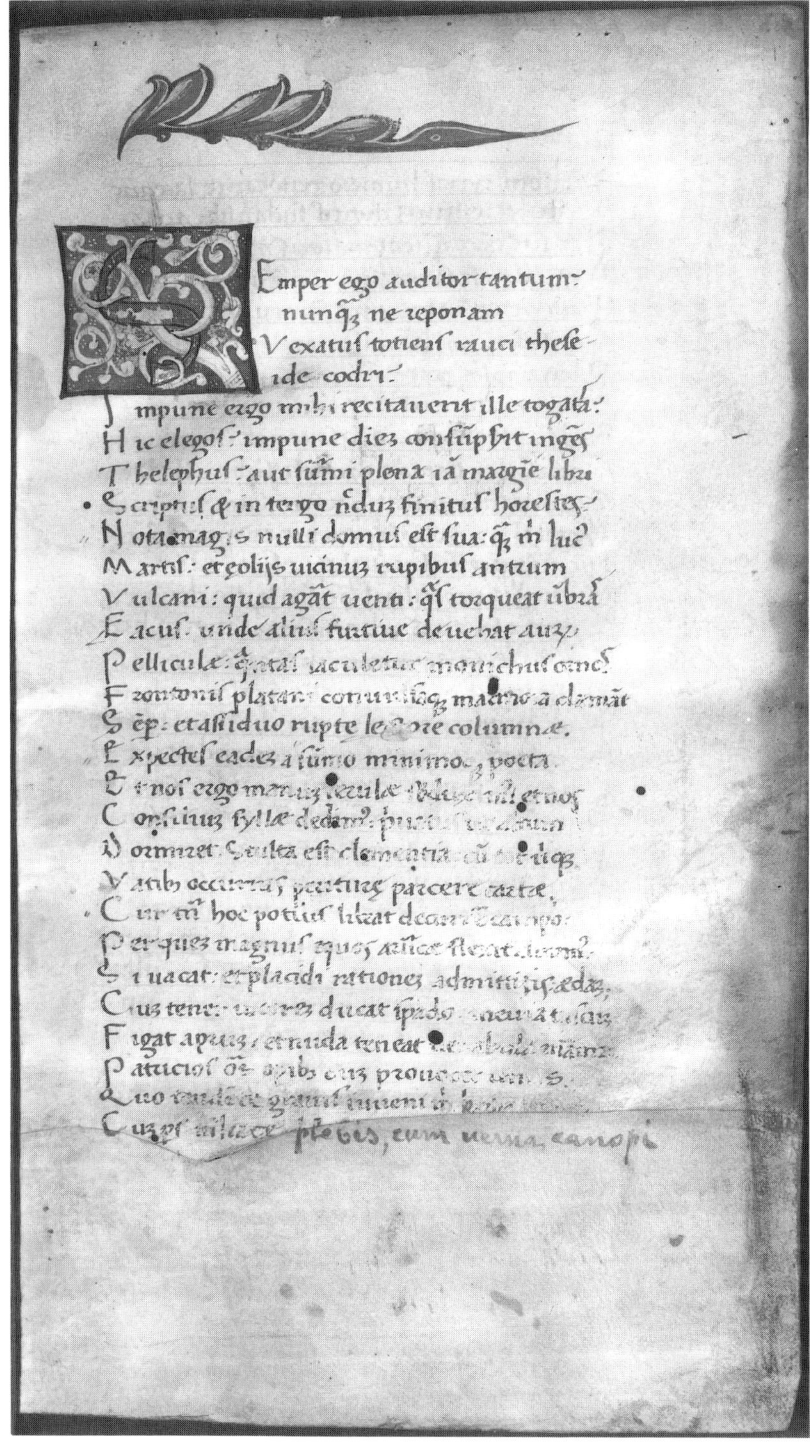

Semper ego auditor tantum? numquamne reponam
Vexatus totiens rauci Theseide codri?
Impune ergo mihi recitauerit ille togatas,
Hic elegos? impune diem consumpserit ingens
Thelephus aut summi plena iam margine libri
Scriptus et in tergo necdum finitus horestes?
Nota magis nulli domus est sua quam mihi lucus
Martis et eolijs uicinum rupibus antrum
Vulcani: quid agant uenti: quas torqueat umbras
Eacus, unde alius furtiue deuehat aurum
Pelliculae: quantas iaculetur monichus ornos
Frontonis platani conuulsaque marmora clamant
Semper et assiduo rupte lectore columnae.
Expectes eadem a summo minimoque poeta.
Et nos ergo manum ferulae subduximus: et nos
Consilium syllae dedimus: priuatus ut altum
Dormiret. Stulta est clementia cum tot ubique
Vatibus occurras, periture parcere cartae.
Cur tamen hoc potius libeat decurrere campo:
Per quem magnus equos aurunce flexit alumnus.
Si uacat: et placidi rationem admittitis, edam.
Cum tener uxorem ducat spado: meuia tuscum
Figat aprum, et nuda teneat uenabula mamma.
Patricios omnes opibus cum prouocet unus
Quo tondente grauis iuueni mihi barba sonabat,
Cum pars niliacae plebis, cum uerna canopi

MS Lat 145, f. 1; Northeastern Italy s. XV 3/4
By permission of the Houghton Library, Harvard University

FRANCISCI BARBARI VE
NETI AD LAVRENTIVM
MEDICEM DE RE VXO
RIA LIBER INCIPIT

MAIORES NO
stri laurenti ca
rissime uel beni
uolentia uel ne
cessitudine sibi co
iunctos a nuptiis
donare consueue
runt ut apud illos amoris et officii
sui monumentum et ornamentum
esset. Hec nunc consuetudo ut ple
raque alia curriculo a maioribus insti
tuto deflexit. Multi n(am) longe diuer
sa sentientes sepe numero ere alieno
grauantur: ut ditissimis donis locu
pletissimos donent. Qui inferendis

MS Lat 163, f. 2; Italy (Florence) s. $XV^{4/4}$

By permission of the Houghton Library, Harvard University

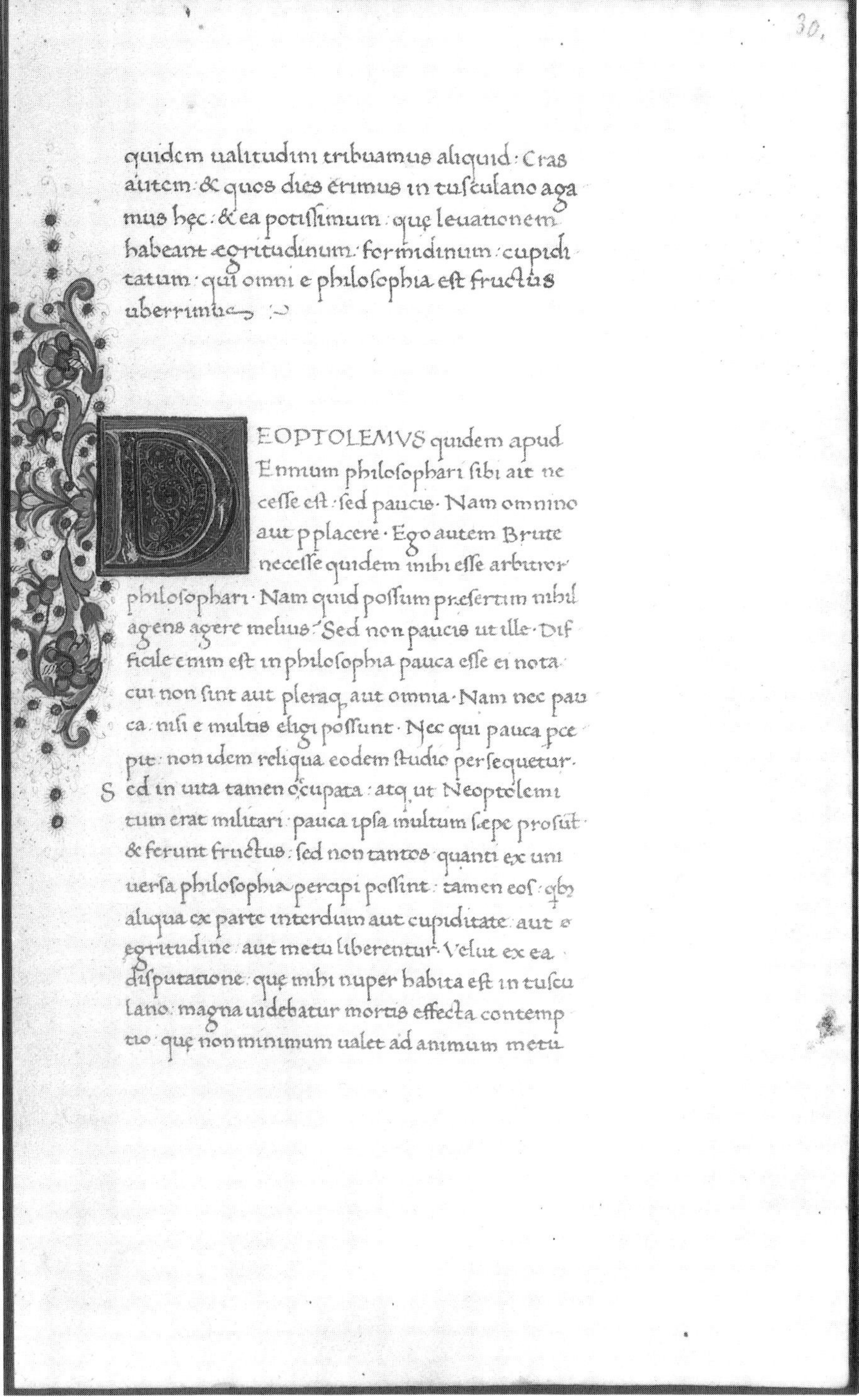

30.

quidem ualitudini tribuamus aliquid: Cras
autem & quos dies erimus in tusculano aga
mus hec: & ea potissimum: que leuationem
habeant egritudinum: formidinum: cupidi
tatum: qui omni e philosophia est fructus
uberrimus.

NEOPTOLEMVS quidem apud
Ennium philosophari sibi ait ne
cesse est: sed paucis. Nam omnino
aut p placere. Ego autem Brute
necesse quidem mihi esse arbitror
philosophari. Nam quid possum presertim nihil
agens agere melius? Sed non paucis ut ille. Dif
ficile enim est in philosophia pauca esse ei nota
cui non sint aut pleraq; aut omnia. Nam nec pau
ca nisi e multis eligi possunt. Nec qui pauca pce
pit: non idem reliqua eodem studio persequetur.
Sed in uita tamen occupata: atq; ut Neoptolemi
tum erat militari pauca ipsa multum sepe prosūt
& ferunt fructus: sed non tantos quanti ex uni
uersa philosophia percipi possint: tamen eos quibus
aliqua ex parte interdum aut cupiditate aut e
gritudine aut metu liberentur. Velut ex ea
disputatione: que mihi nuper habita est in tuscu
lano: magna uidebatur mortis effecta contemp
tio: que non minimum ualet ad animum metu

MS Lat 176, f. 30; Italy (Florence) s. XV[4/4]

By permission of the Houghton Library, Harvard University

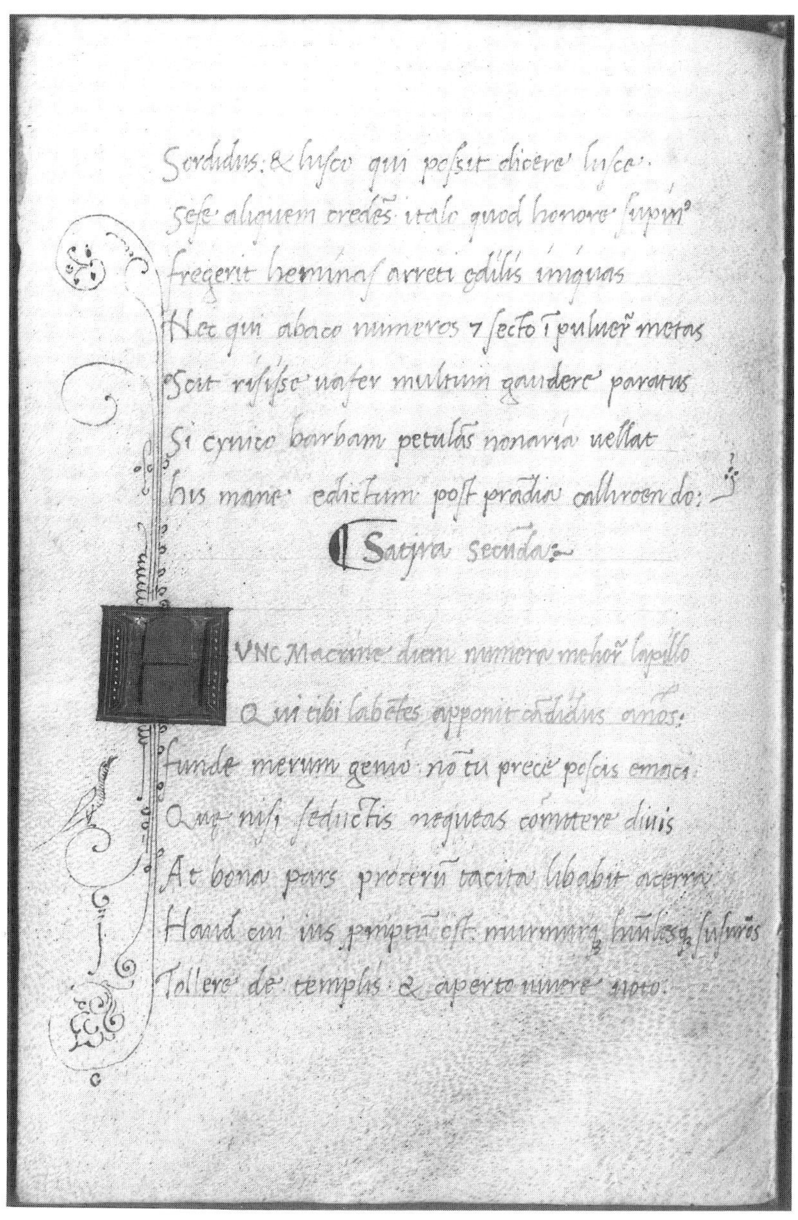

MS Lat 155, f. 5v; Northern Italy (Venice?) s. XV[ex]
By permission of the Houghton Library, Harvard University

pfMS Lat 128, f. 1; Italy s. XVI
By permission of the Houghton Library, Harvard University

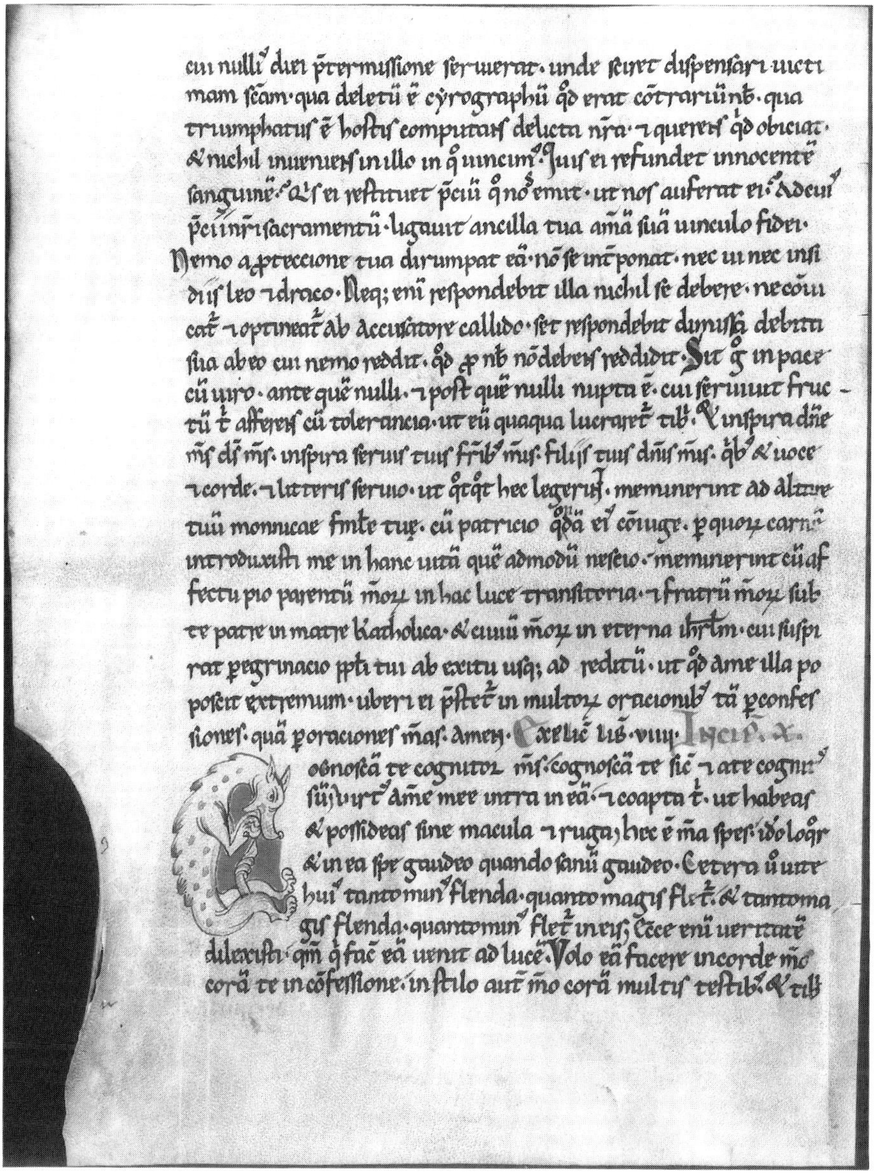

PLATE 60

cui nulli diei ptermissione seruerat· unde scieret dispensari uicti
mam scam·qua deletu e cyrographu qd erat cotrariu nob· qua
triumphatus e hostis computatis delicta nra· 7 queres qd obiciat·
& nichil inueniet in illo in q uincum? Juis ei refundet innocentē
sanguinē· als ei restituet pciu q no emit· ut nos auferat ei· Adcui
pciinr sacramentu· ligauit ancilla tua amā suā uinculo fidei·
Nemo a pteccione tua dirumpat eā· no se inponat· nec ut nec insi
diis leo 7 draco· Neq; eni respondebit illa nichil se debere· ne coū
cat 7 optineat ab accusatore callido· set respondebit dimissa debita
sua ab eo cui nemo reddit· qd q nb no debet reddidit· Sit q in pace
cu uiro· ante quē nulli· 7 post quē nulli nupta e· cui seruiut fructu e affexes cu tolerancia· ut eu quaqua lucraret tib· Inspira dne
mi di mi· inspira seruis tuis frib mis· filiis tuis dnis mis· qb & uoce
7 corde· 7 litteris seruio· ut qtqt hec legerit· meminerint ad altare
tuū monnicae fmte tue· cū patricio qda ei coiuge· p quoz carnē
introduxisti me in hanc uitā quē admodu nescio· meminerint cū af-
fectu pio parentū mou in hac luce transitoria· 7 fratrū mou sub
te patre in matre katholica· & ciuiu mou in eterna ihrlm· cui suspi
rat pegrinacio ppti tui ab exitu usq; ad reditu· ut qd a me illa po
poscit extremum· uberi ei pstet in multox oracionib tā p confes
siones· quā p oraciones mas· amen· Explic lib· viii· Incip· X.
obnosca te cognitor mi· cognosca te sic· 7 a te cogni[?]
sui· uirt Ame mee intra in eā· 7 coapta t· ut habeas
& possideas sine macula· 7 ruga; hec e ma spes ido logr·
& in ea spr gaudeo quando sanu gaudeo· Cetera u uite
hui tanto min flenda· quanto magis flet· & tanto ma
gis flenda· quanto min flet uteis; Ecce eni ueritatē
dilexisti qm q fac eā uenit ad lucē· Volo eā facere in corde mo
corā te in cofessione· in stilo aut mo corā multis testib· & tib

MS Lat 150, f. 64v; Southern Europe s. XII[2/4]

By permission of the Houghton Library, Harvard University

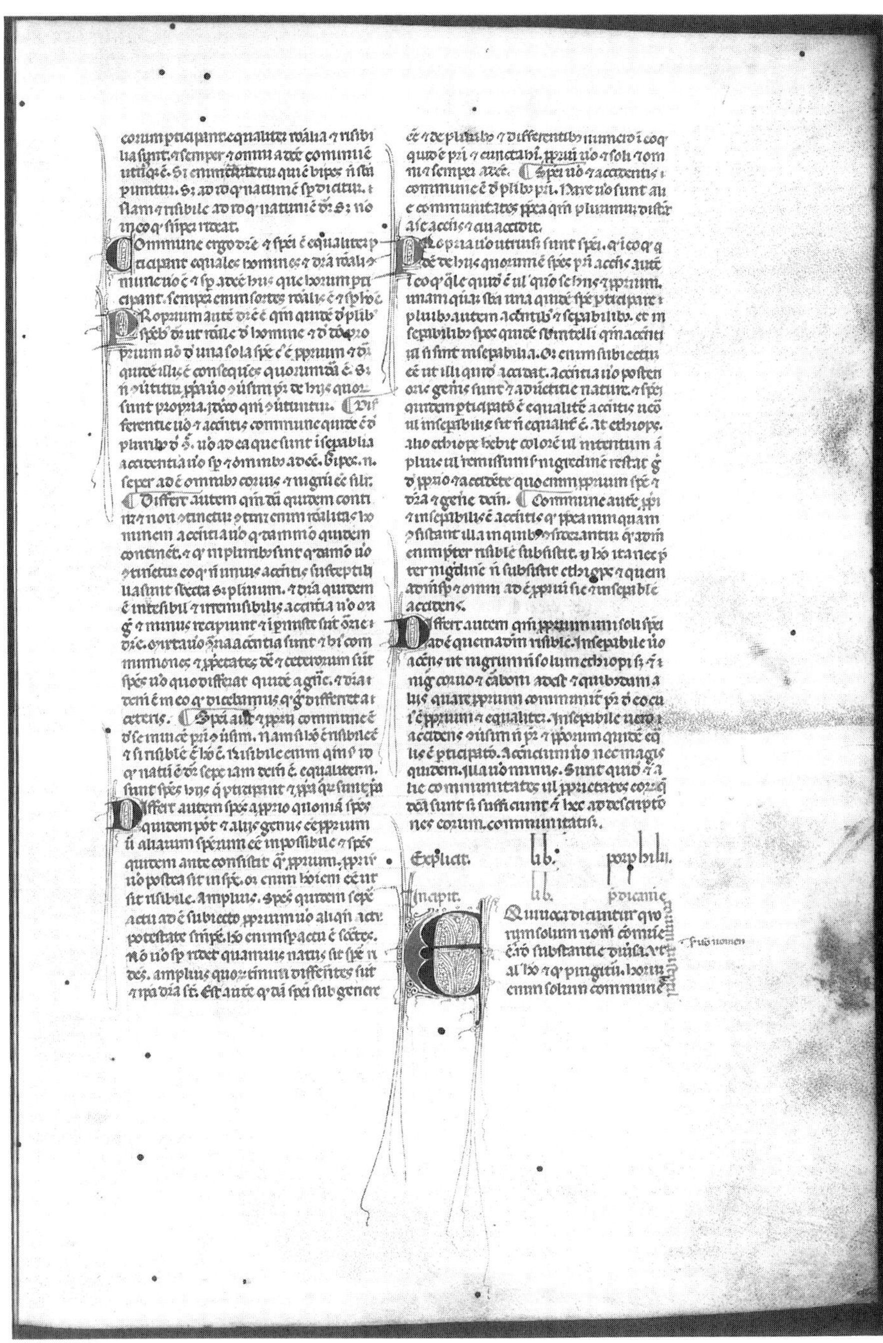

fMS Lat 38, pg. 7; Spain s. XIII$^{4/4}$–XIV$^{1/4}$

By permission of the Houghton Library, Harvard University

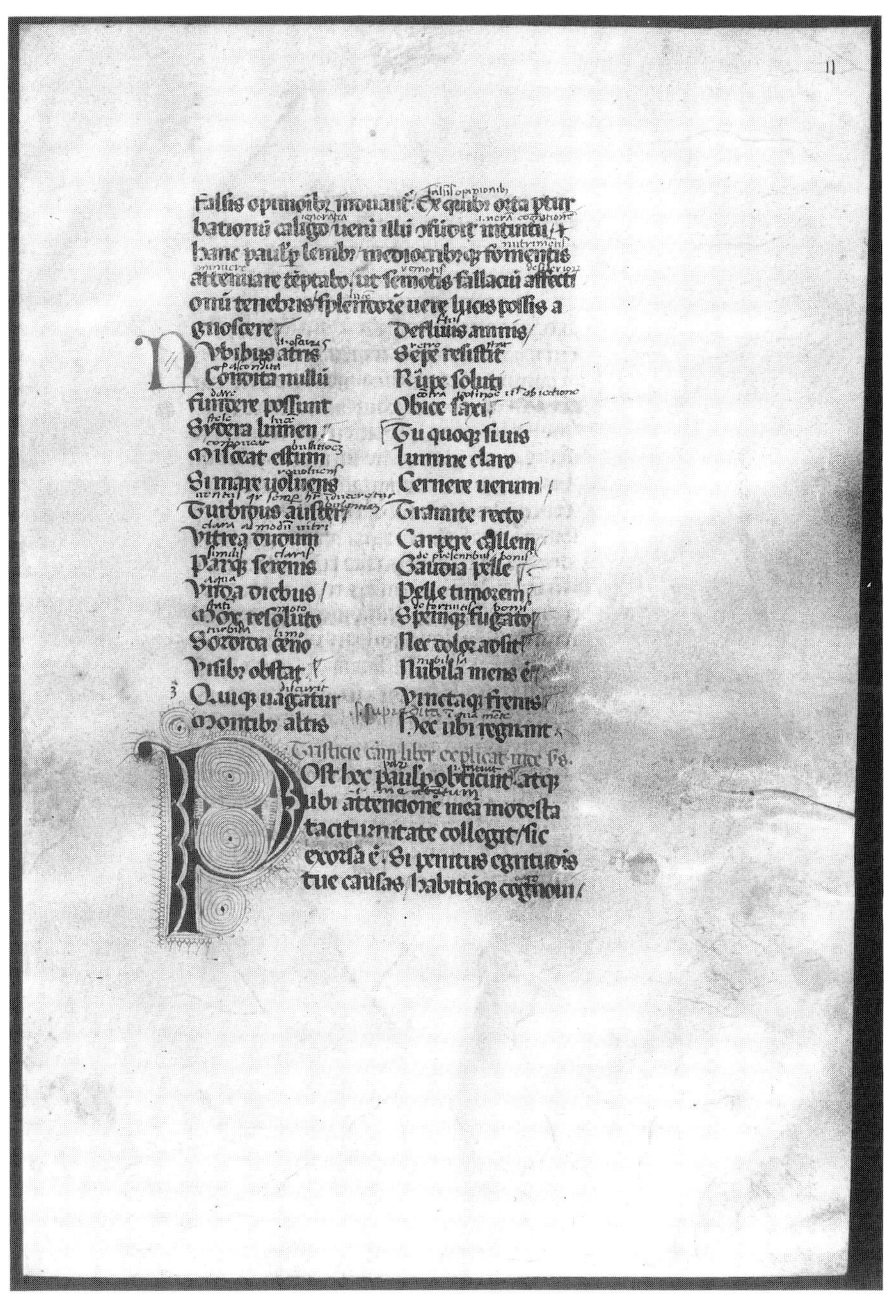

MS Lat 179, f. 11; Southern France or Spain s. XIV[2]
By permission of the Houghton Library, Harvard University

PLATE 63

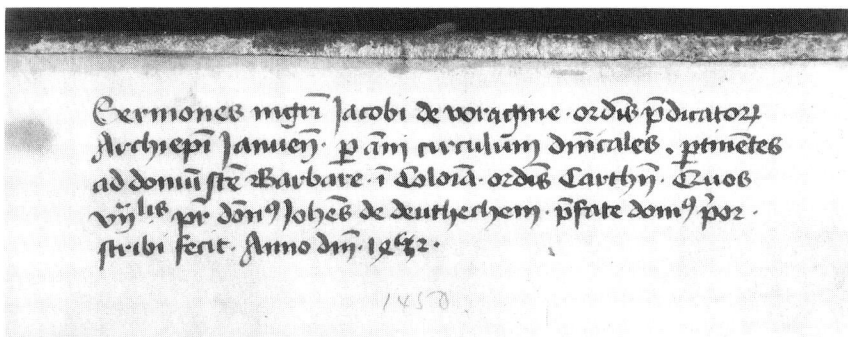

MS Lat 9, inside front cover
By permission of the Houghton Library, Harvard University

PLATE 64

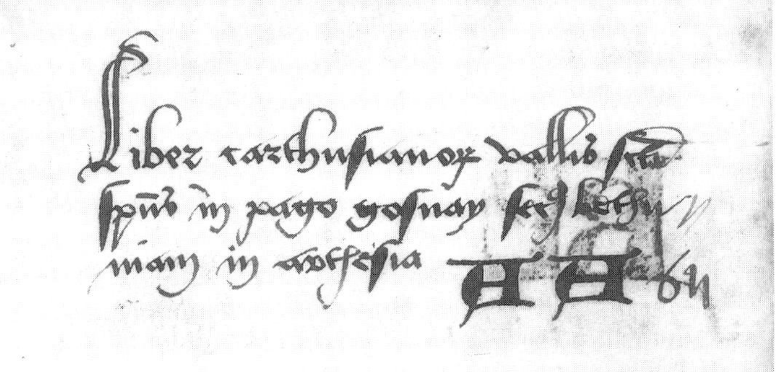

MS Lat 111, f. 1v
By permission of the Houghton Library, Harvard University

PLATE 65

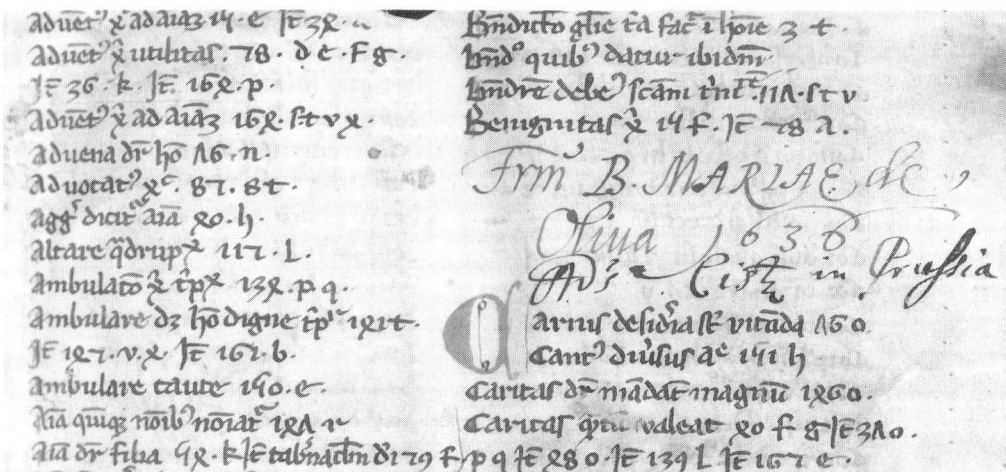

MS Lat 15, f. 1
By permission of the Houghton Library, Harvard University

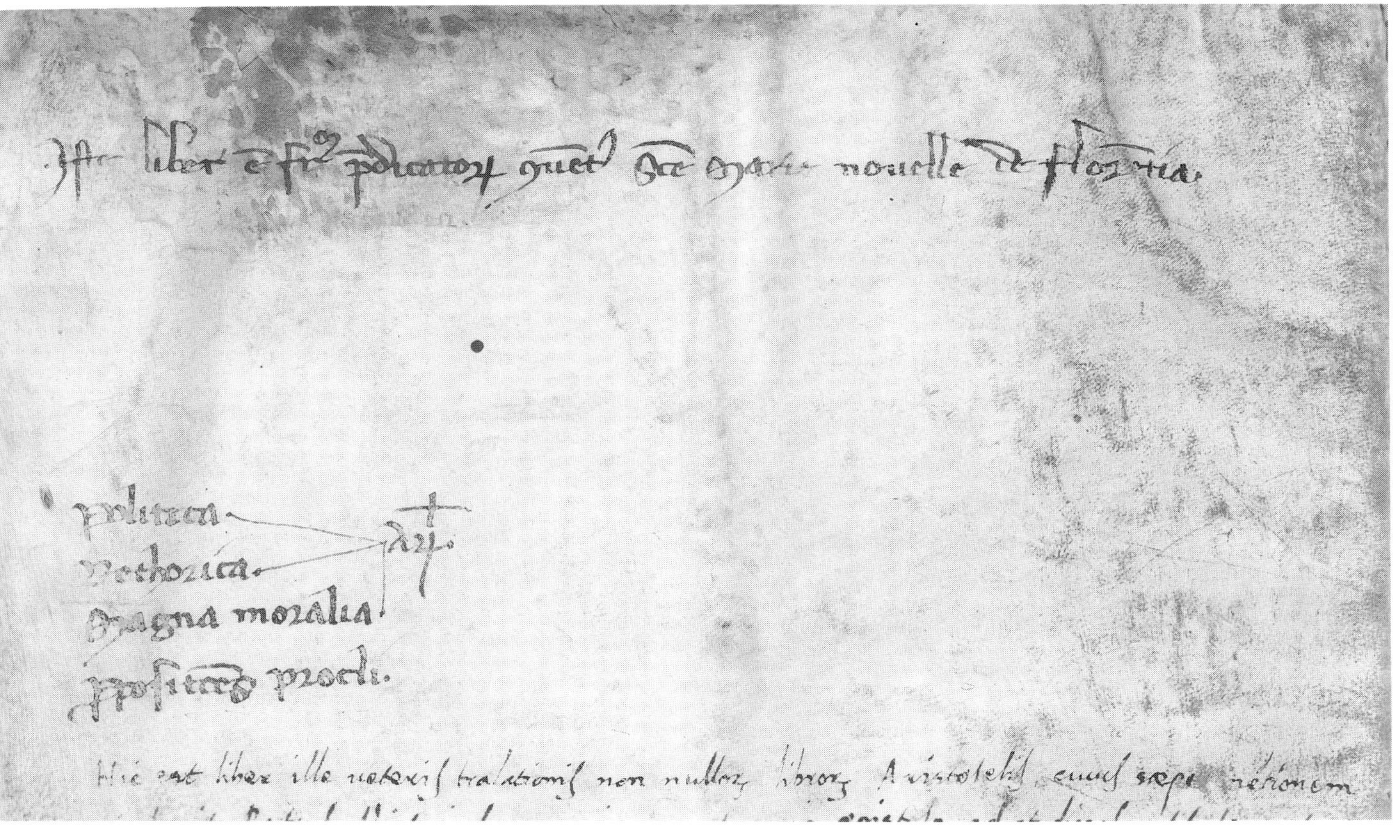

fMS Lat 39, f. i^{v}
By permission of the Houghton Library, Harvard University

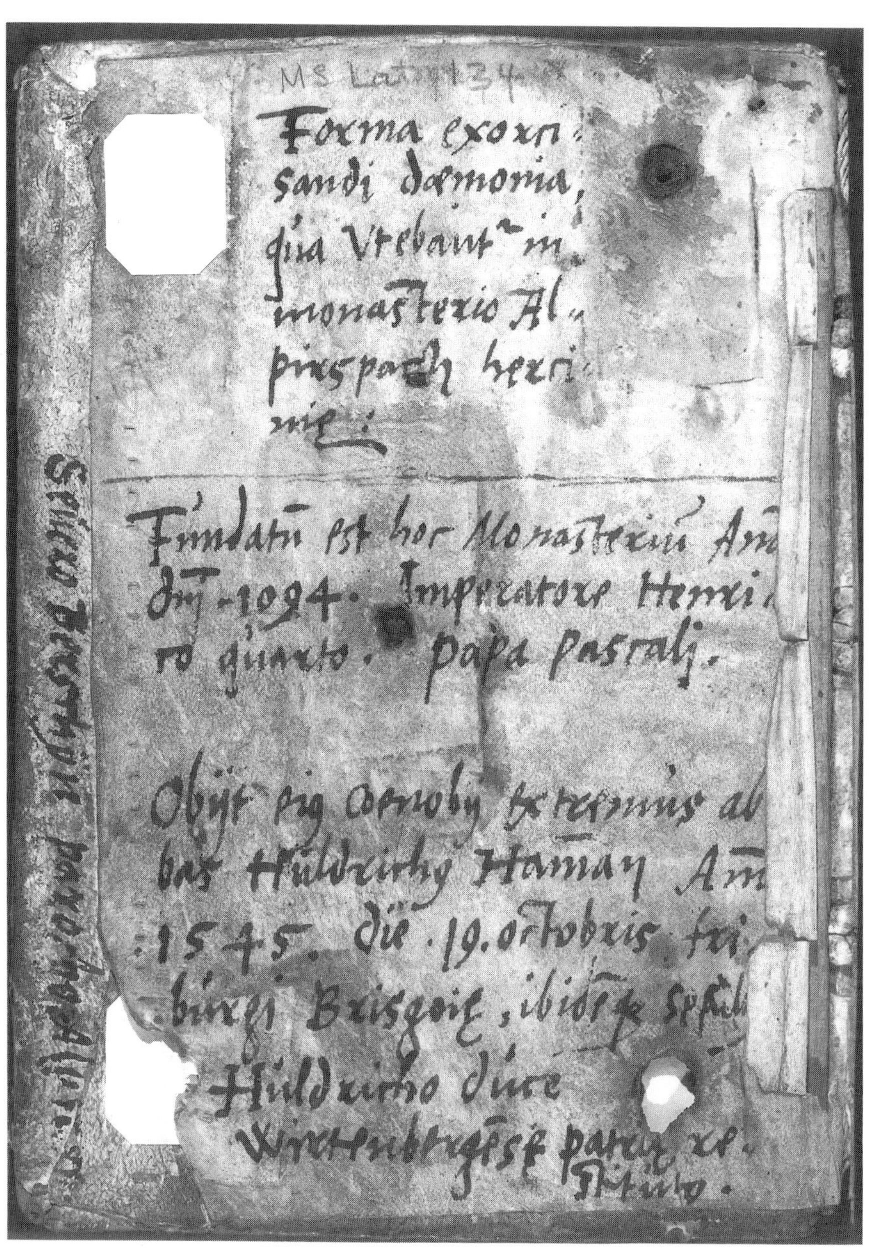

MS Lat 134, front paste down
By permission of the Houghton Library, Harvard University